THE MAKING OF THE MODERN MUSLIM STATE

PRINCETON STUDIES IN MUSLIM POLITICS

Dale F. Eickelman, Series Editor

For a full list of titles in the series, go to https://press.princeton.edu/series/princeton-studies-in-muslim-politics

Malika Zeghal, *The Making of the Modern Muslim State: Islam and Governance in the Middle East and North Africa*

Ismail Farjie Alatas, *What Is Religious Authority? Cultivating Islamic Community in Indonesia*

Sean Roberts, *The War on the Uyghurs: China's Internal Campaign against a Muslim Minority*

Walter Armbrust, *Martyrs and Tricksters: An Ethnography of the Egyptian Revolution*

Muhammad Qasim Zaman, *Islam in Pakistan: A History*

David Kloos, *Becoming Better Muslims: Religious Authority and Ethical Improvement in Aceh, Indonesia*

Alexander Thurston, *Boko Haram: The History of an African Jihadist Movement*

Gilles Kepel, with Antoine Jardin, *Terror in France: The Rise of Jihad in the West*

John R. Bowen, *On British Islam: Religion, Law, and Everyday Practice in Shari'a Councils*

Lihi Ben Shitrit, *Righteous Transgressions: Women's Activism on the Israeli and Palestinian Religious Right*

Bernard Rougier, *The Sunni Tragedy in the Middle East: North Lebanon from al-Qaeda to ISIS*

Nadav Samin, *Of Sand or Soil: Genealogy and Tribal Belonging in Saudi Arabia*

Avi Max Spiegel, *Young Islam: The New Politics of Religion in Morocco and the Arab World*

Ellen Anne McLarney, *Soft Force: Women in Egypt's Islamic Awakening*

Esra Özyürek, *Being German, Becoming Muslim: Race, Religion, and Conversion in the New Europe*

Lara Deeb and Mona Harb, *Leisurely Islam: Negotiating Geography and Morality in Shi'ite South Beirut*

The Making of the Modern Muslim State

ISLAM AND GOVERNANCE IN THE MIDDLE EAST AND NORTH AFRICA

MALIKA ZEGHAL

PRINCETON UNIVERSITY PRESS
PRINCETON & OXFORD

Published by Princeton University Press
41 William Street, Princeton, New Jersey 08540
99 Banbury Road, Oxford OX2 6JX

press.princeton.edu

Library of Congress Control Number: 2023947031

ISBN 9780691259673
ISBN (paperback) 9780691134369
ISBN (e-book) 9780691189031

British Library Cataloging-in-Publication Data is available

Editorial: Fred Appel and James Collier
Production Editorial: Mark Bellis
Jacket Design: Katie Osborne
Production: Erin Suydam
Publicity: William Pagdatoon
Copyeditor: Karen Carroll

Jacket image: Modern Qur'anic School, Sfax, Tunisia, ca. 1920.
From the author's personal archives.

This book has been composed in Arno

Printed on acid-free paper. ∞

Printed in the United States of America

10 9 8 7 6 5 4 3 2 1

To my family

CONTENTS

TABLES

NOTE ON TRANSLITERATIONS

ARABIC AND TURKISH words are transliterated following the system of the *International Journal of Middle East Studies* (IJMES), without the initial *hamza.* I have generally not transliterated terms that are already widely used in English, such as fatwa, madrasa, waqf, Qur'an, hadith, sharia, Sufi, Sunni, and Shiite. The plural forms are usually indicated by adding an "s" to the word in the singular, with the notable exception of the term "ʿulamā" (singular: *ʿālim*), which I do not italicize (and for which I omit the final hamza) because of its frequent occurrence. For historical characters, places, and institutions, I have simplified the transliteration, such as Khayr al-Din (rather than Khayr al-Dīn) and Sahib al-Tabi (rather than Ṣāḥib al-Ṭābiʿ), or adopted the commonly used spelling, such as Abdeljelil Zaouche (rather than ʿAbd al-Jalīl Al-Zāwush), Sfax (rather than Ṣafāqis), or Djemaia (rather than Jamʿīyat al-Aḥbās). I sometimes use the term *Ḥabūs* (capitalized) when referring to the central administration that manages the *ḥabūs*, a term I use for the singular as well as the plural (rather than *aḥbās*).

ACKNOWLEDGMENTS

IN THE COURSE of preparing this book, I have incurred many debts, especially to my colleagues who have generously read and commented on parts or the entirety of the manuscript: Khaled El-Rouayheb, Edward Glaeser, Ellis Goldberg, Baber Johansen, Hedi Kallal, Mary Lewis, Kristen Stilt, Avram Udovitch, Lucette Valensi, and Mohammad Qasim Zaman. As this project took shape, I also benefited greatly from discussions with Latifeh Aavani, Omar Abdel-Ghaffar, Mohamed Abdelsalam, Asma Afsaruddin, Leila Ahmed, Yadh Ben Achour, Mohamed Arkoun, Lamiss Azab, Mahmoud Azab, Régine Azria, Lucy Ballard, Youssef Ben Ismail, Mahmoud Ben Romdhane, John Bowen, Leon Carl Brown, Barbara Lynn Carter, Houssam Chachia, Abdelmajid Charfi, Rachida Chih, Deirdre DeBruyn, Janan Delgado, Hichem Djait, Conor Dube, Diana Eck, Dale Eickelman, Lulie El-Ashry, Mary Elston, Roxanne Euben, Noah Feldman, Abdou Filali-Ansary, Owen M. Fiss, William Graham, Mona Hassan, Hatem Hattab, Bernard Haykel, Robert Hefner, Marwa Henchiri, Izza Hussin, Hédi Jallab, Philip Khoury, Gabriel Koehler-Derrick, Anthony T. Kronman, Kawther Latiri, Rémy Leveau, Johannes Makar, Jessica Marglin, Silvia Marsans-Sakly, Lenore Martin, Françoise Meltzer, Adam Mestyan, Roy Mottahedeh, Tamir Moustafa, Mohamed Naciri, Shady Nasser, Fatih Okumuş, Caitlyn Olson, Lauren Osborne, M'hamed Oualdi, Şevket Pamuk, Claire Parker, James Piscatori, Ayşe Polat, Moshe Postone, Jawad Qureshi, Intisar Rabb, Martin Riesebrodt, Rick Rosengarten, Emmanuelle Saada, Hafsa Saidi, Mohamed Saleh, Noah Salomon, Ari Schriber, Kathryn Schwartz, Nancy Schwartz, Michael Sells, Emad El-Din Shahin, Armaan Siddiqi, Munim Sirry, Winnifred Sullivan, Kathryn Tanner, Himmet Taskomur, Laura Thompson, Houari Touati, Cem Türköz, Guillaume Wadia, Lisa Wedeen, Julian Weideman, Kirsten Wesselhoeft, Leonard Wood, Kimberly Wortman, Béchir Yazidi, and Metin Yuksel.

I have also benefited greatly from comments I received while presenting parts of this research at the Institute for the Transregional Study of the

Contemporary Middle East, North Africa and Central Asia at Princeton University; the Hagop Kevorkian Center for Near Eastern Studies at New York University; the Institute on Culture, Religion and World Affairs at Boston University; Northwestern University Pritzker School of Law; the Graduate Institute of International and Development Studies in Geneva, Switzerland; Yale Law School's Dallah Albaraka Lectures on Islamic Law and Civilization; the Emile Bustani Middle East Seminar at MIT; the Julis-Rabinowitz Program on Jewish and Israeli Law at Harvard Law School; Indiana University's 15th Annual Wadie Jwaideh Memorial Lecture in Islamic Studies; the Tunisian Academy of Sciences, Letters and Arts (Beït al-Hikma); and Duke University's Islamic Studies Center.

Several institutions made this project possible. I would like to thank the Carnegie Corporation for granting me a Carnegie Fellowship in 2009 and the Radcliffe Institute for Advanced Study at Harvard University, where I spent the 2013–14 academic year as the Rita Hauser fellow. I thank Liz Cohen and Judith Vichniac for their support and for their comments on my project during that year. I am also thankful to the Weatherhead Center for International Affairs at Harvard University for supporting and organizing an Author's Conference in October 2014. I am grateful to the Faculty of Arts and Sciences at Harvard University for supporting the late stages of the manuscript preparation with a Faculty Publication Fund grant. I also must extend further thanks to Michael Hopper and Abdelaali Boutaqmanti at the Harvard Widener Library's Middle East, Africa, and Asia Division for helping me find sources for my manuscript. Last but not least, the Tunisia Office at Harvard's Center for Middle Eastern Studies has provided invaluable support. I extend particular thanks to Sihem Lamine for her continuous interest in my project. At the University of Chicago, Lauren Osborne and Jawad Qureshi provided superb research assistance, as did Jan Peter Bockstiegel, Clare Duncan, Faiq Habash, and Nisreen Shiban at Harvard's Radcliffe Institute for Advanced Study. Conor Dube meticulously reviewed the manuscript and offered invaluable comments. I thank Kenz Kallal and Claire Shi for their technical assistance with the tables.

I also thank Lucette Valensi for her generosity in sharing with me part of the vast correspondence written by the *qāʾid*s to the authorities in Tunis regarding the 1864 rebellion. These archives, compiled by Dr. Hachmi Karoui from ANT SH C184 D1034 and SH C184 D1039, provided the sources for a research project they conducted and remained unpublished. Special thanks also go to Şevket Pamuk for his guidance on GDP time series, to Ayşe Polat for helping me navigate the Ottoman and Turkish sources I consulted for chapter 5, to Silvia Marsans-Sakly for introducing me to the topic of the 1864 revolt in the Regency of Tunis, to Béchir Yazidi and Houssam Chachia for sharing with me their knowledge of the Tunisian archives, and to Kawther Latiri for sharing with me her knowledge of the democratization process in Tunisia after 2011.

Chapter 1 is related in part to my previously published article, "The Shaping of the 1857 Security Pact in the Regency of Tunis: A Reappraisal of the Nineteenth Century Constitutional Reforms," *Studia Islamica* 117, no. 2 (2022): 275–334. Chapter 3 is a substantially revised version of my chapter "Constitutionalizing a Democratic Muslim State without Sharia: The Religious Establishment in the Tunisian 2014 Constitution," in Robert Hefner, ed., *Shari'a Law and Modern Muslim Ethics* (Indiana University Press, 2016, 107–134). Chapter 5 is inspired by ongoing research projects with Hedi Kallal and with Ayşe Polat.

I would also like to extend my thanks to Fred Appel of Princeton University Press for his early support of the project as well as James Collier and Mark Bellis, also of Princeton University Press, for seeing the manuscript through the final stages. I am thankful to Karen Carroll for the wonderful copyediting. I am indebted to three anonymous reviewers for their invaluable comments and suggestions for improvement. All remaining errors are mine.

ABBREVIATIONS

AMAE	Archives du Ministère des Affaires Étrangères, La Courneuve, France
ANF-P	Archives Nationales de France, Pierrefitte-sur-Seine, France
ANOM	Archives Nationales d'Outre-Mer, Aix-en-Provence, France
ANT	Archives Nationales de Tunisie, Tunis, Tunisia
BEP	*Bulletin de l'enseignement public,* Morocco
BNF	Bibliothèque Nationale de France, Paris, France
BNT	Bibliothèque Nationale de Tunisie, Tunis, Tunisia
BOEP	*Bulletin officiel de l'enseignement public,* Tunisia
BODIP	*Bulletin officiel de la Direction de l'instruction publique,* Tunisia
CADN	Centre des Archives Diplomatiques de Nantes, Nantes, France
CDN	Centre de Documentation Nationale, Tunis, Tunisia
CHEAM	Centre des Hautes Études d'Administration Musulmane
ECM	École Coranique Moderne
EI[1]	*Encyclopedia of Islam,* first edition
EI[2]	*Encyclopedia of Islam,* second edition
EI[3]	*Encyclopedia of Islam,* third edition
IBLA	Institut des Belles Lettres Arabes
IFPO	Institut Français du Proche Orient
IHEM	Institut des Hautes Études Marocaines
IHET	Institut des Hautes Études de Tunis
ISHTC	Institut Supérieur d'Histoire de la Tunisie Contemporaine, Manouba, Tunisia

JORF *Journal officiel de la République française*

JORF-DP *Journal officiel de la République française: Débats parlementaires*

JOT *Journal officiel tunisien (Al-Rāʾid al-Tūnisī)*

JORT *Journal officiel de la République tunisienne (Al-Rāʾid al-Rasmī li-l-Jumhūrīya al-Tūnisīya)*

RPR *Rapport au Président de la République sur la situation de la Tunisie*

THE MAKING OF THE MODERN MUSLIM STATE

Introduction

IN THIS BOOK, I study how the role of Islam in governance has been conceived in the modern period,[1] how it has been implemented in concrete terms, and what has changed from premodern times. I do so by examining constitutional projects and debates from their onset in the modern Middle East as well as the evolution of public expenditures on religious provisions (Islamic worship infrastructure, Islamic education, Islamic courts and personnel, Islamic forms of public assistance) from the nineteenth to the twenty-first century, with some incursions into the further past. There is a vast literature on the premodern history of Islam in governance, which has notably discussed the distribution of religious authority among rulers and ʿulamā (religious scholars). Despite some scholarly disagreements about specifics,[2] a consensus seems to have emerged that the relationship between Islam and the state in premodern times was characterized by (1) a partnership between political and religious

1. By modern period, I mean the nineteenth to the twenty-first centuries, in a mere chronological sense.

2. For instance, Crone and Hinds (1986) argued that, in early Islam, religious authority was concentrated in the hands of the ruler. In contrast, Tyan (1938) argued that the prophet, as well as the first four caliphs, did not establish a new judicial system and did not act as judges. Also, Lapidus (1975, 364) argued that, by the tenth century, "Muslim states were fully differentiated political bodies without any intrinsic religious character, though they were officially loyal to Islam and committed to its defense." Lapidus (1975) interpreted Islamic history as a process of separation of religion and state through the emergence of a class of ʿulamā and their competition with rulers for religious authority, whereas Crone and Hinds (1986) saw the separation between religious and political authorities as a division of labor under the canopy of Islamic law, which prevented any separation of religion and state. Zaman (1997a, 1997b) showed that, except for the period of the *miḥna* under the Caliph al-Ma'mun, there is little evidence of a competition for religious authority between rulers and ʿulamā in the Abbasid period, whereas there is evidence for the continuity of their partnership.

authorities (notwithstanding confrontations and significant fluctuations in the balance of power in this partnership) and (2) the expectation that the state be what I will call throughout this book the custodian of Islam (the state-preferred religion), of its institutions, and of the Muslim community. Crone (2004, 286–314) enumerates the services medieval Muslims "expected from the state" from the point of view of the revealed law as well as its "non-*sharʿī*" duties: "the validation of the community" by the ruler who had to maintain the normative order of sharia, the "validation of public worship," the "execution of the law," the "execution of the *ḥudūd* [punishments]," the execution of "*jihād*," "commanding right and forbidding wrong," "the preservation of the religion" (*ḥifz al-dīn*), "fiscal services," "internal security," "roads, bridges, inns, walls, mosques, and other infrastructure," as well as "poor help, disability pensions, famine relief," "medical services," "education," and "culture." Many of the "non- *sharʿī*" state duties, such as the building of mosques and madrasas, and Islamic education more broadly, could also be understood as part of the preservation of the religion. Crone (2004, 395) also argues that "there was nothing specifically Islamic about [the rulers]," but that they had "a religious role to play" as "protectors of a religious institution." Stilt (2011, 26) provides another premodern example, that of the Mamluk sultans of Egypt, who, she shows, "undertook the fundamental duties demanded of a ruler of a Muslim polity: establishing prayer, collecting *zakāt* [almsgiving], appointing judges, carrying out punishments, and facilitating the pilgrimage." She underlines that "these are not isolated examples of a political entity taking an interest in the "religious" but rather some of the very core functions of the ruler."[3]

There have also been ample discussions in the literature about what changes the modern period brought to the relationship between Islam and the state. Responses have pointed to imperialism, colonization, nationalism, modernization and to the effect of various forces, such as secularism, to posit a radical rupture to this relationship. This book aims to contribute to these discussions by showing that the premodern partnership between rulers and ʿulamā has generally endured in modern Muslim-majority polities. Moreover, although new techniques of governance have been imported from the West in modern times, the state has generally continued to be expected to act as the custodian of Islam (its preferred religion, in the sense that it protects and supports Islam more than other religions). This has continued through a variety of contexts, including

3. Stilt (2011, 4) also shows, echoing in part Zaman (1997a, 1997b), how "policy concerns and doctrine interacted, cooperated and competed."

precolonial rule, colonial rule, nationalist struggle for independence, independent state building, authoritarian rule, and democratization. This duty is viewed by most political actors as indispensable and inextricably tied to sovereignty, even when exercised by a foreign, non-Muslim ruler. To be sure, the precise list of duties expected from and carried out by the state as the custodian of Islam has varied from time to time and from place to place, but three broad overlapping principles have persisted. The first is the preservation of *the religion*—for example, by guaranteeing worship, the celebration of Muslim holidays, or the organization of the pilgrimage but also by producing, disseminating, and enforcing specific interpretations of Islam articulated by state religious authorities and/or the public school system or limiting freedom of expression. The second principle is the preservation of *the Muslim community*—for example, by defending its borders or shoring it up against erosion through forbidding or preventing Muslims' conversions. Third is the preservation of *Islamic institutions*—for example, by upholding Islamic law, courts, and judges or funding Islamic education, schools, and teachers as well as places of worship and their personnel. Therefore, the state's custodianship of Islam as the preferred religion is a specific type of state engagement with religion. Indeed, state engagement with religion has been shown to be ubiquitous in premodern and modern times (whether supportive, neutral, or hostile), including in polities that aspire to separate religion and state.[4] Moreover, the state's custodianship of Islam does not necessarily imply the conflation between religious and political authorities, which is only one of its conceivable instantiations. Nor can it be reduced to the absence of state neutrality or of separation between Islam and the state: they are only two of its implications. And it does not preclude that the state might also be the custodian of religions other than Islam, even if Islam is the preferred one, or that there can be domains of equality between Muslims and non-Muslims. We do find such domains in modern as well as premodern times.[5]

Equally importantly, Muslims have vigorously debated how to implement the state's custodianship of Islam, and these debates have structured an important part of political life in most modern Muslim-majority polities. To be sure, neither its necessity nor the existence of debates about how to best implement it are distinctive features of the modern period; nor is the import of foreign

4. For a quantitative study of the various forms of contemporary states' engagement with religion worldwide, see Fox (2008, 2011, 2015); for a study of the United States, see Sullivan (2005); for an analysis of state support versus hostility toward religion, see Kuru (2009).

5. For some premodern examples, see Fierro and Tolan (2013) and Delgado (2022).

techniques of governance in Muslim states; nor are other significant changes in governance, such as those historically triggered by severe epidemics, conquests, invasions, economic crises, and so on. However, a central argument of this book is that, notwithstanding previous significant ebbs and flows of centralization and decentralization, at least one transformation of the modern period is truly unprecedented and has had a profound impact on the role of Islam in governance: the significant increase in the size and reach of the state, in absolute terms and in relation to the overall economy. Moreover, some features are distinctive of the modern period. New institutional forms have developed and expanded, old ones have disappeared or been marginalized, and debates about how to implement the state custodianship of Islam have involved new protagonists, such as mass political movements and parties (e.g., nationalist, progressive, or Islamist parties), in addition to old ones (e.g., rulers, state officials, ʿulamā, tribal leaders, ordinary people, or foreign powers). They have been influenced by the salient issues of the time, such as foreign occupation, world wars, the urgency of human and economic development, the integration of religious minorities into the nation, authoritarianism, and democratization. These debates and their concrete outcomes have therefore varied considerably in time and space.

State Custodianship of Islam in Constitutional Debates and in State Expenditures

To clarify the terms of the contemporary political cleavage on Islam in governance, and to retrace the historical continuity of the expectation that the state be the custodian of Islam, I start by examining debates throughout Tunisia's constitutional history since it is one of the oldest and longest among Muslim-majority polities.[6] This allows for a study of the conceptions and implementation of the state's custodianship of Islam in a particularly wide variety of contexts and for the disaggregation of what the debates on Islam and governance owe to historical contingencies from what they owe to the persistence of core principles. Tunisia's first constitution was proclaimed in pre-protectorate Tunisia in

6. The 1839 Ottoman Khatt-i Sherif of Gulkhane, a declaration of principles, and the 1856 Khatt-i Humayun, made up of more than thirty paragraphs, predate the Tunisian 1857 Security Pact and 1861 Constitution. However, they did not have the comprehensive legal reach of a constitution, despite the French use of the term "charter" or "constitutional charter" to characterize them at the time. See Charte des Turcs (1840) and Bianchi (1856).

1861, in a context of imperial competition and European penetration. Its 1959 Constitution was drafted at independence at the onset of an authoritarian regime and after a nationalist struggle against colonization, during which constitutional demands played a salient role. Finally, its third constitution, proclaimed in 2014, was drafted in a post–Arab Spring context of transition to democracy, and its fourth, in 2022, in a context of return to authoritarianism. Therefore, Tunisia's constitutional history is rather unique in that it allows us to examine conceptions of Islam in governance in contexts that span precolonial times, colonial rule, a nationalist fight for independence, the building of an independent state, authoritarian rule, and a transition to democracy. Moreover, since Tunisia is often deemed one of the most "religiously neutral" polities of the Middle East,[7] it is a particularly illuminating case to sustain my argument for the continuity of the state's custodianship of Islam as the preferred religion in most Muslim-majority polities and of the vigorous debates about its concrete implementation.

While it is not my aim to provide a continuous and exhaustive history of constitutional episodes and debates in the Middle East, I also thematically focus on key ones outside of Tunisia to illuminate my argument. I analyze constitutional debates about Islam in governance that took place in the 1920s, a period often described as a "liberal age" (and contrasted with later periods of alleged Islamization), when several Middle Eastern polities first drafted constitutions for their newly sovereign (or quasi-sovereign) states.[8] In particular, I examine the creation of the 1923 Egyptian Constitution by analyzing the debates on Islam in governance in its Constitutional Committee, which to my knowledge have not yet been the object of thorough scholarly attention. This is a particularly important case, not only because of its rich intellectual and political legacy and its paradigmatic status in the historiography but also because it immediately preceded the emergence of the Egyptian Muslim Brothers, one of the first and most influential organized Islamist movements. This allows for a reassessment of the Muslim Brothers' contribution to the conservative political tradition on the role of Islam in governance. In conjunction

7. For instance, Stepan (2012) points to Tunisia's "pioneering role in building constitutional and state structures that were religiously neutral [*sic*]." Similarly, Al-Azmeh (2020, 385–386) curiously claims that Tunisia was one of the very few "Arab state[s] without an official religion."

8. Other examples from this period, not examined in this book, include the 1923 Fundamental Law of Afghanistan, the 1924 Constitution of Turkey, the 1925 Constitution of Iraq, the 1926 Fundamental Law of the Hijaz, and the 1928 Constitution of Transjordan.

with an examination of the debates that took place during the creation of the 1920 Greater Syria Draft Constitution and the 1926 Lebanese Constitution (in two polities that are distinctive because of their large proportion of non-Muslims), it also allows for a study of the impact of the demographic weight of religious minorities on the role religion can play in governance and on the extent to which there can be a state-preferred religion. In addition, these three constitutional episodes provide us with organized and fully-fledged constitutional debates that took place in formal arenas of deliberation in the 1920s, when, in Tunisia, nationalists wrote their first known constitutional draft. In this process, constitutional demands were central to nationalist claims, but colonial authorities foreclosed democratic deliberations.

Lenses other than constitution making could be used—for example, treatises on governance, court decisions, chronicles, mirrors for princes, parliamentary debates, etc.—and I use some of these as a complement.[9] However, the study of constitution making presents the distinct advantage that, in Muslim-majority polities, constitutions are imported tools of governance in which the reaffirmation of the Muslim character of the state is often made evident by their drafters and is therefore discussed explicitly. Moreover, constitutional episodes are often moments of deep introspection by state and intellectual elites about their conceptions of governance. In Muslim-majority polities, they often crystallize existing disputes about how to preserve the state's custodianship of Islam as the preferred religion in the face of ongoing challenges. Therefore, my primary object of study is not the final texts of constitutions[10] but the negotiations and deliberations that took place during their making, unmaking, or modification.[11] The text of a constitution is usually too thin to be used by itself to analyze the conceptions of Islam in governance in a polity and the disagreements about it. It is often more revealing for what it does not say or for how it was deliberately mistranslated in foreign languages, as we will see in several instances. Moreover, constitutional clauses are sometimes not enforceable or not enforced, and are not necessary to implement the state's custodianship of Islam as the preferred religion. For instance, although a 1928 amendment to Turkey's Constitution removed its "Islam is the religion of the state" clause, which was present in the

9. Some works, such as Findley (2010) and Salomon (2016), use cultural productions.

10. Therefore, this book is not about "constitutional Islam" per se, as in Ahmed and Ginsburg (2014), or about Middle Eastern constitutions, as in N. Brown (2002).

11. Another important component in constitutional analysis is the judicialization of constitutions. See Moustafa (2018).

1876 Ottoman Constitution and in the 1924 Constitution of the Republic of Turkey—and although a 1937 amendment proclaimed secularism (*laiklik*) one of the principles at the foundation of the Turkish Republic—the state continued to be the custodian of Islam, the state-preferred religion in Turkey, as shown by the role of the Diyanet within the state bureaucracy, the state's ambition to define correct Islam,[12] and its training of religious personnel, albeit with significant fluctuations in enrollments (see chapter 5). Moreover, debates about the role of Islam in governance continued to animate Turkey's political life.[13] In fact, as of 2010, five Muslim-majority polities with a state-preferred religion[14] (more than 10 percent of them) do not have any establishment, source law, or repugnancy constitutional clauses,[15] and two (Syria and Sudan) have a source law clause but no establishment clause.[16]

In addition, I examine quantitatively the evolution of an important metric of the concrete implementation of the state's custodianship of Islam, aggregate state expenditures on public Islamic provisions (whether funded and dispensed directly, or indirectly—for example, via public religious endowments), in four Muslim-majority polities of the Middle East (Morocco, Tunisia, Egypt, and Turkey) from the nineteenth or twentieth to the twenty-first century, with some incursions into the further past and elsewhere in the Muslim world, such as tenth-century Iraq. This particular metric is appealing because (1) it captures a concrete and objective outcome (how much is actually spent or budgeted), with

12. Berkes (1964, 485).

13. For instance, in 2016, some members of the Islamist Party of Justice and Development expressed their wishes to draft "a religious constitution." The April 25, 2016 "declaration by the speaker of the Grand National Assembly of Turkey, Ismail Kahraman, a representative of the Party of Justice and Development." For a critique of this project, see Halil Karaveli, Turkey's Journey from Secularism to Islamization: A Capitalist Story, *Turkey Analyst*, https://www.turkeyanalyst.org/publications/turkey-analyst-articles/item/542-turkey%E2%80%99s-journey-from-secularism-to-islamization-a-capitalist-story.html, accessed December 9, 2018.

14. I use, as a proxy, the data set of polities with a state-preferred religion (i.e., with an "Official Support" variable named SBX greater than or equal to 8 as of 2010) according to the Religion and State Project, Round 3, which includes 183 of the most populous polities worldwide. Jonathan Fox, Religion and State dataset, http://www.religionandstate.org. Fox (2008, 2011, 2015).

15. Turkey, Northern Cyprus, Indonesia, Guinea, and Gambia.

16. I follow here the terminology of Stilt (2015). Constitutional establishment clauses—that is, clauses enshrining Islam as the religion of the state—are common (although not universal) in Muslim-majority polities. When they are present, they are often (89 percent of the time in the Middle East, and 83 percent overall) combined with clauses making Islamic law a (or the) source of legislation or repugnancy clauses. See table 8 for the frequencies of each type of clause in 2010.

less risk of interpretative bias than alternative metrics; (2) it allows more straightforward comparisons with nonreligious state undertakings, notwithstanding the challenge of determining what counts as religious and nonreligious; and (3) it allows more straightforward comparisons across time (including across centuries) and countries, notwithstanding the challenge of computing accurate relative price levels.[17] This allows for a quantitative identification of historical continuities and ruptures that have previously been overlooked. While my selection of countries for this study is far from exhaustive, their historical, political, and socioeconomic dissimilarities are significant enough to assess the robustness of my findings. That said, it might be illuminating to expand the range of this analysis to include, for instance, theocracies or polities that aspire to separate religion and state. In addition, I do not evaluate the extent of the state financial support of public religious provisions for the non-Muslim populations of Muslim-majority polities (a question that would deserve a study of its own) since my aim is to evaluate historically the extent of the state's custodianship of Islam, the state-preferred religion, and not that of other religions.

The Main Questions at the Heart of the Debates on Islam in Governance

Despite the persistence of a broad agreement on the principle of the state's custodianship of Islam as the preferred religion, at least four core and interrelated questions have shaped the terms of disagreements about the role of Islam in governance in Muslim-majority polities in modern times, regardless of the significantly different contexts and circumstances in which these disagreements arose and regardless of the specific, recurrent, or contingent issues being debated: (1) to what extent should Islamic principles constrain the state (e.g., in legislation or as a philosophy of governance), what I call the *thickness* of the state's custodianship of Islam, or the commitment of the state to Islamic principles in governance; (2) what is the extent of public religious provisions that the state should make available to Muslims (e.g., mosques, imams, Islamic education, Islamic courts and personnel, Islamic forms of public assistance), what I call the *munificence* of the state's custodianship of Islam, or the state's commitment to Islam from a material point of view; (3) to what extent should

17. Alternative metrics, which have their own virtues, include expert coding of laws and regulations and government practices, such as in Fox (2008, 2011, 2015).

the state constrain Islam and its institutions with its coercive and pedagogical apparatus (e.g., by imposing its own interpretations of Islam), what I call the *strength* of the state's custodianship of Islam, or the degree of state control of the religion, the Muslim community, and its institutions; and (4) who can partake in implementing and discussing the state's custodianship of Islam? While the first three questions are mostly about *outcome*, this fourth question is more about *process* and addresses in particular the organization of the partnership between political and religious authorities. Political actors often describe it as the question of the legitimacy of "mixing religion and *politics*," sometimes (and wrongly) confused with the question of separation of religion and *state* in the literature. For instance, an issue often at stake is whether the ʿulamā, the experts in sharia, should engage with politics (*siyāsa*). They might bring religion into politics when reproaching the ruler for his lack of commitment to Islam—for example, a too thin and not sufficiently munificent custodianship of Islam (see chapters 1 and 5). In the face of too strong a state custodian of Islam, they might opt for a quietist attitude, leaving politics to governing elites, which can also lead to tensions (see chapter 1). Other examples we will encounter include debates about the extent to which political competition should be influenced by religion—for example, by organizing political representation along sectarian lines (see chapter 4)—and whether to disallow politics in mosques or political activism based on Islamic principles (see chapter 3). States that are strong custodians of Islam often prohibit civil society from mixing religion and politics in order to enforce their monopoly on this practice.

As we will see, disagreements about these four interrelated core questions—their formulations; their connections with specific, recurrent, or contingent issues; and the answers that were provided—have varied considerably in the history of the modern Middle East. Therefore, we can observe state custodianships of Islam that differ in strength, thickness, and munificence, with varying degrees and forms of the mixing of religion and politics. We also consistently observe political battles between two camps: those who, in response to these four questions, argue for increasing the role of Islam in governance and those who argue for decreasing it in their respective times and places. There is, of course, considerable regional and historical variation in the ideological characteristics of these two camps: arguing for a larger or smaller role for Islam in governance takes different meanings depending on the status quo. Moreover, we can observe ideological diversity as well as ideological evolution within each camp, which will be highlighted throughout this book. Even though these labels are imperfect and might sometimes be anachronistic, I will usually call these two camps "conservative" on the one hand and "liberal" on the other hand. I will also sometimes use common contextual labels for ease of exposition. In real life, in the twentieth century, conservative political actors are often referred to as "conservatives" (*muḥāfiẓūn*), and liberal political actors as "liberals" (*aḥrār*),[18] but also as "progressives" (*taqaddumīyūn*), "modernists" (*ḥadīthīyūn*), or "civil" (*madanīyūn*), three labels that many conservatives have also, at times, claimed for themselves. In the heat of the battle, some in each camp have used other, sometimes inflammatory or self-flattering, labels—such as "atheists" (*mulḥidūn*), "nominal" or "geographical" (*jughrāfīyūn*) Muslims, "nonreligious" (*lā-dīnī*), or "enlightened" (*mustanīrūn*) to refer to liberals; and "reactionaries" (*rajʿīyūn*), "fanatics" (*fanatiques*), or "servants of the religion" (*khadamat al-dīn*) to refer to conservatives. The term "Islamists" (*Islāmīyūn*) is also often used to refer to conservatives when organized into movements or parties.[19] I will only use this label contextually to refer to specific movements labeled as such, and the terms "Islamism" or "political Islam" to refer to their ideologies, without ascribing conceptual definitions to these terms.[20] On the other hand, although political actors (especially conservatives) and scholars and observers (especially in the West) often use the term "secularist" (*ʿilmānīyūn*)[21] to refer to liberals, I refrain from using it because it could imply support for the separation between Islam and the *state*, or for state neutrality, a rarity in most (albeit not all) Muslim-majority polities in the period under

18. On the meaning of the Arabic adjective *ḥurr* in the Arab Middle East in the last decades of the nineteenth century, see Abu-Uksa (2016, 194).

19. Lauzière (2015, 17) points out that the term "Islamism" was used by Hassan al-Banna as early as 1944. The actual Arabic word he used was "*Islāmīya*." See Ḥasan al-Bannā, Bayn al-Qawmīya wa-l-Islāmīya [Between nationalism and Islamism], *Al-Ikhwān al-Muslimūn*, January 29, 1944, vol. 2, no. 27, 3–4.

20. Definitions the literature has given of these terms vary from the narrowest to the broadest, making their use as concepts (as opposed to labels) unhelpful to analyzing the terms of the debate on Islam in governance. Definitions range from the project of implementing sharia and/or rejecting Western liberal ideas, which are specific and contextual instantiations of conservative (and Islamist) articulations about the role of Islam in governance, to, for instance, the definition of political Islam by John Voll and Tamara Sonn in *Oxford Bibliographies Online*—"Any interpretation of Islam that serves as a basis for political identity and action"—which is so broad in scope that it would encompass most political movements and actors in the modern Middle East and would therefore also lead to mischaracterizing the terms of the debate on Islam in governance.

21. We find two pronunciations of the term: *ʿalmānīya* and *ʿilmānīya*, with the latter appearing to be the oldest, dating back at least to 1882 as attested in Steingass (1882, 350). See, for a brief genealogy, Al-Azmeh (2020, 7).

study. In fact, as we will see, many liberals do not even advocate for separating religion and *politics*, for instance when asking for political representation of religious minorities. That said, I will not give unwarranted importance to labels since my aim is to analyze the substance and the history of ideological agreements and disagreements about the role of Islam in governance.

With this in mind, in the debates about Islam in governance in relation to the four aforementioned main questions, conservatives argue for a thicker state custodianship of Islam whereas liberals advocate for a thinner one—that is, for fewer Islamic constraints on the state. Conservatives also argue for a more munificent state custodianship of Islam; they aim to expand the place of Islam in governance by increasing state-funded religious provisions, whereas their liberal adversaries aim to shrink it by decreasing them. On the other hand, on the issues of the strength of the state's custodianship of Islam and the mixing of religion and politics, the picture is more complicated. Liberals, who argue for a thinner state custodianship of Islam often also advocate for a stronger one—that is, for its coercive implementation—and would in that case be better described as illiberal progressives. For instance, they often advocate for specifying and enforcing a "correct Islam" and for imposing limits on their (conservative) political adversaries' freedoms of expression and association—for example, by outlawing the "mixing of religion and politics." However, they seldom argue for separating Islam from the state or for state neutrality, converging in this regard with conservatives. On the other hand, conservatives generally support "mixing religion and politics" since they often argue that policies can and should be derived from religious doctrine. They also often support a weak state custodianship of Islam, in response to the repression some of them endure or have endured from authoritarian regimes in their respective countries. However, they might advocate for a stronger one if the state abides by an Islamic philosophy of governance that is to their liking. Disagreements about the implementation of the state's custodianship of Islam are sometimes accompanied by disagreements about institutional forms (e.g., Islamic education in modern schools vs. in madrasas,[22] direct state funding and delivery of religious provisions vs. indirect via public religious endowments). They are also sometimes accompanied by disagreements about content (e.g., what constitutes Islamic knowledge). And disagreements about

22. I call "modern schools" those established in the modern period for the primary purpose of teaching imported European knowledge, as opposed to the madrasas whose primary purpose is the teaching of the Islamic sciences.

doctrinal matters (e.g., Sufis vs. anti-Sufis) are sometimes salient. However, as we will see in several instances, the liberal vs. conservative political divide over Islam in governance described above does not always overlap neatly with these disagreements about institutional forms, content, and doctrinal matters. In addition, it has recurrently come to the fore in discussions about how to maintain the Muslim character of the state even (and especially) in the face of pressing challenges of a nonreligious nature.

The Concrete Implementation of the State Custodianship of Islam: A Quantitative Evaluation

We can observe that, as of 2010, all twenty or so Muslim-majority Middle Eastern polities—except for highly religiously fractionalized Lebanon, and including Turkey, despite its constitutionalization of "*laiklik*" (secularism)—have a state-preferred religion, Islam.[23] Outside of the Middle East, the only exceptions to this empirical regularity among Muslim-majority polities are those that were formerly part of the Communist Bloc[24] and six out of the ten Muslim-majority West and Central African countries.[25] Overall, 88 percent of the population of Muslim-majority polities around the world, and 99 percent in the Middle East, live under a state that favors Islam (table 8). The fact that there are exceptions to this empirical regularity shows that the state having a preferred religion is not an inevitable or essential feature of Muslim-majority polities. Moreover, this feature is not distinctive of these polities, since 45 percent of other polities have a state-preferred religion. However, it is much more prevalent among Muslim-majority polities (being present in 71 percent of them), a difference that is both substantial and statistically significant.[26] A worldwide statistical analysis of the factors that might influence the odds of a state having a preferred religion strongly suggests that it is a variable of choice,[27] subject to

23. As mentioned above, I use as a proxy the data set of polities with a state-preferred religion according to the Religion and State Project, Round 3. Fox (2008, 2011, 2015).

24. Six former Soviet republics as well as Albania and Kosovo.

25. Niger, Senegal, Mali, Burkina Faso, Sierra Leone, and Chad.

26. P-value = 0.001.

27. Why this particular choice is prevalent is, in my view, a matter of collective preferences, for which I do not have a causal explanation, contrary to M. Cook (2014), who puts forward "the foundational texts" of the Islamic tradition and what he calls "heritage" as an explanation of a related, albeit not identical, question: Why does Islam play "a larger role in contemporary politics than other religions?" While I acknowledge the weight of past choices, I identify one

certain constraints (notably, the demographic weight of religious minorities). Neither GDP per capita, average years of schooling, nor an index of political rights significantly influences these odds, whereas the demographic weight of the religious majority does: it increases them in a substantial and statistically significant way.[28] We will see this effect in action in the constitutional episodes analyzed in this book, when the anxieties of the majority about being governed by the minority have collided with the anxieties of the minority about not having its rights protected. We will see that the larger the demographic weight of religious minorities, the more effective their resistance to the majority's ambition to favor its own religion.

I also find that Muslim states have ensured that their custodianship of Islam is implemented concretely, by providing financial support to religious institutions and by funding public religious provisions.[29] Therefore, such financial support has largely been, and continues to be, a state affair, which the state might provide directly (from the state treasury) or indirectly—notably by way of funding and overseeing religious endowments (waqf or *ḥabūs*) or by subsidizing and leveraging the capabilities of civil society. That said, despite its symbolic prominence in official public records, the extent of this financial support has historically been modest in relation to other public expenditures, and particularly in relation to the overall economy, with significant variations across time and space. In addition, with the massive and unprecedented increase of the size and reach of the state in the modern period—a global phenomenon

element of the Islamic tradition that has remained, the necessity of the state custodianship of Islam as the preferred religion, while many other elements have been abandoned along the way, a fact that M. Cook (2014) does not address.

28. GDP per capita and mean years of schooling from the World Bank, UNDP, and the CIA Factbook; political rights rating (out of 40) from Freedom House; population data from the Pew Research Center and the World Religion Project in Maoz and Henderson (2013). In multivariate analysis, the coefficient on the demographic weight of the religious majority is statistically significant, in contradistinction to the coefficients on these socioeconomic and political rights variables. Its statistical significance is robust to potential measurement error and endogeneity bias correction, and its estimated magnitude is in fact *larger* after such correction. This is important since population censuses often constitute major political issues and are therefore the object of suspicion and manipulation, as this statistical finding would also suggest. Barro and McCleary (2005) obtain a similar result using multiple earlier data sets but interpret it as supporting a market model.

29. In this book, "public provisions" exclude goods supplied within the family as well as those supplied on a user-fee basis.

(albeit not perfectly synchronized across polities)[30]—while the extent of public religious provisions may have decreased in proportion to other state expenditures (as shown for Tunisia in table 2), it has significantly increased in per capita real terms (table 2). This two-pronged, paradoxical, long-term trend has been particularly pronounced in religious education: by implementing universal or quasi-universal public schooling, Muslim states have been able to disseminate Islamic education at an unprecedented scale, reaching the vast majority of their Muslim population and exposing it to an unprecedented number of hours of religious instruction (tables 4a and 4c). Yet, at the same time, the relative share of hours devoted to religious education in school curricula has drastically decreased (table 4c). This trend has fed the (preexisting) debate between conservatives and liberals about the appropriate extent of public Islamic provisions, and policy tugs-of-war between the two camps have led to significant short-term expansions and contractions in the munificence of the state's custodianship of Islam. In addition, these trends and fluctuations have fed academic debates between those scholars who highlight what they see as a process of overwhelming secularization, and who sometimes claim that the modern state annihilated Islamic institutions, and those who highlight what they interpret as an Islamic revival or even a "hegemonic Islam."[31] In reality, (expanding) Muslim states have persisted in their unwavering financial support for religious institutions throughout the modern period. To be sure, Muslim states have provided their support on their own terms, and their means of delivery of public religious provisions have often taken new institutional forms, notably in an effort toward centralization and efficiency. Moreover, some public religious provisions have been drastically deprioritized, or even eliminated, in favor of others. However, these transformations have removed neither the ideal of the state's custodianship of Islam nor the reality of its concrete implementation. Similarly, although they have created new challenges, expectations, and opportunities for both Muslim states and ʿulamā, these transformations have diminished neither the importance of their partnership nor the ʿulamā's ambivalence toward the state (and vice-versa). The ʿulamā have continued to ask for financial support from the state but also for more autonomy. Rulers and state officials have continued in their unwavering financial support for religious institutions but have also continued to strive to

30. Karaman and Pamuk (2010).

31. For instance, Asad (1993) and Hallaq (2013) on the one hand, and Kepel (1985a) and Starrett (1998) on the other.

control them, often while attempting to keep them at a safe distance in order to keep them out of politics and to better manage the expectations of the Muslim community.

Reassessing the Novelty of the Politicization of Islam

Given their importance in the political life of many Muslim-majority countries, and the sustained scholarly and journalistic attention they receive, I also examine and reassess the ideological contribution of organized Islamist movements (at the time they were formed) to the debate about Islam in governance. I find that these movements joined a preexisting intellectual and political battle between conservatives and liberals, rehearsing ideological repertoires formulated by earlier conservatives who sought to expand the role of Islam in governance. I show that the Egyptian Muslim Brothers (founded in 1928 and one of the earliest organized Islamist movements, with the broadest and deepest impact on other such movements) merely repurposed, at their inception, conservative tropes that already resonated in and around the 1922 Egyptian constitutional debates. Therefore, their entry into the political scene marked the advent of mass politics rather than an ideological rupture.[32] If there was a rupture with the past at the time, it was in the means and unprecedented scale of the dissemination of and mobilization around political projects, which can in fact be observed across the political spectrum. Indeed, the thrust of the Muslim Brothers' project was actively promoted, against their liberal adversaries, by conservative ʿulamā in the public and political arena well before Hassan al-Banna established his society, notwithstanding his and other Muslim Brothers' self-serving claims that the ʿulamā were politically (and religiously) passive. Contrary to what is often argued in the literature, the Muslim Brothers'

32. By mass politics, I mean the massive scale of the dissemination of ideas and of the political organization, mobilization, and competition that we observed in the Middle East in the twentieth century. However, I will not venture to date its advent with precision, to fully characterize it, or to describe all its effects. Freeden (2003, 31–33) argues that, in Europe, "the advent of mass politics . . . saw the consolidation of traditions of political thought such as liberalism, conservatism, and socialism." In the same vein, one could argue that the advent of mass politics in the Middle East saw the consolidation of the liberal and conservative traditions of political thought, with their respective projects to expand or reduce the role of Islam in governance, through what Freeden calls the introduction of "programmatic politics" and the "emergence of practical political thinkers who reinterpreted politics not only as a battle among power holders and notables, . . . but as a struggle over the minds of men and women."

project was therefore in continuity with a conservative tradition of political thought, and, as such, it did not result from social, economic, and political factors or dysfunctions,[33] nor was it the unintended consequence of misguided educational or other (indigenous or colonial) policies.[34] Some of these factors might play a role in explaining temporary regional variations or historical ebbs and flows in the strength (electoral or otherwise)—and especially the political and mobilization strategies (such as their use of violence or the moderation of their platforms)—of specific Islamist (and non-Islamist) movements in specific places at specific times. However, they do not explain the presence in the political arena of the political project of a more expansive role for Islam in governance and a thicker and more munificent state custodianship of Islam since this project predates them. And it might be premature to predict its decline.[35] As long as the state custodianship of Islam remains a broadly shared expectation, it is likely to remain a political issue, and disagreements as to how it should be implemented are likely to shape political life, just as those about governance issues of a nonreligious nature.

In the same vein, the impact of colonization, nationalism, independent state building, authoritarianism, secularism, liberalism, and democratization on the relationship between Islam and politics needs to be reassessed. Contrary to what is sometimes argued,[36] these recent historical developments should not be held responsible for the politicization of Islam: the principle of the state's custodianship of Islam and political debates about how to best implement it long preceded them and are inextricably tied to the exercise of sovereignty, including foreign and non-Muslim. This is clear from the history of modern Tunisia, where before, during, and after colonization, as well as under authoritarianism and during a transition to democracy, this principle

33. For such arguments, see, for instance, Ibrahim (1980), Davis (1984), Kepel (1985a), and Burgat (2003). Goldberg (1991) was among the first to question the "dysfunction" explanation of the emergence of Islamist movements. Factors put forward in the literature include economic crises, rapid urbanization, modernization and secularization, authoritarian repression by supposedly "secular" regimes, and exclusion from the political process but also, more recently, a variety of other institutional, organizational, geopolitical, or socioeconomic factors—e.g., in Masoud (2014), Mecham (2017), Brooke and Ketchley (2018), and the bibliography there.

34. For such arguments, see, for instance, Starrett (1998) and Beck (2009).

35. For such predictions, see, for instance, Mitchell (1969, xiii–xiv), Roy (1994), Bayat (1996), and Kepel (2002).

36. E.g., Starrett (1998), Karpat (2001), Nasr (2001), Moaddel (2005, 342), E. Thompson (2015, 2020), Wyrtzen (2015), Mahmood (2016), Fabbe (2019), and Laurence (2021).

was reaffirmed while at the same time its concrete implementation was vigorously debated in the political arena. During colonization, there were competing sovereignties, hence competing custodians of Islam: the state exercising or aspiring to exercise sovereignty was tasked with this custodianship. While these actual or potential custodians were all quite different, what was expected, even if a foreign, non-Muslim occupier was to be custodian, remained broadly the same: the preservation of the religion, the Muslim community, and its institutions. Other cases studied in this book also attest to the persistence of this principle, its tie to sovereignty, and the vigor of its attendant political debates, despite the wide diversity of contexts and circumstances.

Some Remarks on the Literature

One trend in the study of Islam and politics in the modern Middle East has developed in the comparative politics literature, often to explain the democratic deficit of the region and/or to identify ways to reduce it. It analyzes individual attitudes or the strategic choices of political actors under the constraints of institutional structures,[37] sometimes through the lens of social movement theory,[38] or by focusing on the regulation and institutionalization of religion,[39] or on patterns of distribution of religious authority instead,[40] and often by attempting to leverage institutional cross-country differences (rather than focus on persistent historical trends and commonalities across Muslim-majority polities). Works following this trend rarely examine the long history of political ideas and debates regarding Islam in governance. In addition, they rarely examine the liberal side of these ideas[41] and tend instead to disproportionately focus on organized Islamist movements and their conflict with supposedly "secular" governments in the twentieth century. They often reduce the relationship between Islam and politics to this antagonism and ignore the broad and long-standing agreement across the political spectrum that the state be the custodian of Islam, the preferred religion. As a result, they have searched for the institutional and/or

37. E.g., Lust-Okar (2007), N. Brown (2012), Jamal (2012), and Tessler (2015).

38. Notably Rosefsky Wickham (2002, 2013).

39. E.g., Zeghal (1999a, 1999b), Wiktorowicz (2001), Fregosi (2003), Feuer (2018), Fabbe (2019), and Laurence (2021) in a comparison with Catholicism.

40. E.g., Philpott (2007) in a comparison with other religions.

41. Exceptions include Rutherford (2013), who examines liberal Egyptian judges' rulings during the Mubarak era.

social "origins" of political Islam,[42] or of the politicization of Islam, in the development and innerworkings of nation-states and organized Islamist movements in the twentieth century, as if the issue of the role of Islam in governance were not an object of political contentions before that.

Intellectual historians have similarly searched for the intellectual origins of political Islam, but they go slightly further back: starting with the thought of Muslim reformists, typically Jamal al-Din al-Afghani (1838/39–1897) and Muhammad Abduh (1849–1905), transitioning to the writings of one of his students, Rashid Rida (1865–1935), and culminating with the political project of Hassan al-Banna (1906–1949) and the Muslim Brothers. Hourani (1962, 360) argued that the Muslim Brothers "accepted" the "general outlook" of Rashid Rida, although the latter "might have disapproved of [their] political methods." Mitchell (1969, 321–322) wrote that the Muslim Brothers "saw themselves clearly in the line of the modern reform movement identified with the names of Jamal al-Din al-Afghani, Muhammad Abduh, and Rashid Rida," and claimed that this was "a fairly accurate assessment of their role and that of the Society in modernist developments."[43] Dallal (2000, 357–358), Shulze (1990, 2000), Mayeur-Jaouen (2002), and Brunner (2009), in line with conventional wisdom, have also proposed a similar genealogy, presumably inspired by Hourani's (1962) research agenda, selection of authors, and periodization.[44] Albert Hourani's monumental and pioneering modern intellectual history of the Arab Middle East aimed "to relate different thinkers with each other, and to construct a chronological framework within which they could be placed," tracing "a line of descent of four generations of writers" from the 1830s to the

42. E.g., Brooke and Ketchley (2018) have studied the mobilization strategy of the Muslim Brothers at their formation, with the declared aim of finding the "social and institutional origins of political Islam."

43. Carré and Michaud (1983, 14–15 and 35) argue, in the same vein, that Hassan al-Banna was influenced by the "reformist, puritan but also rationalist" ideas of Muhammad Abduh and by Rashid Rida's *Al-Manār*.

44. For instance, Schulze (2000, 18 and 95) speaks of a transition from an intellectual movement that he calls "salafiya," that sought the "return to the 'pure' Islam of the forefathers (*al-salaf al-ṣāliḥ*)" and a "timeless aesthetic and intellectual ideal, derived from an origin that was pure of all temporal circumstances," to what he calls "neo-salafiya," i.e., a movement "of Islamic intellectuals who recognized the failure of the salafiya ulama and sought to found their own independent Islamic public." Mayeur-Jaouen (2002) and Brunner (2009) follow a similar thread, employing a vocabulary that suggests novelty (e.g., "neo-salafiya" and "new ulama"), and speak of a "turning point" or of a "new phase," after 1927–1928. See also P. Shinar and W. Ende, Salafiya, *EI*[2]. For a critique of the use of the notion of *salafīya*, see Lauzière (2015).

mid-twentieth century.[45] However, he treated these thinkers in isolation from their adversaries and therefore seldom explored the terms of the ongoing intellectual debate and political battle over Islam in governance. Taking this broad, linear intellectual history as their starting point, along with the Muslim Brothers' self-serving appropriation of a reformist legacy harking back to Muhammad Abduh,[46] intellectual historians overlooked the writings of those intellectuals who focused on issues of law and governance and who formed, in the words of Hourani (1962), "the first generation" to focus mainly on "the second generation" (revolving around Muhammad Abduh) and its bifurcation into "Muslim fundamentalism," which formed one aspect of "the third generation."[47] They were then left with the challenge of explaining what logically appeared to them as a puzzle: the shift from the sophistication of the earlier intellectual reformism of Afghani and Abduh to the more basic political project of the Islamists of the 1930s and 1940s and its mass appeal.[48] However, this apparent puzzle is an artifact of an approach that diachronically compares stances that are difficult to equate (e.g., the Muslim Brothers' stances on Islam in governance versus Muhammad Abduh's on, say, legal methodology) and that follows a linear succession of writers rather than a synchronic perspective

45. Hourani (1983, v–vi) In the preface of Hourani (1983, iv–x), a reissue of Hourani (1962), the author explains that the first generation he analyzed (1830–1870) was that of proponents and propagandists of the Tanzimat, such as Rifaa Rafi al-Tahtawi (1801–1873) in Egypt, Khayr al-Din al-Tunisi (d. 1890) in Tunis and Istanbul, and Faris al-Shidyaq (1804–1887) and Butrus al-Bustani (1819–1883) in the Levant. The second was represented by Muhammad Abduh (d. 1905), whose task was to "reinterpret Islam so as to make it compatible with living in the modern world," hence moving the analysis away from issues of governance. The third was that of Abduh's "disciples," such as Qasim Amin (d. 1908), Lutfi al-Sayyid (d. 1963), Ali Abd al-Raziq (d. 1966), Rashid Rida (d. 1935), and Taha Husayn (d. 1973), who, he argues, divided in "two strands of thought" represented on the one hand by "a kind of Muslim fundamentalism" and on the other by those who although they accepted Islam "as a body of principles, or at the very least of sentiments, . . . held that life in society should be regulated by secular norms." The fourth generation seems to have been shaped by Arab nationalism and Islamic fundamentalism.

46. Mitchell (1969, 321–322). See also Haddad (1998) on Rashid Rida's appropriation of Muhammad Abduh's legacy.

47. Hourani (1983, iv–x).

48. For instance, Schulze (2000, 93–94) invokes as explanations the economic crisis of the 1930s, the rural exodus to the cities, the exclusion from "the aspirations of colonial society," and the fact that, or so the author claims, Hassan al-Banna "was unable to integrate" and "politicized his own misery when he co-founded the Muslim Brotherhood."

on debates and disagreements.[49] Focusing on a specific issue instead, the role of Islam in governance, and following the history of intellectual and political disagreements on this issue tells us a radically different story: rather than a puzzling shift, we uncover an enduring political battle, one in which the Muslim Brothers simply appear to be new protagonists using the means of their time—that is, mass politics—which certainly made this battle much more noticeable to historians.

Another trend that has enjoyed prominence, inspired by Foucault (1969), Said (1978), and the variegated poststructuralist literature, is notably represented by Asad (1993, 2003), Mahmood (2005, 2016), Agrama (2010, 2012), and Hallaq (2013). It has looked for newly emerging concepts and categories of thought related to religion in modern times as evidence of profound transformations of Islam in Middle Eastern states and societies.[50] When seeking to identify historical ruptures, scholars following this research agenda often deem conceptual reformulations sufficient to explain social transformations. They claim that in modern times the Middle East has become subject to a ubiquitous and hegemonic Western liberal "secularism."[51] This modern condition is at times defined as an aspiration to separate "church and state" or to make the state "neutral in regard to religion,"[52] which, as we will see in this book, are both

49. Albert Hourani was aware of the potential pitfalls of his methodology. Looking back at it in Hourani (1983, iv–x), he underlined the "risk . . . of imposing an artificial unity on [these thinkers'] thought, of making it seem more systematic and consistent than in fact it was," and acknowledged that he started with "a debate which began on the level of political institutions or laws" and continued toward broader questions "about how men and women identified themselves and what they could believe about human life." He also acknowledged that he did not investigate why and how intellectual influences took place and that he was mainly interested to "note the breaks with the past: new ways of thought, new words, or old ones used in a new way." As a result, he focused very little on conservative articulations.

50. For instance, Asad (2003, 25 and 209) argues that "changes in concepts articulate changes in practice" and aims to explore "precisely what is involved when conceptual changes in a particular country make "secularism" thinkable." For a critique of the claim that religion is a distinctively modern epistemological category, see Riesebrodt (2010).

51. For instance, Mahmood (2016, 10 and 208) wants to account for the "epistemological hegemony of European forms of life and historical teleology" and argues that, "as a feature of liberal political rule, secularism characterizes all modern societies." For similar claims, see also Asad (1993, 7–24 and 191) and Asad (2003, 25).

52. Mahmood (2016, 105) defines the "classic framework of liberal secularism" as "how to engineer a system of governance that was neutral in regard to religion while at the same time allowing it to flourish in the social and civic life of the polity." Mahmood (2016, 20–21) also

largely (albeit not completely) absent from the political history of the modern Middle East, as both aspirations and realities. At other times, "secularism" is extended to mean the state regulation of religion and the delimitation of the proper place it must occupy,[53] two features that, as we will see and as is already well-known, are not distinctive of modern times. In other instances, this modern condition is taken to mean the "separation of religion and politics."[54] However, as we will see, in the modern Middle East separation of religion and *politics* has often served as a means for the state to enforce a specific understanding of Islam, and also to keep religious minorities' political ambitions at bay and keep Islam the sole state-preferred religion. This trend in the literature posits (rather than documents) a radical rupture in the role of Islam in governance between premodern and modern times. It overlooks past conceptions of secular domains of human activity in the long history of Islam and ignores the ambitions of premodern Muslim states to regulate and bound specific religious domains, even though these past conceptions and ambitions have been amply documented, in Imber (1997), Zaman (1997b), Hallaq (1997), Dakhlia (1998), Al-ʿAẓma (1998), and Stilt (2011) among others. It also elides most modern Middle Eastern states' duty and ambition to be the custodians of Islam as the preferred religion, a broadly shared expectation, and ignores modern conservative articulations of the role of Islam in governance. It only acknowledges remnants of a premodern Islamic tradition that the inescapable and universal force of Western modern

---

argues that "political secularism is not *merely* the principle of state neutrality or the separation of church and state. It also entails the reordering and remaking of religious life and interconfessional relations in accord with specific norms, themselves foreign to the life of the religions and peoples it organizes." Emphasis is hers.

53. Mahmood (2016, 3) defines "political secularism" as "the modern state's sovereign power to reorganize substantive features of religious life, stipulating what religion is or ought to be, assigning its proper content, and disseminating concomitant subjectivities, ethical frameworks, and quotidian practices." Agrama (2012, 28) defines secularism as "a problem-space," i.e., "the ensemble of questions, stakes, and range of answers that have historically characterized it," with at its center "the question of where to draw a line between religion and politics (and a presupposition that there *is* a line to be drawn)." He acknowledges that "there were certainly discussions and instances of the separation of temporal and spiritual power" in medieval times, but he does not say (or document) what the premodern identifiable stakes were (or were not), only that in modern times the stakes "are the rights, freedoms, and virtues that have become historically identified with liberalism, such as legal equality, freedom of belief and expression, tolerance, as well as the possibilities and justifications for peace and war."

54. E.g., Mahmood (2016, 87) speaks of "the secular promise of the modern state to keep religion and politics separate."

liberal secular governance allegedly annihilated, and it provides scant empirical evidence for this sweeping claim. In fact, Asad (2003, 206) claims that "the issue here is not an empirical one" and that "it will not be resolved simply by more intensive archival research" and "mere ethnographic fieldwork."[55] Hence, these works often read as thought-provoking ruminations on the modern condition, and especially the anxieties it provokes, but do not deliver on their promise to illuminate the rupture they posit.[56]

What This Book Strives to Do Instead

With this in mind, I strive to identify, through empirical (discursive and quantitative) evidence in the *longue durée,*[57] historical continuities as much as ruptures. I also strive to relate the history of ideas about Islam in governance to concrete history—that is, to concrete aspects of the state's custodianship of Islam—and, when relevant, to economic and demographic contexts, since I analyze ideas about Islam in governance as answers to concrete challenges and aspirations. I put the broadly shared expectation that the state be the custodian of Islam as the preferred religion at the center of my analysis and I examine (as much as possible in actual loci of political deliberation, with a particular attention to indigenous protagonists' points of view) intellectual and political debates about how this custodianship should be carried out. This vantage point allows me to broaden the scope of the study of Islam in governance in the modern period beyond (and, when appropriate, in combination with) mechanisms of state regulation, instrumentalization, institutionalization, and control of religion, or distribution of religious authority, and beyond an overly narrow focus on legal procedures and practices.[58] From the vantage point of the state's custodianship of Islam as the preferred religion, these mechanisms and organizational aspects are simply means to an end, although they are certainly often quite salient. They are, in fact, also often at play in polities in which the state is not the custodian of a preferred religion, including those that aspire to separate religion and state. However, they are only an accessory to the

55. However, note that Asad (1993, 167) also promises to "reconstruct in detail the historical conditions in which different projects and motivations are formed."

56. For incisive reviews of this trend in the literature, see March (2015) and Al-Azmeh (2020, xxiii–xxvi).

57. On some of these methodological points, see also Sewell (2005) and Armitage (2012).

58. On the disproportionate emphasis on law in the study of Islam, see S. Ahmed (2016).

question at hand: identifying the core agreements and disagreements about the role of Islam in governance in Muslim-majority polities. This approach allows me to paint a more complete and accurate historical picture of one of the most important political cleavages that animates political life in the modern Middle East and to reappraise claims that have been made in the literature about the ruptures of modern times.

What This Book Does Not Argue

First, while I underline the prevalence and historical persistence of the necessity of the state's custodianship of Islam as the preferred religion (and therefore of the absence of separation between Islam and the state and of state neutrality) in most Muslim-majority polities, I do not mean to essentialize it. I treat it as an empirical observation, by no means universal or inevitable. Notably, I do not argue that Islam is an inherently political religion, or more political than other religions,[59] or that the political in Muslim states is inherently or predominantly religious. In fact, I provide a quantitative evaluation of a well-bounded domain of state involvement in religion—public religious expenditures, relative to nonreligious ones, in modern but also premodern times—which shows just the opposite. I also do not make predictions as to whether the expectation that the state be the custodian of Islam as the preferred religion will continue to be prevalent in most Muslim-majority polities in the future, its historical persistence notwithstanding. In fact, I argue that it is rather a variable of choice, subject to certain constraints such as the demographic weight of religious minorities, and that this choice has been made, in the modern period, in full awareness of a wide array of alternative potential options as to the role of religion in governance. Different choices could therefore be made in the future. Nor do I theorize on the compatibility of Islam with democracy or with liberalism, freedom, or equality, in a scriptural or essential sense, although I study how these questions have been raised, answered, and debated by indigenous and foreign political protagonists throughout the modern period. We will see that such lofty notions have sometimes been embraced and implemented, and at other times qualified or rejected outright, sometimes with the help of religious scriptures and at other times in contradistinction to them.

59. This is, on the other hand, the argument of M. Cook (2014) in a comparative study of Islam, Christianity, and Hinduism.

Second, my focus here is not on individual conduct and subjectivities. It has been shown that there is a wide spectrum of attitudes among Muslims, from assiduous practice to rejection of Islam, including in Muslim-majority polities where Islam is the state-preferred religion.[60] In this vein, while I highlight the prevalence of a broad agreement on the state custodianship of Islam as the preferred religion in Muslim-majority polities, especially in the Middle East, I also find that some voices call (or have called) for a change in this respect, although they are rare and seldom express themselves in formal deliberative arenas.[61] This reinforces the fact that what is prevalent today, as far as the role of Islam in governance is concerned, is by no means ineluctable.

Third, while I begin with a study of the 1857–1861 Tunisian constitutional reforms, I do not argue that nineteenth-century constitutional innovations marked the beginning of "modern" political thought or other modernizing trends in the Middle East.[62] Nor do I argue that this was the first time that severe challenges induced changes in techniques of governance and prompted a reaffirmation of the ideal of the state custodianship of Islam as well as intellectual and political debates about how to best implement it. It is in fact my expectation that earlier debates about Islam in governance can also be illuminated by a conceptualization of change as recurrently prompted by new challenges, met by solutions that may unsettle existing ideals of governance and trigger disagreements.

Fourth, contrary to a recent literature that has interpreted the politicization of the issue of religious minorities in the Middle East as a "modern" phenomenon and/or has argued that minorities are a modern invention,[63] I do not

60. E.g., Mahmood (2005), Lybarger (2007), Schielke (2012), and Zeghal (2013b).

61. See, for instance, for a Sudanese voice, An-Na'im (2008), and, for a Tunisian voice, Mezghani (2011). See also, in chapter 4, earlier voices in 1920s and 1950s Syria.

62. Hourani (1962), Gran (1979), Levtzion and Voll (1987), Schulze (1990), and Dallal (2018), among others, have attempted to date such trends, albeit with scant attention to Islam in governance and to conservative articulations; and so have (with a focus on legal practice) works surveyed in Wood (2018, 554–555n10, and 577) as "revisionist."

63. For instance, Makdisi (2000, 7) relates the advent of sectarianism in Mount Lebanon (1830–1860), which he defines as "the deployment of religious heritage as a primary marker of modern political identity," to the process of modernization ushered in by the nineteenth-century Tanzimat. Similarly, White (2011) argues that modern governance in nation-states, with its principle of popular sovereignty and majority rule, is responsible for "the emergence of minorities in the Middle East." However, majorities and minorities, and, among other mechanisms, the balance of power between them, long preexisted nation-states, if not as analytical categories, certainly as empirical ones.

subscribe to such a periodization. Nor do I blame, as some authors do, "modern secular governance," the "modern liberal state," and "the epistemological hegemony of European forms of life and historical teleology" for the discrimination against religious minorities in Middle Eastern polities such as Egypt.[64] Instead, I analyze the issue of minorities in the early constitutional history of the Middle East as yet another instance in which, as in premodern times, the organization and management of religious differences and hierarchies under a Muslim state have constituted a political and legal issue that was discussed and instrumentalized by all protagonists, indigenous and foreign.[65]

Fifth, my continuity argument notwithstanding, I do not mean to minimize the changes that occurred during the modern period, notably with colonization, nationalism, independence, mass politics, the massification of education,[66] and democratization efforts. In fact, I highlight the implications of one unprecedented development of the modern period, the massive increase in the size of the state in absolute terms and in relation to the overall economy. I argue that however transformative and/or traumatic these historical developments were, two core features of the relationship between Islam and the state have generally remained: the necessity of the state's custodianship of Islam, the preferred religion, and vigorous debates about how to implement it. This is not to minimize the potentially traumatic effects of the displacement of some traditional institutions by new ones, or of the erosion of sharia as a technique and foundation of governance, a much-debated question as to its actual and desired extent. However, I do not venture to take part in this debate like Hallaq (2013), who argues

64. E.g., Mahmood (2016, 1, 2, 10, 26), whose reasoning can be summarized as follows: (1) religious minorities are discriminated against in Egypt; (2) Egypt has adopted "the principle of state neutrality toward religion" (an ambition that is, however, absent from the sources, as we will see in chapter 4); and therefore (3) it is the secular principle of state neutrality toward religion that is to blame for the discrimination against religious minorities in Egypt. Mahmood (2016, 2) also writes, without providing concrete evidence, "While Islamic concepts and practices are crucial to the production of this inequality, I argue that the modern state and its political rationality have played a far more decisive role in transforming preexisting religious differences, producing new forms of communal polarization, and making religion more rather than less salient to minority and majority identities alike." Whether the situation of religious minorities worsened or improved in the modern period in Muslim-majority polities, and in Egypt in particular, is a pertinent question and should be studied with the appropriate tools and metrics.

65. For premodern examples, see Cohen (2008), Rustow (2013, 307–332), and Yarbrough (2019).

66. See Eickelman (1992) for its impact on religious subjectivities in Arab societies.

that modern transformations removed the ideal of sharia from governance and that "*any* conception of a modern Islamic state is *inherently self-contradictory*."[67] Nor do I argue that this debate must be settled once and for all, as urged by some.[68] It is an integral part of political life in most Muslim-majority polities (historians of modern Europe would not, I believe, suggest that the contentious issues that animate political life in European countries should be settled once and for all). Further, I do not argue that the role of Islam in governance is the only issue at stake in the modern Middle East. Political life in this region of the world should be studied by rigorously identifying and historicizing other crucial issues that may be at stake, and that may or may not involve Islam.

Outline

In chapter 1, I study the making and the demise of the Regency of Tunis's 1857 Security Pact and 1861 Constitution, in a context of imperial competition, deep fiscal crisis, and, most of all, a battle for legal sovereignty between the bey's state and the European powers. I find that, with the importation of European techniques of governance and the erosion of sharia as a technique of governance, the state custodianship of Islam was strongly reaffirmed in the new legal framework and that vigorous debates, which have often been overlooked in the historiography, took place about how to best implement this custodianship.

In chapter 2, I examine the demands for a constitution and the constitutional projects articulated in Tunisia under French occupation (1881–1956) as well as the making of its 1959 Constitution. I find that, in continuity with precolonial times, the state's custodianship of Islam continued to be formulated as a duty that had to be fulfilled by the sovereign, be it the Husaynid dynasty for the bey, imperial "Islamic France" for the French and for Tunisian protonationalists and antinationalists, or a sovereign independent Tunisia (or Tunisian people) for nationalists. Once Tunisia became independent, debates focused again on how to best implement this custodianship, and I show that President Bourguiba not only arbitrated but also suppressed these debates by imposing an "authoritarian synthesis" between liberal and conservative conceptions of

67. Hallaq (2013, xi). Note, however, what seems to be a caveat on page 172. Emphasis is his.
68. E.g., Wood (2018, 569).

the role of Islam in governance, as other autocratic leaders have done in much of the contemporary Middle East.

In chapter 3, I turn to the post–Arab Spring democratic transition, and I examine the 2012–2014 debates of the newly elected Tunisian National Constituent Assembly. I show the remarkable persistence not only of the state's custodianship of Islam—the preferred religion—as an imperative but also the main elements of Bourguiba's synthesis, while vigorous debates between Islamists and their adversaries reactivated public expressions of a long-standing cleavage about the role of Islam in governance. I also show that, far from compromising on the substance of their disagreements, they built a framework through which Tunisians could continue to democratically debate and adjudicate them in the future.

In chapter 4, I examine and reassess a paradigmatic case, the making of the 1923 Egyptian Constitution, and the terms of the debate on religion and governance between liberals and conservatives in 1920s Egypt. This period is commonly celebrated as a "liberal age" later spoiled by the emergence of the Society of the Muslim Brothers. I find instead that the Muslim Brothers rehearsed already-resonating conservative tropes and did not innovate ideologically at their inception, and that there was a broad agreement between liberals and conservatives about the state being the custodian of Islam, the preferred religion. I also examine two constitutional episodes in polities with distinctly large proportions of non-Muslims—1920 Greater Syria and 1926 Lebanon—to analyze how the demographic weight of the religious majority influences the role religion can play in governance.

In chapter 5, I measure the concrete implementation of the state custodianship of Islam by estimating aggregate public religious expenditures from the nineteenth or twentieth to the twenty-first century in Tunisia, Egypt, Morocco, and Turkey, with some incursions into the further past, such as tenth-century Iraq. These expenditures have mainly been a state affair, and despite their symbolic prominence and the state's unwavering financial support for religious institutions (albeit on its own terms), they have been modest in relation to other state expenditures and especially in relation to the overall economy. While they may have decreased relative to other public expenditures in the *longue durée*, they significantly increased in per capita real terms, both driven by the unprecedented increase in the size and reach of the state in the modern period. I examine debates related to these long-term trends and to short-term fluctuations due to policy tugs-of-war between liberals and conservatives as well as disputes about the content and institutional form of delivery of public religious provisions. I also analyze the ambivalence expressed by ʿulamā (who yearn for autonomy and state financial support) but also rulers and state officials (who strive to control religious institutions while keeping them at a safe distance) about the state's support of, and meddling in, religious institutions. A summary of sources and methodology for the quantitative aspects of this chapter can be found in the data appendix.

1

The State's Enduring Custodianship of Islam

OLD IDEALS AND NEW TECHNIQUES OF GOVERNANCE IN THE REGENCY OF TUNIS'S 1861 CONSTITUTION

THE EARLIEST CONSTITUTIONAL episode in the Middle East took place in the Regency of Tunis[1] with the drafting and promulgation of the 1857 Security Pact (*ʿAhd al-Amān*) and the 1861 Constitution (*Qānūn al-Dawla al-Tūnisīya*),[2] which was suspended in 1864 after a revolt swept the Regency.[3] These legal reforms

1. For convenience, I often use "Tunisia" and "Tunisians" in lieu of the Regency of Tunis and the bey's subjects.

2. The 1861 Tunisian Constitution was officially named "law of the state" (*qānūn al-dawla*). The European consuls called it (as well as the 1857 Security Pact) a constitution. It was usually called a *qānūn*, and rarely, as in Qabādū (1875–1879, vol. 2, 63), a *dustūr*, a word of Persian origin that came to designate a constitution in Arabic in the early twentieth century. Dustūr, *EI*². The notion of *dustūr* was only evoked at the end of the 1861 Constitution's preamble in the sense of a "set of rules" or a "regulation." It stated that its dispositions "will last as a *dustūr* that will be consulted and that will be the only foundation relied upon." *Qānūn al-Dawla al-Tūnisīya* (1861, 13). Although the French called the Ottoman 1839 Khatt-i Sherif of Gulkhane and the 1856 Khatt-i Humayun "charters" or "constitutional charters," they did not have the comprehensive legal reach of a constitution. See Charte des Turcs (1840) and Bianchi (1856). An Ottoman constitution came in 1876.

3. The 1857–1861 constitutional reforms have notably been studied in Raymond (1953, 1964), Karoui (1973), Amor (1974), Chater (1975), Bdira (1978), Khadar (1989), Womble (1997), and Chekir (2006), and, indirectly, in L. C. Brown (1967, 2005), Slama (1967), Abdesselem (1973), Van Krieken (1976), Green (1978), Bashrūsh (1991), Marsans-Sakly (2010), Oualdi (2011), Ben Slimane (2012), and Al-Ṭayyif (2015).

joined a broader series of earlier reforms (military and fiscal in particular) that also aimed to save the bey's state. They were a response to severe and long-brewing economic, fiscal, judicial, and diplomatic challenges and were negotiated between Tunisian and European officials at a time when the Regency aimed to affirm its autonomy from Istanbul.[4] How did they conceive of the role of Islam in governance? What debates did they trigger? We will see how, in these negotiations, despite a lopsided balance of power with the Europeans (who were focused on facilitating their economic penetration and increasing their political influence in the Regency), the bey and his government continuously defended two central principles: the legal sovereignty of the bey's state (the power to judge all those established on its territory), which was increasingly challenged, and the state's custodianship of Islam—that is, the state's protection and preservation of Islam, the Muslim community, and its Islamic institutions. Therefore, contrary to what is generally assumed, the 1857–1861 constitutional reforms were coproduced by Tunisian and European officials from their inception, rather than entirely shaped by the latter.[5] Tunisian officials managed to introduce (and weaponize in this battle for legal sovereignty) notions of equality irrespective of religion for *all* inhabitants of the Regency, including foreigners, against the French government's wishes that these notions only apply to the bey's subjects. Most notions of equality irrespective of religion introduced by the reforms were rejected by Tunisian conservatives as in contravention to sharia, but Tunisian officials used them to attempt to subsume foreigners under the jurisdiction of the new Tunisian tribunals and hence to affirm the beylical state's legal sovereignty. And they reasserted sharia as an *ideal* of governance, and with it the state's custodianship of Islam, while sharia as a *technique* of governance was being eroded.

There were vigorous debates about whether sharia was also being eroded as an *ideal*, with the introduction of imported techniques of governance, and about how to best implement the state's custodianship of Islam. The reforms'

4. Despite some pressures, the role of the Ottoman state in drafting the 1857 Security Pact and the 1861 Constitution does not seem to have been central, although it would be important to further explore this point and Ottoman views of these reforms.

5. For instance, Raymond (1953, 261–263; 1964, 163) argues that the reforms became a "Tunisian affair" only after the promulgation of the Security Pact. For a review of the historiography on this point, see Zeghal (2022). See Benton (2002) for a broad study of the participation of indigenous people in the formation of new legal institutions in colonial (and imperial) contexts.

defenders employed a conceptual framework for the practice of change that they rooted firmly in the Islamic tradition, by way of expansion of the domain of temporal legislation (*qānūn*) in accordance with revealed law (sharia), but not everyone was convinced of the reforms' Islamic legitimacy. As an ideal—that is, as a philosophy of governance—sharia had no alternative in the eyes of the reforms' advocates. They were confident not only about the necessity to maintain it as an ideal but also about the adequacy of sharia to make room for change, and they described the constitutional reforms as simple reorganizations (*tartībs*). At the same time, they recognized that sharia's role as a technique of governance had to shrink to make space for new ones, including those imported from Europe. For their conservative critics, some of whom were also pragmatic and equally aware of the severe challenges faced by the Regency, this erosion bent the ideal of Islamic governance to an extent that made it unrecognizable and was therefore unacceptable. General Husayn (1826–1887), a Mamluk and high-ranking Tunisian official who participated in the reforms, used a revealing metaphor.[6] He compared Islam to a vessel (*ẓarf*) containing life in this world (*dunyā*) and argued that the vessel was already cracked (*thalmihi*) and could very well break if the reforms went too far.[7]

In contrast, the historiography has generally analyzed the 1857–1861 constitutional reforms as part of a broad and lasting reform process that put Tunisia and other Middle Eastern polities on a checkered path to "modernity."[8] By and large, it has dismissed the place of Islam in these reforms,[9] often arguing that Tunisian reformers used Islamic narratives as a superficial dressing and a ploy to make "westernizing" reforms palatable to traditional elites.[10] It has often overlooked

6. General Husayn studied at the Bardo military school (established circa 1840), as did Khayr al-Din, and was initially an officer under his command. He carried out official diplomatic missions in Italy and France, was president of the Municipal Council in Tunis from its 1858 creation until 1865, and was the president of the civil and criminal tribunal of Tunis from 1861 to 1863. For more details see Oualdi (2011, 2020).

7. BNT, ms. 18775, fol. 8; Bercher (1972, 78).

8. E.g., Chater (1975, 244) speaks of the 1857 Security Pact as "the birth of the liberal state" and as "a true bill of rights." For a review of some aspects of this historiography, see Zeghal (2022).

9. E.g., Van Krieken (1976, 51) argues that the legal reforms "seemed to prompt the principle of separation between state and religion."

10. E.g., L. C. Brown (1967, 63–64), Van Krieken (1976, 51 and 117), Green (1978, 117), Womble (1997, 57) and L. C. Brown (2005, 23–25 and 31).

the internal debates about Islam in governance that surrounded the making of the 1857 Security Pact and the 1861 Constitution,[11] underestimated the role of the Tunisian government in shaping the constitutional reforms,[12] and overestimated the rupture they brought to Tunisian conceptions of governance (particularly their secularization).[13] It generally assumes that these reforms were initially imposed by the European powers (motivated by self-interest but also constitutional idealism) and entirely shaped by them, but that once the Security Pact was promulgated, and despite initial reluctance from Tunisian elites, the reforms were then enthusiastically embraced by those same elites.[14] In this account, it is unclear how this conversion to constitutionalism would have taken place and why so suddenly. By focusing instead on the Tunisians' points of view, on their internal debates, on their negotiations with the Europeans from the very inception of the 1857–1861 legal reforms, and on the diplomatic, legal, economic, and fiscal context, I provide a more coherent picture of this constitutional episode.[15]

I have used documents from the Tunisian National Archives, which have not yet been fully exploited for the purpose of analyzing this constitutional episode, as well as the French, British, and other consuls' correspondence. I also draw on the writings of several important protagonists, notably Ahmad Ibn Abi Diyaf (1802 or 1803–1874),[16] a religious scholar and champion of the constitutional reforms who studied at the Zaytuna, the main Islamic institution of higher learning in Tunis, as did Muhammad Qabadu (1812–1872) and Bayram V (1840–1889), two prominent ʿulamā we will also encounter. Ibn Diyaf was born into a well-known Tunisian family and served as personal

11. E.g., Brown and Revkin (2018).

12. E.g., Raymond (1964, 163) argues that "Tunisian participation [in the drafting of the 1857 Security Pact], regardless of the role played by a few ministers, was limited and the new law came out ready from Roches' and Wood's files." Similarly, Karoui (1973) argues that it was "essentially the work of the French and English consuls." Most subsequent works follow this account.

13. E.g., Raymond (1964, 163; 1953, 261–263) argues that the 1857 Security Pact led to "a brutal change" and started an "irreversible process," and that at that moment "the movement of Reform began in Tunisia."

14. E.g., Raymond (1964), who attributes the 1857 Security Pact to the French consul's initiative and idealism.

15. Raymond (2009, 32–33) sees little coherence in the constitutional reforms and views the precedence of Tunis over Cairo and Istanbul in this regard as a puzzle. He describes them as fortuitous and as a "curious patchwork of the dispositions of the 1839 Charter of Gulkhane and the 1856 Khatt-i Humayun."

16. Hereafter "Ibn Diyaf," in line with the literature.

secretary (*kātib al-sirr*) to the beys from 1827 to 1864.[17] He expressed his views in his multivolume chronicles, *Itḥāf Ahl al-Zamān bi-Akhbār Mulūk Tūnis wa-ʿAhd al-Amān*, or "The History of the Kings of Tunis and the Security Pact Presented to the Contemporaries" (hereafter *Itḥāf*) written in the 1860s.[18] Another important protagonist is Khayr al-Din al-Tunisi (1820–1890), a Mamluk of Circassian origins, who rose to the rank of general in the bey's army, and occupied several important political posts.[19] He defended the spirit of the constitutional reforms in *Aqwam al-Masālik fī Maʿrifat Aḥwāl al-Mamālik*, or "The Surest Path to Knowledge Concerning the Conditions of Countries," which was published in Arabic in 1867[20] and in French in 1868.[21] It elicited interest beyond Tunis and Paris since it was wholly or partially translated into several languages, notably English in 1874, Urdu in 1875, and Ottoman Turkish in 1879.[22]

Section 1 examines the diplomatic, legal, economic, and fiscal context of the Regency of Tunis prior to the 1857–1861 legal reforms. Section 2 analyzes the making of the 1857 Security Pact as a battle for legal sovereignty between the beylical state and the European powers and how the ideal of Islamic governance was reaffirmed with it. Section 3 shows how this battle intensified during and after the making of the 1861 Constitution and was accompanied by narratives and counternarratives about the (in)compatibility of Islam and constitutionalism. Section 4 analyzes disputes among ʿulamā and state officials about the Islamic legitimacy of the reforms. Section 5 contrasts the motives of the 1864 revolt with the explanations provided by contemporaries aiming to justify or condemn the legal reforms. Section 6 explores how, after the reforms, Tunisian reformers conceptualized them in an Islamic framework for change.

17. Abdesselem (1973, 333–334).

18. Ibn Abī al-Ḍiyāf (1963).

19. After a stay in Paris from 1853 to 1857, Khayr al-Din became secretary of the navy (*wazīr al-baḥr*) in 1857, a post from which he resigned in 1862. He was prime minister from 1873 to 1877. In 1878, disillusioned with what he described as "a deplorable administration," he moved to Istanbul where he became grand vizier (1878–1879). Mzali and Pignon (1971, 26–27).

20. Al-Tūnisī (1867). For a critical study and English translation, see L. C. Brown (1967).

21. Al-Tunisi (1868), which was not a direct translation and was written under Khayr al-Din's direction.

22. Al-Tūnisī (2000, vol. 1, 23). For more details on the life and work of Khayr al-Din, see Mzali and Pignon (1971), Abdesselem (1973, 109–110 and 315–331), Van Krieken (1976), and Oualdi (2011).

1. The Road to the 1861 Constitution: The Regency of Tunis's Fiscal Challenges and Europe's Economic and Diplomatic Might

On September 15, 1860, on the advice of the French consul Léon Roches, Muhammad al-Sadiq Bey, the sovereign of the Regency of Tunis, set out on the Mediterranean. The steamship *La foudre* was sent by the French emperor Napoléon III to sail him to Algiers,[23] where he presented a draft of the new "law of the state," or *qānūn al-dawla*, to the emperor. The French called it a "constitution," a term the bey himself used in its Arabic transliteration, *kunstitusiyūn*.[24] In 1857 the bey had promulgated an organic law, the Security Pact (*ʿAhd al-Amān*), based on which the 1861 Constitution reorganized the state and guaranteed security and notions of equality to all inhabitants of the Regency (Tunisian subjects and foreigners), irrespective of their religion. The proclamation of the Constitution was a significant event, at home and abroad. It took place first on November 26, 1860, two months after the bey's visit to Algiers, and then again on April 23, 1861, when the bey convened in his palace his ministers, the ʿulamā from the sharia court, the members of the new tribunals, notables, military officials, and Jewish religious leaders. In a celebratory atmosphere, and in the presence of foreign notables and consuls, they reiterated their allegiance (*bayʿa*) to the bey and took a pledge to follow and defend the new law.[25] Celebrations lasted several days and were orchestrated with great pomp.[26] The bey received congratulations and medals from heads of European nations and was praised in the European press as an enlightened prince.[27] The Constitution was published in Arabic by the Tunisian state presses in 1861,[28] in a French translation that same year,[29] and in Judeo-Arabic in 1862.[30] Yet, behind the celebratory mood in official

23. The French minister of the marine to the French minister of foreign affairs, August 22, 1860, AMAE, Tunis, CP, vol. 19, fols. 236–237. Léon Roches accompanied the bey to Algiers. Roches to Benedetti, September 24, 1860, AMAE, Tunis, CP, vol. 19, fol. 277. This visit had been planned since July 1860 and the sharia court (*majlis al-sharīʿa*) authorized it on September 13, 1860. ANT SH C209 D159, no. 15.

24. The bey to the Italian consul Gambarotta, November 13, 1863, ANT SH C200 D3, no. 23, quoted in Ibn Abī al-Ḍiyāf (1963, vol. 5, 77–78).

25. Ibn Abī al-Ḍiyāf (1963, vol. 5, 42–62). The Constitution was put into effect on April 26, 1861.

26. Ibn Abī al-Ḍiyāf (1963, vol. 5, 46).

27. Ibn Abī al-Ḍiyāf (1963, vol. 5, 63). For instance, *Le Journal des débats* of July 12, 1861, 1.

28. *Qānūn al-Dawla al-Tūnisīya* (1861).

29. *Loi organique ou code politique* (1861).

30. See Valensi (1994, 102).

and diplomatic circles, important and unresolved problems lurked. When the bey sailed to Algiers in 1860, he was actually seeking the emperor's approval of a law that had been drafted after tense negotiations with the French consul Léon Roches and the British consul Richard Wood,[31] in the context of the Regency's long-brewing diplomatic, judicial, economic, and fiscal problems.

The Bey's Quest for Autonomy between Ottoman and European Ambitions

In the nineteenth century, the Regency of Tunis was the arena of a complex diplomatic rivalry between the Ottoman sultan, the French, and the British. The French encouraged the bey to seek autonomy from the Ottomans to bring the Regency under their influence and make it a buffer zone on the eastern border of Algeria, which they had started to conquer in 1830. They wanted Tunisia "to remain a small and almost independent state."[32] The British, on the other hand, sought to reinforce the relationship between the bey and the Ottomans to counter France's influence and economic penetration in the Regency.[33] As for the Ottomans, they had reasserted their sovereignty in nearby Tripoli in 1835. The Regency was therefore squeezed between the French on its western flank and the Ottomans in the east. The French recognized that the Husaynid bey still retained some of the marks of his earlier vassal status of pacha of an Ottoman province:[34] each new bey was officially confirmed by the Ottoman sultan after declaring his allegiance; coins were minted and Friday prayers were pronounced in the name of the sultan.[35] The bey would also occasionally send presents to the sultan as well as soldiers to assist in wars.[36] However, the French argued that these were only the marks of symbolic and religious links between the Regency and the Ottoman Porte. In the 1840s, the

31. Ibn Abī al-Ḍiyāf (1963, vol. 5).

32. Ministère de la Guerre, "Note sur la Tunisie," August 4, 1857, AMAE, Tunis, CP, vol. 17, fols. 154–155.

33. England was notably eager to enforce its 1838 trade treaty with the Ottomans in Tunisia. Bdira (1978, 40) and Raymond (1964, 138–140).

34. The Ottomans conquered Tunisia in 1574. The Husaynid dynasty came to power in 1705: Husayn Ibn Ali took over, suppressed the power of the dey, and obtained the title of pacha from the sultan.

35. Mantran (1959, 319–333) and Valensi (1977, 312). Prayers in the name of the sultan officially ceased with the end of the caliphate in 1924.

36. The bey sent soldiers to Crete (1810), to the battle of Navarin (1827), and to the Crimean War (1856).

French Ministry of Foreign Affairs articulated the argument for the "independence" of the Regency, a term that Tunisian officials embraced and used in Arabic as well (*istiqlāl*). As evidence, the French would argue that consular agents in Tunisia were not accredited by the Ottoman state but by the Regency, which signed treaties with European nations without Ottoman authorization. They also argued that the bey sent occasional presents to the sultan as opposed to paying a tribute, that France had protected the Regency from Ottoman military ambitions, and had received the bey in Paris in 1846 with all the honors due to a sovereign.[37] Contemporaries therefore disagreed (as historians still do) about the nature and strength of the relationship that the Regency of Tunis maintained with the Ottoman state in the nineteenth century.[38] More important for my purpose, however, is the fact that its autonomy was a crucial stake for all actors involved, particularly for the bey. He used the Regency's Ottoman bonds to keep the European powers in check but also embraced the French argument about the Regency's "independence," notably, as we will see, to fight for his state's legal sovereignty.

This competition between the Ottomans, the French, and the British was taking place at a time of increasing integration of Tunisia, and the region as a whole, into the global economy and of increasing European economic might. Small groups of European merchants joined rapidly expanding economic networks, especially after the end of piracy in the Mediterranean in the early nineteenth century opened safer trade routes.[39] The Regency provided raw materials and food staples to the European markets, particularly wheat at first, and by the nineteenth century mostly olive oil (used in the soap factories of Marseilles).[40] The Regency also imported an increasing amount of manufactured products from Europe, displacing traditional local crafts. By 1860 more than 90 percent of the Regency's international trade was transported by French, Italian, and British ships, and France provided half of Tunisia's imports, thanks to its geographical proximity and to the presence in Tunisia of a small but economically significant colony of merchants from Marseilles.[41] Europeans were in search of places in which to invest their capital,[42] and competed to obtain

37. "Preuves à l'appui de l'indépendance et de la souveraineté du bey, 1851," AMAE, Tunis, *Mémoires et documents*, vol. 44.

38. See Valensi (1969b) vs. Moalla (2004) and Oualdi (2011).

39. Valensi (1969b, 62–69).

40. Valensi (1977, 329–344).

41. Ganiage (1968, 49–53).

42. Porter (1984, 70ff.).

concessions on mines, railways, and roads.[43] Through their commercial activities, and also because of their increasing numbers, they now came in more frequent contact with the bey's subjects.[44] There were about 8,000 Europeans in the Regency in 1834, 12,000 in 1856, and 15,000 by 1870,[45] out of a total population of approximately one million,[46] including 25,000 to 30,000 native Jews.[47] Most Europeans practiced humble professions, but there were about thirty wealthy families.[48] Three-quarters of them were concentrated in Tunis, where they represented about one-tenth of the population,[49] and to a lesser extent in the coastal cities of Sousse and Sfax, where a few families from Marseilles and Genoa competed with native producers and merchants.[50] Moreover, their economic presence was considerable: they notably controlled the bulk of the olive oil trade with Europe.[51] Europeans were therefore often perceived by local elites and the populace as an economic threat,[52] at a time when they were increasingly gaining commercial access to the Regency with little reciprocity for the bey's subjects.[53]

The Regency of Tunis's Long-Brewing Economic and Fiscal Challenges

At the time, the Regency faced severe economic and fiscal challenges, which long predated the nineteenth century and the increase in European penetration.[54] The Regency's successive governments had been attempting to address them

43. Ganiage (1968, 55–61).
44. Clancy-Smith (2011) and Planel (2015, 18–19).
45. Ganiage (1968, 41 and 43) and Ganiage (1960, 19).
46. Seklani (1974, 13) and Tabutin et al. (2001).
47. Sebag (1991, 114). According to Ganiage (1968, 41), in 1871 about 1,100 were from Livorno.
48. Ganiage (1959, 48).
49. Ganiage (1960, 19), and Sebag (1998, 280) for the population of Tunis.
50. Chater (1978, 34).
51. Chater (1984, 332–333) estimates that in 1819–1822 the European merchants were responsible for 83 percent of olive oil exported, Muslim Tunisian merchants for 11 percent, and Jewish merchants for the rest. See also Jerfel (2012).
52. Planel (2015, 15–16).
53. Valensi (1969b, 18).
54. In contrast, part of the historiography overemphasizes factors specific to the nineteenth century as the main culprits for the Regency's woes at the time of the reforms. Ibn Diyaf, cited in Chérif (1970, 722), dates them to the great plague of 1818–1819. Some even attribute the Regency's fiscal problems to the expenditures necessitated by the reforms themselves and/or to the conditions of the first external loan contracted in 1863 in response to these problems—e.g., Ganiage (1959, 179–216), Karoui (1973, 80–83), and Sraïeb (1987, 67–69)—based in part on the

since the eighteenth century at least. On the economic front, the Regency was unable to compete with new and cheaper sources of agricultural products, such as the wheat of the Black Sea region, and with European manufactured products, such as the *shāshīya* hats manufactured in France. Things only took a turn for the worse after 1815, with the end of the Napoleonic Wars and with the crash in the price of olive oil.[55] On the fiscal front, state revenues were insufficient,[56] likely due to a deficit in coercive and organizational capabilities, which the beys attempted to mitigate by reorganizing their tax collection and reinforcing their army, since the eighteenth century at least, in the context of similar efforts in Istanbul.[57] As an indication of the Regency's long-standing fiscal challenges and attempts to address them, the Husaynid beys started to debase the Tunisian riyal shortly after they took over in the early eighteenth century and had begun to mint their currency. In 1735 the riyal's pure silver content was already only 64 percent of what it was at the inception of their dynasty in 1705. It dropped

---

conclusions of the French public finances inspector F. Villet's 1872 and 1873 reports against Prime Minister Mustafa Khaznadar, which start with the improbable claim that before Ahmad Bey's reign (1837–1955), "the Regency was relatively prosperous" and "there was no public debt." AMAE, Tunis, *Mémoires et documents*, vol. 12, fols. 245–303.

55. Valensi (1969a, 400; 1981, 722–723) and Chérif (1970, 723, 725, 726, 731, and 737). On the eve of the reforms, olive oil represented more than half of the total Tunisian exports. Chater (1984, 574–575 and 589).

56. In the eighteenth century, monetary state tax revenues did not increase, partly due to the depreciation of the Tunisian currency and to the fact that "the types of taxes remained unchanged as did the tax base and its volume" ("the census of men and of olive and date trees was not brought up to date"). Valensi (1981, 720; 1977, 349–354). This occurred despite a probable demographic expansion—discussed in Chérif (1970) and Valensi (1977), with some words of caution in Chérif (2008, vol. 1, 14–19)—which was made possible by the rarity of epidemics and other disasters until 1776. After that, a succession of bad harvests, plagues, and other epidemics affected the country until 1867, leading to a decrease in population, agricultural production, and state tax revenues in kind. See Valensi (1981, 720; 1977, 302–316 and 290). In addition, "from 1815 onward, the disappearance of privateering and the cessation of tributes previously paid by certain powers decreased the income to the Treasury." Valensi (1981, 722). Privateering revenues were modest to start with, both relative to the overall economy and total state revenues. See Valensi (1967) and Chater (1984, 89n184, 92, tables I and II, and 289).

57. Part of the historiography points instead to external threats as the main reason for reinforcing the army and to the futility of this effort. However, as argued by Moalla (2004, 138), although the bey's army was certainly no match for the European armies' firepower, it was strong enough to tighten the bey's "fiscal control of the countryside from the first decade of the nineteenth century," and "changes in the beylical fiscal policies . . . were already slowly underway during Hammouda Pasha's period of rule [1777–1814]."

to 39 percent in 1766, 32 percent in 1815, and 22 percent in 1825.[58] Although he acknowledges that "the circumstances behind the depreciation of the [Tunisian] riyal are not yet well understood," Pamuk (2000a, 180) argues that, "if the experience of the kurus at Istanbul is any guide, fiscal causes played an important role." And despite a rapid succession of fiscal innovations initiated in 1819,[59] state revenues remained small as a fraction of the overall economy.[60] I estimate that they still only represented less than 5 percent of GDP on the eve of the legal reforms, compared to about 2 percent of GDP in the eighteenth century (see table 1).[61] This was still insufficient. In 1855 the bey lamented to the French consul that he only had a few months of reserves and that he would have to considerably reduce his army's headcount.[62] In the years 1852–55 the state fiscal deficit was about 1.5 million piasters compared to average annual revenues of about 10 million piasters,[63] and the state debt had already reached an unsustainable level

58. Computations based on Candia de Farrugia (1933, 1934, 1935). See also Valensi (1977, 326–327 and 345n19). Pamuk (2000a, 172–185) shows that the Tunisian Riyal debasement broadly followed the currency debasements in Istanbul and Cairo but started earlier. For an account of the 1825 debasement, see Ibn Abī al-Ḍiyāf (1963, vol. 3, 155). For a monetary history of Husaynid Tunisia, see Fenina (2003). See also Bachrouch (1989, 273–307).

59. See Valensi (1977, 354–359). As an illustration, Valensi estimated, for Msaken, that the *dîme* (tithe) introduced in 1818 to replace the *qānūn*, and paid on olive oil production from 1819 to 1838, went from 0.1 percent of production in 1819 to about 1 percent on average for the years 1819–1838, and was replaced after 1840 by a tax that amounted to about 3 percent of production. See also Valensi (1981, 720–721).

60. Ibn Diyaf compared the Regency to a cow that had been milked until it bled. (Ibn Abī al-Ḍiyāf 1963, vol. 5, 113). His subjective assessment reflected a prevalent sentiment at the time. The amount of legal or illegal taxation by local intermediaries that failed to reach central state coffers at that time, as discussed in Karaman and Pamuk (2010), also needs to be ascertained, along with the fraction of the surplus above subsistence levels that overall taxation represented.

61. In line with received wisdom, M. Kraïem (1973, vol. 1, 337–343) and Chérif (1973, 10) put forward much higher (and improbable) evaluations of state revenues as a fraction of aggregate output, largely based on theoretical tax rates or on unsubstantiated assumptions (such as on yields, prices, and labor share).

62. The French consul described it as a "horrible financial situation." Roches to the French minister of foreign affairs, December 18, 1855, AMAE, Tunis, CP, vol. 15, fols. 303–306. That same year, invoking financial pressures, the bey minted a gold coin 20 percent above its intrinsic value, to the dismay of the French merchants' community and their consul. See Fenina (2003, 229–232) and Roches to the French minister of foreign affairs, September 29, 1855, AMAE, Tunis, CP, vol. 15, fols. 254–255. See also the bey to Roches, September 8, 1855, "Annexe à la dépêche du 29 Septembre 1855," fol. 266.

63. Chater (1984, 582–583).

given the beylical state's fiscal capabilities. It reached about 19 million piasters in 1859 and 28 million in 1862 (i.e., around two and three times the average state annual revenues, respectively).[64] These fiscal difficulties were exacerbated by the unsustainably high interest rate the Regency paid on its (internal) debt, some 12 to 13 percent.[65] This meant that state debt would double every six years or so even without additional primary budget deficits. The Regency would have paid a much lower rate, about 7 percent,[66] had it borrowed externally, and it attempted to do so on several occasions (notably in 1844, 1850, and in the winter of 1854) but was unsuccessful.[67] The Regency's fiscal challenges were therefore putting it in danger of collapse and threatened its political integrity,[68] as expressed by the British consul Richard Wood in November 1856. He thought this could be avoided by "political and administrative reforms" and "the introduction of European capital."[69] Similarly, in late 1855 Léon Roches worried that a potential bankruptcy of Tunisia would harm French commerce but could be avoided by adequate reforms spearheaded by France.[70]

Extraterritoriality and the Beylical State's Legal Sovereignty

In theory, Europeans established in the Regency were under consular protection and authority, in accordance with the treaties between the Regency and the European nations, and they expected their consuls to protect and help

64. Roches to Thouvenel, October 21, 1860, AMAE, Tunis, CP, vol. 20, fol. 22, and Emerit (1949, 251).

65. Emerit (1949, 251).

66. Ganiage (1959, 195–197) notes an average interest rate of about 5 percent quoted at the Bourse de Paris at the time as well as the fact that, in 1862, the Egyptian government borrowed externally at 7 percent, as did the Regency of Tunis in 1863. Also, the bey opened an account with Messrs. Rothschild and Moïena in Paris in 1857 to buy "things he orders for himself or his army" and paid an annual interest rate of 6 percent. Roches to the French minister of foreign Affairs, March 17, 1857, AMAE, Tunis, CP, vol. 17, fol. 57.

67. Van Krieken (1976, 22); Raymond (1953, 206–209 and 231); and Béclard to the French minister of foreign affairs, November 16, 1854, AMAE, Tunis, CP, vol. 15, fol. 6.

68. Contrary to common assumptions, given the Regency's fiscal capabilities and debt-to-revenues ratio, keeping the debt strictly internal would have done little to save Tunisia. For domestic debt as the "missing link explaining external default," see Reinhart and Rogoff (2009, 119–120), particularly table 8.1 (120), which shows that defaults routinely occurred with ratios of total public debt to revenue like those of 1850s Tunisia, and little external debt.

69. Raymond (1955, 51).

70. Roches to the French minister of foreign affairs, December 18, 1855, AMAE Tunis, CP, vol. 15, fol. 306.

expand their commercial interests. In the Franco-Tunisian case, successive bilateral treaties invariably confirmed the Ottoman Capitulations, at least until 1830, with additional stipulations that often simply reaffirmed customary practices.[71] According to the treaties, the consul adjudicated all affairs that involved only French nationals and protégés, and assisted them in mixed cases (i.e., cases involving local subjects), which were to be adjudicated by the ruler or a special government appointee (or commission), in the presence of their consul, rather than by the ordinary local courts.[72] However, in practice, local customs that followed neither the Ottoman Capitulations nor the treaties developed on the ground. For instance, in the eighteenth century, we find ad hoc mixed commercial arbitration committees (e.g., consisting of two Tunisian and two French members) for disputes involving French nationals or protégés and subjects of the bey, a practice that was inscribed in the 1802 Treaty.[73] In the nineteenth century, in criminal cases, "it was accepted that Europeans were, in all circumstances, insulated from the local jurisdictions, and were under that of their country,"[74] although a famous 1844 case deviated from this practice: a Maltese resident, accused of murdering a Muslim subject of the bey, was tried by the Maliki *qāḍī* in the presence of the bey and the English consul, provoking the ire of the French consul, who worried about the precedent this would set.[75] There were in fact numerous infringements of treaties' stipulations and customary practices, and case resolutions often required intricate and tense negotiations between the consul and the bey or other Tunisian officials.[76] The French consul was therefore squeezed between the expectations of his nationals and protégés (particularly the important merchants) and his duty to keep good relations with the bey, while answering to his own government.

Moreover, there were tensions between the jurisdictions of the French Nation in the Regency (the Nation Française, originally a body of accredited French merchants, which governed itself in partnership with the consul),

71. Windler (2002, 220).

72. Y. Debbasch (1957, 195–226). For the treaties, see Plantet (1899) and Jerad (2012).

73. Windler (2002, 338). The 1824 Treaty expanded on this practice. For an 1858 example, see Roches to the bey, February 25, 1858, ANT SH C207 D95.

74. Pellissier de Reynaud (1853, 339–340). See Y. Debbasch (1957, 206–212) for a historical account of this practice, which could be understood as delegating to the consul the power of judgment the treaties granted to the bey.

75. See L. C. Brown (1974, 247–251), and Correspondence relating to the trial of a Maltese in the court of the Bey of Tunis, *House of Commons Parliamentary Papers*, May 3, 1844, 1–44. The defendant was found guilty, sentenced to death, and executed.

76. Y. Debbasch (1957), Windler (2002), Clancy-Smith (2011, chapter 6), and Jerad (2018).

France (through its consular and metropolitan justice), and the bey.[77] The bey often gave his protection to French residents who worked for him, or to those who asked for it, whether to remain in the Regency in defiance of France's residency regulations, or simply to avoid consular justice.[78] As for the French consul, he claimed jurisdiction over all French nationals in tension with the bey but also with the Nation Française. With the 1802 Treaty, French consular jurisdiction was extended to those Jewish subjects of the bey and foreigners who worked as agents of the French Nation, and with the 1824 Treaty *all* French nationals, "indiscriminately," had to submit to their consular jurisdiction. In addition, in the 1830s, the European consuls were increasingly able to extend their protection to some Muslim subjects of the bey.[79] To put it in broader terms, there was an ongoing shift in the diplomatic balance of power and the Regency was excluded from the newly emerging system of European sovereign states dealing with each other on a level playing field.[80] This was accompanied by a shift in the judicial balance of power in the Regency in favor of the Europeans, which accelerated in the 1830s after some ebbs and flows.[81] Tunisian elites were acutely aware of this ongoing shift and persistently resisted it. This situation also created resentment in the Regency's Muslim population,[82] not only against Europeans but also against Jewish subjects of the bey who would claim the consuls' legal protection.

2. The Making of the 1857 Security Pact: A Battle for Legal Sovereignty and a Reaffirmation of Islamic Governance

The European consuls, despite their increasing power, and the bey's government both deplored the legal uncertainty and complexity that resulted from the ad hoc resolution of cases involving beylical subjects and foreigners and the

77. Windler (2002, 188–193), who counts 37 (resp. 143) members of the French Nation registered at the consulate in 1782 (resp. 1813), out of a total of about 110 (resp. 373) French souls residing in Tunis. For the relations between the French Nation and the consul, see Y. Debbasch (1957, 274–284).

78. Windler (2002).

79. Windler (2002, 402–403). Article XI of the 1824 Franco-Tunisian Treaty extended French protection to all Tunisians working as agents of French merchants.

80. See, for instance, the battle for tariff reciprocity described in Windler (2002, 227–230).

81. Chérif (1970, 738). For a longer historical perspective, see Y. Debbasch (1957).

82. For instance, Ibn Abī al-Ḍiyāf (1963, vol. 5, 84) writes that the foreign consuls practiced "plunder rather than commerce."

intricate and tense negotiations they necessitated. These cases often put the consuls at odds with the bey and/or their nationals and protégés and compromised their standing and authority. This situation worsened with the accumulation of judicial affairs caused by the demographic and economic expansion of Europeans in the Regency.[83] The consuls and the bey's government also deplored the existence of multiple jurisdictions (there were a dozen consuls representing as many jurisdictions), as well as the absence of clarity about which treaties were in vigor and what they stipulated.[84] In 1857 the deputies of the French Nation described the situation as "a daily struggle" that the consul invariably lost.[85] The French consul, a few years later, still spoke of a "state of uncertainty [that] paralyzed business and worried [the French] colony."[86] Moreover, despite their increasing privileges, Europeans were hindered in their economic activities in the Regency by their lack of property rights (which required them to resort to nominees) and other impediments, such as the bey's monopolies.[87] In February 1856, the British and the French, who were allies in the Crimean War, temporarily put an end to their rivalry in Tunisia to join forces, at least officially, and push the bey toward reforms.[88] The French Ministries of Foreign Affairs and War, the French emperor, the British Foreign Office, the French and British consuls, and the Europeans established in the Regency each had their own political and economic agendas.[89] They intersected in seeking (1) security for Europeans, (2) a predictable justice system for Europeans, (3) free reign for European commerce and industries, (4) property rights for Europeans, and (5) legal *guarantees* on all these points. It seems that some further economic

83. For instance, in 1862, Léon Roches spoke of the "thousands of little irritating questions that absorb most of the time and influence of the consuls and their officers." Roches to the French minister of foreign affairs, February 8, 1862, AMAE, Tunis, CP, vol. 21, fol. 8.

84. Roches to the French minister of foreign affairs, June 20, 1861, AMAE, Tunis, CP, vol. 20, fols. 137–138. For Khayr al-Din's perspective, see his verbal note to Minister of Foreign Affairs Thouvenel, September 4, 1861, ANT SH C118 D408, no. 34.

85. Deputies of the Nation Française to Roches, June 27, 1857, AMAE, Tunis, CP, vol. 17, fols. 116–117.

86. Roches to the French minister of foreign affairs, June 20, 1861, AMAE, Tunis, CP, vol. 20, fol. 138.

87. The August 8, 1830 Treaty guaranteed foreigners and their consuls some freedom of commerce and prohibited the Tunisian government from running monopolies, but they persisted. See Bdira (1978, 26–28, 31, and 33–34). See also Raymond (1964, 147) for the list of impediments enumerated in 1856 by Richard Wood.

88. Raymond (1964, 141).

89. Raymond (1953, 1955, 1964).

concessions, some further adjustments to bilateral treaties, and a simple judicial reorganization should have satisfied the substance of the first four exigencies. However, it was organic laws (a "Security Pact" and a "Constitution") that were able to provide sufficient guarantees and satisfy the Europeans but also the bey. As early as 1855, the French consul envisioned that the legal reforms would be double-edged. He argued that a "kind of Tanzimat" would offer guarantees to Europeans in the Regency while, "at the same time," providing the bey's subjects with guarantees of their own, in addition to reorganizing the Tunisian state and saving it from bankruptcy.[90] Notwithstanding strong European pressures (including military coercion) to enact legal reforms, pressures that left a lasting imprint on Tunisian memory and historiography,[91] these reforms offered the Regency's government an opportunity to obtain economic and political benefits, and the bey actively shaped them from their inception.

The Tunisian Point of View: What Did the Bey Have to Gain from a Constitution?

The bey and his government had a strong incentive to facilitate the deployment of foreign capital, at a crucial time for the survival of his dynasty. In the legal standing and assertion of sovereignty a constitution provided to the Regency, they must also have seen a way to make the Regency a legally credible borrower for international bankers.[92] Recall that the Regency was paying an unsustainably high interest rate of 12 to 13 percent on its internal debt, when it would have paid about 7 percent on external debt. This constituted a significant incentive to borrow externally,[93] and Tunisia repeatedly but unsuccessfully attempted to

90. Roches to the French minister of foreign affairs, December 18, 1855, AMAE, Tunis, CP, vol. 15, fol. 306. Later, Léon Roches also argued that some wealthy Tunisians saw the reforms positively because they would protect their persons and possessions from the arbitrary power of the bey. Roches to Thouvenel, October 21, 1860, AMAE, Tunis, CP, vol. 20, fol. 44.

91. For instance, the correspondence between the bey and the European consuls was archived under the title "Letters . . . which led to the imposition [*ilzām*] of the Security Pact." ANT SH C118 D403, nos. 4 and 51. See also chapters 2 and 3 for how the memory of the 1857–1861 reforms was evoked in subsequent constitutional episodes.

92. For an instance in seventeenth-century England where this kind of institutional change "reflected an explicit attempt to make credible the government's ability to honor its commitments," and led the government to "become financially solvent" by gaining "access to an unprecedented level of funds," see North and Weingast (1989, 804–805).

93. The bey recognized, for instance, that the internal loan contracted in 1862 had been "ruinous," and hence necessitated an external loan in 1863. Roches to the French minister of foreign affairs, February 28, 1863, AMAE, Tunis, CP, vol. 21, fols. 149–153.

do so before the legal reforms, as we saw. It met with reluctance from European bankers, who invoked the lack of Tunisian independence (i.e., its Ottoman vassal status).[94] Moreover, it was only after the 1861 Constitution was promulgated (and before its financial conditions worsened dramatically) that the Regency was able to contract, in 1863,[95] a 7 percent external loan to refinance its internal debt and fund new needs, although there were internal disagreements as to whether borrowing externally threatened its sovereignty.[96]

More broadly, legal reforms in the form of higher laws gave the bey an opportunity to bolster his dynasty's autonomy from Istanbul and to obtain the Great Powers' recognition of his state on a level legal and diplomatic playing field.[97] A constitution was not an Ottoman "Tanzimat" (which the Ottoman state had long pressured the Regency to implement)[98] but a European type of law, and it was a marker of sovereignty. It promised, in the eyes of the bey, "the independence of his family,"[99] and an opportunity to "become a member

94. E.g., during its 1854 loan negotiations. See Béclard to Druyn de Lhuys, November 27, 1854, AMAE, Tunis, CP, vol. 15, fols. 9–11. See also D'Alvarès (likely a representative of the bey in Paris) to Prime Minister Khaznadar, December 16, 1854, ANT SH C220 D350, no. 51.

95. The 1863 loan was contracted despite Ottoman officials' assertions that the bey should have obtained "[Ottoman] Imperial authorization." Başbakanlık Osmanlı Arşivi, HR_SFR_3, 77, 36. The conditions of this loan were discussed by Tunisia's Great Council on February 13, 1863, and on April 17, 1863. ANT, Register #2695, fols. 514–515, 531–532. The French Ministry of Foreign Affairs supported the loan and its official listing against the objections of the French Ministry of Finance, arguing that Tunisia was an independent state (and that its independence was guaranteed by France). French minister of finance to the French minister of foreign affairs, March 27, 1863, AMAE, Tunis, CP, vol. 21, fol. 155. See also French minister of foreign affairs to Roches, June 10, 1863, AMAE, Tunis, CP, vol. 21, fol. 172, and its Arabic translation in ANT SH C220 D350, no. 58. However, I could not find any explicit mention of the Constitution per se facilitating an external loan, only the usual "independence" arguments.

96. Roches to the French minister of foreign affairs, May 17, 1862, AMAE, Tunis, CP, vol. 21, fols. 40–41.

97. As Marsans-Sakly (2010, 33) writes, "The Regency was experimenting with ways to constitute itself as a state with an independent legal personality."

98. The Ottoman state pressured the bey to implement the Ottoman 1839 Khatt-i Sherif of Gulkhane shortly after it was promulgated in Istanbul and received an evasive response. Pressures were reiterated with the 1856 Khatt-i Humayun. In 1857, shortly after the proclamation of the Security Pact, the bey received a letter from the Ottoman grand vizier reproaching him for his actions in the Sfez affair and pressuring him to take inspiration from both edicts. Ibn Abī al-Ḍiyāf (1963, vol. 1, 39, and vol. 4, 37–38, 58–62, 248). ANT SH C117 D390bis, nos. 1 to 9.

99. Roches to Thouvenel, October 21, 1860, AMAE, Tunis, CP, vol. 20, fol. 14. Ibn Abī al-Ḍiyāf (1963, vol. 5, 20).

of the Great Family of Europe."[100] And indeed, by referring to and praising the policies of the sultan of Islam (*salṭanat al-Islām*) and the Great Powers (*al-duwal al-ʿiẓām*), the 1857 Security Pact situated the Tunisian state at the level of other states,[101] all the more so as the Treaty of Paris had recognized the Ottoman state's independence and integrity, formally admitting it into the Concert of Europe, shortly after the proclamation of the 1856 Khatt-i Humayun.[102] In addition, the promulgation of the Security Pact and the Constitution, as higher laws organizing the operations of the state, provided the bey with an opportunity to publicly reaffirm the Muslim character of his state at a time of heightened anxieties among Tunisian Muslims about the erosion of the Islamic tradition brought about by the increasing presence and economic penetration of Europeans. The French consul reported that some Tunisian Muslims reproached Ahmad Bey (1837–1855) for having been "not the bey of the Muslims, but the bey of the Jews and the Christians," and that they hoped that Muhammad Bey (r. 1855–1859) would defend Islam in a more forceful way than his predecessor.[103] The final text of the Security Pact, as we will see, emphasized the Muslim character of the state, although some of its stipulations—such as most of its notions of equality irrespective of religion—triggered vigorous contentions since many viewed them as an unacceptable legal innovation from an Islamic point of view.

Finally, the making of the Security Pact and the Constitution provided the bey with an opportunity to affirm his state's legal sovereignty, and he seized it, as we will see. He insisted that foreigners in the Regency must submit to the country's jurisdictions, weaponizing the Security Pact's notions of equality irrespective of religion for all, although the Europeans originally conceived this equality to apply only to the subjects of the bey. The bey argued that there was no reason why he should "alter the law of [his] subjects, almost all of whom are Muslim," since "there are barely thirty-thousand Jews in the Regency," if "foreigners . . . were not to submit to the same jurisdiction."[104]

100. Wood to Clarendon, September 2, 1857, FO 102, 53, quoted in Raymond (1955, 53).

101. *ʿAhd al-Amān*, in *Qānūn al-Dawla al-Tūnisīya* (1861, 5).

102. Davison (1963, 4). The Treaty of Paris was signed on March 30, 1856. See also Findley (2008, 16–17).

103. Roches to the French minister of foreign affairs, June 29, 1857, AMAE, Tunis, CP, vol. 17, fols. 130–131.

104. Roches to the French minister of foreign affairs, October 21, 1860, AMAE, Tunis, CP, vol. 20, fol. 38. In the same vein, see the bey to Roches, October 3, 1860, ANT SH C118 D408, no. 2.

During the first proclamation of the Constitution on November 26, 1860, the bey publicly explained this quid pro quo. He underlined that the rights given to foreigners were "conditioned [*mashrūṭa*] on their submission to the penal tribunals as defined by the Constitution."[105]

The Bey's Weaponization of Equality for All in a Battle for Legal Sovereignty

In the early summer of 1857 an incident involving a Jewish subject of the bey, Bato Sfez, gave the European consuls the opportunity to finally make the bey yield to their demands for reform.[106] On June 20, 1857, Sfez, an employee of Nassim Shamama (a high-ranking Jewish tax collector), injured a child while riding his cart in the streets of Tunis and, when reprimanded by passersby, allegedly insulted the religion of Islam.[107] In the midst of tense interreligious tensions, the case was presented to the bey, who refrained from ruling on a punishment (*ta ʿzīr*) in his own court. He sent the case to the Maliki sharia court, which punished this type of offense with a death sentence, whereas the Hanafi court would have been more lenient according to Ibn Diyaf.[108] Rejecting advice for caution and leniency from members of his government and yielding to the pressure of the Hanafi Shaykh al-Islam Muhammad Bayram IV, the bey objected that a Muslim soldier had recently been executed for having killed a Jew.[109] Despite the French consul's pressures for clemency, the sharia court sentenced Bato Sfez to death; the sentence was swiftly confirmed by the bey on June 25, 1857, and immediately carried out. A series of attacks by the populace against Jews followed, and Jewish leaders appealed to the European consuls for protection.[110] Facing the discontent of the European consuls, who echoed the fears expressed by their nationals that "a Christian may be at any moment exposed to the same fate as this unfortunate Jew," the bey objected

105. Ibn Abī al-Ḍiyāf (1963, vol. 5, 44).

106. For more details about the Bato Sfez affair, see Zeghal (2022) and the references there.

107. ANT SH C117 B390bis, nos. 29 and 31. Nassim Shamama later became the administrative leader—*qā ʾid*—of the Jewish community and "receiver general and director of finance." For more details, see Marglin (2022, 22–25).

108. Ibn Abī al-Ḍiyāf (1963, vol. 4, 233).

109. Ibn Abī al-Ḍiyāf (1963, vol. 4, 233), who claims that Bayram IV held some resentment against Nassim Shamama.

110. Allagui (2016, 44).

that it was his duty to implement the decisions of the sharia court.[111] French authorities in Paris recognized that the bey could not have acted differently, given the Muslim character of the state and its laws.[112] However, they argued that, in order to "prevent a reoccurrence of such revolting actions," judicial changes had to be implemented in Tunisia.[113]

EUROPEAN PRESSURES AND PRESCRIPTIONS

A July 15, 1857, note from the French Ministry of Foreign Affairs enumerated the recent judicial reforms enacted in Istanbul, including a February 1854 firman that organized mixed criminal tribunals in all Ottoman provinces for affairs between Muslim and non-Muslim Ottoman subjects or between them and foreigners. However, in order to "resolve the difficulty happening in Tunis," this note advised choosing a solution "analogous" to the stipulations of the 1856 Ottoman Khatt-i Humayun, which spoke of mixed tribunals only for affairs between Muslim and non-Muslim (or between exclusively non-Muslim) Ottoman *subjects*.[114] This note contained two caveats to this recommendation. First, it could not be "a special act of the Ottoman authority, and hence something similar [to the 1856 Khatt-i Humayun was] needed, but under a different name." Second, it was not necessary to promulgate a law as broad as the 1856 Khatt-i Humayun, which would be too complex to implement. An "immediate reform of the judicial organization" would be more practical.[115] On July 20, 1857, Walewski, the French minister of foreign affairs, heeded this advice and sent the consul Léon Roches instructions to advise the bey to follow the lead of the Ottoman sultan who established mixed tribunals, "that is, tribunals composed of judges of all religions, to adjudicate all commercial and criminal affairs between Muslims and Christians or other non-Muslim subjects, or between

111. Wood to the bey, July 24, 1857, ANT SH C117 D390bis, no. 23. The bey to Wood, August 11, 1857, ANT SH C117 B390bis, no. 18.

112. "Note: Exécution d'un Israélite à Tunis," July 15, 1857, AMAE, Tunis, CP, vol. 17, fols. 137–143, and French minister of foreign affairs to Roches, July 20, 1857, AMAE, Tunis, CP, vol. 17, fols. 145–147.

113. "Note: Exécution d'un Israélite à Tunis," July 15, 1857, AMAE, Tunis, CP, vol. 17, fols. 137–143, and French minister of foreign affairs to Roches, July 20, 1857, AMAE, Tunis, CP, vol. 17, fols. 145–147. Ganiage (1959, 72–73) and Raymond (1964, 149) claim that such incidents were rare (they mention two cases, in 1824 and 1844). However, the possibility was still feared.

114. "Note: Exécution d'un Israélite à Tunis," July 15, 1857, AMAE, Tunis, CP, vol. 17, fol. 141.

115. "Note: Exécution d'un Israélite à Tunis," July 15, 1857, AMAE, Tunis, CP, vol. 17, fol. 143.

non-Muslim subjects themselves."[116] He argued that by resorting to the sharia court in the Bato Sfez affair, the bey had "exposed the life of all foreigners in the Regency to permanent danger."[117] He hoped that putting Muslim and non-Muslim beylical subjects equally under the jurisdiction of a mixed criminal court, and admitting their testimony indiscriminately, would alleviate the Europeans' fear that as non-Muslims they could be tried in a sharia court in criminal matters (e.g., for blasphemy). However, in this framework, foreigners would continue to fall under the extraterritoriality rules and practices established by the treaties and custom, even in mixed cases.

While rumors were spreading in the capital about an imminent implementation in the Regency of the 1856 Ottoman Khatt-i Humayun, which "would now put Muslims and Jews on an equal footing," the French consul presented to the bey, in early August 1857, a first decree project,[118] which was followed by a month of back-and-forths and tense negotiations about the establishment of mixed criminal and commercial tribunals and codes in particular.[119] The bey did not oppose the establishment of new tribunals and codes, but he resisted the inclusion of non-Muslim judges in these tribunals and strived to submit *all* residents (his Muslim and non-Muslim subjects as well as foreigners) to the Regency's jurisdiction. He responded evasively at first, promising some reforms but explaining that he would only proceed in accordance with the condition (*ḥāl*), customs (*ṭibāʿ ahlihā wa-ʿādāt al-raʿāya*), and interest (*maṣlaḥa*) of his country and his subjects.[120] In the face of the bey's resistance, it took the combined efforts of Léon Roches and Richard Wood (perhaps with the help of some of the bey's advisors), the threat of military European intervention, the arrival of the French fleet led by Admiral Tréhouart near the Regency's coast on August 31, 1857, and the French consul's misrepresentation of the other party's requests to both his superior in Paris and to the bey to come

116. French minister of foreign affairs to Roches, July 20, 1857, AMAE, Tunis, CP, vol. 17, fol. 147.

117. French minister of foreign affairs to Roches, July 20, 1857, AMAE, Tunis, CP, vol. 17, fol. 146.

118. Roches to the French minister of foreign affairs, August 11, 1857, AMAE, Tunis, CP, vol. 17, fol. 158, and "Projet d'ordonnance proposée à S.A. le Bey par le Chargé d'Affaires de France," "Annexe à la dépêche du 10 août 1857," AMAE, Tunis, CP, vol. 17, fols. 171–172. For the Arabic version, see Roches to the bey, August 11, 1857, ANT SH C118 D403, no. 11.

119. For more details on these negotiations, see Zeghal (2022).

120. The bey to Roches, August 11, 1857, ANT SH C117 D390bis, no. 27. For the French translation, see "Annexe à la dépêche du 10 août 1857," AMAE, Tunis, CP, vol. 17, fol. 169.

to a result.[121] In the course of these negotiations, foreigners were added to the jurisdiction of the proposed mixed commercial tribunals, thus expanding the original proposal for mixed tribunals only in affairs involving non-Muslim subjects of the bey.[122] In addition, broad guarantees for all the bey's subjects, akin to constitutional rights, were introduced. The bey then extended these broad guarantees to the foreigners established in the Regency. This resulted in the proclamation of a new law on September 9, 1857, the Security Pact (*ʿAhd al-Amān*), that combined the different and sometimes contradictory guarantees sought by these negotiations' protagonists.[123]

The new law was drafted by the bey's government on the basis of a list of eleven points that Léon Roches, in coordination with Richard Wood, asked the bey to implement on September 7, 1857.[124] The first six consisted of (1) Mixed criminal tribunals for the Jewish and Muslim subjects of the bey when a Jewish subject is involved; (2) Mixed commercial tribunals for affairs involving subjects of the bey (and foreigners, in the Tunisian government's Arabic translation); (3) Civil and religious equality of all the bey's subjects ("*al-musāwāt . . . fī al-umūr al-ʿurfīya wa-l-dīnīya*"—that is, "equality . . . in customary and religious affairs," in the Tunisian government's Arabic translation); (4) Absolute freedom of commerce, including the abolition of monopoly concessions ("*fermes*" or "*lazm*"); (5) Europeans' freedom of industry subject to their submission to the conditions

121. See Zeghal (2022) for more details.

122. Léon Roches seemed more open than his superiors in Paris to submitting foreigners to the jurisdiction of the proposed mixed commercial tribunals. In 1861 he suggested that, in mixed cases in which French nationals were plaintiffs, the French minister of foreign affairs should concede jurisdiction to the new Tunisian tribunals (which would replace in these cases the bey's jurisdiction defined in the treaties). He might have hoped to replace the ad hoc and difficult negotiations with the bey by established tribunals, which, he argued, offered "more serious guarantees than the old order of things." Roches to the French minister of foreign affairs, June 20, 1861, AMAE, Tunis, CP, vol. 20, fol. 137.

123. For more details on the creation of the 1857 Security Pact, see Zeghal (2022).

124. Letters of Léon Roches (September 6, 1857) and Richard Wood (undated), ANT SH C118 D403, no. 51 and no. 53, respectively, which are both in French and nearly identical. For their Arabic translations by the Tunisian government, see ANT SH C118 D403, no. 54 and no. 52, respectively. An undated Arabic rough draft also lists the eleven points in ANT SH C118 D403, no. 12. See also "Annexe à la dépêche du 8 Septembre 1857," AMAE, Tunis, CP, vol. 17, fols. 209–213 ("Note remise le 7 Septembre à Son Altesse Sidi Mohammed Bey par M. Léon Roches, Chargé d'Affaires de France"). As noted by Raymond (1964, 158), Léon Roches and Richard Wood separately submitted to the bey nearly identical lists on September 7, 1857, after the bey asked them to come to a mutual agreement.

imposed on indigenous industries; and (6) Europeans' right to own property, subject to their submission to the obligations incumbent on property owners in the country. To these, the consuls added five points that provided broader guarantees for the bey's subjects and that were understood by the English and French consuls (and the bey) as some sort of constitutional rights:[125] (1) Complete security of life and property; (2) Establishment of an equal tax for all; (3) Equality before the law (*"égalité devant la loi"*; in the Tunisian government's Arabic translation, *"al-musāwāt amām al-sharī ʿa,"* that is, "equality before sharia"); (4) Freedom of worship (*"liberté des cultes"*; in the Tunisian government's Arabic translation, *"kull aḥad yakūn musarraḥ [sic] bi-tamām umūr dīnihi jahran,"* i.e., "every individual is set free to publicly conduct all his religious affairs"); (5) Military conscription with a limit on the length of service. These eleven points therefore included mixed tribunals as desired by the French minister of foreign affairs (although, contrary to his wishes, in the Tunisian government's Arabic translation the commercial tribunals' jurisdiction included foreigners), property rights and freer economic rein for Europeans as desired by their consuls, and some broad language that provided guarantees to the bey's subjects. The bey asked Ibn Diyaf to draft the new law on the basis of these eleven points, and he wrote that he had accomplished this task in one evening, after which the bey's advisors introduced some modifications.[126] He prefaced eleven rules (*qawāʿid*) that broadly followed the consuls' eleven points (but modified them in significant ways), with a preamble that guaranteed the Muslim character of the state.[127] It was proclaimed the day after, on September 9, 1857, and was sometimes called a constitution, although the 1861 Constitution came later and contained the Security Pact as its preamble.[128]

125. Richard Wood had specified in a September 5, 1857, meeting with the bey what was meant by "guarantees" and listed these five "organic laws." See Raymond (1964, 157–158). See also ANT SH C118 D403, no. 12, where the five-point list is described, in an Arabic undated rough draft, as "the conditions [*shurūṭ*], that must be at the foundation of the establishment [*tartīb*] of the constitution [*kustītūsiyūn* (*sic*)]," in convergence with the letter from Léon Roches to the bey, of September 6, 1857, ANT SH C118 D403, no. 51.

126. Ibn Abī al-Ḍiyāf (1963, vol. 4, 240). He does not explicitly mention that the eleven rules were drafted on the basis of the consuls' eleven points but says that they approved the final draft and he does not explain the substance of the modifications introduced by the bey's advisors.

127. In contrast, Raymond (1964, 159) claims that Ibn Diyaf "simply juxtaposed the [consuls'] eleven articles" and merely added a long preamble.

128. Léon Roches wrote, on September 9, 1857, the day of the proclamation of the *ʿAhd al-Amān*, "The bey just solemnly granted a constitution to his people." Roches to the French

THE TUNISIAN GOVERNMENT'S MODIFICATIONS TO THE CONSULS' PRESCRIPTIONS

A scrutiny of the final text of the Security Pact reveals important differences with the consuls' eleven points.[129] Rule #5 (a promise to regulate military conscription) and Rule #9 (freedom of commerce for all without favoritism, and a commitment that the government will not participate in or hinder trade and must facilitate it) closely adhered to the consuls' wishes, as did Rule #6, which stipulated that when a member of the protected minorities (*ahl al-dhimma*) is a defendant in criminal court, the bey will appoint leaders of his community to this court—a clear concession on the bey's part. However, there were important additions and modifications that continued to show the bey's reluctance to establish truly mixed tribunals as well as his determination to subsume foreigners under his state's jurisdiction and to keep it Muslim. Indeed, Rule #7 promised commercial mixed tribunals, whose members would be "selected from among Muslims and subjects of the friendly powers," with no mention of Jewish subjects. Rules #10 and #11 gave foreigners complete freedom of industry and the right to own property, respectively. However, this was conditioned on their submission to existing or future "laws"

minister of foreign affairs, September 9, 1857, AMAE, Tunis, CP, vol. 17, fol. 222. In the same vein, see Roches to the French minister of foreign affairs, September 12, 1857, AMAE, Tunis, CP, vol. 17, fol. 227.

129. The eleven rules of the final Arabic version of the Security Pact can be summarized as follows: (1) Security (*amān*) of life, property, and honor, for all subjects and residents of the Regency of Tunis regardless of religion, language, and color (*al-adyān al-alsina wa-l-alwān*); (2) Equality (*tasāwī*) of all in taxation (*aṣl qānūn al-adā'*); (3) Equality in deserving fairness (*taswiya fī istiḥqāq al-inṣāf*) between Muslims and non-Muslims residing in the Regency; (4) Protected minorities (*dhimmīs*) among the subjects of the bey cannot be forced to change religion, cannot be forbidden to exercise their religion, and their congregations (*majāmi'*) will be protected against harm and humiliation (*idhāya wa-imtihān*); (5) A promise to regulate military conscription; (6) When a member of a protected religious minority (*ahl al-dhimma*) is a defendant in criminal court, the bey will appoint leaders of his community to this court; (7) A promise to establish a commerce tribunal composed of Muslims and subjects of the friendly powers; (8) Equality between Muslim and non-Muslim subjects of the bey under custom and official laws (*al-umūr al-'urfiya wa-l-qawānīn al-ḥukmīya*); (9) Freedom of commerce for all and without favoritism: the government will not participate in, or hinder, trade, and must facilitate it; (10) Foreigners will be free to practice all professions and industries, as long as they submit to current and future laws (*qawānīn*); and (11) Foreigners will be free to buy property as long as they submit to current and future laws.

(*qawānīn*),[130] rather than to the mere "conditions" or "obligations" incumbent on indigenous industry and property, as the consuls had intended. Moreover, the enactment of Rules #7, 10, and 11 was contingent on an "agreement" with the foreign powers about "procedures" and "mode of implementation." As for Rule #8, it stipulated equality of the bey's subjects regardless of religion before customary and official laws (*al-umūr al-ʿurfiya wa-l-qawānīn al-ḥukmīya*, and in the French version *règlements et usages*, i.e., regulations and customs). This was a narrower reformulation of the "civil and religious equality of all the bey's subjects" requested by the consuls, one that steered clear of speaking of full religious equality (since it remained silent about sharia courts) and made it acceptable to the Hanafi and Maliki grand muftis since, they later argued, it remained within the bounds of the discretionary power of the bey.[131] Rule #4 stipulated that protected minorities (*dhimmīs*) among the subjects of the bey cannot be forced to change religion or be forbidden to exercise it, and that their congregations (*majāmiʿ*) will be protected against harm and humiliation (*idhāya wa-imtihān*). This formulation contrasted with the consuls' request for "*liberté des cultes*" (freedom of worship),[132] since it focused on protected minorities, used double negatives, and deliberately omitted the notion of freedom, although it was present in the Tunisian government's Arabic translation of the consuls' eleven points. Last but not least, three of the guarantees that, per the consuls' eleven points, were supposed to apply only to the bey's subjects were extended in the final text of the Security Pact to also cover foreigners: Rule #1, security (*amān*) of life, property, and honor for all subjects and residents of the Regency of Tunis regardless of religion, language, and color (*al-adyān al-alsina wa-l-alwān*); Rule #2, equality (*tasāwī*) of the people (*al-nās*) in taxation (*aṣl qānūn al-adāʾ*);[133] and Rule #3, equality in deserving fairness (*taswiya fī istiḥqāq al-inṣāf*) between Muslims and non-Muslims residing in the Regency. This last rule was far from the consuls' request for "equality before the law," initially translated by the bey's government as "*al-musāwāt amām al-sharīʿa*" (equality before sharia).[134] This reformulation carefully avoided speaking of

130. "*Al-qawānīn al-murattaba wa-allatī yumkin an tatarattab.*" The official French version of the Security Pact spoke of "regulations" (*règlements*) rather than laws, perhaps intentionally.

131. ANT SH C118 D403, Maliki and Hanafi fatwas regarding the Security Pact, no. 2/59 and no. 3, respectively.

132. It is not entirely clear what the consuls meant by "*liberté des cultes.*" In France, this notion was the object of vigorous debates at the time. See Lalouette (2005, 5–18).

133. Rule #2 of the official French version of the Security Pact only mentions subjects.

134. "Muslims and other inhabitants of the country shall be equal before the law," in the official French version of the Security Pact.

equality before sharia, and, as we will see, the Hanafi and Maliki grand muftis would later argue that this rule's notion of equality was acceptable if and only if it meant that the rules of sharia (*al-ḥukm al-sharʿī*) were implemented in affairs between the Muslim and the unbeliever (*kāfir*).[135]

Therefore, the Tunisian government shaped the Security Pact's final contents[136] to stall on some key European demands (and defer difficult negotiations), to affirm the bey's state's legal jurisdiction over foreigners residing in the country, and to preserve its Muslim character as much as possible—albeit not enough for some conservative critics. To this end, the bey's government reformulated some of the consuls' wishes as expressed in their eleven points and extended to foreigners the guarantees, including notions of equality, that the consuls intended to apply exclusively to the bey's subjects.[137] In contradistinction, the 1856 Ottoman Khatt-i Humayun's stipulations initially invoked by the French minister of foreign affairs as a model to follow only concerned Ottoman subjects, with the exception of foreigners' property rights.[138] Although he expressed his satisfaction with the proclamation of the Security Pact, a result that he said "went beyond our hopes," the French minister also expressed his worries about the difficulty of implementing such a broad reform.[139] Admiral Tréhouart of France also noted the radical character of the reforms and the "immense" gap between the "mixed tribunals that M. Roches had long requested" and these "liberal creations."[140] As for Léon Roches, he called the

135. ANT SH C118 D403, Maliki and Hanafi fatwas regarding the Security Pact, no. 2/59 and no. 3, respectively.

136. In contrast, Raymond (1964, 158) describes the text of the *ʿAhd al-Amān* as the collation of the "essential" parts of the 1839 Khatt-i Sherif of Gulkhane and "some dispositions" of the 1856 Khatt-i Humayun. Van Krieken (1976, 6), Van der Haven (2006), and Ben Slimane (2012, 110) make similar claims.

137. This was explicitly articulated by the bey in a letter to Léon Roches on October 3, 1860, ANT SH C118 D408, no. 2. See its translation in AMAE, Tunis, CP, vol. 20, fols. 45–47. This is reminiscent, in its form, of the creation of the 1856 Ottoman Khatt-i Humayun analyzed in Davison (1963, 53), where guarantees of the rights of Christian Ottoman subjects sought by the Europeans were enlarged to apply to all Ottoman subjects in order not to "infringe on the sovereign rights of the Sultan."

138. The Ottoman sultan had formed mixed tribunals to adjudicate cases involving foreigners and Ottoman subjects prior to the 1856 Khatt-i Humayun. See Shaw and Shaw (1977, 118–119).

139. French minister of foreign affairs to Roches, September 23, 1857, AMAE, Tunis, CP, vol. 17, fol. 242. ANT SH C118 D403, no. 14, for the Arabic translation.

140. Tréhouart to the French minister of the marine, September 9, 1857, AMAE, Tunis, CP, vol. 17, fol. 215.

five-point guarantees he and Richard Wood had drafted a "constitution" and a "charter," and he described them as "a true revolution" and "a radical transformation of the old order."[141]

*The Security Pact (*ʿAhd al-Amān*): A Reaffirmation of the State's Custodianship of Islam*

Despite the French consul Léon Roches's confident proclamation of a "radical transformation," the Security Pact incorporated a key institutional element of the Regency's judicial system as it operated before this reform: the distinction between the jurisdictions of *siyāsa* and sharia, a common Islamic legal arrangement.[142]

SIYĀSA AND SHARIA: A TRADITIONAL FRAMEWORK FOR THE LEGAL REFORMS

Before the legal reforms of 1857 and 1861, except for consular justice, courts were under the authority of the bey. He could either dispense justice himself or delegate this task to the *qāḍīs*, the judges who ruled according to sharia in the sharia court, under his authority. Therefore, in addition to customary justice (*ʿurf*) and the rabbinic court, two types of indigenous courts coexisted. On the one hand, there was the sharia court (*majlis al-sharīʿa*, also called *majlis al-ʿulamāʾ* or the ʿulamā's council), where *qāḍīs* heard "cases of inheritance, marriage and paternity" and other kinds of affairs,[143] more often than not without the bey present. On the other hand, the bey's court (*maḥkamat al-bay*) operated under the direct authority of the bey and in his presence and dealt with cases related to public administration and to the *maẓālim* (i.e., cases of public interest related to abuses of power).[144] Plaintiffs could choose either one of these two courts. The sharia court was seen by the population as less arbitrary than the bey's justice, although the latter was thought to work faster. There was great flexibility—and competition—between these two jurisdictions and

141. Roches to the French minister of foreign affairs, September 8, 1857, AMAE, Tunis, CP, vol. 17, fol. 207.

142. On *siyāsa* and sharia, see Abdesselem (1973, 102–104), Heyd (1973), B. Lewis (1984), Peters (1999), Stilt (2011), and F. Vogel, Siyāsa, *EI*².

143. Abdesselem (1973, 102).

144. Y. Ben Achour (1985).

there was no fixed or objectively defined line separating them: it was drawn according to the circumstances and the balance of power between the bey and the jurists.[145] This distinction was often formulated as a dichotomy between *siyāsa* ("the discretionary authority of the rulers, one which they exercise outside the framework of the sharia"),[146] and sharia (the domain of the ʿulamā), and it constituted a major political stake. In addition to designating the laws that were not sharia's injunctions, *siyāsa* also designated the punishment (*taʿzīr*) that was decided by the sovereign outside of the sharia court's purview. Beyond the notions of regulation and punishment by the ruler, *siyāsa* also extended to the description of the conduct of the sovereign, such as the style he adopted in dealing with his subjects and with foreign diplomats.[147] Hence, *siyāsa* could also mean management of the state, or statecraft.[148] Although they represented two distinct legal jurisdictions, *siyāsa* and sharia were not defined in isolation from one another. For one, *siyāsa* had to be in conformity with the principles of sharia (revealed law): "For public affairs . . . the prince was accountable only to God; the duty of the ʿulamā was to remind him of the effects of divine wrath."[149] It was therefore crucial for the government to maintain the appearance of a governance consistent with revealed law. This convergence was maintained pragmatically, in the everyday practice of legal and administrative power. The ʿulamā were mobilized (sometimes reluctantly) to formulate this convergence, and the ruler had to be careful not to act as to stretch his actions too far out of the bounds of sharia. When the panegyric literature and the ʿulamā's fatwas reconciled the bey's legal and political decisions with revealed law, they often used the notion of "government according to revealed law" (*siyāsa sharʿīya*), an expression that harkened back to medieval political theory, particularly to Ibn Aqil (1040–1119), Ibn Taymiya (1263–1328), and Ibn Qayyim al-Jawziya (1292–1350).[150]

In this vein, the Security Pact's preamble underlined the lasting character of revealed law (*sharīʿa*) as a source of justice (*ʿadl*). It commented on the eleven rules (*qawāʿid*, an Arabic term belonging to Islamic law) within the framework of *siyāsa* and sharia and presented the Security Pact as a text pertaining to the domain of *siyāsa*, which meant that its rules were man-made and dealt with

145. Bargaoui (2003).

146. F. Vogel, Siyāsa, *EI*².

147. Abdesselem (1973, 102–103) and Demeerseman (1996, 62).

148. Today it is most often used to mean "politics" or "policy."

149. Abdesselem (1973, 104).

150. For instance, Bayram I (2016). This epistle by Muhammad Bayram I (d. 1800) is in manuscript form at the BNT (ms. 402) and was printed in Cairo in 1886. For a study and translation, see Van der Haven (2006).

statecraft.[151] It also asserted that they obeyed revealed law. "We have established some of the chapters that deal with statecraft [*fuṣūlihi al-siyāsīya*] in a way that, God willing, does not contradict the rules of sharia [*al-qawā ʿid al-shar ʿīya*]. Judgments will continue to be produced in the sharia court and to be obeyed."[152] By describing the innovations in the Security Pact as pertaining to the domain of *siyāsa*, and by arguing that they did not contradict sharia, its drafters explicitly legitimized them in an Islamic framework, although, as we will see, not everyone agreed. That said, even the ʿulamā who were critical of the Security Pact and were staunchly opposed to equality irrespective of religion when it contradicted sharia viewed some of the concessions made to non-Muslim *foreigners* (i.e., Europeans) as a diplomatic agreement under the discretionary power of the bey—that is, as pertaining to the domain of *siyāsa*. And indeed, as expressed in its title, the 1857 *ʿAhd al-Amān* was a protection agreement.[153] It made use of the Islamic legal concept of *amān*, "a safe conduct or pledge of security by which a *ḥarbī* or 'enemy alien,' i.e. a non-Muslim belonging to the *dār al-ḥarb*, becomes protected by the sanctions of the law in his life and property for a limited period," which could be given to "undetermined groups, such as the population of a whole city or territory or to all traders."[154] Although the 1857 *ʿAhd al-Amān* was a broad law in some respects, it contained distinct guarantees for the bey's Muslim and non-Muslim subjects and for foreigners, in the form of an agreement between two parties. The Zaytuna professor Mahmud Qabadu (1812–1872), in his poetry in praise of the Security Pact, compared it to the Pact of Hudaybiya between the prophet Muhammad and his Meccan enemies.[155]

SECURITY OR FREEDOM? AND FOR WHOM? GUARANTEEING MUSLIM WAYS OF LIFE

The explanatory text that followed the Security Pact was drafted in Arabic shortly after its proclamation and included four pillars (security of religion—*dīn*, security of life—*nafs*, security of property—*māl*, and security of honor— *ʿirḍ*).[156] It

151. On *qawā ʿid*, see W. P. Heinrichs, Ḳawā ʿid Fiḳhiyya, *EI*².

152. *Qānūn al-Dawla al-Tūnisīya* (1861, 5–6). The text also describes the new regulations as "*qānūn siyāsī*" (6).

153. N. Brown (2002, 16–17) curiously transliterates it "*ʿahd al-iman*" and translates it into "Charter of Faith" instead.

154. J. Schacht, Amān, *EI*².

155. Qabādū (1875–1879, vol. 1, 80).

156. The committee that drafted the explanatory text and the Constitution was established in November 1857, after the proclamation of the Security Pact. ANT SH C118 D403, no. 24. See also Van Krieken (1976, 38) and section 4.

defined the principle of "security of religion" (*amānat al-dīn*), which was translated as "freedom of worship" (*liberté des cultes*) in the official French version.[157] It guaranteed to non-Muslim subjects that they would not be forced to change religion or be prevented from converting to another religion. However, the right to convert was only given to non-Muslims.[158] Therefore, the new law ensured that the Muslim community would be preserved from erosion. To be sure, the explanatory text also gave the Muslim subjects of the bey some leeway: they could not be forced to follow a specific legal school—and its prescribed way of worship—that was not their own (*madhhabihi fī ʿaqīdatihi al-sanīya*), allowing them some freedom within Islam. Moreover, no Muslim subject could be prevented from performing the pilgrimage to Mecca if he or she had the means to do so.

The Security Pact's explanatory text reaffirmed the implementation of sharia in a jurisdiction that it took pains to define with great precision, as if to reassure the Muslim subjects of the bey and the *qāḍī*s of the enduring of Muslim ways of life: "The commandments of sharia will remain in effect [for Muslims] for all their acts of worship [*ʿibādāt*], their kin [*qarāba*], their endowments [*aḥbās*], their donations [*hibāt*], their charity [*ṣadaqāt*], their marriages [*ankiḥa*], their servants [*tawābiʿ*], their children's upbringing [*ḥaḍānāt*], their inheritances [*mawārīth*], their wills [*waṣāyā*], their orphans [*aytām*], and all similar affairs."[159] Overall, the Security Pact clearly reaffirmed the principle of the state's custodianship of Islam—that is, of the religion, of the Muslim community, and of its institutions. Vigorous internal debates accompanied this, revealing a political cleavage: were the innovations introduced with the Security Pact (and the ensuing Constitution of 1861) mere techniques of governance reorganizing the state but keeping intact the ideal of Islamic governance and of the state's custodianship of Islam, or did they shatter this ideal? Before we turn to these internal debates, let us examine the making of the 1861 Constitution announced by the Security Pact and the narratives and counternarratives about the (in)compatibility of Islam and constitutionalism that Tunisian and French authorities and opinion makers mobilized while the battle for legal sovereignty continued.

157. For the Arabic version, see *Qānūn al-Dawla al-Tūnisīya* (1861, 9), and for the French version, *Loi organique ou code politique* (1861, 12).

158. *Qānūn al-Dawla al-Tūnisīya* (1861, 9–10). Van Krieken (1976, 51), among others, incorrectly states that the legal reforms gave freedom of religion to all inhabitants of Tunisia.

159. *Qānūn al-Dawla al-Tūnisīya* (1861, 9–10).

3. The Making of the 1861 Constitution: Discourses of (In)compatibility of Islam and Constitutionalism in the Continued Battle for Legal Sovereignty

After the 1857 Security Pact was proclaimed, it took two years (with a beylical succession in September 1859 from Muhammad Bey to Muhammad Sadiq Bey) to draft the 1861 Constitution, which was completed and translated into French in September 1860. It was proclaimed on November 26, 1860, and then again on April 23, 1861, and put into effect on April 26, 1861, with a new code for criminal and customary law (*qānūn al-jināyāt wa-l-ahkām al-ʿurfīya*).[160] The 1861 Constitution, which developed and specified the provisions of the 1857 Security Pact, began with praise to God, whose aim is "human flourishing" (*ʿumrān*), and to the sharia, "which is, in itself, safety and security" (*allatī hiya al-amn wa-l-amān*).[161] The text of the Security Pact, as well as its explanation, formed the rest of the Constitution's preamble.[162] Thirteen chapters followed, comprising 114 articles in total.[163] The Constitution detailed the rights and duties of subjects (*raʿīya*) and inhabitants (*sukkān*) of the realm outlined in the Security Pact. It also reorganized the state in several domains, such as its ministries, its courts, its budget, and its civil servants. It established hereditary power for the Husaynid dynasty and made the bey a "king" (*malik*). The Regency was not a "province" (*iyāla*) anymore but a kingdom (*mamlaka*), whose frontiers the king protected, and the Ottoman sultan was not even mentioned. The Constitution defined the bey's succession through primogeniture, whereas in past practice the oldest man in the bey's extended family was appointed by the sultan to succeed him. It regulated the bey's family, over whom he had absolute power, and a Private Council judged affairs that involved its members. A sixty-member Great Council was also established, to which the bey was accountable (*masʾūl*). A third of its members were meant to be either civil servants or members of the military, and the rest notables. They were all chosen by the king and were to be replaced every five years. The Great Council was the guardian of the Security Pact and of the laws,

160. Roches to the French Ministry of Foreign Affairs, July 14, 1860, AMAE, Tunis, CP, vol. 19, fol. 207. See also Van Krieken (1976, 58). For the criminal and customary code, see ANT, Register 2683.

161. *Qānūn al-Dawla al-Tūnisīya* (1861, 1–2).

162. *Qānūn al-Dawla al-Tūnisīya* (1861, 3–13).

163. *Qānūn al-Dawla al-Tūnisīya* (1861, 13–43).

which it debated and on which it voted, and the king was to govern "in association with the Council." A kind of constitutional monarchy was therefore established: the king had to swear an oath, in the name of God, before the Great Council and the sharia court, pledging to respect the Constitution. If he did not respect it, all allegiances to the king would be null. He was commander in chief of the army, could appoint whomever he pleased as ministers, and could pardon convicted criminals. He also had the authority to proclaim the decrees necessary to apply the Constitution. The ministers were accountable to the king and to the Great Council, whose task was to protect the rights (*ḥuqūq*) of the king and of the inhabitants of the realm. Courts were reorganized, with tribunals of first instance (*majālis al-ḍabṭīya*), criminal and customary courts (*majālis al-jināyāt wa-l-aḥkām al-ʿurfīya*), a court of appeals (*majlis al-taḥqīq*), and a court of cassation (*majlis iʿtiyādī*), which coexisted with the sharia court.[164]

The Battle for Legal Sovereignty Continues with the Making of the 1861 Constitution

Chapter 13 of the Constitution defined the rights and duties of "the subjects of the friendly states" residing in the realm. They were granted the same rights and duties as the king's subjects in the import and export of merchandise along with the right to own property (albeit with some restrictions). Moreover, they were to submit to the jurisdiction of the new tribunals, although their consuls would be allowed to be present in the criminal court. Mixed tribunals were not even mentioned, only some "reassurances" as to the smooth operation of the new tribunals.[165] This blatantly contradicted the French consul's wishes and the bey's oral promise—a few weeks before the Constitution was proclaimed for the first time on November 26, 1860—to withhold this jurisdictional provision until a

164. For more details about the judicial reorganization, see Van Krieken (1976, 56–62).

165. Article 114 of chapter 13 read, "Since it was imperative [*wājib*] to establish legal equality [*al-taswiya ladā al-ḥukm*] irrespective of religion and rank, and since the subjects of our allied states had the same rights and benefits [*al-ḥuqūq wa-l-manāfiʿ*] as our subjects, it was imperative that they submit to the decisions of the tribunals we have instituted. We have given to all enough guarantees on the choice of the judges we have appointed and on the attentive study we have made of the dispositions of the code that will be used by these tribunals, and on the various degrees of jurisdiction we have established. To provide even more reassurances, we have established in the criminal and customary law [*qānūn al-jināyāt wa-l-aḥkām al-ʿurfīya*] that for cases involving subjects of our allied states, the presence of their consul or of a delegate of his would be allowed." *Qānūn al-Dawla al-Tūnisīya* (1861, 43).

solution could be negotiated.[166] When Léon Roches wrote to the bey on March 25, 1861 to obtain confirmation that this provision would be excluded from the Constitution,[167] the bey only responded on May 18, 1861, more than two weeks after it was proclaimed for a second time and put into effect, thereby rendering this provision a fait accompli. The battle for jurisdictional sovereignty between French and Tunisian officials that took place during the making of the Security Pact therefore continued with renewed vigor in the fall of 1860 and did not subside. After lengthy negotiations with the French consul in Tunis and the French government in Paris,[168] the bey established, in June 1861, a Provisional Committee made of seven Muslim Tunisian members and presided over by Ibn Diyaf, in the Tunisian Ministry of Foreign Affairs, to examine cases involving Tunisian subjects and foreigners, which would operate until a suitable agreement could be struck.[169] However, this did not satisfy French authorities, who continued to argue with the Tunisian government on this issue,[170] claiming that the submission of their nationals to Tunisian tribunals contravened the Capitulations. When Minister Khayr al-Din met with the French minister of foreign

166. Roches to the French minister of foreign affairs, April 28, 1861, AMAE, Tunis, CP, vol. 20, fol. 99; Roches to the French minister of foreign affairs, June 20, 1861, AMAE, Tunis, CP, vol. 20, fol. 135; and Roches's letter of January 26, 1861, complaining to the bey, ANT SH C118 D408, no. 1.

167. "Annexe à la dépêche de M. Roches du 20 juin 1861, no. 1 (Le chargé d'affaires de France à Son Altesse le bey, Tunis, le 25 mars 1861)," AMAE, Tunis, CP, vol. 20, fols. 140–142.

168. See, for instance, the bey to Roches, October 3, 1860, AMAE, Tunis, CP, vol. 20, fols. 45–47, also in Arabic in ANT SH C118 D408, no. 2; Roches to Thouvenel, October 21, 1860, AMAE, Tunis, CP, vol. 20, fol. 37–44; Roches to Thouvenel, November 3, 1860, AMAE, Tunis, CP, vol. 20, fol. 55–58; Thouvenel to Roches, November 14, 1860, AMAE, Tunis, CP, vol. 20, fols. 62–64; Roches to the bey, January 26, 1861, ANT SH C118 D408, no. 1; the bey to Roches, February 7, 1861, Ibn Abī al-Ḍiyāf (1963, vol. 5, 70); Roches to the bey, March 25, 1861, AMAE, Tunis, CP, vol. 20, fols. 140–142; Roches to Thouvenel, April 28, 1861, AMAE, Tunis, CP, vol. 20, fol. 99; the bey to Roches, May 19, 1861, AMAE, Tunis, CP, vol. 20, fols. 143–146, also in Arabic (draft dated May 14, 1861) in ANT SH C118 D408, no. 14; Roches to Thouvenel, June 20, 1861, AMAE, Tunis, CP, vol. 20, fols. 135–139; Rousseau to Thouvenel, June 23, 1861, AMAE, Tunis, CP, vol. 20, fol. 149–154; "Observations sur la dépêche écrite de Paris par M. Roches, le 20 juin 1861 en réponse à une dépêche ministérielle du 14 novembre 1860," July 6, 1861, AMAE, Tunis, CP, vol. 20, fols. 167–168; Jules de Lesseps, the bey's representative in Paris, to Prime Minister Mustafa Khaznadar, March 13, 1861 (no. 10), March 20, 1861 (no. 12), April 10, 1861 (no. 23), September 11, 1861 (no. 25), September 25, 1861 (no. 27), October 2, 1861 (no. 29), ANT SH C118 D408.

169. "Annexes à la dépêche du 6 juillet 1861, Direction Politique no. 6," AMAE, Tunis, CP, vol. 20, fols. 174–177. Ibn Abī al-Ḍiyāf (1963, vol. 5, 67–68).

170. Rousseau to Thouvenel, July 6, 1861, AMAE, Tunis, CP, vol. 20, fol. 169–173; Khayr al-Din to Prime Minister Mustafa Khaznadar, July 5, 1861, ANT SH C209 D159bis-1, no. 10.

affairs in Paris in September 1861, he objected that if foreigners did not submit to the local Tunisian jurisdiction, there would be inequality before the law and "harm done to the rights of Tunisians" (*ḍarar ʿalā al-tawānisa fī ḥuqūqihim*). It would "contradict the new organizations" (*al-tarātīb al-jadīda*) and would therefore jeopardize the Constitution. He insisted that, contrary to the French interpretation, the Constitution was in continuity with past Capitulations (*shurūṭ*), which "clearly stipulated that the King of Tunis [*malik tūnis*] had the right to judge the subjects of the [foreign] states in presence of the consul of the defendant in criminal affairs." He argued that the bey had simply transferred this right to the new tribunals.[171] In Tunis, the tug-of-war on this issue continued between the bey's government and Léon Roches.[172] The French consul attempted to prevail by modifying the composition of the Provisional Committee and by curtailing its prerogatives.[173] It also seems that Khayr al-Din lobbied European public opinion through the press. The French consul fulminated against a Belgian journal that blamed the slowness of the new tribunals on the foreign consuls' reluctance to submit their nationals to local justice.[174] In May 1862, Léon Roches, in his correspondence with the French minister of foreign affairs, criticized Khayr al-Din and the bey's ministers for thinking and acting as if Tunisia was "a state constituted as the European states."[175]

The French consul also started to complain openly about the Tunisian Constitution and advocated for the elimination of some of its provisions.[176] He

171. Khayr al-Din to the minister of foreign affairs, "Note verbale," September 4, 1861, AMAE, Tunis, CP, vol. 20, fols. 209–216, and ANT SH C118 D408, no. 34.

172. Léon Roches wrote about the Great Council's opposition to consular jurisdictions, "We cannot tolerate such presumptuousness." Roches to the French minister of foreign affairs, January 12, 1862, AMAE, Tunis, CP, vol. 21, fol. 4.

173. Roches to Thouvenel, February 8, 1862, AMAE, Tunis, CP, vol. 21, fols. 6–9.

174. *L'Indépendance belge*, March 5, 1862, in "Annexe 3 à la dépêche du 22 mars 1862, Nouvelles d'Orient," AMAE, Tunis, CP, vol. 21, fols. 20–21. The article stated, about the French demands, "No constitutional government could accept this." Léon Roches attributed this essay to Khayr al-Din and to General Husayn and accused Khayr al-Din "and his friends" of being behind the 1862 publication in Paris of a booklet by Ferdinand Prévost, *La Tunisie devant l'Europe*, which praised the legal reforms and argued for the recognition of Tunisia as a "sovereign and independent state." Roches to the French minister of foreign affairs, May 17, 1862, AMAE, Tunis, CP, vol. 21, fols. 42–44.

175. Roches to the French minister of foreign affairs, May 17, 1862, AMAE, Tunis, CP, vol. 21, fols. 42–44.

176. Roches to the French minister of foreign affairs, May 31, 1862, AMAE, Tunis, CP, vol. 21, fols. 60–62.

faced mounting pressure from European merchants who claimed that the Constitution caused "their ruin."[177] The deputies of the French Nation in the Regency complained to their consul that the Provisional Committee was biased against Europeans.[178] The consuls of several European countries similarly complained to the bey's government about the conduct of the new tribunals (and, as we will see when we examine the 1864 rebellion, so did the bey's subjects), notably the tribunals of first instance (*majālis al-ḍabṭīya*). They complained about the accumulation of cases in the interior of the country; the intentional slowness of judicial procedures to protect the interests of natives; the judges not being paid, not attending their own courts, or declaring themselves incompetent after long delays; as well as cases of corruption.[179] Overall, although the legal reforms established several important institutions successfully (if only briefly, in many cases),[180] they did not achieve most of the Europeans' and Tunisians' initial goals. A code of commerce was drafted in 1863 but never put into effect,[181] and standing mixed commercial tribunals were only established in 1885,[182] after French occupation, to deal with real estate cases.[183] Foreigners obtained property rights only through bilateral treaties—in 1863 with Great Britain, in 1866 with Austria, in 1868 with Italy, and in 1871 with France.[184] As for Tunisian officials, they failed to put Europeans under the Regency's jurisdiction. It seems that the Provisional Committee that operated between

177. "Mémoire des députés du commerce français à Tunis, transmis par la chambre de commerce de Marseille, et qui fait part des griefs de nos nationaux contre le gouvernement tunisien," July 31, 1862, AMAE, Tunis, CP, vol. 21, fol. 81. According to Léon Roches, they were dissatisfied because the Constitution created more competition, reduced monopolies, and the bey could not spend as much for himself as he now had an allowance (*liste civile*). Roches to the French minister of foreign affairs, September 6, 1862, AMAE, Tunis, CP, vol. 21, fols. 89–90.

178. Lettre des premier et deuxième députés de la Nation française à Roches, December 17, 1862, AMAE, Tunis, CP, vol. 21, fols. 139–141.

179. Letters from several foreign consular authorities, ANT SH C141 D512bis. See also Van Krieken (1976, 60–68).

180. Van Krieken (1976), Womble (1997), and Oualdi (2011).

181. Van Krieken (1976, 72).

182. Law of July 1, 1885.

183. Mixed commercial tribunals were proposed by the Tunisian government in 1871 but faced staunch opposition from the Italian consul. A provisional mixed tribunal was established in 1874, for cases between Tunisians and French or British subjects with less than 1,000 piastres at stake, but it does not seem to have lasted long. See Van Krieken (1976, 237–243) and ANT SH C200 D4.

184. Van Krieken (1976, 68–69).

June 1861 and 1864 never judged a single European.[185] Europeans only sent their cases to this tribunal when they were plaintiffs, in the spirit of past practices. For Ibn Diyaf, presiding over the Provisional Committee was an ordeal because foreigners resisted this court.[186] On the other hand, making legal reforms allowed the bey's government to fight for the Regency's legal sovereignty, despite a lopsided balance of power in favor of Europe.

Debates about the (In)compatibility of Islam and Constitutionalism Take On a Life of Their Own

Although the stakes of the legal reforms were, as we saw, of a concrete (jurisdictional and economic) nature, disputes about the flaws and virtues of Muslim government, and about the compatibility of Islam and constitutionalism, took on a life of their own. Léon Roches depicted all existing "Muslim governments" as capricious and absolute, "unlike Qur'anic prescriptions." He often objected to his Tunisian interlocutors that, although their government was Muslim in name, it did not conform to Islam's principles.[187] The French consul nonetheless justified his refusal to see French subjects submit to the Regency's system of justice by both their reluctance to relinquish their privileges and a narrative of religious difference and fear of Islam. For instance, he reasoned that the Tunisian commercial and criminal courts, although outside of the purview of sharia, would be unable to apply the new codes in an unbiased way since all their judges were Muslim. He even referred to these new tribunals as "Muslim tribunals." In an October 1860 letter to the French minister of foreign affairs, he wrote that he was "shaking with fear" when broaching the subject of French nationals falling under the jurisdiction of these tribunals and their Muslim judges, and he could not accept "that a Frenchman could be jailed in Tunisian prisons or galleys and that his head could fall under the Muslim axe." In spite of his argument that the judges in these tribunals were "the most recommendable," that the different degrees of jurisdictions were now "similar to the French ones," and that the civil and criminal codes were "more or less,

185. ANT Register 2897, "Summary of cases brought to the provisional tribunal from Dhū al-Ḥijja 1277 (July 1861) to Jumādā al-Thānī 1279 (November–December 1862)," as well as Registers 2898, 2899, 2900, 2901, and 2902 for the subsequent periods, until April 1864. See also Van Krieken (1976, 68 and 70).

186. Abdesselem (1973, 354) and Ibn Abī al-Ḍiyāf (1963, vol. 5, 106).

187. Roches to Thouvenel, October 21, 1860, AMAE, Tunis, CP, vol. 20, fols. 15–16.

copied on ours," he still feared that "Muslim fanaticism could be awakened."[188] In these narratives, Islam was an obstacle to the constitutional reforms. However, it was also presented (e.g., in the European press) as fully compatible with the values of the Enlightenment, perhaps the result of a public relations effort on the part of the bey's government. *Le Moniteur judiciaire de Lyon* argued in 1861 that the Constitution made the state "civilized" and its prince "as liberal as he is enlightened."[189] The influential *Journal des débats* described the 1861 Constitution as a sign of "good progress" and a model for other Muslim countries.[190] It argued that it formally reaffirmed "most of the essential principles of European and Christian civilization."[191] Certainly, the article continued, the Constitution was not perfect. It did not allow Muslims to change religion, and it did not include the people's control of the executive power or freedom of the press. However, it was proof that, in Islam, it was possible "to separate the spiritual from the temporal, perhaps more easily than in Rome."[192] The foreign consuls themselves had used this type of argument when attempting to persuade the bey and his entourage of the Islamic legitimacy of the reforms. For example, Richard Wood assured the bey in 1857 that the purpose of the legal reforms was to "reach the very foundation of [Islam]."[193] After 1862, however, incompatibility arguments helped French authorities in Tunis express their increasing misgivings about the Constitution.[194]

As for the bey and his ministers, they responded to these incompatibility arguments in the language of legal universalism. The bey envisioned the laws of his state as applying to all, except in matters reserved for the religious courts. He wrote to Léon Roches, "Our most fervent desire is to eliminate the perceived inequality before the law [*mā yatawahham min ʿadam al-musāwāt ladā*

188. Roches to Thouvenel, October 21, 1860, AMAE, Tunis, CP, vol. 20, fols. 39–40.

189. *Moniteur judiciaire de Lyon*, no. 71, 22 juin 1861. Quoted in Prévost (1862, 14).

190. *Le Journal des débats*, July 12, 1861, 1.

191. *Le Journal des débats*, July 12, 1861, 1.

192. *Le Journal des débats*, July 12, 1861, 1.

193. Ibn Abī al-Ḍiyāf (1963, vol. 4, 236). See also, for the same argument by Léon Roches, Roches to the French minister of foreign affairs, August 11, 1857, AMAE, Tunis, CP, vol. 17, fol. 160.

194. For instance, Lieutenant-Colonel Campenon to Maréchal Randon, Ministre de la Guerre à Paris, May 31, 1862, AMAE, Tunis, CP, vol. 22, fol. 45. "Let us remember that in a Muslim tribunal, a hundred witnesses can always be found to accuse the Christian and none can be found to defend him. Let us keep our centuries-old Capitulations, which are fortunately still in effect in Constantinople." See also Roches to Thouvenel, May 31, 1862, AMAE, Tunis, CP, vol. 21, fols. 58–63.

al-ḥukm] that the difference between [our] religions [*ikhtilāf al-diyāna*] seemed to establish."[195] Later, in his 1867 book on governance, *The Surest Path*, Khayr al-Din argued in the same vein that the law could apply to all, independent of religious differences, and that it was what Islam itself prescribed: "The truth is that religious hostility [*al-ʿadāwa al-dīnīya*] does not incline the judge away from the impartiality [*al-inṣāf*] upon which the sharia is based or from deciding in favor of the truth [*al-ḥaqq*], wherever this leads."[196] All these narratives and counternarratives about the (in)compatibility of Islam and constitutionalism resonate in striking ways with present-day journalistic and academic discourses. Then, as now, they were mobilized as resources in enterprises of persuasion and opinion making. Irrespective of whether or not they actually shaped policy decisions during this crisis, it is noteworthy that all protagonists, at all times, described the Tunisian state (and its legal sovereignty) as unmistakably Muslim: an ambition for some, a problem for others, but a reality for all.

4. Debates among ʿUlamā and in the Great Council: Did the Legal Reforms Bend Sharia beyond Recognition?

Legal universalism under a Muslim state was not a straightforward affair. There were strong misgivings within the bey's administration, which was divided over the Islamic legitimacy of the reforms. These misgivings were notably articulated during the deliberations that took place over several months in the Drafting Committee the bey had appointed on November 4, 1857 (initially five government officials and five ʿulamā, including Ibn Diyaf) to explain the Security Pact and draft the Constitution and the new codes that were to be based on it.[197] The ʿulamā were charged with ascertaining whether each of the rules

195. The bey to Roches, October 3, 1860, ANT SH C118 D408, no. 2, and Annex no. 1 to the letter from Roches to Thouvenel, October 21, 1860, AMAE, Tunis, CP, vol. 20, fol. 46. For other examples, see Ibn Abī al-Ḍiyāf (1963, vol. 5, 70 and 75–77), and the bey to Roches, May 19, 1861, AMAE, Tunis, CP, vol. 20, fols. 143–146.

196. Al-Tūnisī (1867, 38). English translation inspired by L. C. Brown (1967, 120).

197. Bey's decree of November 4, 1857, ANT SH C118 D403, no. 24. "The Prime Minister opened the November 5, 1857, meeting by saying that our Lord the bey gathered us here in order to establish [*tartīb*] political rules [*aḥkām siyāsīya*] that will benefit [*nafʿ*] our country [*waṭan*] and that will not contradict sharia." Meeting of the Drafting Committee, November 5, 1857, ANT SH C118 D403, no. 55.

of the Security Pact conformed to sharia.[198] On many occasions, they showed great reluctance to answer this request, but in the face of the insistence of the bey's ministers, they had to comply. For instance, Shaykh al-Islam Muhammad Bayram proposed that the ʿulamā remain silent if a rule required by the public interest (*maṣlaḥa*) contradicted sharia. This quietist approach was firmly rejected by the prime minister, who insisted that they provide all the opinions (*aqwāl*) they could find, "even if weak" (*wa-law al-ḍaʿīfa*).[199] Ismail Sahib al-Tabi–one of the bey's favorite Mamluks, called "al-Sunni" because of his proximity to the ʿulamā[200]—requested that they rely on opinions "even outside of the Hanafi and Maliki schools of law, in the Shafiʿi and Hanbali *madhhabs*."[201] When the shaykh al-Islam protested that the rules of the Security Pact could be interpreted in various ways and that the ʿulamā did not know the outcome of future negotiations between the bey and the foreign powers over the rules of the Constitution, Ismail Sahib al-Tabi answered that the bey had convened the ʿulamā precisely to do this interpretive work.[202]

The New Laws' Revealing Silence on Apostasy and Blasphemy

The Constitution, the Security Pact, and its explanatory text were all silent on the issue of apostasy, whereas an earlier draft of the explanatory text by the Drafting Committee had addressed this issue. This suggests that it was a point of contention.[203] In this earlier draft, under the title "security of religion" (the first pillar), a passage about apostasy read, "whoever, among our Muslim subjects (we have

198. The ʿulamā notably discussed the apostasy of converts to Islam, the penalty for brigandage by bedouins, the regulation of street sellers, the regulation of wine shops, property rights of non-Muslims, blood crimes, and the validity of the testimony of non-Muslims. ANT SH C118 D409 and ANT SH C142 D515. See also Bachrouch (2008, 163–166).

199. Meeting of the Drafting Committee, November 5, 1857, ANT SH C118 D403, no. 55.

200. Ibn Abī al-Ḍiyāf (1963, vol. 8, 153).

201. Meeting of the Drafting Committee, November 5, 1857, ANT SH C118 D403, no. 55.

202. Meeting of the Drafting Committee, November 5, 1857, ANT SH C118 D403, no. 55.

203. According to Léon Roches, the first session of the Drafting Committee was devoted to a discussion of the Ottoman reforms, and a dispute arose on the issues of "blasphemy, apostasy, and Christians' testimony." Roches to the French minister of foreign affairs, November 6, 1857, AMAE, Tunis, CP, vol. 17, fols. 263–265. It is likely that Léon Roches was referring to the session of November 5, 1857, which is also documented in ANT SH C118 D403, no. 55. This document does not speak of a dispute but rather describes an agreement among the ʿulamā about the use of non-Muslim witnesses in courts "in case of necessity" (*ʿind al-ḍarūra*). It also mentions that a stipulation against apostasy was discussed and approved by the ʿulamā.

not applied this to the *dhimma*), apostatized [*irtadda*], falls under the jurisdiction of the sharia court, which will ask for his repentance, and will judge him. We [the bey] can only execute the sharia court's judgment [*tanfīdh mā ḥakama bihi majlis al-shar*ʿ] in this matter since every Muslim knows the sentence for apostasy [*ridda*] in Islam. Our Jewish subjects, if they convert to Islam, will be under the same rules as our Muslim subjects when it comes to apostasy."[204] However, the final version of the Security Pact's explanatory text remained silent on apostasy. It is noteworthy that in Istanbul, in contrast, an 1844 imperial declaration affirmed that "the death penalty for apostasy from Islam would no longer be applied to Muslims [who are] converts from Christianity [and] who wished to revert to their original faith," and an annex to the 1856 Khatt-i Humayun had reasserted this promise.[205] In the same vein, the Drafting Committee discussed the issue of blasphemy,[206] but the new laws (be it the Security Pact, the Constitution, or the criminal code) did not address it. This left French authorities uneasy: they feared that the sharia court would continue to adjudicate blasphemy cases and that Europeans accused of such acts by Muslim witnesses could be sentenced to death, as had happened to Bato Sfez in 1857.[207] The new laws' silence on apostasy and blasphemy therefore appears to have been both a sign of, and a solution to, deep disagreements, internal and external, on these issues.

The ʿUlamā's Conservatism in Islamic Law and Pragmatism in Governance

Two fatwas, written, respectively, by a Hanafi and a Maliki high official, did not shy away from clearly asserting how parts of the Security Pact might contradict sharia, particularly most of its notions of equality between Muslims and non-Muslims.[208] For instance, the Maliki fatwa stated that Rule #1's security for all

204. ANT SH C118 D409, no. 66. The annotation "*Majlis 1*" on the document seems to confirm that this discussion about apostasy took place during the first session of the committee on November 5, 1857. For examples of how converts to Islam were treated in practice if they reverted back to their original faith, see Clancy-Smith (2011, 229–233).

205. Davison (1963, 45 and 55).

206. ANT SH C118 D409, no. 8.

207. French minister of foreign affairs to Roches, November 14, 1860, AMAE, Tunis, CP, vol. 20, fols. 63–64; Roches to the French minister of foreign affairs, June 20, 1861, AMAE, Tunis, CP, vol. 20, fol. 139.

208. The Maliki fatwa seems to have been preserved in its entirety, but it is undated, and the author's name (probably Maliki Bash Mufti Shaykh Ahmad Ibn al-Husayn or Maliki Mufti

inhabitants of the realm was unacceptable if it meant that the punishments stipulated in the sharia (*ḥudūd*)—retaliation in kind (*qiṣāṣ*) and alms giving (*zakāt*)—were abandoned. This fatwa implied that Rule #2's equality of all in taxation was impossible since, it argued, "Muslims cannot be asked to pay taxes that are not obligatory according to the revelation [*sharʿ*]," "no Muslim should pay the *jizya*," and only in cases of need (*ḥāja*) could nonobligatory taxes be raised, as long as they obeyed the conditions of justice and public interest (*maṣlaḥa*) and benefited only Muslims. This fatwa also tersely rejected Rule #3's equality of all inhabitants regardless of religion in deserving fairness (*istiḥqāq al-inṣāf*), if, by it, the drafters of the Security Pact meant to contradict sharia (*al-ḥukm al-sharʿī* and *sharʿ*). In contrast, the fatwas found Rule #8's equality of Muslim and non-Muslim subjects in affairs of custom (*al-umūr al-ʿurfīya*)—they did not mention official laws (*al-qawānīn al-ḥukmīya*)—to be a *siyāsa* prerogative (i.e., part of the discretionary power of the ruler), which caused no harm and did not contradict sharia. Both fatwas rehearsed their authors' understanding of Islamic law's rules regarding protected minorities (*dhimmīs*) and elements of the so-called Pact of Umar.[209] They wrote, regarding Rule #4, that *dhimmīs* should not be prevented from practicing their religion and should not be forced to change religion, but there were limits: for example, they must worship with discretion (they must not be seen in religious processions, they must not ring the bells, and Muslims should not hear them reading their scriptures), must not be allowed to ride horses, must wear a distinguishable dress, and must be humiliated such as when paying the *jizya* (with "a slap on the back of the head," according to the Maliki fatwa, but without any violence according to the Hanafi fatwa). The Hanafi fatwa added to this principle that if a *dhimmī* had converted to Islam and reverted to his original religion, he must be forced to return to Islam. The Maliki fatwa rejected Rule #6's establishment of mixed criminal courts for affairs involving Jewish and Muslim subjects of the bey (it questioned these courts' purpose since judgments had to be made in accordance with sharia in any event) as well as Rule #7's establishment of mixed commercial tribunals, which, it argued, "give power to the

Shaykh Muhammad al-Banna) is missing. The Hanafi fatwa, written by Bash Mufti and Shaykh al-Islam Muhammad Ibn al-Khuja, is also undated, and the commentaries on Rules #1 to #3 are missing. These two texts are not presented as "fatwas" per se but are classified as "fatwas" in the archives. ANT SH C118 D403, nos. 2 and 59 for the Maliki fatwa, and no. 3 for the Hanafi fatwa.

209. An analysis of the older historical context for these kinds of restrictions is beyond our scope. For a discussion, see Cohen (2008, 57–74).

unbelievers over the Muslims in their commerce."[210] Both fatwas developed lengthy and technical commentaries about foreigners' property rights (Rule #11). The Maliki fatwa concluded that the implementation of this rule depended on necessities (*ḍarūrāt*). The Hanafi fatwa summarized the issue of foreigners' property rights as a decision between war and peace which, in the end, had to satisfy public interest (*maṣlaḥa*).

There was therefore in these fatwas a measure of pragmatism regarding the laws regulating foreigners in the Regency,[211] but much less flexibility concerning the hierarchy between Muslims and non-Muslims (e.g., in courts of law, in their religious worship, and in taxation). This pragmatism toward foreigners stemmed in part from an acute awareness of the economic and military imbalance between Tunisia and Europe. For instance, the Maliki fatwa argued that allowing foreigners to own property was necessitated by the current military inferiority of the Muslims, and the Hanafi fatwa, when insisting on *dhimmīs* paying the *jizya*, spoke of the present as a time "when Islam's power [*shawkat al-Islām*] [has] diminished and the religion has become foreign [*gharīb*]."[212] To be sure, their reasoning at times veered off topic, did not always sound relevant to the Regency's context, and remained firmly anchored in their respective schools of law, contrary to the instructions the ʿulamā were given.[213] On the whole, the two fatwas remained conservative in their general spirit

210. Regarding Rules #6 and #7, the Hanafi fatwa stated that it had the same comment as for Rule #1, which is missing from the document.

211. The Hanafi fatwa in particular analyzed Rules #10 and #11 under the canopy of the *Siyar* literature, a branch of sharia dealing with how states should behave with people residing in the abode of Islam (*dạr al-Islām*) or the abode of war (*dār al-ḥarb*). The foreigner is seen as a *ḥarbī* (an enemy alien) or a *mustaʾmin* (a *ḥarbī* who has been given *amān* or safe conduct). Bsoul (2008, 70–81).

212. This sentence is modeled in part on the hadith "Islam began as something foreign and will return as something foreign, so blessed are the foreigners" (*badaʾa al-Islām gharīban wa-sayaʿūd kamā badaʾa gharīban fa-ṭūbā li-l-ghurabāʾ*). *Saḥīḥ Muslim* 145 (*Kitāb al-īmān*). Also, the Maliki fatwa stated that it was impermissible to raise non-sharia compliant taxes for the state to repay a loan, an implicit reference to the economic situation of the Regency.

213. The Maliki fatwa mostly quoted Maliki jurists (e.g., *Al-Miʿyār* by Al-Wansharīsī (1430 or 1431–1508), *Jāmiʿ Masāʾil al-Aḥkām* by Al-Burzulī (ca. 1339–1438), *Al-Mudawwana* by Saḥnūn (776 or 777–854), *Al-Ajwiba* by Ibn Rushd al-Jadd (1058 or 1059–1126), and Al-Ṭurṭūshī (1059–1126)). The Hanafi fatwa mostly quoted Hanafi jurists (e.g., *Kitāb al-Ṣayd*, from *Kitāb al-Fatāwā*, by Khayr al-Dīn al-Ramlī (1585–1671), *Sharḥ Tanwīr al-Ibtiṣār* by Al-Tamartāshī (1532 or 1533–1595 or 1596), *Al-Hidāya* by Al-Marghīnānī (d. 1197), *Al-Fatḥ al-Qadīr* by Ibn al-Humām (1386 or 1387–1457), and the *Fatāwā Hindīya*).

(they did not accept full equality), realistic about the economic and military weakness of the Regency (and therefore pragmatic within the strict bounds of sharia), and deeply pessimistic in their tone.

The ʿulamā eventually withdrew from the Drafting Committee. They argued that their role was to deal with issues related to sharia and that it was "not appropriate for them to deal with matters of policy [*al-umūr al-siyāsīya*]." They added that if the Drafting Committee needed help on a question of Islamic law (*fiqh*), they would remain available to respond in writing.[214] Contrary to what is often argued, neither the tenor of the fatwas they produced nor their withdrawal from the Drafting Committee implies that they were socially and politically passive.[215] Their understanding of Islamic governance was simply too far from that of the advocates of the legal reforms.[216] Moreover, the ʿulamā were not of one voice. Ibn Diyaf, who was a member of the Drafting Committee, regularly contradicted other ʿulamā and criticized them in harsh terms when they withdrew from it.[217] According to him, "they used the pretext that drafting the constitution did not fall under their customary responsibilities related to sharia [*lā tunāsib khuṭaṭahum al-sharʿīya fī al-ʿurf*]."[218] For Ibn Diyaf, the ʿulamā had to relate their knowledge of religion (*dīn*) and sharia to temporal matters (*dunyā*).[219] Deprived of the ʿulamā's involvement as interpreters of sharia, the state was in danger of losing its Muslim character. Ibn Diyaf and other members of the government were convinced that, to justify the reforms, it was possible to interpret sharia in ways more creative than the conservative ʿulamā were willing to do. This debate should therefore not be interpreted as a dispute between proponents of Islamic governance and proponents of

214. Ibn Abī al-Ḍiyāf (1963, vol. 4, 248, and vol. 5, 17).

215. For instance, M. A. Ben Achour (1977, 259) argues that these fatwas were not "political."

216. The ʿulamā might have also perceived the shrinking of sharia's jurisdiction as threatening their livelihood, as argued by Green (1978). However, evidence on this is mixed, and, as observed by M. A. Ben Achour (1977, 256), the ʿulamā would find positions in the new tribunals.

217. Ibn Abī al-Ḍiyāf (1963, vol. 5, 17).

218. Ibn Abī al-Ḍiyāf (1963, vol. 5, 38).

219. See also Ibn Abī al-Ḍiyāf (1963, vol. 4, 248), for his criticism of the ʿulamā not fulfilling their duty of counsel to the ruler (*nasīḥa*). Note that he did not detail the ʿulamā's fatwas about the *ʿAhd al-Amān* in the *Itḥāf*, arguing that they were too long to reproduce. Muhammad Bayram V (1840–1889) argues, in Bayram V (1884–1894, vol. 2, 14), that the ʿulamā withdrew from the Drafting Committee because they claimed the committee was asked to "lean exclusively toward basic policy-making [*al-mayl al-baḥt ilā al-siyāsa al-sādhija*] without getting close to the revealed law [*sharʿ*], and perhaps even contradicting it."

secular governance but rather between competing understandings of Islamic governance—that is, a dispute about the appropriate degree of involvement of the ʿulamā in politics, and (using my nomenclature) about the appropriate thickness and strength of the state custodianship of Islam.[220]

A Debate about the Inclusion of Jews in the Great Council: The Limits of Equality Regardless of Religion in a Muslim State

There was also a divide about how to practically implement the new laws' notions of equality irrespective of religion when it came to the political representation of the Jewish subjects of the bey. A dispute erupted in July 1861 between Ibn Diyaf and General Husayn about the composition of the newly formed Great Council, the highest deliberative state body in the Regency. This dispute, one of many among state officials,[221] shows that even within the pro-reform camp there were disagreements about how to implement the ideal of Islamic governance in the context of new policy imperatives and that the ʿulamā were not always the most conservative voices. The 1857 and 1861 reforms had been welcomed by Jewish notables who saw them as "an act of emancipation" since they abolished the legal status of protected religious minorities (*dhimmīs*) and the religious inequality it sustained. New laws repealed their obligation to wear a distinctive dress (specifically, a black version of the men's skullcap known as the *shāshīya*) and abolished the capitation tax (*jizya*) and the corvée (*sukhra*).[222] Jewish judges were included in the new penal tribunals,[223] although no Jew was included in the Great Council, a fact that Ibn Diyaf deplored. Noting that the Great Council included a non-Muslim (presumably Count Giuseppe Raffo, a Christian who played the role of minister of foreign affairs), Ibn Diyaf requested the addition of a Jewish notable, invoking the rule of equality (*qā ʿidat al-taswiya*) irrespective of religion inscribed in Rules #3 and #8 of the 1857 Security Pact.[224] A fellow Great Council member, General Husayn, responded that the principle of equality would be

220. Bayram V (1884–1894, vol. 2, 14) spoke of two opposite "camps" (*farīqayn*) when recounting the ʿulamā's withdrawal from the Drafting Committee.

221. On the diversity of positions about the reforms among the Mamluks, and within the Great Council of 1861–1864 more broadly, see Oualdi (2011, 245–250).

222. Allagui (2016, 60).

223. Article 1 of the criminal code, ANT, Register 2683, 73.

224. BNT ms. 18775, fols. 1–4; Bercher (1972, 68 and 70–71).

inherently contradicted if one category of subjects (in this instance Jews) were favored over another.[225] He also argued that, contrary to French and English Jews, the Jewish subjects of the bey were untrustworthy because they had no loyalty to their country and did not have the "public interest" (*maṣlaḥa*) in mind.[226] In the end, the Great Council rejected Ibn Diyaf's request.

As has been argued, this rejection was framed by General Husayn as a principled defense of meritocracy, and it also reflected his antipathy toward the Regency's Jews, who were making gains in economic and social status at the time and who were perceived to be allied with the European powers.[227] What has been overlooked, however, is that it also expressed a rejection of the political recognition and inclusion of the Jewish religious minority as such at the highest level of the state, and an affirmation that the state had to be administered mainly by (and for) Muslims.[228] We also find such a defense of the Muslim character of the state in Khayr al-Din's book justifying the Tanzimat, *The Surest Path*: while supporting the principle of limits to executive power, he pronounced himself against electoral democracy, for fear that non-Muslims would want to "replace one race by the other."[229] Analogous defenses of the Muslim character of the state have been reiterated over time in Tunisia and other Muslim-majority polities and framed as a rejection of mixing religion and politics, as we will see.

5. What Went Wrong? Diverging Explanations of the 1864 Revolt and the Legal Reforms' Failure

The 1861 Constitution, born under unfavorable omens, did not last long. It was suspended in 1864 after a rebellion erupted in the spring, swept the country, and almost annihilated the bey's regime. Although the demise of the Constitution was in great part the result of failed negotiations with the Europeans on

225. BNT ms. 18775, fol. 7; Bercher (1972, 76–77).

226. BNT ms. 18775, fols. 11–12; Bercher (1972, 84).

227. Chérif (1994), Oualdi (2011, 250 and 378–380), and Allagui (2016, 60).

228. See Cohen (2008, 65–68) and Yarbrough (2019) for a discussion of religious minorities' appointments to public office in premodern times.

229. He used the words *"le remplacement d'une race par l'autre,"* in Al-Tunisi (1868, 40–41), the French version of *The Surest Path*. For the Arabic version, which is less explicit, see Al-Tūnisī (1867, 36): "If it is deemed permissible to withhold liberty because of an expected attempt to change the dynasty from among those belonging to the same race [*jins*], then it is even more permissible when such a threat comes from another race [*jins*]." L. C. Brown (1967, 117–118).

jurisdictional matters (and not the direct result of disputes about the role of Islam in governance), this rebellion, the "largest, most protracted" in Tunisian history,[230] provides a window into how the bey's subjects experienced and viewed the constitutional reforms and into the breadth of the debates about their legitimacy.[231] It reveals a conservative rejection by the people (*ʿāmma*) of the new judicial organization and their desire to return to the status quo ante (framed as a return to sharia), an aspect of this rebellion that has been discounted by Tunisian reformists (eager to defend the Islamic legitimacy of the reforms) and by the historiography more focused on the social aspects of the rebellion. It also reveals how the French consul distorted the motives of the rebellion to obtain the suspension of the Constitution and framed it as the result of an incompatibility between Islam and constitutionalism.

The 1864 Revolt against the New Taxes

The immediate cause of the rebellion is well-known.[232] In December 1863, the bey doubled the head tax (the *majbā*) from 36 to 72 piasters, the latest blow in five decades of successive fiscal innovations.[233] The bey had decided to increase the tax, against the Great Council's advice, because the state was in urgent need of revenue, notably to service its debt.[234] Although this tax and other state levies represented only a small percentage of aggregate output, the population was already complaining about and often rebelled against its rapidly increasing tax burden. The bey attempted to stop the rebellion in April 1864 by announcing the suspension of the tax increase, and since the rebels also had grievances

230. Marsans-Sakly (2010, 4).

231. Even before the 1864 revolt there was strong opposition to the new tribunals among Tunisians, as evidenced by a demonstration by a large group of residents of the capital in the fall of 1861. ANT SH C119 D413. On these events, see also Ibn Abī al-Ḍiyāf (1963, vol. 5, 89), Karoui (1973, 57–69), Chater (1975), and Van Krieken (1976, 64–66).

232. Slama (1967, 17–18).

233. By 1864 the *majbā* was the tax with the broadest base and, despite tax avoidance, about 222,000 subjects paid it (out of a population of about 1 million), amounting to a revenue of about 8 million piasters (almost half of total state revenue). See Valensi (1977, 359). I estimate that it amounted to 2–3 percent of GDP.

234. Although the internal debt was refinanced in 1863 with a 7 percent external loan as opposed to 12 to 13 percent for the internal debt, its amortization over 15.5 years meant an equivalent annual debt service (since it included principal paydown), and it was surrounded by controversy. See Emerit (1949, 252).

against the new judicial system, he reestablished the old *maẓālim* tribunal (the bey's court) and offered his subjects the option to bring their cases to it "as was done before."[235] On May 1, 1864, the bey announced the suspension of the Great Council, the Criminal and Customary Court, and the Court of Appeals.[236] Nonetheless, the rebellion continued and spread to the cities of the Sahel, particularly Sfax and Sousse, where, in May 1864 (with the support of a wide range of elites, including ʿulamā and *qāḍīs*),[237] the population joined the tribes in their demands, organized a local government, stopped paying taxes, raised the green flag of the Ottoman sultan, and appealed to him.[238] Soldiers in the bey's army hailing from the Sahel refused to fight against their own cities.[239] The (relative) prosperity of the Sahel might have made it more vulnerable to the ongoing fiscal innovations and tax increases.[240] Moreover, European traders had settled there and threatened local interests. With the bey, they dominated the trade in olive oil,[241] and, with the bey's agents, they provided desperately needed credit but at high interest rates that also generated resentment among locals toward Europeans and the government.[242] It was argued that the government hindered free commerce with the bey's monopolies and had sold the country to "the Christians," and that the Europeans had played an important part in the Regency's growing debt and economic ruin.[243] In May 1864, the local French vice-consuls reported to consular authorities in Tunis that their nationals in the Sahel felt threatened by the rebellion,[244] and Italian, British, and Ottoman fleets arrived near the Regency's coast to protect their subjects. Rumors circulated that France was planning to

235. Ibn Abī al-Ḍiyāf (1963, vol. 5, 133).

236. Ibn Abī al-Ḍiyāf (1963, vol. 5, 134). Slama (1967, 4) argues that the Constitution was suspended at that point.

237. On this support, see Slama (1967, 80–82) and Valensi (1977, 363n38).

238. Ibn Abī al-Ḍiyāf (1963, vol. 5, 146) and Slama (1967, 87).

239. Chater (1978, 45) and Slama (1967, 78–79).

240. For the effect of fiscal innovations in the Sahel, see Valensi (1977, 355–357) and Chater (1984, 556). The Sahel provided one-sixth of the Regency's state revenues and a good number of the soldiers in the bey's army. Chater (1978, 17) and Slama (1967, 76).

241. Chater (1978, 17–19, 32–34, and 38).

242. Valensi (1977, 350) and Chérif (1970, 732–733). High interest rates reflected the Regency's scarcity of cash but were described as usurious.

243. Slama (1967, 85 and 128). On the xenophobic feelings of the rebels, see Ibn Abī al-Ḍiyāf (1963, vol. 5, 147–148).

244. E.g., Espina in Sousse to de Beauvál, May 5, 1864, in Grandchamp (1935, vol. 1, 80). Several letters from the local vice-consuls in early May 1864 reported the same fears.

take over the Regency.[245] These rumors seemed to be confirmed by the arrival of a French ship on May 8, 1864.[246] The *qāʾids* (the state's local agents) also reported violence against Jews in some cities, especially against those who, as tax farmers, represented the state.[247] Attacks against Jews wearing a red cap (*shāshīya*) like Muslims—instead of a black one, as they were required to do before the 1857 Security Pact—were also reported in several cities.[248] Tribal rebels in the interior and urban rebels in the Sahel also attacked representatives of the bey's administration and stormed local tax offices on a regular basis during the revolt.[249] At the height of the rebellion, tribes also pillaged each other as well as villages and towns, which they hoped to push into siding with them. In the summer of 1864, all the territory was in rebellion, except for the capital. After partially successful attempts to sow division among the rebels, the bey unleashed his armed forces to ruthlessly repress the Sahel in the fall and winter of 1864, eventually crushing the rebellion.

The Rebels' Lists of Grievances: Return to Sharia and to the Status Quo Ante

The grievances of the rebelling tribes were collected by the *qāʾid*s and transmitted to the bey.[250] It is clear from this correspondence that the rebels did not ask for the suspension of the Security Pact or the Constitution.[251] Rather, they listed a series of eclectic demands that can be organized into three categories: (1) the suspension of the new taxes; (2) more local political autonomy—a right to have a say on the bey's appointment of local authorities; and (3) the repeal of some of the reforms—notably the revocation of the new tribunals, the repeal of the 1846 abolition of slavery,[252] and the repeal of the newly introduced notions of equality

245. E.g., Espina in Sousse to de Beauval, May 31, 1864, in Grandchamp (1935, vol. 1, 151).

246. Grandchamp (1935, vol. 1, 163).

247. E.g., in Sfax, on May 12, 1864, Elie Sabbagh, a tax farmer, was assassinated along with his wife and children, and several houses belonging to Jews were pillaged. Murad, *qāʾid* of Sfax, to the prime minister, May 12, 1864, ANT SH C184 D1034, no. 132.

248. E.g., Jews in Nabeul were attacked by Bedouins on their leader's order to assault them and to remove their red *shāshīyas* and their white turbans. The *qāḍī* of Nabeul to the bey, May 14, 1864, ANT SH C184 D1034, no. 145.

249. E.g., on April 16, 1864, the *qāʾid* Ferhat of al-Kaf was assassinated by the tribal rebels, and in Jendouba, in February or March 1864, "the *qāʾid* was taken, and his clothes and horse stolen." Ali Shair Ibn Mbarek to Ahmad Ibn Brahim al-Juini, February–March 1864, ANT SH C184 D1034, no. 27.

250. ANT SH C184 D1029.

251. This observation was also made by Slama (1967, 36).

252. On the abolition of slavery, see Largueche (1990) and Montana (2013).

between Tunisian Muslims and Jews. The rebels clearly wished to return to the status quo ante—that is, to the *sharī ʿa/siyāsa* paradigm with its traditional system of justice and hierarchy between Muslims and non-Muslims; they often used the phrase "as it was before [*kamā fī al- ʿāda al-sābiqa*]."[253] Consider the grievances formulated by several tribes of the Riyah lands. The reestablishment of sharia "without limitation" was the first demand on their list.[254] The rebels also asked that the tribunals in Tunis be revoked. Although they did not explicitly mention the Constitution, they rejected the new administration of justice established by the legal reforms. They also requested the suspension of the abolition of slavery and asked that Jews return to wearing a black cap as they were required to do before the reforms. The grievances formulated by members of the Majeur and Frashish tribes are also telling: "We do not want to pay anything. What we ask from our master [the bey] is that he follow the path of his fathers and ancestors. Otherwise, we have nothing to give."[255] They viewed the new taxes and the new tribunals as unjust, and they invoked this injustice as the main motive for their rebellion. In the same vein, a letter from Ibn Ghadhahim, the leader of the rebellion, to the prime minister explaining why he and his followers would not obey the bey's orders read, "It is not the bey anymore who renders justice. The people you charged with [rendering justice] have no pity."[256]

The French Explanation of the 1864 Revolt: A Muslim Rebellion against Constitutionalism

Despite the dearth of explicit condemnations of the Constitution as such among the rebels' grievances, the French consul de Beauval, who succeeded Léon Roches in November 1863, reported to his superiors in Paris that it was one of the rebels' main motives. He distorted his vice-consuls' local reports and used the rebellion as a pretext to obtain the suspension of the Constitution. In the local vice-consuls' reports, the revolt was said to have broken out against the tax increase. The rebels were also said to have criticized the Europeans' influence and the corrupt administration of the bey and his Mamluks, and to have asked

253. The demands articulated by the tribes echoed those of cities and towns of the Sahel, although the latter were more embedded economically with European merchants and Tunisian Jews and might have been more affected by the new tribunals than the tribes. For a study of the 1864 revolt in the Sahel, see Al-Ṭayyif (2015).

254. ANT SH C184 D1029, no. 37.

255. Ali Ibn Azuz to the Amiralay Brahim Ibn Abbas, May 15, 1864, ANT SH C184 D1034, no. 146.

256. Ibn Ghadhahim to the prime minister, May 21, 1864, ANT SH C184 D1034, no. 171.

for the intervention of the Ottoman sultan as a last recourse. The vice-consuls rarely mentioned that the rebels criticized the Constitution itself.[257] Consul de Beauval, on the other hand, in his letters to the minister of foreign affairs in Paris, emphasized the Mamluks' corruption and the opposition to the Constitution.[258] In an April 1864 letter to the minister, he summed up the motives for the revolt with the watchword "No Mamluks, no majba, no Constitution!"[259] French officials also framed the rebels' rejection of the legal reforms and their eventual failure in civilizational terms. They claimed that the rebels were against the new laws because they had been conceived by non-Muslims.[260] According to the French consul, the rebels' appeals to the sultan signaled their inability to distinguish "religious supremacy" from "political sovereignty."[261] He also argued that the "liberalism" of the 1861 Constitution had been "precocious and misplaced."[262]

Ibn Diyaf's Refusal to Acknowledge the Return to Sharia as a Motive for the 1864 Revolt

On the other hand, eager to defend the Islamic legitimacy of the legal reforms, Ibn Diyaf refused to concede that a return to sharia and the bey's justice was one of the main demands of the rebels, despite evidence to the contrary. He dismissed reports to this effect as either untruthful,[263] misguided,[264] or

257. See Grandchamp (1935).

258. Oualdi (2011, 330) reassesses the opposition to the Mamluks per se as a motive for the revolt of 1864, also noting that de Beauval "did not take into account the majority of his vice-consuls' testimonies." He speaks of "meddling, exaggerations, forgeries, [and] covert actions," which make "very problematic the use of the writings of Campenon, Mattei, and de Beauval." See also Slama (1967, 36).

259. De Beauval to Drouyn de Lhuys, April 20, 1864, AMAE, Tunis, CP, vol. 22, fol. 163. See also De Beauval to Drouyn De Lhuys, June 14, 1864, AMAE, Tunis, CP, vol. 23, fols. 78–79.

260. Duchesne de Bellecourt to Druyn de Lhuys, March 20, 1865, AMAE, Tunis, CP, vol 25, fol. 29. De Bellecourt succeeded de Beauval as French consul in 1865.

261. De Beauval to vice-consuls and France's consular agents, July 26, 1864, AMAE, Tunis, CP, vol. 23, fol. 263.

262. De Beauval to the French minister of foreign affairs, December 11, 1863, AMAE, Tunis, CP, vol. 21, fol. 275.

263. He wrote, "A market of lies and slanders developed, which led to blaming the Constitution." Ibn Abī al-Ḍiyāf (1963, vol. 5, 125).

264. He asked why the Frashish, Majeur, Hammama, and Unifa tribes (who did not have new tribunals) would be interested in the suspension of the cities' tribunals (Ibn Abī al-Ḍiyāf 1963, vol. 5, 130).

self-interested,[265] although he recognized that the rebels criticized the new tribunals, which they found too slow.[266] As an architect of the 1861 Constitution who recounted these events after its suspension, he was not ready to concede that some of its aspects could be seen as foreign to sharia. He showed contempt for those who failed to understand its merits and regretted that it had been received with indifference by the populace.[267] Ibn Diyaf also devoted a long passage in his chronicles to explaining that the rebels mainly revolted against the high level of taxation and "nothing else." He found the taxes both unfair and illegitimate since they were, in his words, "a cousin of pure physical force," and he criticized the sumptuary expenses of the court and the growing state debt in a country with a stagnant economy.[268] He noted that the rebelling tribes—essentially the Majeur and the Zlass—targeted the representatives of the fiscal authority.[269] He also noted that the leader of the rebellion promised not to attack his brethren since, he said, "our argument is with the state [*kalāmunā ma ʿa al-dawla*]."[270]

The Suspension of the 1861 Constitution

The French seized the opportunity of the rebellion to pressure the bey to suspend the Constitution. During a visit to the bey on April 19, 1864, Consul de Beauval stressed that the French fleet was approaching and could be reinforced soon if he did not comply. The bey objected that he had to continue his brother's task and noted, "The power that imposed it [the Constitution] on us now wants to impose its removal."[271] No official decree suspended the

265. He noted that in September 1861, a few months after the proclamation of the Constitution, a group of men from Tunis, "the most shameless of the uncivilized," led by a lower-rank teacher at the Zaytuna mosque, complained to the bey about the new organization of the tribunals and the rising grain prices and asked (in order to flatter him, according Ibn Diyaf) that the bey continue to judge as he used to (Ibn Abī al-Ḍiyāf 1963, vol. 5, 89–90). See also ANT SH C119 D413.

266. Muhammad Bayram V follows Ibn Diyaf, albeit with slightly different justifications, as underlined by Marsans-Sakly (2010, 80). He argued that the new tribunals were staffed by unprepared individuals with little education. He also claimed that no one had requested the abolition of the laws "because their foundations [*uṣūl*] do not contradict sharia and people only criticized their implementation [*furū ʿ*]." Bayram V (1884–1894, vol. 2, 65).

267. Ibn Abī al-Ḍiyāf (1963, vol. 5, 55).

268. Ibn Abī al-Ḍiyāf (1963, vol. 5, 127–128).

269. Ibn Abī al-Ḍiyāf (1963, vol. 5, 121–122).

270. Ibn Abī al-Ḍiyāf (1963, vol. 5, 121–123).

271. Ibn Abī al-Ḍiyāf (1963, vol. 5, 151).

Constitution.[272] When, in August 1864, the British consul asked the bey what was becoming of the Constitution now that the tribunals were suspended, he responded that the Security Pact was still in effect, particularly its first rule (security of life, property, and honor for all subjects and residents regardless of religion, language, and color).[273] In 1865 the French consul reported that Khayr al-Din, General Husayn, and other high officials had expressed the desire to see the Constitution reinstated at least in part (especially chapter 1, recognizing the bey's sovereignty, and chapter 2, guaranteeing the life and property of the bey's civil servants)—a wish that the French did not support.[274] And, as we will see in the next chapter, later on, during the French occupation (1881–1956), some Tunisian elites also expressed their desire to reinstate the Constitution.

6. An Islamic Framework for Change to Preserve the Ideal of Islamic Governance

Ibn Diyaf, writing his chronicles after these events, looked back at them with disillusion about the beylical rule and its absolutism, which he described as in blatant contradiction to sharia and as one of the main causes of the legal reforms' failure. He deplored the economic and political context of his time—on many occasions he described the Regency of Tunis as poor (*miskīna*) and weak (*ḍaʿīfa*)[275]—but he remained optimistic: he saw the legal reforms, and particularly the 1861 Constitution, as an effective and legitimate tool to improve governance.[276] Like his political adversaries, the conservative ʿulamā who had produced the fatwas on the Security Pact, he had an acute awareness of the difficult conditions

272. General Elias Musalli verbally announced the Constitution's "provisional suspension" to the French consul in 1864. Duchesne de Bellecourt to the French minister of foreign affairs, April 18, 1865, AMAE, Tunis, CP, vol. 25, fol. 102.

273. Ibn Abī al-Ḍiyāf (1963, vol. 5, 169–175).

274. Duchesne de Bellecourt to the French minister of foreign affairs, March 4, 1865, AMAE, Tunis, CP, vol. 25, fols. 5–6; Duchesne de Bellecourt to the French minister of foreign affairs, April 18, 1865, AMAE, Tunis, CP, vol. 25, fol. 101; "Note sur la Constitution," April 22, 1865, AMAE, Tunis, CP, vol. 25, fol. 122; and the French minister of foreign affairs to Duchesne de Bellecourt, April 26, 1865, AMAE, Tunis, CP, vol. 25, fols. 138–139.

275. For instance, Ibn Abī al-Ḍiyāf (1963, vol. 4, 16–17, 156, and 187).

276. The *Itḥāf* quotes the 1839 Khatt al-Sharif in its entirety, vol. 1, 38–43. Ibn Diyaf writes, about the government established by the Ottoman Tanzimat, "The leader of this type of government is loved and obeyed. His hand protects the religion and the realm." Ibn Abī al-Ḍiyāf (1963, vol. 1, 44).

of "the present time" (*ḥāl al-waqt*). In his view, however, these conditions required urgent and radical changes to "prevent harm" (*ḍarar*).[277] For instance, he underlined that the Islamically legal taxes were now insufficient and that rulers needed to add new taxes (although he deplored the use of violence in raising them) because of the increasing complexity of society.[278] He was therefore pragmatic: he wrote that when it came to the *qānūn* (the temporal legislation), "considerations of the ends [*maqāṣid*] influence the means [*wasāʾil*]."[279] At the same time, while he acknowledged his initial misgivings about the legal reforms,[280] he vigorously defended the idea that, although importing foreign techniques might indeed erode sharia as a technique of governance, it was still possible to maintain sharia as an ideal. His defense of the legal reforms used a mechanism that Islamic political theorists had been using since premodern times: the expansion of the domain of *siyāsa* under the framework of sharia.

New (and Appropriate) Techniques of Governance for a Muslim State

Although proponents of the reforms were in favor of introducing new techniques of governance, they were not in search of a new ideal for their state. This can clearly be seen in the vocabulary they used to designate the 1861 Constitution, which they often called a *tartīb* (a reorganization); the Europeans, in contrast, called it a reform and often described it as a revolutionary transformation of the principles guiding governance. In contrast, the notion of *tartīb* was quite prosaic and designated an organizational and technical kind of change. It was used to designate state interventions as diverse as currency debasements, changes in taxation, or the restructuring of the Zaytuna's curriculum in 1842 and then again in the mid-1870s.[281] When changes were perceived

277. Ibn Abī al-Ḍiyāf (1963, vol. 1, 47).

278. Ibn Abī al-Ḍiyāf (1963, vol. 1, 47).

279. Ibn Abī al-Ḍiyāf (1963, vol. 1, 45).

280. When the consul Richard Wood visited the bey at the end of August 1857 to pressure him to implement the Europeans' demands, the bey reportedly asked Ibn Diyaf to talk to the consul "about the issue of religion" (*mā yataʿallaq bi-amr al-dīn*), and Ibn Diyaf told Richard Wood, "The new organization [*tartīb*] you are requesting from us might harm [*yamass*] our religion [*dīnanā*]." Ibn Abī al-Ḍiyāf (1963, vol. 4, 236).

281. Shaykh Mahmud Ibn al-Khuja to the prime minister, June 21, 1876, designates the debasement of currency as a *tartib*, and Shaykh Ahmad Ibn Muhammad Ibn Murad to the prime minister, November 27, 1876, designates the reforms of the Zaytuna as a *tartīb*. ANT SH C63 D733, no. 5 and no. 6, respectively.

as breaking with custom or sharia, official ʿulamā were mobilized by the government to justify them. These justifications took various forms. At times, they were embedded in the official decrees proclaiming new regulations.[282] In other circumstances, fatwas provided legitimacy to new practices such as quarantines or to legal innovations such as the abolition of slavery in 1846.[283] Other notable examples include a fatwa authorizing Ahmad Bey's 1846 visit to Paris[284] and an 1863 fatwa authorizing the use of surplus revenues from public Islamic endowments to finance the military.[285] Official ʿulamā would also write epistles to justify violent repressive measures by the bey, as we will see with Bayram I's *Risāla fī al-Siyāsa al-Sharʿīya*.

Ibn Diyaf and other state officials were clearly familiar with new techniques of governance introduced elsewhere, notably in Europe, the United States, Istanbul, and Cairo. Ibn Diyaf wrote at length about his visits to Istanbul in 1831 and in 1842, where he met with Arif Bey, the Ottoman shaykh al-Islam and a proponent of the Tanzimat, with whom he discussed their legitimacy.[286] Khayr al-Din went on several missions to France and had acquaintances in the Ottoman embassy in Paris. Therefore, they both had an intimate knowledge of the Ottoman Tanzimat; this knowledge came as much from Istanbul as from Paris, where the bey's representative (*wakīl*), Jules de Lesseps, would regularly send news from the Ottoman Porte to the prime minister in Tunis. His letters also mentioned items such as the civil war raging in the United States, Italian politics, and French elections or constitutional disputes.[287] In the 1850s and 1860s, new regulations were often drafted in the Regency with Ottoman and French codes in hand.[288]

282. For instance, the bey's decree of 1856 regarding the *majbā* tax in AMAE, Tunis, CP, vol. 16, fols. 122–129.

283. For instance, the fatwas justifying the abolition of slavery by Hanafi Mufti Abu Abdallah Muhammad Bayram and by Maliki Mufti Abu Ishaq Ibrahim al-Riyahi, both written in January 1846. These documents are cited in Ibn Abī al-Ḍiyāf (1963, vol. 4, 86–90), analyzed in Montana (2013, 115–120) and Van der Haven (2006, 41–74), and translated in Van der Haven (2006, 159–164). See also Larguèche (1990). For the legitimacy of quarantine, see Ibn Abī al-Ḍiyāf (1963, vol. 4, 130).

284. Van der Haven (2006, 86–93).

285. Ibn Abī al-Ḍiyāf (1963, vol. 4, 97).

286. Ibn Abī al-Ḍiyāf (1963, vol. 1, 71) and Van Krieken (1976, 7).

287. Correspondence of the representative [*wakīl*] of Tunisia in Paris from 1848 to 1850, ANT SH C209 D165.

288. Roches to the French minister of foreign affairs, August 13, 1857, AMAE, Tunis, CP, vol. 17, fols. 177–178; Roches to the French minister of foreign affairs, November 6, 1857, AMAE, Tunis, CP, vol. 17, fols. 263–265; ANT SH C118 D403, no. 55; Van Krieken (1976, 72).

Therefore, Tunisian reformers did not follow a specific model from Paris, Cairo, or Istanbul, as is often argued. Rather, they had at their disposal a large body of techniques and references—old and new, and geographically diverse, looking to the East, West, North, and South[289]—from which they could choose in order to solve the specific problems with which they were confronted.[290] In addition, although they were fully aware of republican and democratic techniques of governance, they found them unsuitable for themselves. In the typology of political regimes with which he introduced his chronicles, Ibn Diyaf contrasted absolute power, which he criticized, with republican government (*al-mulk al-jumhūrī*), inspired by "America and other countries."[291] He described republican government as useful for temporal life (*naf ʿ dunyāwī*) but quickly added that the Muslim community, because it already had adequate rules, did not need it.[292] He considered revealed law (*sharī ʿa*) and reason (*ʿaql*) as the best means to limit the ruler's political arbitrariness: combined together, they formed a solid restraint (*wāzi ʿ*) of despotism.[293] Moreover, for Ibn Diyaf, one of the crucial functions of the government was the implementation of policies in conformity with sharia, whose purpose was to ensure its subjects' welfare on earth and their salvation in the other world, a salvation that a republican order could not provide.

The Reformers' Islamic Framework for Change: The Expansion of the Domain of Siyāsa

Ibn Diyaf's chronicles—which have had a strong legacy as a founding text of reformist thought in Tunisia—blended history and political theory with abundant references to the Islamic jurisprudential tradition. For Ibn Diyaf, the science of history (*ʿilm al-tārīkh*) served as "a means to the sciences of the revealed law [*al- ʿulūm al-shar ʿīya*]."[294] He therefore understood revealed law as a necessary constraint on the ruler but also as the enduring source of a malleable set of norms. He remained faithful to classical Sunni Islamic political theory, referring to Abu Hamid al-Ghazali (d. 1111) as well as Ibn Khaldun (1332–1406) to

289. The 1846 Hanafi fatwa justifying the abolition of slavery used the fatwa of Shaykh Sidi Ahmad Baba of Timbuktu. Montana (2013, 115–117) and Van der Haven (2006, 160–161).

290. Van Krieken (1976, 95).

291. Ibn Abī al-Ḍiyāf (1963, vol. 1, 28).

292. Ibn Abī al-Ḍiyāf (1963, vol. 1, 28).

293. Ibn Abī al-Ḍiyāf (1963, vol. 1, 15).

294. Ibn Abī al-Ḍiyāf (1963, vol. 1, 2).

argue that government is necessary and constitutes an Islamic duty and that, although one should not revolt against a prince's tyranny if this leads to disorder, the ruler must be exhorted to be just. Ibn Diyaf did not recommend patience in the face of coercive and unjust power and wrote that speaking the truth to the sovereign was a duty (*wājib*) that the ʿulamā had abandoned.[295] On many occasions, he exemplified this posture by criticizing the beys' policies, without ever putting their dynasty's legitimacy into question. He saw the government of his time as an "absolute government" (*al-mulk al-muṭlaq*), in which the ruler "leads people to do what he pleases with the use of the stick"[296] with no regard for public interest (*maṣlaḥa*). Citing Ibn Khaldun's *Muqaddima* at length,[297] he drew a sharp distinction between justice (*ʿadl*) and civilization (*ʿumrān*) on the one hand and tyranny (*ẓulm*), corruption (*fasād*), and destruction (*kharāb*) on the other.[298] Like Ibn Khaldun, he read political history as a history of decline and corruption,[299] but he also looked with confidence for ways to improve governance under an Islamic framework.

Ibn Diyaf combined references to Ibn Khaldun with quotes from Ibn al-Azraq (1428 or 1429–1491), who compiled and commented on Ibn Khaldun's ideas by integrating them into his own ethical and legal framework.[300] This helped Ibn Diyaf combine the pragmatic understanding of politics he found in Ibn Khaldun with the concept of governance according to revealed law (*siyāsa sharʿīya*), which had also allowed Ibn al-Azraq to give centrality to the notion of *siyāsa* (the discretionary power of the ruler) while at the same time attempting to keep *siyāsa* within the bounds of sharia.[301] Ibn Diyaf quoted Ibn al-Azraq's commentary on Al-Turtushi's *Sirāj al-Mulūk*, which was also quoted in a 1861 article praising the Constitution in the Official Gazette:[302] "The infidel sultan [*al-sulṭān al-kāfir*] who ensures correct policy [*al-siyāsa al-iṣṭilāḥīya*] is more durable and stronger than a just, believing sultan who is neglectful of governance according to revealed law [*siyāsa sharʿīya*]. Well-ordered

295. Ibn Abī al-Ḍiyāf (1963, vol. 1, 12–15).

296. Ibn Abī al-Ḍiyāf (1963, vol. 1, 9).

297. In the *Itḥāf*'s introduction, I counted nine explicit references to Ibn Khaldun, the most-cited author, whereas his Egyptian contemporary Rifaa Rafi al-Tahtawi (1801–1873) is only mentioned once.

298. Ibn Abī al-Ḍiyāf (1963, vol. 1, 16–19 and 33).

299. Ibn Abī al-Ḍiyāf (1963, vol. 1, 7–8 and 35).

300. Muḥammad Ibn al-Azraq, author of *Badāʾiʿ al-Silk fī Ṭabāʾiʿ al-Mulk*.

301. Abdesselem (1983, 29).

302. *Al-Rāʾid al-Tūnisī*, May 6, 1861, vol. 1, no. 33.

oppression [*jawr murattab*] is more durable than neglectful justice [*al-ʿadl al-muhmil*], for there is nothing more suitable to a sultan than effectively ordering affairs [*tartīb al-umūr*] and nothing more corrupt than neglecting them. A sultan, whether a believer or an infidel, will prevail only with strong justice [*ʿadl qawīy*] or good organization [*tartīb iṣṭilāḥī*]."[303] Ibn Diyaf, like many Islamic political theorists before him, recognized the importance of pure policy (*siyāsa*) when correctly devised. For instance, Al-Shatibi's (1320–1388) definition of "civil policy" (*siyāsa madanīya*), came in handy for Ibn Diyaf to argue that, even if a ruler does not have revealed law to conform to, he must follow civil policy, and hence that well-known and well-kept policy (*siyāsa maʿrūfa maḥfūẓa*) is crucial for rule.[304] In a similar vein, the eleventh-century Hanbali scholar Ibn Aqil (1040–1119) provided Ibn Diyaf with a definition of *siyāsa sharʿīya* (governance according to revealed law) that tended toward pragmatism and clearly expanded the domain of *siyāsa*: "The essence of *siyāsa sharʿīya* is the action [*fiʿl*] that brings people closer to righteousness and farther from corruption, even if the revealed law [*sharʿ*] does not lay it out and no revelation came down containing it."[305] Placing *siyāsa* at the center of his writings and expanding its range of action under a framework binding it to sharia helped Ibn Diyaf justify change without renouncing the ideal of Islamic governance.

This was not the first time in the Regency of Tunis that the domain of *siyāsa* was expanded to justify change, and Ibn Diyaf was not innovating in this regard. Ibn Aqil's legal thought had also helped the eighteenth-century Hanafi shaykh al-Islam in Tunis, Muhammad Bayram I, expand the policy-making prerogatives of bey Hammuda Pasha (1777–1814) to meet the necessities of the time; his *Risāla fī al-Siyāsa al-Sharʿīya*, written in 1800,[306] gave the ruler broad powers in policy matters, even if they seemed contrary to justice and sharia. Although Bayram I did not explain the exact motivations behind his work, it came at a time when the bey was attempting to recentralize the tax-raising process that was in the hands of the local governors.[307] Bayram I

303. Ibn Abī al-Ḍiyāf (1963, vol. 1, 45), translation largely inspired by L. C. Brown (2005, 90). See Ibn al-Azraq (1977, vol. 1, 286) and Al-Ṭurṭūshī (1872, 92).

304. Ibn Abī al-Ḍiyāf (1963, vol. 1, 46–47). Ibn Diyaf also quotes, in the same vein, Ibn Khaldun's distinction between religious policy (*siyāsa dīnīya*) and rational policy (*siyāsa ʿaqlīya*).

305. Ibn Abī al-Ḍiyāf (1963, vol. 1, 45). Ibn Diyaf does not explicitly attribute this definition to Ibn Aqil, but it is recognizable. See Johansen (2008, 269).

306. BNT, ms. 402. Bayram I (2016). For a study and translation, see Van der Haven (2006).

307. Van der Haven (2006, 33–35).

broadened the repressive powers of the ruler, allowing him to use tools prohibited to the *qāḍī* by the rules of Islamic law (*fiqh*), such as threats or physical violence to obtain confessions.[308] It is revealing that Ibn Diyaf intentionally did not cite Bayram I's *Risāla* in his justification of the reforms,[309] although, like him, Ibn Diyaf justified innovations by expanding the domain of *siyāsa* and, like him, Ibn Diyaf cited Ibn Aqil's definition of *siyāsa shar ʿīya*, albeit only in passing. Bayram I's use of Ibn Aqil was much more expansive than Ibn Diyaf's. It included the justification of repressive policy decisions implemented by the successors of the prophet, such as the burning of copies of the Qur'an and the burning of heretics: "The executions and exemplary punishments ordered by the Rightly Guided Caliphs . . . are such as not to be denied by anyone who knows the Tradition, even if this involved the burning of the Qur'an—a judgment they based on the welfare of the community—and the burning of the heretics in the trenches by Caliph Ali . . . who said: When I witness something reprehensible, I light a fire [to burn the heretic] and call for a celebration."[310] As underlined by Johansen (2008, 270), Ibn Aqil's definition of *siyāsa shar ʿīya* was a way to "produce larger visions of political decision-making," and it was also approvingly cited by Ibn Taymiya and his student Ibn Qayyim al-Jawziya.[311] However, Ibn Diyaf's method of expanding *siyāsa* could not have been more at odds with the methods and aims of expanding the rulers' discretionary power developed by Ibn Aqil, Ibn Taymiya, Ibn Qayyim al-Jawziya, and, much later, by Bayram I. For Ibn Diyaf, it had to be done through the development of the *qānūn* (temporal legislation) not by simply giving free reign to the repressive

308. Abdesselem (1973, 105–107). Khayr al-Din's *Surest Path* also used references allowing the expansion of *siyāsa* that were deployed by Bayram I. He quoted Ibn Aqil's statement explaining that the proposition "there is no valid administration except that which agrees with revealed law" did not mean that "there is no valid administration except that which is stated explicitly in revealed law" but rather "there is no valid administration except that which does not contradict revealed law." Al-Tūnisī (1867, 42). For an analysis of Khayr al-Din's arguments, and his use of the notion of *ʿurf* (custom), see Zeghal (2022).

309. Ibn Diyaf was aware of the existence of Bayram I's *Risāla* since he mentions it in Ibn Abī al-Ḍiyāf (1963, vol. 3, 82, and vol. 7, 34).

310. Ibn Aqil's quote is from Johansen (2008, 269–70). See also the reference to it in Bayram I (2016, 105–106). It refers to Qur'ans that did not accord with the Uthmanic codex, as part of an effort of standardization.

311. Ibn Qayyim al-Jawzīya (1899–1900, 12–13) cited Ibn Aqil's definition of *siyāsa shar ʿīya*.

powers of the ruler.[312] For him, the *qānūn* was both an instrument for change and a way to reinforce constraints on the arbitrariness of the ruler. And indeed, in his typology of political regimes, Ibn Diyaf rejected absolute rule and wrote that, second to the Caliphate—a type of regime now extinct in his eyes, having given way to hereditary kingships in a more complex civilization with new needs[313]—his favored kind of government was government bounded by temporal legislation (*ḥukm muqayyad bi-l-qānūn*). For him, it was a type of government that could be established through adequate reforms and that would fulfill the aims of revealed law.[314] He argued that the 1861 Constitution came to put an end to the problematic regression of the bey's government to despotism. In his view, the *qānūn* (temporal legislation) had many advantages: "It protects people, removes corruption, and can be trusted to realize our intentions"; with government bounded by the *qānūn*, justice could be realized because "it revolves around reason and revealed law."[315]

To be sure, some of the changes introduced by the 1857–1861 legal reforms were not that easy to reconcile with the existing norms derived from revealed law. In Ibn Diyaf's justification of correct *siyāsa* in accordance with sharia, the *qānūn* had to bear the burden of these transformations. Once more, this was not an innovation on Ibn Diyaf's part; for instance, it echoed a conception of law that sought to bring "the *qānūn* into conformity with sharia," exemplified, in the Ottoman tradition, by the sixteenth-century mufti of Istanbul Ebu's-Su'ud.[316] The *qānūn*'s conformity with sharia was also invoked during the nineteenth century Ottoman Tanzimat and, after Ibn Khaldun's *Muqaddima*, it was the Ottoman 1839 Khatt al-Sharif that was the most cited work in the *Itḥāf*'s introduction to justify the reforms. Ibn Diyaf argued that old techniques

312. Historians disagree on the legacy of Bayram I's *Risāla*. M.A. Ben Achour (1977) argues that its aim was to legitimize the sovereign and his use of violence, whereas Bashir al-Makki Abd al-Lawi argues somewhat rosily, in Bayram I (2016), that it foreshadowed the 1857–1861 reforms.

313. Ibn Abī al-Ḍiyāf (1963, vol. 1, 47).

314. Ibn Abī al-Ḍiyāf (1963, vol. 1, 32).

315. Ibn Abī al-Ḍiyāf (1963, vol. 1, 32).

316. Imber (1997, 269–270). I could only find one reference to Ebu's-Su'ud in Ibn Abī al-Ḍiyāf (1963, vol. 7, 85), in relation to the biography of the Tunisian *ʿālim* Mahmud Maqdish (d. 1813), who wrote a commentary on Ebu's-Su'ud's Qur'anic exegesis. However, we find a reference to the legal thought of Ebu's-Su'ud in Hanafi Shaykh al-Islam Bayram IV's judgment of Bato Sfez in 1857, ANT SH C117 D390bis, no. 31.

of governance had to be replaced, although, he insisted, without sacrificing the ideal of Islamic governance.[317] As an example of the tensions at play in such a project, Ibn Diyaf built a defense of equality irrespective of religion (in what sounded like a strong rebuttal to the ʿulamā's fatwas regarding the Security Pact) by using an established mechanism reflected in the legal maxim, also reproduced in the 1877 Ottoman Majalla, "Necessity permits what is otherwise prohibited."[318] He argued that the purpose behind collecting the capitation tax (*jizya*) from non-Muslim subjects was not to accumulate wealth or to exert tyranny over the Regency's Jews, whom he called "our compatriots" (*ikhwānunā fī al-waṭan*)[319] but rather to incite them to convert to Islam.[320] He reasoned that equality regardless of religion would realize the ideal of justice and therefore make Islam more appealing to religious minorities.[321] As we saw, not everyone agreed with Ibn Diyaf: for some, this meant loosening the constraints imposed by Islamic law on governance to an unacceptable degree—that is, making the state custodianship of Islam too thin. This difference of opinion was not limited to the conservative ʿulamā: recall some of the motives of the 1864 revolt as well as General Husayn's opposition to the inclusion of a Tunisian Jew in the Great Council in 1861. This debate about how to continue to implement the ideal of Islamic governance endured, in various forms, throughout the history of modern Tunisia, as we will see.

Conclusion

The making and unmaking of the 1861 Constitution came at a time of deep and long-brewing economic, fiscal, judicial, and diplomatic challenges for the Regency. This was unlikely to be the first major crisis forcing changes in techniques of governance in the long history of Tunisia. We can assume that earlier

317. Similarly, Mahmud Qabadu, another prominent partisan of the legal reforms of the same generation as Ibn Diyaf, compared the *qānūn* to a glass container protecting the flame of sharia (Qabādū 1875–1879, vol. 2, 67).

318. "*Al-ḍarūrāt tubīḥ al-maḥẓūrāt.*" This legal maxim was coined by Zayn al-Din Ibn Nujaym (d. 1563). Y. Linant de Bellefonds, Ḍarūra, *EI*².

319. Ibn Abī al-Ḍiyāf (1963, vol. 5, 85, and vol. 6, 88), also cited by Chérif (1994, 92).

320. Ibn Abī al-Ḍiyāf (1963, vol. 1, 50).

321. Ibn Abī al-Ḍiyāf (1963, vol. 1, 48–52). Citing *Marātib al-Ijmāʿ* by Ibn Ḥazm (994–1064), Ibn Diyaf also called for the protection of the *dhimma* at any cost. Abdesselem (1973, 377) writes that Ibn Diyaf's demonstration of equality of rights and duties between Jews and Muslims under sharia was "difficult" (*malaisée*). See also Chérif (1994, 92).

challenges—such as foreign conquests, invasions by foreigners, dynastic changes, economic ruptures (due, for instance, to technical innovations or foreign competition), or natural disasters like famines or epidemics—also necessitated important governance adjustments. It remains to be studied in detail how such earlier shocks or slower transformations reshaped the operations of the state in Tunisia, and how political thinkers articulated and theorized the possibility and/or necessity of changes in practices of governance after such transformations. What emerges from the history of the 1857–1861 legal reforms is that Tunisian officials, including some ʿulamā, inscribed themselves in a tradition of Islamic political thought and practice of governance that was able to accommodate change and the expanding secular ambitions of the Muslim state, within the framework of "governance according to revealed law." The importation of new techniques of governance, such as some notions of equality irrespective of religion, helped the Tunisian state put up a fight to defend its legal sovereignty. It also triggered vigorous disputes: intellectual and political debates among state officials and ʿulamā, hard-fought diplomatic negotiations with European powers, and internal armed conflicts with rebelling tribes and cities. The broad set of protagonists involved testifies to the breadth of these disputes, which revealed a deep divide over how to maintain the ideal of Islamic governance amid these transformations (or if it was even possible).

We will see how this was tackled after the 1881 French occupation. Until then, reforms continued, although not of a constitutional nature: for example, in the mid-1870s a modern school, the *Madrasa Ṣādiqīya* (also called Sadiki School), was established; the administration of religious endowments was centralized further; and the sharia justice system was reorganized. With internal and external debt ballooning, and with Tunisia's bankruptcy, an International Financial Commission was established in 1869 to manage its debt. The Regency continued to cautiously navigate its relations with the European powers and the Ottomans, with a period of rapprochement with the latter after 1864. However, neither the Ottomans nor indigenous resistance were able to prevent the French occupation.[322] The Bardo Treaty of May 12, 1881, gave France control over Tunisia's foreign affairs, and the La Marsa Agreement of June 8, 1883, established a French protectorate: it gave France exclusive power to make the reforms it deemed necessary and to authorize loans (Article 2 stipulated

322. Mahjoubi and Karoui (1983). On the relationship between Tunis and the Ottomans, see Ben Ismail (2021).

that the French government would guarantee a loan to pay off or convert outstanding debt, which had soared to more than 142 million francs, more than ten times annual state revenues).[323] The Regency's government was staffed with French officials, retaining only a Tunisian prime minister and a first secretary, and the bey was held in place, "to maintain the appearance of a Muslim ruler,"[324] which, as we will see, did not prevent disputes about who the custodian of Islam should be and what duties it should fulfill.

323. For the 1882–83 and 1883–84 state budgets (which do not include revenues and expenditures handled, for debt service, by the Financial Commission), see *JOT*, October 18, 1882. For the debt service part, see *RPR* (1881–90, 21).

324. Cardinal Lavigerie to Félix Charmetant, April 24, 1881, AMAE, Tunis, CP, vol. 57, fols. 407–408.

2

Competing Custodians of Islam in the 1907–1959 Tunisian Constitutional Episode

ISLAMIC FRANCE, THE BEY, AND INDEPENDENT TUNISIA

HOW DID CONCEPTIONS of the role of Islam in governance change after France occupied Tunisia in 1881? What was the impact, if any, of colonization, nationalism, and independence on the ideal of state custodianship of Islam? To shed light on these questions, I examine a protracted constitutional episode that stretched from 1907, the first year the indigenous journal *Le Tunisien* was published,[1] in which constitutional demands were addressed to the protectorate authorities, until 1959, the year the second Constitution of Tunisia was promulgated. I show that the precolonial ideal of state custodianship of Islam as the preferred religion, and the debate over how this ideal should be implemented, endured throughout the periods of colonial occupation, nationalist struggle for independence, and independent state building, although new issues arose and its articulations changed. Under the French protectorate (1881–1956), different groups of Tunisian elites successively reactivated the memory of the 1861 Constitution, asking for political representation via the channel of a Tunisian constitution at various junctures until independence in 1956. These constitutional projects were tools in a variety of political struggles, including

1. *Le Tunisien* was the first indigenous journal printed in French and appeared between 1907 and 1912, when it was suppressed by the protectorate authorities. Its Arabic version, *Al-Tūnisī*, appeared between 1909 and 1911.

those for equality of rights, emancipation of the Tunisian people, and state independence, and they varied depending on the political tactics of the moment. It is well-known that during this period Tunisian nationalists frequently mobilized Islam as a marker of identity and sovereignty. It is much less often understood, however, that protonationalists and nationalists, the beylical dynasty, Tunisian antinationalists (a constituency seldom considered in the historiography), and French authorities all continued to formulate state custodianship of Islam as a necessity, as in precolonial times. Since they advocated for competing sovereignties, they each put forward competing custodians of Islam: the Husaynid dynasty, imperial "Islamic France," or a sovereign and independent Tunisia or Tunisian people. In other words, the state that was exercising sovereignty, or aspiring to exercise it, was tasked (among other duties) with the preservation and protection of Islam, religious institutions, and the Muslim community. I retrace this continuity by focusing on three distinct junctures.

First, in 1907, before the creation of an organized nationalist movement, a group of protonationalist indigenous elites, the Young Tunisians, asked for a constitution without full sovereignty, as a guarantee of equality between Tunisian natives (*indigènes*) and French settlers (*colons*). At a time when France represented itself as a "Muslim power," the Young Tunisians vocally asked that it respect, support, and help improve Tunisia's Islamic institutions. Although they advocated for a putative equality of all irrespective of religion, they also wanted Tunisia's sixty thousand Jews to be restricted from access to high-level administrative posts, thereby articulating a conception of the Tunisian state as administered mainly by (and for) Muslims. Historians have overlooked this fact. Second, after the Great War, Tunisian nationalists, in their newly created party, made Tunisia's emancipation from the French protectorate part of their political program. Drafted in March 1920, it outlined the main principles of a constitution, including Islam as "the official religion of the country and of its army." When they subsequently petitioned French Parliament for a constitution, Tunisian nationalists did not include this clause. They did not need to since their petitions did not ask for sovereignty. However, a counterpetition, filed by a Tunisian veteran of the Great War that same year, argued that Tunisians did not need a constitution but rather needed "Islamic France" to "maintain the religious status quo" and to protect Tunisians, "especially from the religious point of view." This was followed, in 1922, by the bey's reaffirmation of his dynasty's sovereignty and his role of custodian of Islam as "reigning prince" and "religious leader." Throughout this period, competing for sovereignty also meant competing for the custodianship of Islam. Third, Tunisia became independent in 1956, resolving the question of sovereignty and hence of who was entrusted with the custodianship of Islam. But the 1956–1959 National Constituent Assembly debated what this custodianship entailed. In combination with the 1956 Personal Status Code (which greatly improved women's rights), the 1959 Constitution, and its stipulation that Islam was the religion of the state, formed what I call Bourguiba's postindependence authoritarian synthesis between conservative and liberal conceptions of the role of Islam in governance. In this synthesis, while striving to minimize the constraints of Islamic law (what I call the thickness of the state's custodianship of Islam), the nationalist leader Habib Bourguiba articulated an understanding of the state as the custodian of a religious infrastructure that not only provided for Islamic worship but also disseminated Islamic values through its rapidly expanding public school system. Importantly, neither he nor his political rivals (liberals and conservatives alike) argued at any point for separating Islam and the state or for state neutrality.

This study has at least two broad implications that diverge from the literature on Islam and politics in the modern Middle East. First, examining the 1907–1959 constitutional episode allows us to disentangle what the postindependence role of Islam in governance (and attendant debates) owes to the legacy of precolonial conceptions from what it owes to later historical contingencies. The historiography has held colonization, nationalism, and the formation of nation-states responsible for the "politicization of Islam."[2] While all these (and other) developments have certainly left a distinct mark on debates about the role of Islam in governance in the modern period—and while nationalists and other political protagonists have used Islam as a powerful tool for political mobilization—the principle that the protection of the Muslim community, Islamic institutions, and Islam as the preferred religion is one of the state's duties (and political disagreements about how the state should fulfill this duty) long preceded them. This duty simply continued to evolve in its formulation and implementation, and to be the object of vigorous disputes (joined by new protagonists) about how it should be carried out. And, as in the past, it was inextricably tied to sovereignty, whatever its form, including when overseen by a foreign and non-Muslim power. This leads to a significant reassessment of the ruptures of the colonial and postindependence periods[3] as far as the role of

2. For instance, Starrett (1998), Karpat (2001), Nasr (2001), Moaddel (2005, 342), E. Thompson (2015), Wyrtzen (2015, 5), Mahmood (2016), Fabbe (2019), and Laurence (2021).

3. For a reassessment of the rupture of the colonial period in other dimensions, see Grangaud and Oualdi (2014).

Islam in governance is concerned: while the de facto ruler was France, the expectations of the Muslim community about the state's custodianship of Islam remained, and French authorities had to address them. Likewise, the independent Tunisian state that succeeded the French was also expected to be the custodian of Islam, despite the "secular" label often ascribed to it in the literature. Second, the tail end of this long constitutional episode, the 1955–1959 period of independent state building, offers a rare glimpse into the actual formation of what I call an authoritarian synthesis between conservative and liberal conceptions of the role of Islam in governance. Its study makes more legible one of the central political cleavages in Tunisia and in much of the Middle East, where this type of synthesis has also shaped political life under authoritarianism. I show that Habib Bourguiba's authoritarian synthesis did not make Islam a mere matter of symbolism and identity, as is often argued.[4] Rather, it preserved the state's custodianship of Islam while suppressing the existing debate between conservatives and liberals. Hence, there is no "paradox of liberation" as posited by Walzer (2015), who claims that "campaigns for national liberation in the years following World War II were initially based on democratic and secular ideals," but that "once established . . . the newly independent nations had to deal with entirely unexpected [*sic*] religious fierceness."[5]

During the French protectorate and after independence, debates about religion and governance were often muffled because freedom of expression was severely restricted. It is nonetheless possible to grasp the visions for the role of Islam in governance articulated by the main protagonists of the 1907–1959 Tunisian constitutional episode by using Tunisian and French archives; the Arabic and French periodical press; and the published official Arabic transcripts of the 1956–1959 debates in the Tunisian National Constituent Assembly.

Section 1 examines the Young Tunisians' constitutional demands in the years 1907–1912. Section 2 analyzes the March 1920 constitutional draft in the nationalist party's political program. Section 3 sheds light on the 1920 Tunisian petitions and counterpetitions to French Parliament for and against a Tunisian constitution as well as the eighteen points the bey submitted to the French General Residence in 1922. Section 4 delves into the making of Bourguiba's authoritarian synthesis upon independence during the years 1955–1959.

4. For instance, Salem (1984). For an institutional approach, see Ḥajjī (2004).

5. https://yalebooks.yale.edu/book/9780300223637/paradox-liberation, accessed September 23, 2020. Walzer (2015) presents as evidence an idealized view of the movement of liberation of Algeria, largely based on secondary sources.

1. The Young Tunisians' Demands for a Constitution without Sovereignty and with France's Custodianship of Islam (*Le Tunisien*, 1907–1912)

In 1907 a group of Tunisian elites named the "Young Tunisians," a reference to the Ottoman Young Turks,[6] expressed their grievances against the French protectorate in their newly founded weekly journal, *Le Tunisien* (The Tunisian). They encountered opposition from French settlers, and, after riots by Tunisians in 1911 and 1912, French authorities pushed the group underground and sent its leaders into exile. The literature has highlighted how their short-lived movement foreshadowed the nationalist ideas of the 1920s,[7] but it has paid scant attention to their conceptions of the role of Islam in governance. The Young Tunisians described themselves as "Tunisian Muslims"[8] but formulated their demands within the framework of the protectorate, which they did not condemn as such (at least overtly). Most of them were from well-to-do families and had received a bilingual high school education in Arabic and French, typically at the Sadiki School.[9] Many of them, such as Abdeljelil Zaouche (1873–1947), studied law in France and were exposed to French public law.[10] However, there were some exceptions, such as Abd al-Aziz Thaalibi (1874?–1944), who received a purely Arabic training at the Zaytuna.[11] Most Young Tunisians worked in the Tunisian administration, and Abdeljelil Zaouche in particular held several administrative posts. In the early twentieth century, Tunisian elites often referred to the tradition of Islamic reformism articulated by nineteenth-century Tunisian statesmen such as Khayr al-Din

6. *Le Tunisien*, no. 8, March 28, 1907, Les "Jeunes Tunisiens," 1–2.

7. Tlili (1979) and Ayadi (1986).

8. Ali Bach Hamba, Notre programme, *Le Tunisien*, no. 1, February 7, 1907, 1.

9. Khairallah (1938), Guezmir (1978, 81), and Sraïeb (1995).

10. Zaouche's mother was Italian, and he did not read Arabic well. He belonged to the upper bourgeoisie of Tunis, graduated from the prominent Lycée Louis Le Grand, and obtained a *licence* degree in law in Paris. In *Le Tunisien*, no. 31, September 5, 1907, 1, the Young Tunisians are described as "a bit too specialized in legal studies."

11. Guezmir (1978). See also Goldstein (1978, 18). Thaalibi, of Algerian origins, studied at the Zaytuna but did not graduate. He helped found the Dustūr Party in 1920. The failures of the constitutional demands led to a schism in the party, and he was politically isolated after 1923. He spent the years 1923–1937 in the Mashriq, notably in Iraq and Egypt. Upon his return to Tunis in 1937, he came into conflict with Habib Bourguiba, who had created the New Dustūr Party in 1934. This isolated Thaalibi further and his political legacy was never fully recognized. Dellagi (2013).

and Ibn Diyaf, and this tradition was being enriched by a native periodical press that brought news and ideas from Europe but also from the Middle East and more distant Muslim societies.[12] Tunisians were exposed to European nationalisms, particularly through the flow of Italian immigrants to Tunisia, and to atheism, especially through French socialist ideologies.[13] Tunisian elites were also aware of the debates about the French 1905 law separating churches from the state, although this law did not seem to apply in the protectorates and colonies.

Demands for Equality of Rights, Participation, and Representation not Independence

The Young Tunisians expressed their admiration for French "civilization" and deplored their exclusion from it. They asked for equality with French settlers and for access to more public resources, better opportunities, and particularly education, which they placed "at the forefront of [their] preoccupations."[14] They wanted Tunisians to participate fully in the state administration and to receive wages equal to those of French civil servants in Tunisia. Their de facto exclusion from high-level administrative posts made them feel, they wrote, like foreigners in their own country.[15] They applied the adjective "Tunisian" to their journal, to communities, and to individuals, including Tunisian Jews, whom they called their fellow citizens (*concitoyens*). They also applied it to some institutions, such as their justice system (*justice tunisienne*) and education system (*l'enseignement tunisien*) as well as to the bey's government (*le gouvernement tunisien*). However, they did not apply it to the state since they were not asking for independence overtly and recognized, at least prima facie, the French state's authority. Still, as we will see, this did not prevent them from articulating a conception of their state as having to be administered mainly by (and for) Muslims. The Young Tunisians also asked for "political representation" and "an elected council" under the regime of the protectorate. The French colony had obtained political

12. Chenoufi (1968). See also the Arabic journal *Al-Ḥāḍira*, which appeared from 1888 to 1911.

13. Soumille (1975).

14. *Le Tunisien*, no. 1, February 7, 1907, 1. They asked for compulsory primary education for Tunisians, the development of vocational schools, a reform of the justice system (including codification of law), and tax decreases. See *Le Tunisien*, no. 8, March 26, 1907, Les "Jeunes Tunisiens," 1. They also asked for access to state-owned agricultural property (*terres domaniales*). See, in the same issue, Les indigènes et la colonization, 1.

15. *Le Tunisien*, no. 17, May 30, 1907, 1.

representation through universal suffrage in the Consultative Conference in 1896, but Tunisian natives were excluded from it until 1907 and henceforth given very limited representation. The Young Tunisians fought for the expansion of their role in this representative body.[16] In order to enshrine their political representation in law they asked for a constitution, although they did not put it forward as an overt marker of sovereignty.[17]

Half-Sovereignty, the Tunisian State's Legal Personality, and Tunisian Nationality

The particular legal structure of the French protectorate helped the Young Tunisians conceive of their state and their constitutional project since, in theory, the bey remained sovereign in domestic affairs. The 1881 Bardo Treaty maintained the bey's government, while France had the power to represent and defend Tunisia abroad.[18] However, with the 1883 Agreement of La Marsa the bey's sovereignty became a legal fiction.[19] The bey had the obligation to implement all the reforms judged necessary by the French Government and could not borrow funds without French approval. The French de facto governed Tunisia: they controlled the state's debt, budget, and administration,[20] and the bey "became an instrument in the hands of the French General Resident" (*Résident Général*)[21] since his approval was necessary for the bey's decrees to have legal value. Still, from a legal point of view, Tunisia kept its sovereignty, exercised by the bey, who also represented the "personality" of the Tunisian state.[22] In the late nineteenth century, as France experimented with the protectorate as a more flexible legal formula than annexation (which it had formally implemented in Algeria in 1848), French legal theorists argued that, in a world of nation-states, there could be exceptions to the principle of a state's absolute sovereignty and that the sovereignty of the protected state was "relative"—that is, a "half-sovereignty."[23] The view was that a protectorate was not a "brutal and violent fact" but an agreement signed by two sovereign entities, and that "the personality of the protected

16. *Le Tunisien*, no. 1, February 7, 1907, 1.
17. *Le Tunisien*, no. 1, February 7, 1907, 1.
18. Traité de Ksar Said, May 12, 1881.
19. Convention de La Marsa, June 8, 1883.
20. Fitoussi (1901, 176–177 and 186–195).
21. Mahjoubi (1977, 144).
22. M. Lewis (2014, 101–102).
23. Foucher (1897, 1–3).

state subsists after the signature of the protectorate agreement," although the weak state agrees to be under the "supremacy" of the strong state.[24] In a 1901 book, the Tunisian jurist Elie Fitoussi, citing French legal literature from the 1890s, argued that before French occupation the Regency of Tunis was a fully independent state, freed from Ottoman domination, and that, with the protectorate, the Tunisian state had not entirely lost its sovereignty: "1-The protected state does not disappear from the international community; it keeps its *legal personality* despite the powers of the protecting state. 2-The territory of the protected state is not the same as the territory of the protecting state. *Two sovereignties* apply to it . . . 3-The subjects of the protected state keep their *nationality*."[25] Until their independence in 1956, the theory of two coexisting sovereignties allowed Tunisians to argue that they formed a distinct community of people endowed with a distinct nationality.[26] Although they were unable to administer their own state, which was not fully sovereign, it retained its legal personality and they could still elaborate on how they conceived of it.

Demands for a Constitution without Sovereignty: Islam as a "Moral Sentiment"

The Young Tunisians also showed a strong interest in other constitutional experiences in the Muslim world. In 1907 *Le Tunisien* published excerpts of the 1906 Iranian Constitution.[27] One year later, it reported on the 1908 reinstatement of the 1876 Turkish Constitution, which, it underlined, had been praised in France. In August 1908, Abdeljelil Zaouche reminded *Le Tunisien*'s readers that "the Turkish people . . . have declared that there now must be complete harmony between all Ottomans, without distinction of race or religion."[28] Invoking the memory of the 1861 Tunisian Constitution, he wrote, "Tunisians hope that . . . a constitution will be given to them, which will guarantee individual freedom, the sanctity of their homes, freedom of the press . . . and will

24. Foucher (1897, 24–25).

25. Fitoussi (1901, 135). Emphases are mine.

26. According to M. Lewis (2014, 100, 223n6, and 132), the Quai d'Orsay invented the concept of "cosovereignty" in the 1910s and 1920s "or, rather, refashioned it from its prior usage on the European continent" to become a doctrine. The nationalist leader Habib Bourguiba also used this concept in the 1930s.

27. *Le Tunisien*, no. 1, February 7, 1907, La Constitution persane, 2–3.

28. *Le Tunisien*, no. 78, August 27, 1908, Abdeljelil Zaouche, La Tunisie et la constitution, 1.

proclaim that all citizens are equal before the law."[29] Responding to the French press's negative reactions to his article, Abdeljelil Zaouche argued that Tunisians were not looking for emancipation from the French protectorate: although a constitution would be created "for" Tunisians and would be called a "Tunisian constitution,"[30] it would not be the constitution of a sovereign Tunisian state[31]—an argument consistent with the French theory of half-sovereignty. Similarly, Ali Bach Hamba wrote that had the 1861 Constitution still been in force, the Treaty of 1881 would certainly have confirmed it.[32] For the Young Tunisians, Islam was not an obstacle to having a constitution either.[33] *Le Tunisien* reproduced various articles that had appeared in the French press in this regard.[34] Some asserted that if Islam could be modernized, Tunisians could become mature enough to have a constitution. If the Turks, a "Muslim power," had done it in 1876 and in 1908, then why not Tunisians? In the past, this argument continued, "Muslim liberals had religious orthodoxy against them. Now it has become their ally."[35] In contrast, one of the French opinion essays reproduced in *Le Tunisien* argued that since France had separated church from state in 1905, Tunisians should be given rights independently of religious considerations.[36] It seems that both arguments (a constitution mandated by Islam or one with no relation to Islam) suited the Young Tunisians, and *Le Tunisien* remained silent on the exact place of Islam in their constitutional demands. That said, Islam was very much present in the pages of *Le Tunisien*, although the Young Tunisians took pains to argue that it was not a foundation for their

29. *Le Tunisien*, no. 78, August 27, 1908, Abdeljelil Zaouche, La Tunisie et la constitution, 1.

30. *Le Tunisien*, no. 82, October 8, 1908, La Constitution Tunisienne, 1.

31. He also invoked the 1857 Security Pact: "Is [the Tunisians'] mentality inferior to that of 1857?" *Le Tunisien*, no. 79, October 9, 1906, Abdeljelil Zaouche, Expliquons-nous!, 1.

32. *Le Tunisien*, no. 80, September 24, 1908, Ali Bach Hamba, Encore un mot sur la constitution, 1.

33. *Le Tunisien*, no. 78, August 27, 1908, Abdeljelil Zaouche, La Tunisie et la constitution, 1.

34. *Le Tunisien*, no. 80, September 24, 1908: reproduction of "L'islam et nous" published in *Le Temps*, 1–2; reproduction of an article published in *Le Journal des débats*, 2; reproduction of an article by Camille Pelletan, in *Le Matin*, under the title "La France musulmane et la Turquie française," 2. *Le Tunisien*, no. 81, October 1, 1908, reproduction of an article by Duthil de la Tuque in *La Revue diplomatique* under the title "Les peuples musulmans," 1. *Le Tunisien*, no. 82, October 8, 1908, reproduction of an article in *La Presse coloniale* under the title "La Constitution tunisienne," 1.

35. *Le Tunisien*, no. 80, September 24, 1908, reproduction of "L'islam et nous" published in *Le Temps*, 1–2, and reproduction of Camille Pelletan's aforementioned article in *Le Matin*.

36. *Le Tunisien*, no. 81, October 1, 1908, reproduction of "Les peuples musulmans" by Duthil de la Tuque, in *La Revue diplomatique*, 1–2.

political claims. In 1910 the pro-settler journal *Le Colon Français* accused them of having "friends in Constantinople and Egypt."[37] These accusations stemmed from French fears that allegiance to the Ottoman Caliph, and by extension what they called "pan-Islamism," were causing anti-French feelings that would lead to political demands in Tunisia. The Young Tunisians rejected these accusations, and Ali Bach Hamba responded in an editorial in *Le Tunisien*: "Any Muslim is, by definition, pan-Islamist! . . . It is a banality . . . [Tunisians] venerate the Ottoman dynasty . . . which makes them pan-Islamists and turcophiles . . . and they do not hide it." To reassure the French, he described pan-Islamism as a "sentiment of fraternity," "a purely moral relationship" and not a basis for political claims.[38]

Demands for France's Custodianship of Islamic Institutions and Muslim Personal Status

While the Young Tunisians affirmed their "Muslim individuality," they also proclaimed their loyalty to France.[39] And since France represented itself as a "Muslim power" at the time,[40] the Young Tunisians reasoned that its responsibility was to be a custodian of Islam.[41] They criticized French authorities for being too tentative in developing primary schooling for Tunisians[42] and asked that "an Arabic education based on Islamic morality" be provided to them.[43] They exhorted the protectorate authorities to reform Qur'anic schools (*kuttābs*), and to have the Qur'an taught in a way that it would be properly understood by pupils.[44] They also asked them to help with some

37. *Le Tunisien*, no. 161, October 20, 1910, Procès de tendance, 1.

38. *Le Tunisien*, no. 161, October 20, 1910, Procès de tendance, 1. See ʿAbd al-ʿAzīz al-Thaʿālibī, Al-Ittiḥād al-Islāmī, in *Al-Ittiḥād al-Islāmī*, no. 1, October 19, 1911, reproduced in Duqqī (1999, 182–186).

39. *Le Tunisien*, no. 161, October 20, 1910, 1.

40. Cloarec (1996) and Le Pautremat (2003).

41. For instance, Abdeljelil Zaouche's speech at the North African Congress of 1908 (reproduced in *Le Tunisien*, no. 83, October 15, 1908, 1) in which France is described as a "Muslim Power," echoing René Millet, former general resident in Tunisia.

42. Khairallah Ben Mustapha, in Depincé (1909, vol. 2, 552–572).

43. *Le Tunisien*, no. 77, August 13, 1908, 3. See also Mohamed Lasram, L'enseignement supérieur musulman à la mosquée de l'olivier ou Grande Mosquée, à Tunis, in Depincé (1909, vol. 2, 163).

44. Khairallah Ben Mustapha, L'enseignement primaire des indigènes en Tunisie, in Depincé (1909, vol. 2, 562).

reforms of Islamic institutions of higher learning, such as the Zaytuna, but without hurting Tunisians' Islamic sentiments.[45] The Young Tunisians also asked France to respect their Muslim personal status after the naturalization decree of October 1910 offered French citizenship to foreigners residing in Tunisia and to a narrow category of educated Tunisian Jews and Muslims,[46] an attempt to mitigate what the French called the "indigenous threat" and to bolster the French demographic presence in Tunisia.[47] The Young Tunisians responded to this law by arguing that, since French naturalization required submitting to the French civil code and abandoning Muslim personal status (which the vast majority of Tunisians viewed as a sort of apostasy), naturalized Tunisian Muslims would be ostracized by their community.[48] They insisted that they were well aware that France's civil code had imposed universal laws on all its citizens and that the French republic had separated church and state. However, they argued, since France now extended its domination over millions of Muslims, it had to change the legal regime of French nationality and respect the personal status laws of the Muslim populations it governed. Only then would it be theoretically conceivable for a Tunisian Muslim to become French.[49] Given its hypothetical formulation, we should not interpret the Young Tunisians' reasoning as a demand for French naturalization with Muslim personal status. Rather, it was a demand for the protection and preservation of Muslim personal status in Tunisia.

45. Mohamed Lasram, in Depincé (1909, vol. 2, 172).

46. Decree of October 3, 1910, *JORF*, no. 274, October 8, 1910, 8321–8322. Naturalization of foreigners was conditioned on length of residence. According to *Statistique générale de la Tunisie* (1923, 21), there were 2,069 naturalizations by virtue of this decree (from 1911 to 1923), of which only 261 Tunisians (83 Muslims and 178 Jews).

47. According to the official count of 1911 in *Dénombrement* (1911, 4–6), there were 148,476 European civilians (of which 88,082 were Italians and only 46,044 French) and, according to *Statistique générale de la Tunisie* (1913, 18–19), an "approximate number" of 1,790,611 natives (an official count of the native population was first conducted in 1921). See Seklani (1974) and Tabutin et al. (2001) for the flaws of and corrections to population estimates, official counts, and censuses before and at independence, due to technical limitations and population reluctance. As in the rest of this book, population evaluations and breakdowns should be taken as indicative of orders of magnitude only.

48. Ahmed Essafi, La naturalization des Tunisiens I, *Le Tunisien*, no. 161, October 20, 1910, 1–2; and La naturalization des Tunisiens II, *Le Tunisien*, no. 162, October 27, 1910, 1–2. See the article's Arabic version in *Al-Tūnisī*, October 24 and 31, 1910, cited in Duqqī (1999, 77–82).

49. Ahmed Essafi, La naturalisation des Tunisiens I, *Le Tunisien*, no. 161, October 20, 1910, 1–2; and La naturalisation des Tunisiens II, *Le Tunisien*, no. 162, October 27, 1910, 1–2.

Can Tunisian Jews Administer Tunisia? The Limits of Equality under a Muslim State

The Young Tunisians, who were all Muslim, reproached Tunisian Jews for their readiness to abandon their Jewish personal status to become French citizens and/or to fall under French jurisdiction instead of submitting to the Tunisian justice system. For Tunisian Jews, this consisted in the secular tribunals they shared with Muslims and their rabbinic tribunals.[50] The French government in Paris was not enthusiastic about naturalizing indigenous Jews, as it did in Algeria with the 1870 Crémieux decree. Although French officials recognized that the Tunisian Jews' ambition to become French was "legitimate," they argued that France, a Muslim power (*puissance musulmane*), had to worry about the potential consequences: in Algeria, the Crémieux decree had led to a wave of antisemitic violence from French settlers, and this time protests could arise from Tunisian Muslims. A 1910 report to the French Parliament argued that two reasons motivated Tunisian Jews to become French: the desire to escape the Tunisian justice system and their ambition to be eligible for administrative posts, traditionally inaccessible to them. However, the report urged caution since, it argued, "the Muslim population would be extremely displeased to see public posts progressively being held by French naturalized Israelites of Tunisian descent. France must avoid hurting the feelings of a population of two million Muslims for the benefit of a small minority."[51] As for the Young Tunisians, they encouraged Tunisian Jews to unite with them as "compatriots" in their fight to maintain a Tunisian jurisdiction for both Muslims and Jews and to improve the Tunisian justice system as a whole.[52] They also wanted to "speak as Tunisians, and not as Muslims or Jews," and to fight together for equality with the French in the domains of education, public assistance (*assistance publique*),

50. Ali Bach Hamba, La question juive en Tunisie, *Le Tunisien*, no. 134, December 30, 1909, and *Al-Tūnisī*, no. 1, November 8, 1909, quoted in Duqqī (1999, 72–74).

51. Messimy Report to Parliament, second session of February 8, 1910, quoted in *Le Tunisien*, no. 147, March 31, 1910. In 1910 the Consultative Conference proposed that non-Muslims be given French citizenship en masse. With the Messimy report, the government rejected this option. *Statistique générale de la Tunisie* (1913, 18–19) estimates the native population at 1,740,144 Muslims and 50,467 Jews in 1911.

52. This was also the position of some parliamentarians in Paris. See the Messimy Report quoted in *Le Tunisien*, no. 147, March 31, 1910. The Young Tunisians deplored the state of the Tunisian justice system, which they described as "crumbling" and "frozen in past traditions." See Guellaty (1909, ii–iii and 58–59) and *Le Tunisien*, nos. 11, 12, 15, 16, 18, 51, and 64.

and taxation.[53] Abdeljelil Zaouche was adamant that, as Jewish magistrates were allowed in the secular part of the Tunisian justice system (*juridiction séculière*), Tunisian Jews could not argue it was "Muslim justice."[54] In his November 26, 1909, speech at the Consultative Conference, he exhorted the French to reform the Tunisian justice system rather than shield Tunisian Jews from it and insisted that "Tunisian justice must be one and equal for all Tunisians, irrespective of beliefs."[55] Moreover, the Young Tunisians argued that if Tunisian Jews were to fall under French justice, it would be "a shocking inequality between nationals of one and the same state."[56] For them, the Tunisian system of justice was a marker of Tunisian sovereignty.[57] Paradoxically, as fragmented as it was between its sharia, rabbinic, and secular courts, it became one of the sites where the idea of the nation crystallized: a set of "equal" religious communities each obeying their own religious laws under one Tunisian (and, as we will see, Muslim) state.

The Young Tunisians also explicitly addressed the issue of the unequal status of Tunisian Jews in Tunisia. Although they approved Tunisian Jews' access to the judiciary, they were much less ready to give them access to posts in the Tunisian state administration, from which they were traditionally often excluded, although there were exceptions.[58] For instance, in 1907 Abdeljelil Zaouche wrote an article entitled "What are they?" (*Que sont-ils?*) in response to an article published in the Jewish journal *La Justice*, entitled "What are we?" (*Que sommes-nous?*).[59] In his article, he called Tunisian Jews his "fellow citizens" (*concitoyens*) and criticized *La Justice* for claiming that Jews "were not and never were Tunisians." He argued that they were of Tunisian nationality and had never attempted to renounce it. He underlined that, like Tunisian Muslims, they were natives (*indigènes*), and that the Young Tunisians asked for reforms

53. Ali Bach Hamba, La question juive en Tunisie, *Le Tunisien*, no. 134, December 30, 1909, 1.

54. *Le Tunisien*, no. 86, November 5, 1908. See also *Le Tunisien*, no. 64, April 23, 1908; *Le Tunisien*, no. 126, November 4, 1909; and *Le Tunisien*, no. 130, December 2, 1909.

55. *Le Tunisien*, no. 130, December 2, 1909.

56. Guellaty (1909, 47).

57. Guellaty (1909, 46).

58. Recall high-ranking official Nassim Shamama in chapter 1. On the appointment of non-Muslims to high official positions in premodern Muslim states, see Cohen (2008) and Yarbrough (2019).

59. *Le Tunisien*, no. 18, June 6, 1907. *La Justice*, May 24, 1907. The Jewish journal *La Justice*, created in 1906 by Mardochée Smadja, regularly argued in favor of Tunisian Jews falling under French jurisdiction.

from France "for all natives, regardless of religion." There remained, he acknowledged, one point of contention: the exclusion of Jews from the administration of the state. He framed it as a purely Tunisian issue, as if there were no French occupation and no French domination in the state administration. He argued that it was a long-held tradition in "all Muslim countries" that Jews participated in the administration of the state in "very limited numbers," and that this was because "the majority belonged to the Muslim religion." He also argued that it would be conceivable, in principle, to allow Tunisian Jews to compete for posts on merit. However, in his view, because Jews, "having understood for a long time the necessity of instruction," were much more educated than Muslims, the result would be the exclusion of Tunisian Muslims from the administration of the country, "which would soon fall in the hands of the Jews." He then concluded that Tunisian Jews should be allocated posts in proportion to their demographic weight since, in his view, the state should be administered by the majority—that is, by Muslims.[60] This reasoning illustrates well the tensions that are typically at play between the ideal of state custodianship of Islam as the preferred religion and the principle of equality of all irrespective of religion. We have encountered them in 1861 and we will see them at play again in the making of the constitutions of Tunisia in 1959, right after independence, and in 2014, during its transition to democracy. In fact, the French general resident had articulated an analogous reasoning in 1895 to justify his reluctance to naturalize Tunisian Jews en masse, when he argued that the 60,000 Jews of the Regency, if naturalized, would "overwhelm" the small "core" French community of 16,000 individuals.[61]

2. Islam as the "Official Religion of the Country" and Its "National Army": The March 1920 Dustūr Party Program Constitutional Draft

Although they conceived of their state as having to be administered mainly by (and for) Muslims, the Young Tunisians did not fully elaborate on the role of Islam in the state in their constitutional demands since they did not overtly

60. In *Le Républicain* of June 9, 1907, Dr. Cattan recognized that Jews in Tunisia were of Tunisian nationality but criticized Abdeljelil Zaouche's refusal to open the Tunisian administration to Jews.

61. Hagège and Zarca (2001, 17).

ask for full sovereignty. However, this changed after the Great War, when a younger generation of Young Tunisians openly asked for independence. The Free Tunisian Party (*al-ḥizb al-ḥurr al-tūnisī*) was created in the spring of 1920, renamed the Free Constitutional Party (*al-ḥizb al-ḥurr al-dustūrī*) in 1921, and called the Party of the Constitution (*ḥizb al-dustūr*) or Dustūr Party for short.[62] Calls for independence became public, and the idea of a Tunisian constitution a central theme in this quest. The party was established under the leadership of Abd al-Aziz Thaalibi (1874–1944) and other Young Tunisians, such as Ahmed Essafi (1882–1935), Ahmed Sakka (1891–1957), Sadok Zmerli (1893–1993), Ali Kahia (1879–1956), Hamouda Mestiri (1862–1945), M'hamed Djaibi (1880–1938), and Farhat Ben Ayed (b. circa 1880), who generally belonged to a younger generation than Ali Bach Hamba (1875–1918) and Béchir Sfar (1856–1917) and who had not all participated in the journalistic enterprise of *Le Tunisien*.[63] They were also often educated in the French language, and sometimes in France and in French law, but were generally more overtly intransigent toward France than the earlier generation of Young Tunisians. After the Great War, Tunisians expressed their grievances more vocally, and in a more organized manner.[64] This can be explained, in part, by the post–Great War deterioration of economic conditions in Tunisia and by the heavy casualties among Tunisians who fought in the Great War, which fed urban and rural discontent. The historiography also lists the influence of international events[65] and the circulation of new ideas among possible factors. Tunisian nationalists were certainly attentive to nationalism abroad: among their inspirations were the 1919 Egyptian revolution and the 1919 *Statuto Libico* (a constitution given by Italy to Tripolitania, as we will see). This new generation of Tunisian activists also had greater access to French intellectuals and politicians

62. Goldstein (1978, 295 and 334). In both instances, "*ḥurr*" is usually translated by "liberal," but it also means "free."

63. These are the names found in the letter from Farhat Ben Ayed to Abd al-Aziz Thaalibi in Paris regarding the vote on the program of the newly created party that took place in March 1920. Farhat Ben Ayed to Abd al-Aziz Thaalibi, February 2, 1920, ISHTC, Série Tunisie, Fonds de la Résidence, Bobine R28, C1552B, D2, fols. 378–386.

64. Bernard (1926, 88–89), Tlili (1973), M. Kraïem (1976), Mahjoubi (1982, chapter 3), and Frémeaux (2006).

65. For instance, the Young Tunisians originally thought that the January 1918 statement of principles by the US president Woodrow Wilson could help their cause but soon realized that it did not apply to them. "Lettre apportée par Chédly," February 5, 1920, ISHTC, Série Tunisie, Fonds de la Résidence, Bobine R28, C1552B, D2, fols. 361–368, fol. 363.

in Paris, who were sometimes sympathetic to their claims.[66] Among them were human rights activists, lawyers, and communist- and socialist-leaning French parliamentarians such as MP Marius Moutet (1876–1968),[67] who encouraged them to move forward with their demands for a constitution and publicized their claims in Paris and Tunis.

Martyr Tunisia and the Idea of Muslim Public Law

It was in this context that Abd al-Aziz Thaalibi joined Ahmed Sakka in Paris in July 1919 to sound out French public opinion about a Tunisian constitution. While in Paris, they contacted French socialists in Parliament[68] and wrote what became the manifesto of the early nationalist movement, *Martyr Tunisia—Its Demands* (*La Tunisie martyre—Ses revendications*). In this book, they laid out the main claims of the soon-to-be-formed Dustūr Party against French policies, which led to Thaalibi's arrest in July 1920. It was meant to be "a loyal exposition of the Tunisian problem" to the French public, and it included, at its very end, ten points listed under the title "Our Demands" (*Nos revendications*).[69] It was part of a two-pronged effort to reach out to French elites and parliamentarians[70] and to organize a nationalist party in Tunis. Out of caution, the book did not explicitly advocate for independence from France, although this was clearly its aim. Thaalibi, who studied at the Zaytuna, wrote in Arabic and had no proficiency in French.[71] Ahmed Sakka, a Tunisian lawyer who had written a doctoral thesis titled *Sovereignty in Sunni Muslim Public Law* at the University of Paris Faculty of Law in 1917, apparently wrote

66. In Paris, during the Great War, the newspaper *Le Temps*, as well as the French League for the Rights of Man and the Citizen and MPs such as Marius Moutet, actively advocated for softening the political regime to which Muslim natives were subjected in Algeria. Julien (1952, 34–36).

67. Marius Moutet was a French socialist MP and a member of the French League for the Rights of Man and the Citizen. He represented the district of the Rhône in Parliament from 1914 to 1928 and belonged to the Committee for Foreign Affairs and to the Committee of Algeria, the Colonies, and the Protectorates. He coined the idea of "democratic colonization." Gratien (2006).

68. Sahli (1982, 315–319).

69. Thaalibi (1920, 1 and 207–212).

70. Lettre de Farhat Ben Ayed à Abd al-Aziz Thaalibi, December 3, 1919, cited in Sahli (1982, 322).

71. However, Thaalibi's earlier thought was Francophile, rationalist, and staunchly opposed to the conservative ʿulamā of the Zaytuna. Thaalibi was tried for blasphemy in July 1904 after a coterie of Zaytuna shaykhs accused him of having spoken irreligiously. See A. Kraïem (1986) and L. Thompson (2022).

Martyr Tunisia in French under Thaalibi's direction.[72] In his thesis, Sakka argued that in Muslim public law God was the sovereign but that in the modern Muslim state the nation could elect its sovereign and organize itself.[73] One of his most cited sources was a 1901 French translation of Al-Mawardī's *Al-Aḥkām al-Sulṭānīya* by the French jurist Léon Ostrorog, who, in a long introduction, had analyzed what he called "Muslim public law."[74]

Martyr Tunisia referred to the 1857 Security Pact and the 1861 Constitution as having established the Tunisian constitutional tradition and argued that "no legal text had suppressed or suspended the [1861] Constitution."[75] It claimed that Tunisia had "a parliament" in the form of the Great Council, which the French protectorate had eliminated "in a brutal gesture," and that the protectorate "entirely destroyed our public law and the Tunisian state."[76] It sought the "constitutional guarantees of liberty and justice that International Law recognizes for any people, who, as ours, have a History, a civilization, a territory, a personality."[77] It aimed to persuade French public opinion of both the injustices of the protectorate and the ability of Tunisians to govern themselves. It argued that they had historically possessed a body of "Muslim public law" (*droit public musulman*) similar to and older than French public law, one that respected liberty, personality, and property, contained all the principles of democracy and representative government, and allowed for secular legislation outside of personal status.[78] It spoke of Tunisia before the protectorate as an "Islamic state" (*Etat islamique*) and argued that, in this kind of state, "the principles that are at the foundation of the charter of Muslim society constrain [*disciplinent*] and govern [*régissent*] legislative power." It described the role of legislative power as "very limited" in the domain of personal status but "quite extensive" in the domain of "secular legislation" (*législation laïque*), within "the limits and under the regulation of the Muslim code [*code musulman*]."[79] This

72. Sahli (1982, 311–312).

73. Sakka (1917, 143).

74. Chapter 1 of Ahmed Sakka's thesis is an extensive quote of the introduction to Ostrorog (1901).

75. Thaalibi (1920, 6–9). In 1921 a legal consultation by Barthélémy and Weiss argued that the 1861 Constitution had not been abrogated and could be reinstated. It was published in an annex to Duran-Angliviel (1921). See also ANT SG-SG5 C1 D3-1.

76. Thaalibi (1920, 9).

77. Thaalibi (1920, 2, 208, and 210).

78. Thaalibi (1920, 5 and 17).

79. Thaalibi (1920, 5).

echoed some aspects of the *siyāsa/sharīʿa* paradigm that we saw Ibn Diyaf mobilize in chapter 1. However, *Martyr Tunisia* affirmed the continuity of the Muslim state with a new formulation, the Gallicized concept of "Muslim public law," which was also deployed by other legal experts in and beyond Tunisia in the interwar period (e.g., the Egyptian lawyer Abd al-Razzaq Sanhuri).[80]

Islam as the "Official Religion of the Country and Its Army" in the 1920 Constitutional Draft

In the spring of 1920, a few months after the publication of *Martyr Tunisia*, a group of Tunisians met to create what would soon be called the Dustūr Party.[81] In their program, they included the draft of a Tunisian Constitution. They called it a "Fundamental Pact," an echo of the French official designation of the 1857 Security Pact. Their program, and the correspondence related to it, were secret documents that the French police seized when they searched Thaalibi's lodgings in Paris in June 1920.[82] Unlike *Martyr Tunisia*, they were meant to be discussed internally for the time being, and they did not hold back on independence claims. They provided details about how the soon-to-be-formed party's members imagined and debated the governance of their party and of a future independent Tunisia. They envisaged that the party's members would include "all the Muslim and Jewish residents of Tunisia and those who are not of foreign nationality, as long as they approve its program and its special regulations."[83] The aim of the party was to "obtain the emancipation of the Tunisian people"; a constitution, "which will bestow upon this people to govern itself according to the rules . . . approved by all the civilized world," was said

80. Sanhuri (1926).

81. Farhat Ben Ayed to Abd al-Aziz Thaalibi, March 17, 1920, ISHTC, Série Tunisie, Fonds de la Résidence, Bobine R28, C1552B, D2, fols. 384–386.

82. Large excerpts from this correspondence are cited in French police reports, in French, in ISHTC, Série Tunisie, Fonds de la Résidence, Bobine R28, C1552B, D2. I was not able to find an Arabic version.

83. Farhat Ben Ayed to Abd al-Aziz Thaalibi, May 7, 1920, ISHTC, Série Tunisie, Fonds de la Résidence, Bobine R28, C1552B, D2, fol. 380. Note that this letter is dated March 7, 1920 in Sahli (1982, 325). In his March 18, 1920, letter to Farhat Ben Ayed, Abd al-Aziz Thaalibi reformulated the text of the party's program and constitutional draft. It became the party's charter. He changed the specification of the party's membership to "Any Tunisian who has not become a naturalized foreigner can be a member after committing to adhere to its principles." Cited in Sahli (1982, 325).

to be a particularly important tool for realizing this aim.[84] The party would be charged with sending delegations "to Paris and to other capitals of the civilized world" to persuade these nations of the "legitimacy of its demands."[85] In a faint echo of the eleven rules (*qawā ʿid*) of the 1857 Security Pact, a section titled "What is the Constitution?" listed eleven rules that formed the party's constitutional draft.[86] These eleven rules included the separation of legislative, judicial, and executive powers (Rule #1); respect for individual freedoms "irrespective of race and religion" (Rule #2); recognition of the legitimacy of the bey's dynasty, contingent upon his oath to respect the Constitution (Rule #4); the formation of a Tunisian government responsible to the nation and to a Parliament, with the French general resident as minister of foreign affairs for the time being (Rule #5); and the election of a Parliament in which French representatives might participate until the liberation of the Tunisian people (Rule #6). The eleven rules also included procedures for electing Parliament and local and professional representative bodies (Rules #7 to 10). Rule #3 read, "The Arabic language is the official language of Tunisia, with total freedom for other languages." Finally, Rule #11 stipulated that "the Tunisian budget's revenues will only be allocated to expenditures related to matters of Tunisian public interest and to the upkeep for the national army. Under no circumstance shall this army fight against people of the Muslim faith, which would be a reprehensible attack against *the official religion of the country and of its army*."[87]

As in the Young Tunisians' writings of 1907–1912, the citizenry was conceived of as equals irrespective of religion. This principle went hand in hand with the Muslim character of the state. Since the nationalists' declared aim was the sovereignty of a future independent Tunisian state, it was only natural in their eyes that said state would be entrusted with the custodianship of Islam; with sovereignty, the future independent state would automatically inherit this duty. The responsibility was, of course, incumbent on the state long before the

84. Farhat Ben Ayed to Abd al-Aziz Thaalibi, May 7, 1920, ISHTC, Série Tunisie, Fonds de la Résidence, Bobine R28, C1552B, D2, fol. 380.

85. Farhat Ben Ayed to Abd al-Aziz Thaalibi, May 7, 1920, ISHTC, Série Tunisie, Fonds de la Résidence, Bobine R28, C1552B, D2, fols. 382–383.

86. Farhat Ben Ayed to Abd al-Aziz Thaalibi, May 7, 1920, ISHTC, Série Tunisie, Fonds de la Résidence, Bobine R28, C1552B, D2, fols. 380–382.

87. Emphasis is mine. We find slight variations in formulations in the nationalists' correspondence. Compare Farhat Ben Ayed to Abd al-Aziz Thaalibi, May 7, 1920, ISHTC, Série Tunisie, Fonds de la Résidence, Bobine R28, C1552B, D2, fol. 382, and Abd al-Aziz Thaalibi's March 18, 1920, letter to Farhat Ben Ayed, cited in Sahli (1982, 325–327).

nationalist struggle (as we saw in precolonial Tunisia) and, if necessary, could be entrusted to foreign (including non-Muslim) rulers. The mention of the "official religion of the country and of its army" in the March 1920 Dustūr Party's constitutional draft was simply a reminder of this historical responsibility. In the party leaders' correspondence, there is no trace of a dispute about Rule #11 or its formulation. There was, however, contention over whether to include French citizens in the future Assembly (part of Rule #6),[88] and a majority of the party's leaders originally voted against it. They instead proposed offering Tunisian citizenship to the French who wanted to participate in Tunisian politics.[89] Their inspiration was the 1919 Libyan Statute (*Statuto Libico*), which established a special, local Italian citizenship while preserving the religious personal status of all Muslim, Jewish, and Italian residents of Tripolitania.[90] It also created a Parliament and gave voting rights to male Muslim and Jewish natives and male Italian residents above the age of twenty. The Italian government saw it as establishing a sort of Libyan citizenship that unified all inhabitants of the colony with equal rights, which Tunisian nationalists would have liked to emulate.

The Scale of the Tunisians' Participation in the Great War and the "Blood Price"

It seems that this was the first time that a formulation of this kind, referencing the religion of the country and of its army, was included in a constitutional draft in Tunisia. It implicitly invoked one of the most salient issues of that time: the Tunisian soldiers' participation in the Great War, particularly in Muslim territories (Turkey), and in the French pacification of Morocco. As we will see, subsequent petitions to the French Parliament for a Tunisian constitution referred to this participation at length and to the debt of honor France owed as a result. It is therefore important to understand its scale and the issues it raised. After the protectorate was put in place in 1881, French authorities took advantage of the military conscription reorganized by the 1857 Security Pact. During the Great

88. Farhat Ben Ayed to Thaalbi, May 7, 1920, ISHTC, Série Tunisie, Fonds de la Résidence, Bobine R28, C1552B, D2, fols. 381–382, and Abd al-Aziz Thaalibi's March 18, 1920 letter to Farhat Ben Ayed, cited in Sahli (1982, 326).

89. "Lettre apportée par Chédly," February 5, 1920, ISHTC, Série Tunisie, Fonds de la Résidence, Bobine R28, C1552B, D2, fols. 361–365. They also proposed to establish a "Tunisian Religious Council," but the sources at our disposal do not provide details about its potential role.

90. D.L. 31 ottobre 1919, n. 2401, che approva le norme fondamentali per l'assetto della Cirenaica (Leggi e Decreti, 1919, 5702–5704).

War, Tunisian and other North African troops, called *troupes indigènes*, served in the Army of Africa (*Armée d'Afrique*), a branch of the French army.[91] Although estimates vary, we can evaluate the number of Tunisian recruits for the Great War at about one-seventh of the Tunisian Muslim male population aged eighteen and over.[92] About one-sixth of these men ended up dying or missing in action, and about as many were seriously wounded—a casualty rate comparable to that of French troops, although this was not the perception among Tunisians at the time.[93] Importantly, the number of men who were put through the conscription process was four to five times larger than the number of actual recruits because a large number of conscripts were exempted (non-Muslims, madrasa graduates, students "pursuing degrees," and city dwellers) or declared unfit for service.[94] Moreover, conscription operated via a lottery, which wealthy Tunisians could avoid by paying a fee. Therefore, for the vast majority of (rural) Muslim young men, going to war for France had been ever-present, in a way it had not for most Young Tunisians and leaders of the nationalist movement—as French authorities and antinationalists would often point out.

French authorities justified the use of colonial troops by arguing that France had given natives access to progress and civilization, which they now had to repay in blood.[95] As far as Tunisians were concerned, their educated elites denounced France's use of Tunisian soldiers to fight a war that was not theirs but that of their oppressors.[96] Volunteer soldiers were few, despite monetary

91. Fogarty (2008, chapter 1).

92. Based on *Dénombrement* (1926 and 1931, vol. 2), I estimate at roughly half a million the male Tunisian Muslims aged above eighteen at the time (out of a population of almost 2 million). See also Seklani (1974, 19). Estimates of the number of Tunisian Great War recruits range from about one-sixth to one-eighth of this population. See Bernard (1926, Statistiques et Documents, Annexes, Tableau II), Arnoulet (1984, 48), Goldstein (1978, 164), Frémeaux (2006, 63), and Fogarty (2008, 27). Frémeaux (2006, 63) estimates that about 70 percent of recruits were sent to fight in Europe. DeGeorges (2006, 21) estimates that 12,000 Tunisian soldiers were mobilized for the occupation of Morocco from 1912 to 1914.

93. Bernard (1926, Statistiques et Documents, Annexes, Tableau II) and Goldstein (1978, 176). Figures of dead and wounded Tunisian soldiers comparable to these were acknowledged by the French general resident at the time, whereas the figures put forward by nationalists were more than two times larger. See Mahjoubi (1982, 185).

94. Frémeaux (2006, 63) and DeGeorges (2006, 18).

95. Fogarty (2008, 15–16).

96. Mohamed Bach Hamba, Le Sang Tunisien, *La Revue du Maghreb*, nos. 5 and 6, May–June 1918, 74–75. Quoted in Tlili (1979, 465).

incentives.[97] In the letters Tunisian soldiers sent to their families, among declarations of loyalty to France, there were expressions of multiple grievances.[98] Notably, despite efforts by French authorities, some soldiers complained about their religious needs not being met, especially burial rites.[99] When French forces moved into Ottoman territory in the Battle of Gallipoli in 1915, for fear of a "scandal," the general resident in Tunisia had to remove copies of a French journal reproducing a map of the Dardanelles with the title "After more than four centuries of waiting, Christianity stands up to punish Islam." He also cited the propagation of rumors that cadavers of natives were found on Tunisian shores, which Tunisians took as the sign of a curse resulting from France's attack on the Caliph's capital.[100] As a result, the French initially decided not to deploy Muslim troops to the Dardanelles Front. In 1916 they changed course and sent eight thousand Tunisian troops, from whom only a few deserted.[101] Nevertheless, throughout the war, some French officials continued to have doubts about the loyalty of Muslim soldiers in the fight against the Ottoman sultan, an ally of the Germans. Both sides presented themselves as a "Muslim power" and competed through their propaganda for the allegiance of Muslim troops.[102] In November 1914, the Ottoman sultan proclaimed jihad in all Muslim territories. France replied by having the bey, the heads of Sufi brotherhoods, and Tunisian members of the Consultative Conference call on Tunisians to come to the Allies' defense.[103] Germany, on the other hand, exhorted the French army's Muslim troops to desert and join the Central Powers. Shaykh Salah al-Sharif (1869–1920), a Zaytuna scholar who would later join the Dustūr Party, published a brochure in support of the Central Powers, calling for jihad against "the Russians, the British, and the French" and stating that it was "a duty of the entire Islamic world" to "follow the flag of the Caliph."[104] It accused the French of having

97. Arnoulet (1984, 48) estimates that, on December 1, 1917, there were 71,000 Tunisian troops, of which only 3,900 had voluntarily enlisted. Goldstein (1978, 164) estimates that 73,000 Tunisian soldiers participated in the Great War, of which 10,000 had voluntarily enlisted.

98. Arnoulet (1984) and Fogarty (2008, 182–183), based on the postal censor's archives.

99. Frémeaux (2006, 324) and Fogarty (2008, 183).

100. "Procès-verbal de la séance de la Commission interministérielle des affaires musulmanes du 2 avril 1915," ISHTC, Série Guerre 1914–1918, Fonds Quai d'Orsay, Bobine P82, C1670, fol. 17.

101. Arnoulet (1984, 56).

102. Laurens (1996) and Sbaï (1996).

103. Arnoulet (1984).

104. Al-Sharif (1916). The text of the brochure is reproduced in Abdelmoula (1987, 153–164).

destroyed the religion of the people they conquered.[105] Despite these harsh denunciations, and despite armed revolts against the French in Southern Tunisia between 1915 and 1918,[106] there was no desertion movement large enough to seriously worry the French army.[107]

After the Great War, French authorities continued to see the nationalists' emancipatory project as being "fomented by the emissaries of pan-Islamism" and Ottomanism.[108] In reality, although during this period Abd al-Aziz Thaalibi and his friends made use of anything that could bolster their claims for independence, the Caliphate itself was not an object of political allegiance for them. Rather, it was a model for the Tunisian state they envisioned. As Gabriel Alapetite, the French general resident in Tunis, argued in August 1915, it was not the Ottoman call to jihad per se that had moved the Tunisians' feelings but rather the fact that "Constantinople is the capital of *the only Muslim military power* freed from the yoke of the Christians. Our natives contemplate that power with pride."[109] Alapetite rightly reasoned that Tunisians wanted a Muslim state, with a Muslim army able to defend Tunisia, a Muslim country. The reference to "the official religion" of the "country" and of "its army" in the nationalists' March 1920 constitutional draft implied that, in their view, France had failed in its duty to protect Islam despite its claims to the contrary.

3. Competing Custodians of Islam: France, Independent Tunisia, and the Bey (1920–1922)

Despite the abundant references nationalists made to the Tunisians' contribution to the Great War, the concept of "Islam [as the] official religion of the country and of its army" was absent from two official petitions for a constitution the Dustūr Party presented to the French Parliament in June and December 1920. This was not because the party had abandoned the idea since a similar concept remained in its charter, reappeared in a 1949 constitutional draft, and

105. Al-Sharif (1916, 157).
106. Abdelmoula (1987).
107. Fogarty (2008, 170).
108. "Note sur la Tunisie Martyre," ISHTC, Série Tunisie, Fonds de la Résidence, Bobine R28, C1552B, D1, fols. 29–30.
109. "Procès-verbal de la séance de la Commission interministérielle des affaires musulmanes du jeudi 12 août 1915," ISHTC, Série Guerre 1914–1918, Fonds Quai d'Orsay, Bobine P82, C1670, fol. 4. Emphasis is mine.

was eventually inscribed in Article 1 of the 1959 Constitution. Rather, it was because these petitions did not ask for independence: since a sovereign Tunisia was not evoked, there was no need to specify its "official religion." However, it was not long before the issue of Islam was brought to the fore in the context of constitutional demands and a dispute between three sets of protagonists—Tunisian nationalists, Tunisian antinationalists in an alliance with French authorities, and the bey—about who should be the custodian of Islam: an independent sovereign Tunisian state, France as an imperial "Muslim power," or the bey as a constitutional monarch.

Land Property Politics: The Private Ḥabūs *and Demands for a Constitution*

The official petition the Dustūr Party presented to the French Parliament in June 1920 to ask for a constitution came in the context of political turmoil tied to the issue of *ḥabūs* (pious endowments) land. In 1920 the French general resident planned a new decree forcing the cultivation, and partial expropriation by the Directorate of Agriculture for colonization purposes, of uncultivated or insufficiently cultivated land amounting to 3.5 million hectares (more than a quarter of Tunisia's total acreage). This included private (*milk*) and *ḥabūs* land as well as titleless and collective land. News of this project sparked demonstrations in Tunis and demands for a constitution, connecting the issues of land ownership and political representation.[110] French officials lamented that a lack of caution by some French settlers and the exasperation of religious feelings that the *ḥabūs* issue caused in the Muslim population led Tunisian nationalists to use this issue as a springboard for their constitutional demands.[111] A succinct definition of the *ḥabūs* (or waqf, as it is also called) was given by the Tribunal of Tunis in 1897: "an Islamic legal institution in which the owner of a property makes it inalienable for the benefit of pious works or works of public interest, immediately or at the death of intermediate beneficiaries."[112] Much more often than not, *ḥabūs* beneficiaries were the extended family or descendants of the founder, in which case it was called a "family" (*ahlī*) or "private" (*khāṣṣ*) *ḥabūs*. When the *ḥabūs* beneficiary was a religious institution or a charitable endeavor, it was called a "charitable" (*khayrī*) or "public" (*ʿāmm*) *ḥabūs*, and there were

110. Monchicourt (1920, 62) and Goldstein (1978, 300).
111. J. Reclus, "Note sur les Habous," ANT SC C21 D3-4.
112. De Montety (1927, 13).

also "mixed" (*mushtarak*) *ḥabūs* with both private and public beneficiaries. In any event, the *ḥabūs* was considered by most an Islamic form of property, and it was under the jurisdiction of the sharia court. It was common that a *ḥabūs* contribute to the upkeep of the tomb of a *zāwiya* saint and the well-being of his descendants, blurring the lines between private aims and public provisions.[113] Since 1874, the *Jam ʿīyat al-Awqāf* (Djemaia), a centralized state administration, managed the public *ḥabūs* and some private *ḥabūs* (see chapter 5). There was a great amount of legal diversity and flexibility in the Islamic legal procedures governing the *ḥabūs*, into which I need not delve. Suffice it to say that French and Tunisians alike exploited this flexibility, and that the *ḥabūs*, both private and public, constituted a major political issue.

On May 14, 1920, a demonstration was organized in Tunis to protest against the general resident's project. A delegation of ten notables led by Béchir Fourti (1884–1954), a teacher at the Zaytuna and director of the journal *Al-Taqaddum* (Progress), came to see the general resident. They read a petition arguing that Tunisians were eager to develop their land but needed help, just as French settlers benefited from state support. They also argued that the general resident's project harmed sharia.[114] Shortly after, the journal *Al-Ṣawāb* campaigned against the decree project and claimed that it amounted to the confiscation of private property and to "Bolshevism." It also argued that it disrespected Islam, which Tunisian public opinion would never allow, since "the waqfs . . . are linked to religion like the soul to the body."[115] The repression of the May 14, 1920 demonstration, the initial refusal of the police to let the delegates into the General Residence, and censorship of the Tunisian press sparked a demand, in *Al-Ṣawāb*, for a constitution.[116] The general resident was also warned that "he might want to ponder the issue [of the private *ḥabūs*], which taints France's reputation not only in North Africa, but also in Greater Syria and even in the Muslim world at large."[117] Another *Al-Ṣawāb* article warned that it would be

113. See Bargaoui (2015). A *zāwiya* (literally, "corner") generally designates a small room within a mosque where disciples gather around a Sufi master, or a Sufi convent (also called a *khanqah*). In the Maghrib, the word *zāwiya* may also designate the tomb of a saint, or, more broadly, the members of a Sufi order (*ṭarīqa*) and its religious infrastructure. I use it in this latter, broader sense.

114. General resident to the minister of foreign affairs, May 14, 1920, ISHTC, Série Tunisie, Fonds de la Résidence, Bobine R26, C1551, D1, fols. 18–19. See also *Al-Ṣawāb*, May 21, 1920, and ANT SC C80 D2 no. 1–32.

115. *Al-Ṣawāb*, May 28, 1920.

116. *Al-Ṣawāb*, May 21, 1920.

117. *Al-Ṣawāb*, May 21, 1920.

wrong for the bey, who was "the caretaker and custodian of Islam" (*qayyim ʿalā al-dīn wa-ḥāris ḥimāh*) in the Regency, to let the decree project become a reality, since it violated sharia.[118] According to police reports, some Young Tunisians also criticized the bey in secret meetings. For them, he was already at fault for allowing Tunisians to be sent to fight in the Great War and in the pacification of Morocco, pitting Muslims against Muslims "contrary to the laws of the Prophet." They took this opportunity to shame France, which called itself an "Islamic power," for not fulfilling her so-frequently advertised religious role,[119] and they included the issue of protecting private *ḥabūs* in their political program. The French surveillance reports describe a state of agitation. Some private *ḥabūs* beneficiaries also petitioned for the "status quo in private habous" and raised money to fund a delegation that was about to leave for Paris to ask the French Parliament for a Tunisian constitution.[120] For some French officials and members of the French settlers' lobby, the Young Tunisians were shamelessly instrumentalizing religion for political ends.[121] They portrayed them as "Young Turks" whose well-to-do families had exploited and abused the rural masses with total impunity, even before the protectorate era, and who had avoided conscription during the Great War thanks to the exemptions system. Some also argued that Tunisian nationalists were led by Italy, which pretended to "be the protector of Islam" by offering a constitution (the aforementioned Libyan Statute) to the people of Tripolitania and by naturalizing them without having them renounce their Muslim personal status. It was, they argued, the only way for Italy—given its weak army and lack of settlers—to maintain its presence in Libya.[122] In addition, they underlined blind spots in the Young Tunisians' constitutional demands, such as their silence about the status of Jews and Italians in Tunisia.[123] The nationalists' program, they argued, "submitted entirely to Muslim orthodoxy and prejudices,"[124] while asking for "the people's sovereignty, freedom and equality . . . forgetting what the Revolution did to pious endowments [in

118. *Al-Ṣawāb*, June 4, 1920.

119. "Sûreté Publique, Rapport" (about a meeting in the home of Ali Kahia), June 4, 1920, ISHTC, Série Tunisie, Fonds de la Résidence, Bobine R26, C1551, D1, fol. 30.

120. "Sûreté Publique, Rapport," June 5, 1920, ISHTC, Série Tunisie, Fonds de la Résidence, Bobine R26, C1551, D1, fol. 32.

121. Monchicourt (1920, 63–64). Louis Chappedelaine, Le soleil et les nuages en Tunisie (2), *La Revue mondiale*, February 1, 1921, no. 3, 289.

122. Monchicourt (1920, 51).

123. Monchicourt (1920, 57–58).

124. Monchicourt (1920, 57–58).

France]."[125] Nevertheless, the interests behind private *ḥabūs* were widespread from an economic and social point of view and had an undeniable religious component, especially when it came to the *ḥabūs* of *zāwiyas*. To understand what was at stake and how this issue was linked to constitutional demands, we should briefly examine the French protectorate's *ḥabūs* policy in Tunisia.

From the protectorate's inception, the French searched for the right legislation and administrative reorganization to free the theoretically inalienable *ḥabūs* land from the constraints of Islamic law and to make it more marketable, especially after they had exhausted other options (such as state-owned land) for colonization.[126] From the 1880s, a series of laws and decrees were promulgated, notably to regulate and facilitate perpetual leases at a fixed annual rent ("enzels," essentially a form of quasi-property) and to attempt to relax the stringent legal conditions under which *ḥabūs* property could be exchanged (and therefore put on the market).[127] Since this proved insufficient, an 1898 decree required the Djemaia to sell, in the form of exchanges in kind or in cash, 2,000 hectares of public *ḥabūs* a year through the Directorate of Agriculture, effectively giving preference to French settlers over Tunisian buyers.[128] A 1905 decree authorized the buyback of enzel perpetual leases, effectively making enzeled *ḥabūs* property alienable.[129] Despite all this legislation, and despite the pressure of the French settlers' lobby to encourage the colonization of private *ḥabūs* land,[130] of the roughly 700,000 hectares of land owned by the French, only some 50,000 were acquired from religious endowments, including the sales the Djemaia had been required to make annually by the 1898 decree.[131] These modest numbers notwithstanding, the colonization of *ḥabūs* land continued to be a significant political issue and the

125. Louis Chappedelaine, Le soleil et les nuages en Tunisie (1), *La Revue mondiale*, January 15, 1921, no. 2, 156.

126. Yazidi (2005, 234).

127. De Montety (1927, 34–42, 58, and 62).

128. Decree of November 13, 1898. De Montety (1927, 64) and Poncet (1962, 191).

129. Decree of January 22, 1905. Sicard (1965, 235–236).

130. Notably Edouard de Warren (1871–1962) and Victor de Carnières (1849–1917). De Warren was a member of the Fédération Républicaine, the most important party of the French republican Right at the time. He was a settler and large landowner in Tunisia and a powerful member of the settlers' lobby, which he unofficially represented in the French Parliament. De Carnières, also a settler, was a virulent proponent of annexation and founded the French journal *La Tunisie française*. He was vice president of the Chamber of Agriculture.

131. Sicard (1965, 234 and 251). Only about 25,000 ha in total were made available for colonization by the November 13, 1898 decree, which does not seem to have been applied past 1910. See also Poncet (1962, 287–288).

object of vocal condemnations by many Tunisians.[132] It was brought to the fore after the Great War, when politicians in Paris, in alliance with the French settlers' lobby in Tunisia, sought to make the colonies and protectorates contribute to the economic reconstruction of France and help counter the demographic predominance of the Italian colony.[133] This project was sustained by two persistent, albeit unfounded and contradictory, narratives:[134] (1) *ḥabūs* land supposedly represented an immense area of cultivable land (allegedly up to one-third of the Regency),[135] and (2) it was supposedly impossible to estimate the extent of this area because surveys had allegedly not been conducted. In fact, surveys had been conducted as early as 1890,[136] and more realistic (much smaller) estimates existed at the time.[137] Squeezed between the pressures of French settlers looking

132. For instance, in Zaouche (1906). See also, in chapter 5, the discussions in the 1937 committee that examined the financial situation of the Djemaia.

133. See the discussions of the Commission de l'Algérie, des Colonies et des Protectorats, Chambre des députés, July 13, 1920, ANF-P, C//14640 for arguments in favor of developing a "small colonization." See also Monchicourt (1920). According to *Dénombrement* (1921, 4), there were 156,115 European civilians in Tunisia in 1921, out of which 54,476 were French and 84,799 Italian.

134. On the persistence of these narratives, including in the secondary literature to this day, see chapter 5. Another persistent narrative was the alleged economic inefficiency of the *ḥabūs* form of property, notably due to its supposed inflexibility, as in Monchicourt (1920, 61, and 255). However, Sicard (1965, 252–53), by comparing comparable plots, finds that a deficit in modern agricultural techniques, rather than legal inflexibility, was the determinant factor in the failure of land development by natives.

135. Monchicourt (1920, 258) put forward evaluations of private *ḥabūs* land from 150,000 ha to about one-third of the Regency's 12.5 million ha, although it seems that this high estimate resulted from a confusion between *ḥabūs* and collective land. See Goldstein (1978, 100n40). Earlier, *RPR* (1881–90, 42) spoke of the *ḥabūs* representing "an enormous mass of real estate (perhaps a quarter of the Tunisian territory)."

136. For example, an 1890 note about an experimental survey of *ḥabūs* land by the Public Works Topographical Services reproduced a precise map of *ḥabūs* plots that could be rented or enzeled near Béja and mentioned the existence of additional plots beyond this map. "Note sur la colonisation des biens habous," August 13, 1890, in "Biens habous: Note sur les habous, statut juridique, intérêt pour la colonisation," CADN 1TU-1V-1118. See also ANT SC C23 D2. In 1956 an official report about the dissolution of the Djemaia noted that although an exhaustive inventory of the *ḥabūs* properties it administered had not been completed, "the greatest part of them were well-known and well-delimited." "Rapport concernant la liquidation de la Djemaia des Habous," ANT SC C80 D2, no. 36. See also Yazidi (2005, 241).

137. For instance, 380,000 hectares of private *ḥabūs* land in Pierre Perreau-Pradier, "Rapport au nom de la commission des comptes définitifs et des économies chargée d'examiner le projet de loi portant règlement définitif du Budget de l'Exercice 1913 (Protectorats du Maroc et de la

for more land to colonize on the one hand, and the long-held distrust and discontent of Tunisians on the other,[138] the French government in Paris remained cautious and reluctant to disturb the "status quo."[139] A 1920 note from a French civil servant in the Tunisian Government called for respecting "the religious sentiments of our protected natives" as well as "the principles of Islamic law and custom." This note also argued that all large public *ḥabūs* parcels of land were already colonized, and that the aggregate acreage of available *ḥabūs* land had been overestimated. It stressed that private *ḥabūs* land was occupied by tens of thousands of peasants, most of whom were on "habous land of *zāwiyas*," and that any further colonization of this land would require the use of force and would "threaten Tunisia's security."[140]

Tunisians who objected to the use of private *ḥabūs* for colonization articulated their argument as much in economic as in religious terms. The Young Tunisians had previously broached this issue in *Le Tunisien* between 1907 and 1911. They had denounced the "displacement of natives" (*refoulement des indigènes*), who lived off land for which they did not have titles, to the (infertile) margins of the large agricultural domains sold to the French.[141] They had condemned the "dispossession" of Tunisians,[142] and, responding to French settlers' narratives that Tunisians were too poor and ignorant to cultivate their land efficiently,[143] they had asked to be trained in the latest agricultural techniques

Tunisie)," Chambre des députés, no. 2693, session de 1916, 119, cited in (Goldstein 1978, 100n40). Compare to Tunisia's total area: 12.5MM hectares, of which 3.5MM were not productive, 4.7MM were pastoral and uncultivated lands, 1.1MM were forests, 2.8MM were arable, and 0.4MM were orchards. Goldstein (1978, 95). See also Poncet (1962).

138. See, for instance, the uproar caused by then head of the Djemaia Béchir Sfar's transfer from this post in 1908, in *Le Tunisien*, no. 75, July 16, 1908.

139. Rapport Pédebidou, in *Le Tunisien*, no. 100, February 11, 1909. A cautiousness in "scrupulously respecting 'Muslim conscience'" (*la conscience musulmane*) was already officially articulated in the first decade of the occupation, with the stated aim to guarantee the security of the French settlers in Tunisia. *RPR* (1881–90, 102). See also an 1892 Note by Rey, a French civil servant, which spoke critically of earlier projects submitted in vain to the government of the Regency by some French financial corporations. Rey argued that they aimed to "be a substitute for the Administration of the Djemaia." "Les biens habous en Tunisie," ANT SC C21 D3-4.

140. J. Reclus, "Notes sur les Habous," ANT SC C21 D3-4.

141. *Le Tunisien*, no. 6, March 3, 1907.

142. *Le Tunisien*, no. 161, October 20, 1910.

143. The difference in yield between the lands exploited by Europeans and Tunisian natives was considerable (a factor of three or more). Poncet (1962, 248).

and to be given equal access to land and credit by the state.[144] In addition, for them, the private *ḥabūs*, by and large still untouched by the colonization decrees, remained one of the last strongholds of Tunisian Muslims' personal status, one that "France had promised to respect." They too had argued for maintaining the "status quo."[145] This issue remained sensitive after the Great War, and it was one of the cornerstones of the early nationalist movement. There was a broad convergence of economic interests among many categories of Tunisians against the colonization of *ḥabūs* land,[146] including former, current, or aspiring farmers and landowners (both large and small);[147] *ḥabūs* land managers (*wakīls*); titleless peasants living off *ḥabūs* land who were or might be displaced to its less fertile fringes; high-level and petty functionaries of the Djemaia; and *zāwiya* shaykhs, who were ruling over a significant number of private *ḥabūs* properties and personnel.[148] One third of *Martyr Tunisia* was devoted to land issues,[149] which, like

144. *Le Tunisien*, no. 8, March 28, 1907; *Le Tunisien*, no. 24, July 18, 1907; *Le Tunisien*, no. 25, July 25, 1907; *Le Tunisien*, no. 32, September 12, 1907; *Le Tunisien*, no. 38, October 24, 1907; *Le Tunisien*, no. 44, December 5, 1907; *Le Tunisien*, no. 68, May 21, 1908; and *Le Tunisien*, no. 72, June 18, 1908.

145. *Le Tunisien*, no. 87, November 12, 1908. See also Béchir Sfar's 1903 critiques of the French colonization of public and private *ḥabūs*, "an institution that is at the foundation of the Muslim edifice in Tunisia," cited in Green (1976). Béchir Sfar was reacting to a project facilitating the colonization of public and private *ḥabūs*, detailed in M. L.-J. Pelletier, Commission de Colonisation, *Rapport déposé au nom de la 3ème Sous-Commission (Sous-Commission des Habous)*, Tunis, Imprimerie Rapide, 1903, ANT SC C21 D3-4.

146. Poncet (1962, 190), Mahjoubi (1977, 306–307), and Mahjoubi (1982, 167). See also M. A. Ben Achour (1989, 337–357).

147. Some were ruined by their enzel fixed perpetual rents, made worthless by the high post–Great War inflation, and expressed seller's remorse. Some were unable to exploit their land efficiently, due to financial or other constraints, and had to sell it. Others were unable to buy land because of price increases due to technological innovations and financial speculation. Technological innovations necessitated investments in modern equipment, and therefore capital or credit, which was difficult to access for Tunisians. Moreover, with the mechanization of agriculture during the war, labor needs decreased to the detriment of laborers and of small landowners who used to provide labor to the (French or Tunisian) owners of larger plots. The Young Tunisians, who were mostly of urban and bourgeois extraction, might have defended the interests of their own social group.

148. There is scant aggregate information about the extent of *zāwiyas*' private *ḥabūs* land and personnel. A July 19, 1932, note of the Direction Générale de l'Intérieur estimated that there were roughly 1,000 *zāwiyas* with about 30,000 people, i.e., about 1.4 percent of the Muslim population. ANT SD C97 D5.

149. Poncet (1962, 280).

the issue of the Tunisians' participation in the Great War, were quite prominent in the constitutional petitions that subsequently came to the fore in 1920.

The Young Tunisians' June 1920 Petition to the French Parliament for a Constitution: The Conspicuous Absence of an "Official Religion"

After a month of agitation about the general resident's 1920 land decree project, a Tunisian delegation—three lawyers and two *zāwiya* shaykhs—left Tunis on June 6, 1920, to join Abd al-Aziz Thaalibi in Paris. The delegates presented a petition to the French Parliament asking for a Tunisian constitution, and disseminated, through their personal contacts and the press, an eight-point memorandum describing the new regime they envisioned and "the rights and duties of all."[150] The petition was apparently signed by at least several hundred Tunisians.[151] Although Millerand, then head of the government, refused to see the delegates, they met with the president of Parliament and with some allies in Paris—for example, at the League of the Rights of Man and the League of Education. The June 1920 petition and memorandum were substantially softer than the March 1920 Dustūr Party's program.[152] They did not include (1) anything

150. The petition was also presented simultaneously to the bey and the general resident in Tunis, while Tunisia was under a state of siege, which remained in effect until March 1921. The petition filed to the French Parliament by MP Marius Moutet under #413 was printed in Paris. Titled "Pétition adressée au parlement Français par le peuple tunisien demandant l'octroi d'une constitution. Le Peuple Tunisien au Peuple Français," it was seven pages long. It is referenced in ANF, "Chambre des Députés, Rôle général des pétitions, no. 251 à 487, du 21 mars au 31 juillet 1920," 17, but is missing from ANF-P, C//14721. A copy is in ISHTC, Série Tunisie, Fonds de la Résidence, Bobine R26, C1551, D1, fols. 211–214. It is reproduced in *Revue parlementaire*, July 1, 1920. The eight-point memorandum is partly reproduced in *Le Temps* of July 14, 1920, 1. It seems to be entirely reproduced under the title "La question tunisienne," in "Les délégations destouriennes (1920–1924)," CDN B-3-28.

151. The printed petition included the statement "Several thousand signatures follow from all classes of the population." However, the French General Residence mentioned 800 to 900 signatures only, a "disappointing" result for the Young Tunisians, and claimed that notables had refused to sign. Résidence Générale à Diplomatie, Télégramme 273, no date, ISHTC, Série Tunisie, Fonds de la Résidence, Bobine R26, C1551, D1, fol. 31.

152. The final version of the petition was also softer than its initial draft according to French authorities. General resident to minister of foreign affairs, Télégramme 271, June 3, 1920, and Télégramme 273, no date, ISHTC, Série Tunisie, Fonds de la Résidence, Bobine R26, C1551, D1, fol. 31. I was unable to locate the entirety of this initial draft.

that could be interpreted as a demand for independence and therefore (2) the idea of an "official religion" of Tunisia or of its army. They asked for "a written constitution proclaiming and guaranteeing public rights and freedoms, separation of powers, the full participation of the people in the government of the country without distinction of race or religion."[153] They reminded the French Parliament of the 1857–1861 legal reforms and of France's role in their inception. They deplored the fact that the protectorate had transformed the previous government "which could be called constitutional" into an "autocratic regime," in which Tunisians had virtually no representation.[154] However, they also stressed that their constitutional demands "were not incompatible at all with the situation of France in Tunisia," and notably with its Army of Occupation.[155]

The eight-point memorandum envisioned a regime in which the Tunisian people would share power with the French in a representative electoral democracy with separation of powers (point #3); freedom of the press, of association and assembly (point #7); and a "deliberative assembly" made up of Tunisian and French representatives and elected through universal suffrage (point #1).[156] This greatly moderated the idea in the Dustūr Party's political program of March 1920 of a "legislative council" and a parliament.[157] However, this deliberative assembly, to which the government would be accountable (point #2), would have budgetary powers and would control its own agenda (point #1). French citizens residing in Tunisia and Tunisian natives would have equal access to administrative posts and equal pay (points #4 and #5). The *ḥabūs* issue was evoked only implicitly in point #8, which asked that Tunisians be given the opportunity to purchase land allocated by the Ministry of Agriculture and state-owned land (*terres domaniales*). France was also asked to cease its "policy of displacement" of Tunisian peasants. Yet the surveillance

153. "Pétition adressée au Parlement français par le peuple tunisien demandant l'octroi d'une constitution," ISHTC, Série Tunisie, Fonds de la Résidence, Bobine R26, C1551, D1, fols. 211–214.

154. Memorandum, "La question tunisienne," in "Les délégations destouriennes (1920–1924)," CDN B-3-28.

155. Memorandum, "La question tunisienne," in "Les délégations destouriennes (1920–1924)," CDN B-3-28.

156. Point #6 asked for the election of municipal councils through universal suffrage.

157. For mention of a legislative council, see "Lettre apportée par Chédly," February 5, 1920, ISHTC, Série Tunisie, Fonds de la Résidence, Bobine R28, C1552B, D2, fols. 361–368, fol. 366. For mention of a parliament, see Farhat Ben Ayed to Abd al-Aziz Thaalibi, May 7, 1920, ISHTC, Série Tunisie, Fonds de la Résidence, Bobine R28, C1552B, D2, fol. 381–382.

reports stressed that addressing the private *ḥabūs* issue was indeed one of the main objectives of the delegation.[158] The sacrifices made by Tunisians in the Great War were also prominent in the petition and memorandum. A bit more than half the petition was devoted to reminding France of the debt "of honor" it owed to Tunisian soldiers, arguing that it was its duty to repay this debt by granting Tunisians a constitution.[159] However, there was no mention, in the petition or the memorandum, of the March 1920 constitutional draft's principle according to which the Tunisian army should not fight against other Muslim people because Islam was the religion of the country and of its army.

It has been argued that this was because the Tunisian delegation sought the support of French socialists in Parliament, who were active defenders of French secularism (*laïcité*).[160] The French Section of the Workers' International (SFIO) activists in Tunisia were vocally anticlerical and attacked the representatives of Christianity and Islam in their mouthpiece *Tunis-socialiste*.[161] There is, however, another plausible rationale. Although they did support the project of a Tunisian constitution that would give equal rights to all, French socialists opposed Tunisian sovereignty and independence. Their opposition (and the warnings of the General Residence) are likely to have led the delegation to forego independence claims. For this reason, the principle of Islam as "official religion" was simply not applicable. Indeed, Tunisians did not invoke this principle in their subsequent petitions to the French Parliament that did not mention independence, despite the fact that, on at least one such occasion (when lobbying for the Taittinger motion in the spring of 1922), they were working with right-wing French parliamentarians such as Pierre-Charles Taittinger and Maurice Barrès, an outspoken and staunch critic of French *laïcité*.[162] However, this does not mean that Tunisian nationalists renounced the principle of Islam as "official religion." We find it, for instance, in the "organic statute

158. E.g., General resident to minister of foreign affairs, Télégramme 273, no date, ISHTC, Série Tunisie, Fonds de la Résidence, Bobine R26, C1551, D1, fol. 31.

159. "Pétition adressée au Parlement français par le peuple tunisien demandant l'octroi d'une constitution," ISHTC, Série Tunisie, Fonds de la Résidence, Bobine R26, C1551, D1, fols. 211–214. This theme was ubiquitous in the Arabic press at the time. For instance, see *Al-Ṣawāb*, April 21, 1920.

160. E.g., Tlili (1978, 61).

161. E.g., *Tunis-Socialiste*, October 20, 1923, quoted in Tlili (1978, 65–66). See also Goldstein (1978, 386).

162. "Les délégations destouriennes (1920–1924)," CDN B-3-28; and "Mouvement National Tunisien," CDN B-3-2.

of the Dustūr [Party]," published in 1932,[163] as well as in a 1949 draft Constitution conceived for an independent state[164] and in the 1959 Constitution at independence. Moreover, as we saw, there was no trace of contention over this principle when the Dustūr Party program was drafted in March 1920, and therefore no trace of the ideological disagreement that could have led to its suppression from the petitions. In any event, French authorities in Tunis and Paris were not ready to respond positively to these constitutional demands[165] and were staunchly opposed to the project of a deliberative assembly to which the government would be accountable, a concept they equated with independence. Despite this opposition and internal disputes over which strategy to pursue,[166] Tunisian nationalists continued to send delegations to Paris to ask for a constitution, to no avail. Two such missions occurred in December 1920 and November 1924; on both occasions, a ninth point—compulsory education for all—was added to the eight points presented in June 1920.[167] They continued to invoke the memory of the 1857–1861 legal reforms[168] and

163. It was published in *La Voix du Tunisien* of September 9, 1932, reproduced in Dabbab (1980, 63–65), and stipulated "In no way will it be possible to employ [the national army] to fight against people of the Muslim faith, which would reprehensibly harm the official religion of the country and of its army."

164. A clause made Islam "the religion of the state" in this draft constitution. *Tūnis*, June 15, 1949.

165. See, for instance, the auditions of Ahmed Essafi and General Resident Etienne Flandin by the French Parliament's Committee of Algeria, the Colonies, and the Protectorates. ANF-P, C//14640, Chambre des Députés, Commission de l'Algérie, des Colonies et des Protectorats, 12ème Législature, sessions of June 30, 1920, and July 5, 1920.

166. For instance, for Hassan Guellaty, nationalists had to cease using the terms "constitution," "accountable government," and "parliament." Hassan Guellaty, La Question tunisienne, *Tunis-Socialiste*, August 28, 1921, reproduced in Dabbab (1980, 144–151). Some members of the Dustūr, such as Mohamed Noomane, Béchir Acacha, and Hassouna Ayachi, joined the new Reformist Party he established. See also Goldstein (1978, 333–342).

167. The December 1920 delegation was led by Tahar Ben Ammar, from a family of large landowners. It received the support of the communist MP André Berthon in Paris; the Socialist Party in Tunis; and Duran-Angliviel, a lawyer and director of the journal *L'Avenir social* who wrote a pamphlet arguing that the 1861 Constitution had never been abrogated and that to reinstate it would not contradict the principles of the protectorate. The General Residence spoke of reforms that would increase some of the rights of Tunisian natives, an insufficient response for nationalists. A third delegation led by Ahmed Essafi was sent to Paris in November 1924 to present the same nine points, to no avail. "Les délégations destouriennes (1920–1924)," CDN B-3-28.

168. See, for instance, Ahmed Essafi's speech at the General Residence on August 11, 1921. Dabbab (1980, 126–131) and *Le Courrier de Tunisie*, August 17, 1921.

to face the opposition of the French settlers' lobby, which associated the Young Tunisians with the perils of socialism, communism, and pan-Islamism.

Mohsen Zaccaria's Counterpetition: "Islamic France" as the Custodian of Islam

The June 1920 petition was not unanimously supported by Tunisians either. In late June 1920, the Federation of War Associations in Tunisia objected to this petition's "usurpation of combatant status."[169] In addition, in July 1920, Mohsen Zaccaria (d. 1950)—a member of the beylical family and a decorated Tunisian veteran of the Great War who served in the French army as a "reserve second lieutenant in Sidi Bou Said"—sent a counterpetition to the French Parliament in the name of the "group of Muslim Tunisian veterans of the Great War." It was filed as a petition for "the preservation of the 'status quo' from the religious point of view."[170] It vehemently criticized the Tunisian nationalists' constitutional demands and asked for France's protection, especially from a religious point of view, allegedly on behalf of a majority of Tunisians. Mohsen Zaccaria brought his counterpetition to Paris himself while accompanying Pierre de la Charrière, the president of the Committee of the League of Platoon Commanders and Soldiers of Tunis,[171] to place a wreath on the tomb of the unknown soldier. His counterpetition objected to "the actions of a few Young Tunisian adventurers who are currently in Paris to supposedly defend the interests of our country."[172] It argued that the Young Tunisians, like the Young Turks, were blinded by their ambition and that, in 1881, Tunisians had "joyfully" called on France to protect them from other powers and from the absolutism of the beylical regime, "which put the life and the property of Tunisians in danger." The counterpetition asked for "the preservation of the 'status

169. June 28, 1920, letter annexed to a letter to the General Residence, July 7, 1920, ISHTC, Série Tunisie 1917–1940, Fonds Quai d'Orsay, Bobine 622, C317, fols. 16–17.

170. Petition #459, referenced in ANF, "Chambre des Députés, Rôle général des pétitions, no. 251 à 487, du 21 mars au 31 juillet 1920," 17, but missing from ANF-P, C//14721. However, this petition, presumably handwritten by Mohsen Zaccaria himself, is in ANT SE C550 D30/15-599, "Gens à surveiller, Mohsen Zaccaria, 1907–1922."

171. The league was established in 1919. Pierre Ladreit de la Charrière was a decorated war veteran who later became a member of the right-wing French nationalist league Cross of Fire and the French Social Party. He was the editor of the journal *La Tunisie française,* which was hostile to Tunisian nationalists. See Nataf (2008).

172. ANT SE C550 D30/15-599.

quo' with an improvement in our general situation," and for "our protection, in particular from the religious point of view, as in the question of the private Habous, that the Young Tunisians' party takes as an argument." Mohsen Zaccaria added that he was reassured by the fact that France was, in the end, against the colonization of private *ḥabūs* land, since her leaders knew that it was "a delicate religious issue." He claimed to belong to the "moderate Tunisian party" and harshly criticized the Young Tunisians as "a handful of extremists" who never gave much thought to those who, like him, fought in the Great War with and for France. He wondered if it occurred to them that "a small fraction of these sacred Habous" could be used to reward the Tunisian veterans of the Great War and their families, who had suffered so much. He added that he and a majority of Tunisians had "full confidence in Islamic France."

The French Ministry of Foreign Affairs responded positively to Mohsen Zaccaria's petition, promising France's continuous protection "of the religious, political and economic interests of Tunisians."[173] In January 1921, Mohsen Zaccaria was invited to give a speech at a reception at the French General Residence in Tunis, and he reiterated his demands for "the preservation of the French protectorate . . . and above all an absolute and unconditional respect for our religious institutions" as well as his full confidence in the "representatives of Islamic France."[174] The term "Islamic France" (*France islamique*) he used was employed by French authorities and had gained broad currency in newspapers and periodicals before the Great War.[175] It went hand in hand with the notion of "Muslim policy" (*politique musulmane*), which designated France's diplomatic activities in Muslim countries as well as its policy toward Muslims in its colonies, protectorates, and zones of influence. The terms "Islamic France" and "Muslim policy" were often used together to project France's diplomatic power and prestige in its competition with the British and the Ottoman Empires (until the latter's demise after the Great War). In this context, these terms also

173. ANT SE C550 D30/15-599.

174. *Le Progrès de Tunis*, January 13, 1921. ANT SE C550 D30/15-599.

175. For instance, Ladreit de Lacharrière called France a "great Islamic power" (*grande puissance islamique*) in an article about the role of France in Morocco in *Le Temps*, August 19, 1910. See also mentions of the concept of "*France islamique*" in periodicals as diverse as *Revue de géographie*, 25ème année, December 1901, 506; *La Croix de l'Algérie et de la Tunisie*, April 19, 1903; *L'Echo d'Alger*, March 2, 1914; *Le Radical*, November 11, 1921; *L'Homme libre*, March 6, 1924; *L'Intransigeant*, July 1, 1925; *Revue des deux mondes*, tome XLVI, 1928, 74 and 781–811; and *Journal des mutilés, réformés et blessés de Guerre*, September 8, 1929. We find these terms since the 1890s at least. See Laurens (1996) and Le Pautremat (2003).

projected France's ambitions to both administer and protect Islam.[176] But Mohsen Zaccaria's petition to the French Parliament and his public speech in Tunis in support of the protectorate made him a traitor in the eyes of the nationalists and triggered the resignation of several members of the Muslim section of the League of Platoon Commanders and Soldiers, who declared that he had committed a "political mistake."[177] Several Arabic journals also criticized him, and he did not seem to find much public support among Tunisians. A French police report about a Young Tunisians' meeting in March 1921 noted that the cries of "Long live the constitution, long live France" and "Down with Zaccaria" were heard.[178] Moreover, despite his apparent connections in high places in Tunis and Paris and his various administrative posts, he seems to have had financial and other troubles, at times on the fringes of legality.[179] Although the French colonial press had only praise for Mohsen Zaccaria's "unwavering loyalty to France,"[180] he does not seem to have left an enduring political imprint, and he disappeared from the political limelight in the early 1920s. That said, since his request for Islamic France's protection of Islamic institutions was in line with official French policy in Tunisia, it represented a tangible alternative to the custodianship of Islam by a Tunisian independent state envisioned in the nationalists' March 1920 constitutional draft.

The Bey's Eighteen Points: The Husaynid Dynasty as Custodian of Islam

In 1922 it was the bey's turn to articulate a quasi-constitutional project in which he reasserted his role of custodian of Islam. That year, on the occasion of a parliamentary debate in Paris about a potential 225-million-franc loan to

176. For examples of various understandings of the French "*politique musulmane*," see Alfred Le Châtelier, Politique musulmane, *Revue du monde musulman*, juillet–décembre 1910; Louis Massignon, Introduction à l'étude des revendications islamiques, *Revue du monde musulman*, juin 1920; and Louis Milliot, Notre politique musulmane, *Année politique française et étrangère*, juin 1926, 113–155. See also Sbaï (1996), and on the roles played by Louis Massignon and Robert Montagne, Sbaï (2018).

177. Letter of January 12, 1921, ANT SE C550 D30/15-599.

178. Note of March 25, 1921, ANT SE C550 D30/15-599.

179. ANT SE C550 D30/15-599.

180. Notes of June 18, 20, 21, 1921, ANT SE C550 D30/15-599. For an example of praise of Mohsen Zaccaria, see *La Tunisie française*, May 28, 1922, at the occasion of his appointment as *qā 'id* of Tunis's suburbs.

Tunisia, perhaps encouraged by the February 28, 1922, abolition of the British protectorate in Egypt, Tunisians again attempted to pressure the French Parliament to motion for a Tunisian constitution as a condition for the approval of this loan. A group of twenty-five French MPs of various political persuasions, headed by the right-wing MP Pierre-Charles Taittinger, signed the motion.[181] However, on May 15, 1922, the MP and advocate for French settlers Edouard de Warren objected to the Taittinger motion in the French Parliament's Committee on Algeria, Colonies, and Protectorates, arguing that reforms would be sufficient to avoid independence and that communists, who were allied with nationalists, were "the real danger."[182] The death of the Taittinger motion followed, and on July 5, 1922, Parliament voted (507 to 64) for an indissoluble alliance between France and Tunisia, reaffirming France's political authority in Tunisia.[183] However, during these discussions in Paris, a crisis in Tunis was sparked by a March 22, 1922, interview in *Le Petit Journal* with the reigning Naceur Bey, in which he condemned the ideology of communism and the nationalists' constitutionalist program.[184] Probably pressured by nationalists, the bey claimed subsequently that *Le Petit Journal* had mischaracterized his words. On April 3, 1922, he summoned the general resident to his palace and threatened to abdicate.[185] The news of his imminent abdication spread like wildfire the next day. The bey won acclaim from the nationalists for standing up to France, and on April 5, 1922, demonstrators holding Tunisian flags and portraits of the bey marched from the capital to his palace.[186] On the same day, the general resident, while planning for succession in the event of the bey's abdication, requested that he sign a public declaration announcing that he was not abdicating and that

181. "Proposition de résolution de Charles Taittinger no. 3820 sur l'emprunt Tunisien," ANF-P, C//14640, Commission de l'Algérie, des Colonies et des Protectorats de la Chambre des Députés, session of March 2, 1922, and "Mouvement national tunisien," CDN B-3-2.

182. ANF-P, C//14640, Commission de l'Algérie, des Colonies et des Protectorats, session of May 15, 1922. The socialist MP André Berthon criticized the motion as too tentative and objected to those who likened them to communists that the constitutionalists were "bourgeois." *JORF-DP* Année 1922-No. 63, 2ème séance du 4 juillet 1922, 2265–2283.

183. Despite the socialist MP André Berthon's objections in Parliament, Edouard de Warren insisted that Tunisia was "an extension [*prolongement*] of France." *JORF-DP* no. 80, du 6 juillet 1922; 1ère séance du 5 juillet 1922, 2313; and 2ème séance du 5 juillet 1922, 2317–2328.

184. *Le Petit Journal*, March 22, 1922.

185. General resident to minister of foreign affairs, April 4, 1922, ISHTC, Série Tunisie, Fonds de la Résidence, Bobine R281, C1976, fol. 45.

186. *Al-Ṣawāb*, April 6, 1922. General resident to Raymond Poincaré, April 8, 1922, ISHTC, Série Tunisie, Fonds de la Résidence, Bobine R281, C1976, fols. 150–153.

he had full confidence in the French protectorate in Tunisia.[187] The bey initially conditioned his signature on France agreeing to a list of eighteen points.[188] However, he was eventually coerced (and perhaps bribed) by the protectorate authorities into renouncing his abdication as well as his eighteen points, which he did on April 15, 1922.[189] Although the bey did not ask for a constitution in his eighteen points, the general resident claimed they reproduced "and aggravated" the Dustūr Party's constitutional demands and that they amounted to "the total eviction of France."[190] In the face of public unrest, the first of this magnitude since the May 1920 protests about the private *ḥabūs*, he asked for *non-Muslim* military reinforcements from the French government in Algiers.[191] The general resident's account of these events, our only source, presents the bey as weak, senile, indecisive, financially vulnerable, and easily manipulated by his entourage and by the nationalists. Nonetheless, the bey's eighteen points—whoever may have written or inspired them—were a resolute assertion of the Husaynid dynasty's claim to power and to the custodianship of Islam.[192]

The bey's eighteen points, presented as a "program" (*lā'iḥa*), were first and foremost meant to assert his dynasty's power, and to make him the central representative of Tunisian sovereignty. The bey would be charged with appointing

187. General resident to minister of foreign affairs, April 5, 1922, ISHTC, Série Tunisie, Fonds de la Résidence, Bobine R281, C1976, fol. 59.

188. Letter in Arabic from Naceur Bey to the general resident, April 9, 1922, which is followed by the bey's eighteen points. ISHTC, Série Tunisie, Fonds de la Résidence, Bobine R281, C1976, fols. 267–270. It seems that the bey handed his eighteen points to the general resident's interpreter on April 5, 1922, after a long and heated meeting with him (Bobine R281, C1976, fols. 154–155) and that he sent him a letter on April 9, 1922, accompanied by his eighteen points in Arabic. Goldstein (1978, 408–409) incorrectly dates this meeting to April 8, 1922. I was not able to locate the original April 5 list, only its French translation by the General Residence, which is virtually identical to the April 9 version in Arabic in general resident to Raymond Poincaré, April 8, 1922. ISHTC, Série Tunisie, Fonds de la Résidence, Bobine R281, C1976, fols. 156–157.

189. Goldstein (1978, 412). See also French minister of foreign affairs to general resident, April 7, 1922, ISHTC, Série Tunisie, Fonds de la Résidence, Bobine R281, C1976, fol. 118. For the general resident's account of the recanting of the bey, see general resident to Raymond Poincaré, April 15, 1922, ISHTC, Série Tunisie, Fonds de la Résidence, Bobine R281, C1976, fols. 272–281.

190. General resident to Raymond Poincaré, April 8, 1922, ISHTC, Série Tunisie, Fonds de la Résidence, Bobine R281, C1976, fol. 156.

191. General resident to the general governor of Algeria, April 7, 1922, ISHTC, Série Tunisie, Fonds de la Résidence, Bobine R281, C1976, fol. 119.

192. General Resident Lucien Saint himself wrote that the bey's senility "is at times animated by outbursts of obstinate energy." General resident to Raymond Poincaré, April 15, 1922, ISHTC, Série Tunisie, Fonds de la Résidence, Bobine R281, C1976, fol. 273.

the prime minister (point #3), who would in turn appoint the other ministers, "following the traditions of great states."[193] This was a prerogative claimed by the protectorate, and for the French general resident it was an unacceptable demand; he called it a definite "act of sovereignty."[194] There was a strong nationalist flavor to the bey's program, as at the time there was increasing hope that the Taittinger motion would be adopted by the French Parliament. The eighteen points stipulated that the ministers, as well as their advisors, would all be Tunisian (point #4); that French naturalization of Tunisians, whether they served in the French army or not, would be abolished (point #9); and that Tunisian soldiers could carry only the Tunisian flag (and not the French flag) (point #10). The bey asked that Tunisians receive "an equitable distribution of the proceeds of the loan [of the Taittinger motion]" (point #7), compulsory education, access to higher education (points #12 and #13), and access to agriculture and commerce (point #15). He also asked that freedom of the press and of assembly be guaranteed (point #16). As for the political organization of the Regency, the bey put himself at the center of a constitutional monarchy and declared that he would physically preside over a legislative assembly elected through universal suffrage, which he would approve and to which the government would be accountable (points #1, #2, and #5). This went much further than the demands for a deliberative assembly in the memoranda successive Tunisian delegations brought to Paris in 1920. In his eighteen points, the bey also insisted on the necessity of protecting religious institutions: all *ḥabūs*, public (*ʿāmma*) and private (*khāṣṣa*), would be respected (point #11), as would the sharia court and judges, who would receive proper training (point #14). The protection of the *ḥabūs* was also implicit in point #8, which abolished the purchase of land with public funds for the purpose of colonization. The bey's eighteen points emphatically reaffirmed his role as chief of the Husaynid dynasty and custodian of Islam. In his infamous interview with *Le Petit Journal* condemning the idea of a constitution as a communist ploy, he was quoted as having said, "Not only as the reigning prince, but also as a religious leader, . . . I cannot tolerate . . . attempts . . . to harm the principles of Islam that it is my imperative duty to defend."[195]

193. Although the prime minister would preside over the Cabinet, the bey would have the power to summon it when deemed necessary (point #6).

194. General resident to Raymond Poincaré, April 15, 1922, ISHTC, Série Tunisie, Fonds de la Résidence, Bobine R281, C1976, fols. 278–279.

195. *Le Petit Journal*, March 22, 1922.

State Custodianship of Islam's Inextricable Tie to State Sovereignty (Whoever Rules)

These successive political programs put forward competing visions of the state and show that, during the colonial period (in continuity with precolonial times), the principle of the state custodianship of Islam was inextricably tied to state sovereignty, even if exercised by a foreign and non-Muslim power. Whether it was the independent Tunisian state imagined by nationalists, Mohsen Zaccaria's "Islamic France," or the bey's Husaynid constitutional monarchy, the sovereign (or aspiring sovereign) state had to be the custodian of Islam, as in the past. This necessity was not merely a symbolic matter. It related to some of the concrete duties incumbent on the state, such as the protection of Muslims' life (cf. the issue of the participation in the Great War) and property (cf. the issue of the colonization of private *ḥabūs*). In the years 1857–1861, we saw that it was formulated using idioms such as *siyāsa* and sharia, and that its attendant debates reflected the economic and diplomatic challenges of the time. In the 1920s, contemporary issues (e.g., war and land) and contemporary rival political agendas (the nationalist fight for independence, the bey's fight for the survival of his dynasty, or the antinationalists' call for France's protection) also shaped its formulations and attendant debates, with new idioms (e.g., "Muslim public law," "official religion of the country," or "Islamic France"). Despite all these changes, the ideal of the state custodianship of Islam endured.

This ideal also proved to be a formidable instrument in the 1930s, in a context of economic crisis, nationalist mass mobilization, and abundant press coverage of grievances of a religious and nonreligious nature.[196] The salience of this period of turmoil in the historiography has led some scholars to incorrectly attribute the politicization of Islam to nationalism, whereas this period was yet another instantiation of this politicization. For example, the 1930 International Eucharistic Congress of Carthage, organized by the Catholic Church,[197]

196. See, for instance, *La Voix du peuple*, April 8, 15, 22, 29, and May 6, 13, 20, 27, 1933; *L'Action tunisienne*, May 2, 3, 4, 5, 8, 9, 13, 1933; and *Al-ʿAmal*, July 8, 24, 1934. For fatwas on naturalization, see Mahjoubi (1982, 486–500) and El-Ghoul (2009). As another example of the nationalists' use of religious narratives, in the late 1920s Habib Bourguiba made Tunisian Muslim women's wearing the veil a symbol of Tunisian identity, against French encouragements to unveil, although after independence he encouraged its removal as a mark of "modernism." See Marzouki (1988) and Zeghal (2012).

197. It was held under the bey's patronage and financed by the Tunisian budget.

provided nationalists with a rallying opportunity, especially the "parades of Catholic youths dressed as crusaders, the distribution of pamphlets in Arabic promoting conversion, and the rhetoric of the papal legate, who characterized the Islamic era in North Africa as 'fourteen centuries of desolation and death.'"[198] Moreover, in 1932–1933, the Dustūr Party leaders organized large demonstrations against the Muslim burials of Tunisians who became naturalized French citizens, claiming that, by submitting to the French civil code, they had relinquished their Muslim personal legal status and had therefore apostatized (an issue that had also been raised in earlier decades as we saw).[199] In the midst of the unrest over naturalization, the Dustūr Party drafted a new charter on the occasion of its Congress of May 1933.[200] In alignment with the strategy advocated by Habib Bourguiba, who had recently joined the Dustūr Party Executive Committee,[201] this charter envisioned a strictly Tunisian Parliament (a point vigorously debated, and eventually rejected, by the drafters of the 1920 Dustūr Party Program, as we saw) and went beyond the language of equality with the French, speaking of "ineluctable emancipation" and the "sovereignty" of the Tunisian people.[202] It also stressed that the constitution must "safeguard the Tunisian personality,"[203] and Muslim personal status, echoing the issue of naturalizations. Therefore, it reaffirmed the ideal of state custodianship of Islam (albeit with a different formulation than in the 1920 Dustūr Party Program, which centered on the sovereignty of "the country" instead). Compared to the previous constitutional demands by the protonationalist Young Tunisians' writings in *Le Tunisien* and by the Dustūr Party itself, the 1933 Dustūr

198. Perkins (2014, 95). For a detailed description of the polemics around this event, see Mahjoubi (1982, 466–479).

199. While the number of Tunisian Muslim naturalizations always remained low, it reached its peak in the 1920s. According to the *Annuaire statistique*, there were fewer than 100 naturalizations of Tunisian Muslims before 1920, about 1,000 from 1920 to 1932 (they peaked at 248 in 1927 out of a Tunisian Muslim population of more than two million), and only very few after that. On naturalizations during the interwar period, see El-Ghoul (2009).

200. Mahjoubi (1982, 502–505).

201. At the occasion of the Dustūr Party Congress of May 12 and 13, 1933.

202. Declaration of the Tunisian Liberal Constitutional Party, *La Voix du peuple*, May 20, 1933.

203. Perkins (2014, 98) claims that this concept gave a new "twist" to the Dustūr constitutional demands. However, as we saw, neither this concept (which we find in *La Tunisie martyre*, published in 1920, as well as in *Le Tunisien* more than a decade earlier) nor religious issues in constitutional demands were new.

Party Charter could be viewed as more radical toward France, as Bourguiba claimed at the time.[204] However, it did not invoke markers of a sovereign state such as a "national army," and hence it did not speak of an "official religion," as the 1920 Dustūr Party Program and 1932 organic statute had. This should not be interpreted as a preference for a secular regime on Bourguiba's part. In a highly constrained political context, the language and stances of these successive programs and charters were strategic choices.[205] Hence, the formulations that invoked the principle of state custodianship of Islam (or the omission of the same) varied with the circumstances. As we saw, this principle was absent from the constitutional demands taken to Paris by the three successive Dustūr Party delegations of June 1920, December 1920, and November 1924 since they did not invoke any project of sovereignty, be it for the state, for the country, or for the people. However, it was present in the March 1920 Dustūr Party Program, in Mohsen Zaccaria's 1920 counterpetition, in the bey's eighteen points of 1922, and in the May 1933 Dustūr Party Charter (joined, respectively, with sovereignty for the country, for "Islamic France," for the bey, and for the people). When the New Dustūr Party—established by Bourguiba in March 1934 after seceding from the Dustūr Party, which was subsequently called the Old Dustūr Party—formed a political committee in 1949 to draft the main principles of a future constitution, it proposed an article (#6) which read "The religion of the state is Islam and all other religions will be respected."[206] The drafters of the 1959 Constitution of independent Tunisia discussed and used a similar formulation, as we will see.

204. *L'Action tunisienne*, May 15, 1933.

205. For example, when asked by a military tribunal in 1939 whether his aim was Tunisian independence, Bourguiba answered that since the 1861 Constitution had not been suspended, a constitution was compatible with the protectorate, and that the 1933 Charter did not aim to separate Tunisia from France (at least not immediately). The tribunal also pointed to a more moderate "Charter" put forward in 1937 without abrogating the 1933 Charter, and underlined Bourguiba's strategic use of both versions. ANT SG-MN C64 D2. The 1937 document articulating a more moderate strategy is in ANT SG-MN C35 D1.

206. Worried about Bourguiba's possible return from Cairo, the party's general secretary Salah Ben Youssef formed this committee in February 1949 to affirm the principle of a constitutional monarchy and support the bey's dynasty. H. Cornet, "Note sur un projet de constitution tunisienne (30 juillet 1949)," ANF-P, CHEAM, vol. 62, no. 1651. The committee discussed this formulation at length, with some arguing that it should be integrated into Article 1, which stated that the Tunisian state was a constitutional and democratic monarchy. *Tūnis*, June 15, 1949, 1.

4. Islam as the Religion of the State in the 1959 Constitution of Independent Tunisia: Bourguiba's Authoritarian Synthesis

By the end of the 1940s, despite the opposition of French settlers, the idea of an autonomous Tunisia, if not of an independent one, was envisaged by French authorities. A succession of proposals about Tunisia's relation with France were negotiated with the New Dustūr in the first half of the 1950s, with episodes of nationalist resistance and colonial repression. There were also conflicts, and competition for power, between Tunisian organizations such as the Old Dustūr and New Dustūr Parties, the Tunisian Communist Party, and the Tunisian Labor Union (UGTT). In addition, there were conflicts within the New Dustūr, especially over the compromises that could be made with France. Tunisia eventually gained its internal autonomy in June 1955 and its independence on March 20, 1956,[207] and the second constitution in its history was promulgated in 1959. Tunisia was not a monarchy anymore[208] but a republic with strong presidential powers, as in the recently proclaimed 1958 French Constitution (which served in part as a model). Although the regime was already on the fast track to authoritarianism, the Constitution stated that sovereignty came from the people, who were represented by an assembly elected through universal suffrage.[209] For the elites in power, the 1959 Constitution was first and foremost the mark of Tunisia's newly acquired full sovereignty, and it explicitly ascribed the custodianship of Islam to the new sovereign state, although, in contrast with the 1861 Constitution, it did not mention sharia. Article 1 read, "Tunisia is a free, independent, and sovereign state. Islam is its religion, Arabic is its language, and the republic is its system [of government, *niẓām*]."[210]

207. On March 20, 1956, the independence of Tunisia, in "interdependence" with France, was proclaimed. Although Bourguiba proclaimed Tunisia's full sovereignty in the National Constituent Assembly on April 8, 1956, full independence was not achieved until later. See C. Debbasch (1959).

208. The end of the monarchy was debated in the National Constituent Assembly on July 25, 1957, and the Republic was proclaimed on the same day. In the long speech he gave in the Assembly, Bourguiba accused the bey of favoring a constitution drafted by a committee appointed by himself, rather than by an elected assembly, and of wanting to keep his prerogatives concerning sharia courts. Al-Jumhūrīya al-Tūnisīya, *Munāqashāt* (2009, vol. 2, 24), July 25, 1957.

209. Constitution of Tunisia, 1959, Articles 3 and 19. The 1959 Constitution also had other democratic features, including separation of powers, freedom of the press, and free elections; see, e.g., the preamble and Article 8.

210. Al-Jumhūrīya al-Tūnisīya, *Munāqashāt* (2009, vol. 2, 355).

This article, combined with an earlier and quasi-constitutional text (the 1956 Personal Status Code, or PSC, which considerably improved women's rights), formed what I call Tunisia's postindependence "authoritarian synthesis." With this synthesis, the New Dustūr Party's leader, Habib Bourguiba, sought to achieve two major imperatives: (1) as the bey had attempted in vain in 1857–1861 (see chapter 1),[211] to "facilitate the unification of national courts with exclusive jurisdiction over all residents in Tunisia,"[212] a unification that the June 1955 internal autonomy agreement with France subjected to the introduction of a "modern code" in Tunisian tribunals and to "complete equality . . . irrespective of religion,"[213] and (2) to arbitrate the dispute between Tunisian liberals and conservatives, or rather "progressives" and "conservatives," as Habib Bourguiba called them when he urged all nationalist forces to unify in 1932.[214] In 1955 this dispute mainly revolved around three interrelated questions. First, to what extent should postindependence governance be based on and constrained by sharia? Second, was it legitimate to introduce an optional "secular" personal status not related to sharia? Third, should the legal system keep different personal status jurisdictions and codes for different religious communities, or should it be unified (to foster the cohesion of the nation)? Bourguiba—who took on the positions of prime minister, minister of defense, and minister of foreign affairs in the Tunisian government on April 9, 1956, and who then became president of the Republic in 1957—arbitrated between liberal and conservative views on these questions, imposed his synthesis, and silenced all sides of the debate. He decided that (1) the system of governance would not be based on sharia, although some personal status legal provisions would be; (2) there would be no optional "secular" personal status (and hence no freedom *from* religion); and (3) there would be a unique personal status for all, irrespective of religion. Although Bourguiba's synthesis, taken as a whole, failed to satisfy liberals and conservatives alike, it seems that both camps embraced some of its central tenets: the rejection of both the separation of religion and state and state neutrality, and

211. Interestingly, in the last National Constituent Assembly session, Bourguiba argued that the new Constitution was nothing like the 1861 Constitution, a law Tunisians should not have been proud of since "the people" did not ask for it, the bey did not believe in it, it was drafted under the pressures of European powers, and it ended in a violent revolt and foreign occupation. He did acknowledge, however, that it was quite helpful as a tactical tool during the nationalist struggle. Al-Jumhūrīya al-Tūnisīya, *Munāqashāt* (2009, vol. 2, 349–50).

212. Anderson (1958, 265).

213. For the text of the agreement, see Ladhari (1956).

214. *L'Action tunisienne*, November 1, 1932. This was the first issue of his journal.

the affirmation of the state's duty to provide a religious infrastructure for Muslim worship and for the dissemination of Islamic values (e.g., in the public school system), as part of a project of human development.[215]

Can Tunisia Be Secular (lā ʾikīya)? Laïcité *as Endangering the Muslim Community*

After Tunisia's June 3, 1955 agreement on internal autonomy with France, a proposal was put forward by some leaders of the New Dustūr Party's French Federation; on July 24–25, 1955, their constitutional program was discussed in a public meeting in Tunis in the presence of ministers of the government, dignitaries of the sharia and secular courts, a Husaynid prince, and some ʿulamā, as well as numerous youth.[216] This program stated that "the Tunisian Constitution must establish a secular regime [*niẓām lā ʾikī*], given the diversity of beliefs of its inhabitants [*ikhtilāf al-mutasākinīn fī ʿaqāʾidihim*]."[217] By a "secular regime," it meant: "1) the preservation of each religion's personal status and 2) the creation of a secular Tunisian personal status [*statut personnel tunisien laïque*], which each Tunisian would be free to adopt."[218] A chain of condemnations ensued, from the Zaytuna's ʿulamā and the Old Dustūr Party but also from the New Dustūr Party itself, revealing a broad opposition to a "secular regime" that would give Tunisian Muslims freedom *from* religion and therefore allow them to fall into apostasy. All agreed that the state had to continue to protect the national Muslim community by preventing its members from leaving it. The breadth of this agreement highlights the fact that the supporters of what was called a "secular regime" (although in this context it meant only freedom *from* religion, and certainly not separation of Islam and the state or state neutrality) represented a fringe, minority position.

This dispute must be read against the background of the June 1955 internal autonomy agreement that Habib Bourguiba had negotiated with France, which conditioned the unification of the various Tunisian legal jurisdictions, and therefore the removal of French legal jurisdiction, on the introduction of

215. Tunisian leftist movements do not seem to have been too concerned by the relationship between Islam and the state, but more research is needed on this point.

216. French Ministry of Foreign Affairs report, ISHTC, Série Tunisie, Fonds Quai d'Orsay, Bobine 719, C455, fols. 262–265.

217. *Al-Majalla al-Zaytūnīya*, vol. 4, no. 9, September 1955, 220–222.

218. *Le Petit Matin*, July 28, 1955.

"a modern code" in Tunisian tribunals. Tunisia had to guarantee "rights in conformity with the Universal Declaration of Human Rights for all residents," a clause that aimed to protect the French settlers' community still residing in Tunisia at the time. In addition, Tunisia had to guarantee, "*in conformity with its traditions,* complete equality between [its] nationals, irrespective of ethnic origin or religious faith."[219] The official mouthpiece of the Zaytuna strongly objected to the proposal of the New Dustūr's French Federation and, without criticizing the internal autonomy agreement per se, argued that this was going too far in yielding to French pressures. The Old Dustūr, on the other hand, had objected to the autonomy agreement in an alliance with the New Dustūr leadership member Salah Ben Youssef, who was vehemently opposed to Bourguiba's piecemeal approach to the negotiations with France. Contrary to conventional analysis that presents Ben Youssef as a traditionalist and Bourguiba as a modernist—their opposition had more to do with political strategy and foreign policy than with religious differences.[220] And notwithstanding the labels that rival nationalist factions threw at each other during this tumultuous period of intense rivalries for the pursuit of power, the same can be said about the opposition between the Old and the New Dustūr.[221] Despite their divergence on the issue of the internal autonomy agreement, both parties, in tune with the ʿulamā of the Zaytuna, unambiguously rejected the proposal of the New Dustūr's French Federation, the freedom from religion it would allow, and the erosion of the Muslim community it could lead to.

In September 1955, the journal of the Zaytuna, *Al-Majalla al-Zaytūnīya,* reported and commented on the proposal of the New Dustūr's French Federation and on the reactions it elicited.[222] It argued that Tunisia's legal regime could not legitimately be built on the principle of secularism (*lā'ikīya*), which would amount to extremism (*taṭarruf*), and that an Islamic government should be established instead. It added that Islam was a foundation as solid as the principle of sovereignty, that "it must be the official religion," and that "the

219. Ladhari (1956, 98 and 118). Emphasis is mine.

220. Oualdi (2022) shows that the Zaytuna milieu was itself divided—e.g., Shaykh Djait was a Youssefist, whereas the Ben Achour and Al-Nayfar families were closer to Bourguiba.

221. Mahjoubi (1982, 528–529) and El-Méchat (2002) show that both the Old and New Dustūrs made Islam a central element of their nationalist narratives. The New Dustūr often accused the Old Dustūr of being frozen in a "conservative" interpretation of Islam, but this does not make the New Dustūr a party of "secular" activists, as claimed by Julien (1952, 75–74) and Perkins (2014, 97).

222. *Al-Majalla al-Zaytūnīya,* vol. 4, no. 9, September 1955, 220–222.

government must be an Islamic government for a Muslim people [*ḥukūma Islāmīya li-sha ʿb muslim*], who have at their head a Muslim king who watches over [*yar ʿā*] Islam and protects it [*yaḥmī ḥimāh*]." The journal of the Zaytuna claimed that the protectorate authorities themselves would never have dared to make such a proposal. It conceded, somewhat charitably, that the young members of the New Dustūr Party's French Federation had merely intended to please "people abroad" (read "the French") in order "to accelerate independence." However, it added, this was dangerous because tradition (*taqlīd*), "and only tradition"—echoing the careful wording of the autonomy agreement—had to guide the drafting of the Constitution. It argued that in order to mitigate the effects of a state religion on religious minorities, it was sufficient to have an article guaranteeing "the protection of [their] material and moral interests." It reminded its readers that "our brothers in Islamic countries" drafted constitutions in which the religion of the state is Islam and that the presence of other religious groups (such as Copts in Egypt, the Hindus in Pakistan, or Jews in all these countries) did not prevent them from maintaining this principle. In the same issue of the journal of the Zaytuna, the sermon of the Maliki shaykh al-Islam, Muhammad al-Aziz Djait (1886–1970),[223] pronounced on the occasion of Eid al-Adha in the presence of the bey, was reproduced. He proposed to inscribe in the Constitution that "the government is Islamic and follows the precepts of Islam" (*ḥukūma Islāmīya tadīn bi-l-Islām*), and argued that inscribing "a regime of *laïcité*" (*lā ʾikīyat al-niẓām*) in the Tunisian Constitution would produce discord (*fitna*).[224]

The Old Dustūr's Executive Committee also published a statement opposing the proposal of the New Dustūr's French Federation. It deplored the fact that some Tunisians were submitting to the pressures of the French government to establish a "modern code"—that is, "a code not inspired by heavenly religions."[225] It condemned *laïcité* because it leads to "the violation of sacred things" and "allows Muslims the freedom to fall into apostasy." It added that Qur'anic laws provided minorities "a fair share of freedom," even more so than modern

223. Shaykh Muhammad al-Aziz Djait was the Maliki shaykh al-Islam from 1945 to 1956 and minister of justice from 1947 to 1950. Green (1978, 266), biography no. 69.

224. *Al-Majalla al-Zaytūnīya*, vol. 4, no. 9, September 1955, 218–219.

225. The statement was reproduced in French in *Le Petit Matin*, August 27, 1955, but I was not able to find the version *Le Petit Matin* claimed had appeared in the Arabic journal *Al-Zuhra*. Salah Farhat (1894–1979), the Free Constitutional Party Executive Committee's president, signed it. He became general secretary of the party after the death of Abd al-Aziz Thaalibi in 1944.

constitutions. It concluded, "since the Tunisian state is Muslim, it should remain Muslim for eternity. The Constitution must be inspired by Islam in consideration of the majority and must not be secular in consideration of a small minority."[226] As for the New Dustūr Party, it also argued that the proposal from its own French Federation amounted to "extremism" (*taṭarruf*).[227] Through the voice of Ali Belhaouane—a high-ranking member of the party and close ally of Bourguiba—it argued that a secular personal status had been proposed by "some young Dustūr Party members who studied in France" and who "were unaware of the meaning [of the word *laïcité*]." Ali Belhaouane claimed that these youngsters were the instruments of French colonialism and that the use of the word *laïcité* was not justified. He added, "Our sovereign is the commander of the faithful. Public prayers are pronounced in his name. Laws and decrees are also pronounced in his name. It is obvious that our Tunisian state is a Muslim state."[228] Although the New Dustūr accepted—and, as we will see, called for—freedom *of* religion (freedom to practice one's religion), it emphatically rejected freedom *from* religion (freedom to choose one's religion or no religion).[229]

The 1956 Personal Status Code: Sharia Lives on in a Quasi-Constitutional Text

Habib Bourguiba intervened in this debate and formed his synthesis. In August 1956, ten days after having abolished sharia courts,[230] he imposed, without discussion, a Personal Status Code (PSC, in Arabic *Majallat al-Aḥwāl al-Shakhṣīya*). It was presented as an implementation of Islamic law, and it did preserve some

226. *Le Petit Matin*, August 27, 1955.

227. *Al-Majalla al-Zaytūnīya*, vol. 4, no. 9, September 1955, 220. The accusation of extremism was articulated by Taieb Mehiri (1924–1965), who held an important position in the New Dustūr Party and became its director in November 1955. He was minister of the interior from 1956 to 1965.

228. Ali Belhaouane, speech on the occasion of the first day of the Hegirian year (August 20, 1955), at a conference organized by the Association of Young Muslims. Cited in *Le Petit Matin*, August 25, 1955.

229. As another illustration of the New Dustūr state elites' opposition to freedom from religion, an agreement was signed between the Vatican and the Tunisian government in 1957 in which the Catholic Church agreed to abstain from religious proselytism, restrict its activities to Catholics residing in Tunisia, and cater to Muslims only for health and education. Boissevain (2013, 3).

230. Decree of August 3, 1956 (*JOT* no. 64, August 10, 1956, 1101) abolished sharia courts. Decree of September 25, 1956 (*JOT* no. 77, September 25, 1956, 1286) integrated their personnel into the unified courts.

elements of sharia.[231] Starting in 1957, it applied to all Tunisians irrespective of their religion.[232] Although the PSC constituted progress toward gender equality compared to the rabbinic and sharia laws as they applied in Tunisia, some jurists disapproved of a code of Muslim inspiration being applied indifferently to Jews and Muslims.[233] With the 1956 PSC, Bourguiba put an end to a legal system that had long been strongly criticized by Tunisians for being fragmented, disorderly, and arbitrary.[234] The French protectorate had attempted to codify personal status law and had given this task to the minister of justice and Maliki shaykh al-Islam Muhammad al-Aziz Djait, in 1948. The "Djait code"[235] was drafted by a committee composed of ʿulamā, lawyers, journalists, and intellectuals working under the patronage of the Ministry of Justice. It summarized the main provisions of the Maliki and Hanafi schools of law on personal status.[236] The French did not institute this code because they took issue with several of its articles, such as the ones permitting polygamy, and Shaykh Djait refused to modify it accordingly. He argued that the French wrongly thought that the code's aim was the same as that of "positive laws" (*al-qawānīn al waḍʿīya*)—that is, "to create new laws" (*inshāʾ tashrīʿ jadīd*).[237] Still, his code largely inspired the 1956 PSC, although the latter did not explicitly mention sharia and regulated family matters in a way that significantly departed from Islamic law. It made repudiation a legal impediment to the husband remarrying, criminalized polygamy, and

231. Decree of August 13, 1956, which began to be applied in January 1957.

232. Initially, the PSC did not apply to Tunisian Jews, who were under the rabbinic court's jurisdiction. This court was abolished with law 40 of September 27, 1957. Its personnel were integrated into the unified courts, and the PSC was applied to all Tunisians irrespective of religion starting October 1, 1957. See Borrmans (1977, 327–328).

233. Sebag (1991, 291) and Haddad De Paz (1977, 27). During the negotiations over internal autonomy, Tunisian Jewish elites had been of two opinions. One group, under the leadership of Charles Haddad, the president of the Jewish community of Tunis, favored a specific legal and political status for Tunisian Jews and quotas to guarantee Jewish representation in assemblies. Another group, led by Elie Nataf, as well as Albert Bessis (who was a member of the Tunisian delegation negotiating with France), Serge Moati, André Barouch, and Léon Moati, favored equal rights and duties for all Tunisians irrespective of religion and no Jewish minority status. The wording of the June 3, 1955, agreement was in line with the latter and with the editorials of *Le Petit Matin*. See Nataf (2013).

234. Thaalibi (1920, 52–53).

235. *Lāʾiḥat Majallat al-Aḥkām al-Sharʿīya* (n.d.).

236. As with other codes in Tunisia and in the Middle East, the process of *talfiq* (combining material from various schools of law) was used. See, for instance, Commission de Codification des Lois Tunisiennes (1899).

237. Exchange of letters between Shaykh Muhammad al-Aziz Djait and the offices of the Tunisian Ministry of Justice, June–July 1953, published in Derouiche-Ben Achour (1996, 351–355).

mandated that all divorce requests go through the courts.[238] Although Schacht (1960, 106) called it "the most radical document of modern Islamic legislation," official state narratives described it as conforming to "sharia" and even as being derived from it, the result of *ijtihād* based on Islamic texts.[239] They also emphasized the legacy of the 1949 Djait Code.[240] Moreover, the articles concerning descent, dowry, and inheritance adhered to Islamic law. In addition, details of interpretation were left to the judges, who were instructed to refer to "the main reference books and fundamental texts, if need be,"[241] a statement conservative judges often interpreted as allowing them to refer to Islamic law when the code was silent on a particular issue; this put them at odds with liberal judges.

Although the 1956–1959 National Constituent Assembly (NCA, in Arabic *al-majlis al-qawmī al-taʾsīsī*), which also operated as a legislative body, began to convene as early as April 1956, its members never discussed or voted on the text of the PSC.[242] Had it been brought before the NCA, it would have triggered heated discussion: although Bourguiba and his successor Ben Ali gave it a quasi-constitutional status, in reality the PSC was the object of deep contention at its inception, as shown by the opposition expressed in the press at the time. The Old Dustūr's mouthpiece, *Al-Istiqlāl*, voiced the strong disapproval of many ʿulamā of the Zaytuna.[243] Responding to a request by a group of eighty-three

238. The PSC also abolished constraint (*jabr*) in marriage, replacing it with mandatory mutual agreement of the prospective spouses, a provision that Shaykh Djait accepted. For a comparative description and analysis of these transformations in North Africa, see Charrad (2001).

239. To this effect, the first editions of the code included numerous footnotes that referred to Hanafi and Maliki interpretations of sharia. For more details, see Zeghal (2013a). Ahmed Mestiri, the minister of justice (1956–1958) at the time of this reform, later wrote, "Whereas Mustapha Kemal totally disregarded Muslim law and copied almost literally the Swiss Civil Code, the Tunisian legislator took direct inspiration from the principles of sharia law as they are articulated in the Qur'an, the hadith, the jurisprudence, and the doctrine, according to a novel conception of ijtihad." *Révolution africaine*, no. 157, January 29, 1966.

240. August 3, 1956, communiqué of the Ministry of Justice. République Tunisienne, Ministère des Affaires Religieuses (2008, 34).

241. August 3, 1956, communiqué of the Ministry of Justice. République tunisienne, Ministère des Affaires Religieuses (2008, 34).

242. Women's right to vote was discussed during the February 3, 1958 session of the NCA. After a long debate, it was approved by a bare majority. Al-Jumhūrīya al-Tūnisīya, *Munāqashāt* (2009, vol. 2, 83–92).

243. For example, on August 31, 1956, *Al-Istiqlāl* published an open letter to the bey and to Bourguiba, with 137 signatures, thanking the government for its reforms but criticizing it for not involving ʿulamā and experts in Islamic law in the elaboration of the PSC, whereas it had involved experts in all other domains such as the economy and the budget.

readers for a fatwa on the PSC, Shaykh Muhammad al-Aziz Djait—the author of the Djait Code who had expressed himself against a "secular regime" and in favor of inscribing the principle of an "Islamic government" in the constitution—published a legal opinion in the fall of 1956 and reassured his readers that he had requested "the revision of the [seven] articles [of the PSC] that contradicted sharia rules [*ḥukm shar ʿī*]" from the Ministry of Justice.[244] Despite requests that the PSC be discussed, Bourguiba and his close aides essentially imposed it without deliberations.[245] They argued that they had to act quickly because the nationalization of the justice system, which was still in the hands of the French, was at stake. Bourguiba needed to prove to France that Tunisia had a "modern" system of justice—that is, tribunals that "would be perfectly fit to decide cases involving all residents, Tunisian and foreign."[246] Since Bourguiba had the upper hand, conservatives did not go very far in their opposition to the PSC. In the meantime, the discussions in the NCA were leading toward the recognition of Islam as "the religion of the state." Shaykh Muhammad al-Tahar Ben Achour, a preeminent religious scholar who had just been appointed dean of the Zaytuna, approved of the PSC, giving his "full confidence to a government that has declared itself a Muslim government in its first fundamental law, to proclaim laws that are accepted by the elite and the whole community."[247] It therefore seems

244. The readers' request was published in *Al-Istiqlāl*, no. 45, August 31, 1956. It asked Shaykh Djait and other religious dignitaries and professors to "give their opinion and explain the judgment of God [*ḥukm Allāh*] on the content of the Personal [Status] Code. Is it in conformity with the commandments of the Qur'an, the Sunna of the Prophet and the consensus [*hal huwa muṭābiq li-nuṣūṣ aḥkām al-Qur ʾān wa-sunnat Rasūl Allāh wa-l-ijmā ʿ*]?" For the legal opinion, see Muḥammad ʿAbd al-ʿAzīz Jʿayyiṭ, Jawāb ʿan al-Istiftā ʾ, *Al-Istiqlāl*, no. 47, September 14, 1956, 1.

245. During the NCA session of April 17, 1956, Shaykh al-Nayfar requested, to no avail, that the Assembly discuss whether family law should be under an "Islamic" or a "non-Islamic" regime. Al-Jumhūrīya al-Tūnisīya, *Munāqashāt* (2009, vol. 1, 27–28). This issue was only discussed obliquely in the NCA. For instance, during the June 19, 1957 NCA session, in the absence of Shaykh al-Nayfar, Mohamed Bellalouna criticized the incomplete codification of the law of contracts and obligations, saying "Islam, which is my religion, does not guide [*yar ʿā*] the PSC anymore but guides the contracts and obligations." Still, he added, the code of contracts and obligations is called a "secular" code. The minister of justice Ahmed Mestiri responded, "Islam guides everything, no one has gone too far in anything, there is only ignorance about Islam." Al-Jumhūrīya al-Tūnisīya, *Munāqashāt* (2009, vol. 2, 303). See also *Al-Istiqlāl*, no. 52, October 19, 1956, which condemned the decision to proclaim the PSC and unify the justice system without parliamentary deliberation.

246. Mestiri (2011, 114–115).

247. Quoted in République Tunisienne, Ministère des Affaires Religieuses (2008, 103–104).

that Bourguiba gave the ʿulamā Islamic guarantees with Article 1 of the Constitution, and that, in exchange, they were forced to accept breaches to Islamic law in the PSC since the contentious articles were never modified toward a more "Islamic" interpretation as Shaykh Djait and many others had hoped.

The 1956 PSC antagonized conservatives, notably because it prohibited unilateral repudiation and polygamy. Yet, because some regulations such as inheritance still conformed to Islamic law, liberals wished for the code to be further modernized. Bourguiba's and Ben Ali's authoritarian regime, especially when it began confronting its Islamist opposition in the 1970s, gave the PSC a quasi-constitutional status and made it untouchable. For those in power, it could not be amended—neither to accommodate conservatives' demands to make it conform more strictly to Islamic law, nor to satisfy those who wanted to make it more progressive and to further gender equality. It was enshrined in the 1959 Constitution through a 1997 amendment that made "respect" of the PSC's principles by political parties a condition for their legality, justifying the exclusion of the main Islamist political movement, al-Nahdha, from the legal opposition.[248] Bourguiba and Ben Ali promoted the PSC as a distinctive symbol of Tunisian modernity,[249] with tropes underlining its exceptionality in the Arab world. Simultaneously, they insisted on its conformity with sharia. This allowed them to maintain a balance between liberal and conservative interpretations of the code, but no real open, public debate took place on this question, and the authorities kept a lid on it until 2011.

Islam as "Religion of the State" in the 1959 Constitution

The 1956–1959 NCA was elected through universal male suffrage on March 25, 1956, just five days after independence, and held its first session on April 8, 1956. Its ninety-eight members all came from the National Front, a coalition of the Labor Union, Farmers' Union, and Employers' Union[250] in alliance with the New Dustūr Party. The electoral process was far from free and fair, and results were tailored ex ante to cement the New Dustūr's hegemony.[251] The overwhelming majority of the NCA consisted of men who had links with the

248. Constitutional law 97-65, October 27, 1997, in *JORT*, no. 87, October 31, 1997.
249. S. Ben Achour (2007).
250. Union Générale Tunisienne du Travail, Union Nationale des Agriculteurs Tunisiens, and Union Tunisienne de l'Industrie, du Commerce et de l'Artisanat.
251. Toumi (1989, 30).

party.[252] Two Tunisian Jews who were members of the New Dustūr were elected, Albert Bessis and André Barouch, in almost exact proportion to the demographic weight of the Tunisian Jewish community at that time.[253] Overall, half the Assembly was made up of men educated at the Zaytuna.[254] There was a broad agreement in the NCA about the necessity to affirm in the Constitution that Islam was the religion of the state, although there were disagreements about how to formulate this principle. On April 14, 1956, in its third session, the NCA debated a draft of the Constitution's Article 1, which was to define the "pillar [*di ʿāma*] of the Tunisian state."[255] Its initial draft read, #1 "Tunisia is an Arab, Muslim, independent, and sovereign state"; #2 "The Tunisian people are sovereign. The people exercise this sovereignty as specified in this Constitution"; #3 "The Tunisian state guarantees freedom of belief [*ḥurrīyat al-mu ʿtaqad*] and protects the freedom to exercise religious worship [*ḥurrīyat al-qiyām bi-l-sha ʿā ʾir al-dīnīya*] as long as it does not harm order [*al-niẓām*] and does not contradict propriety [*al-ādāb*]."[256] As soon as this proposal was announced, Habib Bourguiba—president of the council and future president of the republic—countered it with, #1 "Tunisia is an independent and sovereign state"; #2 "Sovereignty belongs to the Tunisian people. They implement it as determined in this Constitution"; and #3 "Islam is the religion of the state and Arabic is its language. The state guarantees freedom of belief and protects the freedom to exercise religious worship as long as they do not violate the law [*qānūn*]."[257] This counterproposal, which avoided the term "Muslim state," encountered some resistance in the NCA,[258] but Bourguiba turned increasingly authoritarian as discussions progressed, and it was difficult to contradict him. The NCA member Béhi Ladgham, one of his close political allies, argued that what was most important was "to make clear the state's characteristic quality [*ṣifa*], which is independence before anything else." In fact, he went even

252. There were 99 members with links to the New Dustūr Party out of a total of 108 who were elected to the NCA over time (on March 25, 1956, and in by-elections). Jazi (1971, 83).

253. There were about 58,000 Tunisian Jews in 1956, out of a Tunisian population of about 3,520,000. Seklani (1974, 24 and 27) and Sebag (1991, 279).

254. Half of the 108 members of the NCA who were elected (on March 25, 1956 and in by-elections). Jazi (1971, 54).

255. Al-Jumhūrīya al-Tūnisīya, *Munāqashāt* (2009, vol.1, 13–19), session of April 14, 1956.

256. Al-Jumhūrīya al-Tūnisīya, *Munāqashāt* (2009, vol. 1, 13), session of April 14, 1956.

257. Al-Jumhūrīya al-Tūnisīya, *Munāqashāt* (2009, vol. 1, 13–14), session of April 14, 1956.

258. For instance, Shadhili al-Nayfar, a Zaytuna trained scholar, objected to Bourguiba's counterproposal. Al-Jumhūrīya al-Tūnisīya, *Munāqashāt* (2009, vol. 1, 14), session of April 14, 1956.

further than Bourguiba, proposing the formula "Islam is *its* religion,"[259] which, he argued, meant "that the religion of the state is Islam," contending that this was more "correct legally and more precise in its meaning." For Ladgham, the concept of an "Islamic state" had no legal definition (*al-ta ʿrīf al-qānūnī*) or specific form because, he argued, "Islamic states are all different. There is a republic such as Syria, or a monarchy such as Morocco, or [other] . . . intermediate kinds [of political systems] that have succeeded one another in history."[260] Bourguiba supported Béhi Ladgham's proposal and, in response to Shaykh al-Nayfar's insistence that the term "religion of the state" be kept, he reiterated that "Islam is its religion" meant that Islam is "the religion of the state," "without ambiguity," and not merely "the religion of Tunisia."[261] He also invoked his legal training and expertise, arguing that a constitution was primarily a legal document, and that the reference to an "Arab and Muslim state" belonged to the order of "sentiments" (*ʿawāṭif*), and not to the law.[262] The discussions were rushed: independence had to be approved quickly because of the tense political context of the Youssefist insurrection,[263] which might have served as an excuse to pass this article without much deliberation. Indeed, that same day, Habib Bourguiba and Béhi Ladgham's proposal was approved in its first reading. After the monarchy was abolished in July 1957, the final form of Article 1 in the Constitution read, "Tunisia is a free, independent, and sovereign state; Islam is its religion, Arabic is its language, and the republic is its system of government."[264]

A MUSLIM STATE UNCONSTRAINED BY SHARIA: ISLAM AS A USEFUL SET OF VALUES

As Béhi Ladgham retrospectively explained in 1984, a decision was made not to delve too deeply into the debate related to Article 1 because "we would have had to decide what sort of an Islamic state we wanted and if it is Islamic because of religious practices [*ʿibādāt*] or because of the social relationships

259. Emphasis is mine.

260. Al-Jumhūrīya al-Tūnisīya, *Munāqashāt* (2009, vol. 1, 14–15), session of April 14, 1956.

261. Al-Jumhūrīya al-Tūnisīya, *Munāqashāt* (2009, vol. 1, 17), session of April 14, 1956. A High Islamic Council was created in 1987, shortly before Ben Ali's takeover, to examine, among other issues, the implementation of Article 1, which was then also described as meaning that "Islam is the religion of the state." Decree 87–663 of April 22, 1987, *JORT*, April 28–May 1, 1987, 574–575.

262. Al-Jumhūrīya al-Tūnisīya, *Munāqashāt* (2009, vol. 1, 17), session of April 14, 1956.

263. Al-Jam ʿīya al-Tūnisīya li-l-Qānūn al-Dustūrī (1986, 142–144).

264. Al-Jumhūrīya al-Tūnisīya, *Munāqashāt* (2009, vol. 2, 355).

[*mu ʿāmalāt*]."[265] It is clear that Bourguiba and his allies did not want to be constrained by a constitutional formula that could easily be interpreted as requiring the implementation of sharia, and they sought to avoid accumulating references to Islam in the Constitution. They argued that it was not useful "to talk about the eternal meanings of Islam [*al-ma ʿānī al-khālida al-Islāmīya*] all the time, unless we relate them to specific things [*ashyā ʾ*]." They preferred making the "lofty principles of Islam" (*al-mabādi ʾ al- ʿulyā allatī atā bihā al-Islām*), particularly "religious tolerance" (*al-tasāmuḥ al-dīnī*) and the equality of human races (*al-ajnās al-basharīya*) "in which states pride themselves" (*allatī tubāhī bihi al-duwal*), a foundation for "human development" (*al-taqaddum al-basharī*).[266] In the same vein, in his closing speech on June 1, 1959, the last day of the NCA's deliberations, Bourguiba firmly rejected the idea, put forward by some, that "the Constitution in Islam is the Qur'an." He added that the Qur'an did not specify issues of governance in constitutional terms.[267] Therefore, he unambiguously rejected what I call a thick conception of the state's custodianship of Islam. Moreover, immediately after Article 1 was voted on in the 1956–1959 NCA, Bourguiba insisted that "since we have proclaimed that the religion of the Tunisian state is Islam, as the religion of the majority," and "since there are Israelites," it is urgent to "immediately" guarantee freedom of belief (*ḥurrīyat al-mu ʿtaqad*) and the protection of religious rites and rituals (*al-sha ʿā ʾir wa-l-ṭuqūs al-dīnīya*) in the Constitution and to proclaim it "to the whole world." However, the introduction of the principles of freedom of belief (not freedom of conscience, which would only come in the 2014 Constitution) and protection of worship—with the purpose, in Bourguiba's words, of respecting "the religion of the other" (*dīn al-ghayr*)—did not erase the substance of Article 1.[268] It simply mitigated some of, but far from all, its potentially adverse effects on individual rights and freedoms. Moreover, Article 37 of the Constitution reinforced Article 1 by stipulating that

265. Al-Jam ʿīya al-Tūnisīya li-l-Qānūn al-Dustūrī (1986, 208). This is a conventional pairing (e.g., ʿIbādāt and Mu ʿāmalāt, *EI*²).

266. Béhi Ladgham, Al-Jumhūrīya al-Tūnisīya, *Munāqashāt* (2009, vol. 1, 127), session of July 17, 1956.

267. Al-Jumhūrīya al-Tūnisīya, *Munāqashāt* (2009, vol. 2, 349), session of June 1, 1959. For example, Bourguiba received a letter dated June 4, 1956, from a fellow named Muhammad Ibn al-Arbi al-Rizqi, requesting that the NCA "establish their laws according to the path of Islam" (*yasunnū sunanahum ʿalā ṭarīqat al-Islām*), adding, "A people whose religion is Islam and who follow the Book and the Sunna, should not follow for their lives the model of the unbelievers." ANT SD C230 D133.

268. Al-Jumhūrīya al-Tūnisīya, *Munāqashāt* (2009, vol. 1, 18–19), session of 14 April 1956.

non-Muslim Tunisians were ineligible for the post of president. It was at odds with the principle of equality of all citizens (Article 6) but in alignment with the privileges accorded to Islam as the religion of the state.

THE STATE AS THE CUSTODIAN OF A RELIGIOUS INFRASTRUCTURE

Although they rejected the idea of too many Islamic constraints on the state, Bourguiba and his allies agreed with most NCA members that it was the responsibility of the state to organize the infrastructure of Muslim worship for its citizens. To make this point, an NCA member argued that, although the Constitution was silent on this issue, it did say that "Islam is the religion of the Tunisian state."[269] Béhi Ladgham, echoing several other NCA members,[270] also argued that this was "an issue of principle," mandated by Article 1, and that "the state not only respects religious values but also works to reinforce them and considers this to be among the rights [*ḥaqq*] of its citizens."[271] In a reference to the Bourguiba government's abolition of the private and public *ḥabūs* upon independence (an ironic turnaround given the importance the *ḥabūs* issue took in the nationalist struggle for independence),[272] he added, "When the state revised its laws about the waqfs, it . . . promised to take charge of the expenses necessary for religious worship."[273] There were disagreements, however, on the form and extent of the state's religious provisions (i.e., the munificence of the state's

269. Hassan Shafroud, Al-Jumhūrīya al-Tūnisīya, *Munāqashāt* (2009, vol. 1, 225), session of June 17, 1957. He argued that "Islam is about religious obligations [*wājibāt dīnīya*], such as the performance of prayer in mosques," and advocated for the creation of an administration in charge of imams.

270. For instance, MP Rachid Driss: "Since the NCA has decided that the state is an Islamic state, we think that the functionaries of religious worship should be taken care of and that there should be an administrative structure for them with a line in the budget so that we can specify their number and improve their situation." Also, MP Ahmed Drira: "This issue must be dealt with by the government and the NCA because the government is founded on articles decided by the NCA, [one of them being] that the religion of the state is Islam." Al-Jumhūrīya al-Tūnisīya, *Munāqashāt* (2009, vol. 1, 212–213, and 216), session of June 17, 1957.

271. Al-Jumhūrīya al-Tūnisīya, *Munāqashāt* (2009, vol. 1, 226), session of June 17, 1957.

272. The May 31, 1956 decree abolished the public *ḥabūs* and suppressed the *Ḥabūs* Administration (Djemaia). Existing ones were transferred to the state (Domaine de l'État). A July 18, 1957 decree abolished the establishment of new private and mixed *ḥabūs*, and existing properties were distributed to the *ḥabūs* beneficiaries.

273. Al-Jumhūrīya al-Tūnisīya, *Munāqashāt* (2009, vol. 1, 225–226), session of June 17, 1957.

custodianship of Islam), especially the number of mosques. For instance, a few voices were heard in the NCA in favor of limiting it and instead prioritizing health and education in the state budget, including religious education in public schools.[274] As for Bourguiba and his allies, their utmost priority, in addition to independence, was economic and social development. Therefore, armed with a developmentalist philosophy of governance, Bourguiba articulated a conception of the state's custodianship of Islam as first and foremost devoted to the moral and financial support of a religious infrastructure that not only provided for Islamic worship but also disseminated Islamic values, notably in its public schools. These state religious provisions were viewed as an inalienable right of Muslim citizens and as a public provision (among others, such as housing, health care, and schooling) that fostered human development with inevitable trade-offs in budgetary discussions.[275] To be sure, to deliver on several of these provisions, the state removed or marginalized traditional institutions (e.g., the sharia courts, the Zaytuna, and the religious endowments). However, it ensured the continuity of public religious provisions (from precolonial and colonial times), and in fact continued to expand them in per capita real terms in the long run, as we will see in chapter 5. In addition, Bourguiba sought to preserve the religion and the Muslim community by keeping provisions related to sharia in the PSC and by rejecting freedom from religion. For conservatives, such as some ʿulamā and (starting in the 1970s) the Islamist opposition, this was insufficient. They wished for what I call a thicker and more munificent state custodianship of Islam. For liberals, it was too much, and they wished for a thinner and less munificent one.

Suppressing the Debate between Conservatives and Liberals

The debate about Islam in governance did not completely die out after the 1959 Constitution was promulgated. It remained muffled, with the regime at times allowing for a modicum of discussions in limited spheres of deliberation, in an attempt to manage the Islamists' opposition. For instance, in 1984, former members of the 1956–1959 NCA were invited, along with legal scholars, to an academic conference about the making of the 1959 Constitution. On that occasion, they recognized that the interpretation of Article 1 of the Constitution had

274. Al-Jumhūrīya al-Tūnisīya, *Munāqashāt* (2009, vol. 1, 225), session of June 17, 1957.

275. See, for instance, Shaykh Kamel Tarzi, director of the Office of Religious Affairs (Directeur du Culte), cited by Souriau (1979, 357).

been contentious in the NCA,[276] and a vigorous exchange took place between the legal scholar Ali Mezghani and the Zaytuna scholar Shaykh al-Nayfar. The former pointed out the contradiction between the principles of Islam as the official religion of the state and freedom of belief and equality, while pushing the latter to delve into the meaning of an Islamic state that did not implement sharia. Shaykh al-Nayfar responded, "If we adopt Islam, we adopt it entirely, not some things without others," recognizing that he was as dissatisfied as the liberal Mezghani with Bourguiba's synthesis.[277] The lines of this debate remained essentially frozen until the drafting of the third Constitution of Tunisia (from 2012 to 2014) fully reopened the discussion, leading this time to a freer, and therefore richer but deeply polarizing, debate. However, as we will see in the next chapter, despite all the transformations initiated by the post-2011 democratic transition, the 2012–2014 constitutional drafting process kept the substance of Bourguiba's synthesis essentially intact, only specifying its meaning a bit further and keeping the debate alive. In early 2011, Yadh Ben Achour, a high-profile Tunisian expert on public law and Muslim political theory and head of the Committee for Political Reforms charged with organizing the political transition,[278] underlined the centrality of the two key elements of this synthesis. In the construction of "a new state,"[279] he argued, two crucial legal texts had to remain unchanged: Article 1 of the 1959 Constitution and the 1956 Personal Status Code, which, he added, was "the real Constitution of Tunisia."[280]

Conclusion

From the first decade of the twentieth century until 1959 (i.e., during the formation, maturation, and implementation of the Tunisian nationalist project), in continuity with the precolonial period, the custodianship of Islam by the (sovereign) state continued to be formulated as a necessity by protonationalist,

276. Al-Jamʿīya al-Tūnisīya li-l-Qānūn al-Dustūrī (1986, 208).

277. Al-Jamʿīya al-Tūnisīya li-l-Qānūn al-Dustūrī (1986, 310).

278. After the fall of President Ben Ali on January 14, 2011, the interim government charged the Committee for Political Reforms with proposing a path for the political transition. Its tasks included drafting any necessary new legal texts, such as amendments to the Constitution and laws on political parties, elections, and the press.

279. The point that a "new state" was being built after the fall of President Ben Ali in January 2011 was reiterated to me by Ajmi Lourimi, a member of the al-Nahdha Party's Political Bureau, during our meeting in Tunis on June 9, 2011.

280. Yadh Ben Achour, interview on Nessma TV, February 3, 2011.

nationalist, and antinationalist Tunisian elites alike, as well as by the bey and French authorities. During the colonial period, however, several sovereignties were in competition: a Husaynid dynastic sovereignty (the bey), French imperial sovereignty ("Islamic France"), and a Tunisian national sovereignty (independent Tunisia). As a result, there were several competing custodians of Islam. At each juncture, the state that was exercising sovereignty or that was aspiring to exercise it was tasked with ensuring the protection of Islam, the Muslim community, and its religious institutions. When independence was not invoked, such as in the 1920 nationalists' petitions to the French Parliament for a constitution, the state custodianship of Islam was not mentioned either, a testament to its inextricable link with sovereignty. Moreover, as in the 1857–1861 constitutional episode, the necessity and ideal of state custodianship of Islam were reaffirmed by all political protagonists, including foreigners. To be sure, the context was different, and the formulations of this ideal reflected the salient issues of the time, such as the Tunisians' participation in the Great War and the French colonization of *ḥabūs* land. They included newly available idioms (e.g., "Muslim public law") and the language of the existing systems of governance (e.g., "Imperial rule," "dynastic monarchy," "independent constitutional republic"). However, behind the polarizing debates and the opportune use of religious narratives for political mobilization (something French colonial authorities and subsequently the postindependence authoritarian regime routinely condemned when originating from their opposition), a robust agreement always persisted, that of state custodianship of Islam, often challenged as to its implementation, never on its principle. Two of the instantiations of state custodianship of Islam we have encountered in this chapter have lived on, on each side of the Mediterranean, into the twenty-first century. Although there is no longer an "Imperial Islamic France," the French Republic is still grappling with what "French Islam" is and with the extent to which it should be sustained, but this time within its own borders, for the benefit of a significant French Muslim minority, and in a context of separation of churches and state.[281] In Tunisia, Bourguiba's authoritarian synthesis that borrowed from conservative and liberal conceptions of the state custodianship of Islam essentially persisted (with its attendant political cleavage) through the Arab Spring and the political challenge that followed: how to constitutionalize a Muslim *and* democratic state. It is to this constitutional episode that I now turn.

281. Zeghal (2005).

3

State Custodianship of Islam in the Tunisian 2014 Constitution

DEBATING A MUSLIM AND DEMOCRATIC STATE

WHAT BECAME OF past conceptions of the role of Islam in governance during the democratic transition that followed the fall of the Tunisian authoritarian regime in 2011? What happened to Habib Bourguiba's authoritarian synthesis, and how did the terms of the debate between liberals and conservatives change, if at all, with democracy and the participation of Islamist parties in electoral politics? The 2012–2014 National Constituent Assembly debates provide us with a rare window into contemporary political discussions about Islam in governance in a context of extensive freedom of expression, after the first free and fair elections in the history of Tunisia. Since the political transition was not brought on by an Islamic revolution or by a pact between Islamists and their political adversaries but rather by uprisings caused by severe economic problems, it simply removed the lid on the debate about the role of Islam in governance frozen under authoritarianism. After several weeks of uprisings followed by the fall of President Ben Ali on January 14, 2011, the 1959 Constitution was abrogated, and a National Constituent Assembly (hereafter NCA or Assembly) was elected. The Assembly, composed of a plurality (but not an absolute majority) of Islamists, reexamined, in a deep introspective moment, the relationship between the state and Islam, and Bourguiba's authoritarian synthesis was fully reopened for discussion. This issue dominated the Assembly and public debates from 2012 to 2014, despite the dire economic situation and what seemed to be more pressing challenges. In continuity with the past, throughout the democratic transition, the ideal of state custodianship of Islam, the preferred religion, remained the object of a broad agreement. As in the previous constitutional discussions of 1955–1959, neither a separation between Islam and the state nor state neutrality were considered an option for Tunisia. Moreover, in a highly polarized debate that opposed Islamists and their adversaries, the constituents vigorously disagreed about the role Islam should play in governance. They disagreed about the degree to which Islam as a philosophy of governance should constrain the state (what I call the thickness of the state's custodianship of Islam) and the degree to which the state should constrain Islam (what I call the strength of the state's custodianship of Islam)—for example, with its coercive and/or pedagogical apparatus. They also disagreed about the legitimacy of mixing religion and *politics*—for example, of allowing Islam in political competition or politics in places of worship. Given their irreconcilable views, the constituents left Bourguiba's synthesis largely unchanged from its 1959 formulation, although they specified it a bit further. Despite the novelty brought by what Tunisians liked to call a revolution (*thawra*) at the time, past constitutional history weighed heavily on the Assembly. The constituents' main innovation was a new framework for their debate to endure and be adjudicated democratically in the future. This framework provided guarantees to each camp by imposing limits on their respective freedoms. It does not seem to have been premeditated and it emerged progressively as a solution to their disagreements.

Three important points should be underlined. First, the Assembly worked at establishing Islam *and* democracy together and making them coexist without compromising on their substance in the Constitution. That the Islamist party al-Nahdha's leadership renounced the invocation of sharia in the Constitution, after initially insisting on it, should not be interpreted as a "dilution" of their political project brought about by their inclusion in the newly democratic political process. Indeed, they did not abandon their project of a thicker state custodianship of Islam nor did they renounce the implementation of sharia. Since the agreement they reached with their adversaries was not on substance but on the framework that would organize the debate going forward, a wide array of conceptions of the role of Islam in governance, from the most liberal to the most conservative, were discussed during and after the constitutional drafting process. This means that the inclusion of Islamist parties in the democratic process, instead of leading to the moderation of their political project (as argued by the proponents of the "moderation hypothesis")[1] has instead helped

1. There is a vast literature on the potential "behavorial" and "ideological" moderation of Islamists through political inclusion, which is mostly informed by authoritarian contexts. For

deepen and polarize, but also organize, the debate with their political adversaries. I do not mean to say that al-Nahdha's leadership lacked pragmatism in their political behavior or that they refused to play by the rules of the democratic game nor do I mean to say that they used doublespeak, as is sometimes argued. Rather, I argue that they acknowledged that they could continue to pursue the ideal of a democratic state constrained by Islam without invoking sharia in the Constitution. In fact, all the constituents acknowledged that the thickness and strength of the state's custodianship of Islam could fluctuate according to future electoral outcomes and seemed intent on implementing their own conceptions of this custodianship if they were to govern. Second, the disagreements and political battle between Islamists and non-Islamists in the Assembly about the role of Islam in governance must be put in a historical perspective, including the 1857–1864 disputes about the constitutional reforms (chapter 1) and the 1956–1959 NCA debates after independence (chapter 2). Islamist movements inserted themselves into this long-standing debate, and challenged Bourguiba's authoritarian synthesis, by borrowing from past conservative ideological repertoires about the role of Islam in governance. Like the Egyptian Muslim Brothers, examined in the next chapter (and who inspired them in part), Tunisian Islamists' main contribution, when they sprung onto the political scene in the 1960s and 1970s, consisted of mobilizing and organizing their constituency around an earlier conservative project: the expansion of the role of Islam in governance. Third, there has been much speculation in the academic literature and other forums about the compatibility of Islam and democracy[2] as well as debates about whether a modern state can truly be a Muslim state. Hallaq (2013) argues that modern states cannot be authentic Muslim states, notably because they are devoid of the moral content essential to Islamic governance. On the other side, Mezghani (2011) argues that modern states in the Muslim world are "incomplete," because their legal systems rely too much on Islamic principles. He too concludes that a modern and Muslim state is impossible. In this chapter, I do not evaluate the Islamic authenticity of the solutions the constituents provided, although I do underline the tensions and contradictions they grappled with while making the two imperatives—state

a review, see Schwedler (2011). Interestingly, few studies, if any, explore the potential "moderation" of non-Islamist parties under democratic conditions.

2. E.g., Hefner (2000), in a study of Islam in Indonesia's democratization process in response to skeptics like Samuel Huntington. This type of inquiry is not limited to Muslim states. For instance, Gavison (2011) argues that a Jewish and democratic state is feasible, coherent, and justifiable.

custodianship of Islam as the preferred religion and democracy—coexist, a task they claim they have realized.

The main sources I use are videos and transcripts of the NCA debates that took place from February 3, 2012, when the NCA started its deliberations, until the NCA's adoption of the new constitution on January 26, 2014.[3] I also use some documents and data related to the October 2011 election of the NCA as well as interviews I conducted during this period with political actors in Tunis.

Section 1 describes Tunisia's political context going into the democratic transition and the main political actors in the 2012–2014 NCA. Section 2 discusses the main points of agreement in the NCA and the main points of disagreement on nonreligious issues. Section 3 analyzes the Islamist al-Nahdha Party's renunciation of sharia in the Constitution. Section 4 delineates the competing conceptions of the role of Islam in governance envisioned by the constituents as well as the divide within al-Nahdha on this issue. Section 5 highlights how the constituents reached an innovative compromise that, far from conceding on the substance of their disagreements, organized their conflict going forward.

1. The 2011 Election of the National Constituent Assembly: Power-Sharing between Islamists and Non-Islamists

The drafting of a new constitution in a democratic context gave Tunisians the opportunity to express themselves fully and publicly. Under the authoritarian regimes of Bourguiba (1956–1987) and Ben Ali (1987–2011), there were few spaces for debates about governance. The lid that Bourguiba had put at independence on the disputes about the role of Islam in governance (the prohibition of the "mixing of religion and politics," combined with a strong but thin custodianship of Islam) remained firmly in place.[4] With democracy, religion fully entered the political debate.

3. These debates are available in video format on the NCA website at http://www.anc.tn/site/main/AR/docs/vid_debat.jsp?id=03022012&t=t and transcripts were published in *JORT*. When I started my research, only a small number of transcripts had been published, and most of the debates I used were available only in video form.

4. One rare, and short-lived, public discussion took place with the various petitions published in the press in 1988 shortly after Ben Ali's takeover. They discussed separation (or lack thereof) between Islam and "politics," and are reproduced in Al-Ma'rūfi (1988). They foreshadow some of the lines of disagreements in the 2012–2014 NCA. A broad spectrum of political activists and

The Pre–Arab Spring Political Landscape: A Co-Opted or Illegal Political Opposition

Before 2011, only sham elections took place, and political parties were either co-opted by the regime (assigned a few seats in the legislature as well as financial and other resources) or repressed and living on the margins of political life.[5] Opposition parties, legal and illegal, remained small and unable to participate in politics fully given the strong constraints imposed on them. Most of them were situated on the left or the center-left, ranging from communists and various shades of pan-Arabists to social democrats. They were generally progressive and developmentalist in their understandings of the role of Islam in governance and did not (overtly at least) challenge the synthesis Bourguiba imposed at independence on this issue. As for the Islamic Tendency Movement (founded in 1981, although it had existed informally since the late 1960s), it took the name al-Nahdha Movement (*ḥarakat al-nahḍa*) in 1989 and remained illegal until 2011. Its emergence as an organization of political opposition turned the historical debate on Islam in governance into a broader conflict, violent at times, with the authoritarian regimes of Bourguiba and Ben Ali. This conflict deepened the divide between the proponents of a larger role for Islam in governance (such as the al-Nahdha Movement's supporters) and those opposed to it (such as those in power and part of the opposition). When al-Nahdha became a political party after the fall of Ben Ali in 2011, its protracted conflict with the regime gave way to an open political competition that polarized political parties into two camps.[6]

The Post–Arab Spring Political Landscape: Unprecedented Freedom of Expression

When the democratic transition started in the spring of 2011, a large number of newly created political parties quickly crowded the political landscape, and there were some one hundred parties participating in the electoral process. The main parties, in addition to the newly created Islamist "Party of al-Nahdha

---

intellectuals, from leftists to Islamists, supported a project of "democratic coexistence" and proposed to amend Article 1 of the 1959 Constitution to "Islam is the religion of the state."

5. Braun (2006).

6. As a caveat, the 2012–2014 NCA deliberations did not include Salafi parties, who were not allowed to, or decided not to, compete in the 2011 NCA elections.

Movement" (hereafter al-Nahdha), were the few parties that attempted to reconstitute Ben Ali's RCD,[7] such as al-Moubadara, and the main pre–Arab Spring opposition parties of the left and center-left, whether they had been co-opted by the previous regime or not. In this group, four parties emerged as important political forces competing with al-Nahdha. Two of them were led by longtime defenders of human rights and opponents to Ben Ali's regime who had refused to be co-opted: Moncef Marzouki's center-left Congress for the Republic (CPR)[8] and Mustapha Ben Jaafar's social democratic party Democratic Forum for Labor and Liberties (Ettakattol).[9] A third was a leftist party with old Baathist roots, the Progressive Democratic Party (PDP),[10] and a fourth was the Modernist Democratic Pole (PDM), a coalition of leftist parties such as al-Tajdid, a remnant of the Communist Party, which had been co-opted under Ben Ali.[11] In addition to these parties, an important new force turned out to be al-Aridha al-Chaabiya (The Popular Petition), a coalition of populist electoral lists whose leader had been a member of al-Nahdha until he left the movement in 1992.[12]

7. The RCD (Rassemblement Constitutionnel Démocratique) was created by Ben Ali in 1988 shortly after he took over and was the direct heir of Bourguiba's New Dustūr Party and its various successive incarnations.

8. The CPR, founded by Moncef Marzouki in 2001, had no recognizable ideology except for a critique of authoritarianism. It united opposition activists from different movements, including al-Nahdha. Its platform remained vague and did not evoke religion, although Moncef Marzouki himself made public declarations in favor of the Arab and Muslim identity of Tunisia. See Dodge (2013). Moncef Marzouki was forced into exile in 2001.

9. Mustapha Ben Jaafar, a medical doctor and member of the single labor union UGTT under the previous regime, founded his party in 1994, although it was not legalized until 2002. It is affiliated with the Socialist International. He started his political career as a dissident when he cofounded the Mouvement des Démocrates Sociaux in 1978.

10. The PDP was founded under the name Rassemblement Socialiste Progressiste in 1983 with a Marxist platform by former members of the leftist movement Perspectives-L'ouvrier Tunisien, with the aim of unifying the Tunisian left. See Khalfaoui (2012). It became PDP in 2001 when it removed its reference to socialism. It ran in legislative elections in 1989, 1994, and 1999 but was not allocated any seats. It subsequently boycotted the legislative elections of 2004 and 2009. Its leader Néjib Chabbi participated in hunger strikes to protest the regime in 2005. Contrary to CPR, al-Nahdha, and Ettakattol leaders, Néjib Chabbi accepted a post in the two Mohammed Ghannouchi transitional governments after the fall of Ben Ali.

11. The Tajdid Party harked back to the 1920s. In the 2009 legislative elections, it was allocated two seats. It was the only party co-opted under Ben Ali whose share of seats declined over time (from 2.5 percent in 1994 to 0.9 percent in 2009).

12. Al-Aridha al-Chaabiya's full name was the "Popular Petition for Liberty, Justice, and Development." This coalition of lists was led by al-Hachmi Hamdi, a wealthy businessman who hailed

The electoral campaign was largely dominated by a highly polarized debate between al-Nahdha and al-Aridha al-Chaabiya (referred to as Islamists) and their political adversaries. The latter are commonly called "secularists" in the literature, which is misleading: very few, if any, would call themselves " *'ilmānīyīn*" (secularists), even though some of them were at times so labeled by Islamist activists in inflammatory rhetoric. Moreover, the views of a small minority of intellectuals notwithstanding,[13] these political actors did not argue for the separation of religion and state or for state neutrality: they shared with their Islamist political opponents the view that the state must be the custodian of Islam, the preferred religion.[14] They often called themselves "modernists" (*ḥadīthīyīn*) and "progressives" (*taqaddumiyīn*), but these labels were also claimed by some Islamists. Since among Islamists' adversaries there were liberal progressives influenced by universal human rights principles, such as Ettakatol and CPR—but also illiberal progressives in the mold of the previous authoritarian regime, such as PDM and al-Moubadara—I will favor calling them "non-Islamists" rather than "liberals" in this specific context. Beyond the labels and epithets that political parties were appropriating for themselves or throwing at each other, there was a wide ideological spectrum within each camp, as we will see in our examination of the Assembly's deliberations.

The 2011 National Constituent Assembly Election: Al-Nahdha Wins a Plurality of the Seats

On October 23, 2011, a 217-member Assembly, comprising 61 women and 156 men, was elected. Despite some reported irregularities, the results were widely accepted by public opinion and by international observers, and we can consider this election free and fair.[15] This was a first in Tunisia's history, as electoral

---

from Sidi Bouzid, where the 2011 revolt had originated. He owned a London-based TV channel, al-Mustakilla, which used to broadcast the voices of many opponents to Ben Ali and was accessible via satellite in Tunisia. He ran his campaign from London via his TV channel. For more details about the electoral campaign, see Zeghal (2013b) and Latiri and Zeghal (forthcoming).

13. Notably the position of legal scholar Ali Mezghani in Mezghani (2012).

14. Some Tunisians certainly held the opposite view, but they were largely absent from political competition.

15. See ATIDE, Les élections de l'Assemblée Nationale Constituante ont elles été transparentes et intègres? http://www.atide.org/rapport-preliminaire-les-elections-de-l%E2%80%99assemblee-nationale-constituante-ont%E2%80%90elles-ete-transparentes-et-integres/; MOE UE. *Mission d'observation électorale de l'Union européenne en Tunisie, Rapport final, Election de l'Assemblée*

outcomes were previously determined ex ante by those in power. The Islamist party al-Nahdha won 89 seats (41 percent of the total), of which 41 were won by women. The electoral law enforced gender parity by requiring electoral lists in each district to alternate between men and women, but the vast majority of the lists (93 percent) placed a male candidate in first position. Because al-Nahdha was the only party to win multiple seats in more than two districts (thirty of thirty-three districts), no other party actually came close to gender parity. The center-left party CPR won 29 seats (13 percent of the total), the Islamist coalition of lists Al-Aridha al-Chaabiya (The Popular Petition) won 26 seats (12 percent of the total), and the social democratic party Ettakattol won 20 seats (9 percent of the total). The leftist party PDP, a media darling during the campaign, campaigned on an anti-Islamist platform and saw itself as the main non-Islamist contender. It was comforted in this view by favorable preelection polls[16] but obtained only 16 seats (7 percent of the total). Al-Moubadara (The Initiative), a vestige of the former ruling single-party RCD, obtained 5 seats (2 percent of the total). In addition, the coalition of leftist parties PDM also explicitly campaigned against Islamism on a "modernist" platform but won only 5 seats (2 percent of the total). Overall, these electoral results reflected a clear rejection of the previous authoritarian regime as well as a popular endorsement of al-Nahdha and, to a lesser extent, political opposition parties that had not been previously co-opted by Ben Ali's regime.[17] Thus, the Assembly was fairly evenly split between Islamists and non-Islamists, although the latter were highly fragmented. Importantly, al-Nahdha did not win an absolute majority of seats and was forced to govern in a coalition, which created a divide among non-Islamists about the legitimacy of forming a coalition with them. This was not by chance. The Assembly was elected pursuant to a system of proportional representation with closed lists in one round, using the largest remainder method (also called Hare's method) and with no formal vote threshold. Transitional elites deliberately chose this particular electoral system (among other readily available and more commonly used options): aware of the potential electoral strength of al-Nahdha,

---

Nationale Constituante (2011). http://www.eueom.eu/tunisie2011/rapports; Mourakiboun, http://www.mourakiboun.org/docs/pdf/DP-Mourakiboun-Final.pdf, October 28, 2011; NDI, *Final Report on the Tunisian Constituent Assembly Election*, National Democratic Institute (2012), http://www.ndi.org/node/18588; Carter Center, *Final Report: Observing the Oct. 23, 2011, National Constituent Assembly Elections in Tunisia*, May 24, 2012, http://www.cartercenter.org/news/publications/election_reports.html#tunisia, accessed March 1, 2013.

16. Khalfaoui (2012, 104–105).

17. An electoral sociology of the divide between liberals and conservatives is beyond the scope of this book. For more details, see Latiri and Zeghal (forthcoming).

and afraid of a winner-takes-all scenario, they sought to constrain the likely winner into a coalition and compromise.[18] Had the much more common highest averages Jefferson method (also called D'Hondt method) been used, al-Nahdha would most likely have won a comfortable majority.[19]

After the October 2011 elections, the "Troika," an alliance between al-Nahdha, CPR, and Ettakattol, governed the country from December 14, 2011, to January 9, 2014. In a context of unprecedented freedom of expression, renewal of political elites, and acute economic crisis and social unrest, the issue of the role of Islam in governance, including the role of sharia in legislation, came to the fore in both public discussions and the media, and it took on a life of its own. The Assembly—as well as Tunisian society more broadly—was split into two seemingly irreconcilable camps. On the one hand, Islamists argued that Islam had been muted by more than fifty years of authoritarianism and that it was now time to reassert it as the foundation of governance and legislation. On the other hand, non-Islamists wanted to preserve some, if not all, elements of Habib Bourguiba's authoritarian synthesis about Islam in governance, which they saw as embodying progress and modernity. Some of them advocated for reducing the role of Islam in governance even further. This debate crystallized around several key issues, notably references to Islam and sharia in the constitution, freedom of conscience and expression, and women's rights. Even the governing coalition reflected this divide, with the Islamists (al-Nahdha) opposed to the non-Islamists (CPR and Ettakattol) in the Troika on many issues—although, as we will see, some CPR MPs leaned toward an understanding of the role of Islam in governance close to that espoused by al-Nahdha.

2. The Broad Agreements in the National Constituent Assembly: A Democracy, a Muslim Identity, a "Modern" Islam

The constituents chose not to resort to an experts' draft and instead consulted broadly with civil society and with Tunisian and international legal and political experts, giving MPs and civil society ownership of the process and thus of its outcome. An al-Nahdha MP pointed out with satisfaction that, in contrast with

18. See Latiri and Zeghal (forthcoming).

19. See the simulations performed by Amin Khechin in 2012: al-Nahdha would have won 69.1 percent of the seats, assuming that voters and parties would not have changed strategy as a result (a plausible assumption in this first election). https://aminkh2.wordpress.com/2012/10/22/et-si-le-23-octobre-2011-on-avait-vote-avec-un-autre-mode-de-scrutin/, accessed June 30, 2017.

earlier constitutional episodes, the new constitution was "not written in the corridors of foreign embassies."[20] This was certainly inaccurate history, as we saw in previous chapters, but it captured the desire to claim popular legitimacy for the new constitution, and according to Mustapha Ben Jaafar, president of the Assembly and leader of Ettakattol, it made compromises more acceptable to all parties.[21] However, these broad consultations had the disadvantage of lengthening the drafting process. Committees were set up to draft specific chapters of the constitution. Their composition mirrored the Assembly's, featuring an Islamist plurality in each committee. This produced tensions and delays. Recognizing that the constitution could only be drafted by finding sufficient common ground, a consensus committee equally representing all political sensibilities in the Assembly was formed in 2013, paving the way for an agreement.

Polarization, Theatrics, and Sense of Fatigue: "Each camp fears for its identity"

Although an agreement was eventually reached, divisions, particularly over the role of Islam, ran deep in the Assembly, reflecting the polarization of society.[22] As an MP acknowledged, "Each camp fears for its identity."[23] The political events taking place in Tunisia and elsewhere in the Middle East at that time influenced the debates, particularly the assassination of two leftist members of the Tunisian political opposition in 2013, allegedly by radical Islamists, and the emergence of Salafi groups that advocated for more Islamization.[24] The news of the Egyptian military coup against the Muslim Brothers' government in the summer of 2013 also pressured the constituents to reach an agreement and to hasten the drafting process. The fear of an "Egyptian scenario," reminiscent of the January 1992 coup by the Algerian military against the imminent electoral victory of the Islamic Salvation Front, was palpable in the Assembly and prompted its members to find a way forward on the most contentious issues, particularly those involving Islam. It was not easy, however. There were

20. Nabiha Torjmane, NCA session of July 11, 2013.

21. NCA session of July 1, 2013.

22. Y. Ben Achour (2016, 316–326).

23. Al-Nahdha MP Nabiha Torjmane, NCA session of July 11, 2013.

24. Chokri Belaid, leader of the Democratic Patriot Movement (left, 1 NCA seat) was assassinated on February 6, 2013. Mohamed Brahmi, a member of the NCA and leader of the People's Movement (Arab nationalist left, 2 NCA seats) was assassinated on July 25, 2013. The Ministry of the Interior blamed radical Salafi groups for both assassinations.

numerous vehement disputes, and many sessions were interrupted and adjourned. For instance, a leftist MP accused al-Nahdha of "monopolizing" Islam and accused the president of the Assembly of giving preference to Islamists during the debates.[25] An al-Nahdha MP addressed the opposition harshly (before the president of the Assembly interrupted her for being too polemical): "Say it honestly! You refuse Islam! Say it with courage! Say that you want to uproot Islam from society and that you want to remove it from all laws to build a secular state [*dawla lā 'ikīya*]! . . . Aren't the MPs ashamed?"[26] In late July 2013, tensions reached their apex. After the assassination of the leftist MP Mohamed Brahmi and while the repression against the Muslim Brothers was raging in Egypt, a group of about seventy opposition MPs suspended their participation in the Assembly and asked for the removal of the Troika government. There were also tense moments during which MPs traded insults, and in at least one instance the national hymn was sung by non-Islamists while Islamists responded by reciting the Qur'an.[27] These theatrics were encouraged by the debates' transmission on live, public television, which made the Assembly's sessions perfect opportunities for MPs to stage political spectacles and publicize their political stances.[28] As some MPs I interviewed told me, the drafting committees discussions, which were held behind closed doors, were more conciliatory than the Assembly's public debates.[29] That said, some MPs eventually expressed a sense of fatigue about the discussions about religion, which they thought had become fruitless, if not downright absurd. A center-left CPR MP argued, "If we accept that in Islam there is no religious state [a statement made many times by both Islamist and non-Islamist MPs], then the Islamists versus secularists conflict is sterile. This is a struggle that threatens to divide our society."[30] In the same vein, a leftist PDP MP argued that when the Tunisian people rose for their revolution, they did not ask themselves "Who are we?" In his view, "too much effort was wasted in sterile discussions about identity.

25. Mongi Rahoui, NCA session of January 3, 2014. Mongi Rahoui was the only MP elected on the list of the Movement of the Democrats Patriots, which was led by Chokri Belaid, who was assassinated on February 6, 2013.

26. Mounira Omri, NCA session of July 8, 2013.

27. NCA session of July 1, 2013.

28. The Tunisian NGO Albawsala also tweeted the debates and collected and published information about the activities of the NCA on its website; see http://www.marsad.tn/.

29. Fieldwork notes, Tunis, June 2012.

30. Hasna Marsit, NCA session of July 6, 2013.

Since the Tunisian people are attached to their Islamic identity and history, these discussions are irrelevant."[31]

The Main Points of Agreement in the National Constituent Assembly

To be sure, Islam was far from being the sole point of contention debated in the Assembly. The main divisions on nonreligious issues revolved around whether the regime should be presidential or parliamentary, with al-Nahdha leaning toward a parliamentary system as a shield against a presidential takeover and as a way to preserve the Islamist party's presence and weight in future legislatures. Some non-Islamists leaned toward a mixed system or a strong presidential system. There were also divisions over the extent of state welfare provisions. Although no MP argued against state intervention in the economy or against state welfare provisions, the Islamist Popular Petition and the parties on the far left argued for more economic redistribution. The Assembly was also divided on Tunisia's stance toward the state of Israel. Arab nationalists and Islamists were particularly vocal in wanting to constitutionalize a prohibition on the normalization of Tunisia's relations with Israel. However, the debates also revealed several important points of agreement: breaking with the authoritarian past, building an electoral democracy based on the separation of powers and the independence of justice, allowing for political alternation, and establishing a constitutional court. For the constituents, the new democratic regime should guarantee individual rights and freedoms—although, as we will see, the issues of freedom *of* religion and freedom *from* religion proved highly contentious.

When it came to Islam in the constitution, the constituents all spoke of Islam as shaping "the identity [*huwīya*] of Tunisia" and the "personality" (*shakhṣīya*) of its people, a concept that we encountered earlier in the context of constitutional demands during French occupation. The constituents all associated—or equated—the values of Islam (*qiyam al-Islām*) with universal values (*qiyam kawnīya*) and human rights (*ḥuqūq al-insān*), two concepts that were championed by the Tunisian Human Rights League (established in 1977) and appropriated by the authoritarian regimes of Bourguiba and Ben Ali in an enterprise of democratic window dressing. The kind of Islam envisioned by all was a "modern Islam"—or, phrased differently, an Islam compatible with modernity. Bourguiba and Ben Ali had invoked the notion of modernity (*ḥadātha*) to describe their

31. Mohamed Gahbich, NCA session of July 11, 2013. The center-left CPR MP Béchir Nafsi made a similar statement during the same session.

progressive and developmentalist projects and to justify their repression of al-Nahdha. During that time, it was also used by the non-Islamist political opposition, which advocated for democracy. After the fall of Ben Ali, Islamists returned to that same concept, refusing characterization as "antimodern." Thus, almost all MPs agreed that Islam had to be "modern" in one sense or another. For instance, Néjib Chabbi, leader of the leftist PDP, and longtime opponent of the authoritarian regime, spoke of Islam as a religion "of this age [ʿ*aṣrī*]," consciously avoiding speaking of "modernity" (*ḥadātha*). For him, Islam was to be present in the constitution as a civilization in dialogue with others and as an identity but also as a set of values. He also argued, in line with Bourguiba's synthesis, that women's legal rights could not be altered—although some might think that they contradicted a "sacred heritage" (*mawrūth muqaddas*).[32] Al-Nahdha's MPs also insisted that the constitution speak of a "modern Islam," for instance claiming, "These battles about the constitution are imaginary [*wahmīya*]. We heard those who spoke about their fear for Islam, and we heard those who fear for modernity [*ḥadātha*]. I say that there are no contradictions between the spirit of Islam and the spirit of modernity."[33] Sadok Chourou, a preeminent member of al-Nahdha, had initially advocated for sharia as a "source for the codification of the law";[34] a year later, he underlined the convergence of Islam and "modernity" when he accepted Article 1 in its 1959 formulation without sharia. However, he made it explicit that he interpreted Article 1 as meaning that the state "derived its principles from Islam."[35] Therefore, although there was broad agreement on a "modern Islam," there was a diversity of interpretations as to what that meant. That said, there were a few critiques of the notion of "modernity," and especially its instrumentalization by Bourguiba's and Ben Ali's regimes against the Islamist opposition. For instance, a center-left CPR MP spoke of the 1959 Constitution as having established "a decor of modernity."[36] In contrast with the leftist PDP leader Néjib Chabbi, he disagreed with the image of a Tunisia situated "at the crossroad of civilizations," a formula he described as having been "imposed by the tyranny [of the previous regime]." He added, "Our constitution must start with our identity, our Arab and Islamic identity."[37] Regarding the issue of Islam in

32. NCA session of July 11, 2013.
33. Ahmed Mechergui, NCA session of July 11, 2013.
34. NCA session of October 24, 2012.
35. NCA session of January 4, 2014.
36. Abdelraouf Ayadi, NCA morning session of February 28, 2013.
37. NCA morning session of February 28, 2013.

governance, Islamists and non-Islamists agreed that the state should not be theocratic—that is, not be administered by religious specialists—and thus should be explicitly defined as a civil state. However, no MP clearly argued for the separation of Islam and the state or for state neutrality.[38] This distinction was most clearly articulated by an al-Nahdha MP who explained that she agreed with the notion of a "civil state" (*dawla madanīya*) because "the civil character of the state [*madanīyat al-dawla*] does not mean that religion is separate from the state."[39]

3. Renouncing Sharia in the Constitution

As the drafting committees began their work on the new constitution in early 2012, a public debate that had started a year earlier about sharia in the constitution gained traction. The Salafi currents—organized after January 14, 2011,[40] but excluded from the 2011 elections—as well as the conservative wing of al-Nahdha asked that sharia be mentioned as "a" or "the" source of legislation in the constitution, and demonstrated in front of the Assembly in spring 2012. In addition, as in most other Arab countries, several opinion polls showed that the overwhelming majority of Tunisian men and women alike (almost 80 percent) said that they wanted legislation to be partially or wholly founded on sharia.[41]

The Debates on Sharia as a/the "Source of Legislation"

On February 28, 2012, political parties, coalitions, and independent MPs presented their conceptions of the future constitution of Tunisia, providing a window into their visions for the role of Islam in governance. While the expositions of each party revealed a broad agreement on the Muslim identity of Tunisia and on the

38. MP Salaheddine Zahaf (*Voix de l'Indépendant*, 1 seat) argued in the July 2, 2013, NCA session that Tunisians had revolted for temporal and not for ideological or religious aims and that this required a "clear separation [*faṣl*] between religion and state." However, he contradicted himself in the same session when, criticizing Article 6 of the draft under examination, he rejected the principle of a state "custodian of Islam" and argued that the state should be the custodian of "all religions."

39. Soulaf Ksantini, NCA session of July 6, 2013.

40. See Nwīra (2012).

41. For instance, Sigma Conseil, Les Tunisiens, la politique et la religion, poll of May 3–4, 2012, and Dalia Mogahed, Arab Women and Men See Eye to Eye on Religion's Role in Law, June 25, 2012, http://www.gallup.com/poll/155324/Arab-Women-Men-Eye-Eye-Religion-Role-Law.aspx.

state's custodianship of Islam as the preferred religion, they showed a clear divide between Islamists and non-Islamists on the specifics of this custodianship and, in particular, on the role of sharia (or of Islam) in legislation. MP Sahbi Atiq spoke for al-Nahdha. This graduate of the Zaytuna University, born in 1959, presented al-Nahdha's ideal state as an "Islamic" and "civil" state, in which sharia would play a central role. He did not specify, however, what the institutional workings of such a state would be. In a style reminiscent of the Muslim Brothers' ideology (see chapter 4), he invoked Islam as "a doctrine [*ʿaqīda*], an act of worship [*ʿibāda*], a morality [*khuluq*], a complete sharia [*sharīʿa mutakāmila*], and a way of life [*manhaj li-l-ḥayāh*]." He added, "Politics, as we conceive of it, is an activity situated at the most elevated level of worship, and religion cannot be a private affair in the internal conscience of the individual person [*shaʾn khāṣṣ fī al-ḍamīr al-dākhilī li-l-insān*]." For him, Islam needed to be present "in the structures of the state, and not be a mere slogan." He argued that "Islam relates to individuals' lives, to family affairs, to society's rules, to the foundations of the state, and to relations with the world."[42] He also made a reference to the seventh-century Charter of Medina as the first "constitution" of Islam. Overall, he presented a more comprehensive conception of Islam in governance than could be found in al-Nahdha's October 2011 electoral platform, which did not include references to sharia, perhaps to avoid frightening parts of the electorate and derailing the transition. Although he did not explicitly argue in favor of mentioning sharia as a/the source of legislation in the future constitution, his argument could easily be interpreted in such a way. Representatives from the (Islamist) Popular Petition articulated a similar view and envisioned a state and a legal system founded on "Islam." One of its MPs, Mohamed Hamdi, proposed to make "Islam the main source of legislation" and presented a vision of the political system in al-Nahdha's vein but with a more pronounced focus on social justice and economic redistribution. He argued for the use of the word "Islam" rather than sharia, "because Islam's meaning is broader than . . . the meaning commonly given to the term sharia."[43]

In contrast with Islamists, non-Islamists either rejected explicitly mentioning sharia in the constitution or kept silent on this issue. The social democratic Ettakattol MP Mouldi Riahi rejected including sharia in the constitution as "the" or "a" source of legislation because, he argued, the content, sources, and limits of sharia were subject to too many different interpretations, which could threaten the unity of the nation and its religious integrity. In his view, it was

42. NCA morning session of February 28, 2012.
43. NCA afternoon session of February 28, 2012.

sufficient to use Article 1 of the 1959 Constitution and to know that Tunisian legislation had been founded in part on sharia, such as the Personal Status Code. On the other hand, the leftist PDM MP Fadhel Moussa, a former dean of the University of Tunis Law School, did not address the issue of sharia and only spoke of the Islamic and Arab identity of the country. Rather than invoking an early Islamic constitutional genealogy, as al-Nahdha did, he anchored the constitutional history of Tunisia in the 1857–1861 legal reforms. In contrast, the center-left CPR MP Abdelraouf Ayadi criticized the 1857 Security Pact as having been drafted "under foreign pressures," a common trope also employed by some Islamists. He insisted on the Islamic and Arab identity of the nation without invoking sharia and, to justify this stance, underlined that the constitution had to be founded on general principles rather than on overly specific ones.[44]

Al-Nahdha's Renunciation of Sharia in the Constitution

In late March 2012, contradicting the spirit of al-Nahdha MP Sahbi Atiq's declarations, al-Nahdha's president, Rached Ghannouchi, announced that his party would not ask for a reference to sharia in the new constitution. This decision came after a vote in the Founding Committee of the party. According to Rached Ghannouchi, thirteen committee members voted to keep the reference to sharia, and fifty-three against it.[45] Before this vote, an al-Nahdha preamble draft that included sharia as "one of the main sources of legislation" had been circulated.[46] Al-Nahdha's renunciation of sharia in the constitution was openly opposed by some of its preeminent members. On social networks such as Facebook and in street demonstrations, Islamist activists also insisted that sharia be the source of legislation and that the constitution inscribe this principle as a perennial rule, as in many Muslim-majority countries (see table 8).

What drove al-Nahdha leaders' renunciation of sharia in the constitution, going against some of its preeminent members and public opinion? First, al-Nahdha did not win an outright majority of the Assembly's seats, and its two center-left coalition partners were not in favor of mentioning sharia in the constitution. This electoral outcome, and therefore the necessity for the eventual

44. NCA morning session of February 28, 2012.

45. *Al-Sharq al-Awsaṭ*, March 29, 2012, no. 12175.

46. Al-Nahdha Party, Draft of a Constitution, Tunis, n.d. In this draft, Article 1 remained the same as in the 1959 Constitution. Article 10 read: "The Islamic sharia is one of the main sources of legislation [*al-sharīʿa al-Islāmīya maṣdar asāsī min maṣādir al-tashrīʿ*]."

winner to compromise as part of a coalition, had been engineered ex ante through the new electoral law crafted after Ben Ali's fall, as we saw. Second, al-Nahdha faced resistance from a great number of adversaries, not only in the political arena but also in civil society, such as organizations for the defense of women's and human rights and the UGTT labor union (Union Générale Tunisienne du Travail), which was staunchly opposed to al-Nahdha. It often organized strikes and demonstrations against the Troika government, and there were several episodes of violent conflicts in the street between rival political constituencies.[47] Al-Nahdha thus pragmatically aimed to minimize tensions in a period of political transition and social instability, especially considering the high unemployment rate.[48] However, this came at the cost of producing divisions between the party's more liberal and pragmatic wing on the one hand and its more conservative and radical wing on the other. Third, al-Nahdha's leadership recognized that they could implement the kind of Muslim state they had in mind without mentioning sharia in the constitution, using (like their political adversaries) Bourguiba's authoritarian synthesis embodied in the quasi-constitutional 1956 Personal Status Code (PSC) and in Article 1 of the 1959 Constitution.[49] Immediately after returning from exile, al-Nahdha's leader Rached Ghannouchi had declared that his party would not call for any modifications to the PSC, although he remained very critical of Bourguiba's progressive policies regarding women's rights,[50] and al-Nahdha firmly resisted

47. E.g., the mob attack against the Nessma Television offices on October 9, 2011, and the violent street conflict between UGTT labor union members and the Leagues of Protection of the Revolution on December 4, 2012.

48. In the first quarter of 2012, official unemployment reached 18.1 percent nationally and was as high as 28.4 percent in the interior regions, according to the National Institute of Statistics of Tunisia. See Institut National de la Statistique (2012). For more realistic (much higher) estimates, see Latiri and Zeghal (forthcoming).

49. As an example of how non-Islamists also kept to Bourguiba's synthesis, in the spring of 2014, three months after the proclamation of the 2014 Constitution and two months after the resignation of the Troika government, the non-Islamist-led Tunisian Government notified the secretary-general of the United Nations of its decision to remove Tunisia's reservations to the principles of the Convention on the Elimination of All Forms of Discrimination against Women (CEDAW), but with a declaration that "it shall not take any organizational or legislative decision in conformity with the requirements of this Convention where such a decision would conflict with the provisions of Chapter I [Articles 1 to 20] of the Tunisian Constitution," and hence with the establishment clause in Article 1.

50. NCA discussions about gender did not seem as prominent as debates about sharia or about freedom of conscience. One exception was the vehement August 2012 debate that set

initiatives to remove Islamic stipulations about inheritance in the PSC. It remained unchanged and in the following years continued to play a central role as an instrument for mobilizing conservative and liberal constituencies.[51] Moreover, despite the vigorous disagreements about how to interpret Article 1 of the Constitution and about whether and how to modify it, it also remained unchanged from its 1959 formulation, as we will see.

4. Disagreements about the Thickness and Strength of the State Custodianship of Islam

Although there was no disagreement over the principle of the state's custodianship of Islam as the preferred religion, the most significant and visible contentions in the Assembly revolved around its thickness and strength and the degree to which religion and *politics* should be allowed to mix. Given the constitutional nature of their deliberations, MPs did not debate the munificence of the state custodianship of Islam (the topic of chapter 5). On the issue of thickness—that is, the degree to which Islamic principles constrain governance—the liberal Afek Party MP Rym Mahjoub criticized al-Nahdha's vision of the state and described it as a "doctrinal state" (*dawla ʿaqāʾidīya*).[52] Indeed, as we saw, the al-Nahdha

---

supporters of a clause guaranteeing gender equality against those who wanted to invoke "complementarity" between men and women in the Constitution. The committee in charge of drafting Chapter I of the Constitution on rights and freedoms proposed, in a project dated August 3, 2012, an article that read, "The state guarantees the protection of women's rights and defends women's gains [*makāsibahā*] as a true partner [*sharīk*] of men in the building of the nation. Their roles in the family are complementary [*yatakāmil dawruhumā dākhil al-usra*]." The concept of complementarity was rejected, and Article 20 of the Constitution read, "Men and women citizens have equal rights and duties. They are equal before the law without any discrimination." The NCA passed this article on January 6, 2014 (159 in favor, 7 against, 3 abstentions); 77 al-Nahdha MPs (out of 87 present) voted in favor of this formulation, and only one al-Nahdha MP voted against. https://majles.marsad.tn/vote/52ced46d12bdaa09ac3f3a7b, accessed May 27, 2018.

51. For instance, in August 2017, the Committee for Individual Liberties and Equality (COLIBE) was formed by President Béji Caid Essebsi to reflect on issues such as equality in inheritance, the death penalty, and the decriminalization of homosexuality. The COLIBE published its report in June 2018, recommending in particular citizens be free to choose an Islamic system of inheritance or one based on equality, which is reminiscent of the proposal of the French New Dustūr Federation in 1955 (see chapter 2).

52. NCA session of July 8, 2013. This was in response to the al-Nahdha MP Sana Mirsni's argument that proposed (and later dropped) Article 141 ("No constitutional amendment can

MP Sahbi Atiq had presented Islam as "a doctrine, a worship, a morality, a complete sharia, and a way of life."[53] A few years earlier, he had advocated for "the liberation of religion from the state's control [*taḥrīr al-dīn min sayṭarat al-dawla*] and not the liberation of the state from religion [*taḥrīr al-dawla min al-dīn*]."[54] The issue of the strength of the state custodianship of Islam—that is, the degree to which the state constrains Islam—was shaped by more than fifty years of authoritarianism and repressive enforcement of Bourguiba's synthesis that curtailed Islamists' freedom *of* religion and many non-Islamists' freedom *from* religion. Islamists and non-Islamists therefore sought guarantees about their respective ways of life.[55] As for the degree to which religion and *politics* should be allowed to mix, Islamists advocated for the separation of religion and politics when criticizing how non-Islamists might govern but in favor of mixing religion and politics when it came to bringing religion into political competition and bringing politics into mosques, which non-Islamists often opposed. On the rejection of separation of religion and *state*, however, there was broad agreement. Common to the many varieties of state custodianships of Islam as the preferred religion discussed in the Assembly was the state's duty to provide a minimum level of support and protection of Islam, the Muslim community, and its institutions, which included a religious infrastructure for Muslims to live their lives as Muslims, as already envisioned by the 1956–1959 NCA (see chapter 2).

The State Custodianships of Islam Envisioned in the National Constituent Assembly

The social democratic Ettakattol Party advocated for a thin and weak state custodianship of Islam—that is, for a merely bureaucratic, identity-related, and nonlegislative one, in which the state would provide a religious infrastructure and manage religious institutions without imposing its own interpretation of Islam, while ensuring religious freedom and keeping political activism and religion as separate as possible. Although they saw Islam as having religious

harm [*nāla min*] Islam as the religion of the state") "represented the spirit and the philosophy of the constitution." The social democratic Ettakattol MP Salma Mabrouk also argued in the same session that this article threatened women's rights.

53. NCA session of February 28, 2012.

54. *Al-Mawqif*, December 18, 2009, 5.

55. On Islamists' and non-Islamists' ways of life, see Zeghal (2013b).

and moral importance, for Ettakattol's MPs Islam was neither a source of legislation nor a philosophy at the foundation of governance. A young member of Ettakattol's leadership told me, "Article 1 does not mean much more than what it says. Whoever invented it was a genius. But it is out of the question that there be any article on sharia being a source of legislation."[56] In other words, the very idea of sharia was frightening for Ettakattol's leadership, whereas the broader notion of "Islam" was not, because it referred to a collective identity and to a set of shared values rather than to specific legal prescriptions. In the February 28, 2012 Assembly session during which each party presented its conception of the future constitution, Ettakattol's general position was voiced by MP Mouldi Riahi, a high school teacher who held a master's degree in Islamic philosophy from the University of Tunis. For him, Islam was "the source of [Tunisians'] unity"; represented "the identity of the people," which interacted "with the universal values [*qiyam kawnīya*] described in the Universal Declaration of Human Rights"; and needed to be kept away from "doctrinal contentions and from all political instrumentalizations." He underlined that the Tunisian Republic needed to be defined as "civil," that it should not bear any resemblance to "republics that call themselves "Islamic republics," and that it should not be a military republic either. However, in his view, the state needed to protect the people's identity, and he did not question the state's management of religious institutions. In fact, he also emphasized that the state should enforce the political neutrality of places of worship and prohibit the use of religion in political activities. Yet he argued against a state monopoly on religion and religious interpretations: for him, there was a risk that this monopoly might take the form of a "rigid and extremist reading of our religion," with the state "meddling with coercive methods in the private lives of citizens" and thereby threatening to "harm their rights and freedoms." Here, he seemed to refer to "Islamic republics." On the other hand, he also argued that this monopoly might take the shape of an authoritarian "interpretation of modernity, which could lead to the elimination [*ilghā'*] of religion from public life in coercive ways," a description that seemed to refer to Bourguiba's and Ben Ali's regimes. He also categorically opposed the introduction of sharia in Article 1, arguing that sharia had many interpretations, that Tunisians would be divided on its legal implementation, and that, in any event, they had "based all [their] legislation on Article 1 since independence" in accordance with the values derived from the Qur'an and the hadith.[57] Everything considered,

56. Interview with a member of Ettakattol, Tunis, June 18, 2011.

57. NCA morning session of February 28, 2012.

Ettakattol argued for leaving Article 1 unchanged from its 1959 formulation. The party shared with Bourguiba's authoritarian synthesis a thin conception of the state's custodianship of Islam, as well as a condemnation of the mixing of religion and politics, but advocated for a weak (i.e., noncoercive) version of this custodianship. That said, as thin and weak as this conception was, it was an ideal, and we cannot presume that in actual government practice Ettakattol might not seek to constrain Islam or be constrained by it.

Within the opposition to the Troika, some non-Islamist parties advocated for a thin and strong state custodianship of Islam that would be bureaucratic and identity-related and that would operate as a tool for the management and control of Islam. For instance, for MP Samir Taïeb, a member of the Political Bureau of the Tajdid Party (formerly the Communist Party) in the PDM coalition, the state had to manage and regulate religious institutions in a way that would explicitly restrict the influence of Islamists and that would ban the mixing of religion and politics. When I met with him in the summer of 2012 at the Assembly, he told me, "We are against secularism defined the French way. We are against separation between religion and state. The state cannot abandon the regulation of mosques. These mosques would fall into the hands of Islamists. If we did the same with education, we would have the Taliban. However, we want to separate religion and politics. . . . One can refer to religion in a political platform but should not say that this or that verse of the Qur'an prescribes this or that behavior."[58] Therefore, although he firmly argued against separating Islam and the state, he advocated for keeping Islam out of "politics," a pervasive trope of authoritarian Middle Eastern regimes, including Bourguiba's and Ben Ali's. In these contexts, this is often meant to exclude political opposition, such as activists who advocate for a larger role of Islam in governance, but also (as we will see in chapter 4) to exclude religious minorities who might be seen as having political ambitions that threaten the Muslim character of the state.

On the other hand, Islamists advocated for a thick state custodianship of Islam.[59] The al-Nahdha MP Sadok Chourou provided the following interpretation of Article 1: "Islam legislates all aspects of life and guarantees justice and dignity."[60] He added that Islam limits freedoms in order to prevent obscenity

58. Interview with Samir Taïeb, NCA, Le Bardo, June 15, 2012.

59. As did the al-Moubadara (an offspring of the single-party RCD formerly in power) MP Mouna Ben Nasr. She argued that civil servants should conform to Islam by respecting the prayer schedule and argued against freedom of conscience. NCA session of January 4, 2014.

60. NCA session of July 6, 2013.

(*fāḥisha*) and apostasy (*khurūj ʿan al-dīn*). He argued that the sovereignty of the people derived from the sovereignty of God and that "our highest constitution is the Qur'an." He urged that the sovereignty of God be inscribed in the constitution, as in Canada, asking "Are we less Muslim than they are?"[61] Although some of them did argue for restricting their political opponents' individual freedoms, Islamists did not explicitly advocate that the state constrain Islam and religious institutions, as envisioned by the leftist PDM MP Samir Taïeb. However, it is clear that they would approve of a strong state custodianship of Islam if (and only if) the state abided by an Islamic philosophy of governance. We have seen earlier how al-Nahdha MP Sahbi Atiq argued for Islam playing an integral role in the state. He also argued that legislation should not contradict the certainties contained in the Qur'an and the Sunna. To sustain his argument, he invoked freedom of religion and argued that "a democratic state does not have the right to meddle in people's lives, impose ways of life, doctrines, or tastes [*anmāṭ al-ḥayāh, ʿaqāʾid wa-adhwāq*]."[62] This conception of a state that should remain neutral with regard to ways of life, doctrines, and tastes converged with social democratic Ettakattol's conception of a thin state custodianship of Islam, and was in fact shaped by al-Nahdha's and the center-left's shared fight against authoritarianism before the Arab Spring (notably in the 2005 "October 18 Movement").[63] However, it was strikingly at odds with his own argument in favor of a "doctrinal state." Sahbi Atiq did not seem to be aware of this contradiction, in all likelihood because by "the meddling of the state" in people's lives he meant al-Nahdha's repression under Bourguiba and Ben Ali in the context of a strong but thin state custodianship

61. The Canadian Charter of Rights and Freedoms begins, "Whereas Canada is founded upon principles that recognize the supremacy of God and the rule of law."

62. NCA session of February 28, 2012.

63. The 2005 "October 18 Movement" members debated the issue of religion and state, foreshadowing the 2012–2014 NCA divides. Their common position stated, "A democratic state must award a special place to Islam, because it is the religion of the majority of the people, without monopolizing or instrumentalizing Islam, and must guarantee the rights of all beliefs and convictions, and the freedom of religious practice." It did not specify what this "special place" would be but spoke of a "creative interaction" between Islam and individual human rights. Sahbi Atiq explicitly dissented from the common position at the time: although he similarly condemned the excessive strength of the authoritarian state's custodianship of Islam, he also condemned the vagueness of the "special place" accorded to Islam in the common position, and he defended a thicker role for Islam as "the religion of the state" and as a source of legislation. *Al-Mawqif*, December 18, 2009, 5.

of Islam. It must be that, in his view, a state constrained by Islam could not be construed as "meddling" in individuals' lives since, in that case, they would (or ought to) adhere to the state's religious doctrine.

Al-Nahdha's Compromise: Implementing a Thick State Custodianship of Islam without Constitutionalizing Sharia

Sahbi Atiq represented a conservative current within al-Nahdha that elicited strong reactions from non-Islamists in the 2012–2014 NCA. For instance, in reference to the al-Nahdha MP Sadok Chourou's call, during the January 23, 2012 session, for the implementation of Islamic *ḥudūd* (corporal punishments) against street demonstrators, a social democratic Ettakattol MP argued, "It is not acceptable that under the roof of this assembly there be calls to cut hands and legs. Tunisia must not be the country of the Taliban!"[64] To defuse this tension, some al-Nahdha MPs often used the terms "*maqāṣid al-sharīʿa*" to signal that they were not intent on implementing the specific legal rules of sharia, particularly the *ḥudūd* penalties, but rather on implementing "sharia's purposes." To reassure their political opponents, they argued that by sharia they meant the spirit of Islamic law, rather than its letter. However, the al-Nahdha MP Abdelmajid Najar vocally condemned his party's decision to renounce sharia in the constitution and to keep to the spirit rather than the letter of Islamic law. He argued that sharia was not a set of "purposes" but rather "a set of rules" and he criticized his own party for contradicting one of the central tenets of its ideology.[65] The (Islamist) Popular Petition MP Skander Bouallegui, on the other hand, argued for including "Islam as source of the law" in the constitution without invoking sharia.[66] Some sessions later, he stated that in his view Islam was already the source of "99 percent of the laws" in Tunisia.[67] Later, during the January 4, 2014, session, when Article 1 was discussed for the final vote, the Popular Petition continued to defend this position, whereas al-Nahdha had already agreed to renounce the mention of sharia. Even the most conservative al-Nahdha MPs who had explicitly argued in favor of sharia as the source of legislation in the constitution—such as Habib Ellouze and Sadok Chourou—voted for Article 1 in its 1959

64. Ali Bechrifa, NCA session of July 8, 2013.

65. NCA session of January 3, 2014.

66. NCA session of February 28, 2012. In the same session, another group argued in favor of "the Qur'an and the Sunna" as a main source of law.

67. NCA session of July 11, 2013.

formulation.[68] This was a political compromise, not only between Islamists and their political opponents but also within al-Nahdha. Indeed, the view that Islam was an integral set of rules to be implemented in all domains of life was not shared by all members of al-Nahdha's leadership. Moreover, it became clear within al-Nahdha that implementing a thicker state custodianship of Islam did not require constitutionalizing sharia, and that Article 1 in its 1959 formulation was sufficient to achieve this goal. Sana Haddad—a female MP for al-Nahdha and member of the Preamble Committee[69] who was also a lawyer with her own practice and a doctoral student in private law—explained to the Assembly her party's compromise on sharia.[70] She interpreted Article 1 as meaning that Islam was the religion "of the state." This, she added, did not make the state a "religious state": "In our Committee, we have defined the civil nature of the state. It means the supremacy of the law and the sovereignty of the people. Never ever will it mean that the state is secular, which means that religion and state are separate and that religion and law are separate!" She insisted that Article 1 should be interpreted as meaning that Islam "is the religion of the people and of the state, not just of the people," because to do otherwise "would mean that Islam does not constrain the state in any way."[71] She also put the Preamble Committee's renunciation of Islam as a source of legislation into perspective: "I do not want to say that we have changed the principle that Islam is a source of legislation, but I say that the party of the majority in the Assembly [al-Nahdha] has decided that *Article 1 was enough by itself to compel the state, with its institutions and its three branches of government, to respect Islam.*"[72] In particular, in Sana Haddad's view, a constitutional court seemed to be a key body that would interpret Article 1 in a way that could advance al-Nahda's agenda. She also argued that an independent justice system would protect "against extremism . . . would anchor society in its values and would protect us from the imposition of a specific way of life." This

68. http://www.marsad.tn/fr/vote/52c9ba0712bdaa7f9b90f436, accessed December 22, 2016.

69. The Preamble Committee was in charge of drafting the Constitution's preamble.

70. It is noteworthy that al-Nahdha's female MPs played a crucial role in building compromises with al-Nahdha's political adversaries, as well as within al-Nahdha, when it came to religious issues. About half of al-Nahdha's female MPs were new members of the party in 2011, although they had affinities with al-Nahdha's movement prior to their political careers in the NCA, as argued by Ben Ismail (2014). As a result, and in contrast with most al-Nahdha male MPs—who had been molded, often for decades, by the movement's doctrines—as newcomers to political life al-Nahdha female MPs displayed more versatility in articulating al-Nahdha's conception of a thick state custodianship of Islam without invoking sharia in the Constitution.

71. NCA session of July 6, 2013.

72. NCA session of July 6, 2013. Emphasis is mine.

would be a new development as before 2011 the "religion of the state" formulation had not been democratically adjudicated. In Sana Haddad's conception of governance, Islam constituted an essential constraint on the state *and* an essential ingredient of democratic governance that guaranteed the continuity of Islamic prescriptions and ways of life. It had its contradictions, however: it was democratic (it respected the desire of the majority of citizens to live as Muslims), but it might also limit some important freedoms (non-Muslim ways of life).

5. Organizing Intra-Muslim Conflicts in a Democratic Muslim State: The State as "Custodian of Islam" and Defender of "Freedom of Conscience"

In the face of the strong disagreements in the Assembly about the thickness and strength of the state's custodianship of Islam and each camp's fears of their adversaries manipulating insufficiently specific constitutional language in future legislatures,[73] the constituents drafted mutually limiting clauses about Islam and freedoms in a newly introduced Article 6, which organized the conflict between Islamists and non-Islamists in a democratic setting. The end result of a negotiation, this was an innovative compromise, albeit one that left the door open to potential future conflicts and deferred interpretative issues for future adjudication in courts of law (such as the future constitutional court) and other arenas.[74] Far from moderating Islamist (and non-Islamist) views, it organized their future debates.

The National Constituent Assembly's Reluctance to Specify Article 1

The June 1, 2013, provisional constitutional draft reflected some of the contentions in the Assembly about Islam in governance, with several articles invoking Islam explicitly or implicitly. Article 1 was left identical to its 1959 version. Article 2 was new ("Tunisia is a civil state [*dawla madanīya*] founded on citizenship

73. Some MPs from various political parties notably objected to the absence of clear definitions of terms such as "freedom of conscience," "the constants and aims of Islam," and "sacred things." CPR MP Samia Abbou, NCA session of January 18, 2013; CPR MP Hasna Marsit, NCA session of July 6, 2013; al-Nahdha MP Adel Ben Attia, NCA session of July 8, 2013; al-Nahdha MP Samia Toumia, al-Nahdha MP Mounia Gasri, and PDP MP Mohamed Baroudi, NCA session of January 4, 2014.

74. In her study of Israel, India, and Ireland, Lerner (2011, i) similarly notes that "ambivalent legal language and the inclusion of contrasting provisions in the constitution . . . allow the deferral of controversial choices."

[*muwāṭana*], on the people's will [*irādat al-sha ʿb*], and on the supremacy of the law [*ʿalawīyat al-qānūn*]"), and so was Article 6 ("The state is the custodian of the religion [*rā ʿiyat al-dīn*], guarantees freedom of belief and conscience [*ḥurrīyat al-mu ʿtaqad wa-l-ḍamīr*], and freedom of religious practice [*al-sha ʿā ʾir al-dīnīya*]. It protects sacred things [*muqaddasāt*] and guarantees the neutrality [*ḥiyād*] of mosques and places of worship with respect to partisan instrumentalization [*al-tawẓīf al-ḥizbī*]"). Finally, to clarify the 1959 formulation of Article 1—which could be interpreted as "Islam is the religion of the state" or "Islam is the religion of Tunisia"—al-Nahdha's MPs introduced Article 141, which included "No constitutional amendment can harm [*nāla min*] Islam as the religion of the state." All these articles remained in the final draft of the 2014 Constitution, with some modifications, except for Article 141, which was removed in the face of strong opposition. Although there was broad agreement on the principle of state custodianship of Islam as the preferred religion, non-Islamists did not accept specification of Article 1 and rejected Article 141.

The issue of whether to interpret Article 1 as meaning that Islam was the religion "of the state," "of Tunisia," or "of the people" therefore remained unresolved, and Islamists and non-Islamists rehearsed their own various interpretations until the very end of the drafting process. A few weeks before the final draft was passed, the center-left CPR MP Rafik Tlili argued, "Is it the religion of the people or of the state? Article 141 was proposed to lift this ambiguity by explaining that it is the religion of the state, but it almost caused the disintegration of the Assembly and, with it, the political experiment we are living right now."[75] For him, it was necessary to add to Article 1—"Islam is the religion of its people"—because "it is the people who will have to face the Final Judgment, not the state." Al-Nahdha MPs rejected this suggestion, arguing that Islam was also the religion of all the institutions of the state, not merely the religion of the people.[76] In the end, out of the 149 MPs in attendance (of a total 217), only 3, all from the Popular Petition, refused to vote for Article 1 in its 1959 formulation (1 against and 2 abstentions).[77] The only change from 1959 was the addition of "This article cannot be amended." The constituents accepted Article 1's ambiguity, perhaps

75. NCA session of January 4, 2014.

76. Notably Warda Turki and Sana Haddad. NCA session of January 4, 2014.

77. This included all 74 al-Nahdha MPs in attendance (83 percent al-Nahdha MPs were present, compared to 59 percent of all other MPs, which was a typical attendance differential). NCA session of January 4, 2014, http://majles.marsad.tn/vote/52c9ba0712bdaa7f9b90f436, accessed May 29, 2017.

because they knew from past experience what to expect from it. Jawhara Tiss, a female al-Nahdha MP from a younger generation, recognized that it was impossible to define once and for all what "Islam" meant in Article 1, and that the constituents had to live with this ambiguity. She argued, "The issue of religion remains, the issue of what Islam is, and of how Tunisian elites represent Islam today. *It is impossible to solve this issue in the constitution.* The Assembly's debates have revealed that there are those who see Islam as mere rituals [*ṭuqūs*] and teachings that only matter for the relation between the individual and God. There is another view, however, that sees Islam as one of the sources of knowledge, and therefore, as one of the sources of the law."[78] She did not offer an answer to the issue of, in her own words, "what Islam is" and was willing to leave it at that. In that sense, she was at odds with an older generation within al-Nahdha.

Ensuring the Coexistence of Freedom of *Religion and Freedom* from *Religion*

The Assembly was also divided on how to define religious freedom, and this cleavage did not strictly follow the Islamist/non-Islamist divide. One camp wanted to limit freedom *of* religion in the constitution—for example, by banning *takfīr* (accusations of apostasy). Their opponents wanted to limit freedom *from* religion—for example, by refusing to inscribe freedom of conscience in the constitution.[79] Rather than leave this unresolved, as they did with Article 1, each camp crafted explicit limits on the other camp's conception of freedoms in Article 6 to ensure that they could coexist, an example of drafting by accretion. The content of Article 6 was owed to highly publicized, and at times violent, events that took place during the drafting process.[80] For instance, in the 2011 "Persepolis" affair, a television director who had broadcast the animated movie Persepolis (dubbed in dialectal Tunisian) was taken to court by plaintiffs who argued that the movie harmed Islam. Violence also erupted in the streets in relation to the controversy. As another example, on March 28, 2012, the Mahdia correctional court sentenced two young men who published caricatures of the prophet Muhammad on social networks to seven years in prison

78. NCA session of July 8, 2013. Emphasis is mine. Jawhara Tiss, born in 1985, was one of the youngest constituents.

79. What the PDM MP Fadhel Moussa referred to as "rights of conscience" (*ḥaqq al-ḍamīr*), which he supported. NCA morning session of February 28, 2012.

80. For more details, see Zeghal (2013b).

for "disseminating publications disturbing public order" and "offense to morality." The complaint against the two young men was brought to court by a lawyer who denounced their atheism.[81] Also, on June 11, 2012, artists exhibiting their works in the hall of the Abdelliya palace, in the posh suburbs of La Marsa, saw a bailiff ask them to remove pictures some Salafists considered "blasphemous." After the artists refused to let the bailiff in, the exhibit was attacked by Salafists who destroyed some of the artwork.

The final version of Article 6 complemented and fleshed out Article 1. It stated, "The state is the custodian of the religion [*rā ʿiyat al-dīn*]. It guarantees freedom of belief, of conscience, and of religious worship [*ḥurrīyat al-mu ʿtaqad wa-l-ḍamīr wa-mumārasāt al-sha ʿā ʾir al-dīnīya*]. It ensures the neutrality of mosques and places of worship and protects them from partisan instrumentalization. The state shall commit to spreading the values of moderation and tolerance, to protecting sacred things [*muqaddasāt*], and to preventing attacks on them. It shall also commit to prohibiting accusations of apostasy [*takfīr*] and incitements to hatred and violence, and to confronting them." As in its June 1, 2013, version, this article designated the state as the custodian of Islam ("*rā ʿiyat al-dīn,*" i.e., custodian of *the* religion, literally "shepherd of the religion," echoing a concept in classical Islam, that of the ruler who watches over and leads his flock). However, it was augmented by prohibiting *takfīr* (accusations of apostasy, presumably against those making use of their freedom of conscience and expression), while making the state the protector of sacred things (allowing the state to limit freedom of conscience and expression). Also related to the idea of the state's custodianship of Islam, Article 39 stipulated that Islamic values should be disseminated to the youth in public education ("the state ensures that the Arab and Muslim identity is rooted in the youth") in combination with "nationalism" and with "the values of human rights." In addition, as in the 1959 Constitution, only Muslims were eligible to the post of president of the republic (Article 74). Although Tunisian citizenship was not defined in relation to religion, there was no absolute equality between religions; this article excluded Tunisian Jews, the main religious minority, from the highest post in the state.[82]

81. http://tobegoodagain.wordpress.com/2012/04/05/affaire-mahdia-lenquete-atheisme-delit-de-pensee-atteinte-au-sacre/, accessed October 21, 2012. For more details on this and other similar affairs, see L. Thompson (2022).

82. Tunisia's Jewish population had started to decline before independence, reaching about 2,000 citizens in 2011 (0.2 percent of the Tunisian population). In 1946 there were about 71,000

Freedom of Conscience: A Contentious Innovation

The notion of freedom of conscience was a novelty, unlike the notions of freedom of belief and of worship, which were part of the earlier constitutional vocabulary of Tunisia. We saw how, although it did not use the concept of freedom, the 1861 Constitution protected the right to worship and allowed non-Muslims to convert, albeit by employing negative formulations such as "cannot be forbidden" or "cannot be forced to." The 1959 Constitution, on the other hand, employed the terms "freedom of belief" (*ḥurrīyat al-muʿtaqad*) and "freedom of religious worship" (*ḥurrīyat al-qiyām bi-l-shaʿāʾir al-dīnīya*)." It did not mention freedom of conscience, although its French version (which had no legal standing since only the Arabic version was, by law, the official constitution) translated "*ḥurrīyat al-muʿtaqad*" (freedom of belief) as "*liberté de conscience*" (freedom of conscience), in a common and often deliberate pattern of mistranslation of this term in the Middle East.[83] In contrast, the 2014 Constitution introduced freedom of conscience, rendered in Arabic by "*ḥurrīyat al-ḍamīr*." Therefore, Article 6 added a radically new element to Tunisia's constitutional tradition: in addition to the freedom to exercise one's own religion, it gave Tunisians, including Tunisian Muslims, freedom from religion—that is, the freedom to choose their religious convictions or no religious conviction at all. However, Article 6 also limited this freedom. In its formulation, the state was "custodian of Islam" and "protector of sacred things," which freedom of and especially from religion could potentially threaten. In addition, Article 39, as we saw, made explicit the pedagogical role of the state in inculcating Islamic values in all its citizens. Therefore, in the face of the possibility of freedom of conscience eroding the Islamic community, the thickness of the state custodianship of Islam was reaffirmed.

Freedom of conscience was a contentious issue for Islamists as well as for some non-Islamists in the Assembly, being generally understood as freedom *from* Islam and thus in blatant contradiction to Article 1 and with the principle of the state custodianship of Islam inscribed in Article 6 itself. Discussing the June 1, 2013, provisional constitutional draft, the Fidélité (an independent electoral list from Kasserine) MP Mabrouk Hrizi, who later joined the center-left

Tunisian Jews (2.5 percent of the Tunisian population, a similar percentage as a decade earlier), compared to 58,000 (1.6 percent) at independence in 1956. Seklani (1974, 24 and 27) and Sebag (1991, 186 and 279).

83. E.g., see, in chapter 4, the 1923 Constitution of Egypt and the 1926 Constitution of Lebanon.

CPR, argued that Article 1 (Islam as the religion of the state and/or Tunisia), Article 2 (the state as civil), Article 6 (the state as custodian of Islam and guarantor of freedom of conscience), and Article 141 (later dropped; Islam as the religion of the state) should be interpreted as a whole and that they imposed necessary limits to freedom of conscience: "Can freedom of conscience be without a conscience? Can freedom of expression be left without an overseer [*raqib*]?"[84] Mabrouk Hrizi and nineteen other MPs from al-Nahdha and CPR, some of whom articulated similar sentiments,[85] proposed an amendment to Article 6 that would suppress freedom of conscience.[86] Later on in the deliberations, Azed Badi, a CPR MP who refused to accept expressions of atheism in public, argued that freedom of conscience was "imposed by foreign agendas," an implicit reference to the drafting of the 1861 and 1959 Constitutions.[87] The leftist PDP MP Iyed Dahmani as well as the liberal Afek Party MP Rym Mahjoub opposed Azed Badi on this issue, with Rym Mahjoub arguing against any limits to human rights.[88] In the same vein, the Afek Party MP Chokri Yaich had earlier underlined the contradiction between a state that protects freedom of conscience and is at the same time the "custodian of the religion." "Here," he added, in a rare explicit mention of religious minorities during the 2012–2014 NCA debates, "minorities are ignored, even though they are very few."[89] The statements of some CPR MPs against freedom of conscience were similar to those made by al-Nahdha MPs. For instance, the al-Nahdha MP Kamel Ben Amara argued, "When we speak of the civil nature of the state, we speak about it in the framework of civil universal human values, but not in the framework of the global universal values founded on absolute liberalism and on the principles of secularism and *laïcité*."[90] For him, it was unacceptable to allow an individual to renounce his religion or choose any religion, and Article 1 served to limit this freedom. The al-Nahdha MP Khaled Belhaj also argued for limiting freedoms by invoking moral norms, which he considered absent from secular constitutions: "Secular constitutions assert the absolute freedom of the individual without relating it to morality [*akhlāq*]. The freedom we want is a freedom constrained by our culture

84. NCA session of July 11, 2013.

85. For instance, the CPR MP Rabii Abdi, NCA session of July 6, 2013.

86. NCA session of July 11, 2013.

87. NCA session of January 4, 2014.

88. NCA session of January 3, 2014.

89. NCA session of July 8, 2013.

90. NCA session of July 11, 2013. See also the July 8, 2013, remarks of the al-Nahdha MP Adel Ben Attia against freedom of conscience.

and our morals."[91] Despite a divide in the Assembly, freedom of conscience was eventually introduced in the 2014 Constitution. Article 6 made freedom *of* religion and freedom *from* religion limit each other and coexist: its final version was a compromise that kept the "extremists" of each camp in check—those who might accuse fellow Muslims of apostasy or restrict the freedoms of religious minorities on the one hand, and those who might publicize anti-Islamic statements and practices on the other. Article 6 could seem incoherent because of the contradictory duties it ascribed to the state—custodian of Islam and protector of "sacred things" on the one hand, and protector of freedom of conscience on the other. However, it was coherent insofar as it reflected the existence of an important political cleavage in Tunisian society.

Moderation of Islamism or Organization of the Debate?

Indeed, Article 6 was a political compromise, not a compromise on the substance of democracy or of Islam in governance. No effort was made during the constitutional process to make Islam or democracy less stringent, to "reconcile" them or "adapt" them to each other to make them "compatible" (a question that has, on the other hand, been the object of much scholarly attention). Rather, the Assembly worked at guaranteeing both democracy and the state's custodianship of Islam as the preferred religion, making them coexist. Therefore, Article 6 simply organized the conflict between Islamists and their adversaries in a democratic setting by banning the most extreme manifestations of this conflict. In fact, various interpretations of Islam and its custodianship by the state were heard in the Assembly, from the most conservative to the most liberal, and the Constitution did not articulate a "moderate" (or, for that matter, a "radical") role for Islam in governance since it left this issue unresolved. And al-Nahdha's compromise should not be interpreted as a "moderation" of its brand of Islamism. Despite al-Nahdha's renunciation of sharia in the 2014 Constitution, the project to implement sharia was not explicitly excluded from the 2012–2014 NCA compromise. For al-Nahdha, the Constitution left open the possibility of implementing a thicker state custodianship of Islam, even if it did not mention sharia. Recall an intervention by a member of al-Nahdha in the Assembly arguing that "Article 1 was enough by itself to compel the state, with its institutions and its three branches of government, to respect Islam."[92] Courts of law (such as the future

91. NCA session of July 11, 2013.

92. NCA session of July 6, 2013.

Constitutional Court, on which all constituents agreed)[93] and future legislative assemblies would adjudicate how to interpret Article 1, whether with a conservative or liberal bent (i.e., thickening or thinning the state custodianship of Islam). De facto, constituents accepted that the interpretation of Islam and its role in governance would be a matter of democratic debate.

Who Won?

Two years after the 2014 Constitution was proclaimed, al-Nahdha's leader Rached Ghannouchi wrote in *Foreign Affairs* that his party had "moved beyond its origins as an Islamist party and has fully embraced a new identity as a party of Muslim democrats." He argued, "Tunisia's new constitution enshrines democracy and protects political and religious freedoms. Under the new constitution, the rights of Tunisians to worship freely, express their convictions and beliefs, and embrace an Arab Muslim identity are guaranteed, and so Ennahda no longer needs to focus its energies on fighting for such protections." Here again, this declaration, which affirmed that "the party no longer accepts the label of 'Islamism,'" should not be read as a sign of moderation in al-Nahdha's ideology and conception of the role of Islam in governance.[94] Rather, al-Nahdha's leadership signaled that they were satisfied with the (democratic) synthesis inscribed in the 2014 Constitution, and were content to let its ambiguities be adjudicated in courts of law and future legislative assemblies. This was also an attempt by al-Nahdha's leader to tame the debate between Islamists and non-Islamists as well as the debate within his own party, which must be read in the context of the vulnerability of Islamist parties in the Middle East after 2013. He wrote, "Of course, as Muslims, the values of Islam still guide our actions. However, we no longer consider the old ideological debates about the Islamization or

93. The 2014 Constitution (Articles 118–124) stipulates that the Constitutional Court, which did not exist before (and, as it turned out, was never established under this Constitution), is an independent judicial body composed of 12 members, 4 appointed by the president of the republic, 4 by the Assembly of the People's Representatives, and 4 by the High Council of the Judiciary. It reviews the constitutionality of laws. Its decisions must be reasoned, and they are binding. The Assembly voted quasi-unanimously in favor of establishing it, despite important divisions about the appointment of its members and its specific prerogatives. See the sessions of the Assembly of November 14, 2015, November 18, 2015, and its passing on November 20, 2015 (130 in favor, 3 abstentions). http://majles.marsad.tn/2014/fr/vote/56a2bd7912bdaa42423b4e2, accessed November 13, 2016.

94. E.g., as in Feldman (2020).

secularization of society to be necessary or even relevant."[95] Non-Islamists projected the same sense of satisfaction with the synthesis inscribed in the 2014 Constitution. For instance, on October 5, 2017, publicly commenting on a lecture I delivered at the Tunisian Academy of Arts and Sciences in Carthage (Beït al-Hikma) on constitutional debates about Islam in governance in the Middle East, the former NCA leftist PDM MP Fadhel Moussa insisted that the 2014 Constitution was not a "compromise," and that liberals had won by keeping the 1959 formulation of Article 1 intact (which, he insisted, did not say that Islam was the religion of the state) and by introducing the civil character of the state (Article 2) as well as freedom of conscience (Article 6). Therefore, it seems that both camps believed that they had won, in the sense that they were now in a better position to pursue the debate about the role of Islam in governance. The political cleavage around this issue continued to play an important role in political life, and it was still centered on Bourguiba's synthesis, which was given more specificity in a democratic process by the 2012–2014 NCA and opened for discussion and adjudication.

What's Next?

The discussions and compromises of the democratic transition came to an end with the July 25, 2021 coup by President of the Republic Kais Saied, who, invoking the notion of "imminent danger" in Article 80 of the 2014 Constitution,[96] suspended Parliament and took over legislative, executive, and judicial powers. He then dissolved Parliament on March 30, 2022. Saied, a constitutional law scholar, was democratically elected in October 2019. He ran without the support of a political party on a platform focused on antiparliamentarianism, anticorruption, and justice for the economically marginalized, combined with a populist and conservative vision and strong criticism of the 2014 Constitution. His summer 2021 coup took advantage of Tunisians' growing dissatisfaction with the ineffectiveness of Parliament at addressing the economic problems that had led

95. Rached Ghannouchi, From Political Islam to Muslim Democracy: The Ennahda Party and the Future of Tunisia, *Foreign Affairs*, September–October 2016, https://www.foreignaffairs.com/articles/tunisia/political-islam-muslim-democracy, accessed November 13, 2016. For an analysis of Ghannouchi's political writings, see March (2019).

96. According to Article 80 of the 2014 Constitution, in case of "imminent danger threatening national integrity, the country's security or independence, and the regular operations of public powers," the president may take measures "imposed by the state of exception."

to the 2010–2011 protests and came after more than a year of duels with Parliament and with the speaker of the Assembly and leader of al-Nahdha, Rached Ghannouchi. Intent on replacing the post-2011 parliamentary political system with a presidential one, in May 2022 he charged a "National Consultative Commission" headed by the constitutional law expert Sadọk Belaid to write a new constitution, to be submitted to a referendum. In contrast to the creation of the 2014 Constitution, this process was rushed and clad in secrecy. Belaid delivered his constitution draft on June 20, 2022,[97] but President Saied published a significantly different one in the Official Gazette ten days later.[98] It was approved via referendum on July 25, 2022, with a 94.6 percent approval rate (reminiscent of Bourguiba's and Ben Ali's era) and 30.5 percent turnout according to official results.[99] Both Belaid's and Saied's constitution drafts returned to a presidential system, with the aim of mitigating the parliamentary instability of the post–Arab Spring decade; Saied's constitution drastically strengthened presidential powers to the detriment of balancing institutions such as the judiciary and the Parliament.[100] Both envisioned a stronger state custodianship of Islam, but Belaid's made it thinner, whereas Saied's made it thicker. Belaid had announced that stripping the Constitution of references to Islam would help neutralize Islamist parties.[101] In his constitution draft, Articles 1 and 6 of the 2014 Constitution were removed; there was no requirement for the president of the republic to be a Muslim; and Islam was only mentioned in the preamble, which stated that the people were "attached to the teachings of Islam and its purposes of openness [*tafattuḥ*] and moderation [*iʿtidāl*]." On the other hand, the state had to ensure the "neutrality" of educational, judicial, and security institutions, avoiding "religious, ideological, sectarian and partisan instrumentalization." In addition, the principles of freedom of belief, conscience, and religious worship were guaranteed "as long as they do not harm public freedoms, public security, or the administration's neutrality" (Article 20). Reminiscent of pre-2011 times, Article 32 prohibited political parties whose ideologies are founded on "religion, language, race, or region." Therefore,

97. It appeared in *Al-Ṣabāḥ*, July 3, 2022.

98. Presidential Decree 578 of June 30, 2022 (*JORT* June 30, 2022, year 165, no. 74).

99. Initial results published by ISIE (the Independent Institute for Elections), *Qarār*, July 26, 2022.

100. For instance, Article 120 states that the president appoints judges to courts of law (on a proposal from the High Council of the Judiciary), as well as to the Constitutional Court. According to Article 102, he may fire any member of the government. Article 110 stipulates that the president is "not accountable."

101. Interview aired on France24, June 7, 2022.

in Belaid's constitutional draft the state custodianship of Islam was greatly strengthened and thinned, which gave the state the means to eliminate Islamist political parties from political competition and Islam from politics—which does not mean, however, that Islam and the state were separated.

As for the president's constitution, it introduced certain innovations to the way Islam was treated legally although with some nods to precolonial constitutional history. The preamble underlined the people's "attachment to the humanistic features of the Islamic religion." Article 88 stipulated that the president had to be a Muslim (and Tunisian by uninterrupted paternal and maternal lineages for two generations, a new twist). The educational system had to reinforce Islamic identity (Article 44). As in Belaid's draft, Articles 1 and 6 of the 2014 Constitution were removed, but Article 5 reintroduced Islam with a new formulation: "Tunisia is part of the Islamic umma. The state, and only the state, must work toward realizing the purposes of Islam in preserving life, honor, property, religion, and freedom [*al-nafs wa-l- ʿirḍ wa-l-māl wa-l-dīn wa-l-ḥurrīya*], under the auspices of a democratic system." The reference to a democratic system was added only after the president's draft faced opposition from democratic activists.[102] Moving away from the ambiguities of Article 1 of the previous two constitutions, this clause gave the state a full monopoly on the custodianship of Islam, hence strengthening it. It defined Islam by rehearsing a set of tenets that echoed the traditional categories known as "the purposes of sharia," although it pointedly avoided using the term "sharia."[103] Therefore, it thickened the state custodianship of Islam, although freedom of conscience (*ḥurrīyat al-ḍamīr*) remained in Article 27. Saied's formulations used the vocabulary of an older tradition that he knew well.[104] Recall that security of life, honor, property, and religion were guaranteed to all in the explanatory text of the 1857 Security Pact (see chapter 1). And indeed, Kais Saied's preamble referred to the 1857–1861 constitutional texts but did not mention the 1959 or the

102. Presidential Decree 607 of July 8, 2022 (*JORT* July 8, 2022, year 165 no. 77). Other symbolic nods to democracy were also added.

103. The list of sharia's purposes in the legal literature varies, but they often include the preservation of life, property, progeny, religion, and intellect (*ʿaql*). Note that the latter is missing from Saied's list. Also note that he added the preservation of freedom, a modification some modernist Islamic thinkers had made in the past. For instance, Muhammad al-Tahar Ben Achour (d. 1973), added "equality and freedom to al-Shāṭibī's [d. 1388] list of the five elements necessary for human existence to prosper [i.e., the five purposes just mentioned]." R. M. Gleave, Maḳāṣid al-Sharīʿa, *EI*^{2}.

104. As shown by his coauthoring ʿAmur and Saʿīd (1987).

2014 Constitutions. His expanded vision of the role of Islam in governance might entice part of al-Nahdha's constituency (with whom Saied shared conservative ideas, despite his political quarrels with al-Nahdha's leadership) to accept authoritarianism. Returning to authoritarianism, on the other hand, might appeal to the illiberal progressives who see in the rupture with the democratic experiment an opportunity to weaken Islamist parties. As for liberals, they criticized Article 5 (and the undemocratic features of the president's draft).[105] This is more evidence that the divide on the role of Islam in governance is likely to endure, regime changes notwithstanding, and that it does not overlap neatly with the divide on democracy vs. authoritarianism.

Conclusion

The 2014 Constitution contained all the elements of a democratic polity—for example, the sovereignty of the people, free elections, individual freedoms, separation of powers, judicial independence, and a constitutional court. Article 1 ("its religion is Islam") remained ambiguous and unchanged from the 1959 Constitution, with the addition that it could not be changed. The drafters in each camp avoided opening it up to changes, for fear of losing some ground. In addition, as in 1959, sharia was not explicitly mentioned in the Constitution—in large part because this was deemed unnecessary by al-Nahdha (and undesirable by its political adversaries) in order to implement their conception of the state custodianship of Islam as the preferred religion. Although there was broad agreement among Islamists and non-Islamists that Islam and the state should not be separated, there were strong disagreements about the appropriate strength and thickness of the state's custodianship of Islam, and on the degree to which Islam and politics should be allowed to mix. In particular, freedom of conscience (i.e., freedom *from* religion)—absent from past constitutions—was a point of contention, and eventually adopted. A compromise was reached with Article 6, which restricted freedom *of* religion and freedom *from* religion, although it left much to be defined and adjudicated in the future. Far from moderating the content of the Islamists' and non-Islamists' positions, it sought to organize their potential future disputes by prohibiting extreme behavior on both sides. The constituents understood that their debate about Islam in governance was an integral part of Tunisian political life, and that it was therefore

105. Belaid described the Constitution as establishing a dictatorial regime and as "distorting Tunisian identity." *Al-Ṣabāḥ*, July 3, 2022.

important to keep it alive for the sake of the democratic transition and of a healthy democratic life. Echoing numerous polls that showed that most Tunisians wanted "Islam and democracy," the 2014 Constitution reflected the desire for a democratic state whose custodianship of Islam, the preferred religion, set limits on freedom *of* and *from* religion. It provided an answer to a difficult question, one that is not unique to Tunisia or Muslim polities: How do you make the state both democratic *and* the custodian of a preferred religion?[106] More broadly, a similar question can also arise in secular states that struggle to maintain neutrality toward religion, such as France. French *laïcité*, as an imperative, has coexisted since 1905 with the imperative of democracy, and this coexistence has triggered vigorous debates about how to realize them both simultaneously. The main takeaway of this brief comparison is that states' non-neutrality toward religion (or toward a specific identity) limits the thickness of their democracy and forces them into contortions to simultaneously affirm this non-neutral stance and their democratic aspirations. The mutual limits that democracy and non-neutrality put on each other can be alleviated by reducing democracy to a "one man one vote" procedural mechanism,[107] or by articulating a state theology that draws from the preferred religion resources that align with a thick conception of democracy.[108] Inevitably, the search for such a solution leads to disputes that feed political life if they are allowed to express themselves.

106. For instance, the state of Israel grapples with the same issue. See Gavison (2011).
107. Gavison (2011).
108. For examples of such liberal Muslim theologies, see Zeghal (2008a).

4

The Political Cleavage about Islam in Governance in the Modern Middle East

A REAPPRAISAL

WE HAVE SEEN the persistence of broad agreement on the necessity of the state's custodianship of Islam as the preferred religion throughout the modern history of Tunisia, in continuity with earlier times and through drastically different contexts that included precolonial beylical rule, colonial rule, a fight for independence, independent state building, authoritarian rule, and a transition to democracy. How exceptional is Tunisia's experience among Muslim-majority polities with respect to this broad agreement and the attendant debates as to its implementation? As of the early twenty-first century, Islam as the state's preferred religion is prevalent in Muslim-majority polities, with a variety of constitutional formulations and institutional arrangements (table 8). However, a common view is that this is the result of an "Islamic revival" that sealed the failure of the "liberal experiment" of the early 1920s, the beginning of constitution making in the Mashriq and a period often romanticized in the historiography.[1] By examining three constitutional episodes of this period—the creation of the 1920 Greater Syria Draft Constitution, the 1926 Lebanese Constitution, and the 1923 Constitution of Egypt, which is regarded as paradigmatic of this "liberal age" and has a rich intellectual and political legacy—I show instead that there was broad agreement at the time among liberals and conservatives alike about the necessity of continuing the state's custodianship

1. Notably by Al-Sayyid Marsot (1977).

of Islam as the preferred religion, except when the demographic weight of religious minorities prevented it. To be sure, liberals and conservatives also shared the aim of implementing other governance imperatives such as freedom and equality. I therefore delineate what actually separated them ideologically: which of these imperatives they thought should be thickened or thinned.

Findings in this chapter contrast with claims that have been made in the literature about separation of religion and state (or state neutrality) as a project for which liberals in the Middle East allegedly advocated and with other claims about the presumed novelty of the Muslim Brothers' ideology, when their movement developed in the 1930s. By redirecting attention to debates that took place in deliberative arenas in 1920s Egypt, particularly in the 1922 Egyptian Constitutional Committee (as opposed to focusing on writings by intellectuals, diplomatic reports, newspapers, or secondary sources),[2] I find that discussions about religion were more important than is generally assumed and further that they were not mainly about identity (as is commonly argued) but about governance issues.[3] Moreover, contrary to often-heard claims,[4] liberals and conservatives alike firmly rejected the separation of religion and *state* as

2. For instance, Kedourie (1968), in his analysis of the creation of the 1923 Egyptian Constitution, focuses on the negotiations involving Egyptian and foreign political actors, mostly based on U.S. diplomatic archives. For a cultural approach, see Maghraoui (2006). Others, such as Mahmood (2016), rely on Sharīf (1938), an incomplete selection of the transcripts of the 1922 constitutional deliberations, which omits some crucial parts and was published fifteen years after the fact by a member of the Egyptian Senate, Muhammad al-Sharif.

3. The main lenses of study for this period have been nationalism and liberalism, with scant attention to Islam in governance. For instance, in Gershoni and Jankowski (1986, 4), an important study of the formation of the Egyptian nationhood, the focus is on the "nature of the political community." In the same vein, Mahmood (2016, 12, 18) views Islam as "the collective identity of the nation" or as shaping the "Islamic identity of the state." Others reduce Islam to a symbolic element that helped imagine and reinforce national identity or to window dressing adopted to ensure social order, to cater to the sentiments of the masses, or to mobilize public opinion in a time of "religious passions," as in Smith (1983, 72, 83, 113) and Safran (1961, 119–120). Gershoni and Jankowski (1986, 54) claim that the 1923 Constitution "[referred] to Islam and the Arabs [*sic*] only in Article 149." Similarly, Brown and Revkin (2018) claim that "issues of Islamic law did not arise in constitutional discussions" in 1922 Egypt.

4. For instance, Mahmood (2016, 105), in line with Asad (2003, 209), describes the modern Egyptian state (or governance) as secular-liberal and the 1923 Constitution as a law for secular governance, i.e., in her words, "a system of governance that was neutral in regard to religion." Al-Sayyid Marsot (1977, 222, 228) makes similar claims. Gershoni and Jankowski (1986, 43) argue that the nationalist Wafd party was "explicitly secular" because it united Copts and Muslims. Lia (1998, 79) calls Taha Husayn an advocate of "secular Egyptian nationalism."

well as state neutrality toward religion. What many liberals did is argue against mixing religion with *politics*, and more specifically with political competition, in order to protect the state as custodian of Islam against, for instance, the political ambitions of the ʿulamā or the religious minorities as such. Public calls for separating Islam and the state or for state neutrality were extremely rare at the time (and still would be a century later) in Egypt and other predominantly Muslim polities of the Middle East, although we will hear such voices in the Levant.[5] In fact, we will hear a prominent Egyptian liberal intellectual argue that the Egyptian state had to have only one religion (Islam), and that it would be "monstrous" if it had more than one[6]—a view that was not disputed by other liberals—and we will hear another speak of Islam as "the national religion."[7] I also analyze conservative conceptions of the role of Islam in governance in 1920s Egypt, rebalancing the literature's exclusive focus on the liberal side until the emergence of the Egyptian Muslim Brothers, who are commonly viewed as the spoilsports of this liberal experiment. I show that the Muslim Brothers did not innovate ideologically concerning the role of Islam in governance when they created in 1928 what would become, a decade or so later, one of the first and most influential mass-organized Islamist movements.[8] They merely repurposed

5. Even Ali Abd al-Raziq (1888–1966), whom the historiography generally describes as a "secularist" because of his 1925 book *Islam and the Foundation of Government*, firmly condemned the separation of Islam and the state. He only argued that Islam did not specify rules for governance and that Muslims could choose whichever political regime they found convenient. See ʿAbd al-Rāziq (1925) and ʿAlī ʿAbd al-Rāziq, Al-Jumhūrīya al-Lā-Dīnīya fī al-Islām [The secular republic in Islam], *Al-Siyāsa*, May 13 and June 17, 1928. See also Hatina (2000). In contrast, Al-Sayyid Marsot (1977, 228) incorrectly argues that, for Ali Abd al-Raziq, "secularism in government was in time to become an established principle. Secularism meant . . . that Islam as a religion did not need a counterpart in government, that government had nothing to do with religion."

6. Ahmad Lutfi al-Sayyid. In contrast, Al-Sayyid Marsot (1977, 222) argues that he "believed that religion should concern man's relations with God and that government should be secular." Similarly, see Gershoni and Jankowski (1986, 14).

7. Taha Husayn.

8. Hassan al-Banna's lack of ideological sophistication has been noted in the literature. For instance, Mitchell (1969, 237, 324) argues that he did not provide "any reliable intellectual roadmaps"; Krämer (2010, 84) argues that he "did not invite theorizing," and could be described as "anti-intellectual"; March (2019, 73) finds that he provided no "ideological or doctrinal formation"; and Lia (1998, 2, 72) argues that "the Society's ideology was of a fairly rudimentary nature during most of the 1930s." Wood (2011, 125) makes a similar argument from the point of view of "Islamic legal revivalism." Like their competitors, the Muslim Brothers and other Islamist movements later articulated ideological innovations—e.g., with Sayyid Qutb in the 1950s and 1960s. See Kepel (1985a), Carré (2003), Shepard (2003), and March (2019), and on the legal side, Wood (2016, 256–257).

conservative tropes that were already resonating with the 1922 Egyptian constitutional debates, joining organizational prowess to a political battle that preexisted them and that pitted those who argued for a larger role of Islam in governance, and for a thicker and more munificent state custodianship of Islam in particular, against those who argued for the opposite.[9]

While Islam as the state's preferred religion is prevalent in Muslim-majority polities, there are exceptions (table 8); it is therefore not inevitable but rather a matter of choice. We saw in the introduction to this book that socioeconomic and political rights indices do not significantly impact the odds of a state having a preferred religion but that the relative size of the religious majority does: it significantly increases them. As a case in point, the three constitutional episodes and debates examined in this chapter occurred in polities in which discussions about the issue of religious minorities were significant very early in their constitutional history but in which the demographic weights of non-Muslims differed greatly, leading to different outcomes for the role of Islam in governance. Egypt in 1922 was about 90 percent Muslim, Greater Syria in 1920 about three-quarters Muslim, and Lebanon in 1926 about half Muslim. The examination of these episodes illuminates the role the size of religious minorities might play on the choices made as to the role of religion in governance. In all three cases (including Lebanon, the only one not to have a state-preferred religion), religious communities' anxieties about other religious communities' political competition, combined with fears of conflict and a desire for national cohesion, led to rejecting the separation of religion and state.

The main primary sources I use in this chapter include the transcripts of the 1922 Egyptian Constitutional Committee debates, which met in fifty-four sessions between April and October 1922, and the transcripts of the subcommittee in charge of drafting the general principles of the constitution, which met in eighteen sessions between April and May 1922. I also make use of the 1911 Egyptian Congress Report, the 1920s and 1930s Egyptian press, and writings by liberal and conservative intellectuals. On the liberal side, in addition to members of the Constitutional Committee such as Tawfiq Duss (1882–1950),[10] Abd

9. For an in-depth analysis of the early organizational aspects of the Society of the Muslim Brothers, see Lia (1998). Note, however, that there is little analysis in the literature on how their organizational abilities compared to their competitors' and adversaries'.

10. Tawfiq Duss hailed from a well-to-do Coptic family and played an important role in the 1911 Coptic Congress. He was appointed minister of agriculture for six months in 1925 and later became a senator.

al-Aziz Fahmy (1870–1951),[11] Abd al-Hamid Badawi (1887–1965),[12] Husayn Rushdi (1863–1928),[13] and the preeminent intellectual Ahmad Lutfi al-Sayyid (1872–1963),[14] who was considered by many of his followers as the "teacher of the generation" (*ustādh al-jīl*), I examine the arguments of the journalist Mahmud Azmi (1889–1954), who edited several liberal Egyptian newspapers in the 1920s,[15] and the man of letters Taha Husayn (1889–1973),[16] who was, according to Hourani (1962, 326), "the last great representative of a [liberal] line of thought, the writer who has given the final statement of the system of ideas which underlay social thought and political action in the Arab countries for three generations." On the conservative side, I examine the arguments of two preeminent conservative ʿulamā trained at al-Azhar: Shaykh Muhammad Bakhit (1856–1935), who was mufti of Egypt from 1914 to 1920 and a member of the 1922 Constitutional Committee,[17] and Shaykh Yusuf al-Dijwi (1870–1948),[18] a member of the Great Council of the ʿUlamā

11. Abd al-Aziz Fahmy studied at al-Azhar and in the government school system. He held several high posts in the administration, worked in the judiciary and the Waqfs Administration, and opened his own law office in 1903. He was elected to the Legislative Assembly in 1913 and headed the Egyptian Bar Association. One of the founders of the Wafd Party, he broke from it in 1920 and helped found the Liberal Constitutional Party, becoming its president in 1924. See Goldschmidt (2000, 49).

12. Abd al-Hamid Badawi was a judge and legal expert trained at the Khedivial School of Law and at the University of Grenoble in France, where he earned a doctorate in 1912. He was a law professor at the Egyptian University in Cairo from 1912 to 1916 and then worked in the judiciary. He held several government portfolios after 1940.

13. Husayn Rushdi studied law in Geneva, Cairo, and Paris and was a member of the Cabinet (justice and foreign affairs) before the Great War. He was appointed prime minister four times. See Goldschmidt (2000, 169–170).

14. Ahmad Lutfi al-Sayyid graduated from the Khedivial School of Law in 1894. For more biographical details, see I. Gershoni, Lutfi al-Sayyid, Ahmad, *EI*^{3}; J. Ahmed (1960, 85–112); and Hourani (1962, 170–182).

15. Mahmud Azmi graduated from the Khedivial School of Law in 1909, and earned a law doctorate in Paris in 1912. He notably edited *Al-Maḥrūsa* and *Al-Istiqlāl*, which he founded in 1921, as well as the magazine *Al-Jadīd*. He became the editor-in-chief of *Al-Siyāsa al-Usbūʿīya* in 1922. He worked at Baghdad's Law College in the 1930s, came back to Egypt in the 1940s, and worked in the Human Rights Commission of the United Nations in the 1950s. On Mahmud Azmi and his liberal leanings, see Nasīra (2006).

16. Taha Husayn studied at al-Azhar, at the Egyptian University, and at the Sorbonne in Paris, where he obtained a doctorate in 1919. For more details, see Cachia (1956), and H. Ahmed (2018).

17. Muhammad Bakhit made his career in the judiciary and played an important role in nationalist politics. For a biography, see Skovgaard-Petersen (1997, 133–141).

18. Yusuf al-Dijwi obtained his doctorate (*ʿālimīya*) from al-Azhar in 1899 and was a prolific Maliki author. He was appointed the Maliki member of the Great Council of the ʿUlamā of al-Azhar in August 1920. Al-Dijwī (2006).

of al-Azhar (*Hay'at kibār al-'ulamā'*). I also consider other prolific contributors to the *Majallat al-Azhar*, such as Shaykh Muhammad Khidr Husayn (1876–1958),[19] and writings by modern school–trained conservatives such as Hassan al-Banna (1906–1949), the founder and leader of the Egyptian Society of the Muslim Brothers, and Rashid Rida (1865–1935), a Syrian émigré who lived in Cairo and was an active participant in Egyptian intellectual debates as well as in the making of the Greater Syria Draft Constitution of 1920. In addition, I examine printed material related to the creation of this Draft Constitution and the Lebanese 1926 Constitution, including the transcripts of the debates of the Lebanese Representative Council and archival material from the French Ministry of Foreign Affairs on the Organic Statutes of the French Mandates of Syria and Lebanon.

Section 1 examines the creation of the 1920 Greater Syria Draft Constitution and the 1926 Lebanese Constitution, two Middle Eastern polities that are distinctive because of their large non-Muslim population. Section 2 analyzes the debates about Islam in governance in the 1922 Egyptian Constitutional Committee, notably as they relate to the political representation of religious minorities. Section 3 sheds light on the key agreements and disagreements about the role of Islam in governance that united or divided conservatives and liberals in 1920s Egypt. Section 4 shows how the Muslim Brothers, in their early decades, merely rehearsed elements of a preexisting conservative ideological repertoire on Islam in governance.

1. The Demographic Weight of Minorities in Action: The 1920 Greater Syria Draft Constitution and the 1926 Lebanese Constitution

Two episodes of the early constitutional history of the Levant are distinctive because they took place in polities with a particularly large fraction of non-Muslims: the draftings of the 1920 Greater Syria Draft Constitution and the 1926 Lebanese Constitution. Contrary to the rest of the Middle East (such as the 90 percent–Muslim Egypt of 1923, the constitutional episode examined in the next section),[20] these polities were quite diverse in religious terms: non-Muslims constituted slightly more than one-quarter of the population of 1920

19. Muhammad Khidr Husayn, of Tunisian origin, was shaykh of al-Azhar from 1952 to 1954.

20. The 1917 Census of Egypt reports about 91.4 percent Muslims, 8.1 percent Christians (mostly Copts), and 0.5 percent Jews.

Greater Syria and slightly more than half the population of 1926 Lebanon.[21] These episodes showcase how the issue of religious minorities shapes outcomes and debates about the relationship between religion, state, and politics much more explicitly than what we could learn from Tunisia's history and from what we will learn from Egypt. The religious demographics made it too difficult to explicitly signal a state-preferred religion with an establishment clause, a type of clause otherwise present in *all* the constitutions promulgated or already in effect in the Middle East at the time, all of them in polities with a predominantly Muslim population.[22] The ambition to give Islam (or another religion) such a role had to be restrained, given the more balanced religious demographics. However, this does not mean that a choice was made to separate religion and state in 1920 Greater Syria and 1926 Lebanon, notwithstanding some voices arguing for it, a rarity in the Middle East. Religion and politics were not separated either since political representation along sectarian lines was constitutionalized in both cases, unlike in less demographically balanced 1923 Egypt where the anxieties of the majority (of being governed by the minority as such) trumped those of the minority (of not having their rights protected). Yet constituents in all three constitutional episodes invoked the goals of preserving national unity and avoiding discord, protecting the rights of minorities, and keeping foreign powers at bay, arguments that were used both in favor of and against proportional political representation of minorities.

21. Aggregating the censuses conducted by the French and British Mandate authorities in the early 1920s in the territories that composed Greater Syria in 1920, we count about 72 percent Muslims (59 percent Sunnis, 4 percent Shiites, 8 percent Alawites, and 1 percent Isma'ilis), 3 percent Druzes, 21 percent Christians, and 4 percent Jews. République Française, Ministère des Affaires Etrangères, *Rapport sur la situation de la Syrie et du Liban pour 1926–1927*, 190–194; and Palestine, *Report and General Abstracts of the Census of 1922*, 4–5). For the demographic breakdown of 1926 Lebanon, see the next section.

22. The 1906–1907 Constitution of Iran ("The official religion of Persia is Islam, according to the orthodox Twelver Ja'fari school, which the Shah of Persia must profess and promote," Art. 1 of the complement of 1907); the 1923 Constitution of Egypt ("Islam is the religion of the state," Art. 149); the 1923 Fundamental Law of Afghanistan ("The religion of Afghanistan is Islam," Art. 2, amended in 1924 to specify the official Hanafi school); the 1876 Ottoman Constitution ("The Ottoman state's religion is Islam," Art. 11); the 1924 Constitution of Turkey ("The religion of the Turkish state is the religion of Islam," Art. 2, amended in 1928 to suppress this clause); the 1925 Constitution of Iraq ("Islam is the official religion of the state," Art. 13); the 1926 Fundamental Law of the Hijaz ("The Arab Hijazi state is a monarchical, consultative, Islamic, and independent state," Art. 2); and the 1928 Constitution of Transjordan ("Islam is the religion of the state," Art. 10).

The 1920 Greater Syria Draft Constitution: "Islam Is the Religion of the King"

The stillborn 1920 Greater Syria Draft Constitution was conceived for a democratic constitutional monarchy. It was written by the General Syrian Congress, which met between June 3, 1919, and July 19, 1920, but it was never proclaimed or put into effect. Its drafting took place in the tumultuous context that immediately preceded the dismembering of Greater Syria into French Mandates in Syria and Lebanon and a British Mandate in Palestine.[23] The soon-to-be-king Amir Faysal advocated for the principle of equality irrespective of religion, which was not contentious in the General Syrian Congress.[24] In what seems to be the final 1920 Draft Constitution,[25] freedom of belief and worship were guaranteed, and it was left to future legislation to define the mode by which the leaders of religious communities, sharia courts, and religious endowments would be appointed.[26] The Draft Constitution did not include an establishment clause—leading some historians to describe it as "the most secular" constitution in the Middle East[27]—but it did obliquely assert a state-preferred status for Islam: Article 1 read, "The government of the Syrian Arab Kingdom is a representative, civil [*madanī*], monarchical government. Its capital is Damascus in Greater Syria [*Shām*] and the religion of its king is Islam

23. The literature does not refer to transcripts of the entirety of the constitutional debates, only to what was reported in the Syrian press and the Syrian Official Gazette, *Al-ʿĀṣima*. I could not locate comprehensive transcripts, if they are extant. In addition, Rashid Rida, who (as reported in *Al-ʿĀṣima*, no. 123, May 6, 1920) was elected president of the General Syrian Congress on May 5, 1920, wrote in 1934 in *Al-Manār* as well as in his 1925 correspondence with Shakib Arslan, about some of the discussions in the General Syrian Congress.

24. Shahrastān (2000) and Rabbath (1986). Many of the petitions addressed to the American King-Crane Commission underlined the necessity of protecting religious minorities.

25. The original text of the 1920 Greater Syria Draft Constitution does not seem to exist. According to Atassi (2018, 69–70), "Some non-Arabic-speaking commentators question whether an original version of the 1920 constitution is still extant. They refer to the French translation of the text in the 1923 thesis by Philippe David, which it is claimed was subsequently translated back into Arabic." Rabbath (1986, 335) claims that there was no official publication of the 1920 Syrian Draft Constitution. The first published version I found appeared in Maʿhad al-Dirāsāt al-ʿArabīya al-ʿĀliya (1955, 3–22), which does not provide any reference for its sources.

26. Articles 14 and 15.

27. E. Thompson (2015, 244).

[*dīn malikihā al-Islām*]."[28] Moreover, in contrast with the 1923 Egyptian Constitution, the 1920 Greater Syria Draft Constitution stipulated proportional representation of religious minorities in national and local legislative assemblies,[29] although it appears that there was some disagreement in the General Syrian Congress about this principle.[30] Under the French Mandate, the formula "the religion of its president is Islam," rather than an establishment clause, was included in the 1930 Constitution of Syria, which also stipulated that the electoral law would ensure representation of religious minorities.[31] All subsequent constitutions of Syria also included this "the religion of its president is Islam" formula, but mention of the political representation of religious minorities was eventually dropped.[32]

A COMPROMISE BETWEEN LIBERALS AND CONSERVATIVES

The absence of an establishment clause in the 1920 Greater Syria Draft Constitution resulted from a compromise between its proponents (some ʿulamā and Muslim conservatives) and their adversaries (representatives of religious minorities and some Muslims who wanted to avoid such state favoritism toward Islam), as recounted by Yusuf al-Hakim (1879–1979), a prominent official and member of the General Syrian Congress, in his memoirs. He spoke of a virulent opposition between the conservative ʿulamā and the "progressives" (*taqaddumīyūn*) who advocated for separation of "religion and politics," a pattern they argued was adopted by advanced nations.[33] In a quid pro quo, conservatives

28. The French version of Article 1 in David (1923, 135) differs from the known Arabic version reproduced in *Al-ʿĀṣima*, no. 140, July 15, 1920, 2, in Maʿhad al-Dirāsāt al-ʿArabīya al-ʿĀliya (1955, 3–22) and in Khūrī (1989, 23), and states "The government of the Syrian Arab Kingdom is a civil and representative monarchy. Its capital is Damascus and its state religion is Islam." Philippe David might have misread *malik* (king) as *mulk* (government).

29. Articles 89 and 129.

30. *Al-ʿĀṣima*, no. 131, June 10, 1920, 3, and no. 134, June 24, 1920, 3. Philippe David (1923, 113) interpreted proportional parliamentary representation of minorities as "the 'reward offered' to religious communities other than the Sunni Muslims in exchange for their attachment to the Sharifian dynasty."

31. Article 3 of the 1930 Constitution of Syria read: "Syria is a parliamentary republic. The religion of its president is Islam. Its capital is Damascus." Article 37 mandated the representation of religious minorities.

32. We do not find it in the final draft of the 1950 Constitution of the independent Republic of Syria passed by the Constituent Assembly.

33. Al-Ḥakīm (1966, 95–96).

agreed to renounce an establishment clause but obtained the stipulation that Islam is "the religion of the king," the sole (if oblique) reference to the Muslim character of the state in the Draft Constitution. This was also recounted several years later, in 1934, by Rashid Rida, who was a member of the 1920 General Syrian Congress and participated in the negotiations.[34] According to his account, some non-Muslim members of the General Syrian Congress had asked that the government of Syria be "nonreligious [*lā-dīnīya*] and secular [*lā ʾikī*]." He added, "Some nominal [*jughrāfīyīn*] Muslims agreed with them. Others opposed this view and advised that it be stated that Syria's government is an Islamic and Arab government, or that its official religion is Islam. The dispute [*jidāl*] became heated. I did not see a solution other than advising to remain silent on this issue."[35] Rashid Rida claims that he facilitated a compromise by arguing that the "religion of the king is Islam" clause was sufficient to prevent the constitutionalization of a secular state, which he viewed as "a government of unbelief [*kufr*]" to which allegiance "would not be obligatory." Even assuming that the constitution were not to stipulate that Islam was the religion of the state, he insisted that "sharia must be the greatest foundation of the laws that the nation needs." In the end, he recounted, "the majority agreed with this view and that it would suffice that Islam be the official religion of its king."[36]

Yusuf al-Hakim and Rashid Rida did not explain what the "progressives" in the General Syrian Congress meant by separation of "religion and politics,"[37] what was meant exactly by a "nonreligious and secular" government, and how prevalent these aspirations were. However, the consultations that the French

34. Rashid Rida also wrote that he negotiated the aforementioned Article 15 with Christian leaders. Rashid Rida to Shakib Arslan, December 11, 1925, in Arslān (1937, 427–430).

35. Rashīd Riḍā, Al-ʿIbra bi-Sīrat al-Malik Fayṣal [Lessons from the life of King Faysal], *Al-Manār*, vol. 34, no. 1, May 1, 1934, 68–73. Rashid Rida also claimed that members of the General Syrian Congress were opposed to him and to Shaykh Abd al-Qadir al-Khatib because they were ʿulamā. Rashīd Riḍā, Al-ʿIbra bi-Sīrat al-Malik Fayṣal, *Al-Manār*, vol. 34, no. 5, October 7, 1934, 393. Khoury (1981, 446–448) argues that Abd al-Rahman Shahbandar and Michel Lutfallah were "among the leading advocates of a purely secular nationalism" and that Shakib Arslan and Rashid Rida emphazised "an Arab nation whose underlying moral principles were based on the Divine Law of Islam."

36. Rashīd Riḍā, Al-ʿIbra bi-Sīrat al-Malik Fayṣal, *Al-Manār*, vol. 34, no. 1, May 1, 1934, 68–73.

37. The explanation of the 1920 Syrian Draft Constitution—reproduced in Shahrastān (2000, 229–244) and written by Uthman Sultan, a representative of Tripoli and member of the General Syrian Congress—described the state as "civil" and as one in which "purely religious factors will not be given a role in politics." Note, however, the political representation of religious minorities.

organized a few years later for the drafting of Organic Statutes for their Mandates in the Levant (which encompassed 1920 Greater Syria except for Palestine) provide us with some clues.[38] Out of a total of 138 responses received between early August and early November 1925, almost half (63, i.e., 46 percent) broached the subject of religion in governance.[39] None explicitly argued for full separation of religion and state,[40] although 14 responses (10 percent) argued for a state that is neutral, secular, or without a religion and either rejected or did not mention proportional representation of religions in elected assemblies or in government.[41] These fourteen responses came from Muslims and Christians alike, in a proportion that approximately reflected their demographic weight in Syria and Lebanon.[42] Ten of them used the Arabic "ʿilmānīya" or French "laïcité," albeit without fully developing their meaning. For example, one response advocated for a "separation between the policy of the government and religion" (*faṣl siyāsat al-ḥukūma ʿan al-dīn*), against the

38. The censuses conducted in the French Mandates of the Levant in the early 1920s reported about 70 percent Muslims (53 percent Sunnis, 5 percent Shiites, 11 percent Alawites, and 1 percent Ismaʿilis), 4 percent Druzes, 25 percent Christians, and 1 percent Jews in these territories. Therefore, Muslim demographic preponderance was slightly less pronounced than in the whole of 1920 Greater Syria since, according to the British Mandate census, there was a clearer Muslim majority in Palestine with about 78 percent Sunni Muslims, 1 percent Druzes, 10 percent Christians, and 11 percent Jews. République Française, Ministère des Affaires Etrangères, *Rapport sur la situation de la Syrie et du Liban pour 1926–1927*, 190–194; and Palestine, *Report and General Abstracts of the Census of 1922*, 4–5.

39. AMAE, Levant 1918–1940, "Réorganisation de la Syrie. Gouvernement et administration des pays sous Mandat français, Elaboration du Statut Organique de ces pays," vols. 219 to 224. French Mandate authorities, afraid of deliberative elected assemblies, organized individual consultations of handpicked Lebanese and Syrian personalities. Two broad questions were asked: (1) the organization of the future states (Syria, Lebanon, and the Alawite state); and (2) their mutual relations. The response rate seems to have been high: I counted 155 names French authorities claimed they solicited.

40. However, I was able to locate a petition addressed to the Peace Conference on March 15, 1919, in favor of "the absolute separation of Church and State" in an independent Syria based on federalism, written by the Greek Orthodox Abraham Mitrie Rihbany (1869–1944), who represented the New Syria National League. http://dcollections.oberlin.edu/cdm/search/searchterm/Doc_Ribhany_Syria_1919_3_15.tif.

41. Seven of these fourteen responses explicitly rejected sectarian representation. In addition, there were four responses that argued for a state that is neutral or without a religion but also for proportional representation of religions in elected assemblies or the government.

42. Among these 14 responses, 10 were sent by Muslims, and 4 by Christians: 3 Muslims and 3 Christians for Lebanon, 6 Muslims and 1 Christian for Syria, and 1 Sunni for the Alawite state.

representation of religious communities in the Cabinet, and for a "secular" (*ʿilmānī*) system of education,[43] and another, written in French, argued for the absence of a state religion and for a legislation of "secular inspiration" (*d'inspiration laïque*).[44] Another response advocated for a "purely secular government [*ḥukūma ʿilmānīya maḥḍ*] that does not meddle with religion" and elections based on merit only, for the Alawite state,[45] and another two responses for "a principle of nonsectarian secularism" (*qāʿidat al-ʿilmānīya al-lā-ṭāʾifīya*) at the foundation of governance for Syria.[46] A response in French argued for a "civil, secular and constitutional" (*civil, laïque et constitutionnel*) Syrian government, rejected sectarian political representation, and added that no student in private or public schools should be forced to attend religious ceremonies.[47] Another argued for a "secular government" (*gouvernement laïque*), for the removal of sharia courts, and for ending the relation between religious leaders and the government.[48] Arguments of this kind have rarely been heard in the modern Middle East, especially in public deliberative arenas. It is therefore noteworthy that they were heard among a small but nonnegligible number of individual responses to this consultation, in this limit-case

43. Arif Alouani, a Sunni lawyer from Aleppo, for Syria. AMAE, Levant 1918–1940, "Réorganisation de la Syrie. Gouvernement et administration des pays sous Mandat français, Elaboration du Statut Organique de ces pays," vol. 222, fols. 150–151.

44. Sami al-Sulh, a Sunni civil servant in the Lebanese justice system, for Lebanon. AMAE, Levant 1918–1940, "Réorganisation de la Syrie. Gouvernement et administration des pays sous Mandat français, Elaboration du Statut Organique de ces pays," vol. 221, fols. 5–7.

45. Abd al-Wahid Harun, a Sunni Muslim and former member of the Ottoman Parliament. AMAE, Levant 1918–1940, "Réorganisation de la Syrie. Gouvernement et administration des pays sous Mandat français, Elaboration du Statut Organique de ces pays," vol. 223, fol. 9. A similar response was sent for Lebanon by Musa Namur, a Maronite lawyer from Zahlé and president of the Representative Council of Lebanon. AMAE, Levant 1918–1940, "Réorganisation de la Syrie. Gouvernement et administration des pays sous Mandat français, Elaboration du Statut Organique de ces pays," vol. 221, fols. 296–309.

46. Jamil Shuman, a journalist in Lattaquieh, and Abd al-Qadir Shraytah, president of the Chamber of Commerce of Lattaquieh, both Sunni Muslims. AMAE, Levant 1918–1940, "Réorganisation de la Syrie. Gouvernement et administration des pays sous Mandat français, Elaboration du Statut Organique de ces pays," vol. 223, fols. 34 and 40.

47. Muhammad Makhzumi, a Muslim from Beirut. AMAE, Levant 1918–1940, "Réorganisation de la Syrie. Gouvernement et administration des pays sous Mandat français, Elaboration du Statut Organique de ces pays," vol. 223, fols. 206–207.

48. AMAE, Levant 1918–1940, "Réorganisation de la Syrie. Gouvernement et administration des pays sous Mandat français, Elaboration du Statut Organique de ces pays," vol. 222, fols. 170–172.

where the demographic (and political) weight of non-Muslims was greater than elsewhere in the region.

In time, Syria moved in the opposite direction. Article 3 of the 1950 Constitution of the independent Republic of Syria not only stated that "the religion of the President of the Republic is Islam" but also that "Islamic *fiqh* shall be the main source of legislation." This was, once again, the result of a hard-fought political battle between conservatives (notably the Syrian Muslim Brothers and some ʿulamā), who were in favor of inscribing Islam as the religion of the state in the constitution, and Muslim and Christian Syrians, who were against it and even, in some instances, argued in the Constituent Assembly in favor of "separation of religion and state" (*faṣl al-dīn ʿan al-dawla*).[49] By that time, the demographic makeup of the Syrian republic, more than 80 percent Muslim,[50] had tilted further in favor of the Muslim majority, which facilitated this outcome.

49. Article 3 of the Constitution Draft presented to the Constituent Assembly (*al-lajna al-taʾsīsīya*) in April 1950 stipulated, "(1) Islam is the religion of the state; (2) The heavenly religions [*al-adyān al-samāwīya*] are respected and sacred; (3) The personal status of the religious communities [*al-ṭawāʾif al-dīnīya*] is protected and preserved; (4) Citizens have equal rights and obligations, irrespective of religion." Mustafa al-Sibaʿi (1915–1964), leader of the Syrian Muslim Brothers and member of the Constituent Assembly, had vocally defended these stipulations in the press in early March 1950, in an essay reproduced in Zarzūr (2000, 251–266) and translated in Winder (1954). This proposal, supported by several ʿulamā, was criticized in the press and in the Constituent Assembly, as illustrated by the July 24, 1950 (session 38) intervention of the Christian member Elyas Damr, who advocated for the separation of religion and state, argued that the establishment clause was contrary to nationalism, and rejected any religious "constraint" (*qayd*) on the state. A new version of Article 3 was discussed and passed on July 29, 1950 (session 41) and included in the Constitution approved in September 1950. It read, "(1) The religion of the president of the republic is Islam; (2) Islamic *fiqh* [*al-fiqh al-Islāmī*] shall be the main source of legislation; (3) Freedom of belief [*ḥurrīyat al-iʿtiqād*] is guaranteed. The state respects all heavenly religions and provides freedom of worship as long as this does not harm public order [*al-niẓām al-ʿāmm*]; (4) The personal status of the religious communities is protected and preserved." Mustafa al-Sibaʿi spoke of this outcome as a "natural right" (*ḥaqq ṭabīʿī*) of the Muslim majority and the result of a compromise between proponents of an establishment clause and their adversaries. See *Al-Jumhūrīya al-Sūrīya, Al-Jarīda al-Rasmīya, Mudhākarāt Majlis al-Nuwwāb*, June 22, 1950, vol. 33, Annex, 12–27 (for the Constitution Draft), vol. 32, no. 57, November 9, 1950 (for session 38), 629–644, and vol. 32, no. 62, December 14 (for session 41), 1950, 659–684.

50. According to the Syrian Republic, Ministry of National Economy, *Statistical Abstract of Syria for 1951 and 1952*, 20, there were, in 1950, about 82 percent Muslims (including 69 percent Sunnis and 11 percent Alawites), 3 percent Druzes, 14 percent Christians, and 1 percent Jews.

DID RASHID RIDA CHANGE HIS MIND OR WAS HE SIMPLY BEING PRAGMATIC?

Why did Rashid Rida—who so consistently advocated for the Islamic character of the state before and after this episode—agree to forego an establishment clause in the Greater Syria 1920 Draft Constitution? In 1911 he had virulently opposed the idea of proportional representation of Copts in elected assemblies in Egypt, arguing that "they only represented 5 or 6 percent of the nation" whereas they "consumed about 30 percent of its harvest."[51] He insisted that "Muslims consider themselves a nation whose nationality is Islam and that it is imperative for them to have a government that is Islamic."[52] A few years earlier, in 1908, he had similarly argued that in Egypt the Copts "who work in the government outnumber the Muslims," even though "it is known that [they] are around half a million, whereas the Muslims are 11 million." He then concluded, "It is important here to examine the character of the Egyptian government and its official religion. If it continues to remain an Islamic government, contrary to what some Copts affirm, it becomes obvious that the demands of this community [*ṭāʾifa*] for equality with Muslims in everything is misplaced."[53] Therefore, Rashid Rida's stance concerning Greater Syria in 1920 is not a sign of "liberalism" on his part, contrary to claims that he radicalized only later.[54] He explicitly advocated for the Islamic character of the state

51. Rashīd Riḍā, Al-Muslimūn wa-l-Qubṭ [Muslims and Copts], *Al-Manār*, vol. 14, no. 3, March 30, 1911.

52. Rashīd Riḍā, Al-Muslimūn wa-l-Qubṭ, *Al-Manār*, vol. 14, no. 4, April 29, 1911. In this article, Rashid Rida also argued, "This nationality of theirs [Islam] is capacious and just and does not differentiate between the Muslim and the non-Muslim. It contains tolerance and freedom and it does not forbid its people to include others in all dimensions of life, despite the fact that the Copts, in the past and in the present, and up to this day, have too many positions in the government, in their real estate and land, and in their waqfs."

53. He continued, "If [the government] has abandoned the principles of being Islamic and that its ruler is the representative of the Muslims' Caliph, then why does [the government] appoint Islamic judges, [employees in] its administration of the Muslims waqfs, and preachers and imams in mosques and other legal [*sharʿī*] issues of this kind? Does the ruler possess these legal rights [*ḥuqūq sharʿīya*] today or does he possess these rights by force over the Copts and others without the sovereignty given to him by revealed law [*wilāyat al-sharʿ*]? Has the country lost its existence as the abode of Islam [*dār al-Islām*]?" Rashīd Riḍā, Al-Muslimūn wa-l-Qubṭ, *Al-Manār*, vol. 11, no. 5, June 29, 1908.

54. E. Thompson (2015, 245) does not consider Rashid Rida's earlier stances and claims that Rashid Rida's rejection of "liberalism as a universal model of just governance" was triggered by his disappointment with the imposition of the French Mandate on Syria and concludes that

whenever possible, and he did so adamantly both before and after his participation in the drafting of the 1920 Greater Syria Draft Constitution. He simply adapted to what was feasible in Greater Syria in 1920, given the significantly larger fraction of non-Muslims than in Egypt.[55]

The 1926 Constitution of Lebanon: Similar Questions, Different Outcome

The making of the 1926 Constitution of Lebanon, which was drafted by the thirteen-member Lebanese Organic Statute Committee (*Commission du Statut Organique*)[56] under the tutelage of the French Mandate authorities,[57] is also telling. Given the religious makeup of Lebanon at the time—about half Christian, of various denominations, and the other half mostly Muslim with a significant Druze minority[58]—it would also have been difficult to include an establishment

---

"the rise of modern Islamism [is] the product of a contingent moment rather than the inexorable expression of a timeless force." In the same vein, E. Thompson (2020, 124) claims that an "organic law" drafted in 1915 by Rashid Rida envisioned a "future Syrian Arab state . . . that would separate religion from state." However, this text explicitly stipulates that the "official religion" of this would-be "Arabian Empire" is Islam. See Haddad (1997, 269).

55. In contrast with most of the literature, which sees an ideological shift in his support of the Wahhabis starting in the 1920s, Lauzière (2015, 62) similarly argues that "Rida tried to rehabilitate the Wahhabis primarily for reasons of sociopolitical expedience—that is, more out of necessity than conviction."

56. The Lebanese Organic Status Committee was elected by the Lebanese Representative Council on December 10, 1925. There were 4 Maronite (including the president of the committee), 2 Greek Orthodox, 1 Greek Catholic, 1 Latin, 2 Sunni, 2 Shiite, and 1 Druze—a composition not too far, percentage-wise, from that of the 30-member Representative Council from which it was elected (10 Maronite, 4 Greek Orthodox, 2 Greek Catholic, 1 Latin, 6 Sunni, 5 Shiite, 2 Druze).

57. Article 1 of the 1922 League of Nations Mandate Charter of Syria and Lebanon gave French Mandate authorities three years to elaborate an Organic Statute for Syria and for Lebanon "in agreement with native authorities" and taking into account "the rights, interests and wishes of all the populations residing in these territories." There were disputes within, as well as between, French authorities and Lebanese elites about territorial divisions, about the meaning of an Organic Statute, and about the drafting process. After protracted tergiversations on the part of the French authorities in Paris and Beirut, and after the 1925 Syrian revolt, order was reestablished militarily, and the elected Lebanese Representative Council was tasked with drafting the Constitution. The Boncour Commission—made up of French legal experts and officially appointed in June 1925—worked closely with the Lebanese Organic Statute Committee. See Rabbath (1982, 1986), and Hokayem (1996).

58. According to the census conducted in the French Mandates of the Levant in the early 1920s, counting residents and temporary absents only, there were about 38 percent Muslims

clause in the Constitution: even the largest community according to the censuses conducted around that time, the Christians, had a precarious, fragmented, and disputed majority. The Organic Statute Committee drafted the 1926 Constitution on the basis of an initial draft provided by the French Mandate authorities.[59] Article 7 stipulated the full equality of all Lebanese. In the initial French authorities' draft,[60] later echoed by the official French-language version of the Constitution, Article 9 guaranteed "freedom of conscience" (*liberté de conscience*). The final, official Arabic version rendered this as "freedom of belief" (*ḥurrīyat al-iʿtiqād*), part of a common, deliberate pattern of mistranslation.[61] It also stated, "The state respects all faiths and confessions [*adyān wa-madhāhib*] and guarantees and protects their free worship, as long as public order is not harmed. The state also guarantees populations of any sect [*ʿalā ikhtilāf milalihim*] respect for their personal status and for their religious interests."

The Organic Statute Committee also based its work on the answers to twelve questions sent to 240 delegates chosen among Lebanese elites to represent the religious communities, as well as political, administrative, and

---

(21 percent Sunnis and 17 percent Shiites), 6 percent Druzes, 55 percent Christians, and 1 percent Jews in Lebanon. République Française, Ministère des Affaires Etrangères, *Rapport sur la situation de la Syrie et du Liban pour 1926, 1927*, 190–194. According to the 1932 Census of the Republic of Lebanon, there were about 42 percent Sunni and Shiite Muslims, 7 percent Druzes, 50 percent Christians, and 1 percent Jews, but counting emigrants who retained Lebanese citizenship, there were about 40 percent Sunni and Shiite Muslims, and 53 percent Christians. For a summary of the 1932 census results, see Himadeh (1936, 408–409) and Maktabi (1999, 222). For a discussion of the degrees of accuracy of, contentions about, and political manipulations involved in the censuses in Lebanon, see Himadeh (1936, 3–4), Faour (1991), and Maktabi (1999).

59. The French and Arabic official versions of the 1926 Lebanese Constitution were, respectively, published in the 1926 French and Arabic Lebanese Official Gazettes. The French version is also in *Revue générale de droit international public*, November–December 1930, vol. 4, no. 6, 672–683. The Arabic version is reproduced in Khūrī (1989, 438–442).

60. Hokayem (1996, 235–240).

61. This mistranslation seems deliberate since "*liberté de conscience*" (freedom of conscience) in Article 8 of the 1922 League of Nations Mandate Charter of Syria and Lebanon was properly translated into "*ḥurrīyat al-ḍamīr*." See *Al-Bashīr* of October 18, 1923, reproduced in Khūrī (1989, 210). An undated handwritten draft in French by Michel Chiha, member of the Organic Statute Committee (available at http://www.michelchiha.org/statehood/constitution-and-amendments/62/1/) also uses the term "freedom of conscience." It seems that Arabic and French were both used during the drafting process, notably in the deliberations of the May 22, 1926, extraordinary sessions of the Representative Council as evidenced by the transcripts of the deliberations, where Paul Souchier intervened several times (in all likelihood in French) and the presence of a translator is mentioned. See Zayn and Mājid (1995, 73–85).

professional groups.[62] The Committee received written answers from 132 delegates (a 55 percent response rate), which were summarized in a report drafted by Cheble Dammous, a member of the Organic Statute Committee. This very low response rate, especially considering that the delegates were hand-picked, indicates that the constitutional process, even at this later stage, was contentious among Lebanese elites. During earlier phases some had already expressed their refusal to recognize the state of Lebanon in its 1920 borders and their reservations about the mode and degree of consultation.[63] The Dammous Report mentions that among the 240 delegates, 59 of them (25 percent) did not respond at all, and 49 of them (20 percent) replied that they would not answer the Committee's questionnaire. Of these, 32 delegates (13 percent) refused because they supported a United Syria (which, it should be noted, would have led to a clear Muslim majority) or because they refused to recognize the state of Lebanon's borders as drawn by the Mandate; 13 delegates (5 percent) because they objected to the consultative method; and 4 delegates (2 percent) for health reasons.[64] The Dammous Report is nevertheless illuminating since two of the questions the Organic Statute Committee asked pertained to the representation of religious minorities in politics and in the state: "Must the sectarian principle be adopted as the criterion to distribute seats in Parliament?" (Question #6) and "Must the representation of communities be taken into consideration in the attribution of public posts and in particular in the composition of the Cabinet?" (Question #12).[65]

French authorities in Paris and Beirut had been deeply divided on these issues. For instance, sectarian political representation had been condemned by Henry de Jouvenel's predecessor at the post of high commissioner, the staunchly anticlerical General Sarrail, who (arguing that it would appease "religious antagonism") attempted to eliminate it from the electoral rules in 1925

62. I derive this number from the Dammous Report, reproduced in Hokayem (1996, 342–353) and analyzed in Rabbath (1982, 12–32) and Hokayem (1996, 222–231). Some of the figures in the Dammous Report are inconsistent. It claims that the questionnaire was sent to 189 delegates and provides a list, organized in 24 categories, which adds up to 228 delegates. However, the number of responses, written responses, and nonresponses listed in the report add up to 240. It turns out that 189 is the number of delegates of the first 10 categories listed. In addition, 12 delegates are missing from the list, probably due to a typo in one of the categories or to a missing category. It must be kept in mind that this list was augmented over time.

63. Hokayem (1996, 225–231).

64. Dammous Report, reproduced in Hokayem (1996, 342–353).

65. Dammous Report, reproduced in Hokayem (1996, 348 and 352).

but renounced in the face of strong opposition in Paris.[66] In addition, the Dammous Report revealed a divide among Lebanese elites on both of these questions, although the *principle* of proportional representation of religious communities in Parliament was unanimously condemned by the delegates, who "expressed their desire to see the prejudices that have made us attached to this system disappear."[67] Still, 121 delegates (50 percent of all delegates, 92 percent of those who answered) answered that they advised, "although not without great reluctance," that the confessional system be at the basis of political representation, and invoked several reasons: without it, some communities would gain dominance over others; all communities had to be fairly represented and their rights guaranteed to avoid any recriminations; it was too early to attempt to erase the persistently sectarian mentality of the Lebanese who were not yet ready to abandon their religious allegiances for patriotic solidarity; and "communities in Lebanon play the role of political parties."[68] Against these arguments, 11 delegates (5 percent of all delegates, 8 percent of those who answered) argued that sectarianism was "a malady," that it was antithetical to constitutional government, and that communities could not be considered political parties: "One voluntarily adheres to a party, but does not choose to be born in a religious community."[69] In the end, Article 24 of the 1926 Constitution stipulated that, until a new law could be passed, parliamentary elections would be conducted according to current regulations, which specified quotas for each religious community in the Representative Council.[70] Hence, Article 24 implicitly inscribed sectarian representation in Parliament. In addition, Article 96 explicitly distributed seats in the Senate according to quotas for each community.

As for Question #12, which dealt with the distribution of the state's administrative posts, 100 delegates (42 percent of all delegates, 76 percent of those who answered) answered positively, "while recognizing the faults of a system that refused to give consideration to competence and merit," against 32 delegates

66. Hokayem (1996, 166–176).

67. Dammous Report, reproduced in Hokayem (1996, 348).

68. Dammous Report, reproduced in Hokayem (1996, 348–349). See also Rabbath (1982, 26).

69. Dammous Report, reproduced in Hokayem (1996, 349). See also Rabbath (1982, 27).

70. Members of the Chamber of Deputies would be elected, for the time being, in accordance with Arrêté no. 1307 of March 10, 1922, which stipulated how to compute each community's number of seats in the Representative Council based on census results. *Recueil des actes administratifs du haut-commissariat de la République française en Syrie et au Liban*, 1922, vol. 3, 195–229.

(13 percent of all delegates, 24 percent of those who answered) who gave preference to merit alone.[71] After vigorous debates in the Representative Council on the eve of the May 23, 1926, promulgation of the Constitution, a choice was reluctantly made to inscribe in Article 95 the distribution of posts in the state administration along sectarian lines, and to underline this reluctance by making this principle provisional.[72] The discussion showed deep divisions, which cut across sectarian lines.[73] Those against Article 95 argued that it was incompatible with "national unity" (*waḥda waṭanīya*)[74] and that the "sectarian spirit" (*al-rūḥ al-ṭā ʾifīya*) was "the cause of our backwardness," was "harmful," and was "killing" the Lebanese.[75] It was a "disease" and the reason for the Mandate.[76] These arguments also appeared in the press. In April 1926, the cover of the journal *Al-Aḥrār al-Muṣawwara* (The Liberals Illustrated) presented the Lebanese Constitution as a book from which emerged a seven-headed creature, labeled as "a demon" (*shayṭān*), each of its heads representing a religious community.[77] Referring to

71. Dammous Report, reproduced in Hokayem (1996, 352).

72. The draft of the Constitution was discussed during eight extraordinary sessions of the Representative Council, from May 19 to May 22, 1926, and Article 95 during the last session. Arabic transcripts of the deliberations are reproduced in the Official Gazette of Greater Lebanon (*Jarīdat Lubnān al-Kabīr al-Rasmīya*), Annex no. 1968, year 1926, 17–48, in *Al-Nashra al-Qaḍā ʾīya al-Lubnānīya*, January 1970, year 26, no. 1, 1–65, and in Zayn and Mājid (1995, 16–85). Article 95 reads: "As a temporary measure, and in accordance with the dispositions of Article 1 of the Mandate Charter and with the aim of justice and peace, the communities will be equitably represented in public service posts and in the composition of ministries, without causing, however, any harm to the interest of the state." See also Rabbath (1982, 37).

73. Sixteen (53 percent) of the thirty members of the Representative Council voted in favor of Article 95, whereas six (20 percent) voted against and eight (27 percent) abstained or were absent (the transcripts of the deliberation do not indicate the number of absent members). For the seventeen Christian members, these percentages were 53 percent, 23.5 percent, and 23.5 percent, respectively. For the thirteen Muslim and Druze members, they were 54 percent, 15 percent, and 31 percent, respectively. The ten Maronite members seem to have been the most divided on this issue in the council, with 40 percent for, 30 percent against, and 30 percent abstentions. These figures are derived from Zayn and Mājid (1995, 77).

74. Georges Tabet (Maronite), Representative Council, afternoon session of May 22, 1926, in Zayn and Mājid (1995, 74–77).

75. Ibrahim Mundhir (Greek Orthodox), Representative Council, afternoon session of May 22, 1926, in Zayn and Mājid (1995, 74–77). Georges Zuwayn (Maronite) makes the same argument during the same session.

76. Georges Zuwayn (Maronite), Representative Council, afternoon session of May 22, 1926, in Zayn and Mājid (1995, 74–77).

77. *Al-Aḥrār al-Muṣawwara*, no. 16, April 27, 1926.

the 1922 Egyptian Constitutional Committee's rejection of proportional representation for religious minorities as a model to follow, an article in the same issue, in all likelihood authored by the Greek Orthodox Gibran Tueni, the chief editor of the journal, urged the Representative Council not to inscribe sectarianism in the Constitution.[78] However, the prevalent view in the Representative Council was that, although sectarianism was incompatible with nationalism, Article 95 provided security to all religious communities and prevented discord.[79] It was a way to limit any religious community's potential ambition to take over the state to the detriment of others.[80] It also meant that the state could not have a preferred religion. During the Representative Council debates, Cheble Dammous, who voted in favor of Article 95, argued, "The country is a group of religions [*adyān*] and they are all minorities [*aqallīya*]. The state does not belong to any one of them, but is rather 'areligious' [*lā-dīnīya*], although it respects all religions."[81] In the end, the thirty-member Representative Council approved Article 95 by 16 votes against 6,[82] and this principle, as well as sectarian political representation, endured with some variations into the twenty-first century in Lebanon, while continuing to be declared provisional.

2. Building a Cohesive Nation of Political Equals under a Muslim State: The 1922 Egyptian Constitutional Debates

In Egypt, where Muslims constituted a much clearer majority, the terms of the debate were similar to 1920 Greater Syria and 1926 Lebanon, but the outcome was different. After Egypt gained quasi-independence from England in 1922, Egyptians drafted a constitution, affirmed their state's sovereignty,[83] and (in

78. Al-Ṭā'ifīya fī al-Dustūr [Sectarianism in the Constitution], *Al-Aḥrār al-Muṣawwara*, no. 16, April 27, 1926, 3.

79. Petro Trad (Greek Orthodox), Representative Council, afternoon session of May 22, 1926, in Zayn and Mājid (1995, 74–77).

80. Cheble Dammous (Greek Orthodox) and Jamil Talhuq (Druze), Representative Council, afternoon session of May 22, 1926, in Zayn and Mājid (1995, 74–77).

81. Cheble Dammous (Greek Orthodox), Representative Council, session of May 20, 1926, in Zayn and Mājid (1995, 26).

82. Zayn and Mājid (1995, 77).

83. The 1923 Constitution could be considered the first constitution of Egypt, although on February 7, 1882, a fundamental law (*qānūn asāsī*), which the British at the time along with some of the historiography since called a "constitution," was adopted by the Assembly of Delegates (*majlis al-nuwwāb*). It was also called the Regulation of the Assembly of Delegates (*Lā'iḥat*

a broad agreement between conservatives and liberals alike) strongly reasserted the role of the state as the custodian of Islam, which they enshrined in an establishment clause: Article 149 of the 1923 Egyptian Constitution read, "Islam is the religion of the state and Arabic is its official language."[84] At the same time, the 1923 Constitution stipulated that "Egyptians are equal before the law [*al-miṣrīyūn ladā al-qānūn sawā*] . . . regardless of differences of origin [*aṣl*], language [*lugha*] and religion [*dīn*]"[85] and guaranteed "individual freedom" (*ḥurrīya shakhṣīya*)[86] as well as "freedom of belief" (*ḥurriyat al-muʿtaqad*), which was to be "absolute" (*muṭlaqa*).[87] It also described the Egyptian state as the protector of "freedom of religious worship and beliefs [*ḥurrīyat al-qiyām bi-shaʿāʾir al-adyān wa-l-ʿaqāʾid*] in accordance with the customs [*al-ʿādāt*] observed in Egypt, as long as they do not violate public order [*al-niẓām al-ʿāmm*] and do not contravene propriety [*ādāb*]."[88] And indeed, at the opening session of the thirty-two-member Constitutional Committee (*lajnat al-dustūr*) that he had appointed, the prime minister had stressed that the constitution would be based on "the most modern principles of public law" (*aḥdath mabādiʾ al-qānūn al-ʿāmm*) while respecting Egypt's "local traditions and customs" (*taqālīd al-bilād al-maḥallīya wa-ʿādātahā*).[89]

Contrary to received wisdom, discussions about religion occupied a significant fraction of the deliberations of the Constitutional Committee: one-third of its sessions dealt with religion, although only one-twentieth of the articles of the Constitution did.[90] The majority of the constituents were "socially and

---

Majlis al-Nuwwāb) and mainly regulated its operations, whereas the 1923 Constitution was much broader in its scope. See Schölch (1981, 214) and Naqqāsh (1994, vol. 4).

84. *Al-Waqāʾiʿ al-Miṣrīya*, no. 42, April 20, 1923. This was Article 138 of the 1923 final Constitution Draft Project. Al-Ḥukūma al-Miṣrīya, Lajnat al-Dustūr (1924, 237).

85. Article 3 of the 1923 Constitution, *Al-Waqāʾiʿ al-Miṣrīya*, no. 42, April 20, 1923.

86. Article 4 of the 1923 Constitution, *Al-Waqāʾiʿ al-Miṣrīya*, no. 42, April 20, 1923.

87. Article 12 of the 1923 Constitution, *Al-Waqāʾiʿ al-Miṣrīya*, no. 42, April 20, 1923.

88. Article 13 of the 1923 Constitution, *Al-Waqāʾiʿ al-Miṣrīya*, no. 42, April 20, 1923.

89. Speech by Prime Minister Abd al-Khaliq Tharwat, session 1, April 11, 1922, Al-Ḥukūma al-Miṣrīya, Lajnat al-Dustūr (1924, 1–3). These "modern principles" included the establishment of democratic elections, governmental accountability before Parliament, and equal rights and duties for all Egyptians. The Constitutional Committee had thirty members plus a president and a vice president.

90. I counted that 18 out of the total of 54 sessions (33 percent) of Constitutional Committee deliberations dealt with religion in one way or another, in any proportion, and that 40 out of a total of 218 pages (18 percent) of the transcripts of these deliberations mention religion. These percentages are even higher for the subcommittee in charge of drafting the general principles

politically conservative," with an active "liberal minority," represented by personalities who had left the nationalist Wafd Party, whose leadership refused to participate in the drafting process to protest against the fact that the Committee had not been democratically elected. This "liberal minority" would join the Liberal Constitutional Party (LCP, *ḥizb al-aḥrār al-dustūrīyīn*) when it was created in October 1922, after the Constitutional Committee ended its deliberations.[91] It was represented by men such as Abd al-Aziz Fahmy and Tawfiq Duss, who opposed each other concerning the legitimacy of proportional representation of religious minorities in Parliament, even though they both agreed that there was a tension to address between the principle of a state-preferred religion and equality irrespective of religion. Among conservatives, Shaykh Muhammad Bakhit played an important role in the constitutional debates.[92] It was at his request that Article 149 was introduced in the Constitution Draft and apparently adopted without discussions or contentions.[93] He supported democratic institutions and equality irrespective of religion, but he opposed the principle of freedom *from* religion when it was discussed in the Constitutional Committee: at his and Azhari shaykh Khayrat al-Radhi's request, the word "religious" was removed from the original formulation of Article 12, which initially read

of the Constitution: 7 out of its 18 sessions (39 percent) dealt with religion, and 14 out of the 54 pages (26 percent) of the transcripts of its deliberations mention religion. In contrast, only 9 out of a total of 170 articles (5 percent) of the 1923 Constitution do. Al-Ḥukūma al-Miṣrīya, Lajnat al-Dustūr (1924, 1–218) and Al-Ḥukūma al-Miṣrīya, Lajnat al-Dustūr (1927, 1–54).

91. Cantori (1966, 320, 336 and 341). "Virtually all the most prominent of those present [at the founding meeting of the LCP] had been members of the constitutional committee." The LCP was more moderate in its demands for full independence and more elitist than the Wafd. See also Landau (1953, 169).

92. Like his liberal Constitutional Committee fellow members, Shaykh Bakhit had been a member of the Wafd Party and joined the LCP when it was created in 1922. Cantori (1966, 398). He resigned from the LCP after the scandal triggered by Ali Abd al-Raziq's 1925 book, which argued that the institution of the Caliphate was unnecessary. On this controversy, see Hassan (2016, 225–236).

93. Initially, Shaykh Bakhit presented two separate clauses, one about the Arabic language and the other about Islam. They were combined for the final draft. Shaykh Bakhit proposed the establishment clause to the subcommittee in charge of drafting the general principles of the Constitution on May 19, 1922, and it was accepted without discussions. Al-Ḥukūma al-Miṣrīya, Lajnat al-Dustūr (1927, 51), session 17, May 19, 1922. The Constitutional Committee adopted it, again apparently without discussions, as part of the "general rules" on August 14, 1922, and once again on October 3, 1922. Al-Ḥukūma al-Miṣrīya, Lajnat al-Dustūr (1924, 70 and 145), session 18, August 14, 1922, and session 38, October 3, 1922.

"Freedom of religious belief is absolute" and was changed to "Freedom of belief is absolute."[94] In a common mistranslation pattern, the official French version rendered it as "freedom of conscience is absolute" (*La liberté de conscience est absolue*), and English translations as "Liberty of religious opinion is absolute."[95] Shaykh Bakhit notably warned against allowing "the invention of new religions."[96] Both shaykhs' stated aim was to prevent the erosion of the Muslim community, preserve the religious makeup of Egypt, maintain "order" (*niẓām*), and avoid "chaos" (*fawḍa*).[97] The shaykhs' objections were supported in the Constitutional Committee by the Coptic clergy member (and future patriarch) Metropolitan Yoannis. The prominent Azharite shaykh Muhammad Shakir, a former vice-rector of al-Azhar, also lent his support to their arguments in a letter to the president of the Constitutional Committee published in *Al-Ahrām*.[98]

The Official Explanation of the Establishment Clause: Modernity, Necessity of Public Order, and Historical Continuity

An official report by the Constitutional Committee explained Article 149 and how the principles of equality regardless of religion, individual freedoms, and Islam as the religion of the state would work together coherently.[99] First, it underlined that this type of clause was common in contemporary states, such as in the "constitutions of Italy, Spain, Denmark, Turkey, Sweden, Norway, Romania, Greece and others,"[100] a list in which the only Muslim-majority

94. Al-Ḥukūma al-Miṣrīya, Lajnat al-Dustūr (1924, 77), session 19, August 15, 1922.

95. For the official French translation, see Gouvernement Egyptien, *Rescrit Royal no. 42 de 1923*, Imprimerie Nationale, Le Caire, 1923, 2. For an unofficial English translation, see Peaslee (1950, 722).

96. Al-Ḥukūma al-Miṣrīya, Lajnat al-Dustūr (1924, 115), session 29, August 28, 1922.

97. Al-Ḥukūma al-Miṣrīya, Lajnat al-Dustūr (1924, 115), session 29, August 28, 1922. In the same vein, see Shaykh Bakhit's intervention in the subcommittee in charge of drafting the general principles of the Constitution. Al-Ḥukūma al-Miṣrīya, Lajnat al-Dustūr (1927, 51), session 17, May 19, 1922.

98. Muḥammad Shākir, Al-Dustūr wa-l-Iʿtiqād al-Dīnī [The Constitution and religious belief], *Al-Ahrām*, August 24, 1922.

99. Al-Ḥukūma al-Miṣrīya, Lajnat al-Dustūr (1924, 228). Safran (1961, 110) surprisingly claims that Article 149's meaning was not clarified "anywhere."

100. It must have referred to Italy's 1848 Fundamental Law (Article 1): "The Catholic, Apostolic and Roman religion is the sole religion of the state"; Spain's 1876 Constitution (Article 11): "The Roman Catholic Apostolic religion is the religion of the state"; Denmark's 1915 Constitution (Article 3): "The Evangelical Lutheran Church is the Danish national church, and as such,

country was Turkey.[101] In other words, the Egyptian state, like Turkey's, could be Muslim and as "modern" as European states.

Second, it explained that Article 149 was drafted in affirmation of "one of the accepted necessities of public order" (*ḍarūra min ḍarūrāt al-niẓām al-ʿāmm al-musallam bihā*). *Ḍarūra*, or necessity, is a well-known legal and theological concept in the Islamic tradition. The medieval theologian Abu Hamid al-Ghazali (d. 1111) equated "necessities" (*ḍarūrāt*) with the five indispensable purposes of sharia, the first of which is the preservation of religion.[102] Similarly, the concept of "public order" has an analogue in the Islamic tradition: *ḥifẓ al-niẓām*, or preservation of order. We find it defined in medieval political treatises as one of the aims of justice.[103] We also find it inscribed in earlier laws in Egypt, such as in the 1882 regulation of the Egyptian Assembly of Delegates,

---

it shall be supported by the state"; Sweden's 1809 Form of Government (Article 2): "The king shall always belong to the pure Evangelical faith, as adopted and explained in the unaltered Augsburg Confession and in the resolution of the Upsala Synod of the year 1593"; Norway's 1814 Constitution (Article 2): "The Evangelical Lutheran religion shall remain the official religion of the state"; Romania's 1866 Constitution (Article 21): "The Eastern Orthodox religion is the dominant religion of the Romanian state"; and Greece's 1911 Constitution (Article 1): "The established religion in Greece is that of the Eastern Orthodox Church of Christ."

101. Article 11 of the 1876 Ottoman Constitution starts with "The Ottoman state's religion is the religion of Islam [*Devlet-i ʿOs̱māniyyenin dīni, dīn-i İslāmdır*]," although Brown and Sharif (2004, 60) claim that this clause was only "implicit." It continues: "While protecting this principle, the free application and practices [*Serbestī-i icrā*] of all the religions recognized in the Ottoman domains, and continuity [*cereyān*] of communal privileges accorded to the various religious communities are (as it used to be) under the protection of the state on the condition that they are not disturbing communal order [*āsāyiş-i ḫalḳ*] and public etiquette [*ādāb-ı ʿumūmiye*]." I thank Himmet Taskomur for his translation and explanation of this article. Article 2 of the 1924 Constitution of the Republic of Turkey would also include, "The religion of the Turkish state is the religion of Islam" (*Türkiye devletinin dini, dini İslâmdır*).

102. Al-Ghazālī (1904–1906, vol. 1, 287). The five indispensable purposes of sharia are the protection of a person's religion, life, intellect, lineage, and property (*dīn, nafs, ʿaql, nasl, māl*). Hierarchically placed under the *ḍarūrāt* are the *ḥājīyāt* (needs) and the *taḥsīnīyāt* (improvements). Hallaq (1997, 168–70).

103. Ahmad Ibn Ahmad Zarruq (d. 1493) lists the preservation of order (*ḥifẓ al-niẓām*) as a rule (*qāʿida*) and writes, in Zarrūq (1992, 69), "Preservation of order is a duty and consideration of the public welfare [*al-maṣlaḥa al-ʿāmma*] necessary." Muhammad Ibn al-Azraq also speaks, in Ibn al-Azraq (1977, vol. 1, 252), of "preservation of order and repudiation of public harm" (*ḥifẓ al-niẓām wa-dafʿ al-ḍarar al-ʿāmm*) as the reason for the legitimacy of the judgeship. Agrama (2010) nonetheless claims that public order in Egyptian law is "central to the liberal rule of law."

and elsewhere, as in the 1861 Constitution of the Regency of Tunis.[104] It appears, however, that the constituents might have also borrowed the term "public order" from the French legal tradition.[105] In French international private law, the exception of "public order" is invoked when there is a large discrepancy between foreign and national law: it "defines the limits of tolerance of our [national] juridical system vis-à-vis foreign institutions"[106]—that is, what a society can accept even if it does not approve. In relation to Article 149, it meant that the state had to act as the guardian of Islamic norms and remove anything that would be intolerable from an Islamic point of view. In addition, in French administrative law, the notion of public order means "public security" (*sécurité publique*)—that is, "security, tranquility, safety, or public morality."[107] A norm of public order (*une norme d'ordre public*) is an imperative rule (*une règle impérative*), which echoes the notion of the "necessity of public order" mentioned in the explanatory text of Article 149. In the 1923 Egyptian Constitution, this meant that shared Muslim norms could set limits on certain rights, such as freedom of worship, in order to preserve order.[108]

Third, the explanatory text underlined that, according to Egyptian law, the king must be Muslim,[109] and that government takes recess during Muslim holidays. A ministry of religious endowments (waqfs)—"one of the ministries in the government"—is in charge of mosques and religious endowments, about which "the constitutional text forecloses all discussion."[110] Fourth, it argued that "this text does not create a new situation. All the customs and rules followed in affairs of religious worship [*al-shaʿāʾir al-dīnīya*], in religious education [*al-taʿlīm al-dīnī*], and in religious courts and communities [*al-maḥākim wa-l-anẓima al-millīya*] remain as they were and will continue to evolve on the path they had

104. "Preservation of public security (*al-muḥāfaẓa ʿalā al-amn al-ʿumūmī*)" in Naqqāsh (1994, vol. 4, 231) and "preservation of order (*ḥifẓ al-niẓām*)" in *Qānūn al-Dawla al-Tūnisīya* (1861, 3).

105. Article 1 of the French 1905 Law of Separation of Churches and State stipulates: "La République assure la liberté de conscience. Elle garantit le libre exercise des cultes sous les seules restrictions édictées ci-après dans l'intérêt de l'ordre public."

106. Bodin (2002, 2).

107. Bodin (2002, 66).

108. E.g., Article 13 of the 1923 Constitution reads, "The state protects freedom of religious worship and beliefs in accordance with the customs observed in Egypt and as long as they do not violate public order and do not contravene propriety."

109. Article 6 of Decree no. 25, of April 13, 1922, *Al-Waqāʾiʿ al-Miṣrīya* of April 15, 1922. It stipulates that the king has to be "endowed with reason and Muslim, with two Muslim parents."

110. Al-Ḥukūma al-Miṣrīya, Lajnat al-Dustūr (1924, 228).

already taken."[111] Hence, the drafters understood Article 149 as an affirmation of the historical continuity of the state's custodianship of Islam, which they argued was a necessity, although they acknowledged that its form and content had continuously evolved in the past and would continue to do so. Fifth, the explanatory text stated: "As for the second chapter [of the Constitution, titled "The Rights and Duties of Egyptians"]—which affirmed equality of public rights [*al-musāwāt fī al-ḥuqūq al-ʿāmma*] for Egyptian individuals regardless of their religion and freedom of language [*ḥurriyat istiʿmāl al-lughāt*]—it guarantees that no injustice [*ḥayf*] can be inflicted on anyone because of [Article 149]."[112] Therefore, in order for the principle of Islam as the religion of the state to coexist with the principles of freedom and equality, they had to limit each other (a line of reasoning that we also encountered in the constitutional history of Tunisia).

For the Constitutional Committee, the notion that the state had a religion was not simply a matter of identity. It meant that, under a Muslim sovereign, one of the functions of the state was to tend to Islamic institutions such as sharia courts, mosques, religious education (at al-Azhar and in the modern school system), and religious endowments—that is, to provide Muslims with the infrastructure required for their religious life. These concrete obligations, some of which were subsequently reaffirmed by the addition of Article 153,[113] gave more substance to Article 149 and were also inextricably tied to sovereignty: they were incumbent either on the king or on the people (represented by Parliament).[114] They could also set strong limits to freedom of and from

111. Al-Ḥukūma al-Miṣrīya, Lajnat al-Dustūr (1924, 228).

112. Al-Ḥukūma al-Miṣrīya, Lajnat al-Dustūr (1924, 228).

113. A Consultative Legislative Council (*Lajna Istishārīya Tashrīʿīya*) added Article 153 to the final Constitution Draft since, it was argued, it "remained completely silent about the established personal rights of the king from the religious point of view." Majlis al-Shuyūkh (1940, vol. 3, 3405). Article 153 stated, "The law regulates the manner in which the king exercises his powers, in conformity with the principles of the present Constitution, as it pertains to religious institutions [*maʿāhid dīnīya*], the appointments of the heads of religious bodies [*al-ruʾasāʾ al-dīnīyīn*], the religious endowments managed by the Ministry of Waqfs, and, in general, to matters concerning the faiths authorized [*al-masmūḥ bihā*] in the country. Absent any legislative provision, these powers will continue to be exercised in accordance with the rules and usages currently in force." *Al-Waqāʾiʿ al-Miṣrīya*, no. 42, April 20, 1923.

114. With the flourishing of parliamentary life after 1924, disputes about the powers of the king on religious institutions (versus those of the elected Parliament) and disagreements about how to interpret Article 153 of the Constitution did not alter the principle that whoever was the sovereign, the king or the people, had to be the custodian of Islam. For more details about these disputes, see Majlis al-Shuyūkh (1940, vol. 3, 3405–3437).

religion and to equality irrespective of religion. As we will see, this tension was highlighted in the Constitutional Committee by the Coptic member Tawfiq Duss, among others, and formed an important point of contention during the drafting process when a dispute arose about the legitimacy of proportional representation of religious minorities in Parliament. The terms of this disagreement reveal that liberals embraced Article 149 or at the very least accepted it, but that they sought to mitigate its effects on religious minorities, although they disagreed on how to achieve this goal.

Rejecting Proportional Representation of Religious Minorities: Building a Cohesive Nation of Political Equals under a Muslim State

In their February 28, 1922, unilateral declaration of Egyptian independence, the British had carved out as one of their domains of discretion the protection of minorities.[115] They also made the new constitution's protection of minorities a condition for future negotiations.[116] For most in the Constitutional Committee, this could be achieved by introducing guarantees of equality and freedom for all regardless of religion into the Constitution, and some argued that it would prevent British meddling in Egyptian affairs.[117] Three years after the 1919

115. Cantori (1966, 331). Britain's role would remain in "(1) The security of the communications of the British Empire in Egypt; (2) The defense of Egypt against all foreign aggression or interference, direct or indirect; (3) The protection of foreign interests in Egypt and the protection of minorities; and (4) The Sudan."

116. In response, six articles were voted in the subcommittee in charge of drafting the general principles of the Constitution, session 13, May 7, 1922. Al-Ḥukūma al-Miṣrīya, Lajnat al-Dustūr (1927, 36). They guaranteed, (1) To all residents, protection of their persons and freedom, regardless of origin, nationality, language, or religion; (2) To the same, full freedom of private and public worship irrespective of religion, within the limits of public order; (3) To all Egyptians, equality before the law irrespective of race, language, or religion; (4) To the same, equal civil and political rights, such as public posts, honorific titles, and the participation in and development of industries, regardless of religion; (5) That no Egyptian can be forced to use a particular language in his private affairs, in commerce, religion, newspapers and printed material of any kind, or in public gatherings; (6) To all Egyptians belonging to religious or linguistic minorities, legal rights, and also in reality, the same treatment and guarantees as other Egyptians, such as the right to establish, manage, and surveil, with their own resources, charitable, religious, and social institutions, as well as schools and other institutions of education. They have the right to use their own language in these institutions and to freely worship in them.

117. See the discussion of the principles of absolute freedom of belief (Article 12), and equal rights regardless of religion (Article 3), which were, respectively, numbered Articles 11 and 12

revolution, which had brought Copts and Muslims together in the nationalist movement, no one in the Constitutional Committee (not even conservatives, such as Shaykh Muhammad Bakhit) rejected these guarantees since they were indispensable for keeping potential British interventions at bay and for ensuring the cohesion of the nation. According to the 1917 Census, the Copts, Egypt's largest religious minority by far, represented about 7 percent of the population, as against Muslims' 91 percent.[118] Copts had been assimilated since the mid-nineteenth century. They ceased to pay the *jizya* tax in 1855 and their exemption from military conscription was lifted after that. They also served in "appointed and elected representative bodies from the time the first Consultative Council was established in 1866."[119] After the Great War, they participated actively in nationalist politics with Muslim Egyptians, notably in the Wafd Party, in which they were quite influential. However, Copts were perceived by some Muslim political and intellectual elites as being unduly privileged due to their overrepresentation in the state's administration as compared to their demographic weight, although this could be explained by their higher-than-average level of schooling.[120] For instance, the 1911 Egyptian Congress Report underlined that 59 percent of all employees in the Ministry of Interior and in the state offices attached to it, as well as in the local administration of governorates and directorates, were Christians.[121] On the flip side, some Copts complained that their community faced discrimination, notably in administrative appointments. They asked that "appointments to Egyptian government posts be made subject to merit and capacity only, without any heed to the numerical proportion between Moslems and Copts," and that Copts be given more weight in representative assemblies. In addition, they asked that Christian religious education be provided in public schools, and that Sunday become the official weekly holiday for Copts (instead of Friday).[122] In a nutshell, Copts wanted more involvement in

during the deliberations of the Constitutional Committee. Al-Ḥukūma al-Miṣrīya, Lajnat al-Dustūr (1924, 77), session 19, August 15, 1922. See also Al-Ḥukūma al-Miṣrīya, Lajnat al-Dustūr (1924, 9), session 2, April 13, 1922.

118. Christians overall represented about 8 percent of the population, and Jews 0.5 percent.

119. Carter (1986, 9).

120. Muslims represented only about two-thirds of higher education enrollments in the first two decades of the twentieth century. Estimation based on Sāmī (1917) and *Statistique scolaire de l'Egypte* (see the data appendix for more details). See also Saleh (2015, 2016).

121. Percentages varied depending on ministries: for instance, 15 percent of the employees of the Ministry of Justice were Copts at that time. Al-Mu'tamar al-Miṣrī (1911, 197–200 and 203).

122. Egyptian Congress (1911, 8–10, 22–25, 65, and 41–47).

government, more access to public resources, and more recognition. When the Constitutional Committee was appointed, it included, in addition to twenty-six Muslim members, one Jewish and five Christian members, which was not too far from Egypt's religious makeup at the time.

In March 1922, as the Constitutional Committee was about to start its deliberations, and then in April, two interrelated issues were raised separately in the press. First, the Coptic paper *Al-Waṭan* (*The Nation*) asked that the principle of proportional representation of religious minorities in the future Parliament be inscribed in the Constitution, arguing that Copts were loyal citizens and wanted to participate in future legislatures to serve their country.[123] Second, two weeks into the Constitutional Committee deliberations, the Maliki scholar and Azharite shaykh Yusuf al-Dijwi, a member of the Great Council of the Ulama of al-Azhar, called on the Constitutional Committee to take from sharia what was necessary for the welfare of the national community since, he argued, "Islam contains the rules of civilization and development that suffice for the advancement of nations and the happiness of humanity."[124] He criticized those who argue that the ʿulamā are "the most remote from and ignorant about politics [*siyāsa*]," and "those ignorant persons who claim that there is no relationship between religion and politics [*lā ʿalāqa bayn al-dīn wa-l-siyāsa*]."[125] Other Azharites echoed his request: in an article titled "Heavenly Revelation and Positive Law," Shaykh Abd Rabbih Miftah (d. 1938)—a mosque imam in Cairo trained at al-Azhar—argued that the "Qur'an is the basic Constitution" (*al-dustūr al-asāsī*).[126] Interestingly, none of these appeals to the Constitutional Committee to draw on sharia broached the issue of religious minorities.

123. *Al-Waṭan*, March 8, 1922, cited in Carter (1986, 139). On these debates in the press, see also Ṭāriq al-Bishrī, Miṣr al-Ḥadītha bayn Aḥmad wa-l-Masīḥ [Egypt between Muhammad and Christ], *Al-Kātib*, no. 119, February 1971, 106–132.

124. *Al-Ahrām*, April 29, 1922. See also *Majallat al-Azhar*, vol. 7, 1936, 460–467.

125. *Al-Ahrām*, April 29, 1922. Shaykh al-Dijwi also proposed a quota of ʿulamā in the future elected Parliament.

126. ʿAbd Rabbih Miftāḥ, *Al-Ahrām*, May 12, 1922. He quoted Edward Gibbon's *History of the Decline and Fall of the Roman Empire*: "From the Atlantic to the Ganges, the Koran is acknowledged as the fundamental code [translated by Shaykh Miftah as *al-dustūr al-asāsī*], not only of theology, but of civil and criminal jurisprudence; and the laws which regulate the actions and the property of mankind are guarded by the infallible and immutable sanction of the will of God." In 1928, Shaykh Abd Rabbih Miftah was appointed director of the newly established Department of Preaching at al-Azhar. For his biography, see *Majallat al-Azhar*, vol. 64, no. 10, April 1992, 1230–1233.

However, the two issues were linked in the subcommittee in charge of drafting the general principles of the Constitution. In May 1922, the Coptic member Tawfiq Duss proposed to inscribe in the Constitution the principle of proportional representation of religious minorities in the future Parliament around the same time that some ʿulamā called for the implementation of sharia.[127] His proposal triggered a long and tense debate in the subcommittee, which prompted further discussions in the press.[128] Subcommittee members recognized this matter was important and delicate and so decided against settling it, bringing it to the full Constitutional Committee.[129]

In his plea to the subcommittee, Tawfiq Duss argued that proportional representation of minorities in Parliament, rather than dividing Egyptians (as his adversaries claimed), would instead ensure their cohesion; as things stood, if Parliament passed a law that was "unintentionally" unfavorable to Copts, or if no Copts were elected in Parliament, Copts might believe (with or without justification) that they had been wronged. Some subcommittee members objected to Tawfiq Duss's argument, countering that it would be enough to guarantee equality and freedom to all in the Constitution.[130] He insisted that although he was glad as an Egyptian that efforts were being made to achieve equality, "unfortunately the reality is different from our hopes. Yesterday, the royal decree regulating the succession to the throne was proclaimed . . . [stating] that the successor to the throne must be an Egyptian Muslim." Husayn Rushdi, who was presiding over the subcommittee, responded, "This is because the state is Islamic [*li-anna al-dawla Islāmīya*]." Tawfiq Duss immediately conceded that this fact was not in dispute, only to be reprimanded by the president and tersely asked to move

127. Al-Ḥukūma al-Miṣrīya, Lajnat al-Dustūr (1927, 37), session 13, May 7, 1922.

128. For instance, articles in *Al-Ahrām*, by Tawfiq Duss, Abd al-Hamid Badawi, and an anonymous "scholar of law and society," respectively, on May 15, May 16, and May 18, 1922. Tawfiq Duss later argued in the Constitutional Committee that the debate had taken an unfortunate turn "because I was the one who brought it up, and I am a member of [the minority]. It was natural that it was believed that I proposed it to benefit the interests of the Copts in particular." Al-Ḥukūma al-Miṣrīya, Lajnat al-Dustūr (1924, 108), session 27, August 25, 1922.

129. Al-Ḥukūma al-Miṣrīya, Lajnat al-Dustūr (1927, 41 and Annex #1, 1 and 13). Some constituents hoped to postpone settling the debate: they argued that this issue was not within their competence and could, if needed, be legislated in the future. See also the intervention of Abd al-Hamid Badawi in the subcommittee. Al-Ḥukūma al-Miṣrīya, Lajnat al-Dustūr (1927, 42), session 14, May 11, 1922.

130. Al-Ḥukūma al-Miṣrīya, Lajnat al-Dustūr (1927, 37–42), sessions 13 and 14, May 7 and May 11, 1922.

away from the topic.[131] Later in the summer of 1922, Tawfiq Duss reiterated his plea in the full Constitutional Committee, invoking once again two widely celebrated principles at the time: religious equality and national unity.[132] According to the transcripts of the deliberations, Shaykh Bakhit, quickly followed by Ibrahim al-Halbawi, left in the middle of Tawfiq Duss's long speech.[133] This was a delicate matter, and it had already provoked, as we saw, intense debates in the subcommittee in charge of drafting the general principles of the Constitution and in the press. Tawfiq Duss reminded the Constitutional Committee that the Egyptian legal system was structured along religious lines, which contravened the ideal of national unity, and argued that it was necessary to guarantee the representation of Copts in the future Parliament in order to protect their rights. In the end, despite Tawfiq Duss's renewed insistence and the support of a few fellow members, his proposal was vocally condemned by conservatives and liberals alike in the Constitutional Committee, notably by the liberal Abd al-Aziz Fahmy. It was formally rejected by a majority vote.[134]

The constituents invoked five main reasons to justify rejecting the proportional representation of religious minorities in the future Parliament: (1) It would introduce divisions in the national community, whereas the 1919 revolution's unity between Christians and Muslims had shown that "the Egyptian people do not differentiate between Copts and Muslims";[135] (2) It would found political representation on religious considerations and would turn political

131. Al-Ḥukūma al-Miṣrīya, Lajnat al-Dustūr (1927, 41–42), session 14, May 11, 1922.

132. Al-Ḥukūma al-Miṣrīya, Lajnat al-Dustūr (1924, 105–113), session 27, August 25, 1922.

133. Al-Ḥukūma al-Miṣrīya, Lajnat al-Dustūr (1924, 110), session 27, August 25, 1922.

134. Al-Ḥukūma al-Miṣrīya, Lajnat al-Dustūr (1924, 113), session 27, August 25, 1922. From the mid-1920s to the end of the 1940s, the percentage of Copts elected in Parliament fluctuated between about 8 percent, when the Wafd won an election, and about 2 percent, when the Wafd lost, or when, in 1950, the Wafd won but Copts were much less represented in it. See Carter (1986, 142–143).

135. Ali Mahir, Al-Ḥukūma al-Miṣrīya, Lajnat al-Dustūr (1924, 112–113), session 27, August 25, 1922. The Coptic member Fahmy Qillini (1862–1918) expressed himself along similar lines during this session. Abd al-Hamid Badawi, in the subcommittee in charge of drafting the general principles of the Constitution, argued that the deep religious divides of the past had disappeared and that, as was now the case in Europe, people did not base their civil affairs on religious considerations anymore. Also, proportional representation of religious minorities would attract demands from other minorities (Jews, Syrians, Bedouins) and the country would then become "a theater of strife [*munāzaʿāt*] between religions and races." It was as if, he argued, another constitution was drafted for the minorities. Al-Ḥukūma al-Miṣrīya, Lajnat al-Dustūr (1927, 35–42), sessions 13 and 14, May 7 and May 11, 1922. See also Carter (1986, 135).

competition into religious competition, mixing religion and politics,[136] whereas "a representative assembly is not a religious assembly, but a political assembly";[137] (3) The constitution should not be shaped by sentiments, especially not those of the minority (i.e., the resentment it would supposedly feel if its members were not elected), without consideration for the anxieties of the majority (as it turns out, of being governed by the minority as such);[138] (4) It would go beyond British demands, which only required equality regardless of religion, not proportional representation;[139] and (5) It would fall into a typical ploy by foreign occupiers to divide and rule, as exemplified by the French Mandate in Syria.[140] In a similar vein, it was argued that the introduction of minimum quotas for minorities in the Legislative Assembly in 1913, supported by the British, had been a mistake.[141] These arguments invoked the reluctance to mix religion and *politics* (i.e., in this context, political competition) as well as the broader necessity of keeping the nation united and independent (under a Muslim state). They did not rely on the principle of separation of religion and

136. Abd al-Hamid Badawi and Abd al-Aziz Fahmy, Al-Ḥukūma al-Miṣrīya, Lajnat al-Dustūr (1924, 110–111), session 27, August 25, 1922. See also Abd al-Hamid Badawi, subcommittee in charge of drafting the general principles of the Constitution, Al-Ḥukūma al-Miṣrīya, Lajnat al-Dustūr (1927, 40), session 14, May 11, 1922.

137. Abd al-Hamid Badawi, subcommittee in charge of drafting the general principles of the Constitution, Al-Ḥukūma al-Miṣrīya, Lajnat al-Dustūr (1927, 38), session 13, May 7, 1922. In its final report, the subcommittee stated: "Political minorities evolve and change and can become political majorities, contrary to racial and religious minorities, which remain constant." Al-Ḥukūma al-Miṣrīya, Lajnat al-dustūr (1927, Annex #1, 13).

138. Abd al-Hamid Badawi, subcommittee in charge of drafting the general principles of the Constitution, Al-Ḥukūma al-Miṣrīya, Lajnat al-dustūr (1927, 42), session 14, May 11, 1922.

139. Abd al-Hamid Badawi and Mahmud Abu al-Nasr, Al-Ḥukūma al-Miṣrīya, Lajnat al-Dustūr (1924, 112–113), session 27, August 25, 1922. Earlier in the Constitutional Committee deliberations, Husayn Rushdi had clarified that the protection of minorities required by the British merely meant guarantee of liberty and equality of rights for all. Al-Ḥukūma al-Miṣrīya, Lajnat al-Dustūr (1924, 9), session 2, April 13, 1922.

140. Mahmud Abu al-Nasr, Al-Ḥukūma al-Miṣrīya, Lajnat al-Dustūr (1924, 113), session 27, August 25, 1922.

141. Abd al-Hamid Badawi, subcommittee in charge of drafting the general principles of the Constitution, Al-Ḥukūma al-Miṣrīya, Lajnat al-Dustūr (1927, 40), session 14, May 11, 1922. He was referring to Law 29 of 1913, *Al-Waqāʾiʿ al-Miṣrīya*, no. 83, July 21, 1913, which stipulated that of the seventeen appointed members, fifteen would ensure the representation of "minorities and other interests not represented among the elected members," as follows, Copts: 2; Arab Bedouins: 3; Merchants: 2; Medical doctors 2; Engineers: 1; Representatives of public or religious education: 2; Representatives of municipalities: 1.

state, or on state neutrality toward religion. As for Tawfiq Duss, he did not dispute the Islamic character of the state when it was brought up. He described the example of France—which had put an end to "recognized religions" in 1905 with a law separating churches and state and with the principle of civil equality—as an unattainable model.[142] Unfortunately, he argued, in Egypt the disappearance of religious differences (*al-fawāriq al-dīnīya*) and the aspiration to national unity were "a beautiful utopia" (*markaz khayālī jamīl*).[143]

The Fear of "Coptic Ambitions" in Government in the 1911 Egyptian Congress

Although it was only obliquely broached in the 1922 constitutional discussions, the majority's fear of being governed by the minority as such if it were to be represented politically (which would threaten the Islamic character of the state) had been explicitly expressed by liberals a decade earlier, at a time of heightened tensions between Muslims and Copts. After the murder of the Coptic prime minister Butros Ghali in 1910, a group of prominent Egyptian Copts, including Tawfiq Duss, organized a Coptic Congress to express their grievances, notably the lack of representation of Copts in representative assemblies. In response, a group of Egyptian Muslims organized the Egyptian Congress of 1911 to publicly reject the demands of the Coptic Congress, and a report was read to its participants by Ahmad Lutfi al-Sayyid,[144] the epitome of the Egyptian liberal intellectual,[145] assisted by, among others, the future

142. He argued, "As long as we continue to base our personal status affairs on religious rules and principles, our political life will remain colored with religion to a certain extent." Al-Ḥukūma al-Miṣrīya, Lajnat al-Dustūr (1924), session 27, August 25, 1922, 110. In this context, "political life" had a broader meaning than political competition. Some intellectuals used the term "religion and politics" in the sense of "religion and state" (i.e., religious power and political power). See, for instance, Muḥammad Khiḍr Ḥusayn, Ḍalālat Faṣl al-Dīn ʿan al-Siyāsa [The error of separating religion from politics], *Nūr al-Islām*, vol. 2, no. 5, September–October 1931, 323–337.

143. Al-Ḥukūma al-Miṣrīya, Lajnat al-Dustūr (1924, 111), session 27, August 25, 1922.

144. Al-Muʾtamar al-Miṣrī (1911) for the Arabic version of the 1911 Egyptian Congress Report, and Egyptian Congress (1911) for its English version, which is not a literal translation of the Arabic.

145. Lutfi al-Sayyid only briefly belonged to the Wafd and disengaged from politics in the early 1920s, although he had affinities with members of the LCP. See Cantori (1966, 342). Lutfi al-Sayyid's liberalism (what he called *madhhab al-ḥurrīya*) emphasized the centrality of individual freedoms in the domains of economics, politics, and intellectual expression (as well as teaching), on which the state should not encroach. See Al-Sayyid (1945, 55–98). Lutfi al-Sayyid does not seem

Constitutional Committee member Abd al-Aziz Fahmy. Three main arguments were put forward in this report to reject proportional political representation of religious minorities. The first two—namely, equality of political rights between all Egyptians irrespective of religion[146] and separation of religion and *politics*[147]—were also explicitly presented in the 1922 Constitutional Committee, as we saw. The third argument was that the state had, and could only have, a single official religion, that of the majority—that is, Islam, which was referred to as "the religion of the Egyptians" in contradistinction to "the religion of others."[148] The 1911 Egyptian Congress Report claimed that the Coptic Congress had the ambition to see Copts take over the government as Copts. This meant that Copts hoped to form a political majority harboring Coptic ambitions that they would bring into government—an absurdity according to the report since Islam was the religion of the majority and of the state[149] and since Coptic ambitions could not conceivably be at the basis of a government that was Muslim.[150] This logic was summarized in the introduction to the report, as follows: "That a state should have more than one religion is perfectly unthinkable, and it would be absurd to admit that religious minorities can exist animated by political ambitions toward exercising public rights, other than those of an essentially religious nature as guaranteed by freedom of worship [in the Arabic version, *ḥurrīyat al-i'tiqād*]. The religion of the Egyptian people is Islam, for Islam is both the religion of the Government and that of the majority."[151] Although they defended equality of political rights, the Egyptian Muslim liberals who participated in the report could not envisage being governed by the religious minority as such—that is, the 1911 Egyptian Congress Report argued, "unless the still more monstrous hypothesis be

---

to have published on the issue of Islam in governance. According to Hourani (1962, 182–183), "The Islamic umma is almost beyond the horizon of his thought, the theory of the Islamic State he does not condemn but ignores, by implication denying its relevance to the problems of the modern world." This, however, seems a stretch considering the 1911 Egyptian Congress Report.

146. Egyptian Congress (1911, 7) and Al-Mu'tamar al-Miṣrī (1911, 5).

147. Egyptian Congress (1911, 6) and Al-Mu'tamar al-Miṣrī (1911, 5).

148. Al-Mu'tamar al-Miṣrī (1911, 5). The English version, Egyptian Congress (1911, 7), calls it "the religion of the occupying power" instead.

149. Egyptian Congress (1911, 25) and Al-Mu'tamar al-Miṣrī (1911, 16).

150. "For the Copts as a religious minority, to convert themselves into a political majority, is impossible so long as they mingle religion and politics, and that their motto is: 'Copts above all.'" Egyptian Congress (1911, 23) and Al-Mu'tamar al-Miṣrī (1911, 15).

151. Egyptian Congress (1911, 6). For the Arabic version, Al-Mu'tamar al-Miṣrī (1911, 5).

admitted that two state religions can exist side by side in one country."[152] The report also affirmed the unity of the Egyptian nation with the slogan "Religion belongs to God and Egypt to the Egyptians" (*al-dīn li-Llāh wa-Miṣr li-l-Miṣrīyīn*).[153] One could imagine that another slogan, "Islam belongs to the state and Egypt to the Egyptians," could have accompanied it.

Separating Religion and Politics to Preserve the Islamic Character of the State

It has been argued that, when they invoked separation of religion and *politics* to reject proportional representation of religious minorities, the 1923 Egyptian Constitution drafters understood it as guaranteeing "neutrality" of the state toward religion.[154] However, the presence of this ambition in the Constitutional Committee, even among the most liberal of the liberals, is not supported by the sources.[155] On the contrary, the Egyptian drafters' project of separation of religion and *politics* (i.e., in this context, political competition) was motivated by the anxieties of the Muslim majority (about being governed by the minority as such, if it were to be represented politically), which, it was argued, trumped the anxieties of the minority (about not having their rights protected). It was a way to guarantee the continuity of the principle of the state's custodianship of Islam as the preferred religion, a project entirely elided by a large segment of the literature. To be sure, this modern instantiation of the organization and management of religious differences in a Muslim state inevitably brings to light tensions that bear family resemblances with those present

152. Egyptian Congress (1911, 6). For the Arabic version, Al-Muʾtamar al-Miṣrī (1911, 5), which speaks of two state religions as "totally incomprehensible" (*ghayr mafhūm bi-l-marra*).

153. Egyptian Congress (1911, 28) and Al-Muʾtamar al-Miṣrī (1911, 17).

154. Mahmood (2016, 25–26) argues, "Ultimately, the proposal for Coptic proportional representation was rejected because of the secular assumption that to give religious minorities a political voice was to compromise the principle of state neutrality toward religion." Mahmood (2016, 105) also argues that the debate of "1923" [*sic*] "occurred almost exclusively within the classic framework of liberal secularism: how to engineer a system of governance that was neutral in regard to religion while at the same time allowing it to flourish in the social and civic life of the polity." See also Mahmood (2016, 68).

155. I could not find any argument in favor of "state neutrality" in the transcripts of the debates of the 1922 Constitutional Committee or of the subcommittee in charge of drafting the general principles of the Constitution. When the state was invoked in these discussions, it was to underline its Islamic character.

in Western polities that aspire to, but struggle with, remaining neutral toward religion.[156] However, these resemblances have more to do with the ubiquity of prejudices against the other and of the majority's fear of being governed by the minority as such than with the hegemony of the project of "secularism" as understood in this segment of the literature,[157] since this project is absent from most Muslim-majority polities. The project we do find consistently is that of national cohesion, and we saw that it was in fact used as an argument both for and against the political representation of religious minorities.

Scanning constitutional debates in other Muslim-majority polities, in the Middle East and beyond, would uncover analogous aspirations and anxieties.[158] Disputes about Islam and governance are in great part shaped by the majority's anxieties about the possibility that the minority, as such, might govern them. They are also often shaped by the challenge of how to reconcile two contradictory and nonnegotiable aspirations: building a cohesive nation of political equals irrespective of religion under a state that guarantees individual freedoms while keeping the state Muslim in the sense that it is governed mainly by (and for) Muslims and performs its duty as custodian of Islam, the preferred religion. In Egypt, liberals and conservatives alike continued to acknowledge and support this dual aspiration, contrary to what is commonly assumed about their antagonism over the role of Islam in governance. Some, such as the liberal Abd al-Aziz Fahmy, explicitly recognized the challenges involved in making them work simultaneously: he argued that, since all Egyptians are equal in the eyes of the law and since it is necessary for "all governmental structures [to] be, as much as possible, in accordance with the official religion, Islam, . . . there will inevitably be a conflict between these structures and the other religions" present in Egypt.[159] In the next section, I examine what actually distinguished liberals and conservatives' conceptions of the role of Islam in governance during this key period.

156. On the tensions inherent to secularism in the United States, see for instance Sullivan (2005).

157. For instance, Mahmood (2016, 6–8, 168, and 170).

158. For example, see Koçunyan (2018) for the Ottoman 1876 Constitution, Hassan (2016, 242–243) for its 1928 amendment; Enayat (2013) for Qajar Iran's 1906 Fundamental Law and its Supplementary Law of 1907; Lau (2012) for the three constitutions of Pakistan from 1947 to 1973; Mo (2014) for the constitutional history of Sudan; and Stilt (2015) for the Federation of Malaya 1957 Constitution.

159. Al-Ḥukūma al-Miṣrīya, Lajnat al-Dustūr (1924, 101), session 26, August 23, 1922.

3. The Liberal-Conservative Cleavage in the "Liberal Age": Competing Interpretations of the State's Custodianship of Islam

In the words of Albert Hourani, in the 1920s and 1930s, Egyptian liberal thinkers conceived of their country as "an Egypt where Muslims and Copts were united in the sacred bond of national loyalty, government was constitutional, individual rights respected, where women were free, national education was universal and national industry raised the standard of living," and where religion and *politics* were separate.[160] Although it is difficult to find fault with this carefully worded description, it can easily mislead, due to what it omits. As we saw, Egyptian liberals embraced national unity and equality between Muslims and religious minorities, but under a state that was and could only be Muslim: they advocated neither for separation of Islam and the *state* nor for state neutrality, although some (but not all) advocated for separation of religion and *politics*. Because Hourani's study paid little attention to issues of governance or to actual loci of political deliberations, it did not fully flesh out the specific terms of the debates opposing liberals to conservatives on the role of Islam in governance in 1920s and 1930s Egypt. It is particularly important to clarify these terms since this political cleavage is central to the political history of Egypt and much of the Middle East (with some fluctuations as to its public expressions, such as its noticeable reactivation by organized Islamist movements and their opponents since the 1970s). In this section, using discussions in Parliament, the press, and other writings, I identify its main fault lines. For liberals and conservatives alike, the principles of a state (preferred) religion—Islam—and of its custodianship by the state had to coexist and operate together with individual freedoms and equality, but they disagreed on which of these principles had to be thickened or thinned. Moreover, within each camp, there were internal disagreements on how to accomplish these goals.[161]

160. Hourani (1962, 324–325).

161. There were also theological disputes that did not align neatly with the divide on Islam in governance—for instance, the virulent theological disputes between Rashid Rida and Shaykh Yusuf al-Dijwi, who were both in favor of a thick state custodianship of Islam. See Al-Dijwī (1929 or 1930) and Al-Dijwī (n.d.).

A Debate among Liberals: Is the (Indispensable) Establishment Clause Innocuous?

As an example of internal disagreement, in June 1922, during the drafting of the 1923 Constitution, two prominent Egyptian liberals, Mahmud Azmi and Taha Husayn, had an argument about the establishment clause in the press. It seems that they both wished that Egypt could do without it but that they both felt that it was indispensable. However, they differed on how to assess and possibly mitigate its effects. When heated public discussions about proportional representation of religious minorities in the future Egyptian Parliament reached their climax in the press in the spring of 1922, they both connected this issue with the establishment clause in a much more explicit and precise way than the Constitutional Committee had done. Mahmud Azmi argued in favor of proportional political representation of religious minorities, echoing the Constitutional Committee member Tawfiq Duss's arguments. He wanted civil laws, including personal status laws, to apply equally to all Egyptians irrespective of religion and advocated for "the purest civil character of our public life for us all," although he conceded that this was unrealistic. He deplored what he saw as a lack of courage on the part of "some of the progressives among us [*ba ʿḍ al-mutaqaddimīn ʿindanā*]" in the Constitutional Committee, who, despite themselves not feeling very "reassured about it" (*lā yaṭma ʾinnūn kabīr al-iṭmi ʾnān*), agreed to Article 149. However, he also argued that "the Egyptian reality would contradict them if they attempted to reject [it]." He conceded that this article translated "ancient social principles" that had become "natural" (*mutaṭabbi ʿa*), and that "it is not easy to fight against nature."[162] Taha Husayn agreed with Mahmud Azmi's main objective, which was to ensure the unity of the nation by guaranteeing equality between Christians and Muslims.[163] However, he disagreed on the means to achieve it. He objected that proportional political representation of religious minorities gave a political meaning to religious differences and "mixed religion and politics," echoing one of the arguments presented in the Constitutional Committee. He also claimed that Article 149 of the 1923 Constitution was "a Platonic [*iflāṭūnī*] text that will probably have no

162. Maḥmūd ʿAzmī, Madanīyat al-Qawānīn Jamīʿan wa-Tamthīl al-Aqallīyāt [The civil character of the laws in their entirety and the representation of minorities], *Al-Ahrām*, June 3, 1922, 1.

163. Ṭāhā Ḥusayn, Aqallīya wa-Aktharīya [Minority and majority], *Al-Ahrām*, June 8, 1922, 1 and 2.

impact of importance," that its value was "merely symbolic," and that it was therefore not justified to be afraid of it. In addition, in a striking echo of the official explanation of Article 149, he argued that this article was "flexible" enough to be adapted to the new reality of Egypt, a reality in which Christians and Muslims were now acquiring equal political rights. In his view, it could be neither interpreted nor adopted "in its true legal meaning." Hence, he took a radically different stance from that of the likes of Shaykh Yusuf al-Dijwi, who wanted the drafters of the Constitution to take inspiration from sharia. Taha Husayn argued that "the religious idea" (*al-fikra al-dīnīya*) had taken on a "spiritual meaning" (*maʿnā rūḥī*) and had become "devoid of any relation with practical life." On the other hand, he insisted that the establishment clause "can and should be accepted" because people were "attached" to it despite its merely symbolic character.[164] Husayn envisioned it disappearing in the long run—a process he viewed as progress—but recognized that this popular symbolism rendered it indispensable for the moment. Moreover, a few years later, in 1927, Taha Husayn argued that opposition to Article 149 by some of the Constitution's drafters subsided when they recognized that "this article is a way to please the sentiments of the masses [*al-sawād*] and to reassure the *shuyūkh* [i.e., the ʿulamā]"; he continued, "but it is not harmful. It might even be useful."[165]

The Establishment Clause in Action: Conservative against Liberal Interpretations of the State's Custodianship of Islam

In fact, Taha Husayn experienced the practical significance of the establishment clause when, in 1926, some Members of Parliament (MPs) advocated for his exclusion from the Egyptian University after he published a book on pre-Islamic poetry, in which he argued that the Qur'an could not be taken as an objective source of history.[166] Their justification was based on Article 149 of the 1923 Constitution. Some MPs interpreted the clause as establishing an "Islamic state" (*dawla Islāmīya*), which justified imposing limits to freedoms. Importantly, this interpretation was not openly contradicted by other MPs, including liberals.[167]

164. Ṭāhā Ḥusayn, Aqallīya wa-Aktharīya [Minority and majority], *Al-Ahrām*, June 8, 1922, 1 and 2.

165. Ṭ. Ḥusayn (1958, 235).

166. Ṭ. Ḥusayn (1926).

167. Al-Dawla al-Miṣrīya, Majlis al-Nuwwāb (1924–1952), session 55, September 13, 1926, 951–955. About Taha Husayn's trial, see Shalabī (1972).

MP Abd al-Khaliq Atiya brought up the issue of Taha Husayn's book in Parliament in September 1926 and contended that he had insulted the Jewish and Christian religions as well as Islam, "the religion of the Egyptian state according to the Constitution." For him, the 1923 Constitution's notion of "public order" had inscribed limits on freedom of education and freedom of opinion. He continued, stirring the applause of the Assembly: "Those who want to burn the incense of atheism [*ilḥād*] may do so in their hearts, because they are free in their beliefs [*ʿaqāʾidihim*]. As for giving it free reign in our schools and from the pulpits of the university, this is inconceivable [applause]." In his view, the fact that Taha Husayn was a civil servant made his book even more problematic.[168] The Wafd MP and Azharite shaykh Mustafa al-Qayati agreed: "The state has proclaimed in its constitution that it is an Islamic state [*dawla Islāmīya*]. God forbid that Egypt be an Islamic state that does not protect its religion from being violated and its dignity from being injured."[169] Similarly, the public prosecutor's office referred to Article 149 when it examined the affair. Although the court ruled that Taha Husayn was not guilty and that he had simply exercised his right to academic research, his book "was banned, only to reappear in superficially emended form."[170] After "a revival of the controversy," he was dismissed in 1932 "from all government service," and hence from his post as dean of the Faculty of Letters at the Egyptian University, which he had occupied since 1930.[171] The establishment clause was therefore not so innocuous after all, and conservatives could and did use it. For instance, Rashid Rida wrote in 1926, "We must take advantage of the force of the majority of the people [*quwwat akthar al-shaʿb*] and of the force of the constitution [*quwwat al-dustūr*], in a regime led by leaders who bring Islam back to its origins [*fī al-ṣadr al-awwal*]."[172] And he invoked the establishment clause to condemn the abolition of private religious endowments, which was being discussed in Parliament.[173]

168. Al-Dawla al-Miṣrīya, Majlis al-Nuwwāb (1924–1952), session 55, September 13, 1926, 951–955.

169. Al-Dawla al-Miṣrīya, Majlis al-Nuwwāb (1924–1952), session 55, September 13, 1926, 951–955.

170. P. Cachia, Ṭāhā Ḥusayn, *EI*[2].

171. P. Cachia, Ṭāhā Ḥusayn, *EI*[2].

172. Rashīd Riḍā, Diʿāyat al-Ilḥād fī Miṣr [Atheism's propaganda in Egypt], *Al-Manār*, vol. 27, no. 2, May 13, 1926, 119.

173. Rashīd Riḍā, Iqtirāḥ Ibṭāl al-Awqāf al-Ahlīya [The proposal concerning the abolition of family waqfs], *Al-Manār*, vol. 29, no. 1, March 22, 1928, 75.

The State's Custodianship of Islam According to Taha Husayn: An Empty Shell Devoid of a Philosophy of Governance

Whereas in his 1922 article in *Al-Ahrām* Taha Husayn had argued that the establishment clause was innocuous, in a 1927 series of essays he reflected on its meaning with the benefit of hindsight.[174] He exposed the main elements of his liberal conception of the role of Islam in governance and described the ideological line that separated liberals from conservatives. This provides an important complement to transcripts of constitutional and parliamentary debates. Taha Husayn rejected Islam as a philosophical or legal *foundation of governance* but insisted that Islam was *an object of governance*; it was very much a state affair since the state had to guarantee a minimum level of support and protection for Islam, the Muslim community, and its institutions in order for Egyptians to live their lives as Muslims. Therefore, his project was far from one of separation of religion and state or of state neutrality. Taha Husayn's argument about Islam in governance was embedded in a broader stance about the relationship between religion and scientific knowledge. Contrary to the theorization of some conservatives (later repeated by the Muslim Brothers), in his view, Islamic knowledge was not the basis of all knowledge.[175] This notably implied that men of religion be excluded from science and from politics, whereas science could contribute to improving *techniques* of governance.[176] He virulently rejected al-Azhar's censorship of scientific writings, opposed the ʿulamā's interpretation of Article 149 (they had invoked it to condemn his book), and deplored what he described as their political instrumentalization of religion. In the 1920s, the ʿulamā were quite vocal on the public scene and actively participated in the political passions of the time.[177] Taha Husayn was the target of conservative Azhari ʿulamā, and his rejection of the ʿulamā's involvement in science (and therefore in politics) was undoubtedly a response to their attacks. Taha Husayn's

174. This series of essays was published in the Syrian periodical *Majallat al-Ḥadīth* in 1927. It was republished in 1935 and again in Ṭ. Ḥusayn (1958).

175. Ṭ. Ḥusayn (1958, 227–228).

176. Ṭ. Ḥusayn (1958, 229). Taha Husayn argued that the ʿulamā were not at the frontier of scientific innovation and had lost their previous monopoly over knowledge. At the time, students of al-Azhar, forced to compete with modern school graduates, protested vocally against their lack of access to administrative and teaching posts. However, Taha Husayn argued that the ʿulamā should not have the ambition to engage with nonreligious knowledge, that this was not their trade, and that teaching posts in modern schools should be reserved for graduates of modern schools.

177. Bruner (2009) and Hatina (2010).

conception of science as the only domain relevant for governance also meant that, for him, governance was not to be constrained by Islamic law, by Islamic principles more broadly, or by any other philosophy. Nor could Islam be an object of state protection beyond the nation's borders. He saw the state as now confined to the governance of the Egyptian nation and strictly tasked with ensuring the nation's political and economic welfare.[178] In other words, he replaced religion and "metaphysical and philosophical theories" with "the idea of the nation [*waṭanīya*] and all the essentially economic and political benefits that derive from it," placing them at the foundation of governance in a strictly nationalist and developmentalist philosophy.[179]

Taha Husayn also made it clear that, for liberals, the 1923 Constitution gave the government "a few obligations [*wājibāt*] related to [Muslim] traditions" and that Article 149 "did not add anything more than what exists already in reality." He enumerated the components of this reality: "The leader of the state in Egypt must be Muslim. The worship of Islam must continue to be performed after the proclamation of the Constitution in the same way as it was before: the mosques will not close their doors, the pilgrimage will not be interrupted, the government will take its holidays on Muslim holidays, the canons will be fired during Ramadan [to mark the end of the daily fast], the celebrations of the *maḥmal* [the departure of the caravan sent by the ruler to Mecca for the pilgrimage] and the Prophet's birthday will not be interrupted. The revenues of the Islamic endowments [waqfs] will continue to be spent according to the donors' wishes." He insisted that liberals did not imagine that "one day [the establishment clause] would prescribe new duties [*wājibāt*] to the Egyptian government or that new regulations [*nuẓum*] that did not exist previously would be enacted."[180] For Taha Husayn, the state's provision, maintenance, and respect of a religious infrastructure, a minimum that allowed (Muslim) Egyptians to live their lives as Muslims, was both necessary and sufficient as far as the role of Islam in governance was concerned since Egyptians also had other imperatives of a nonreligious nature and religion represented only one part of Muslims' lives. However, this did not mean that, in his view, Islam was a private affair. On the contrary, it remained a state affair and a public one, but it had a specific and limited role to play and was to be lived,

178. Ṭ. Ḥusayn (1958, 230–231).
179. Ṭ. Ḥusayn (1958, 230–231).
180. Ṭ. Ḥusayn (1958, 233).

in his words, "the way moderate people [*al-nās al-muʿtadilīn*] [live] it. They do not overdo their piety, nor do they overdo their disobedience and sin."[181]

Did Taha Husayn Change His Mind in the 1930s?

In the same vein, in *The Future of Culture in Egypt* (published in 1938, a decade after his 1927 essays), Taha Husayn argued that though the extent of religious education should be shrunk to make space for modern education (*al-taʿlīm al-ḥadīth*),[182] it should not be eliminated. He insisted that religious education at the primary and secondary levels of modern schools and in al-Azhar's institutes was the responsibility of the state, which had to have oversight over curricula "in accordance with the national welfare [*maṣlaḥa waṭanīya*]."[183] For him, it was not reasonable to "leave the task of religious education to families." Students in private (including foreign) and public schools alike had to learn "the national religion [Islam], the national language, the national history."[184] Therefore, although in the 1920s Taha Husayn saw the state as a mere set of governance procedures stripped of any philosophical foundation (except for a nationalist and developmentalist one), in the 1930s he called for the dissemination of (his own conception of) Islam to all Muslim pupils in Egypt. In 1933 he also asked the government to protect "Egyptian morals," "Egyptian nationalism," and "the official religion of the state" in the face of alleged attempts by foreign Christian school missionaries to convert Muslim pupils.[185] In addition, although Husayn was critical of the ambition of the ʿulamā of al-Azhar to be autonomous from the state in his 1938 book, arguing that al-Azhar could not remain a "state within a state" and "a private power [*sulṭān khāṣṣ*] that defied public authority [*al-sulṭān al-ʿāmm*],"[186] he also argued that the three main Islamic institutions in Egypt—al-Azhar, the religious endowments, and the sharia courts—had to remain,[187] and that they were and should stay part of the state and "under its care."[188]

181. Ṭ. Ḥusayn (1958, 232–233).

182. Ṭ. Ḥusayn (1938, vol. 2, 372–397).

183. Ṭ. Ḥusayn (1938, vol. 1, 89).

184. Ṭ. Ḥusayn (1938, vol. 1, 82). He seems to mean that it is Muslim students who must learn "the national religion."

185. Ṭāhā Ḥusayn, *Kawkab al-Sharq*, June 12 and 16, 1933, reproduced in Ṭ. Ḥusayn (2002–2004, vol. 3, 431–445, at 445).

186. Ṭ. Ḥusayn (1938, vol. 1, 75 and 88).

187. Ṭ. Ḥusayn (1938, vol. 1, 33).

188. Ṭ. Ḥusayn (1938, vol. 1, 85–86).

Therefore, in the 1930s, Taha Husayn specified that the state had an Islamic pedagogical role to play and that it had to play it with a firm hand. This went hand in hand with his long-standing aim of constraining the ʿulamā's influence and deprioritizing religious education *in relative terms*. It would be tempting to argue that his vision shifted from a thin state custodianship of Islam to a thicker one. In reality, Taha Husayn simply made more explicit his long-standing thin but strong conception of the state's custodianship of Islam and nationalist, developmentalist philosophy of governance. To relegate the ʿulamā to their proper theological place and to keep religious curricula (and the ʿulamā) under the control of the state was a way to keep conservative interpretations of Islam at bay and to disseminate his own understanding of Islam instead. Therefore, we should not interpret Taha Husayn's and other liberals' Islamic narratives in the 1930s as evidence of a change of mind on their part regarding the role of Islam in governance (as is common),[189] but rather as a contextual specification of their long-standing views. Why, then, did Taha Husayn feel that this specification was necessary in 1938? In 1927 he defended his academic work against his detractors, whereas his 1938 book exposed his vision for the future of culture in Egypt. This was not just a literary exercise but rather a policy roadmap as Egypt was gaining greater independence. Recall how, in 1927, he had already argued that the establishment clause was not only "not harmful" but that "it might even be useful."[190] Taha Husayn's views are all the more relevant since he played an important role within the Egyptian Ministry of Education, first as an advisor, and then as minister of education in the last Wafd government (1950–1952) before the Free Officers coup.

The Liberal-Conservative Cleavage in Taha Husayn's Words: "Enlightened" vs. "Reactionaries"

Taha Husayn recognized that although there was broad agreement about its necessity, Article 149 "was an object of dispute among Muslims themselves, because they did not all understand it in the same way and did not agree on

189. Among others, Safran (1961) and Smith (1983, 61) make such a claim. Some argue that Taha Husayn's apparent turn was merely tactical. Ayalon (2009) argues that he emended his book on pre-Islamic poetry in order to reach the masses. Hourani (1962, 333–334) argues that his attention to Islamic themes in his literary writings in the 1930s "do not mark a change in his view of Islam" but rather were "an attempt to retell the story of Islam in ways which will appeal to the modern Egyptian consciousness."

190. Ṭ. Ḥusayn (1958, 235).

its implementation."[191] In the interwar period, he and others used a rich and sometimes inflammatory vocabulary to describe the two opposite camps, liberals and conservatives. For Taha Husayn, there were "two kinds of Egyptian Muslims. On one side are those who are enlightened [*mustanīrūn*] and civil [*madanīyūn*]. On the other are the ʿulamā [*shuyūkh*] of al-Azhar and men of religion [*rijāl al-dīn*],"[192] whom he also called the "reactionaries" (*rajʿīyūn*) of al-Azhar.[193] For Rashid Rida, one of the most vocal critics of Taha Husayn, there were, on the one hand, the supporters of Islam—that is, those who served the religion (*khadamat al-dīn*)—and, on the other hand, the apostates (*murtadds*) and atheists (*mulḥids*).[194] In the 1920s, he harshly criticized Ali Abd al-Raziq and Taha Husayn, and portrayed them as supporters of *lā-dīnīya* (areligiosity) and *ilḥād* (atheism) who sought to emulate "the Kemalists in Turkey."[195] He also portrayed them as representatives of the Egyptian University, which he contrasted with what al-Azhar ought to be, in his mind: a defender of Islam.[196] Beyond all these epithets, however, two distinct conceptions of the role of Islam in governance were discernible.

Taha Husayn described liberals as defenders of the status quo for the role of Islam in governance: for them, the state already guaranteed a sufficient level of Islamic infrastructure and legal provisions.[197] However, he also acknowledged that liberals sought to reduce the constraints that Islam might put on the state and found it necessary to bend Islamic legal principles to an extent that could make them unrecognizable. He argued that Egypt had to develop socially and economically and that its government "needed to

191. Ṭ. Ḥusayn (1958, 232).

192. Ṭ. Ḥusayn (1958, 233).

193. For the use of the terms "reactionary" and "reaction" by Taha Husayn and their association with al-Azhar, see Ṭ. Ḥusayn (1958, 238 and 242) as well as Ṭāhā Ḥusayn, Aḥrār wa-Muḥāfiẓūn [Liberals and conservatives], *Al-Ahrām*, August 25, 1922.

194. Rashīd Riḍā, Diʿāyat al-Ilḥād fī Miṣr [Atheism's propaganda in Egypt], *Al-Manār*, vol. 27, no. 2, May 13, 1926, 119.

195. Rashīd Riḍā, Diʿāyat al-Ilḥād fī Miṣr [Atheism's propaganda in Egypt], *Al-Manār*, vol. 27, no. 2, May 13, 1926, 119.

196. He also advocated for a "religious revolution" (*thawra dīnīya*) and criticized the ʿulamā for their passivity. Rashīd Riḍā, Diʿāyat al-Ilḥād fī Miṣr, *Al-Manār*, vol. 27, no. 2, May 13, 1926, 119. A dispute between *Al-Manār* and *Al-Siyāsa*—the mouthpiece of the Liberal Constitutional Party in which Ali Abd al-Raziq and Taha Husayn often wrote—became particularly virulent in May 1927. Rashid Rida described the Liberal Constitutional Party as the "party of atheists" (*ḥizb al-malāḥida*), *Al-Manār*, vol. 28, no. 3, May 2, 1927, 240.

197. Ṭ. Ḥusayn (1958, 233).

govern modern life, which led it to make licit what Islam made illicit before."[198] This meant that if the constitutional principles of equality irrespective of religion and freedom of opinion were to be taken seriously, some Islamic legal principles had to be contradicted: "Islam did not authorize atheism, and does not authorize the atheist to proclaim his atheism publicly. The punishment of atheism is well-known in Islam, and Islam does not make the Muslim and non-Muslim equal in a country in which Islam is the official religion," he argued.[199] However, for him this contradiction of Islamic principles was possible thanks to Islam's "flexibility and softness," which had helped it endure.[200]

On the other hand, Taha Husayn described conservatives as having taken the opportunity of the drafting of the 1923 Constitution to ask for the expansion of Islam in the Egyptian state and society, for an Islamic state "in the old sense," and for "things that they did not even request before the constitution was drafted." He wrote that conservatives "understood [Article 149] in a different way [from liberals]," that "they argued that the state must take upon itself obligations [*wājibāt*] that it did not even have before," and that "a group among them, headed by a party from the Great Council of the ʿUlamā of al-Azhar [*Hayʾat kibār al-ʿulamāʾ*]," did not want a constitution since, they reasoned, "Muslims have God's book and the Sunna of the prophet."[201] Taha Husayn also claimed that conservatives "did not accept the principles of freedom and equality" and understood Article 149 as limiting freedom of opinion (and particularly public expressions of atheism) since, they argued, "the state is charged by the Constitution with the protection of Islam from anything that can harm it or endanger it."[202] Therefore, conservatives aimed to thicken the state's custodianship of Islam—that is, to constrain the state further with Islamic principles to better protect Islam, the Muslim community, and its institutions, including at the expense of individual freedoms. They also aimed to prevent liberals from bending the principles of Islam in their effort to make the state's custodianship of Islam thinner. Taha Husayn also conceded that Article 149 could be used by liberals and conservatives alike to implement their respective conceptions of the role of Islam in governance.

198. Ṭ. Ḥusayn (1958, 234).
199. Ṭ. Ḥusayn (1958, 234).
200. Ṭ. Ḥusayn (1958, 234).
201. Ṭ. Ḥusayn (1958, 235).
202. Ṭ. Ḥusayn (1958, 236–237).

The Persistent Political Cleavage about Islam in Governance and Its Authoritarian Synthesis

Indeed, the inclusion of an establishment clause in the 1923 Constitution and its reiteration (with some modifications) in all subsequent constitutions of Egypt did not settle the debate between liberals and conservatives. In post-1952 Egypt, as in much of the Middle East, this debate was mainly shaped and dominated by authoritarian governments.[203] They produced their own interpretations and implementations of the state's custodianship of Islam by borrowing from both the liberal and conservative camps while also repressing and silencing them, in what I call an authoritarian synthesis.[204] Still, a brief look at the changes of the role of religion in the successive constitutions of Egypt attests to the importance of the disputes about Islam in governance, an analysis that could be refined by studying the drafting processes and subsequent judicial interpretations in detail.[205] It can only be briefly mentioned here that while the establishment clause remained in all subsequent constitutions, it was specified further over time: in 1971, a new clause attached to it in Article 2 made "the principles of Islamic sharia [*mabādi' al-sharīʿa al-Islāmīya*] . . . a main source of legislation [*maṣdar raʾīsī li-l-tashrīʿ*]." In the 1980 revision of the 1971 Constitution, Article 2 remained the same, except the principles of sharia became "the" main source of legislation, a change that was made in part under pressure from Islamists and from the Academy for Islamic Research at al-Azhar.[206] After the Arab Spring, democratic elections in 2012 gave the upper hand to the Muslim Brothers and to the Salafist Party al-Nur. They dominated the Constitutional Assembly and drafted the short-lived 2012 Constitution, which specified the establishment clause even further without much consideration for the liberal side of the debate about the role of Islam in governance.[207]

203. Some scholars, such as Rutherford (2013, 29 and 131–140), speak of "statism," in the context of Mubarak's era, as a distinct ideology on par with liberalism and Islamism. It was rather an authoritarian synthesis of the different sides of the political cleavage on Islam in governance.

204. To study this post-1952 period is challenging given the authoritarian context. I have delved into some of the competing interpretations of Islam in governance during this period—e.g., in Zeghal (1996, 119–124), where I analyze Nasser's conservative tropes to justify his reform of al-Azhar.

205. This has been initiated, for judicial interpretations, in Lombardi and Brown (2006) for the 1970s onward, and Rutherford (2013) for the Mubarak era.

206. See Zeghal (1996, 156–159) and Lombardi (2013).

207. Article 2 from 1980 remained, and a clause noting that religious minorities followed their personal status laws (Article 3) was added. The existence of al-Azhar, an "independent" Islamic institution (yet still financed by the state) whose leadership was to be consulted on matters "related to sharia," was underlined (Article 4). "The principles of sharia" were defined

On the other hand, the 2014 Constitution, which came after the 2013 military coup, exhibited a remarkable continuity with pre-2012 Constitutions and pre-Arab Spring authoritarian syntheses.[208]

4. The Emergence of the Egyptian Muslim Brothers: Rehearsing Existing Conservative Tropes and Continuing an Old Political Battle

Historians of modern Egypt have argued that the 1920s were a period of "liberal experiment" (particularly with the 1923 Constitution) and that the Muslim Brothers (the first organized Islamist mass movement in the Arab Middle East, founded by Hassan al-Banna in 1928) shaped their ideology as a reaction against it, thereby politicizing Islam, as if the role of Islam in governance had not been an object of contention earlier.[209] It is clear from the above analysis that the 1920s were, instead, a period of intense political battle between liberals and conservatives on the role of Islam in governance, and that, despite their disagreements, they shared the ideal that the state must be the custodian of Islam, the preferred religion. It is also clear that this political battle preceded the Muslim Brothers' entry onto the political scene. This recharacterization leads to a significant reassessment of the ideological contribution of the Muslim Brothers in the interwar period. Hassan al-Banna certainly did innovate in the sense that he popularized the conservative side of the existing debate on the role of Islam in governance in an era of mass politics. The movement he created arguably became one of the most influential in the twentieth century. Movements inspired by the Muslim Brothers developed between the 1930s and 1940s in Palestine, Syria, and Jordan, and toward the end of the 1960s in Tunisia, Algeria, and Morocco (although in the Maghrib their influence was less direct than in the Mashriq). They and other organized Islamist movements have played and continue to play an important political role in Egypt as well as in much of the Middle East, which explains the considerable attention they have received in

(Article 219) after intense bargaining between the different Islamist sensibilities in the Constitutional Committee. See Clark Lombardi and Nathan Brown, Islam in Egypt's New Constitution, *Foreign Policy*, December 13, 2012, http://foreignpolicy.com/2012/12/13/islam-in-egypts-new-constitution/, accessed December 13, 2016.

208. The interpretation of sharia was given back to the Supreme Constitutional Court (rather than al-Azhar), sharia was not defined, and Article 180 stated that local councils should "include a proper representation of Christians."

209. E.g., Al-Sayyid Marsot (1977, 219, 231) and Gershoni and Jankowski (1986).

the literature and in the media.[210] However, as we will see, at their inception, at the ideological level the Muslim Brothers merely repurposed already existing conservative tropes, such as those of Muhammad Bakhit, Rashid Rida, and Yusuf al-Dijwi. They used these tropes for mass political activism by exploiting newly available mobilization tools (as did their political adversaries) and made them resonate broadly, including beyond Egypt. Their early intellectual and ideological contribution, as shaped in the 1930s and 1940s, was therefore very limited, although in subsequent decades, to be sure, they would participate in the ideological evolution of conservative ideas about Islam in governance.

The Muslim Brothers' Rehearsal of Existing Conservative Tropes

In what follows, I identify three interrelated, core elements of the Muslim Brothers' early doctrine and show that they were indeed culled from an already existing conservative repertoire. I also underline the ways in which these doctrinal elements contrasted or overlapped with the liberals' conception of Islam in governance.[211]

SHAPING A NATION OF PIOUS CITIZENS: EXPANDING ISLAMIC EDUCATION

First, the Muslim Brothers' project was a pedagogical enterprise, which aimed to reshape individual preferences and behavior to form a nation of pious citizens. The attention to Islamic education was of course in line with Taha Husayn's and other liberals' religious pedagogical ambitions, although they sought to decrease its extent in relative terms, whereas the Muslim Brothers wanted to expand it. They sought to redirect Egyptians toward a piety that they had allegedly lost by teaching them the scriptures and making them conform to their injunctions, a dimension that was also central in later Islamist movements in the Middle East.

210. The literature on the Egyptian Muslim Brothers and the organized Islamist political movements they influenced has mostly focused on the causes of their emergence and/or success, their organizational and mobilization prowess, their electoral and other strategies, their conflicts with authoritarian governments, and the evolution of their ideology. See, for instance, Mitchell (1969), Kepel (1985a, 1985b), Lia (1998), Rosefsky Wickham (2002, 2013), El-Ghobashy (2005), N. Brown (2012), Rutherford (2013), Masoud (2014), and Brooke and Ketchley (2018) and the bibliography there. However, there has been comparatively little work analyzing their ideology within a longer and broader history of political ideas.

211. I draw the core elements of the Muslim Brothers' doctrine from Mitchell (1969) and Lia (1998) as well as from disparate primary sources, such as pamphlets or lessons given by their leader Hassan al-Banna, and journal articles and writings by other members of the movement.

A teacher himself, Hassan al-Banna insisted on putting the Qur'an (and its memorization) at the center of the education system, and he sent letters to the representatives of al-Azhar and to the minister of education to that effect.[212] He spoke of his project as that of the "formation of souls" (*inshā ʾ al-nufūs*).[213] In his project, education was to take place through the discipline instilled by spiritual and bodily exercises that Hassan al-Banna, the Supreme Guide, enjoined the Muslim Brotherhood members to follow.[214] He also clearly sought to reshape the preferences and behavior of the Muslim masses more broadly through the power of a state that he envisioned as "Islamic" and that would give Islamic knowledge and education, including rote learning of the Qur'an, a more expansive role. This was not a new project, however; for instance, more than a decade earlier, conservative ʿulamā such as Shaykh Yusuf al-Dijwi had written in favor of expanding Qur'anic teaching and deepening individuals' piety via schooling and print, calling on the state and the ʿulamā to help in this endeavor.[215]

ISLAM'S EFFICACY IN LIFE: UNIFYING RELIGION (*DĪN*) AND WORLDLY LIFE (*DUNYĀ*)

Second, the Muslim Brothers insisted on the unification of Islam and "worldly life" and argued that "the Qur'an is the Constitution,"[216] echoing earlier ʿulamā's injunctions (such as Abd Rabbih Miftah's in 1922).[217] The Muslim Brothers'

212. E.g., Ḥasan al-Bannā, Wasā ʾil al-Muḥāfaẓa ʿalā al-Qur ʾān al-Karīm [Means of conserving the noble Qur'an], *Al-Fatḥ*, January 16, 1931, 12–15.

213. Hassan al-Banna wrote: "The solution is the education and molding of the souls of the nation in order to create a strong moral immunity, firm and superior principles and a strong and steadfast ideology." Cited in Lia (1998, 67).

214. For instance, see Al-Bannā (1965, 20) as well as "Our credo," a list of beliefs held by the members, published in *Jarīdat al-Ikhwān al-Muslimīn*, no. 13, July 9, 1935, and the prayers, invocations, and litanies published in Al-Bannā (1965, 423–498). Al-Bannā (1965, 139) also enjoined his disciples to be "monks by night and knights by day."

215. For instance, Al-Dijwī (1914, 150–155 and 170). Yusuf al-Dijwi was on a committee established by al-Azhar to report on a 1919 Ministry of Education's project to expand elementary schooling. The committee praised this project but argued that it did not pay enough attention to the rote learning of the Qur'an and that it was detrimental to the al-Azhar system of institutes. See *Al-Ahrām*, December 4, 1919. For other instances of the debate about the extent of religious education in Egypt, see chapter 5.

216. Mitchell (1969, 193–194).

217. Recall Shaykh Abd Rabbih Miftah's statement in *Al-Ahrām*, May 12, 1922. In a 1935 article, titled "Will the Islamic sharia replace the positive laws in Islamic countries?," Hassan al-Banna cited this statement in the journal *Al-Īmān* arguing that al-Azhar only recognized the legitimacy of sharia in Egypt, and not that of secular courts. *Jarīdat al-Ikhwān al-Muslimīn*, June 4, 1935, 31–34.

slogans often took the form of dichotomies that were meant to convey, for instance, that Islam was simultaneously abstract and concrete, private and public, or institutional and emotional. They clamored that Islam was "religion and state" (*dīn wa-dawla*), "spirituality and action" (*rabbānīya wa-ʿamal*),[218] "judgment and implementation" (*ḥukm wa-tanfidh*),[219] "state and nation" (*dawla wa-waṭan*),[220] and "morality and force" (*akhlāq wa-quwwa*),[221] echoing familiar conservative tropes such as those of the Constitutional Committee member Shaykh Bakhit. Indeed, in his 1925 condemnation of fellow Azharite Ali Abd al-Raziq's book *Islam and the Foundations of Government* (*Al-Islām wa-Uṣūl al-Ḥukm*),[222] Shaykh Bakhit had explicitly advocated for expanding the role of Islam in governance and likened early Islamic governance to constitutional governance based on popular sovereignty.[223] He insisted that Islam was both "a religion" (*dīn*) and "a state" (*dawla*), "a message and a government" (*risāla wa-ḥukm*).[224] He argued that "in Islam . . . religious and political power [*sulṭa dīnīya wa-sulṭa siyāsīya*] are united . . . contrary to other religions."[225] These tropes were particularly powerful for

218. Al-Bannā (1965, 244).

219. Al-Bannā (1965, 272).

220. Al-Bannā (1965, 7).

221. Al-Bannā (1965, 7).

222. ʿAbd al-Rāziq (1925).

223. Bakhīt (1925, 108).

224. Bakhīt (1925, 292–293). Skovgaard-Petersen (1997, 137) notes, albeit without drawing the full implications of this observation, that Shaykh Bakhit's refutation of Abd al-Raziq's book "has no doubt been powerful in formulating the contemporary Islamic dogma of *dīn wa dawla* (that Islam is both a religion and a state)."

225. Bakhīt (1925, 292–293). In the 1930s, similar tropes were rehearsed in the press by other prominent ʿulamā, such as Yusuf al-Dijwi (who, in 1922, had urged the drafters of the Constitution to take inspiration from sharia), Muhammad Khidr Husayn (who was at the time the chief editor of the mouthpiece of al-Azhar, *Nūr al-Islām*), as well as by less well-known ʿulamā. See Yūsuf al-Dijwī, Al-Dīn Ḍarurī li-l-ʿUmrān [Religion is necessary for prosperity], *Nūr al-Islām*, vol. 1, no. 3, July–August 1930, 180–187, and vol. 1, no. 5, September–October 1930, 332–337; Ḥājat al-Insān ilā al-Sharīʿa [A person's need for sharia], *Nūr al-Islām*, vol. 8, no. 4, June–July 1937, 253–256; Al-Muwāzana bayn al-Sharīʿa wa-l-Qawānīn al-Waḍʿīya [Comparing the sharia to positive law], *Majallat al-Azhar*, vol. 8, no. 5, July–August 1937, 332–336; Ḥadath Jalal Lā Yumkin al-Ṣabr ʿAlayhi [A momentous incident that cannot be abided], *Majallat al-Azhar*, vol. 8, no, 7, September–October 1937, 487–491, vol. 8 no. 8, October–November 1937, 548–551, and vol. 8, no. 9, November–December 1937, 612–615; Muḥammad al-Khiḍr Ḥusayn, Al-Sharīʿa al-Islāmīya Ṣāliḥa li-Kull Zamān wa-Makān [The Islamic sharia is apt for every time and place], *Nūr al-Islām*, vol. 1, no. 3, July–August 1930, 204–210, Ḍalālat Faṣl al-Dīn ʿan al-Siyāsa [The error of separating religion from politics], *Nūr al-Islām*, vol. 2, no. 5, September–October 1931, 323–337. Members of

mobilization purposes: the Muslim Brothers and other Islamist movements often reused them. They conveyed the idea that Islam was comprehensive and that it had "a broad meaning that regulated all life affairs."[226] In his exhortations to teach the Qur'an in schools, Hassan al-Banna presented it as the foundation of knowledge (*ʿilm*).[227] He saw it as the "lexicon of knowledge [*qāmūs al-ʿilm*], the foundation of law [*qānun tashriʿ*], the editor [*muḥarrir*] of the Muslims' doctrine and rituals, the constitution [*dustūr*] of [the Muslims'] manners [*ādāb*] and social relations [*muʿāmalāt*], [and] the guide [*murshid*] of their rulers and governments."[228] He presented Islam as an "idea" (*fikra*) that could shape the world and be the engine for social and political transformation.[229] For him, law had to be in conformity with the teachings and principles of Islam, which he saw as a system that had to be taught, understood, and applied, while imported Western laws had to be removed if in contradiction to it.[230] Hassan al-Banna's notions of "applied Islam" and social efficacy of Islam have been at the heart of most Islamist movements' projects but had also been widely embraced by conservatives as well as by many liberals before him.[231] They figured prominently in the reforms of religious institutions that the Egyptian state had designed and implemented with the support of many ʿulamā,[232] and, as we saw, the liberal Taha Husayn

---

the sharia courts also expressed themselves in favor of sharia and against separation between what they called religious and political powers. For instance, ʿAbd Allāh Ṣiyām, ʿAlāqat al-Akhlāq bi-l-Sharīʿa al-Islāmīya wa-l-Qānūn al-Waḍʿī [The relationship of morals with the Islamic sharia and positive law], *Nūr al-Islām*, vol. 1, no. 3, July–August 1930, 217–220; and ʿAbbās Ṭāhā, Al-Sulṭatān al-Dīnīya wa-l-Dunyāwīya Kamā Yarāhā al-Islām [The religious and secular powers as Islam sees them], *Majallat al-Azhar*, vol. 8, no. 9, November–December 1937, 657–658.

226. Al-Bannā (1965, 100–101).

227. Ḥasan al-Bannā, Wasāʾil al-Muḥāfaẓa ʿalā al-Qurʾān al-Karīm [Means of conserving the Noble Qur'an], *Al-Fatḥ*, January 16, 1931, 12–15, at 12.

228. Ḥasan al-Bannā, Wasāʾil al-Muḥāfaẓa ʿalā al-Qurʾān al-Karīm [Means of conserving the Noble Qur'an], *Al-Fath*, January 16, 1931, 12–15, at 12.

229. Al-Bannā (1965, 224 and 230). We also find the term "*fikrat al-Islām*" in ʿAbd Allāh Ṣiyām, ʿAlāqat al-Akhlāq bi-l-Sharīʿa al-Islāmīya wa-l-Qānūn al-Waḍʿī [The relationship of morals with the Islamic sharia and positive law], *Nūr al-Islām*, vol. 1, no. 3, July–August 1930, 217–220, at 219.

230. *Jarīdat al-Ikhwān al-Muslimīn*, June 4, 1935, no. 8, 31–34.

231. In contrast, Lia (1998, 74) seems to attribute the notion of "applied Islam" to Hassan al-Banna.

232. For instance, in his project to reform al-Azhar in 1928, the grand imam of al-Azhar Shaykh Mustafa al-Maraghi articulated a conception of Islam as an efficient instrument for reform: "the most efficient remedy for reforming the people's morals" (*anjaʿ dawāʾ li-islāḥ akhlāq*

argued that the establishment clause in the 1923 Constitution could play a "useful" role. However, unlike conservatives (including the Muslim Brothers), who sought to give a more expansive role to Islam, liberals sought to make more space for the secular ambitions of the state and to expand the share of secular knowledge. They also aimed to circumscribe the role of Islamic law in governance and to free the state from some of the constraints imposed by Islamic principles. Another notable difference was that the conservatives' and Muslim Brothers' conception of Islamic governance went beyond the national borders and was to be implemented in the whole Muslim *umma*,[233] a project resisted by liberals, who kept their conception of Islam in governance within strict national borders, as articulated by Taha Husayn in his 1927 essays, as we saw.[234]

THE STATE AS AN ADAPTABLE INSTRUMENT TO EXPAND THE ROLE OF ISLAM IN GOVERNANCE

Third, Hassan al-Banna conceived of the state as an instrument for the implementation of Islam and the enforcement of ways of life he deemed "Islamic,"[235] but he did not elaborate on the specific operations of an "Islamic state" (*dawla Islāmīya*). He saw constitutional government as acceptable, in the sense that it could be put to use to accomplish his Islamic project. He did not oppose the codification of law either, as long as it was in conformity with sharia, which, he argued, was universal in scope but also "flexible"[236] (a quality that was also invoked by the liberal Taha Husayn, as we saw, but with the aim of freeing the state of too many Islamic constraints). Hassan al-Banna stressed that political elites had already promised the principle of an Islamic state with Article 149 of the 1923 Constitution,[237] and he often referred to the establishment clause to push for Islamic policies[238] (as had other conservatives before him, such as Rashid Rida

al-jamāhīr). Muṣṭafā al-Marāghī, Iṣlāḥ al-Azhar al-Sharīf [Reforming al-Azhar], *Al-Manār*, vol. 29, no. 5, September 14, 1928, 325–335, at 326.

233. Riḍā (1922) and Mitchell (1969, 266–269).

234. Ṭ. Ḥusayn (1958, 230–231).

235. For instance, in a letter sent to King Faruq in 1936, al-Banna exhorted "King Faruq, his prime minister, . . . and the heads of all Arab governments" to use state institutions to reinforce private and public Islamic behavior. Although in Al-Bannā (1965, 164–199) this letter is dated 1947, Mitchell (1969, 15) correctly dates it to 1936.

236. Mitchell (1969, 238).

237. Al-Bannā (1965, 337).

238. For instance, Ḥasan al-Bannā, Fī al-Iṣlāḥ al-Azharī [About the reform of al-Azhar], *Jarīdat al-Ikhwān al-Muslimīn*, July 9, 1935, no. 13, 7.

in *al-Manār*, and some ʿulamā).[239] For Hassan al-Banna, what remained to be done for the state to become fully Islamic was to ensure that the laws of the land were in conformity with Islam. This did not necessarily imply revolutionizing the structures of the state, and he did not question the structures and historical foundations of the Egyptian state as it was organized at the time.[240] This does not mean that the Muslim Brothers and other Islamists (some of whom have sought to remove and replace existing state structures) have not considered violence at times and used it as a means to achieve their political aims. It only speaks to the fact that specific forms of state and government were not of deep concern to the early doctrine of the Muslim Brothers. This flexibility was in fact commonplace in Egypt at the time. It was central to the liberal or conservative ʿulamā's conception of their partnership with the state,[241] and according to the liberal Azharite Ali Abd al-Raziq, Egyptians in general did not theorize about alternatives to their state structures.[242] Liberals and conservatives (including the Muslim Brothers) alike recognized that they could implement their respective conceptions of the state's custodianship of Islam (a thinner or a thicker one, respectively) within their current state structures and using various techniques of governance, including imported ones.

Redirecting Attention to the History of Political Ideas

In sum, at their inception, the Muslim Brothers' three aforementioned core tenets had already been rehearsed by Muslim conservatives before them. To be sure, liberals also shared several principles with them: they also rejected the separation of Islam and the state as well as state neutrality and argued that the

239. For instance, Rashīd Riḍā, Diʿāyat al-Ilḥād fī Miṣr [Atheism's propaganda in Egypt], *Al-Manār*, vol. 27, no. 2, May 13, 1926. For similar injunctions by the ʿulamā in the 1930s, see, for instance, Muḥammad al-Aḥmadī al-Ẓawāhirī, Nidāʾ Ṣāḥib al-Faḍīla al-Ustādh al-Akbar bi-Izāʾ Ḥawādith al-Tabshīr [An appeal to the honorable shaykh of al-Azhar regarding instances of proselytism], *Nūr al-Islām*, vol. 2, no. 10, February–March 1932, 716; Muḥammad al-Khiḍr Ḥusayn, Al-Taʿlīm al-Dīnī fī Madāris al-Ḥukūma [Religious education in government schools], *Nūr al-Islām*, vol. 2, no. 6, October–November 1931, 395–401; and Yūsuf al-Dijwī, Ḥadath Jalal Lā Yumkin al-Ṣabr ʿAlayhi [A momentous incident that cannot be abided], *Majallat al-Azhar*, vol. 8, no. 7, September–October 1937, 487–491. For an example of the ʿulamā's insistence on the implementation of sharia in the early 1930s, see Muḥammad al-Khiḍr Ḥusayn, Ḍalālat Faṣl al-Dīn ʿan al-Siyāsa [The error of separating religion from politics], *Nūr al-Islām*, vol. 2, no. 5, September–October 1931, 323–337.

240. Al-Bannā (1965, 337).

241. Zeghal (1996).

242. ʿAbd al-Rāziq (1925, 22–24).

state had to provide a religious infrastructure for its Muslim citizens; that Islam had to play, via public education, a pedagogical role; and that it had broad efficacy for society. They also shared the notion that the state was a key instrument for implementing their respective projects. However, like conservatives before them and unlike liberals, the Muslim Brothers sought a thicker and more munificent state custodianship of Islam: they aimed to give Islam an all-embracing role in knowledge, in society, and in governance, and to impose more significant Islamic constraints on the state. Therefore, the emergence of the Muslim Brothers did not introduce as deep an ideological rupture into the "liberal age" as is commonly assumed. To be sure, the Muslim Brothers and the movements they inspired have subsequently evolved in their mobilization strategies, commitments, organizational structures, and in their interpretations of Islam, and new types of movements that similarly aimed to expand the role of Islam in governance have developed. However, this should be framed as the continuation of an old political battle about the role of Islam in governance. In addition, these movements, rather than constituting a "countersociety" or a "parallel sector,"[243] represent one of many participants in this long-standing political battle.

As I have shown in Zeghal (1996), in the second part of the twentieth century, conservative ʿulamā continued to advocate for the expansion of the role of Islam in governance, as they had before the emergence of the Muslim Brothers, and some of them demonstrated affinities with this movement. The difference between conservative ʿulamā and the Muslim Brothers is not so much about their project but rather about the means through which they express themselves (such as their writing style) and about how they conceive of their mission. Conservative ʿulamā do not have an organized movement at their disposal (although they often leverage their own structures of schooling and religious institutions), and they generally do not aim to govern directly. Taking at face value the Muslim Brothers' self-serving criticisms of the Egyptian ʿulamā as secluded and apolitical, the literature has often portrayed them as aloof from any type of political engagement.[244] However, this is inaccurate, as shown, for instance, by their engagement with the 1922 constitutional debates and, more broadly, by their writings—in the magazine that served as the mouthpiece of al-Azhar since its first publication in 1930.[245] This stereotypical representation of the ʿulamā might be

243. Kepel (1985b) inspired by Bourdieu (1971) and Rosefsky Wickham (2002), respectively.

244. E.g., Lia (1998, 285–286). Exceptions include Zeghal (1996) and Hatina (2010).

245. *Nūr al-Islām*, which subsequently became *Majallat al-Azhar*, contained articles about religion and politics, jurisprudence, Muslim demographics in the world, fatwas in response to

due to their (often tense and ambivalent) partnership with the state, and therefore to the rarity of their overt opposition to governmental policies. In reality, they have held and expressed a variety of political views, and the political cleavage about Islam in governance I have described in this book cuts across their professional body. This cleavage should therefore be studied in a broader framework than social movements theory, to include a larger set of protagonists than organized movements such as those designated as "Islamist," and be framed in a much longer and broader history of political ideas and debates than is customary.

Conclusion

Although organized Islamist movements, in all their varieties, are certainly important protagonists of the politics of the modern Middle East, it is crucial to attend historically and more broadly to the terms of the political cleavage over Islam in governance, which predates them, in order to deepen our understanding of Middle Eastern politics. In Egypt, as in Tunisia and in most Muslim-majority polities, the main fault lines of this political cleavage do not fall along whether the state should be the custodian of Islam as the preferred religion: there has generally been a broad and long-standing agreement about this principle among conservatives and liberals alike. However, *how* the state must perform this duty has been an object of contention, notably regarding the rights of religious minorities and freedom of expression. It is important, in my view, to take seriously and examine deeply the history of this political cleavage over Islam in governance (as well as other governance issues of a nonreligious nature) in this part of the world, much the same way political cleavages have been studied for Western polities. In addition, it must be stressed that a state-preferred religion is not an inevitable or essential reality in Muslim-majority polities. It is merely an empirical regularity which is by no means universal, and there is no reason why it should or should not endure, except for the choices made by people and the governing elites. It should be studied as a variable of choice, subject to constraints such as the demographic weight of religious minorities, or the weight of past choices, and not as the inevitable consequence of external factors such as colonization, imperialism, or the alleged hegemony of Western "secular liberalism" in the Middle East.

---

questions sent by readers, reviews of books (including foreign ones), and polemics, in addition to Qur'anic exegesis, history, literature, and poetry.

5

The Concrete Implementation of the State's Custodianship of Islam in the *Longue Durée* and Its Discontents

HOW HAS THE imperative of the state's custodianship of Islam in Muslim-majority polities translated at the material level? What broad trends can be discerned in this concrete implementation and in the munificence of the state's custodianship of Islam during the modern period? What debates accompanied these trends? What might have driven fluctuations over time and variations across polities? To answer these questions, I examine state expenditures devoted to public Islamic religious provisions (infrastructure and personnel dedicated to Islamic worship, Islamic education in madrasas and modern schools, sharia justice, and public works and assistance when provided in an Islamic form) and their attendant debates in Tunisia, Egypt, Morocco, and Turkey in the *longue durée.* I find that a similar picture is discernible in these four countries, despite their significant historical, political, and socioeconomic dissimilarities. Morocco was not an Ottoman province, and its monarchical regime (and prophetic legitimacy) has endured since the seventeenth century. Ottoman Tunisia and Egypt were virtually autonomous from Istanbul by the nineteenth century, and they transitioned from monarchies to republics in the twentieth century, as Turkey did. These four countries' histories of foreign occupation contrasted greatly, and so did their socioeconomic development trajectories, as illustrated by the trajectory of their school enrollments per capita, GDP per capita, and state expenditures as a percentage of GDP (tables 1, 4a, and 4b).

The data I examine include aggregate state expenditures devoted to public Islamic provisions (defined as religious goods made available free of charge to the public) measured in per capita real terms (i.e., adjusted for inflation and purchasing power parity) as well as relative to other state expenditures and to the size of the overall economy from the late nineteenth century or early twentieth century to 2020, with some incursions into the further past. I also analyze how various protagonists decided and debated the aims, institutional forms, extent, and content of public religious provisions. Importantly, I consider the state's aggregate religious expenditures by its religious *and* nonreligious institutions, administrations, and ministries, and I disaggregate expenditures on public religious provisions from those that went toward operating, maintaining, and managing the revenue-generating assets of public religious endowments. Some studies have examined direct state expenditures by parts of the official religious bureaucracy (which might only constitute a small fraction of total state religious expenditures)—for example, to gain insight into institution building.[1] Others have analyzed religious endowments (or their deeds) and other religious institutions in great detail as inputs for social history, sometimes quantitatively, gaining invaluable insight into topics such as family life, estate planning, gender issues, poverty, attitudes toward charity, religious endowment management practices, and wealth accumulation.[2] Overall, however, these studies have not examined *aggregate public religious provisions* at the country level in the *longue durée* and their attendant debates but have rather focused on institutional and operational aspects of the supply of these provisions.

Estimating aggregate public religious expenditures and following them through time leads to a striking initial conclusion: despite the persistence and prominence of the state's custodianship of Islam as an ideal—displayed, for example, in the large number of lines devoted to religious expenditures in state budgets, or in the sizable economic apparatus of public religious endowments when measured in terms of employment and economic output (only a small part of which went to fund public religious goods)—these expenditures have

1. E.g., Fabbe (2019) on state co-optation of religious elites and Laurence (2021) on state religious legitimacy.

2. E.g., Baer (1962), Faroqhi (1976), Amīn (1980), Pascual (1983), Deguilhem (1986, 1995), Powers (1990), Yediyıldız (1990), Ferchiou (1992), Behrens-Abouseif (1994), Bilici (1994), Petry (1994), Çizakça (1995), Michel (1996), Doumani (1998), Ghānim (1998), Ghazaleh (2011), Hoexter (1998), Raymond (1998), Hénia (1999), Sabra (2000), Deguilhem and Hénia (2004), Bilici (2006), and Kogelmann (2009).

historically been relatively small as a percentage of overall public expenditures, and especially in relation to the overall economy (table 2).[3] Second, public religious provisions, which include neither religious goods produced and consumed in the home or by the family nor religious goods accessible to the public on a user-fee basis, have largely been a state affair. They can be directly paid for and attended to by the state treasury or other parts of the state administration, by the ruler himself, or by other state officials. They can also be indirectly paid for and attended to by the same, via the funding, management, and regulation of institutions such as public religious endowments (waqfs, or *ḥabūs* as they are also commonly called in North Africa), a common decentralizing mechanism. This has not precluded civil society's financial contributions, but these are smaller, and in fact often controlled, guided, supported, and leveraged by the state. Third, in the *longue durée*, while aggregate public religious expenditures may have decreased as a fraction of overall public expenditures (as shown for Tunisia in table 2), they have massively increased in per capita real terms. A core reason enabling this two-pronged trend is that, in the nineteenth and twentieth centuries, Middle Eastern states increased their revenues and expenditures by an order of magnitude relative to the size of their economies, which themselves expanded by an order of magnitude in per capita real terms in the twentieth century. As a result of their expanding size and reach, while they significantly increased their supply of public religious (and nonreligious) provisions in per capita real terms, Muslim states were able to deprioritize religion in public life relative to other domains and to allocate a smaller share of state resources to public religious provisions. Fourth, Muslim student school enrollments (combined with the fraction of Islamic instruction in the curricula of state and state-subsidized[4] "modern schools" and "specialized Islamic tracks") has been an important driver of state religious expenditures in the twentieth and twenty-first centuries. I call "modern schools" those schools established in the modern period for the primary purpose of teaching imported European knowledge. They can include what is commonly called

3. Singer (2008, 183–184) argues, against Inalcik and Quataert (1994), albeit without quantification, that there was no "welfare state" in the Ottoman Empire in the modern sense of the term but rather a "welfare society." It might be more accurate to talk of a "welfare ideal," for the state and society alike.

4. In the period and countries under study, state and state-subsidized schools represented the majority of Muslim students' school enrollments, with the possible exception of nonmodernized Qur'anic schools in the earlier part of the period.

"traditional" structures, such as Qur'anic schools, when they are repurposed to this end. "Specialized Islamic tracks" refers to those institutions whose primary purpose is the teaching of the Islamic sciences. They include madrasas[5] such as the Moroccan Qarawiyin, the Tunisian Zaytuna, the Egyptian al-Azhar, and the Ottoman medreses but also modern incarnations thereof, such as Imam-Hatip schools, Higher Islamic Institutes and Ilahiyat in Turkey, or "original schooling" (*taʿlīm aṣlī* or *aṣīl*) and Islamic Studies departments in modern universities in Morocco. Importantly, Islamic subjects are usually taught in modern schools, and nonreligious ones in specialized Islamic tracks. In some rare cases, the latter might even dispense a higher fraction of nonreligious instruction than the former.[6] Eschewing the usual "modern and secular" vs. "traditional and religious" school distinction, I focus instead on the aggregate per capita number of hours of Islamic instruction modern schools and specialized Islamic tracks both provide. I find that, in the modern period, thanks to the expansion of school enrollments, Muslim states have been able to disseminate Islamic instruction at an unprecedented scale in per capita terms (table 4d), even as its share was declining in curricula (table 4c), and even when specialized Islamic tracks were drastically shrunk (tables 4a and 4b). Islamic education therefore went from representing a small fraction of total state religious expenditures to the largest portion (table 3).

The expansion of per capita public religious expenditures (and religious instruction) was enabled by a broad agreement, throughout the modern period, among state and other elites (including ʿulamā) about the state's duty to sustain religious institutions and dispense public religious provisions (including Islamic instruction), often as part of a broader project of human and economic development. However, there were also significant disagreements and political disputes about the extent of public religious provisions to be dispensed, that is, about what I call the munificence of the state's custodianship of Islam (insufficient for some, excessive for others); about the reprioritization of financial resources from some provisions to others (desirable for some, illegitimate for others); about their content and the institutional form of their delivery (e.g., what constitutes Islamic knowledge, and whether Islamic education should be

5. Madrasas developed after the tenth century. Makdisi (1961, 1981). On their geographical spread from east (Nishapur) to west (Morocco), see Brunschvig (1931). See also Mottahedeh (1997).

6. E.g., see table 4c for 1880 Tunisia, an estimation based on the Sadiki School teachers' specialization and the number of classes taught by subject at the Zaytuna.

taught in madrasas or modern schools); as well as about the direct involvement of the state in the management and reorganization of religious institutions. They complement the political debates about the role of Islam in governance analyzed in the previous chapters. Various protagonists participated in these discussions, such as state officials, conservative and liberal ʿulamā, madrasa and modern school students, colonial authorities, and the broader public. These debates are not exclusive to the modern period,[7] but new interlocutors such as organized movements, associations, and parties gave them a new resonance in the twentieth century thanks to the advent of mass politics. Conservatives lament what they view as excessive deprioritization of religion in public life and insufficient munificence of the state custodianship of Islam; liberals, just the opposite. Unsurprisingly, political competition and conflicts between the two camps, which predate the emergence of organized Islamist movements, have led to tugs-of-war over policy and hence to significant short-term fluctuations in the supply of public religious provisions (tables 2, 4a, 4b, 4c, and 4d).

These disputes have also had some resonance in the academic literature since the 1980s. Some scholars, failing to place recent developments in a wider historical context, emphasize what they see as an Islamic revival (or a process of "Islamization"), in particular since the 1970s. They sometimes interpret it as the unintended consequence of misguided policies, educational or otherwise.[8] Others emphasize instead what they see as a process of secularization and marginalization or even destruction of religious institutions, and of Islam in public life more broadly. They often hypostatize the Islamic past, contrast it with a secularized present, and see a deep rupture within Islamic tradition and Islamic institutions, which they attribute to the loss of their (alleged) former autonomy from the state and (supposed) economic self-sufficiency.[9] I highlight instead the long-standing custodianship of Islam by the state and its unwavering financial support of Islamic institutions or, at the very least, of their mission, notwithstanding disputes about and fluctuations in this mission's content, extent, and institutional forms.

There has been inevitable ambivalence about this financial support: on the one hand, the ʿulamā's ambivalence about the state's meddling in their affairs (such as their simultaneous demands for more autonomy and state support); on the other hand, rulers' or state officials' ambivalence about the institutional

7. For premodern examples, see J. Pedersen and G. Makdisi, Madrasa, *EI*[2]; Bel (1938, 326); Rodríguez-Mañas (1996); Makdisi (1981, 75–152); and Harrak (1989, 33–71 and 297–375).

8. E.g., Barbar and Kepel (1982), Kepel (1985), Starrett (1998), and Nasr (2001).

9. Asad (1993) and Hallaq (2013), among others.

forms (and degree of centralization) this support should take, given their conflicting ambitions to both control religious institutions and its ʿulamā and keep them at a safe distance (in part to better manage the demands and expectations of the ʿulamā and the Muslim community). Such ambivalence is not distinctive of the modern period, and neither are the debates over—for example, the sustaining of religious institutions by the state; their frequent reorganizations, including waves of centralization and decentralization; the introduction of new institutional forms for the delivery of religious provisions and the elimination of old forms; or constant reprioritizations within public religious provisions. Rather, what is distinctive of the modern period is the unprecedented increase in the size and reach of the state. Despite its sheer magnitude, it has not precluded continuity in the concrete implementation of the state's custodianship of Islam. It has rather facilitated its expansion in per capita real terms and presented the ʿulamā with both new challenges and new opportunities.

I mainly use printed and archival material detailing state budget expenditures, the expenditures of important state religious institutions whose budgets are kept separate from those of the state, and the enrollments in specialized Islamic tracks and modern schools administered or subsidized by the state as well as their curricula. I also examine material pertaining to the elaboration of such budgets and to the content, extent, and institutional forms of the supply of public religious provisions. More details can be found in the data appendix.

Section 1 discusses the accuracy of my estimation of aggregate state religious expenditures and probes the scale of nonstate contributions to public religious provisions. Section 2 highlights the symbolic prominence, but modest size, of state religious expenditures in relation to other expenditures and to the overall economy. Section 3 discusses their two-pronged long-term trend of relative decrease alongside absolute per capita expansion. Section 4 analyzes historical debates related to Islamic education's content, extent, and institutional forms of delivery. Section 5 shows the state's unwavering support for religious institutions or their missions and its meddling in their affairs. Section 6 analyzes the resulting ambivalence in the partnership between the ʿulamā and the state.

1. Estimating Aggregate Expenditures on Public Religious Provisions

Public religious expenditures can be classified in five categories: worship (e.g., mosques' personnel and maintenance, public religious celebrations, the organization of the pilgrimage to Mecca, and allowances to descendants of the

Prophet), sharia justice (e.g., sharia courts' personnel and maintenance), Islamic education (e.g., madrasa personnel and maintenance, and more recently religious education teachers in modern schools), assistance (e.g., charity, hospices, and hospitals), and public works (e.g., fountains, wells, and fortifications). To be sure, the boundaries separating these categories and distinguishing them from nonreligious ones can be porous and constitute political issues. The exact content of these categories, their designations, their visibility, and in which budget they are located—that of a religious affairs ministry; a waqfs ministry; another ministry such as health, justice, or education that also has nonreligious expenditures; or that of a religious institution or administration whose budget is kept separate from that of the central state—have changed over time. Tallying aggregate public religious expenditures by the state is therefore challenging since they are scattered and not always neatly labeled as such in public records, which are themselves not always extant or complete. However, for the period under study, a forensic analysis of detailed central state budgets and the accounts of important state religious institutions (such as public religious endowments and madrasas), when these accounts were kept separate from the state budget, as well as estimations based on school enrollments and curricula, provide a sufficiently accurate picture to draw some conclusions. Focusing instead on state expenditures by the religious bureaucracy, omitting the separate accounts of state-managed religious institutions and expenditures on religious education in modern schools, could lead to omitting the bulk of state religious expenditures. Other sources of state expenditures could still be added to my estimate to improve its precision. However, given their relatively modest size, they would not alter my results nor impact long-term trends in significant ways. I have notably omitted the expenditures of the Bayt al-Mal (a fund with a definite religious character constituted of the revenues of the *jizya* when it was in force, some religious endowments, and unclaimed inheritances of Muslims), which, despite their symbolic importance, were comparatively small.[10]

Another question is the contributions of nonstate actors. Civil society might contribute—for example, by funding public religious endowments—but we will

10. E.g., in Tunisia, the Bayt al-Mal's religious expenditures for 1873–77 (resp. 1907), amounted to about 4 percent (resp. 3 percent) of the Djemaia's religious expenditures. Later, this fraction was even smaller. ANT SH C63 D701, ANT SH C63 D702, ANT SH C63 D708, ANT SD C191 D1-11, ANT SC C26 D1-13, ANT SD C191 D1-14, and ANT SD C191 D1-36. Djemaia budgets in ANT SC C26 D1-1 and ANT SC C26 D1-8. For studies of the Bayt al-Mal in Tunisia and beyond, see Chérif (1986), Larguèche (1999), Bashrūsh (1999, 91–94), Abū Ghāzī (2000), Lajili (2007), and Grangaud (2015).

see in section 5 that this has mostly been the domain of rulers and state officials. Civil society might also contribute via private (or, as they are often called, family) endowments, or the endowments and other activities of *zāwiyas*,[11] and more recently via private voluntary associations. All these might involve a significant number of people and carry considerable economic and political weight (as we saw in chapter 2 for *zāwiyas* and private *ḥabūs* in 1920s Tunisia). However, despite the scarcity of information about their finances, we can conclude that their monetary contributions to *public* religious provisions have been small compared to those directly or indirectly made by the state. Often, *zāwiyas* and Islamic private voluntary associations are in large part economic enterprises, and their activities sustained by user fees. In addition, they are often funded, wholly or in part, by the state, to control but also to leverage their contributions. As for private endowments, they predominantly serve private aims. Therefore, public religious provisions have been and continue to be mainly (albeit not exclusively) a state affair.

Zāwiyas' *and Family Endowments' Modest Contributions to Public Religious Provisions*

Zāwiyas are religious organizations par excellence, since they operate thanks to their founders' (the saints) and their descendants' charisma.[12] However, they are also economic and political units that sustain and protect entire communities materially: the saint's family, his disciples, laborers, and also visitors (notably during saintly pilgrimages, albeit usually on a user-fee basis).[13] Therefore, when *zāwiyas* grow, they may come into conflict with the state or receive its support. Rulers have endowed properties for the benefit of *zāwiyas* and have sustained them through the state budget and through tax exemptions for purposes of legitimacy building and/or political co-optation.[14] However, the size of a *zāwiya*'s economic activities, the significance of its political power, and the numerical importance of the community it serves[15] should not be conflated with the extent

11. For the meaning of *zāwiya*, see chapter 2.

12. Elboudrari (1985, 499). For an analysis of the social role of the saint, see Chih (2021).

13. Valensi (1977, 254), Tawfiq (1978, 231–32), Johansen (1988), and Zarcone (1994, 237–238).

14. Amri (2000, 117–136) and Johansen (1988, 238–239). Eickelman (1976, 48) speaks of a "substantial traffic in influence with the Makhzen." See also Pascon (1983, vol. 1, 256–257 and 271–274).

15. Estimates of the number of members of *zāwiyas* at the country level vary greatly and should be taken as orders of magnitude only. *Annuaire du monde musulman* (1955–56, 244) claims that, in 1922, the 476 *zāwiyas* of Tunisia had about 58,000 "affiliated" members, i.e.,

of the tangible public religious provisions it sustains, such as Qur'anic schools, madrasas, and worship infrastructure. Indeed, the rare studies that have attempted to evaluate the charitable/religious provisions of important *zāwiyas* suggest that most of their revenues were dedicated to sustaining the family of the saint and the economic enterprise, that religious activities were themselves a source of revenues (via donations from the faithful), and that public religious provisions constituted only a sliver of their overall (mostly economic) activity.[16] *Zāwiyas* that grew to become large and powerful enough were in fact akin to small local states—for example, in Morocco, "miniature makhzens"[17]—and it is therefore not surprising that, like central states, *zāwiyas* would only devote a small fraction of their resources to public religious provisions.

Yet archived Tunisian government documents suggest that aggregate revenue from *zāwiyas*' private *ḥabūs* were on the order of 3 million francs in 1925,[18] which would mean that *zāwiyas* supplied about 20 percent of aggregate public religious provisions, if we were to assume that, in line with the Djemaia (the Tunisian *Ḥabūs* Administration), slightly less than half their revenues went to public religious expenditures. These documents also contain a hypothetical (i.e., aspirational) budget template that provides, at first glance, some support for this assumption. It assumes that about 42 percent of the revenues of a *zāwiyas*' private *ḥabūs* would go to religious expenditures, 9.5 percent to administrative costs (including 6.25 percent for the shaykh's compensation), and 48.5 percent to "beneficiaries," presumably the descendants of the founder.[19] However, this is not realistic: at the time, more than half the revenues of the

3 percent of the Muslim population. Bachrouch (1989, 76) counts more than one thousand *zāwiyas*, including subsidiaries, on the eve of colonization and in 1932, but does not provide headcounts. Spillman (2011, 117–118) reports on a 1939 survey of the largest *zāwiyas* in Morocco that counted 227,400 "followers" (excluding "sympathizers" and most women), i.e., 3.8 percent of the Muslim population. *Annuaire du monde musulman* (1955–56, 257) estimates the overall number of "affiliates" to 10 percent of the Moroccan population in the mid-1950s. De Jong (2000, 197) estimates that there were six million *zāwiya* members (*adhérents*) in early 1980s Egypt, i.e., about one-seventh of the total population.

16. Hammoudi (1980), Pascon (1983, vol. 1, 255–291), Pascon (1984), and Amri (2000).

17. Laroui (1977, 54).

18. "Note de la Direction Générale de l'Intérieur," March 8, 1927, ANT SD C97 D5, and April 5, 1927, ANT SD C97 D5-5. A July 19, 1932 note estimated that there were about 1,000 *zāwiyas* that "could produce" an annual revenue of 20 million francs (to be distributed to about 30,000 people), but it is not clear what was meant by revenues (gross or net) and how far this hypothetical was from reality. ANT SD C97 D5.

19. ANT SD C97 D5-5.

Djemaia were absorbed by administrative and other costs essentially devoted to operating, maintaining, and managing its revenue-generating assets.[20] Therefore, it is likely that only a sliver of the *zāwiyas*' private *ḥabūs* revenues were dedicated to *public* religious provisions, and that their revenues were more or less evenly split between their (private) beneficiaries and the costs of operating, maintaining, and managing their revenue-generating assets. It might be objected that *zāwiyas* were religious in their very essence and that, as a result, all their activities, including their agricultural work and the management of their revenue-generating assets were perceived by their followers as having a religious character of a public nature. But if so, it could be similarly argued that as the state is Muslim, all its expenditures are religious. In this chapter, I strive to measure expenditures devoted to tangible public religious provisions (infrastructure and personnel dedicated to worship, sharia justice, Islamic education, and public works and assistance).

Similarly, because family (*ahlī* or *khāṣṣ*, i.e., private) *ḥabūs* become public (*ʿāmm* or *khayrī*, i.e., charitable) only after the extinction of the family lineage, they generally do not translate into tangible public religious provisions before that time (even though they often provide charity within the family and signal a pious intention). Some do include public provisions and are called mixed (*mushtarak*). However, overall, they tend to serve predominantly private aims and their contribution to public religious provisions is therefore modest in relation to that of the state.[21]

Private Voluntary Associations' Modest Contributions to Public Religious Provisions

Islamic private voluntary associations, especially from the second half of the twentieth century, have also been discussed as playing an important role in compensating for an alleged withdrawal of the state. In Tunisia, until 2011, there were few legally sanctioned religious associations. It is therefore difficult

20. 1925 Djemaia budget, ANT SC C26 D1-47.

21. E.g., in Egypt, 84 percent of the total disbursements of the family waqfs managed by the Ministry of Waqfs (about one-fifth of all family waqfs, and likely a sample biased toward public provisions) went to private beneficiaries (as opposed to public provisions) during the period 1926–1927 to 1949–1950 (right before family waqfs were abolished). See the Ministry of Waqfs Budgets in *Al-Waqāʾiʿ al-Miṣrīya* and Sékaly (1929). Extrapolating from this biased sample to estimate public religious expenditures made by all family waqfs during this period of popularity of this form of property would lead to about a quarter of state religious expenditures, a likely high upper bound.

to quantify their actual weight in the supply of public religious provisions with accuracy, but it has presumably been very small. Since then, private voluntary associations (including some with religious aims) have multiplied, but it seems that few have disclosed their financial statements. To make an assessment, we can look at other countries. For instance, a 2007 official survey of "nonprofit institutions" in Morocco estimated their overall expenditures at what amounted to about 2.5 percent of state expenditures, and the expenditures of those operating in the religious sector[22] at what amounted to 1.7 percent of state religious expenditures. In addition, almost 30 percent of nonprofit institutions' resources came from the public sector, significantly mitigating their nonstate character, a feature that was even more pronounced for those operating in the religious sector: the state contributed 54 percent of their resources.[23] An even more telling example is that of Egypt, which is often cited as having one of the oldest and most active traditions of private voluntary associations.[24] A 1960 official survey of all registered associations[25] reported aggregate expenditures that amounted to about 1.3 percent of state expenditures, and shows that only 7.9 percent of what they provided was religious.[26] From this I estimate that their religious expenditures amounted to only about 6.5 percent of state religious expenditures.[27] The same survey reveals that about 20 percent of their resources came from government aid, 20 percent from user fees, and only 40 percent from dues and donations. After that, the number of associations increased significantly, and so did the share of associations with an Islamic aim,[28] but there is scant aggregate

22. Group 10 in the International Classification of Non-Profit Organization (ICNPO) classification.

23. Royaume du Maroc, Haut Commissariat au Plan (2011). The survey sampled about 10 percent of the estimated 44,771 active "nonprofit institutions," 1.3 percent of which operated in the religious sector.

24. The funding of private schools (excluding state aid and user fees), as well as the charitable contributions of the many Islamic zakat committees, and expenditures on private mosques could also be added to this discussion.

25. Wizārat al-Shu'ūn al-Ijtimā'īya (1964?), also analyzed by Berger (1970). Of the 3,715 registered associations surveyed, 3,195 responded, including private members associations. Registration was and still is mandatory.

26. The quantity labeled "value" (*qīma*) in the survey.

27. Prorating aggregate associations' expenditures by the fraction of the "value" they provided in the religious sector.

28. The number of associations quadrupled from 1960 to about 15,000 in the early 1990s. Qindīl and Ibn Nafīsa (1994, 111–114) find that associations with an Islamic reference represented 17 percent, 31 percent, 33 percent, 27 percent of all associations in 1960, 1970, 1980, and 1991,

information about their finances.[29] However, a rare study based on a representative sample of all associations' financial statements for 1992 estimated their overall revenues (and expenditures) at what amounted to about 1 percent of state expenditures.[30] From this I estimate that all associations' religious expenditures amounted to 7–8 percent of state religious expenditures in 1992[31] (and it seems that this percentage was similar twenty-five years later, despite the number of associations having continued to increase).[32] Moreover, at the time, about 10 percent of nonprivate membership associations' revenues came from government aid; 40 percent from user fees, notably due to the success of health clinics of Islamic associations; and only about 30 percent from dues and donations. Finally, the presence of the state has been overwhelming in terms of legislation and control, and it has provided other types of support, such as tax and other financial exemptions, as well as assistance (and surveillance) by a large number of civil servants.[33] In other words, available evidence suggests that the extent of public religious provisions that associations financially sustain (outside of state aid or user fees they might receive) is small when compared to state religious expenditures, although country-to-country differences and fluctuations are to be expected (a topic for further research). Notwithstanding often-heard

---

respectively, and those with an Islamic reference and a religious aim (not exclusive of other aims) 12 percent, 25 percent, 27 percent, and 21 percent, respectively. Masoud (2014, 35) finds that, in 2007, 20 percent of all private voluntary organizations had "Islamic characteristics."

29. CAPMAS publishes annual surveys but only based on samples of selected associations. By the 1990s they only included less than 10 percent of registered associations.

30. LaTowsky (1997, 13). This amounted to about 0.4 percent of GDP, as in the 1960 survey above.

31. Applying the increase in the percentage of associations with an Islamic reference and a religious aim (not exclusive of other aims) from 1960 to 1991 reported in Qindīl and Ibn Nafīsa (1994) to my previously estimated share of aggregate associations' expenditures deployed in the religious sector in 1960, and multiplying it by the range of all associations' 1992 expenditures in LaTowsky (1997, 13).

32. According to a declaration of the minister of social solidarity to *Al-Ahrām*, November 9, 2017, there were 29,043 active associations (out of the 48,300 registered), and 12,000 of them spent about 10 billion LE annually for associative work. These associations were presumably the largest and prorating as above we find that all associations' religious expenditures amounted to 5–12 percent of state religious expenditures in 2017.

33. Qindīl and Ibn Nafīsa (1994, 265–285). According to a November 5, 1992, *Al-Wafd* article cited in Qindīl and Ibn Nafīsa (1994, 94), about 60,000 civil servants were "delegated" (*muntadabīn*) to associations to staff them, a substantial fraction of their salaries being paid from the state budget, the association only paying them a salary complement. See also Berger (1970), Clark (1995), and LaTowsky (1997).

narratives of the state's withdrawal, it has in fact supplied and continues to supply the lion's share of public religious and other provisions while leveraging (as well as guiding and controlling) civil society.

2. The Symbolic Prominence and Modest Extent of Public Religious Expenditures

In aggregate, in the period under study, public religious expenditures—including those sustained by public religious endowments and other religious institutions whose budget might be kept separate from that of the central state—have been and remain rather modest in relation to other state expenditures and particularly in relation to the size of the economy (see table 2). In Tunisia, they represented about 5 percent of total state expenditures in the late nineteenth century, and only about 1 percent since 1960. We find similar orders of magnitude in twentieth-century Egypt, Morocco, and Turkey as in Tunisia, and in none of these countries did they exceed 1 percent of GDP. Moreover, the focus of state religious expenditures has changed considerably. Earlier in our datasets, they were mostly devoted to sustaining a worship infrastructure (providing mosques and mosque personnel, imams, and preachers, and tending to Muslim holidays and the pilgrimage to Mecca). In the early 1880s in Tunisia, worship expenditures represented about two-thirds of total public religious expenditures, compared to 16 percent for sharia justice, 10 percent for public works and assistance, and only 7 percent for Islamic education. We find comparable proportions in 1900 Egypt and in 1915 Morocco. While worship expenditures remain important, their share of overall religious expenditures has significantly decreased. In 2020 they represented 30–40 percent of total public religious expenditures in Egypt, Tunisia, Turkey, and Morocco. Moreover, some public provisions—such as public works (e.g., fountains, wells, bridges, and fortifications) and public assistance (e.g., hospitals, hospices, and charity)—have often lost their religious character. Traditionally provided (albeit to a modest extent) by public religious endowments, they became too overwhelming an expenditure and therefore largely fell under the increasingly large welfare provisions directly provided by the state, thereby losing their waqf designations (whether waqfs were abolished, as in Tunisia in 1956,[34] or remained, as in Morocco and Egypt, or were westernized, as in Turkey). As for sharia courts, when they were

34. See chapter 2.

abolished, in Turkey in 1924, in Egypt in 1955, and in Tunisia in 1956, they disappeared from the state budget, reducing the scope of state religious expenditures,[35] although, to be sure, this did not translate universally to the disappearance of the sharia from legal adjudication, as we saw in chapter 2. On the other hand, Islamic education has massively increased in scale. In 2020 it absorbed the largest portion (close to two-thirds) of public religious expenditures in Egypt, Tunisia, Morocco, and Turkey (table 3).

Mosques and Madrasas as Absentee Landlords in the Waqf System

Is the modest size of public religious expenditures relative to other public expenditures and to the overall economy a recent phenomenon? An examination of the 1730–31 Tunisian central state budget combined with some basic economic analysis suggests that it is not.[36] First, this budget (summarized in table 6) shows that the state did pay for religious provisions directly from its treasury, but that these payments only represented 2.7 percent of its expenditures,[37] that is, about 0.05 percent of GDP since total state expenditures only amounted to about 2 percent of GDP at the time. The bulk of the state budget (slightly more than 70 percent) was devoted to military expenditures. Second, although I could not estimate aggregate religious provisions by public waqfs from public records until the creation of the Djemaia in 1874, Lucette Valensi's work provides us with a clue. Her examination of eighteenth-century tax records in a sample of localities in several regions of Tunisia suggests that roughly 10 percent of agricultural property (e.g., olive and date trees) was in waqf form.[38] She also calculates, based on a sample of actual contracts and agricultural yield estimates, that absentee-landlord rent amounted to about 2 to 10 percent of output, a percentage that might seem low but that should be put in the context of rudimentary agricultural

35. In Turkey, the April 8, 1924 decree abolished sharia courts. In Egypt, the September 21, 1955 law abolished the sharia courts and integrated sharia judges into unified national courts. For Tunisia, see chapter 2 and Zeghal (2013a). For Morocco, see Schriber (2021).

36. There are few extant registers of detailed state budgets before 1730–31. See Fakhfākh (1990). The 1730–31 budget, in ANT Register #11, is 160 pages long with 3,663 lines of expenditures. It does not provide details about Dar al-Basha expenditures (the pay of the Turkish militia and prominent Hanafi men of religion) which constituted 47.2 percent of the total. I have assumed that the religious expenditures of Dar al-Basha were negligible.

37. 5.1 percent of state expenditures exclusive of Dar al-Basha. See also Chérif (2008, vol. 1, 315) for a rough upper bound, which is consistent with my evaluation.

38. Valensi (1977, 104, 111, 114–117, and 128).

techniques, scarce manpower, and comparatively abundant land.[39] Since waqf beneficiaries (mosques, madrasas, etc.) should be analyzed as absentee landlords, aggregate waqfs' religious provisions could only amount to about 0.2 to 1 percent of GDP at most (since only a fraction of waqf beneficiaries were public religious provisions, as discussed below). The exact percentage is a topic for further research, but using the average of the absentee-landlord rents reported in Valensi (1977, 140), we find that they would have amounted to 0.5 percent of GDP—that is about 25 percent of aggregate state expenditures (including public waqfs' expenditures). And if we assumed instead that waqfs' religious provisions amounted to the same share of GDP (0.25 percent) as in 1880 (when we have waqfs' centralized accounts at our disposal), we would find that these provisions represented about 15 percent of aggregate state expenditures in 1730. I use these two estimates to display in table 2 an estimated range for total state religious expenditures in 1730 (as a percentage of total state expenditures and GDP as well as in per capita real terms). Similar orders of magnitude are to be expected in other countries in premodern times,[40] with country-to-country variations due to variations in absentee-landlord rents and in the fraction of land and built property devoted to public waqfs (also topics for further research).

Misconceptions about the Extent of Public Religious Provisions by Religious Endowments

Despite its modest size, the supposedly vast wealth generated and disbursed by the waqfs in the form of public provisions in the past has fed the imagination of locals and foreigners alike, from those urging for a return to this alleged past prosperity[41] to those, on the contrary, lamenting their proliferation.[42] Some scholars credit religious endowments with driving the development of cities and/or institutions of learning in premodern times, as if waqfs were agents in their own right rather than malleable instruments in the hands of

39. Valensi (1977, 140).

40. Yediyıldız (1990, 123–124) estimates waqfs' total expenditures "in Turkey" in the eighteenth century at about one-third of state revenues, based on a sample of deeds (rather than accounts), likely a high upper bound.

41. E.g., Çizakça (2000).

42. E.g., Michel (1996, 182–183) shows that, after the Ottoman conquest, some authors exaggerated the importance of waqf and *rizaq iḥbāsīya* lands in Egypt, as the Ottomans proceeded to inspect and register them.

their founders.[43] Others instead blame them for all the Muslim world's economic woes.[44] Regardless, scholarly works usually assume that, in aggregate, waqfs supplied very large amounts of public provisions.[45] They often point, for concrete evidence, to the large fraction of overall landholdings that were (or were alleged to be) in waqf form. Following the chain of authors they cite, we often arrive at Heffening's 1936 article in the first edition of the *Encyclopedia of Islam*, which uncritically relies on observers' accounts.[46] Hence, the prominence of waqfs as a form of property is often vastly exaggerated in the literature. Exaggerations of the amount of aggregate public provisions they disbursed are even greater and are driven, in large part, by a confusion between waqfs as revenue-generating properties (typically land and buildings)[47]—which might have had a significant weight in the economy in terms of output and people employed (albeit not as large as is often claimed)—and the religious beneficiaries of these waqfs (e.g., mosques and madrasas). As we saw, as absentee landlords, these beneficiaries only received a small fraction of the

43. E.g., Raymond (1985, 226), Behrens-Abouseif (1994, 4 and 146), and Makdisi (1981, 28) who credits "the law of waqfs" for bringing "institutions of learning into existence" in the tenth century.

44. E.g., Kuran (2001, 2011), mainly on theoretical grounds. Common criticisms include the problems caused by the (alleged) absence of the concept of legal personality, the (unquantified) transaction costs due to the de jure inalienability of the waqfs, the coordination problem caused by their high number of beneficiaries, their managers' graft, and other agency problems that are hardly specific to waqfs or Islamic institutions.

45. Exceptions include Stöber (1986), Michel (1996, 182–183), Hénia (1999, 348), Shatzmiller (2001, 70), and Crone (2004, 313–314).

46. Fractions often quoted are one-third of Tunisia or of its agricultural land, and one-third, more than half, two-thirds, or even three-quarters of the Ottoman Empire or Turkey. For example, Singer (2008, 186) refers to Kuran (2001, 849) who reports this fraction for 1883 Tunisia, citing Heffening's 1936 article on "Waḳf" reprinted in Gibb and Kramers (1953, 627), which cites, without caveats, Terras (1899, 169), which refers to a report by Alfred Dain published in *Revue algérienne et tunisienne de législation et de jurisprudence*, 1885, vol. 1, 285–356, 288, who stresses that this figure, based on hearsay, is to be used with "extreme caution," and is "excessive." Terras (1899, 169–170) also cautions that this figure is "a bit exaggerated." He points to an actual survey conducted a few years earlier for Northern Tunisia, which found that *ḥabūs* land acreage was 150,000 ha out of a total of 4,000,000 ha (3.75 percent). As we saw in chapter 2, the one-third figure is indeed vastly exaggerated, and more realistic estimates were produced shortly after Terras wrote his thesis. Behrens-Abouseif (1994, 146) reports similarly implausible figures for the Ottoman Empire citing Barnes (1986, 42), who cites Barkan (1939, 237), who cites, but with some words of caution, Heffening's 1936 article. Similarly, Hallaq (2009, 402) cites Barnes (1986, 83), who cites Ubicini (1853–1854, vol. 1, 271).

47. Cash waqfs were popular in certain places, but their legitimacy was the object of debates. See Çizakça (1995).

output of waqfs' properties—for example, 2 to 10 percent in eighteenth-century Tunisia.[48] Therefore, even if the entirety of the country were a public waqf, less than 2 to 10 percent of GDP could possibly be devoted to public religious expenditures at the time. Indeed, public waqf beneficiaries only received the residual revenues of their waqf properties, net of their operating costs (labor and other input costs as well as maintenance and management costs). Examining the Djemaia's budgets from its early days to its liquidation, I estimate that these costs absorbed at least 50 percent of its reported revenues (even though the Djemaia rented out some of the properties under its management, it exploited others). We find similar percentages for the public Waqfs Administrations of the other three countries examined in this chapter.[49] In addition, not all waqfs had public provisions as their main beneficiaries. In fact, very often most did not: the vast majority were private or mixed with few to no public beneficiaries.[50] Moreover, even public waqfs often served private interests rather than public ones, as argued (but not quantified) by Baer (1997).[51] All told, despite their economic, political,

48. Valensi (1977, 140).

49. Variations in the ratio of net to gross reported revenues are to be expected due to variations in the ratio of revenue-generating assets that are directly managed as against those rented out, as well as from variations in the type of rental contract, in the type of property, and in technological and managerial capabilities.

50. In twentieth-century Tunisia and Egypt, public waqfs' land only represented a small fraction of total waqf land (which in turn represented about one-tenth of total productive land). At Tunisia's independence in 1956, after which all waqfs were abolished, this fraction was about 15 percent according to Sicard (1965, 239–240). In Egypt it was about 11 percent in 1928–29, and 8 percent in 1951–52, after which private waqfs were abolished. See Sékaly (1929, parts 1, 2, 3), Mulḥaq li-Maḍbaṭat Majlis al-Nuwwāb, Al-Dawla al-Miṣriya, Majlis al-Nuwwāb (1924–1952), session 36, July 23, 1951, 90, and *Annuaire statistique de l'Egypte* 1951–1952, 1952–1953, and 1953–1954. Earlier in time, Yediyıldız (1990, 21) studied a randomized sample of 330 waqfs created between 1699 and 1839 (out of a total of 6,000 waqfs created during that period and 20,000 that existed at the time), in the area of today's Turkey and estimated that only 18 percent were public (*khayrī*), and 75 percent were mixed (*mushtarak*). His description of a "typical" mixed endowment deed leaves little doubt as to its predominantly family character. Doumani (1998, 11–12) finds that "roughly 79 percent of the 211 waqfs endowed in Tripoli and over 96 percent of the 138 waqfs endowed in Nablus between 1800 and 1860 are of the family (*dhurrī*) type," and that if one counts mixed endowments, the percentage is close to 100 percent in both places. Grangaud (2004) analyzes an eighteenth-century large urbanistic complex in Algiers, composed of waqf properties with the Sidi al-Kittani mosque, the main religious edifice, at its center, and shows that this project mostly served the endowers' private economic aims. Morocco, on the other hand, seems to have had relatively few private *ḥabūs*, according to Luccioni (1982, 6) and Pascon (1983, vol. 1, 389–390).

51. See also the examples of Sultans Qaytbay and al-Ghawri in Mamluk Egypt described in Petry (1994, 196–205).

and religious significance, the aggregate amount of public religious provisions the waqfs supplied was therefore much smaller than has been claimed and perceived, both in relation to overall state expenditures and especially in relation to the overall economy. To come to this realization, it is important to focus the analysis on these provisions and not bundle them with all the economic components of the waqfs. Still, nostalgia for a past prosperity supposedly related to the allegedly vast, but nowadays dilapidated, wealth of the waqfs remains to this day, and it is often reactivated as a solution to all sorts of social and economic woes,[52] generating debates about the waqfs' worth as a legal form of property[53] and as an instrument for human and economic development.[54] It also has increased the Muslim community's expectations as to the amount of public religious provisions that the waqfs could possibly support, often putting governments in a difficult position.[55]

52. E.g., in Morocco, S. Idllanlène, Le habous, instrument de protection de la biodiversité?, *Développement durable et territoires*, vol. 4, no. 1, April 2013, and in Egypt, the proposal of Dr. Ibrahim al-Bayyumi Ghanim to introduce waqfs legislation in the new constitution in order to reinforce civil society, in *Al-Ahrām*, August 5, 2012, 10. Similarly, in 1872, the French consul in Tunis argued that the *ḥabūs*, if managed more efficiently, could raise "considerable revenue" for the state. "Situation financière, Remèdes à y apporter," January 7, 1872, CADN, Direction Politique no. 604, 712PO/1, 1870–1873, Tunis, Consulat Général 1582–1887, vol. 106, fol. 317.

53. E.g., the 1920s debates in Egypt about the project to abolish private waqfs, deemed by some to be inefficient, reported in Sékaly (1929, part 1, 78–79 and part 4, 636–639), and the 1940s debates about the Islamic character of private waqfs analyzed in Baer (1962, 215–219). See also, for debates in French Mandate Syria, Deguilhem and Hénia (2004, 414).

54. E.g., the post–Arab Spring political debates in Tunisia, in Le gouvernement décide de rétablir le régime du waqf: Utilité sociale ou islamisation rampante?, *La Presse*, May 31, 2013, and Mashrūʿ Qānūn al-Awqāf Yukhaffif al-ʿIbʾ ʿan al-Dawla [The bill on waqfs will relieve the state's burden], *Al-Shurūq*, November 12, 2013; and in Egypt, the disagreements about whether returning its waqfs to al-Azhar would bring it back to its past cultural prominence, in *Al-Ahrām*, December 30, 2012, 21. In Turkey, the official narratives of the Directorate General of Foundations highlight the role of foundations for society's development, but the legitimacy and extent of their contribution is often the topic of political disagreements. See, for instance, Halil Deligöz, The Legacy of Vakıf Institutions and the Management of Social Policy in Turkey, *Administrative Culture*, vol. 15, no. 2(2014): 179–203.

55. E.g., in French-occupied Morocco, *Ḥabūs* Administration officials complained that French and Moroccan public opinion assumed that the *Ḥabūs* were "a very wealthy institution, with unlimited resources," whereas the reality was that their resources were far from sufficient to accomplish their mission. "Patrimoine Rural des Habous: Note pour le Vizirat," December 22, 1948, ANOM, Fonds Luccioni, 52APOM7; "Note d'ensemble au sujet des habous de Meknes," 1953, ANOM, Fonds Luccioni, 52APOM3; and Luccioni (1982, 225).

Going Back Further in Time: A Model Budget of the Abbasid Court

Going back further in time is challenging since extant premodern state budgets for Islamic polities are rare, but an "exceptional document"[56] provides us with a glimpse into the extent to which Abbasid monarchs funded (or were expected to fund) religious expenditures out of state tax revenues, although it only informs us on court revenues and expenditures. This document was included in Hilal al-Sabi's *Kitāb al-Wuzarāʾ*, which was composed sometime between 1031 and 1041 AD.[57] Hilal al-Sabi presented it as a budget of the Caliph Al-Muʿtadid's court (r. 892–902).[58] However, given the references to a later period, it seems that it was in fact presented to the Caliph Al-Muqtadir (r. 907–932) and might have been "intended as a memorandum" at a time of "financial difficulties."[59] It should therefore be read as a model for state expenditures.[60] It contains thirty-eight distinct paragraphs of expenditures, whose arrangement follows more of an accounting logic than a thematic one,[61] and a thirty-ninth paragraph that details savings that Hilal al-Sabi claims were made by the caliph after two years of his reign. Making a few assumptions, I have reordered and summarized this budget thematically (table 5).[62] As in 1730–31 Tunisia, state expenditures were very small in relation to the overall economy[63] and most of them (more than

56. Sourdel (1958, 278).

57. I use the version in Al-Ṣābī (1958). See also Busse (1967), and the data appendix for more details.

58. Hilal al-Sabi (d. 1056) was the grandson of a famous secretary. *Kitāb al-Wuzarāʾ* essentially covers the caliphates of Al-Muʿtadid and Al-Muqtadir, and the administration of their viziers Ali Ibn al-Furat, Muhammad al-Haqqani, and Ali Ibn Isa.

59. Busse (1967, 13–14 and 30).

60. Martin Hinds argues that, in ninth-century Iraq, there was "an apparent normative rather than descriptive character of certain lists [of tax rolls]"; quoted in Waines (1977, 284).

61. Most paragraphs list a monthly expenditure, but with months of different lengths over which this amount was to be paid (30, 35, 45, 50, 60, 70, 90, or 120 days) depending on the place of the recipients in the hierarchy. This made computations and recordkeeping quite complex, and dictated the structure of the budget to a large extent. See Busse (1967, particularly 33–35).

62. When religious expenditures are mixed with nonreligious ones in the same paragraph, I prorate them according to the proportion of religious items mentioned. Because the sums in the paragraphs concerned by this assumption (6, 10, and 11) are very small (less than 3 percent of the budget as a whole), alternative assumptions would not alter my conclusions.

63. Although there are no aggregate headcounts or detailed salary lists, daily salaries range from 0.1 to 0.3 dinars in paragraph 12 (military men not allowed to work in the palace). In paragraph 31 daily payments to each of 4,000 Hashemites of Baghdad were cut from 1 to 0.25 dinar by Al-Muʿtadid. We can therefore infer that this budget (7,000 dinars per day) supported tens

70 percent) went to the military,[64] while religious expenditures constituted a very small fraction of the overall budget (only slightly more than 1 percent). This budget's religious expenditures can be organized in three categories: justice (19 percent), charity and public assistance (34 percent), and worship (47 percent), the largest. Worship expenditures consisted in the equipment and personnel (imams and muezzins) of Baghdad's two Friday mosques (Al-Mansur and Al-Rusafa), payments to senior Hashemites (who were honored as being part of the Prophet's family), as well as to Qur'an readers, muezzins in the caliphal palace, and servants who prepared the ritual ablutions for palace officials and the caliph himself.[65] Charity and public assistance consisted in alms (*ṣadaqa*) to women in need (*al-ḥuram al-muḥtājāt*) and in the expenditures of the Sa'idi Bimaristan, the only hospital in Baghdad under Al-Mu'tadid according to this budget, where doctors, nurses, and ophthalmologists as well as personnel caring for the mentally ill worked.[66] Justice expenditures went to pay a *qāḍī* and his deputy, their sons, and ten jurists (*fuqahāʾ*).[67] This budget was drafted before the establishment of madrasas as institutions in their own right in the eleventh century, and it does not contain expenditures for Islamic education,[68] although chief physicians and their students (*ruʾasāʾ al-muṭabbibīn wa-talāmidhatahum*), senior scribes (*akābir al-kuttāb*), archivists (*khuzzān*), state administration officials (e.g., *aṣḥāb al-marātib*), *qāḍīs* and jurists, entertainers (*mulhīn*), and astrologers (*munajjimīn*), all of whom are mentioned in the budget, were clearly educated.[69]

---

of thousands of people, consistent with numbers in ʿAwwād (1964, 13–14). Compare to a taxed population probably two orders of magnitude or so larger.

64. Military expenditures (paragraphs 1–5, 8, and 12) match those in Busse (1967, 35), notwithstanding a typo in his paragraph numbers.

65. Paragraphs #30, #35, part of #6, part of #10, and part of #11, in Al-Ṣābī (1958, 25, 26, 19, and 20–21).

66. Paragraphs #26 and #38, in Al-Ṣābī (1958, 24–25 and 26–27). From the expenditures devoted to the Bimaristan, we can estimate that there were 50 to 150 patients, compared to a court population in the tens of thousands and a total population of Baghdad probably an order of magnitude or so higher at that time.

67. Paragraph #34 in Al-Ṣābī (1958, 26).

68. This budget is silent about the payments to Islamic scholars by rulers mentioned in M. Ahmed (1968, 253) and Makdisi (1981, 162–163). For institutions of education before the establishment of madrasas, see Makdisi (1981). For the relationship between Abbasid rulers and the ʿulamā, see Zaman (1997b).

69. Al-Ṣābī (1958, 15–27). For a description of the caliph's court life, see Kennedy (2004).

Showcasing the Ideal of the State Custodianship of Islam in Central State Budgets

In his *Muqaddima*, Ibn Khaldun (1332–1406) recounts that it was only after showing a skeptical contemporary "stray leaves from the account books of the government offices in the palace of Al-Ma'mun [Abbasid caliph, r. 813–833]" that he was able to convince his interlocutor that the share of religious officials' pay in the ruler's budget is generally small, since the ruler "gives them their share in accordance with the general need and the demand of the population (for them)." As for the importance of the religious professions and institutions, Ibn Khaldun relates them to the ruler's "duty to look after the public interest [*maṣāliḥ*]."[70] Ibn Khaldun's anecdote illustrates an enduring quality of the state's custodianship of Islam: its modest demand on the state budget, alongside its central role as an ideal and as a duty the ruler owed to the ruled. And indeed, in the Abbasid court's "model" budget in Hilal al-Sabi's *Kitāb al-Wuzarā*ʾ, the percentage of budget lines that are devoted to religious expenditures exceeds by an order of magnitude the percentage these expenditures represent in monetary terms.[71] The same goes for the 1730–31 Tunisian central state budget (table 6). In the latter, a large number of lines signaled the bey's interest in sustaining religious institutions, especially the public display of religiosity—for example, in the vein of what Largueche (1999, 117) calls the "theater of princely charity."[72] Worship expenditures,[73] about two-thirds of which were dedicated to Muslim holidays celebrations, accounted for almost 80 percent of religious

70. Ibn Khaldun speaks of "persons who are in charge of offices dealing with religious matters, such as judge, mufti, teacher, prayer leader, preacher, muezzin, and the like." F. Rosenthal (1967, vol. 2, 334–335).

71. In this budget, 13 percent of the paragraphs are fully dedicated to religious expenditures, and an additional 8 percent only partially, although religious expenditures only represent about 1 percent of the total state expenditures in monetary terms.

72. For example, in Tunis, the Tekia (a hospice) and the Sadiki Hospital founded in 1776 and 1879, respectively, had about 100 patients each in the late 1800s (when the population of Tunis was about 80,000) according to Largueche (1999, 122–135). They helped the ruler showcase his attention to charity. See also, for Mamluk Egypt, Fernandes (1988).

73. Excluding payments to ʿulamā whose function was not specified, which amounted to about 13 percent of religious expenditures, and 0.8 percent of the overall central state budget. These ʿulamā (e.g., *fuqahā*ʾ who accompanied the bey's *maḥalla* and/or *zāwiya* shaykhs) seem to have been paid as state officials.

expenditures.[74] In comparison, public assistance accounted for about 3 percent, with a large number of small individual charitable givings (*ṣadaqāt*) interspersed throughout the budget, and justice 1 percent (for support to select *qāḍīs*). Education accounted for only 4 percent,[75] including expenditures for *kuttābs* (Qur'anic schools) for boys and girls and support to select madrasa professors and students in *zāwiyas*. Although it was not an explicit *shar'ī* duty, Islamic education was part of the preservation of the religion,[76] and attention to it was one of the virtues of the ruler in the hagiographic literature.[77] It was therefore an object of particular attention from the state, despite the extremely modest sums devoted to it: in the 1730–31 budget, these sums only represented the equivalent of about fifteen annual salaries of an imam-preacher, a muezzin, or a Qur'an teacher (*mu'addib*), for a country of one million people or so.[78] And judging from the financial accounts of public *ḥabūs* in the late nineteenth century, few of them were devoted to education, and only a small fraction of aggregate public *ḥabūs* expenditures were devoted to it. However, it seemed particularly important as a signal and, like that of other public religious

74. About 70 percent of worship expenditures went to Muslim holidays (the organization of public and court celebrations and the daily breaking of the fast during Ramadan), 20 percent to worship equipment (e.g., the illumination of mosques) and personnel (e.g., imams and muezzins), including the costs related to the personal piety of the bey (e.g., his prayer rug and the repair of his prayer book), and 10 percent by donations (*ṣadaqa*) to the holy cities of Mecca and Madina (*Ḥaramayn*) and to a much lesser extent by donations (*ṣadaqa* and *iḥsān*) to Mecca pilgrims.

75. About 70 percent of state expenditures on education sustained a few madrasa professors, 5 percent students in *zāwiyas*, 20 percent the Qur'anic teacher of the bey's children, and 5 percent Qur'anic schools and their teachers. This is especially noteworthy since these schools had few *ḥabūs* and their teachers were paid mostly by parents, as shown by Al-Mājrī (2014, 198) for the city of Tunis: in 1756 (resp. 1875), 76 (resp. 61) *kuttābs* out of 117 (resp. 106), i.e., 65 percent (resp. 57 percent), were not financed by any *ḥabūs*. Those that were could seldom cover their costs with *ḥabūs* revenues alone. Crone (2004, 312–313) notes that, in the classical age, rulers patronized scholars and madrasa education much more than primary education. For *maktabs* in Mamluk Egypt, see Sabra (2000, 80–83).

76. Crone (2004, 313).

77. E.g., for Tunisia, Ibn Yūsuf (1998, 18–25); for Morocco, Ibn Zaydān (1937); and for Egypt, Al-Jabartī (1879–1880, vol. 1, 418–420).

78. In the budget, the annual salaries of the imam-preacher and muezzin of the Bardo Mosque, or the annualized pay of a *mu'addib*, were on the order of 30 to 40 piasters. ANT Register #11, pp. 64 and 73.

expenditures, its share of the 1730–1731 budget lines far exceeded its monetary weight (table 6).

3. The Drastic Expansion of the State's Size and Reach in the Modern Period and Its Consequences: Islamic Revival or Secularization?

In the modern period, aggregate public religious expenditures massively increased in per capita real terms, although they remained modest in relation to GDP and other state expenditures, and although they may have in fact decreased relative to other state expenditures (making room for nonreligious ones). This two-pronged evolution was driven by the unprecedented expansion of the size of the state in the modern period, in relation to the overall economy and in per capita real terms. The literature on the modern period has been ambivalent, some authors highlighting what they interpret as a process of secularization, and others what they interpret as a process of Islamization. However, all along, as they expanded in size, states in Muslim-majority polities have generally and consistently tended to the supply of public religious provisions, which therefore also expanded.

State Religious Expenditures' Absolute Expansion and Relative Decrease: Mechanistic Effects and Deliberate Choices

In Tunisia, state revenues and expenditures increased significantly in the nineteenth century in relation to GDP, an expansion that seems to have started in earnest with the rapid succession of fiscal innovations initiated in 1819.[79] This increase continued in the twentieth century (during and after colonization), when real GDP per capita also increased by an order of magnitude, thereby magnifying the expansion of state expenditures in per capita real terms (table 1). The expansion in the size of the state in Tunisia is broadly consistent with the experience of the Ottoman Empire's state finances studied by Karaman and Pamuk (2010). They attribute the spectacular increase in the ability of the Ottoman central state to raise tax revenues in the second half of the nineteenth century to "changes in military technology and related organizational innovations" that allowed for a successful fiscal centralization. They show that the expansion in the size of the state started even earlier in Europe, especially in its northern part.

79. See Valensi (1977, 354–359; 1981, 720–721) for more details on these fiscal innovations.

Other polities in the Middle East followed a similar pattern, although there are significant country-to-country variations as to when this expansion started in earnest and its pace.

The massive expansion in the size of the state in relation to the size of the economy, combined with the equally massive increase in real GDP per capita, enabled a significant increase in public religious expenditures in per capita real terms in the modern period (tables 1 and 2).[80] However, it may also have enabled an even more important increase in other (nonreligious) types of expenditures, and hence a relative deprioritization of state religious expenditures, as shown in table 2 for Tunisia. In Tunisia, public religious expenditures decreased by an order of magnitude as a percentage of total state expenditures (from ~15–25 percent to about 2 percent) from 1730 to the early 1900s. Indeed, total state expenditures increased by an order of magnitude as a percentage of GDP, while GDP and public religious expenditures increased only modestly in per capita real terms. Nonreligious state expenditures in Tunisia therefore increased by an order of magnitude in per capita real terms while religious ones increased only modestly during that period. It is as if there was not enough economic growth for a much more munificent state custodianship of Islam and hard choices had to be made as to how to allocate the additional state resources in the face of new needs of a secular nature. It remains a topic for further research to ascertain the timing and extent of such a relative deprioritization of state religious expenditures in other countries prior to the twentieth century.

In the twentieth and twenty-first centuries, the picture is different: the percentage of public religious expenditures relative to total state expenditures remained in the low single digits in Tunisia from 1900 to 2020, as it did in Egypt, Morocco, and Turkey. Moreover, these four countries not only experienced a significant increase in total state expenditures as a percentage of GDP, but their GDP per capita increased by an order of magnitude or so in real terms. Hence, public religious expenditures increased by an order of magnitude in per capita real terms.[81] Of particular note is that this pattern holds for the period of French

80. How much of this increase is attributable to changes in the relative prices of religious goods and to quality enhancements (as opposed to quantity increases) is yet to be ascertained. We do observe a shift toward more human-capital intensive religious provisions such as religious education and increasingly educated teachers and imams.

81. Since per capita public religious expenditures can be expressed as the product of (1) the fraction of total state expenditures that public religious expenditures represent, (2) the fraction of GDP that total state expenditures represent, and (3) GDP per capita.

colonization in Tunisia and Morocco. During that period, state religious expenditures remained little changed as a percentage of total state expenditures, while they increased significantly in per capita real terms and as a percentage of GDP, since total state expenditures as a percentage of GDP increased significantly and so did real GDP per capita (tables 1 and 2).

Behind this broad trend of expansion in public religious expenditures, there are significant short-term fluctuations and country-to-country differences. Some can be traced to historical heritage or to policy choices that were specific to the religious domain (e.g., how many mosques per capita there should be relative to other public infrastructure; what fraction of total enrollments should specialized Islamic tracks represent; or what fraction of modern school curricula should religion constitute),[82] but others are the natural result of differences in the pace of economic development. For instance, we recognize in table 2 the short-term effect of some well-known watershed policy choices on state religious expenditures (in per capita real terms and as a percentage of total state expenditures and GDP), such as the decrease in such expenditures in the 1930s and 1940s in Turkey (the effect of Ataturk's reforms), or in the decade after independence in Tunisia (the effect of Bourguiba's reforms). Some periods of increase in the same metrics were also the effect of policy choices such as after 2000, when, after the "lead years," the Moroccan monarchy integrated Islamist parties into the political arena, and when Islamists governed in Turkey. Of note is the increase in state religious expenditures in per capita real terms and as a percentage of GDP in 1960s Egypt, in the context of Nasser's 1961 reform of al-Azhar, which runs counter to conventional wisdom.[83] Still, in general, these short-term fluctuations are overwhelmed by the long-term trends I described above, and it would be fruitless, in my view, to rank these countries on an "Islamic" scale by comparing them at one time or

82. E.g., see the 1956–1959 Tunisian NCA debates about the appropriate extent of worship infrastructure, and about whether mosques or schools were more important for the dissemination of Islam (*Munāqashāt*, vol. 1, 225). In Turkey, in 1924, MPs debated whether mosques were to be closed. See the debate of April 17, 1924, https://www5.tbmm.gov.tr/tutanaklar/TUTANAK/TBMM/d02/c008/tbmm02008040.pdf, accessed September 10, 2020. For a recent debate about the size of the Turkish Diyanet, see https://www.duvarenglish.com/domestic/2019/09/25/directorate-of-religious-affairs-exceeds-budget-by-3-billion-tl and https://www.dw.com/en/diyanet-the-turkish-religious-authority-that-makes-millions/a-50517590, accessed September 10, 2020.

83. I highlighted the important resources Nasser provided to al-Azhar with its 1961 reform in Zeghal (1996).

another: consider the year 1955 (when Tunisia would be deemed the most "Islamic" and Turkey the most "secular" on the basis of per capita state religious expenditures) and then 2020 (when we have just the opposite). The takeaway is that these short-term fluctuations and country-to country differences are in fact fickle. They can be quickly reversed by policy choices made in relation to the vigorous debates about the concrete implementation of the (enduring) state custodianship of Islam. As we will now see, in the twentieth and twenty-first centuries, the education system has been a formidable tool for various governments to implement this custodianship.

Religious Education's Absolute Expansion and Relative Decrease: Mechanistic Effects and Deliberate Choices

The expansion in the size and reach of the state was particularly pronounced in the realm of education and, in 2020, state expenditures on Islamic instruction represented the bulk of public religious expenditures in Tunisia, Morocco, Egypt, and Turkey (table 3). States generally introduced and financially sustained modern schools in the nineteenth century and drastically expanded their reach in the twentieth century, aiming to make schooling available to all, and in some cases compulsory.[84] Here also, while Tunisia, Morocco, Egypt, and Turkey all experienced this broad expansion pattern (and convergence to quasi-universal schooling), the starting points and paces varied from country to country (tables 4a and 4b). For instance, in the mid-1920s, Egypt's and Turkey's per capita Muslim student enrollments at all levels in state or state-subsidized schools were three times higher than in Tunisia and twenty times higher than in Morocco. Despite these initial differences, all four countries' per capita enrollments reached comparable levels by the end of the twentieth century (table 4a).[85]

84. For Tunisia, see Lelong (1971), Sraïeb (1974, 1995), and Ayachi (2003). For Egypt, Sāmī (1917), Heyworth-Dunne (1939), ʿAbd al-Karīm (1945), Boktor (1963), Reid (1990), Alleaume (1993), Farag (1999), De Lavergne (2004, 2007), Crozet (2008), and Saleh (2016). For the late Ottoman Empire, Somel (2001) and Fortna (2002). For Morocco, Gaudefroy-Demombynes (1928), Manūnī (1985), Rivet (1988), Marrūnī (1996), and Vermeren (2002).

85. Tables 4a, 4b, 4c, and 4d present enrollments and school hours per capita of the total population rather than that of a specific age group since my focus is on public provisions from the point of view of the state. Some cross-country and intertemporal differences are therefore due to differences in population age structure. The same goes (to a lesser extent since the population of the four countries under study is in its vast majority Muslim) for differences in the population's religious composition.

We should also note that, contrary to common assumptions, this expansion was not a story of colonization, nationalism, or independent state building as far as indigenous Muslim students are concerned. In Tunisia, for instance, it started before the French occupation, with an expansion of the Zaytuna and the opening of state or state-subsidized modern schools;[86] did not materially increase with occupation (thirty years after French colonization began in 1881, less than 5 percent of primary school–age Muslim children were enrolled in such schools); and significantly accelerated in the late 1940s, a decade or so before independence.[87] Morocco's experience was similar.[88] In the same vein, in Egypt, state or state-subsidized schools' per capita Muslim student enrollments expanded significantly before the onset of the British occupation (they more than doubled between 1865 and 1880). Under occupation it took twenty years before they started to increase significantly again, an expansion that continued after the quasi-independence of 1922 (table 4a).

Public religious expenditures were often seen by policymakers as contributing to overall human development, an important aspect of which was education. The twentieth-century trend toward universal education in state or state-subsidized schools, combined with the continuous presence of specialized Islamic tracks and Islamic education in modern school curricula (except in 1930s–1940s Turkey), led to an absolute expansion of per capita hours of Islamic instruction (table 4d), in conjunction with a relative decrease when compared to other subjects (table 4c). On the one hand, the proportion of hours of Islamic education decreased significantly in modern school curricula (table 4c), and the relative share of specialized Islamic tracks in overall school enrollments also declined with the expansion of modern schools (table 4a).[89] On the other hand, an even more significant expansion in per capita overall school enrollments led to an increase in the per capita hours of Islamic instruction in state

86. The Zaytuna counted 445 students in 1863 (ANT SH C63 D738), and about double that in the late 1870s according to Bayram V (1884–1894, vol. 2, 126). The Bardo military school and the Sadiki School were established in 1840 and 1875, respectively, albeit with very small enrollments.

87. In the 1940s, French authorities elaborated projects of universal education. Although some progress was made in urban areas, the pace was such that it would have taken decades to reach this goal. See Sraïeb (1974, 31–43).

88. For the establishment of Madrasat al-Makhzen in 1844, well before colonization, see Rollman (1983, 575). Thirty years after colonization began in 1912, less than 4 percent of primary school–age Muslim children were enrolled in state or state-subsidized schools.

89. Tables 4a and 4c do not show data for Turkey before the closure of the medrese system and the drastic reduction of hours of Islamic instruction in modern schools.

or state-subsidized schools (table 4d). Concretely, in stylized terms, during their lifetimes Muslim children born in 2020 will be exposed to *an average* of about 500 hours of Islamic instruction in Tunisia, and to about 1,000 hours in Egypt, Turkey, and Morocco. This is, respectively, 7, 6, 15, and 100 times more average lifetime exposure than for Muslim children born a century earlier.[90] At the same time, the number of hours of exposure to other subjects has increased much more. To be sure, the pace of this evolution varied depending on policy choices specific to Islamic education (e.g., the doubling of weekly hours of religious education in modern schools in Tunisia from the mid-1970s to the mid-1980s, or the drastic reduction of specialized Islamic tracks enrollments in 1958 and 1989), but also, mechanistically, on the pace of development of the education system overall. Also, while in Tunisia, Egypt, Morocco, and Turkey the bulk of state or state-subsidized Islamic instruction nowadays takes place in modern schools rather than in specialized Islamic tracks, there are significant fluctuations and country-to-country differences as to the extent of this shift (table 4d). For instance, by 1925 more than 90 percent of Islamic instruction was already dispensed in modern schools in Turkey and Egypt (following the 1924 closure of the medreses in Turkey and the comparatively high development of modern schools in both countries at the time), versus less than 80 percent in Tunisia and Morocco, where modern schools were not as developed. On the other hand, in 2020, this fraction was only about 60 percent in Turkey and Egypt compared to 95 percent in Morocco, and 99 percent in Tunisia, due to the much higher share of enrollments of Muslim students in specialized Islamic tracks in Turkey and Egypt (after four decades of expansion) as compared to Morocco (whose government has been timidly developing these tracks) and Tunisia (where specialized Islamic tracks were shrunk drastically after independence). These fluctuations and differences have therefore been the natural result of variations in the pace of expansion of the modern school system as much as the result of policy choices specific to the religious domain.

Despite country-to-country differences, historical fluctuations, and reversals, per capita enrollments in specialized Islamic tracks have also increased significantly in all of these countries in the twentieth century, except in Tunisia. In higher education, they increased even in Tunisia (tables 4a and 4b). We would

90. This is a simplified computation based on table 4c. It assumes that the population age structures as well as the curricula and school enrollments remained constant over the children's years of schooling for each of the generations considered. Lifetime exposure is an average exposure of all Muslim children, whether they are schooled or not.

therefore expect to find significant numbers of their graduates in political positions, the education system, and state administration, and not just in the religious domain. For instance, in 1965–66, several years after Bourguiba had drastically shrunk the Zaytuna's enrollments, more than 40 percent of the primary public school teachers held a degree from it.[91] Zaytuna graduates have also constituted a significant fraction of the legislatures: 49 percent of the 1956 National Constituent Assembly, 43 percent of the National Assembly in 1959, and 46 percent in 1964.[92] They still constituted 6 percent of the National Constituent Assembly elected in 2011.[93] We would expect an even larger presence of graduates of specialized Islamic tracks in Morocco, and especially in Egypt and Turkey, given their considerably higher per capita enrollments in specialized Islamic tracks since the 1970s (tables 4a and 4b). It has been argued that the scale of Islamic education in the modern Middle East has caused the "Islamization" of state and society, and that this was unintended.[94] I argue instead that the causality is reversed: the scale of such education has resulted from deliberate (and negotiated) policy choices to sustain specialized Islamic education tracks (albeit shrinking in relative terms) and some amount of religious education in modern school curricula (albeit in a shrinking proportion relative to other subjects), combined with the expanding scale of the overall education system.

4. Debates and Policy Tugs-of-War about the Extent, Form, and Content of Islamic Education

Indeed, the number of hours of religious instruction in modern schools, its content,[95] the size of specialized Islamic education tracks, their curricular scope, and their institutional form, have been the result of negotiations and debates about the concrete implementation of the state custodianship of Islam. Significant fluctuations and reversals in the extent of Islamic education have ensued

91. Sraïeb (1974, 180). Lelong (1971, 735–739) reports that, in 1968–69, about half the civic and religious education teachers in secondary public schools were Zaytuna graduates (about 5 percent of secondary teachers across all subjects).

92. Figures are from Jazi (1971). Although graduates of the Sadiki School occupied most prominent political and administrative posts in postindependence governments, significant numbers of Zaytuna graduates participated in the New Dustūr Party. Sraïeb (1995, 306).

93. Latiri and Zeghal (forthcoming).

94. E.g., Starrett (1998), Langohr (2005), Beck (2009), and Charfi and Redissi (2010).

95. On religious education textbooks, see Carré (1979), Borrmans (1988), and Doumato and Starrett (2007).

from policy tugs-of-war during the modern period (tables 4a, 4b, 4c, and 4d) and have exacerbated already present anxieties. However, debates about Islamic education are not distinctive of the modern period: what is distinctive is its unprecedented scale in terms of per capita enrollments and hours of instruction.

What Should Be Taught in Madrasas? A Long-Standing Debate

In modern times, there were many attempts by state officials to introduce modern science in madrasa curricula, as well as backtracking, reversals, and vigorous debates. There is also a premodern history of state involvement and vigorous debates about what constitutes Islamic knowledge and what can legitimately be taught in madrasas.[96] Madrasas were an "instrument of state power,"[97] and premodern rulers might have sought to sustain an official religious doctrine and legitimize their rule, or to create a small educated elite of civil servants (e.g., *qāḍīs*, muftis, and scribes),[98] all of which helped them perform their duties of custodians of Islam and make it known that they fulfilled them.[99] Debates addressed the importation of foreign sciences (called *ʿulūm al-awāʾil,* the sciences of the ancients). Some subjects, such as logic (*manṭiq*), astronomy (*hayʾa*), or arithmetic (*ḥisāb*), were taught in madrasas as instrumental for the Islamic sciences, notwithstanding important variations in time and space.[100] Modern debates about curricular content should therefore be read as part of this longer history: although they emerged at a time when imported European knowledge became vital for policymakers to inculcate, these debates continued to be premised on the absolute necessity of the transmission of Islamic knowledge. They focused in great part on what constituted this knowledge, on how to teach it correctly, and on its relationship with other types of knowledge. In the nineteenth

96. For examples of premodern debates, see Makdisi (1981, 79), F. Rosenthal (1967, vol. 3, 300–305), and F. Rosenthal (2007). For examples of premodern state involvement, see Harrak (1989, 346–354 and 423–426), Ahmed and Filipovic (2004), and Şen (2021).

97. Chamberlain (1994, 51–54).

98. Brunschvig (1931), Makdisi (1961, 1981), and Bulliet (1972).

99. See, for instance, Chérif (2008, vol. 1, 247–248, and vol. 2, 109–114) for Tunisia, Shatzmiller (1976) for Marinid Morocco, and Pascual (1983, 117–118) for Ottoman Damascus.

100. Makdisi (1981, 78–80) speaks of a discreet presence of rational sciences outside of madrasas in medieval times and the general triumph of traditionalism in premodern history. For a study of the role of the rational vs. traditional sciences in the seventeenth century that reassesses this conventional view, see El-Rouayheb (2015). For variations in time and space in the teaching of logic, see El-Rouayheb (2019).

century, modern science—that is, knowledge imported from Europe—was generally not contentious: it was recognized as being part of knowledge more generally and as being important and necessary for economic competition, and many madrasa students wanted access to it.[101] However, there were debates about where it should be located: in the existing system of Islamic education (e.g., the Zaytuna in Tunisia, al-Azhar in Egypt, the Qarawiyin in Morocco, or the Ottoman medrese system in Istanbul and its provinces), or in new schools established for this purpose.

Supporting the introduction of modern science in madrasas, we often find arguments of efficiency (to compete with modern schools) and unification (to bring together Islamic and modern knowledge, which were, this argument goes, united in the past). At a time when school enrollments were increasing, it was argued that madrasa students must be trained in modern science to be able to compete with modern schools' graduates, and that the ʿulamā must not be isolated in the ivory tower of their Islamic knowledge but rather integrate Islamic and modern science. For instance, we find such arguments in the early twentieth-century Shaykh Muhammad al-Tahar Ben Achour's exhortations to introduce what the ʿulamā called at the time the "foreign sciences" (*ʿulūm ajnabīya*) at the Zaytuna;[102] in the Egyptian chronicler Al-Jabarti's (1753–1825) account of the Ottoman governor of Egypt's surprise to find mathematics (*al-ʿulūm al-riyāḍīya*) only taught in some ʿulamā's homes and not at al-Azhar in 1748–49;[103] in the narratives accompanying Muhammad Abduh's efforts to introduce modern subjects at al-Azhar in the last two decades of the nineteenth century;[104] as well as in Nasser's official justification of the 1961 reform of al-Azhar, which established modern faculties within the old institution

101. E.g., in Tunisia, Zaytuna students went on strike and signed petitions in support of curricular reforms since at least the early twentieth century. See Iṣlāḥ al-Jāmiʿ al-Aʿẓam [The reform of the Great Mosque], *Al-Ḥāḍira*, vol. 23, no. 1059, March 15, 1910; M. Ṭ. Ibn ʿAshūr (1967, 144–151); and ANT SD C36 D1-10. For an earlier critique of the absence of rational sciences in the Zaytuna curriculum, see ʿAlī Bushūsha, Al-Jāmiʿ al-Zaytūna [The Zaytuna mosque], *Al-Ḥāḍira*, vol. 6, no. 242, April 11, 1893.

102. Term used in an 1899 report about the Zaytuna curriculum, ANT SE C262 D13-2. See also M. Ṭ. Ibn ʿĀshūr (1967). For the reforms of the Zaytuna more broadly, see Green (1978, 113–115), Abdelmoula (1984), Sraïeb (1992, 206–207), ʿAyāshī (2003), and Weideman (2021).

103. Al-Jabartī (1879–1880, vol. 1, 186–187).

104. Gesink (2010, 79–82 and 165–230). On astronomy in al-Azhar's curriculum, see Stolz (2018). For Egyptian critics of the ʿulamā who resisted the introduction of modern science, see Bayram (1903) and Ṣaʿīdī (1965).

with the declared aim of bringing together the science of religion (*'ilm al-dīn*) and the science of the world (*'ilm al-dunyā*).[105] When the medrese curriculum was augmented with modern subjects in Istanbul between 1910 and 1917, it was under the official premise of reconciling Islam and modernity.[106] In Morocco, advocates of the modernization of the curriculum of the Qarawiyin—such as Muhammad Hassan al-Hajwi (1874–1956)—also argued in favor of efficiency and unification of all knowledge.[107] As for Allal El-Fasi (1910–1974), one of the most politically prominent Moroccan 'ulamā of the twentieth century, he argued, in support of his project of a modernized and expanded Qarawiyin, that "all sciences are Islamic."[108] For these reformers, these transformations were not deep ideological reorientations but mere reorganizations intended to enhance the system of education on the basis of the existing madrasa structures, in continuity with the past.

On the other hand, the reformers' critics argued that the new sciences, although legitimate, were not part of the madrasas' mission, which they saw as strictly confined to the transmission of the Islamic sciences and their auxiliary disciplines (e.g., grammar), a mission that the ruler had the duty to perpetuate. Also, in the name of efficiency, they often argued that madrasas could not take on the additional responsibility of transmitting modern sciences.[109] For instance, in Morocco, in the 1930s, Abd al-Hayy al-Kattani claimed that projects of reform of the Qarawiyin were akin to eradicating the soul of the institution.[110] In the same vein, for some 'ulamā of al-Azhar, the 1961 reform of their institution, which was designated as an evolution (*taṭwīr*) in official declarations, was but a destruction (*tadmīr*) that diluted and weakened its mission.[111] Nostalgia for the pre-1961 exclusively "Islamic" al-Azhar is often expressed to this day by many of

105. Zeghal (1996, 98–99). See notably Law no. 103, *Al-Jarīda al-Rasmīya*, July 10, 1961, no. 153.

106. Aksit (1991, 157–160) and Bein (2006, 286–288, 294, and 297).

107. On the reforms of the Qarawiyin in the modern period, see Tāzī (1972, vol. 3), Sraïeb (1984), Ibn 'Addāda (2003), and 'Imrānī (2016). On Hajwi's failed attempts to reform the Qarawiyin, see Ibn 'Addāda (2003, 260–278).

108. Zeghal (2008b, 39–49).

109. For these arguments for the Zaytuna, see the transcripts of the sessions of the 1898 committee reorganizing its curriculum, ANT SE C262 D13-3. A prior compromise led to the 1896 creation of a separate institution, the Khalduniya, to complement the Zaytuna curriculum with modern subjects. See M. Ṭ. Ibn 'Āshūr (1967).

110. 'Imrānī (2016, 100).

111. For more details, see Zeghal (1996, 98–124 and 301–302).

its ʿulamā,[112] despite the fact that al-Azhar's ensuing much larger scale and scope are the object of envy of many other ʿulamā around the world.

Policy Vacillations and the Issue of the Size of Specialized Islamic Tracks' Enrollments

Debates about the content of madrasa education have often been accompanied by disputes about its size (in a context of demand-driven enrollment pressures, and of some policymakers' fears of training too many ʿulamā) and by significant policy-driven fluctuations in enrollment. For instance, in Morocco, the Qarawiyin has remained mostly specialized in Islamic knowledge,[113] and, in 1963, its primary and secondary tracks, in addition to its doctoral program, were removed. At the same time, after independence, a primary and secondary specialized track in Islamic education (which also dispensed a blend of religious and modern knowledge with a higher amount of Islamic education than in other schools) expanded, but under the name "*aṣlī*" or "*aṣīl*" (original), and at times "*taqlīdī*" (traditional), and with fluctuations. It seems that its primary level was gradually phased out in the 1960s and 1970s, only to restart after that.[114] As it developed, it was criticized by some Moroccans who claimed it was too traditionalist and had become "an apparatus in the hands of a traditional intellectual elite that strongly defended its interests."[115] Others have lamented the state's neglect of this specialized Islamic track.[116] Departments of Islamic Studies were also established in modern universities in the early 1980s, further expanding Islamic higher education in Morocco, to the discontent of some intellectuals.[117] In Egypt, while al-Azhar's specialized Islamic tracks were rapidly expanding, modern

112. Zeghal (1996, 119–124 and 297–304), and for more recent debates Elston (2020).

113. Zeghal (2008b, 39–49).

114. Email communication from Dr. Chafiqi, director of the curricula at the Ministry of Education, September 3, 2022. See also Baina (1981, vol. 1, 236–237). The *Annuaire Statistique du Maroc* reports zero enrollment (or no data) from 1971–1972 to 1979–1980.

115. See Zeghal (2008b, 52–56).

116. E.g., Jābirī (1978); Muḥammad al-Thaʿālibī al-Ḥajwī, Wāqiʿ al-Taʿlīm al-Aṣīl [The state of original education], *Daʿwat al-Ḥaqq*, no. 260, November 1986, 58–61; *Al-Maḥajja*, no. 194–195, June 9, 2003; the Moroccan government's description of its policy regarding this specialized track in *Mudāwalāt Majlis al-Nuwwāb*, session of October 2018, December 10, 2018, 24–25; and the intervention of the Party of Justice and Development in Parliament on May 13, 2019, www.chambredesrepresentants.ma/ar.

117. E.g., Mohamed Tozy, La Reproduction des clercs, *Lamalif*, no. 190, July–August 1987, 40–42.

faculties (such as a business school and a school of medicine) were gradually introduced at the institution after its 1961 reform,[118] thereby responding to reformists' demands while helping meet the broader demand for access to higher education. Yet this dual expansion has been criticized internally as detrimental to the quality and religious identity of al-Azhar's education.[119] In Tunisia, after several decades of pressures from students (who petitioned and went on strikes[120]), internal debates, timid attempts to modernize the curriculum,[121] and flip-flops by French protectorate authorities, the Zaytuna's secondary level was augmented with a Modern Section in 1950.[122] It was taught in Arabic and included, along with Islamic sciences, courses in mathematics and physics.[123] Many ʿulamā saw this modernized Zaytuna as the embryo of a future modern Tunisian university.[124] However, although Bourguiba initially pursued this path,[125] he radically changed course in 1958, two years after independence, and unified the educational system. "Traditional schooling"—that is, the *kuttāb*s (Qur'anic schools) and the Zaytuna—was described by state officials as "unsuited" to Tunisia's needs and realities and as "destined to disappear."[126] The Zaytuna system was reduced to a small Faculty of Sharia and Theology (*kullīyat al-Zaytūna li-l-sharīʿa wa-uṣūl al-dīn*) within the University of Tunis, which was created in 1960.[127] It unofficially continued to be called "Zaytuna," but its

118. Tables 4a and 4b show the expansion of al-Azhar's specialized Islamic tracks, but not its modern faculties. As a percentage of all al-Azhar's faculties, its modern faculties' enrollments peaked at about 60 percent in 1966, and have hovered around 30 percent since the 1980s.

119. See Zeghal (1996, 278–284).

120. Students organized committees and, in 1949, a union, "The Voice of the Zaytuni Student" (*ṣawt al-ṭālib al-Zaytūnī*). See ANT SD C36 D1-10, and Abdelmoula (1984, 152–153).

121. E.g., the March 30, 1933 decree. Subjects such as arithmetic, geometry, and history would only be taught outside the Grand Mosque. *Al-Rāʾid al-Tūnisī*, vol. 76, no. 35, May 3, 1933.

122. This section was selective and only 150 students were admitted between 1950 and 1957, out of a total annual Zaytuna enrollment larger than 10,000. Acceptance rates ranged from 3 to 5 percent annually. Abdelmoula (1984, 170–174).

123. "Al-Lajna al-farʿīya li-l-taʿlīm al-ʿaṣrī bi-l-jāmiʿ al-aʿẓam wa-furūʿihi," ANT SD C36 D1-12.

124. Abdelmoula (1984, 170–174 and 224).

125. Decrees of March 29, 1956 (*JOT* no. 27, April 3, 1956), and April 26, 1956 (*JOT* no. 34, April 27, 1956).

126. République Tunisienne, "Nouvelle Conception" (1958–1959, 66), and Law of November 4, 1958 (*JORT*, no. 89, November 7, 1958), which unified all the public school curricula. See also Lelong (1971, 71–73).

127. Decree of March 31, 1960 (*JORT* no. 16, March 31, 1960). The Decree of March 1, 1961 (JORT no. 9, March 3–7, 1961) incorporated the Zaytuna in it. See Lelong (1971, 420). Zaytuna secondary education enrollments were gradually reduced to almost zero by the mid-1960s, and marginally increased after that, only to disappear from official statistics in 1989.

enrollments would reach a low of about 600 students in 1966, compared to close to 12,000 at their peak before independence (all levels included). Complaints about this narrow specialization of the Zaytuna system continue to be heard to this day—for example, from some ʿulamā who look at the modernized al-Azhar as a model.[128] In fact, in the mid-1950s in Egypt, Taha Husayn proposed, to no avail, to radically shrink and specialize madrasa education, provoking vehement reactions among the ʿulamā.[129]

One even more radical version of the 1958 Tunisian reform had been, of course, the modernization of the Ottoman medrese curricula in the early twentieth century, culminating in their closure by the Turkish government in 1924 after decades of significant decreases in enrollment.[130] In 1924 a new specialized Islamic track, the Faculty of Theology in the University of Istanbul, was opened,[131] and new secondary schools, called Imam-Hatip schools, were established to train imams and preachers—that is, professionals tending to the religious infrastructure. This was nonetheless seen as a traumatic rupture by many; since the medrese closure coincided with the abolition of the caliphate and other Islamic institutions, the debate was global, as attested by vehement critiques abroad.[132] Moreover, the Imam-Hatip schools and the Faculty of Theology were closed in the early 1930s, only to reopen two decades later. Therefore, the end of the formal medrese system, and subsequent policy vacillations, did not mean the end of Islamic education, nor did it mean the end of the debate about the extent of modern knowledge in curricula for the training of religious professionals. The sizable expansion of the Imam-Hatip schools after the 1950s continued to produce debates and policy tugs-of-war between their advocates and critics,[133]

128. E.g., Houcine Labidi, a self-proclaimed imam who refused to recognize governmental authorities and occupied the physical space of the Zaytuna Grand Mosque in 2015 with the ambition to transform it into an expanded university on the model of al-Azhar, with modern faculties, only to be dislodged by the authorities.

129. Ḥusayn (1938) and *Majallat al-Azhar*, vol. 17, no. 4, November 1955, notably ʿAbd al-Laṭīf al-Subkī, Khuṣūm al-Azhar [Al-Azhar's opponents]. For more details, see Zeghal (1996, 119–124).

130. In Istanbul, medrese enrollments decreased from about 10,000 students in 1892 to 850 in 1920–1921. Parmaksızoğlu (1966, 19–22), Bein (2006, 289 and 297), Güldüren (2017, 36), and Yıldız (2017, 46 and 172–186).

131. On the Faculty of Theology and prior existence of a "Section of higher religious sciences" in the Faculty of Letters from 1900 to 1916, see Jacob (1982, 92).

132. E.g., Rashīd Riḍā, Al-Inqilāb al-Dīnī wa-l-Siyāsa fī al-Jumhūrīya al-Turkīya [Religious upheaval and politics in the Turkish Republic], *Al-Manār*, vol. 25, no. 4, May 4, 1924, 273–299.

133. Jacob (1982), Aksit (1991), Öcal (1999), Çakmak (2009), and Clayer (2015). For a defense of the Imam-Hatip schools, see Öcal (2007),

resulting in significant fluctuations in per capita enrollments, such as in the late 1990s and early 2000s (table 4a). Similarly, the expansion of per capita enrollments in specialized Islamic tracks of higher education (mainly faculties of theology, also called "divinity" in the literature, and Higher Islamic Institutes)—a trend that started in earnest in the 1960s and significantly accelerated in the late 2000s—fed intense debates.[134] However, in relative terms, in 2020 their share of overall (specialized and nonspecialized) higher education enrollments was 1.7 percent, close to what it was in 1970 and 1985; compare to a share of 1.1 percent, 5.7 percent, and 10.6 percent in Tunisia, Morocco, and Egypt, respectively (table 4b).

While Bourguiba's 1958 reform of the Zaytuna was also quite radical, since it shrunk enrollments some twenty-fold, he liked to contrast it with the 1924 Turkish reform and distance himself from Mustapha Kemal.[135] Yet, in 1958, when many Zaytuna teachers and professors were appointed as instructors of religious education in the modern school system, they felt marginalized: "It broke their lives as Zaytunis. . . . They experienced it as a moment of strong social demotion," and it created "tragic personal traumas."[136] Some MPs also deplored Bourguiba's reform during parliamentary debates in the early 1960s. They saw it as an attack against Islam.[137] The government responded with harsh critiques of the ʿulamā, their lack of relevant training, and their excessive numbers, for which it blamed the French protectorate.[138] All the same, while the Zaytuna's pre-university enrollments never recovered and eventually went to zero, its higher education per capita enrollments returned to their 1956 level in the second half of the 1960s, and by the end of the 1980s they more than doubled from there (table 4b). Although President Ben Ali "reopened"[139] the Zaytuna with great fanfare in 1989, shortly after his 1987 takeover, his minister of education Mohamed Charfi (1936–2008) cut its enrollments by two-thirds and imposed

134. For a denunciation, see Kemal Gözler, "Where Is Theology Going? (2) Observations on the Number of Masters and Doctorates in Theology," www.anayasa.gen.tr/ilahiyat-yl-doktora.htm, accessed December 9, 2021.

135. Ḥajjī (2004, 29–41).

136. Interview with a university professor, son of a Zaytuna professor, La Marsa, June 21, 1997.

137. *Al-Rāʾid al-Rasmī li-l-Jumhūrīya al-Tūnisīya, Mudāwalāt Majlis al-Umma,* vol. 3, 1961–1962, no. 15, year 3, March 15, 1962, afternoon session of December 28, 1961, 233.

138. *Al-Rāʾid al-Rasmī li-l-Jumhūrīya al-Tūnisīya, Mudāwalāt Majlis al-Umma,* vol. 3, 1961–1962, no. 15, year 3, March 15, 1962, afternoon session of December 28, 1961, 250.

139. In reality, it only meant that it regained its status as a "university" as opposed to a Faculty in the University of Tunis.

textbooks of his liking.[140] He claimed that public school teachers, badly trained at the Zaytuna, created a breeding ground for the Islamist movement's ideology.[141] He confined Zaytuna graduates to teaching Islamic education, renamed "Islamic thought" (*tafkīr Islāmī*), in public schools and excluded them from teaching civic education (now a separate topic in the curriculum).[142] Zaytuna students deplored both the cuts in enrollment and the government imposing what they were taught at the Zaytuna and what they would teach once they graduated.[143] For instance, a Zaytuna student I interviewed in 1997 told me, "This is not a reform [*iṣlāḥ*]. It is a destruction [*tadmīr*]. At al-Azhar, there are 60 different schools. Here we have 60 students."[144] However, a few years after Mohamed Charfi's 1994 resignation, enrollments at the Zaytuna steadily increased again in absolute and per capita terms (while decreasing relative to overall higher education enrollments), an increase that continued after the democratic transition began in 2011. In 2012, while the Zaytuna campus in Tunis was in full effervescence after the Arab Spring, its dean told me about ambitious projects of expansion.[145] These only translated into modest increases in enrollments, despite the participation of the Islamist al-Nahdha Party in the subsequent governments (table 4b).

Where Most Religious Education Is Dispensed: The Modern Education System

The most significant change in the realm of Islamic education in Egypt, Morocco, Tunisia, and Turkey took place in the modern schooling system that developed in the nineteenth century, by virtue of a massive expansion in enrollments in the twentieth century (tables 4a and 4b) coupled with the continuous presence of Islamic education in curricula (with the exception of a twenty-year hiatus in Turkey during which it was essentially eliminated). It is therefore in modern schools that the bulk of Islamic education is dispensed

140. Mohamed Charfi, a law professor and former leftist activist, was minister of education (1989–1994) under Ben Ali.

141. Charfi and Redissi (2010, 152 and 168–169).

142. It had also been made separate in 1968. See Lelong (1971, 294).

143. Zeghal (2011).

144. Interview with a 1992 Zaytuna graduate who taught in a private religious school, Montfleury, June 30, 1997.

145. Interview with the dean of the Zaytuna University, Tunis, December 12, 2012.

in 2020 (table 4d). It should also be noted that in Egypt, Morocco, and Tunisia neither foreign occupation nor, later, independence altered the principle that public modern schools' Muslim students must be taught Islam (table 4c). And vigorous debates about the extent, content, and form of delivery of Islamic education continued during occupation and after independence.

Among the first schools established by Muhammad Ali in Egypt in 1816, the Cairo Citadel school's curriculum included the Qur'an in addition to reading, writing, Turkish, and military disciplines.[146] Egyptian governmental primary schools, first created in the 1830s, and elementary schools never ceased to provide Islamic education.[147] When, in 1867, the Egyptian government developed a project for a regional network of primary schools, their curriculum included the "doctrines of unicity [*ʿaqāʾid al-tawḥīd*] and the obligations of worship [*wājibāt al-ʿibāda*]."[148] In governmental primary schools, Islam was originally taught under the label "Qur'an" and then "religion" (*diyāna*) starting in the 1890s.[149] The fraction of the curriculum it constituted fluctuated greatly, although it trended downward (from 25 percent in 1863 to 5.5 percent in 1950, right before primary and elementary schools, which generally had more hours of religious instruction, were unified).[150] And there were debates about it. Amin Sami (1857–1941)—author of a history of modern education in Egypt—deplored the government's 1907 decision to increase the hours of religious education in primary schools and argued that, despite its "utmost necessity" (*ashadd luzūm*) for societies, religious sentiment did not correlate with the quantity of religious

146. Sāmī (1917, 7).

147. The governmental primary schools created in the 1830s floundered, but an effort was restarted in the 1860s. In the 1890s, the government also expanded public instruction via the transformation of Qur'anic schools into what would soon be called elementary schools (they were also labeled *kuttābs* in official statistics and sometimes *maktabs*). They received government subsidies in exchange for accepting governmental inspection and adhering to some standards. The 1923 Constitution made elementary schooling compulsory for boys and girls, paving the way for the state project of mass education. See Sāmī (1917), Boktor (1936), Salama (1939), ʿAbd al-Karīm (1945), and De Lavergne (2004, 2007) for more details. By 1905 and until 1948, more than 90 percent of the Muslim children enrolled at the pre-secondary level in state or state-subsidized schools attended elementary schools.

148. Sāmī (1917, 21–22).

149. Sāmī (1917, Annex 3, 2–4). In 1897 the subject "religion, discipline, and morals" (*diyāna tahdhīb wa-tarbiya*) was added to the primary school curriculum and "Qur'an" was phased out to disappear entirely in 1907.

150. Sāmī (1917, Annex 3, 2–4). For this fraction in the broader modern school system before and after 1950, see table 4c.

instruction provided in schools.[151] He also argued that it was now impossible to teach both the rational (*al-tarbiya al-ʿaqlīya*) and religious subjects in depth.[152] This debate continues in Egypt to this day.[153] We also find a similar pattern in Turkey. The modern schools that developed in the second half of the nineteenth century taught a blend of modern and religious subjects. Under Abdelhamid II (r. 1876–1909), state elites viewed them as a system of "Muslim schools," which "while ostensibly interdenominational, featured their own mosques, observed the Muslim calendar, taught Qur'anic interpretation, emphasized a specifically Islamic notion of morality," and were staffed "with healthy numbers of ulema."[154] In the 1930s and 1940s, religious education in public schools was essentially eliminated, but it was reintroduced as an optional subject in primary schools in 1949 and in secondary schools in 1956, and made compulsory in 1982,[155] in a policy tug-of-war between those who wanted to shrink or eliminate religion from curricula altogether and those who wanted to expand its presence.[156]

Similarly, although Tunisia's modern system of schooling started later and expanded more slowly at first, it also included Islamic education in the Bardo military school (est. 1840) and the Sadiki School (est. 1875), as well as in the schools that developed under the French protectorate. As in French-occupied Morocco, Islamic education had generally been provided in these schools since the early days of colonization,[157] but was not always part of the official curriculum. It was sometimes taught outside of the school premises and/or hours, or as part of the Arabic language classes.[158] The number of hours of Islamic

151. Sāmī (1917, Annex 3, 7). Amin Sami Pasha graduated from the Egyptian School of Engineering and held several posts in the Ministry of Education—e.g., that of principal of one of the most important governmental schools.

152. Sāmī (1917, Annex 3, 7). See also how Shaykhs Ali Yusuf and Muhammad Abduh debated the share and aims of Qur'anic memorization in the curriculum of Egyptian elementary schools in 1905. Salama (1939, 305–307) and De Lavergne (2007).

153. See Toronto (1992, 136 and 295–297) and B. J. Cook (2000).

154. Fortna (2000, 369 and 375–376) and, for examples of curricula before 1924, Pehlivan Ağırakça (2013).

155. Şimşek (2013). These optional courses were overwhelmingly attended—e.g., by 99 percent of students in fourth and fifth grades of primary schools in 1949–50 according to Parmaksızoğlu (1966, 31).

156. See Jacob (1982) and, for more recent debates, Genç (2018).

157. Exceptions include the Berber Azrou Collège in Morocco. AMAE CADN 1MA-300-112.

158. It could be taught in nearby Qur'anic schools, or by a *fqih* or *muʾaddib* (a Qur'an teacher in Morocco and Tunisia, respectively) outside of class hours. For Tunisia, see *BOEP*, no. 18,

education was also the object of debate and policy fluctuations. It seems that French authorities in Tunisia felt it was necessary but sought to keep it to the minimum they had to provide to Muslim pupils in the Franco-Arab schools,[159] the main schools for Muslims until independence.[160] They also strove to shape its content to prevent, they claimed, "fanaticism."[161] On the other hand, some Tunisians asked for more hours of Islamic education and instruction in Arabic. Indeed, Islamic education represented a higher fraction of the curriculum in Modern Qur'anic Schools (Écoles Coraniques Modernes or ECMs),[162] which were privately created by Tunisians starting in the early 1900s as an alternative to Franco-Arab schools, and, in their majority, soon significantly state-subsidized.[163] In Morocco, a similar pattern took place with the free school movement (and the creation of "renovated *msids*," i.e., renovated Qur'anic schools) starting in the early 1920s in response to strong demand for education for Moroccan Muslim children. They would supplement the *Écoles franco-arabes* (Franco-Arab schools), *Écoles de fils de notables*, and *Collèges musulmans*.[164] As

2ème année, 1888, 271–272. For Morocco, see AMAE CADN 1MA-300-112 and *BEP* no. 24, September 1920, 396. However, in what they called the "purely Berber" regions, French authorities in Morocco argued that if there were no Qur'anic schools, they would not establish any. See *BEP* no. 24, September 1920, 413.

159. "Note sur le développement des écoles indigènes en Tunisie," undated, ANT AP1 C1 D7-3, and *BOEP*, June 1909, no. 88, 23rd year, 640–653.

160. These schools were often a section of a French school with distinct classes for Tunisians and Europeans.

161. *BOEP*, June 1909, no. 88, 23rd year, 640–653.

162. Their curricula varied from school to school, and this fraction seemed to range between 15 percent and 25 percent (1.0 to 1.5 hours a day, compared to about 40 minutes a day in the Franco-Arab schools at the time). See the "Modèle d'horaires dans les Écoles Coraniques Modernes" modeled on Sfax's schools in 1948–49, ANT AP1 C1 D5-10, and two (undated) Écoles Coraniques Modernes curricula in Sraïeb (1967, 48–49). Interviews I conducted in July 2018 with former pupils in the city of Sfax in the 1940s and the 1950s confirmed this range. For an example of disagreement about their main mission—to teach the Qur'an for a Tunisian inspector vs. French, arithmetic, history, and geography, for French authorities—see "Statut des Écoles Coraniques Modernes (1938)," ANT SG-SG2 C87 D8-1. The Qur'an came first in the Decree of June 28, 1938.

163. Ayachi (2003, 287–323). ECMs were rapidly expanding, but their aggregate enrollments remained smaller than those of the Franco-Arab schools. At independence, in 1956 (resp. 1948, at their peak in relative terms), they still only represented less than a fifth (resp. a quarter) of aggregate modern primary school Muslim students' enrollments, or about 8 percent (resp. 5 percent) of the primary school–age Muslim population.

164. Free schools received some aid from the *Ḥabūs* Administration and the sultan in the 1940s, and direct state subsidies in the 1950s (which continued after independence). See Damis

in Tunisia and Egypt, the amount and content of Islamic education taught in modern schools (rather than its presence) were vigorously debated in Morocco during colonization and after independence; they are still debated to this day.[165] In Tunisia, the ECMs were folded into a unified national public school system at independence. The average number of weekly hours of Islamic education in primary school curricula was reduced from 2.0 (the level the French protectorate reduced it to in the Franco-Arab schools in 1949),[166] to 1.67, but the fraction of the curriculum it constituted remained virtually unchanged, about 5 percent, because total school hours were also reduced (table 4c). The postindependence Ministry of Education envisioned it as a complement to the learning of sciences and modern subjects, "according to the needs of the personality [*shakhṣīya*] of the Tunisian nation [*al-umma al-Tūnisīya*], whose religion is Islam."[167] However, in parliamentary debates in the early 1960s, some MPs advocated for increasing this fraction, arguing that the youth had become ignorant of "the most basic rules of Islam" (*absaṭ qawāʿid al-Islām*), to which the government responded that it was not an issue of quantity but of improving the quality of the content and of the teachers, a common trope among governmental officials at the time about the ʿulamā being ill-trained.[168] Islamist movements, which started organizing at the end of the 1960s, reiterated these requests for more Islamic education in public schools as one of their central mobilizing themes. In the early 1970s, the Islamist activist Rached Ghannouchi denounced the "progressives" (*taqaddumīyūn*), who, he argued, had not provided students with moral criteria in school curricula, creating a "lost generation."[169] He wrote, "We should use the Western sciences but cleanse them of the Western values,

(1970, 125–160 and 225–226). Renovated *msids* enrollments peaked at about 30 percent of aggregate modern primary school Muslim students' enrollments in the 1940s, and 3 percent of the primary school–age Muslim population in 1956.

165. E.g., AMAE CADN 1MA-300-112, Merrouni (1993, 125–126), and Jābirī (1978).

166. This was implemented gradually in the early 1950s. See ANT AP1 C1 D5-9, CADN 1TU-1V-2074 and Sraïeb (1967, 56).

167. *Al-Barāmij, Al-Ṣaff al-Sādis, Al-Tarbiya al-Dīnīya wa-l-Madanīya*, 1959, 5, cited in Lelong (1971, 230).

168. *Al-Rāʾid al-Rasmī li-l-Jumhūrīya al-Tūnisīya, Mudāwalāt Majlis al-Umma*, vol. 3, 1961–1962, no. 15, year 3, March 15, 1962, afternoon session of December 28, 1961, 232–233. See also the debates in the Ministry of Education about Islamic education in primary schools reproduced in *Al-Jumhūrīya al-Tūnisīya, Al-Nashra al-Tarbawīya li-l-Taʿlīm al-Thānawī wa-l-Iʿdādī*, no. 10, April 1962, 17–21.

169. R. Ghannūshī, Barāmij al-Falsafa wa Jīl al-Ḍiyāʿ [The philosophy curricula and the lost generation], *Al-Maʿrifa*, September 10, 1973, reproduced in Ghannūshī (1988, 11–14).

of their philosophy, and of their way of life [*niẓām ḥayāh*]."[170] Under pressure from conservatives, the fraction of Islamic education in school curricula was increased significantly in the 1970s, only to be reduced again in the early 1990s, while the Charfi reforms were also shrinking the Zaytuna's enrollments (tables 4a, 4b, and 4c). Islamic instruction in primary schools was reduced further to one hour per week (about 4 percent of the curriculum) on average in the late 2000s, a level that did not change throughout the democratic transition (during which the Islamist party al-Nahda was part of the government). Similarly, in Egypt, Hassan al-Banna, after founding the Society of the Muslim Brothers in 1928, wrote to the government in the early 1930s to request more Qur'anic education in public schools.[171] Turkish and Moroccan Islamist activists have also put these demands at the center of their mobilizing slogans.[172] Their adversaries have denounced the expansion of Islamic education in all its forms,[173] as well as the modernization of its forms of delivery, as responsible for the development of Islamism. A return to the *ḥalqa* and traditional modes of transmitting knowledge is often invoked and implemented as an alleged antidote to this development by civil society and state actors alike.[174]

5. The State as the Main Financial Caretaker of Religious Institutions or Their Missions

It is often assumed that public religious provisions used to be predominantly supplied by civil society, via religious endowments, rather than by the state in its role of custodian of Islam. The waqf system has been depicted as the foundation of a "civil society" working alongside and sometimes against rulers for the "improvement of the public space,"[175] in an idealized portrayal of past Islamic

170. Ghannūshī (1988, 25).

171. Ḥasan al-Bannā, Wasā'il al-Muḥāfaẓa 'alā al-Qur'ān al-Karīm [Means of conserving the Noble Qur'an], *Al-Fatḥ*, January 16, 1931, 12–15. See also the various projects of "Islamization of knowledge" that developed internationally in the 1970s, and their criticism by Fazlur Rahman, in Islamization of Knowledge: A Response, *American Journal of Islamic Social Sciences*, vol. 5, no. 1, 1988, 3–11.

172. E.g., Kattānī (1982) in Morocco. For the debates in Turkey after 1947, see Jacob (1982, 344–417).

173. E.g., in Morocco, El Ayadi (2004).

174. For Egypt, see Elston (2020).

175. Hoexter (2002, 134) argues that the waqfs were the foundation of an "informal civil society" and a "public sphere," and, as does Singer (2008), underlines the importance of rulers'

societies. This system is said to have provided large amounts (though unquantified in aggregate) of public goods, religious and otherwise, independently from the state based on an overarching moral system linked to sharia that made rulers (as individuals) and subjects equally attentive to supplying public provisions.[176] This idealized vision of the past is often contrasted to nineteenth- and twentieth-century reforms of religious institutions. Sometimes relying on observers' accounts and/or stakeholders' narratives,[177] some scholars depict these reforms as the ransacking of the waqfs' vast wealth (real or imagined) by the modern state, which allegedly deprived civil society of its traditional role as the provider of religious and other public goods[178] and the ʿulamā of their main source of revenue and their autonomy.[179] Islamist activists often make similar claims, arguing that before the reforms the waqfs were at the foundation of a vibrant and autonomous civil society.[180] For them, these waqf reforms, in particular their abolition, where it occurred, are anti-Islamic. They periodically bring back the project to reinvigorate (or reintroduce) the waqfs as a solution to what they see as state deficiencies and as a means to develop private initiative. Their political adversaries, on the other hand, often argue that this institution is inherently inefficient and causes economic backwardness.[181]

---

own personal charitable endowments as part of the moral economy of Muslim societies, without quantifying it.

176. E.g., Ghānim (1998), Ibn Bilghayth (2005), Singer (2008), and Hallaq (2013).

177. A favorite is the Scottish writer Charles MacFarlane, who underlined the state of ruin of religious and other public infrastructure in late 1840s Ottoman Turkey as compared to the 1820s, which he attributed to governmental reforms, cited, for instance, in Barnes (1986, 118), Singer (2008, 190), and Hallaq (2009, 403). Another is the firsthand account of Mustapha Nuri Pasha (1824–1890), a minister in the Ministry of Imperial Waqfs (1886–1890), who argued that waqf reforms were prejudicial to the waqfs, cited, for instance, in Köprülü (1942, 32–33), Barnes (1986, 120–121), and Yerasimos (1994, 46–47).

178. E.g., Ghānim (1998), Çizakça (2000), Ibn Bilghayth (2005) and Raysūnī (2014).

179. E.g., Crecelius (1972, 107), Al-Sayyid Marsot (1972, 151, 154, and 163), Bilici (1994, 11), Ghānim (1998, 17), and Singer (2008, 190–191). Taking for granted the historiography, I did not challenge such claims in Zeghal (1996, 25).

180. E.g., Tamimi (2001, 125 and 157) and Ghannūshī (2001, 51–53) in Tunisia, Raysūnī (2014) in Morocco, and in Egypt, Muhammad Imara in *Al-Ahrām*, December 30, 2012, 21, aligned with the broader argument of Ghānim (1998). For an analysis of Islamists' narratives in Turkey, see Bilici (1993).

181. For instance, on October 17, 2013, the Islamist party al-Nahdha introduced a bill in the Tunisian National Constituent Assembly in favor of reestablishing waqfs (*khayrī, ahlī,* and *mushtarak*), provoking heated controversies in the media. See *La Presse,* May 31, 2013, and *Al-Shurūq,* November 12, 2013.

However, the evidence suggests that rulers and state officials have historically (1) funded the lion's share of public religious provisions, either directly, for example from the state budget, or indirectly, for example by establishing religious endowments (a decentralization mechanism); (2) managed and regulated religious institutions, including religious endowments, with fluctuating degrees of centralization; and (3) consistently come to the rescue of religious institutions, or at the very least of their missions, when they ran into financial difficulties, in order to ensure the continuity of public religious provisions and the state custodianship of Islam. What factors drove bouts of decentralization and centralization, and whether certain types of religious provisions were more prone to decentralization than others, remains to be studied in greater detail. We can suspect that physical distance, agency problems, and most of all state capabilities played a role. What is certain is that this engagement often occurred on the state's own terms, with frequent, and sometimes drastic, reorganizations of religious institutions and reprioritizations within religious expenditures, in response to new or growing needs such as education or the defense of the territory. Moreover, reorganizations have sometimes led to radical modifications in how religious provisions are delivered, entailing the marginalization or disappearance of some traditional forms of delivery and even some religious institutions and engendering anxieties and debate.

The Predominant (and Fluctuating) Role of the State

In Tunisia, in the later part of the colonial period and after independence, virtually all public religious expenditures were funded directly from the state budget, a pattern we also find in Egypt, Morocco, and Turkey, with variations as to when it took hold. Prior to that, the largest portion came from public religious endowments. For instance, when the Djemaia was established in the 1870s, public waqf revenues funded more than 80 percent of aggregate public religious provisions in Tunisia. In 1915 Morocco this fraction was also about 80 percent, and in early 1900s Egypt about 50 percent. However, there is compelling evidence that most public religious endowments were established over time by rulers and state officials. Although it has been debated whether these endowments should be considered as state provision or individual charity, it can be argued that the private and public faces of the ruler were indistinguishable.[182] In Tunisia, Muhammad

182. See, for instance, Chamberlain (1994, 51–54), Grangaud (2004), Afsaruddin (2014), and Berkey (2014, 11–12). Berkey (2014, 57) argues that rulers made these foundations as individuals

Ibn al-Khuja's (1869–1942) data about the identity of the founders of Friday mosques and madrasas in the city of Tunis that were in existence in 1939 (summarized in table 7) informs us on the predominance of such state actors.[183] During the period covered by this dataset (698–1939), 64 percent of the mosques and madrasas were founded by state officials or their families (77 percent of them were rulers, 14 percent government officials, and 9 percent members of the ruler's family, a sultan's daughter or wife), and this percentage is almost identical for mosques and madrasas.[184] However, there were significant fluctuations over the centuries: for instance, under the Hafsid dynasty (1229–1574) and during the transition period of the Ottoman deys (1574–1637) this percentage was 52 percent, and it increased to 87 percent under the Muradite (1637–1705) and Husaynid (1705–1881) beys, only to decline to 30 percent after France took over in 1881 since, during this latter period, public religious provisions were increasingly financed by the state directly from its budget, in a decisive centralization away from religious endowments. Elsewhere, the same pattern is prevalent. In a list of madrasas created in Egypt's capital city from 1170 to 1805, compiled by Amin Sami,[185] 82 percent of them were created by rulers, government officials, or their families. Even accounting for the fact that this list is not exhaustive, there is little doubt about the predominant role of state actors.[186] Similarly, Yediyıldız (1990, 132) estimates that 80 to 90 percent of a randomized sample of 330 waqfs created between 1699 and 1839 in the "territory corresponding to contemporary Turkey" were founded by state officials (including rulers) or by their relatives.

---

but nonetheless calls these institutions "royal." For Singer (2008, 214), "Although rulers gave *ṣadaqa* as individuals, there was also an element of obligation inherent in their giving, and it is perhaps this obligation of office that constitutes a link between the long-familiar personal, individual charity of rulers and the impersonal, bureaucratic welfare of modern states." Moreover, rulers sometimes used state resources to establish public religious endowments, although it was a controversial practice. See Amīn (1980, 61–63 and 95), Cuno (1999), and Sabra (2000, 70–71).

183. Ibn al-Khūja (1939). Based on chroniclers' works (e.g., Shaykh Ibn Nājī, d. 1433; Ibn Abī Dīnār, d. 1681; and Bājī al-Mas ʿūdī, d. 1880), official reports, and oral transmissions, this list seems reliable, despite limitations (it only covers the city of Tunis, it stops in 1939, it does not include the madrasas and Friday mosques that disappeared before that, and it does not provide the amount of the financial contributions made by the founders).

184. Their difference is not statistically significant.

185. Sāmī (1917, Annex 5, 10–32).

186. E.g., Berkey (2014, 46) counts over 100 madrasas for the Mamluk period, compared to 87 in Sāmī (1917). See also Petry (1983, 190). Berkey (2014, 61) still finds that "the Mamluk elite . . . undertook the construction and endowment of the lion's share of religious and educational institutions."

Abdel Nour (1982, 189–192) finds that, in Ottoman Syria, the large public waqfs were mainly financed by the "transfer of tax rights by the state," and that rulers and local governors used the waqf as an instrument for the development of cities and towns. And Chamberlain (1994, 52n81) finds that in the years 1154–1155 and 1223–1224, in Damascus, "almost all madrasas and dār al-ḥadīths were founded by members of households of rulers and amīrs."

To be sure, the role of the state was more salient in periods of centralization. In Tunisia, the 1874 establishment of the Djemaia increased the centralization of the state regulation and management of the *ḥabūs* in a search for efficiency. Khayr al-Din, then prime minister, explained this motivation in his memoirs published in 1888, in which he laments that, prior to that, the administration of the *ḥabūs* had been "deplorable."[187] In truth, many of the flaws of the pre-Djemaia management of the public *ḥabūs* he deplored persisted, such as the payment of ordinary expenditures from the proceeds of the sales of *ḥabūs* properties that were meant to be exchanged, which we often find in the Djemaia's archives (contrary to common arguments that attribute it to graft, this pattern often resulted from necessity). Judging from the Djemaia's dire financial situation in the late 1800s, examined in the next section, it is unlikely that his reforms were as effective as he (and some historians) claimed.[188] Yet, with the establishment of the Djemaia, the government definitely sought to facilitate (1) the management of the *ḥabūs* according to best-known practices and (2) the reprioritization of public religious expenditures as it saw fit. The 1874 beylical decree that established the Djemaia gave to its representatives, the *nā ʾibs*, the task of managing local agents (*wakīls*), who operated under the watch of the local governors, all over the Regency.[189] This decree submitted the accounts of the *ḥabūs*, as well as the salaries for the Djemaia's personnel, for the bey's approval and dictated how the Djemaia should employ its surplus revenues.[190] Therefore, the Djemaia, despite its budget being kept separate from the central state budget, was definitely a state institution. Even before that, public *ḥabūs* were already under the purview of the ruler, who, by virtue of his role as custodian of Islam, had to ensure that they were managed according to the will of the founders. He appointed their managers among ʿulamā, *qāḍīs*, or other notables,

187. Mzali and Pignon (1971, 35–36).
188. E.g., Smida (1970, 270–281).
189. Decree of March 19, 1874.
190. ANT SH C59 D670 and Zeys (1901, vol. 1, 440–441).

and retained the right to authorize *ḥabūs* constitutions.[191] He was also directly involved in the management of some public *ḥabūs*.[192] In the Ottoman Empire, Imber (1997, 156–159) similarly points to the courts' and the sultan's important roles in the verification of the waqfs' legitimacy, their registration, and the supervision of their management, restricting their autonomy. In the same vein, İnalcık (1976, 52) underlines that "*Waqfs* were under close official control."

The creation of the Djemaia was not the first effort toward centralization in Tunisia. For instance, Ibn Diyaf points to the 1819 revitalization of the institution of the Ḥisba to control the waqfs' management.[193] In 1861, after having been under the purview of the Sharia Council for three years,[194] the management of all public waqfs in Tunis was assigned to the recently created Municipality of Tunis; their accounts were to be submitted to the bey annually.[195] In 1863 the management of all public waqfs outside the capital was assigned to General Rashid, who was also charged to use the surplus revenues "for the needs of the army."[196] And there were also recurrent centralizations of the waqfs' management elsewhere—for example, in Mamluk Egypt, in Ottoman Egypt in the early sixteenth century, and again with Egypt's centralizing reforms of the nineteenth and twentieth centuries,[197] in Istanbul in the eighteenth century, and, before that, with "the development of the office of the Chief Black Eunuch" in the late sixteenth century.[198] In Ottoman Algiers, Johansen (1999, 118) finds that, in the years

191. M. A. Ben Achour (1992, 67–68). For examples of official letters of appointments of *ḥabūs* managers by the bey in the mid-1800s, see ANT SH C59 D672.

192. As shown by the correspondence (dated 1857–1869) in ANT SH C59 D675.

193. Hénia (2004, 291–294).

194. Hénia (2004, 293), citing Al-Sanūsī (1983, 77).

195. Decree of July 19, 1861, ANT SH C55 D603-1 no. 21.

196. ANT SH C59 D670BIS, Ibn Abī al-Ḍiyāf (1963, vol. 5, 97), Smida (1970, 260–262), and M. A. Ben Achour (1992, 68).

197. Behrens-Abouseif (2009, 60) argues that, in Mamluk Egypt, "the endowed colleges and monasteries . . . remained essentially state institutions centrally controlled by the ruling establishment." For sixteenth-century Egypt, see the Qanuname of 1524–25 of Ibrahim Pasha analyzed in Shaw (1962, 44ff.) and in Behrens-Abouseif (1994, 151). For nineteenth-century Egypt, see Baer (1962, 169–185) and for a history of the Egyptian Ministry of Waqfs, Ghānim (2007). See also Michel (1996) for a study of the *rizaq iḥbāsīya*, through which local notables and well-off peasants funded mosques and *zāwiyas* in the countryside of Mamluk Egypt. They were authorized by the ruler, in an enterprise of decentralization that helped Islamize the countryside.

198. For the Ottoman centralization of waqfs and the establishment of a ministry in the eighteenth century, see Barnes (1986, 67–86). For the office of the chief black eunuch, see Inalcik and Quataert (1994, 562).

1811–1814, "the more important religious institutions were administered by centralized organizations, such as the *subul al-khairat* for the Hanafite religious institutions." He also shows that new Hanafi *fiqh* rules that emerged in the Mashriq in the eleventh and twelfth centuries took pains to "protect the autonomy of private donors,"[199] which I take as evidence of possible past centralizations that triggered contention. Outside of the Ottoman Empire, in Morocco, there were projects of centralization of the management of the *ḥabūs* right before the French established their protectorate in 1912, and the vizierate of the *ḥabūs* in 1915.[200] Earlier, under the Alawite sultans, it seems that the management of the waqfs was centralized by Sultan Ismail (r. 1672–1727) and that they were firmly under the sultans' control thereafter, as exemplified by an 1885–1886 decree ordering an increase in rents and salaries.[201]

The Unwavering State Financial Support of Religious Institutions or Their Mission

An examination of the Djemaia's budgets and its attendant correspondence with the Tunisian government over the years reveals its frequent interventions in the management of public *ḥabūs* revenues and expenditures. It also reveals that the government unwaveringly provided its financial support to the Djemaia's mission over the course of its existence (e.g., in the form of cash advances, loans, debt forgiveness, direct assumption of some of its areas of responsibilities that had become too costly, and explicit subsidies), including after its liquidation in 1956.[202] Since Djemaia administrators and state officials were often hesitant about the form state financial support should take, and even about acknowledging it, it was not always clearly mentioned in the Djemaia's budgets. However, already in 1891, the Djemaia was carrying a liability that amounted to more than twice its annual *net* revenues, and hence to more

199. Johansen (1999, 127–128). In the same vein, Ibn Nujaym (1520–1563) wrote against taxation of waqfs after a 1553 sultanic order was issued to tax waqfs in Egypt. Johansen (1988, 86–91).

200. For the 1906 project of *ḥabūs* centralization in Morocco, see Manūnī (1985, vol. 2, 435–438).

201. El-Mabkhout (1980, 15–16), Nāṣirī (1992, 17–24 and 195–200), and Bilmuqaddam (1993, 127–169). The lists of *ḥabūs* properties (*ḥawālas*) established since 1698 in various Moroccan cities are also evidence of earlier centralizations. See "Liste des principes [*sic*] haoualas," ANOM 52APOM2.

202. Annual budgets of the Djemaia, and related correspondence, from 1874 to 1956 in ANT SC C26.

than two years' worth of its aggregate religious expenditures.[203] Therefore, even at this early date, *ḥabūs* revenues could not sustain the Djemaia's mission, and the state had to come to its rescue.[204] By 1937 the Djemaia's accumulated liability, essentially to the state (e.g., in the form of cash advances, or unused *ḥabūs* properties' "exchange" proceeds, i.e., proceeds that were meant to be used for the purchase of a replacement property), and which was eventually de facto forgiven, amounted to about seven times its annual net revenues, and hence to about seven years' worth of its religious expenditures.[205] By 1945 state subsidies to the Djemaia represented 50 percent of its religious expenditures and at independence, in 1956, this percentage exceeded 100 percent since the Djemaia was spending more in operating, maintaining, and managing its revenue-generating assets than it was earning from them.[206] Moreover, by the late 1940s, after decades of strong growth in the demand for their services,[207] and of increasingly large central state subsidies to these institutions, the expenditures of the sharia courts, the Sadiki Hospital, and the Zaytuna had already disappeared from the Djemaia's budget and had been folded entirely into the state budget (in the 1920s,[208] 1931,[209] and 1948, respectively). At that point, these three direct state

203. 1,320,000 francs (600,000 of which required for urgent repairs), compared to an expected annual revenue of about 1.2 million francs, about half of which the Djemaia spent on operating, maintaining, and managing its revenue-generation assets. Djemaia Budget of 1891, ANT SC C26 D1-1.

204. Even in the early days of the Djemaia, institutions such as the Sadiki Hospital and the Tekia (a hospice), despite being very small (one hundred beds or so each), had insufficient *ḥabūs* revenues to sustain themselves and were subsidized by the central state budget or other foundations. Djemaia Budget of 1889, ANT SC C26 D1-1, and Djemaia Budgets of 1896 and 1897, ANT SC C26 D1-2.

205. 27.4 million francs in 1937, séance du 17 Avril 1937, ANT SC C1 D14-6. This compared to an expected annual revenue of about 11 million francs, two-thirds of which the Djemaia spent on operating, maintaining, and managing its revenue-generation assets. Djemaia Budget of 1937, ANT SC C26 D1-59.

206. Djemaia Budget of 1945, ANT SC C26 D1-67 and Djemaia Budget of 1956–57, ANT SC C26 D1-75.

207. Tunisians often complained that public assistance provisions were insufficient to meet their needs. See, for instance, Béchir Sfar's speech at the 1905 inauguration of the new Tekia. *La Dépêche tunisienne*, March 25, 1905.

208. Starting in 1925 the Djemaia only paid a contribution to the state budget for a portion of the cost of the sharia justice system. This was gradually phased out over the next five years.

209. The Sadiki Hospital was increasingly state-subsidized and when it was transferred to the state budget in 1931 with its dedicated *ḥabūs* revenues, the latter covered less than 1 percent of its expenditures. The Tekia remained under the Djemaia's budget until independence but

expenditures alone amounted to more than five times the Djemaia's religious expenditures. And by the early 1930s, the state public assistance budget (including medical assistance) was already about twenty times bigger than the Djemaia's, a pattern we also find in other countries. Whether by narrowing down the scope of the Djemaia's responsibilities or by providing direct financial assistance to it (two solutions Tunisians deemed acceptable and/or necessary),[210] the state ensured the continuity of its mission. The principle of the unwavering support of the state was clearly expressed in a 1950 letter from the government to the Djemaia: "It is irrelevant whether the budget is balanced or not, since the main thing is to know whether it exhibits a surplus or a deficit, so that the higher authority may use the surpluses or cover the shortfall as is its right."[211]

We find a similar pattern in Morocco. In a trope reminiscent of Khayr al-Din's memoirs, Joseph Luccioni, a high-ranking French civil servant in the office (Service du Contrôle des Habous) which oversaw the *Ḥabūs* Ministry (Vizirat des Habous), described the nineteenth century as a period of decline for the religious endowments.[212] He praised the French rationalization of their administration as a salutary reform that allowed *ḥabūs* revenues to contribute to state finances, although he also conceded that the state had to contribute to the expenses of the *Ḥabūs* Administration.[213] In reality, although his personal archives abound with graphs displaying the exponential growth in the *Ḥabūs* Administration's nominal revenues under the French protectorate, this growth was almost entirely due to the high inflation of the period, and the rest merely reflected the overall country's economic growth. Hence, during this period, although the *Ḥabūs* Administration's religious expenditures fluctuated as a percentage of GDP, they finished where they started, at about 0.05 percent of GDP. Yet total

received substantial direct state subsidies from 1940 onward (about 50 percent of its expenditures in 1945 and 70 percent on the eve of independence).

210. E.g., a report, likely by Tahar Ben Ammar in 1937, argued that the Zaytuna and the Tekia did not have a "*ḥabūs* character" and that keeping them in the Djemaia's budget "harmed the public *ḥabūs* beneficiaries." "L'Administration des Habous: Ses besoins, ses moyens, ce qu'elle attend du gouvernement tunisien," ANT SC C1 D14-6.

211. General secretary of the Tunisian Government to the Djemaia, October 28, 1950, Djemaia Budget of 1950, ANT SC C26 D1-72.

212. Luccioni entered the Service du Contrôle des Habous (under the Direction des Affaires Chérifiennes) in 1919 and was its director from 1942 to 1955.

213. Luccioni (1982, 13). Kogelmann (2009) similarly claims that these reforms "put an end to squander and abuses" and organized an "efficient" administration but does not quantify their benefits.

state religious expenditures, including those funded directly from the state budget, quadrupled as a percentage of GDP during colonization, and reached 0.24 percent of GDP at independence (table 2). In a familiar pattern, the *Ḥabūs* Administration had to narrow its scope.[214] It also had to ask for state subsidies, and the state had to come to the rescue of its mission, despite Luccioni's resistance and claims to the contrary to make it appear that the *Ḥabūs* Administration was self-sufficient.[215] The state budget directly contributed about 50 percent of aggregate public religious expenditures by 1945, more than 80 percent by 1955, and more than 90 percent by 1979. By 2009 *ḥabūs* net revenues only contributed 5 percent of aggregate public religious expenditures.[216]

In the same vein, in Egypt, as far back as 1897, the official Waqfs Administration[217] budgets published in the Egyptian Official Gazette included aid from the central state budget.[218] This aid represented more than 20 percent of the religious expenditures of the Waqfs Administration in 1897. In 1944 it was about a third, triggering tensions in Parliament.[219] In 1951, on the eve of the Free Officers' coup, it was more than a half. And as in Tunisia and Morocco, the scope of the Waqfs Administration's public provisions was curtailed while total state religious expenditures continued to expand in per capita real terms (table 2). By 2020 waqfs' net revenues only contributed about 4 percent of total state religious expenditures

214. This has been a fixture of Morocco's colonial and postindependence *Ḥabūs* Administration alike, as also highlighted by Kogelman (2009).

215. For examples of state subsidies requested and obtained by the *Ḥabūs* Administration, see "Audience du Sultan," December 19, 1950, ANOM, Fonds Luccioni, 52APOM1 as well as "Note au Palais," 1951 and "Demande de subvention," August 6, 1953, ANOM, Fonds Luccioni, 52APOM2. For Luccioni's opposition to requesting state subsidies for the *Ḥabūs* Administration budget, see "Note d'ensemble," March 15, 1951, ANOM, Fonds Luccioni, 52APOM2. El-Mabkhout (1980, 28), echoing Luccioni (1982, 13) and referring to this March 15, 1951, "Note d'ensemble," incorrectly claims that "during the Protectorate, the *Ḥabūs* Administration only used its own funds to cover its expenditures; the state budget did not provide any subsidies."

216. Estimation based on Al-Mamlaka al-Maghribīya, Wizārat al-Iqtiṣād wa-l-Mālīya (n.d.).

217. It was called an "administration" (*dīwān* or *niẓāra*) or a "ministry" (*wizāra*) with vacillations that accompanied recurrent reorganizations. Its name was also the object of fierce debates with the partisans of the label "administration" arguing in favor of its autonomy from the state. With the law of November 20, 1913, it became a "ministry" and its was stated that it would "retain its autonomy" and that its budget would be "independent." See Sékaly (1929, part 1). For convenience, I often call it the Waqfs Administration even if it was a ministry.

218. Mīzānīyat Maṣlaḥat ʿUmūm al-Awqāf, *Al-Waqāʾiʿ al-Miṣrīya*, no. 24, March 2, 1898, and subsequent yearly Waqfs Administration's budgets published therein.

219. Al-Dawla al-Miṣrīya, Majlis al-Nuwwāb (1924–1952), session 36, July 23, 1951, 88–120. See also Ghānim (1998, 412).

(from about half in the early 1900s and less than 20 percent by the 1940s). This pattern of direct state involvement in sustaining religious institutions or their missions can also be found much earlier in Egypt, however. Al-Jabarti recounts that when Ibrahim Pasha, Muhammad Ali's son, decided to tax mosque waqfs in 1812, complaints arose that this "would ruin the mosques." He answered that he would "repair the ruined mosques and arrange for sufficient means to do it."[220] Michel (1996, 120–121) showed that, prior to Muhammad Ali's era, the Ottomans, while centralizing the management of the religious foundations in Egypt, also "considered the general interest of the Muslims" and took charge of the *rizaq iḥbāsīya* (mainmort agricultural land) when they were failing in their religious mission.

The unwavering support of the state was particularly evident for Islamic education. Few *ḥabūs* were generally devoted to it in Tunisia, but the state continuously sought and found various sources of funding to supplement or improve the ʿulamā's salaries; the ʿulamā expected as much, as shown by nineteenth-century state decrees and by the Zaytuna ʿulamā's correspondence with the Tunisian government.[221] Later, the drastic increase in the Zaytuna's enrollments (tables 4a and 4b) was made possible by a significant increase in direct state financial support. By the mid 1930s, three-quarters of the Zaytuna's expenditures came directly from the central state budget, and by the mid-1940s it was almost the entirety. When the Zaytuna was folded into the central state budget in 1948, it absorbed about 40 percent of overall public religious expenditures, compared to less than 10 percent in the late nineteenth century. Even at that earlier time, however, for its Islamic education mission the Zaytuna relied almost exclusively on either direct state funding or on surpluses from other *ḥabūs* redirected to it by the Djemaia, as ordered by the 1874 beylical decree. In 1895, for instance, its own dedicated *ḥabūs* only went toward its worship expenditures (the Zaytuna, like other madrasas such as al-Azhar and the Qarawiyin, was also a mosque). The net revenues of these *ḥabūs* only covered about a third of its total religious expenditures on worship and education combined.[222] We find a similar pattern

220. Al-Jabartī (1879–1880, vol. 4, 141–142). See also Al-Jabartī (1879–1880, vol. 4, 184).

221. Notably the decrees of 1842 and the 1870s. We also frequently find letters addressed to the prime minister or to the bey by ʿulamā asking for financial assistance (*iʿāna mālīya*)—e.g., in 1860, ANT SH C63 D732. As another example, in 1876, under pressure from professors who had not received their salaries, the Agha of the Bayt al-Mal called on the prime minister, and the government came to the rescue, ANT SH C63 D708.

222. Djemaia Budget of 1895, ANT SC C26 D1-2. This is without even counting extraordinary expenditures such as those incurred for major renovations. In 1895 the reconstruction of the Zaytuna's minaret was planned for a cost that amounted to twice its dedicated *ḥabūs* net revenues. In some years, we also find payments to the professors of the Zaytuna made by the Bayt al-Mal.

in the twentieth century at al-Azhar, whose aggregate (budgetary and extrabudgetary) revenues came, for the most part, from the Ministry of Finance and the Waqfs Administration rather than from waqfs dedicated to it. These waqfs only contributed about 40 percent of al-Azhar's total expenditures in 1901, 1910, and 1915, 20 percent in 1925, 15 percent in 1930, 8 percent in 1940, and 3 percent on the eve of Nasser's 1961 reform of al-Azhar, after which its budget was put into the central state budget. The relative share of the Ministry of Finance's contribution increased over time, and at times the ministry channeled its payments through the Waqfs Administration.[223] Similarly, in 1915 Morocco, the state budget already contributed a significant part of the specialized Islamic tracks expenditures, and more than half by 1950 despite claims of self-sufficiency by the *Ḥabūs* Administration.[224]

Unwavering State Custodianship of Islam, with or without Waqfs

At Tunisia's independence, when public and private *ḥabūs* were outlawed, public *ḥabūs* assets became part of the State Domain (Domaine de l'État),[225] and the Djemaia was liquidated,[226] its religious expenditures (which were already more than entirely covered by a state subsidy, as we saw) were simply transferred to the state budget. This was reminiscent of what the French had done in Algeria at the onset of occupation, when they transferred *ḥabūs* properties to the state

---

For some examples, see ANT SH C63 D701 and ANT SH C63 D708. After 1919 it seems that the Bayt al-Mal became a mere "consignments fund of unclaimed inheritances" and could no longer afford these payments. See "Note au sujet des revendications des professeurs et du personnel administratif de la Grande Mosquée," undated but probably from 1943, ANT SD C36 D1-14.

223. The Ministry of Finance alone provided about 30 percent of al-Azhar's total revenues in 1901, 40 percent in 1930, 80 percent in 1940, and more than 95 percent in 1959. For 1901, see Calame (1903). For 1910, see Commission de la Réforme de l'Université d'El-Azhar (1911, 61–69), which lists al-Azhar's formal budget revenues (only about half its total revenues) but also its extrabudgetary revenues (such as in-species and in-kind revenues from its dedicated waqfs). For al-Azhar's annual budget in 1915, see Majlis al-Azhar al-Aʿlā (1915), and for the years 1925–26 to 1960–61, *Al-Waqāʾiʿ al-Miṣrīya*.

224. For the pressures of the sultan and Moroccan state officials to increase direct state contributions to the Qarawiyin's budget, see "Audience du Sultan," June 19, 1948, and "Audience du Sultan," October 30, 1948, ANOM, Fonds Luccioni, 52APOM1.

225. They represented about 20 percent of state-owned agricultural land, which itself represented about 10 percent of total agricultural land. Elloumi (2014, 50–51).

226. Decree of May 31, 1956 (*JOT* no. 44, June 1, 1956) and Decree of July 18, 1957 (*JOT* no. 58, July 18, 1957). Private waqfs' assets were transferred to their beneficiaries.

and, in exchange, paid for the expenditures related to places of worship, religious education, and Islamic justice from the French state budget.[227] In replacement of the Djemaia, a state Office of Religious Worship (*Maṣlaḥat al-Sha ʿā ʾir al-Dīnīya*) was created in 1956 and put under the purview of the prime minister (or Président du Conseil at the time). The functions of this office, which eventually became the Ministry of Religious Affairs (*Wizārat al-Shu ʾūn al-Dīnīya*) in 1991,[228] included the appointment and management of religious personnel such as imams and the construction and maintenance of mosques. Despite the Djemaia's liquidation and the shrinking of the Zaytuna system to a small Faculty of Theology upon independence, the decrease in aggregate public religious per capita expenditures was only temporary: they surpassed, in real terms, their high-water mark of the mid-1950s by 1980, although as a percentage of overall public expenditures or GDP they never recovered (table 2). As with its creation, the Djemaia's liquidation was therefore a mere reorganization of the state's management of religious institutions and expenditures and was motivated, at least in part, by a search for efficiency. To be sure, this reform also marked the end of the *ḥabūs* as a form of property in Tunisia and of a public administration in charge of managing them. However, it does not seem that it triggered strong criticism, perhaps because the dire financial situation of the Djemaia was well-known. For the ʿulamā, the state was responsible for public religious provisions, as before, and some of them wrote to the newly independent government to make sure that, "in a country whose government professes Islam" (*balad tadīn ḥukūmatuhu bi-l-Islām*), places of worship would be taken good care of.[229] The government gave the local governors the task of paying mosque personnel[230] and added a line in the state budget to this effect. Zaytuni shaykh Kamal Tarzi, the first director of religious worship (*mudīr al-sha ʿā ʾir al-dīnīya*) to occupy this position in 1967, explained what the religious personnel were hoping to gain from the new arrangement: a predictable revenue stream in the form of a government salary, as opposed to uncertain waqf revenues.[231]

227. Saidouni and Saidouni (2009).

228. Until then, it remained an office (under various names) under the prime minister, except for a one-year hiatus in 1987 when it was put under the Ministry of the Interior, in a broad reorganization of the administration that was put under tighter surveillance due to tensions with the Islamists.

229. "Epuration de la Djemaia des Awqaf 1944–1957," ANT SC C80 D2. Letter from the Maliki Mufti to Habib Bourguiba, July 30, 1956.

230. ANT SD C230 D133.

231. Cited by Souriau (1979, 357).

We find a similar pattern in other countries: the ʿulamā are understandably often more attached to the prospect of regular and dependable revenues than to any specific form of delivery. The correspondence of the *Ḥabūs* Administration in French-occupied Morocco often points to the desire of imams and preachers who received their stipends from the *Ḥabūs* to be paid directly from the state budget instead and to become state functionaries.[232] In Egypt, in 1920, the ʿulamā of al-Azhar argued that it was part of the Islamic tradition that the Bayt al-Mal—in the sense of the *state treasury* and not in the sense of the (much smaller) consignment fund of unclaimed inheritances—should provide salaries to the ʿulamā, as state functionaries.[233] In any case, with or without waqfs, governments put in place institutional arrangements to sustain religious institutions and their ʿulamā. While much ink has been spilled on the ineptitude and greed of waqf managers (*wakīl*s) and/or of state officials (among other institutional flaws), the main reason explaining the downfall of the institution of the waqfs in many places is simpler: states funded fewer waqfs and increasingly sustained public religious provisions directly from their treasury (with country-to-country variations in the pace of this trend), a change often welcomed by the ʿulamā. Although in some cases waqfs were abolished or curtailed (as in Tunisia and Egypt, respectively), and sometimes the law regulating them was westernized (as in Turkey), the state continued to ensure the delivery of public religious provisions and to do so as it saw fit.

The State Reprioritization within Religious Expenditures

Long before the Tunisian government folded all public religious expenditures into the central state budget, it provided religious provisions on its own terms, reprioritizing public *ḥabūs* expenditures, and therefore redefining the *ḥabūs*' aims, in accordance with its own priorities. Sometimes, the new aims the ruler decreed diverged blatantly from the founder's will. For instance, *ḥabūs* revenues were used to finance conquests or the defense of the territory, which might have been justified as an urgent necessity falling under the rubric of jihad.[234] In 1872

232. For instance, "Note d'ensemble," March 15, 1951, ANOM, Fonds Luccioni, 52APOM2.

233. "Mudhakkira bi-bayān maṣādir rawātib al-ʿulamā'" [Report clarifying the sources of the ʿulamā's salaries], April 6, 1920, which was sent to the government. Majlis al-Azhar al-Aʿlā (1919–1920, 492–506).

234. E.g., in Tunisia, an 1863 fatwa authorized the use of public waqfs' surplus revenues for the military. Ibn Abī al-Ḍiyāf (1963, vol. 4, 97). See also, in the Ottoman Empire, Inalcik and Quataert (1994, 98), and, in Egypt, Al-Jabartī (1879–1880, vol. 4, 211).

the French consul recommended using them to pay down the Tunisian debt.[235] In many instances, however, the state reprioritized *ḥabūs* expenditures toward an aim that was related to the founder's wish or remained broadly religious. For example, when Ahmad Bey formally introduced the category of second-class professors at the Zaytuna Grand Mosque and increased their salaries in 1848, he used surplus revenues from *ḥabūs* originally devoted to the recitation of prayers in praise of the Prophet in the Grand Mosque. Two professors continued to "realize the wish of the donor" by reading the aforementioned prayers, although "with time, the prayers were forgotten, and these two professors joined the rest of the class."[236]

On a larger scale, the Djemaia was in and of itself an instrument for reprioritizing religious expenditures. Per the decree that created it, its surplus revenues were to be used to pay the *qāḍī*s who were previously paid for managing *ḥabūs*. They henceforth received regular salaries, in a quid pro quo for accepting the transfer of their public *ḥabūs* management functions to the newly created Djemaia.[237] The remaining surplus was to be used to complement the salaries of the Zaytuna's first-class professors and the Zaytuna's imam and library personnel "in replacement of what they previously received from the state budget."[238] Although the reprioritization of public *ḥabūs* revenues was not a distinctive feature of modern times, the Djemaia certainly facilitated it by virtue of its degree of centralization. For example, we can see the scale of its reprioritization from its 1916 detailed budget:[239] more than 40 percent of the overall net revenues of the Djemaia were diverted from the foundations for which they were meant. Sharia justice, Islamic education, and public assistance in Tunis, which all had insufficient *ḥabūs* dedicated to them, absorbed most of the other foundations' surpluses. It is also illustrated by the change in the structure of the Djemaia's budgets. They initially reported the revenues and expenditures of the foundations dedicated to specific aims (e.g., Hanafi mosques in Tunis, Maliki mosques in Tunis, the Haramayn, fountains and wells), whereas starting in the early twentieth century, expenditures were

235. "Situation financière, Remèdes à y apporter," January 7, 1872, no. 604, CADN, 712PO/1, Direction Politique 1870–1873, vol. 106, fol. 317.

236. Ibn al-Khūja (1939, 87–88).

237. Decrees of April 6 and December 22, 1874, and "Note sur les Habous" (Étude de Béchir Sfar, Président de la Djemaia des Habous, sur "Les Habous"), CDN B-1-48.

238. Decree of March 19, 1874, Art. 23. See also Khayr al-Din's account in Mzali and Pignon (1971, 35–36).

239. ANT SC C26 D1-13.

organized by broad categories (e.g., worship, education, public assistance), and revenues were aggregated by revenue source only (harvest proceeds, enzels income, urban rental income, or rural rental income), omitting most remnants of the founders' will. In Egypt, the yearly budgets of the Waqfs Administration published in the Official Gazette after 1897 were similarly structured in a way that obviated the individual foundations' revenues and their aims.[240] In Morocco, the *Ḥabūs* Administration's yearly budgets under the French protectorate did not specify revenues and expenditures by foundation either but by type of revenue-generating property and type of expenditure, a pattern that continued after independence.[241] And as in Tunisia and Egypt, the need to finance religious education (and more broadly to rationalize the management of the *ḥabūs*) led the *Ḥabūs* Administration to use revenues from foundations with other beneficiaries.[242]

While reprioritizations were frequent and ubiquitous, so were complaints about them. For instance, in Morocco in 1913, Muhammad Hassan al-Hajwi, a graduate of the Qarawiyin and author of a project for its reform, complained to French authorities about the difficult material situation of its ʿulamā and accused the *Ḥabūs* Administration of having diverted the revenues of the waqfs of the city of Fez, which, he argued, were significant and generally earmarked for education.[243] With demand for schooling increasing, Moroccan administrators such as Mohamed Mouline (delegate of the grand vizier and previous vizier of the *Ḥabūs*) insisted that *ḥabūs* revenues be allocated to education, independently of the wishes of the founders, and even to the expense of worship. This proposal was received with alarm by French authorities, in part because it aligned with nationalist demands.[244] These complaints and disputes about the reprioritization of *ḥabūs* revenues toward aims deemed illegitimate by some did not cease with independence. For example, in 1964, during a parliamentary discussion of the budget of the Ministry of Waqfs and Islamic Affairs, Allal El-Fasi accused the government of having neglected the

240. *Al-Waqāʾiʿ al-Miṣrīya*, no. 49, May 11, 1898, appendix, Maṣlaḥat al-Awqāf al-ʿUmūmīya, Ḥisāb Khitāmī ʿan Sanat 1897.

241. For an early example, see Al-Iyāla al-Sharīfa, Wizārat ʿUmūm al-Aḥbās (1916).

242. "Note au sujet du recasement des tolbas effectués à Fès en 1950, sur l'ordre du Résident Général," August 9, 1951, 3–4, ANOM, Fonds Luccioni, 52APOM4.

243. Ibn ʿAddāda (2003, 261 and 273).

244. "L'institution des habous menacée," November 24, 1947, 6, ANOM, Fonds Luccioni, 52APOM6.

building of mosques and allowed the establishment of too many churches (built on *ḥabūs* land).[245]

6. Longing for State Support and Religious Institutions' Autonomy: The Ambivalent Partnership between the ʿUlamā and the State

The state's unwavering financial support of religious institutions, as well as its meddling in their affairs and ambition to control them, have not gone without tensions and ambivalence. In the twentieth century, increased direct state subsidies to the operations of public religious endowments signaled the decline of this organizational form, leading to criticism of the state not doing enough to protect it and the religious institutions the endowments sustained. This explains why state officials have often strived to project the economic self-sufficiency of the waqfs as evidence of the state adequately protecting them. To this end, they have frequently publicized the waqfs' achievements and have generally provided little budgetary transparency about direct state aid. As for the ʿulamā, they have requested and welcomed state financial support, but they have also complained about what they perceived as the government's hoarding of their resources and as an erosion of their autonomy. Cultivating the fiction of the autonomy and economic self-sufficiency of religious institutions and ʿulamā (despite increasing direct state subsidies) has helped state officials keep them at a safe distance for fear of their becoming "a state within a state" (to reuse Taha Husayn's expression) and meddling in politics. They have also used this fiction as a buffer of sorts between the government and the demands and expectations of the ʿulamā and the Muslim community.

Budgetary Tensions and Ambivalence toward State Support

In Tunisia, state financial support was not always explicitly mentioned in the Djemaia's budgets, as if there was a reluctance to recognize it, since it would explicitly underline the Djemaia's lack of autonomy and perhaps threaten its existence. Djemaia administrators often asked for "cash advances" from the government, and we also find recurrent wishful forecasts of the coming harvest

245. Cited in *Annuaire de l'Afrique du Nord*, March 1964, 212. For complaints in the 1930s, see Nāṣirī (1992).

(a significant and particularly volatile source of the Djemaia's revenues) in order to "balance" provisional budgets, delaying the inevitable financial intervention of the state.[246] On the other side, the government kept pressuring the Djemaia to reduce its operating costs, particularly its payroll. Having its own budgetary problems, it also frequently tried to make the Djemaia pay for some public expenditures, invoking the traditional role of the *ḥabūs* as providers of public services such as hospitals, fortifications, fountains, and wells.[247] In 1891 Béchir Sfar (president of the Djemaia from 1900 to 1908) complained about the hardship caused by the "contributions" asked of the Djemaia.[248] He claimed that even before the protectorate, a large part of the Djemaia's revenues "went to public coffers," which was an "anomaly" and a very serious one "from the religious point of view" since this prevented the Djemaia from accomplishing its religious tasks.[249] For him, priority had to be given to "worship, public assistance, public education, and the various foundations [the Djemaia] is responsible for."[250] Béchir Sfar did acknowledge, however, that the state budget provided the Djemaia with an annual subsidy to pay "allowances to religious figures" (this subsidy far exceeded, in fact, what the Djemaia was asked to pay in "contributions").[251] The Djemaia eventually (and reluctantly) paid only a small fraction of the contributions requested by the government, which were eliminated after 1898.[252]

246. A 1925 letter by the president of the Djemaia refers to this as "the usual way." ANT SC C26 D1-47. See also "Note sur le budget de la Djemaia, 1923" in ANT SG-SG2 C21 D10, which states that this subterfuge notwithstanding, "it is not less true that the Djemaia has a deficit of 1.6 million francs [i.e., more than half its religious expenditures for that year]."

247. The early budgets of the Djemaia included contributions it owed to the Municipality of Tunis, the Official Printing Press, and the government (about 3 percent, 1 percent, and 8 percent of its annual budget, respectively, in 1895) since the Djemaia now managed (and received revenues from) waqfs previously managed by the municipality, which continued to perform the public works these waqfs were meant to sustain. "Habous: Budget de 1882–1887 (1294–1299/1877–1882)," ANT SC C26 D 1-1.

248. "Rapport sur le budget de l'Administration des Habous pour l'Exercice 1309," ANT SC C26 D1-1.

249. Béchir Sfar, "Origine des embarras de la Djemaia," ANT SC C26 D1-1.

250. "Rapport sur le budget de l'Administration des Habous pour l'Exercice 1309," ANT SC C26 D1-1.

251. The government paid 160,000 piasters in allowances to religious figures, versus the 100,000 piasters it asked the Djemaia to pay, or rather reimburse, the municipality and the government. ANT SC C26 D1-1.

252. The French minister of foreign affairs to the general resident in Tunis, October 10, 1898, Djemaia Budget of 1315–1897, ANT SC C26 D1-2. The government would later also make the

And, as we saw, Béchir Sfar's list of priorities (worship, public assistance, and education) turned out to be far too much for the *ḥabūs* and the Djemaia to handle.

"Where did the Ḥabūs *Wealth Go?" A Common and Persistent Trope*

Despite the state's financial support for the Djemaia's mission, accusations against the state of meddling in the *ḥabūs* and stealing their wealth continued and resonated widely.[253] These became even louder with the rise of nationalism. By 1937 the financial situation of the Djemaia had become so dire, and the issue so politically charged, that French authorities established a committee formed of French high officials, Djemaia administrators, and two Tunisian members of the Great Council (Grand Conseil) to address it.[254] This committee unanimously acknowledged the severity of the Djemaia's difficulties: a debt of 27.4 million francs with expected annual (gross) revenues of only 11 million francs. Several explanations were put forward,[255] such as adverse economic circumstances, bad management decisions (in hindsight), the (alleged) inadequacy and rigidity of waqf and contract law, the difficulty of managing scattered waqf properties efficiently, the excessive scope of the Djemaia's mission, and the (allegedly) sizable acreage the Djemaia was forced to sell via "exchanges" by the 1898 Decree for colonization purposes (see chapter 2).[256]

Djemaia pay for provisions such as newly established schools for Tunisians—e.g., the Muslim Girls School (École de Jeunes Filles Musulmanes), or the food for the students of the Professional School (École Professionnelle). Djemaia Budget of 1925, ANT SC C26 D1-47.

253. E.g., a November 17, 1905, *Al-Ṣawāb* editorial accused French authorities of seeking to hoard the *ḥabūs* properties, "which fulfill most of our religious interests," by putting the Djemaia under the Finance Administration.

254. Sessions of April 17, April 27, May 11, May 19, May 27, 1937, ANT SC C1 D14-6. French authorities handpicked this committee's members, excluding some Tunisian figures who had been nominated (e.g., Salah Farhat).

255. Séance du 17 Avril 1937, and "Lettre du Directeur des Habous au Premier Ministre," May 4, 1937, ANT SC C1 D14-6.

256. The director of the *Ḥabūs* Administration retorted that, since 1898, the Djemaia had only sold 35,549 hectares of farmland, of which 16,869 ha went to French settlers, and the rest to the State Domain (Domaine de l'État). Séance du 11 Mai 1937, ANT SC C1 D14-6. Sicard (1965, 234 and 240) provides a similar estimate, which he compares to the 700,000 ha total acreage used for colonization purposes, and to the 1,200,000 ha total acreage of *ḥabūs* land, public and private. In a prior session, it was also noted that the foregone annual revenues were a small fraction of the Djemaia's deficit, which "should temper the emotions attached to this

One of its members also exhorted the committee to examine the past to understand "where the *ḥabūs* wealth went."[257] Pointing to the government's mistakes, he explained that it now had to "pay back what it had squandered."[258] After much finger-pointing, many suggestions for improvement were made by committee members. In a common pattern, they inevitably converged toward (1) narrowing the scope of the Djemaia's expenditures further by transferring even more of its responsibilities to the state budget and (2) providing it with even more state loans and subsidies.

Indeed, complaints about the state encroaching on the administration of the waqfs and stealing their resources, combined with frequent (and often unacknowledged) requests for financial support from the government and regular bailouts or direct takeovers by the state budget of some of its most significant missions, were a pattern in the history of the Djemaia, which we find throughout the history of other countries' religious institutions as well. In Morocco, for instance, although the state was already subsidizing the *Ḥabūs* Administration, its French officials often expressed reluctance to formally request further state subsidies because, they argued, it would publicly signal the *Ḥabūs*' decline.[259] A 1930 note complained about rumors that the *Ḥabūs* revenues were reaching the state's coffers instead of benefiting mosques and their personnel.[260] Moroccan nationalists accused the protectorate of diverting the *Ḥabūs*' mission and presented the sultan as the guarantor of their autonomy.[261] French authorities complained in turn that the sultan used the *Ḥabūs* as his own personal coffer and a political instrument in his alliance with the nationalists.[262] While foreign occupation

issue," and that "exchanges" were frequent even before the protectorate. Séance du 27 Avril 1937, ANT SC C1 D14-6.

257. Abderrahman Lazzam, also a member of the Grand Conseil, séance du 17 Avril 1937 (inaugural session), ANT SC C1 D14-6.

258. Séance du 17 Avril 1937, ANT SC C1 D14-6.

259. See Luccioni, "Note d'ensemble," March 15, 1951, ANOM, Fonds Luccioni, 52APOM2.

260. "Situation financière des habous," June 6, 1930, 4–5, ANOM, Fonds Luccioni, 52APOM3.

261. See the petition to the sultan, signed by about one thousand Moroccans, requesting that the *Ḥabūs* Administration be under the makhzen's control (*murāqaba*) and the sultan's custodianship (*riʿāya*) as the "commander of the faithful and the highest spiritual leader of the Muslim community" (*amīr al-muʾminīn wa-l-raʾīs al-rūḥī al-aʿlā li-jamāʿat al-Muslimīn*), in *Al-Ḥayāh*, no. 1, March 1, 1934, 6, in ANOM, Fonds Luccioni, 52APOM1. The petition reminded the sultan that the Jewish community freely administered its own waqfs.

262. See, for instance, "Notes sur les biens habous, 1945–1952," ANOM, Fonds Luccioni, 52APOM6.

shaped these narratives in Morocco, we find analogous tropes before and after colonization and elsewhere.[263]

Are Religious Institutions State Institutions? Yearning for State Support and Autonomy

Although Djemaia administrators were often ambivalent about the form of state financial support, they were vocal about its necessity, since the Djemaia could not survive without it. To justify this support, Tunisian members of the 1937 committee argued that the Djemaia was a state institution, and that in Muslim countries the ruler has, "among other prerogatives, the role of leader of the Muslim community's worship."[264] At the same time, they argued that the Djemaia must be autonomous in its budgetary choices. As for French officials, they were as ambivalent as their fellow Tunisian committee members. They resisted calling the Djemaia a state institution and argued that it was autonomous. They oscillated between confining the *ḥabūs* to a stereotypical religious function entirely sustained by civil society and conceding the central role of the state since, they argued, "Islam is the religion of the sovereign and of his subjects."[265] They did not want all public religious expenditures to explicitly fall under the state budget (mainly for financial reasons), but they also recognized that, in continuity with the past, it was the state's unquestionable duty to sustain religious institutions. They also explained that the government had already stepped in to provide financial assistance to the Djemaia, and that it would continue to do so, perhaps even more massively, but only in the form of "subsidies."[266] It seems that they thought of the Djemaia as a buffer that kept the government at a safe distance from the Muslim community's expectations and from demands for more public religious provisions, making it easier to resist these demands. Also, French

263. E.g., in precolonial Tunisia, Ahmad Ibn Abi Diyaf deplored the meddling of rulers in managing the *ḥabūs*. Ibn Abī al-Ḍiyāf (1963, vol. 5, 88). And in 2013 Egypt, requests were made to return its waqfs to al-Azhar in *Al-Ahrām*, April 11, 2013.

264. Séance du 19 Mai 1937, ANT SC C1 D14-6. For earlier arguments that the Djemaia was not independent from the state, see for instance a note dated 1922, but probably written earlier, "Note sur les Habous" (Étude de Béchir Sfar, Président de la Djemaia des Habous, sur "Les Habous"), CDN B-1-48.

265. Séance du 27 Mai 1937, ANT SC C1 D14-6.

266. A "massive" state subsidy was suggested. The government objected on the grounds that the *Ḥabūs* Administration was independent from the state and was financially autonomous, previous state interventions notwithstanding. Séance du 27 Mai 1937, ANT SC C1 D14-6.

authorities hoped not to be held responsible for the (mis)management of the *ḥabūs,* and not to be seen as meddling in the Djemaia's affairs—hence their efforts to maintain the illusion that religious institutions had a large degree of autonomy. Regardless, the government had to provide the necessary financial support when it was needed, since it was its duty.

Similar ambivalence was evident at the Zaytuna. In the first part of the twentieth century, the ʿulamā of the Zaytuna pressured the government to increase its financial support and to align their status and salaries with those of the teachers of the Directorate of Public Instruction (Direction de l'Instruction Publique). They did not view their requests for state financial support to be at odds with their ideal of autonomy,[267] and in any event, they were eager to be paid regular salaries from the state treasury rather than rely on the revenues of the Djemaia, which ran chronic deficits. When these demands became particularly vocal in the 1930s, and as enrollments were increasing (tables 4a and 4b), French authorities countered that the Zaytuna was autonomous and had never been a state institution. They invoked the idealized historical independence of the ʿulamā from the state,[268] which rulers had always attempted to maintain, albeit often as a fiction.[269] They also deplored the fact that the government had followed a slippery slope by agreeing to routinely complement the salaries the ʿulamā received from the Djemaia.[270] Although the state treasury already paid

267. For instance, in 1945, the shaykh of the Zaytuna asked for additional funds from the government and oversight prerogatives over the Grand Mosque budget. Letter from the shaykh of the Zaytuna to the prime minister, December 11, 1945, ANT SL C11 D1-1. Simultaneous demands for state financial support and budgetary autonomy were also expressed in the press. For instance, Mīzānīyat al-Kullīya al-Zaytūnīya [The budget of the Zaytuna faculty], *Al-Nahḍa,* January 4, 1946.

268. Some French officials even argued that, as scholars, ʿulamā should not be concerned with material gratification and had to safeguard their doctrinal independence. "Note du 22 février 1937 au Délégué à l'Administration Tunisienne," ANT SD C36 D1-10.

269. Article 5 of the March 19, 1874 Decree establishing the Djemaia gave it "absolute control over all the Regency's *ḥabūs* except those of the Grand Mosque, which would continue to remain under the care of its imam." The accounts of the Grand Mosque (as well as those of the foundations for the Ḥaramayn, the Qur'an reciters, and the muezzins) were kept separate from those of the Djemaia until 1904.

270. "Note confidentielle sur la Grande Mosquée du 3 novembre 1937," ANT SD C36 D1-10. See also "Note au sujet de la Grande Mosquée, 1er Avril 1936," ANT SD C36 D1-10. It argued that the Zaytuna should be kept "outside of the state's limits." See also Lettre du Résident Général au Général de l'Armée et Commissaire aux Affaires Etrangères d'Alger (December 6, 1943), ANT SD C36 D1-14. It argued that the Zaytuna was "private and autonomous from the state"

the bulk of the professors' salaries, French authorities insisted that they receive them from the hand of the Djemaia (which was therefore to continue to serve as a buffer), in order to appear to respect the "private" character of the Grand Mosque and avoid an outright nationalization of Islamic education (and the costs it would imply). As for the ʿulamā, they protested and asked to be paid directly by the state treasury instead.[271] Eventually, in 1947, a decree aligned the salaries of the professors of the Grand Mosque with those of civil servants and also established the principle of its budgetary autonomy.[272] However, this autonomy was not realized in practice,[273] a state of affairs that continued after independence, in conjunction with a total lack of budgetary transparency from 1960 to 2015.[274]

We find similar tensions between the ideal of autonomy and state financial support in Turkey,[275] Morocco,[276] and Egypt, irrespective of the presence of an occupying foreign power. The Egyptian waqfs' waves of centralization and decentralization in the nineteenth and twentieth centuries were accompanied by demands for more autonomy *and* more state aid, both before, during, and after British occupation. A telling example is the waqf reforms under Presidents Nasser and Sadat. Whereas after their 1952 coup, the Free Officers had aimed to

---

under the Husaynids, and that making ʿulamā civil servants "would result in an enormous cost for the state budget."

271. In 1938, the Great Council's Tunisian Section argued for "the direct payment by the General and Central Administration of the salaries of the professors of the Zaytuna." "Du Directeur de l'Administration Générale et Centrale à Résident Général," May 18, 1938, ANT SD C36 D1-14. See also "Note du Directeur de l'Administration Centrale et Communale au Secrétaire Général du Gouvernement Tunisien," November 5, 1938, ANT SD C36 D1-10. It proposed paying the Zaytuna professors from a special fund fed by the Djemaia and state coffers since they wanted to be paid by the state and not by the Djemaia, which was running a deficit.

272. Decree of June 1, 1947.

273. The shaykh of the Zaytuna complained that the protectorate authorities, despite having proclaimed its autonomy, had not allowed him to establish its budget for 1948–49. He presented an official request for a supplement, in "Bayān min Mashyakhat al-Jāmiʿ al-Aʿẓam," 9, ANT SL C11 D1-3.

274. From 1960 onward, the expenditures related to the Zaytuna were either entirely, or almost entirely from 1970 onward, subsumed under those of the University of Tunis. It was only in 2015, after the Arab Spring, that the published state budget listed all the expenditures of the Zaytuna University.

275. For the issue of the autonomy of Turkey's Diyanet, see Bein (2011, 155–166).

276. Such ambivalence in the Ministry of Waqfs and Islamic Affairs were highlighted and deplored in El-Mabkhout (1980, 109), a 1980 School of Administration study. For the tense relationships between the Moroccan monarchy and the ʿulamā, see Zeghal (2008b, 1–76).

transfer public waqfs' revenue-generating properties to the Organization of the Agrarian Reform, to the governorates, and to the local councils, in 1971 Sadat ordered their transfer to a new institution, with its own section in the state budget: "the Waqfs' Organization" (*hayʾat al-awqāf*). It was (and still is) entrusted with managing the waqfs' properties and with disbursing their net revenues to the Waqfs Ministry to be spent "according to the donors' wishes."[277] However, seeking efficiency and publicizing the waqfs' alleged self-sufficiency in this manner did not prevent complaints that the donors' wishes were not respected[278] nor requests for more state aid since the Waqfs' Organization's net revenues from the religious endowments were far from sufficient to sustain the Islamic missions of the Waqfs Ministry. In 1973 they only contributed 31 percent of the Waqfs Ministry expenditures—that is, about 9 percent of total state religious expenditures. By 1984–85 these percentages had dropped to 13 percent and 3 percent, respectively (approximately what they were in 2019–20). Similarly, in twentieth-century Morocco, the revenues of the *ḥabūs* properties proved increasingly insufficient to tend to their missions (even as their scope kept being reduced), a fact that has not been widely advertised. It has rather been buried in the yearly reports published by the Ministry of Waqfs and Islamic Affairs that publicize the many achievements of the *Ḥabūs* institution, as if it was self-sufficient.[279] However, by 2009—the only time since 1979 for which the specific budget of the *Ḥabūs*, which lists the revenues and expenditures of their productive apparatus and is distinct from the budget of the Ministry of Waqfs and Islamic Affairs has been made publicly available, it seems—the state budget fed the vast majority of the revenues of the *Ḥabūs*' specific budget. On its own, it only contributed a sliver of overall state religious expenditures, as we saw.[280] In this case too, the Moroccan government seeks to maintain the appearance of the institution's self-sufficiency and flourishing to project the accomplishment of its duty as custodian of Islam and to maintain a buffer of sorts between the state and the expectations of the Muslim community.

277. Law no. 80 of 1971. See Barbar and Kepel (1982, 31–43) and Ghānim (1998, 485–493).

278. Barbar and Kepel (1982, 58).

279. Al-Mamlaka al-Maghribīya, Wizārat al-Awqāf wa-l-Shuʾūn al-Islāmīya, *Nashrat al-Munjazāt* (2003–2020).

280. The specific budget of the *Ḥabūs* was published yearly in the *Annuaire statistique du Maroc* from 1925 until 1979. For 2009 and 2010, see al-Mamlaka al-Maghribīya, *Mashrūʿ Qānūn al-Mālīya li-Sanat 2009*, Wizārat al-Awqāf wa-l-Shuʾūn al-Islamīya, Al-Mīzānīya al-ʿĀmma, Al-Mīzānīya al-Khāṣṣa, and the 2009 report by the parliamentary committee on external affairs, defense, and Islamic affairs for the 2010 budget.

Al-Azhar between State Patronage and Ambitions of Autonomy

Yet the most telling example of ambivalence over autonomy and state financial support in a religious institution is that of al-Azhar, given its importance and singular expansion in the twentieth century. The ʿulamā of al-Azhar, although they welcome state financial support, often also lament the loss of their (real or imagined) former independence from the state. As is the case for other madrasas, this past independence needs to be strongly qualified: as we saw in nineteenth-century Tunisia, in their partnership with the ruler, autonomy was not always easy to achieve for the ʿulamā, although it was viewed as an ideal. The ruler appointed them to high positions, made them waqf beneficiaries, and gave them waqfs to manage, as well as direct gifts in kind and in cash. To be sure, autonomy must have increased in periods of decentralization and waned with recentralization. The late nineteenth century was, for al-Azhar, another period of centralization. With recurrent curricular and administrative reforms came the need for more financial help from state coffers, and this help increased steadily. In 1895 the Ministry of Finance promised a yearly subsidy (*iʿāna*) of 2,000 Egyptian pounds conditioned on the organization of a standardized salary scale. This was in addition to allowances in kind and in cash that already existed, such as yearly gifts of *kiswas* (robes of honor) to high ʿulamā that were now to be converted into cash allowances, as well as monthly allowances to select ʿulamā (and their sons after their fathers' death), also provided from the state budget. In 1897 at the request of the Council of al-Azhar's Administration, the Khedive ordered additional yearly funds to be paid by the Waqfs Ministry to sustain the curricular reforms.[281] Direct subsidies by the Finance and Waqfs Ministries both continued to increase as a fraction of al-Azhar's total revenues, reaching more than 80 percent overall in the early 1930s. Although the ʿulamā welcomed these additional resources[282] (and being paid from the state treasury, as we saw), they were also wary of the centralization of the revenues and distributions they controlled. Officials had long complained that the ʿulamā who managed waqfs dedicated to al-Azhar outside the purview of the Waqfs Ministry followed their own whims when distributing these waqfs' proceeds, and that many ʿulamā had to endlessly struggle and negotiate with them for their livelihood.[283] They had also long underlined the necessity to centralize *all* the revenues of al-Azhar under

281. *Aʿmāl Majlis Idārat al-Azhar* (1905, 2–38).

282. *Aʿmāl Majlis Idārat al-Azhar* (1905, 9).

283. *Aʿmāl Majlis Idārat al-Azhar* (1905, 2–38) and Lajnat Iṣlāḥ al-Azhar al-Maʿmūr (1910).

one transparent and comprehensive budget.[284] However, a formal al-Azhar budget was published in the Official Gazette starting only in 1927. And, even then, it omitted "extrabudgetary" revenues that still represented almost 20 percent of total revenues.[285] With law no. 15 of May 31, 1927, which transferred the king's powers over religious establishments to Parliament, al-Azhar's budget was to be examined and approved by the legislature. MPs reiterated the request that it include its previously "extrabudgetary" waqf revenues,[286] and it was only starting in 1931–1932 that the budgets published in the Official Gazette included them.

All these pressures led to misgivings about the disappearance of old forms of financial support, as illustrated by complaints that the donors' wishes were ignored.[287] This explains why official requests for al-Azhar to centralize its revenues under one unified budget, to follow the same rules of accounting as the state budget, to integrate al-Azhar's own waqfs with those of the Waqfs Ministry, and to ensure equity among ʿulamā in the distribution of waqf proceeds went hand in hand with assurances that this could be done in compliance with the wishes of the waqfs' founders.[288] There was also a tension, among state elites, between two aims: (1) to moderate al-Azhar's ambitions of autonomy—for example, by financing it directly from the state budget since they feared that it could otherwise become too powerful and akin to "a clergy" (*kahānūt*); and (2) to provide it with some degree of autonomy to keep it at a safe distance from "politics"—for example, by paying its ʿulamā exclusively from the Waqfs Ministry's budget (which was kept separate from that of the state) to ensure, it was argued, their "independence."[289] The Waqfs Ministry would serve—as the Djemaia in Tunisia, and the *Ḥabūs* Administration in Morocco—as a sort of buffer protecting the state from the ʿulamā's financial and other requests and from their meddling in politics.

284. *Aʿmāl Majlis Idārat al-Azhar* (1905), Lajnat Iṣlāḥ al-Azhar al-Maʿmūr (1910), and Majlis al-Nuwwāb (1927).

285. *Al-Waqāʾiʿ al-Miṣrīya*, no. 66, August 4, 1927, 1926–27 and 1927–1928 provisional al-Azhar budgets, and Majlis al-Nuwwāb (1927, 1).

286. Majlis al-Nuwwāb (1927, 1–2).

287. E.g., some ʿulamā's reluctance to accept the transformation of bread rations into cash, in Majlis al-Nuwwāb (1927, 13).

288. Majlis al-Nuwwāb (1927).

289. E.g., see the parliamentary debate between MPs Ahmad Abd al-Ghaffar, of the Liberal Constitutional Party, and Abd al-Rahman Azzam, member of the Wafd Party, in Al-Dawla al-Miṣrīya, Majlis al-Nuwwāb (1924–1952), sessions 30 and 31 of August 11 and 14, 1926, 441–457. See also Al-Dawla al-Miṣrīya, Majlis al-Nuwwāb (1924–1952), session 61 of July 1, 1924, 758, and session 66 of July 7, 1924, 829–830.

Be that as it may, as with other preeminent madrasas examined in this book, al-Azhar only survived (and thrived) with increasing direct state financial support, as shown by the evolution of its revenue sources until its full integration into the budget of the state with the reform law no. 103 of 1961 (see section 5). Some accounts of the modern history of al-Azhar have deplored this evolution toward full and direct financial support by the state and interpreted it as the state's hoarding of the revenues of the waqfs dedicated to the institution. Others have welcomed it and interpreted it as the state's rescue of an al-Azhar that was in a situation of general "decline" due in part, the argument goes, to the mismanagement of its waqfs by corrupt individual managers left without state control.[290] The reality is that the remarkable expansion of al-Azhar's size and scope in the twentieth century (tables 4a and 4b) has been overwhelmingly funded by the state budget and decreasingly so by the creation of religious endowments.[291] Whether in the form of waqfs or through direct financial support, the state has continued to play the role of the main financial caretaker of al-Azhar.[292] To be sure, periods of centralization and authoritarianism can only reinforce the myth of (and the yearning for) a past autonomy. It is not surprising that, after the fall of Mubarak following the Arab Spring, during the two years of freedom of expression that ended in 2013 with a military coup, the issue of al-Azhar's autonomy and political role was so salient in public debates. It was asked whether the law of 1961 could be modified to make al-Azhar independent from state control and, *at the same time*, whether the budget of al-Azhar could be aligned with that of other Egyptian universities.[293] The shaykh of al-Azhar also asked that the state give back the waqfs that belonged to al-Azhar.[294] Along with the ideal of the duty of the state's

290. E.g., Mubārak (1886–1889, vol. 1, 87–88) and Bayram (1903, 14), which is rehearsed by Eccel (1984, 243) among others.

291. The 1961 law that reformed al-Azhar allowed for gifts and endowments for the benefit of al-Azhar, but the creation of waqfs in general slowed down considerably after the 1950s. See Ghānim (1998, 105–107).

292. In contrast, Al-Sayyid Marsot (1973, 137–148) argues that Muhammad Ali's centralization efforts led to the end of the ʿulamā's "golden age" in terms of economic and political influence, and that "his new administration was to culminate in a secular bureaucracy under his successors which had little use for the ulama [*sic*]."

293. *Al-Ahrām*, March 20, 2011, 8. In this article, the al-Azhar grand imam Ahmad al-Tayyib condemned the proposed abolition of the Waqfs Ministry but supported the appointment of a representative of al-Azhar in that ministry. He also supported the election of the shaykh of al-Azhar by the ʿUlamā High Council. On the project of modifying the 1961 law of al-Azhar, see also *Al-Ahrām*, February 2, 2012.

294. *Al-Ahrām*, May 2, 2012, 21.

custodianship, that of the religious institution's autonomy and economic self-sufficiency also endured.

Conclusion

Examining public religious expenditures in Tunisia, Morocco, Egypt, and Turkey, in the *longue durée*, reveals the continuity of the state's custodianship of Islam as both a principle and a concrete reality in these four countries, despite their significant historical, political, and socioeconomic differences. This chapter's core findings can likely be generalized, in their broad strokes, to Muslim-majority polities in which the state is expected to be the custodian of Islam since the key factors driving them are not country-specific—for example, the inextricable tie of this duty to sovereignty, the diversity of views as to how it should be performed, the drastic expansion of the reach and size of the state in the modern period, and the organizational mechanisms and ambivalence (e.g., about self-sufficiency/state support and autonomy/state control) that are often at play in public and other institutions. The four countries studied in this chapter certainly exhibit significant differences and fluctuations—in the extent of public religious provisions, in their scope, in their content, in the institutional form of their delivery, and in their attendant debates. And studying public religious provisions in more Muslim-majority countries would certainly bring to light more differences and fluctuations. Some could be traced to policy choices specific to the religious domain made by rulers over time given their resources, capabilities, need for legitimacy, and other constraints they may face (including policy debates). Other differences could be the mechanistic effects of dissimilarities in human and economic development trajectories, notably in the domain of education. All these fluctuations and country-to-country differences notwithstanding, a similar picture should be discernible. The concrete implementation of the state's custodianship of Islam has continued to be the object of sustained attention on the part of rulers and state officials, although its size has been modest relative to other public provisions, and especially compared to the overall economy (though still larger than civil society's contribution). And, despite its unwavering financial support for the mission of religious institutions, in many instances in the modern period the state transformed them by eliminating or marginalizing part of the traditional structures through which it provided, directly or indirectly, public religious goods (e.g., the institutions managing public religious endowments, the Bayt al-Mal, the sharia courts, and the madrasas). These transformations in the scope and institutional form of delivery of public religious provisions by the state, and the debates that accompanied them, makes the continuity of the concrete reality of the state custodianship of Islam even more striking. However, such reorganizations were not unprecedented. From a *longue durée* perspective, the unprecedented transformation was related to the drastic absolute and relative (to the size of the economy) increase in the size and reach of the state in the modern period. This transformation certainly exacerbated preexisting debates about the role and extent of religion in governance. The policy tug-of-war between those who wanted to expand it and those who wanted to reduce it has continued unabated, while new entrants such as organized mass movements and parties have entered the discussion. In this long-term process, although the partnership between the state and the ʿulamā has evolved, religious institutions have generally continued to be both a constraint and a resource for Muslim states. Hence the continued ambivalence about the state financial support of religious institutions on the part of ʿulamā but also rulers and state officials. On the one hand, the ʿulamā often ask for more autonomy from state control and, at the same time, for more financial support from the state budget. On the other hand, rulers and state officials often strive to tighten their control of religious institutions while maintaining the appearance of these institutions' autonomy and economic self-sufficiency, in part to buffer themselves from the demands and expectations of the ʿulamā and the Muslim community. They also seek civil society's financial participation, leveraging it to alleviate the financial burden of their duty as custodians of Islam. The expansion of the size and reach of the state therefore created more opportunities but also more challenges for governments and ʿulamā alike, and their ambivalence continues to produce tensions over the distribution of religious authority, as in the past.

Conclusion

I HAVE HIGHLIGHTED the continuity in most (but not all) Muslim-majority polities of the broadly shared expectation that the state be the custodian of Islam, the preferred religion, and this duty's inextricable connection to sovereignty, whether exercised by indigenous or foreign non-Muslim rulers. I have found it in a wide variety of contexts, including precolonial rule, colonial rule, independent state building, authoritarian rule, and democratization, a testament to its endurance. I have also highlighted the persistence of vigorous debates and political battles about how this custodianship should be implemented between those who advocate for the expansion of the role of Islam in governance and their adversaries. Their disagreements revolve around what I call the thickness and munificence of the state custodianship of Islam but also around its strength, around the relationship between Islam and politics, and around the content and means of delivery of religious provisions. They have involved a remarkably broad spectrum of protagonists in the modern period: foreign and indigenous, state and nonstate, elites and common folk, ʿulamā and other intellectuals as well as—with the advent of mass politics—organized movements and parties, among them those commonly referred to as "Islamist." Notwithstanding the remarkable persistence of a broad agreement on the principle of the state custodianship of Islam as the preferred religion, I find it to be a matter of choice—by no means essential or inevitable. I have also found the borrowing of Western techniques of governance in the modern period to be a reasoned and selective choice (albeit often a heavily constrained and contentious one) rather than the mere result of Western hegemony, as is sometimes argued. These techniques were in fact well-known and well-understood by indigenous protagonists, and vigorous debates took place about whether and how much they threatened or changed the existing ideals of governance, particularly the state custodianship of Islam.

Political elites sifted through them to keep what they thought was relevant or necessary.

I have also shown that the continuity of the principle of the state's custodianship of Islam in most Muslim-majority countries has meant that the state has given unwavering financial support to religious institutions or, at the very least, to their missions (such as worship and Islamic education). To be sure, it has done so on its own terms, reorganizing religious institutions, reprioritizing their aims, introducing new means of delivery, and sometimes replacing old ones. Moreover, although states have often ostentatiously advertised this support, in practice this has translated into a modest amount of state religious expenditures in relation to other public expenditures and especially to the overall economy. In addition, while the drastic and unprecedented increase in the size of the state in the modern period may have enabled a relative deprioritization of state religious expenditures relative to nonreligious ones in the *longue durée*, it also led to their massive increase in per capita real terms. Moreover, debates and policy fights about the munificence of the state's custodianship of Islam have engendered short-term fluctuations in this munificence. These long-term trends and short-term fluctuations have often been interpreted by scholars of the modern period as either part of a process of Islamization or, on the contrary, of secularization and marginalization of religious institutions, whereas they really are only the results of the vigorously negotiated implementation of the custodianship of Islam by states that have expanded in size and reach on an unprecedented scale.

It is also notable that in the modern period, amid major transformations in techniques of governance, in the size and reach of the state, and in the means of delivery of public religious provisions, the partnership between states and the ʿulamā has persisted under various systems of governance: precolonial, colonial, and postindependence authoritarian or democratic. In this always tense and ambivalent partnership, the ʿulamā have continued to simultaneously long for the financial support of the state and yearn for an allegedly lost autonomy. As for rulers and state officials, they have continued to concurrently seek to control religious institutions and to keep them and their ʿulamā (some of whom actively participate in the debates about the role of Islam in governance when they can) at a safe distance, to better manage their expectations and those of the Muslim community and keep them out of politics. To this end, they often cultivate and manipulate the myth of the autonomy and economic self-sufficiency of Islamic institutions. Although the ʿulamā have confronted deep challenges in modern times, a significant one being the expanding domain of secular knowledge, they have also had new opportunities to strengthen their influence in the public arena, thanks to the masses' unprecedented access to education. It is therefore incorrect to assume, as is common, that the transformations of modern times have only marginalized and weakened the ʿulamā. In fact, it is likely that some premodern ʿulamā might have welcomed such a broad access to the masses to facilitate the dissemination of what they viewed as correct beliefs and practices.[1]

While I have mostly focused on debates among Muslims about the state's custodianship of the majority religion, Islam, our understanding of the relations between religion and state in the Middle East, and in Muslim-majority countries more broadly, could be further deepened by examining religious minorities' viewpoints on the enduring principle of the state's custodianship of Islam as the preferred religion and on the state's custodianship of other religions in more detail. It would notably be fruitful to measure the state's financial support (or lack thereof) for public religious provisions devoted to non-Muslims in Muslim-majority countries (in absolute terms and compared to those devoted to Muslims) and to examine the debates this support, or the lack thereof, may have triggered among the Muslim majority and non-Muslim minorities.

While I have mostly focused my analysis on the modern period, it would be fruitful to go back in time to deepen our understanding of ruptures and continuities with the past. Questions about how to implement the state's custodianship of Islam as the preferred religion were also posed in earlier times and were shaped by their distinct political and socioeconomic contexts.[2] For instance, in Fatimid Cairo, in matters of *siyāsa*—that is, in *maẓālim* courts—Muslims and *dhimmīs* were "subject to similar treatment by the state,"[3] a principle that we also found at the heart of the Regency of Tunis's 1857 Security Pact but this time around expressed in constitutional form. In both cases, the question of minorities' rights under a state that was the

1. See, for instance, the analysis of the disputes among theologians of the Maghrib from the fifteenth to the seventeenth century regarding how and to what extent the common people should be taught and learn the creed, in Olson (2020).

2. M. Cook (2000) analyzes the moral duty of "forbidding wrong" in premodern times, uncovering a whole range of positions about how to accomplish this duty, and various perspectives about the role of the state in it. Zaman (1997b, e.g., 91–101) and Crone (2004, 148–164) analyze mirrors for princes. For a history of rebellions and state formation based on religious criticism and reform, see García-Arenal (2006). For a study of premodern debates about the role of Christian officials in a Muslim state administration, see Yarbrough (2019).

3. Rustow (2013, 326).

custodian of Islam, the preferred religion, was addressed. And in both cases, we can discern a tension between the realm of policy making by rulers and that of the interpretation and implementation of sharia by *qāḍīs* and ʿulamā. I would like to suggest that there are many more continuities with the past than is conventionally assumed, notwithstanding radical contextual changes. It would be fruitful, in my view, to expand our understanding of such continuities when studying Islam in governance in the modern period, rather than simply assuming that modern times have distorted Islamic thought and practice to such an extent that they have become entirely unrecognizable from premodern times. In other words, it might not be necessary to posit radical epistemological ruptures to illuminate recent changes in the relationship between Islam and the state. As far as the state's custodianship of Islam (as an aspiration and a concrete reality) is concerned, it has in fact solidified thanks to the expanding size and reach of the state in the modern period.

TABLES

TABLE 1. Total population, real GDP per capita, and state expenditures as a percentage of GDP

	Total population[a] (millions)				GDP per capita in purchasing power parity (PPP) adjusted 1990 USD (thousands)				Total state expenditures[b] as a % of GDP			
Year	Egypt	Tunisia	Turkey	Morocco	Egypt	Tunisia	Turkey	Morocco	Egypt	Tunisia	Turkey	Morocco
1730	4.4	0.8		1.9	0.6	0.5		0.5		~ 2%		
1800	4.2	0.9		2.5		0.5				~ 2%		
1850	5.7	1.0		3.3		0.6				~ 5%		
⋮	⋮	⋮	⋮	⋮	⋮	⋮	⋮	⋮	⋮	⋮	⋮	⋮
1880	7.5	1.3		4.1		0.7				6%		
1885	7.9	1.4		4.2		0.7				7%		
1890	8.6	1.5		4.3		0.7				8%		
1895	9.4	1.5		4.5		0.8				11%		
1900	10.1	1.6		4.7	0.8	0.8			18%	11%		
1905	10.9	1.7		4.8	0.9	0.8			15%	20%		
1910	11.7	1.8		5.0	0.9	0.9			15%	16%		
1915	12.4	1.9		5.3	0.9	0.9		0.8	15%	15%		3%
1920	13.1	2.1		5.7	0.8	1.0		0.9	17%	8%		4%
1925	13.9	2.3	14.1	6.2	1.0	1.1	0.9	0.9	18%	8%	12%	5%
1930	14.7	2.4	14.9	6.6	0.9	1.2	1.2	1.0	25%	14%	13%	8%
1935	15.4	2.6	16.2	6.9	1.0	1.2	1.4	1.1	18%	20%	19%	14%

1940	17.0	2.9	17.8	7.6	0.9	1.1	1.7	1.2	23%	12%	22%	5%
1945	19.0	3.2	18.8	8.4	0.9	1.1	1.1	1.3	15%	13%	11%	5%
1950	20.7	3.5	21.1	9.3	1.0	1.1	1.6	1.5	21%	22%	17%	8%
1955	23.9	3.8	24.1	10.8	1.0	1.2	2.2	1.5	21%	23%	14%	16%
1960	26.8	4.1	28.2	12.4	1.1	1.2	2.4	1.3	30%	27%	12%	20%
1965	30.3	4.6	32.0	14.1	1.3	1.7	2.7	1.4	52%	24%	14%	23%
1970	33.6	5.1	35.8	15.9	1.3	1.8	3.4	1.6	50%	31%	17%	26%
1975	37.0	5.6	40.5	17.7	1.5	2.3	4.5	1.8	57%	27%	17%	51%
1980	44.2	6.4	45.0	19.1	2.1	2.9	4.7	2.1	64%	33%	20%	43%
1985	50.1	7.2	51.0	21.9	2.5	3.1	5.4	2.4	41%	39%	17%	33%
1990	55.3	8.2	56.6	24.7	2.5	3.3	6.5	2.6	31%	42%	20%	32%
1995	61.2	9.0	62.3	27.0	2.6	3.7	7.1	2.5	32%	42%	20%	33%
2000	67.3	9.5	67.8	28.7	3.1	4.6	8.1	2.8	29%	36%	35%	34%
2005	76.3	10.0	72.2	30.4	3.5	5.4	9.5	3.3	35%	31%	31%	34%
2010	83.5	10.5	77.2	32.4	4.0	6.4	10.5	4.0	29%	28%	37%	35%
2015	94.9	11.1	82.6	34.4	4.5	6.6	11.2	4.6	42%	32%	33%	39%
2020	106.2	11.7	88.0	36.4	5.0	6.1	10.9	4.6	34%	33%	35%	45%

Note: See the data appendix for sources, fiscal and calendar years alignment, and more details.

[a] Total population of the country, including non-Muslims

[b] State expenditures include all recurrent and nonrecurrent expenditures of the central state budget and its annexed budgets (including debt service, social security, and capital expenditures) as well as those of the administration of state-managed public religious endowments and other religious institutions when kept separate from the central state budget.

TABLE 2. State religious expenditures as a percentage of total state expenditures, as a percentage of GDP, and in per capita real terms

	State religious expenditures as a % of total state expenditures[a]				State religious expenditures as a % of GDP				State religious expenditures per capita[b] in purchasing power parity (PPP) adjusted 1990 USD			
Year	Egypt	Tunisia	Turkey	Morocco	Egypt	Tunisia	Turkey	Morocco	Egypt	Tunisia	Turkey	Morocco
1730		~ 15%–25%				~ 0.3%–0.5%				~ 1.5–2.5		
1800												
1850												
⋮	⋮	⋮	⋮	⋮	⋮	⋮	⋮	⋮	⋮	⋮	⋮	⋮
1880		5.4%				0.31%				2.1		
1885												
1890		3.0%				0.24%				1.8		
1895		3.3%				0.36%				2.7		
1900	2.0%	3.2%			0.37%	0.35%			2.8	2.8		
1905	3.0%	2.0%			0.44%	0.41%			4.1	3.4		
1910	3.1%	2.4%			0.46%	0.39%			4.2	3.3		
1915	3.4%	2.6%		1.6%	0.50%	0.40%		0.06%	4.7	3.6		0.4
1920	2.1%	1.9%		1.1%	0.37%	0.15%		0.05%	3.0	1.5		0.4
1925	3.2%	1.8%	1.8%	1.2%	0.58%	0.14%	0.21%	0.06%	5.6	1.5	1.9	0.6
1930	3.0%	2.0%	1.3%	1.0%	0.74%	0.28%	0.17%	0.09%	6.7	3.2	2.1	0.9
1935	4.0%	2.1%	0.6%	1.0%	0.73%	0.41%	0.12%	0.14%	7.1	4.8	1.6	1.5

1940	3.0%	2.3%	0.3%	1.7%	0.70%	0.29%	0.07%	0.09%	6.6	3.3	1.2	1.1
1945	3.2%	1.5%	0.3%	1.2%	0.49%	0.19%	0.03%	0.06%	4.6	2.2	0.4	0.8
1950	2.0%	2.2%	0.5%	1.6%	0.42%	0.48%	0.09%	0.13%	4.1	5.4	1.4	1.9
1955	2.4%	3.0%	0.7%	1.6%	0.51%	0.71%	0.09%	0.24%	4.9	8.3	2.0	3.6
1960	1.6%	1.2%	1.1%	2.6%	0.47%	0.33%	0.14%	0.53%	5.0	4.0	3.2	7.0
1965	1.4%	1.2%	0.9%	3.1%	0.71%	0.30%	0.12%	0.71%	9.1	4.9	3.4	9.9
1970	1.3%	1.0%	1.1%	2.3%	0.67%	0.32%	0.18%	0.59%	8.7	5.8	6.3	9.6
1975	1.3%	1.2%	1.4%	1.1%	0.75%	0.32%	0.24%	0.55%	11.0	7.5	10.7	10.0
1980		1.0%	1.2%	1.5%		0.31%	0.25%	0.65%		9.3	12.0	13.9
1985	1.7%	1.0%	1.1%	1.5%	0.68%	0.37%	0.18%	0.49%	16.8	11.5	9.6	11.7
1990	1.9%	0.9%	1.7%	1.4%	0.58%	0.39%	0.34%	0.46%	14.6	12.9	22.4	12.0
1995		0.9%	1.4%	1.4%		0.37%	0.28%	0.45%		13.7	19.7	11.1
2000		0.9%	0.8%	1.4%		0.31%	0.29%	0.49%		14.2	23.1	13.8
2005	2.5%	1.0%	0.9%	1.6%	0.86%	0.31%	0.30%	0.54%	29.8	16.9	28.0	18.2
2010	2.8%	0.9%	1.1%	2.3%	0.82%	0.25%	0.40%	0.82%	32.7	15.8	42.2	32.9
2015	2.5%	0.8%	1.7%	2.1%	1.02%	0.27%	0.56%	0.83%	45.6	17.7	62.5	38.5
2020	1.8%	1.1%	1.6%	2.2%	0.59%	0.35%	0.56%	0.97%	29.8	21.6	61.0	44.9

Note: State religious expenditures (Islamic worship, sharia justice, Islamic education, and Islamic public assistance) include direct religious expenditures from the central state budget (including an estimation, based on the fraction of the curriculum it represents, of state expenditures on Islamic instruction dispensed in modern schools) as well as the expenditures of the administration of state-managed public religious endowments and other religious institutions when kept separate from the central state budget (excluding expenditures devoted to the operations of their revenue-generating assets when applicable). See the data appendix for sources, fiscal and calendar years alignment, and more details.

[a]Total state expenditures include all recurrent and nonrecurrent expenditures of the central state budget and its annexed budgets (including debt service, social security, and capital expenditures) as well as those of the administration of state-managed public religious endowments and other religious institutions when kept separate from the central state budget.

[b]Per capita computation using the total population of the country, including non-Muslims

TABLE 3. State expenditures on Islamic education as a percentage of total state religious expenditures

Year	State expenditures on Islamic education in modern schools[a] as a % of total state religious expenditures				State expenditures on specialized Islamic tracks[b] and on Islamic education in modern schools as a % of total state religious expenditures			
	Egypt	Tunisia	Turkey	Morocco	Egypt	Tunisia	Turkey	Morocco
1865								
1870								
1875								
1880		1%				7%		
1885								
1890		5%				10%		
1895		5%				14%		
1900	3%	4%			14%	13%		
1905	4%	4%			14%	16%		
1910	7%	7%			29%	13%		
1915	11%	14%		6%	33%	27%		20%
1920	15%	8%		10%	48%	16%		23%
1925	25%	26%	22%	13%	55%	39%	25%	23%
1930	23%	26%	14%	25%	44%	39%	14%	35%
1935	42%	26%	4%	24%	61%	47%	4%	34%
1940	37%	24%	0%	20%	59%	56%	0%	29%
1945	38%	26%	0%	36%	62%	52%	0%	46%
1950	33%	22%	23%	64%	61%	63%	24%	75%
1955	33%	20%	18%	64%	68%	62%	20%	72%
1960	37%	50%	16%	79%	71%	81%	17%	90%
1965	30%	59%	22%	68%	64%	63%	27%	88%
1970	39%	68%	15%	75%	72%	73%	25%	86%
1975	35%	80%	15%	77%	68%	83%	23%	89%
1980		75%	15%	76%		78%	37%	89%
1985	29%	72%	24%	77%	77%	75%	44%	96%
1990	27%	69%	22%	73%	79%	72%	39%	94%
1995		69%	21%	75%		70%	46%	95%
2000		69%	31%	74%		70%	41%	95%
2005	21%	70%	32%	68%	70%	72%	38%	86%
2010	19%	67%	28%	58%	71%	69%	37%	71%
2015	18%	61%	19%	48%	67%	64%	52%	60%
2020	16%	63%	20%	46%	66%	66%	59%	61%

Note: State religious expenditures (Islamic worship, sharia justice, Islamic education, and Islamic public assistance) include direct religious expenditures from the central state budget (including an estimation, based on the fraction of the curriculum it represents, of state expenditures on Islamic instruction dispensed in modern schools) as well as the expenditures of the administration of state-managed public religious endowments and other religious institutions when kept separate from the central state budget (excluding expenditures devoted to the operations of their revenue-generating assets when applicable). See the data appendix for sources, fiscal and calendar years alignment, and more details.

[a] "Modern schools" designates schools established in the modern period for the primary purpose of teaching imported European knowledge.

[b] "Specialized Islamic tracks" designates madrasas (or modern incarnations thereof), the institutions whose primary purpose is the teaching of the Islamic sciences.

TABLE 4a. Muslim student enrollments (at all levels) in state or state-subsidized schools

	Muslim students (at all levels[a]) in modern schools or specialized Islamic tracks per 1mm total population[b]				Muslim students (at all levels[a]) in specialized Islamic tracks per 1mm total population[b]				% of Muslim student enrollments (at all levels[a]) specialized Islamic tracks represent			
Year	Egypt	Tunisia	Turkey	Morocco	Egypt	Tunisia	Turkey	Morocco	Egypt	Tunisia	Turkey	Morocco
1865	917	398			588	398			64.1%	100.0%		
1870	1,582	321			1,308	321			82.7%	100.0%		
1875	2,516	390			2,066	390			82.1%	100.0%		
1880	2,243	733			1,726	617			76.9%	84.2%		
1885	2,488	660			1,617	431			65.0%	65.4%		
1890	1,992	1,673			1,466	450			73.6%	26.9%		
1895	2,453	2,860			1,421	549			57.9%	19.2%		
1900	3,075	2,938			1,492	563			48.5%	19.1%		
1905	11,214	2,252			1,434	477			12.8%	21.2%		
1910	19,436	4,118			1,194	558			6.1%	13.6%		
1915	25,860	9,299		514	1,237	551		123	4.8%	5.9%		24.0%
1920		6,952		759	1,140	720		97		10.4%		12.7%
1925	28,043	11,762	29,588	1,389	793	779	124	184	2.8%	6.6%	0.4%	13.2%
1930	40,747	15,902	34,753	2,120	660	1,039	12	148	1.6%	6.5%	0.0%	7.0%
1935	59,022	19,908	45,130	3,044	685	1,776	-	168	1.2%	8.9%	0.0%	5.5%
1940	71,621	22,449	59,950	4,034	810	2,059	-	146	1.1%	9.2%	0.0%	3.6%
1945	59,276	19,022	75,792	5,694	754	1,828	-	250	1.3%	9.6%	0.0%	4.4%
1950	59,615	32,649	85,212	13,241	744	2,690	4	317	1.2%	8.2%	0.0%	2.4%

(*continued*)

TABLE 4a. *(continued)*

	Muslim students (at all levels[a]) in modern schools or specialized Islamic tracks per 1mm total population[b]				Muslim students (at all levels[a]) in specialized Islamic tracks per 1mm total population[b]				% of Muslim student enrollments (at all levels[a]) specialized Islamic tracks represent			
Year	Egypt	Tunisia	Turkey	Morocco	Egypt	Tunisia	Turkey	Morocco	Egypt	Tunisia	Turkey	Morocco
1955	82,390	53,383	89,795	22,930	1,348	2,979	86	523	1.6%	5.6%	0.1%	2.3%
1960	103,557	97,819	109,081	55,514	1,508	1,473	155	1,389	1.5%	1.5%	0.1%	2.5%
1965	136,120	164,217	143,092	85,008	2,473	239	386	2,351	1.8%	0.1%	0.3%	2.8%
1970	147,638	215,449	177,024	87,948	2,675	244	1,277	943	1.8%	0.1%	0.7%	1.1%
1975	164,360	196,334	183,187	102,746	3,467	158	1,291	794	2.1%	0.1%	0.7%	0.8%
1980	174,359	206,576	183,761	144,636	8,410	221	4,169	1,077	4.8%	0.1%	2.3%	0.7%
1985	187,492	232,118	194,054	158,540	8,316	350	4,745	1,482	4.4%	0.2%	2.4%	0.9%
1990	202,462	238,015	200,386	149,901	13,982	391	5,211	1,253	6.9%	0.2%	2.6%	0.8%
1995	223,584	253,188	195,363	166,145	18,890	137	7,901	1,251	8.4%	0.1%	4.0%	0.8%
2000	230,074	266,524	205,828	182,797	21,573	92	2,225	1,262	9.4%	0.0%	1.1%	0.7%
2005	221,411	260,796	218,249	194,821	24,300	120	1,443	1,244	11.0%	0.0%	0.7%	0.6%
2010	210,842	225,626	243,003	186,279	26,296	152	2,802	1,196	12.5%	0.1%	1.2%	0.6%
2015	207,048	203,536	270,586	190,645	21,678	222	13,914	1,606	10.5%	0.1%	5.1%	0.8%
2020	216,602	202,010	277,295	199,247	18,284	220	17,378	1,803	8.4%	0.1%	6.3%	0.9%

Note: "Modern schools" designates schools established in the modern period for the primary purpose of teaching imported European knowledge. "Specialized Islamic tracks" designates madrasas (or modern incarnations thereof), the institutions whose primary purpose is the teaching of the Islamic sciences. They include in Egypt, the al-Azhar system (primary and secondary Institutes and al-Azhar University without its modern faculties); in Tunisia, the Zaytuna system; in Turkey, the Imam-Hatip schools, the Islamic Higher Institutes, and the Ilahiyat Faculties; in Morocco, the Qarawiyin system, "original schooling (*ta ʿlīm aṣlī*)," and Islamic Studies departments in modern universities. See the data appendix for sources and more details.

[a] "All levels" = primary, secondary, and undergraduate higher education, excluding preschools [b] Total population of the country, including non-Muslims

TABLE 4b. Muslim student enrollments in higher education in state or state-subsidized schools

Year	Muslim students (in higher ed[a]) in modern schools or specialized Islamic tracks per 1mm total population[b]				Muslim students (in higher ed[a]) in specialized Islamic tracks per 1mm total population[b]				% of Muslim student enrollments (in higher ed[a]) specialized Islamic tracks represent			
	Egypt	Tunisia	Turkey	Morocco	Egypt	Tunisia	Turkey	Morocco	Egypt	Tunisia	Turkey	Morocco
1865	44	19			38	19			87.0%	100.0%		
1870	104	15			85	15			82.0%	100.0%		
1875	161	19			135	19			83.8%	100.0%		
1880	148	29			113	29			76.0%	100.0%		
1885	143	21			106	21			74.0%	100.0%		
1890	128	21			96	21			75.0%	100.0%		
1895	127	26			93	26			72.9%	100.0%		
1900	121	27			98	27			80.9%	100.0%		
1905	135	23			94	23			69.2%	100.0%		
1910	158	27			78	27			49.4%	100.0%		
1915	189	89		3	86	26		3	45.4%	29.4%		100.0%
1920	177	81		2	74	32		2	41.7%	39.2%		100.0%
1925	279	120	249	5	103	36	20	4	36.9%	29.9%	8.2%	87.2%
1930	311	102	250	5	71	28	2	4	22.8%	27.9%	1.0%	79.0%
1935	409	170	416	6	87	70	-	4	21.3%	41.1%	0.0%	71.2%
1940	560	182	692	6	156	92	-	4	27.9%	50.5%	0.0%	55.2%
1945	706	261	1,049	12	146	73	-	6	20.7%	27.9%	0.0%	52.0%
1950	1,066	270	1,216	21	128	95	4	8	12.0%	35.1%	0.3%	36.1%

(continued)

TABLE 4b. (*continued*)

Year	Muslim students (in higher ed[a]) in modern schools or specialized Islamic tracks per 1mm total population[b]				Muslim students (in higher ed[a]) in specialized Islamic tracks per 1mm total population[b]				% of Muslim student enrollments (in higher ed[a]) specialized Islamic tracks represent			
	Egypt	Tunisia	Turkey	Morocco	Egypt	Tunisia	Turkey	Morocco	Egypt	Tunisia	Turkey	Morocco
1955	2,005	314	1,196	30	150	146	2	10	7.5%	46.5%	0.2%	33.7%
1960	3,188	359	1,977	157	190	91	6	16	5.9%	25.4%	0.3%	10.1%
1965	4,489	1,751	2,701	597	240	128	35	27	5.3%	7.3%	1.3%	4.6%
1970	5,150	2,517	4,211	829	268	185	63	55	5.2%	7.3%	1.5%	6.7%
1975	9,181	2,422	6,638	1,948	575	91	54	45	6.3%	3.7%	0.8%	2.3%
1980	11,357	4,801	6,120	4,838	729	139	138	182	6.4%	2.9%	2.3%	3.8%
1985	13,017	5,405	7,989	7,014	1,665	294	151	545	12.8%	5.4%	1.9%	7.8%
1990	9,517	7,777	11,627	8,315	1,111	343	113	765	11.7%	4.4%	1.0%	9.2%
1995	10,923	11,618	18,113	9,462	1,342	137	159	749	12.3%	1.2%	0.9%	7.9%
2000	18,926	19,120	21,232	9,232	1,972	92	224	847	10.4%	0.5%	1.1%	9.2%
2005	24,211	31,453	27,594	9,752	3,378	120	86	697	14.0%	0.4%	0.3%	7.2%
2010	23,346	33,352	43,692	9,371	2,787	152	190	625	11.9%	0.5%	0.4%	6.7%
2015	20,787	25,719	69,255	19,582	2,273	222	975	1,154	10.9%	0.9%	1.4%	5.9%
2020	23,081	20,100	86,583	24,638	2,454	220	1,450	1,396	10.6%	1.1%	1.7%	5.7%

Note: "Modern schools" designates schools established in the modern period for the primary purpose of teaching imported European knowledge. "Specialized Islamic tracks" designates madrasas (or modern incarnations thereof), the institutions whose primary purpose is the teaching of the Islamic sciences. At the higher education level, they include in Egypt, al-Azhar University without its modern faculties; in Tunisia, the Zaytuna University; in Turkey, the Islamic Higher Institutes and Ilahiyat Faculties; in Morocco, the Qarawiyin University system and Islamic Studies departments in modern universities. See the data appendix for sources and more details.

[a] "Higher ed" = undergraduate level higher education [b] Total population of the country, including non-Muslims

TABLE 4C. Percentage of hours of Islamic education in state or state-subsidized schools

	% of school hours Islamic education represents for Muslim students[a] in modern schools (at all levels[b])				% of school hours Islamic education represents for Muslim students[a] in modern schools and specialized Islamic tracks combined (at all levels[b])			
Year	Egypt	Tunisia	Turkey	Morocco	Egypt	Tunisia	Turkey	Morocco
1865	13.9%				40.4%	31.4%		
1870	8.9%				44.9%	31.4%		
1875	7.1%				44.5%	31.4%		
1880	7.0%	46.2%			42.5%	33.9%		
1885	7.8%	24.3%			38.1%	28.8%		
1890	6.9%	24.3%			41.2%	26.1%		
1895	20.4%	24.3%			39.6%	25.6%		
1900	36.7%	24.3%			44.2%	30.2%		
1905	39.6%	24.1%			41.3%	30.7%		
1910	40.9%	23.8%			41.6%	27.9%		
1915	40.3%	11.0%		16.7%	40.8%	13.0%		20.8%
1920		11.1%		16.7%		14.5%		18.8%
1925	24.5%	11.0%	5.5%	17.3%	25.3%	13.2%	5.6%	19.5%
1930	15.4%	11.1%	2.1%	17.0%	15.8%	13.4%	2.1%	18.2%
1935	31.1%	11.1%	0.3%	17.1%	31.1%	14.2%	0.3%	18.0%
1940	16.9%	11.4%	0.0%	17.1%	17.2%	14.5%	0.0%	17.7%
1945	14.3%	11.3%	0.0%	17.9%	14.6%	14.6%	0.0%	18.6%
1950	5.0%	8.4%	1.4%	17.4%	5.5%	11.4%	1.4%	17.8%
1955	7.4%	7.0%	1.3%	16.8%	7.8%	8.2%	1.4%	17.2%
1960	7.6%	4.5%	1.5%	19.6%	8.0%	5.0%	1.6%	19.9%
1965	7.4%	4.6%	1.5%	18.9%	8.0%	4.7%	1.6%	19.3%
1970	8.3%	3.8%	1.6%	18.1%	8.9%	3.9%	1.9%	18.2%
1975	8.0%	7.3%	1.6%	13.4%	8.7%	7.3%	1.9%	13.5%
1980	7.8%	7.1%	2.0%	12.3%	10.3%	7.1%	2.7%	12.4%
1985	7.6%	6.9%	3.7%	11.5%	10.2%	6.9%	4.4%	11.7%
1990	7.4%	6.3%	3.7%	9.1%	11.8%	6.4%	4.4%	9.3%
1995	7.6%	5.1%	3.6%	9.4%	13.2%	5.1%	4.6%	9.6%
2000	7.1%	4.7%	3.9%	9.5%	12.8%	4.7%	4.2%	9.8%
2005	6.2%	4.4%	3.8%	8.9%	10.5%	4.4%	4.0%	9.1%
2010	6.2%	3.3%	3.5%	9.0%	11.0%	3.3%	3.9%	9.2%
2015	6.1%	3.4%	3.1%	8.4%	10.1%	3.4%	4.5%	8.7%
2020	6.2%	3.6%	3.4%	7.9%	9.5%	3.7%	4.9%	8.2%

Note: "Modern schools" designates schools established in the modern period for the primary purpose of teaching imported European knowledge. "Specialized Islamic tracks" designates madrasas (or modern incarnations thereof), the institutions whose primary purpose is the teaching of the Islamic sciences. They include in Egypt, the al-Azhar system (primary and secondary Institutes and al-Azhar University without its modern faculties); in Tunisia, the Zaytuna system; in Turkey, the Imam-Hatip schools, the Islamic Higher Institutes, and the Ilahiyat Faculties; in Morocco, the Qarawiyin system, "original schooling (*ta 'līm aṣlī*)," and Islamic Studies departments in modern universities. See the data appendix for sources and more details.

[a] % computed using the aggregate number of hours of instruction dispensed to Muslim students

[b] "All levels" = primary, secondary, and undergraduate higher education, excluding preschools

TABLE 4d. Annual Islamic education hours dispensed in state or state-subsidized schools per capita and the share dispensed in modern schools

	Total annual Islamic education hours dispensed (in modern schools and specialized Islamic tracks combined) per capita[a] (at all levels[b])				Modern schools' share of total annual Islamic education hours dispensed (at all levels[b])			
Year	Egypt	Tunisia	Turkey	Morocco	Egypt	Tunisia	Turkey	Morocco
1865	0.4	0.1			9.8%	0.0%		
1870	0.8	0.1			2.8%	0.0%		
1875	1.2	0.1			2.3%	0.0%		
1880	1.0	0.2			3.2%	23.1%		
1885	1.0	0.2			6.1%	30.9%		
1890	0.9	0.5			3.7%	69.7%		
1895	1.0	0.8			19.0%	78.1%		
1900	1.4	0.9			39.0%	66.1%		
1905	4.5	0.7			81.3%	63.0%		
1910	8.5	1.2			91.9%	74.6%		
1915	11.1	1.3		0.1	93.6%	79.9%		61.1%
1920		1.1		0.2		68.9%		77.2%
1925	7.2	1.7	1.7	0.3	93.7%	78.3%	97.7%	77.3%
1930	4.9	2.3	0.7	0.4	94.7%	78.2%	99.4%	87.2%
1935	13.4	3.0	0.1	0.6	98.0%	71.9%	100.0%	89.7%
1940	8.9	3.5	0.0	0.8	96.4%	71.7%	–	93.1%
1945	7.7	3.0	0.0	1.1	96.2%	70.6%	–	92.0%
1950	3.2	4.0	1.1	2.5	90.7%	67.8%	99.8%	95.4%
1955	6.2	4.7	1.2	4.2	92.8%	81.0%	97.7%	95.5%
1960	8.0	3.9	1.6	11.9	93.4%	88.7%	97.3%	95.8%
1965	10.5	6.2	2.2	17.7	90.9%	99.0%	94.5%	95.2%
1970	11.0	7.8	3.2	17.3	90.8%	99.1%	87.6%	98.0%
1975	12.4	13.4	3.4	15.0	89.4%	99.7%	85.9%	98.0%
1980	16.0	13.8	4.9	19.5	69.8%	99.6%	72.2%	97.9%
1985	17.3	15.3	8.4	20.2	69.6%	99.3%	81.6%	96.9%
1990	22.0	14.6	8.7	14.8	56.7%	99.2%	82.6%	96.6%
1995	27.0	12.9	9.2	16.7	50.1%	99.7%	74.5%	97.1%
2000	27.3	13.0	8.9	18.7	47.6%	99.8%	91.3%	97.2%
2005	24.5	11.8	8.9	18.3	51.0%	99.7%	94.4%	97.3%
2010	24.8	7.7	9.7	18.2	47.2%	99.4%	90.0%	97.4%
2015	22.3	7.1	12.7	17.6	52.5%	99.1%	65.3%	95.9%
2020	21.5	7.3	14.6	18.3	58.5%	99.1%	63.9%	95.4%

Note: "Modern schools" designates schools established in the modern period for the primary purpose of teaching imported European knowledge. "Specialized Islamic tracks" designates madrasas (or modern incarnations thereof), the institutions whose primary purpose is the teaching of the Islamic sciences. They include in Egypt, the al-Azhar system (primary and secondary Institutes and al-Azhar University without its modern faculties); in Tunisia, the Zaytuna system; in Turkey, the Imam-Hatip schools, the Islamic Higher Institutes, and the Ilahiyat Faculties; in Morocco, the Qarawiyin system, "original schooling (*ta ʿlīm aṣlī*)," and Islamic Studies departments in modern universities. See the data appendix for sources and more details.

[a] Islamic education dispensed in modern schools and specialized Islamic tracks combined, per capita of the total population of the country, including non-Muslims, rather than the student population

[b] "All levels" = primary, secondary, and undergraduate higher education, excluding preschools

TABLE 5. A tenth-century Abbasid court "model" budget

	% of total expenditures	% of religious expenditures
Religious expenditures	**1.2%**	**100%**
Worship	0.6%	47%
Justice	0.2%	19%
Charity/Assistance	0.4%	34%
Religious expenditures - budget items		**100%**
Qāḍī, his deputy, their sons, and ten fuqahā' [§34]		19%
Two Friday mosques' personnel and equipment [§35]		4%
Men of religion (Hashimids and Friday preachers) [§30]		23%
Qur'an readers and muezzins (palace) [part of §6]		15%
Ritual ablutions (pageantry and caliph) [part of §10 and §11]		5%
Alms (*ṣadaqa*) to women in need [§26]		17%
Hospital (charity) [§38]		17%
Other expenditures - budget items	**98.8%**	
Military [§1–5; §8; §12]	72.4%	
Public security (police, prison, gatekeepers) [§7; §36]	1.4%	
Public infrastructure (2 bridges) [§37]	0.1%	
Administration [§33]	2.2%	
Vizier and son [§32]	0.7%	
Caliph's family [§27–29; §31]	1.4%	
Pageantry [part of §10]	1.4%	
Harem [§14]	1.4%	
Health (physicians and drugs) [§22]	0.3%	
Entertainers [§21]	0.6%	
Personnel and servants [part of §6; §13; §18; §20; §23–24]	4.6%	
Kitchens, water distribution, and lighting [§9; part of §11; §17; §19; §25]	5.4%	
Animals (buying and upkeep) [§15–16]	6.7%	

Note: Data from Hilāl Ibn al-Muḥassin Al-Ṣābī (970–1056), *Al-Wuzarā', Aw, Tuḥfat Al-Umarā' fī Tārīkh Al-Wuzarā'*, in (Al-Ṣābī 1958, 15–27). For each budget item, the budget's paragraph number is indicated in brackets. I estimated the palace Qur'an readers and muezzins at 2/17 of the figure given in §6, the pageantry ritual ablutions at 1/24 of the figure given in §10, and the caliph ritual ablutions at 1/9 of the figure given in §11. Percentages might not add up to 100 due to rounding.

TABLE 6. Direct state religious expenditures in the Regency of Tunis, central state budget (1730–31)

	Religious expenditures						Worship expenditures				
	Total	Justice	Charity/ Assistance	Education	ʿUlamā[a]	**Worship**	Worship personnel	Worship equipment	Muslim holidays	Mecca pilgrimage	Holy cities (Ḥaramayn)
% of total central state expenditures	**2.7%**	0.03%	0.08%	0.11%	0.36%	**2.1%**	0.18%	0.25%	1.44%	0.03%	0.20%
% of total central state budget lines	**10.9%**	0.14%	3.14%	0.57%	0.82%	**6.3%**	1.64%	0.76%	3.55%	0.30%	0.03%
% of religious expenditures	**100%**	1.1%	3.1%	4.2%	13.3%	**78.3%**	6.8%	9.4%	53.6%	1.2%	7.3%
% of religious budget lines	**100%**	1.2%	28.7%	5.2%	7.5%	**57.4%**	15.0%	7.0%	32.4%	2.7%	0.2%

Note: Data from ANT, Register #11 (3,663 budget lines). Total central state expenditures include those of Dār al-Bāsha (47% of the total) for which we do not have details but which include some religious items (e.g., Hanafi Ottoman men of religion) not counted in this table. Military expenditures represented about 70% of the total budget. I estimate that total central state expenditures amounted to about 10 purchasing power parity (PPP) adjusted 1990 US dollars per capita, and represented about 2% of GDP (see the data appendix for sources and more details). Percentages might not add up to 100 due to rounding.

[a]ʿUlamā whose function is not specified in the budget

TABLE 7. Tunis Friday mosques and madrasas, and percentage founded by state actors

Period	Friday Mosques & Madrasas	Friday Mosques	Madrasas
All observations	**55 (64%)**	**18 (67%)**	**37 (62%)**
Umayyads (670–750)	1 (100%)	1 (100%)	0 (0%)
Hafsids (1229–1574)	15 (53%)	7 (57%)	8 (50%)
Ottoman deys (1591–1637)	6 (50%)	3 (67%)	3 (33%)
Ottoman Muradid beys (1637–1705)	4 (100%)	2 (100%)	2 (100%)
Ottoman Husaynid beys (1705–1881)	19 (84%)	2 (100%)	17 (82%)
French protectorate (1881–1956)	10 (30%)	3 (33%)	7 (29%)

Note: Number of Friday mosques and madrasas in existence in 1939 founded in each period (% founded by state actors in parentheses). Data from Muḥammad Ibn al-Khūja, *Tārīkh Ma ʿālim al-Tawḥīd*, Tūnis, 1939.

TABLE 8. Prevalence of a state-preferred religion in the world and of Islamic constitutional clauses in Muslim-majority polities (2010)

	Number of polities in sample	Total population (in millions)	State-preferred religion		Constitutional Islamic establishment clause		Constitutional Islamic source of law or repugnancy clause	
			% of polities	% of the population	% of polities	% of the population	% of polities	% of the population
All polities	**183**	**6,900**	**52%**	**48%**	**N/A**	**N/A**	**N/A**	**N/A**
Non-Muslim-majority polities	132	5,600	45%	39%	N/A	N/A	N/A	N/A
Muslim-majority polities	51	1,300	71%	88%	57%	58%	49%	47%
Non–Middle Eastern Muslim-majority polities	30	850	52%	82%	38%	47%	28%	33%
Middle Eastern Muslim-majority polities	21	450	95%	99%	82%	78%	77%	74%

Note: Polities with a state-preferred religion (i.e., with an "Official Support" variable named SBX larger than or equal to 8 as of 2010) according to the Religion and State Project, Round 3. Jonathan Fox, Religion and State dataset, http://www.religionandstate.org, Fox (2008, 2011, 2015). Population data (rounded) from the Pew Research Center and the World Bank.

DATA APPENDIX

General Remarks

I ESTIMATE STATE religious expenditures from central state budgets (and their annexed budgets) as well as from the budgets of important state religious institutions such as the administration(s) of public religious endowments (e.g., the Waqfs Administration in Egypt,[1] the Djemaia in Tunisia,[2] or the *Ḥabūs* Administration in Morocco[3]) and institutions of Islamic learning (such

1. It was called an "administration" (*dīwān* or *niẓāra*) or a "ministry" (*wizāra*), with vacillations that accompanied its recurrent reorganizations in the nineteenth century. The budgets published in the late 1890s in *Al-Waqā'i' al-Miṣrīya* called it *Maṣlaḥat 'Umūm al-Awqāf.* With the law of November 20, 1913, it became a "ministry," and it was stated that it would "retain its autonomy" and that its budget would be "independent." See Sékaly (1929, part 1). For convenience, I often call it the Waqfs Administration even if it was a ministry. There were separate Waqfs Ministry budgets in *Al-Waqā'i' al-Miṣrīya* until 1958–59, after which they became part of the state budget.

2. *Jam'īyat al-Awqāf* or *Jam'īyat al-Aḥbās* (commonly transliterated into "Djemaia"). After the Djemaia's liquidation in 1956, its religious expenditures were transferred to the state budget. In replacement, a state Office of Religious Worship (*Maṣlaḥat al-Sha'ā'ir al-Dīnīya*), perhaps a translation of the French *Bureau des Cultes*, was created in 1956 and put under the purview of the prime minister (or Président du Conseil at the time), except for a brief hiatus, in 1987, when it was put under the Ministry of Interior. It took the name of Office of Worship Affairs (*Idārat Shu'ūn al-Sha'ā'ir*) in 1967, Office of Religious Affairs (*Idārat al-Shu'ūn al-Dīnīya*) in 1970, State Secretary of Religious Affairs (*Kitābat al-Dawla li-l-Shu'ūn al-Dīnīya*) in 1989, before becoming the Ministry of Religious Affairs (*Wizārat al-Shu'ūn al-Dīnīya*) in 1991.

3. From the first years of the French protectorate, the *Ḥabūs* Administration (*Idārat al-Aḥbas al-'Umūmīya*) was overseen by the Ministry of *Ḥabūs* (*wizāra*, or *vizirat* in French). We find the expenditures of the Ministry of *Ḥabūs* (called Ministry of Waqfs after 1958, and Ministry of Waqfs and Islamic Affairs after 1965) in the state budget, which reports expenditures on high-level administrative personnel of the ministry as well as on some religious expenditures (generally in the form of subsidies) that increased over time. There is also a separate budget (later called the Waqfs "specific" budget, or *al-Mīzānīya al-khaṣṣa li-l-awqāf*) for the *Ḥabūs* Administration that contains expenditures on the management of its revenue-generating properties as

as the al-Azhar[4] and Zaytuna[5] systems in Egypt and Tunisia, respectively), when their budgets are kept separate from that of the central state budget. I include in total state expenditures the expenditures devoted to operating, maintaining, and managing the waqfs' revenue-generating assets, but I exclude them from my estimate of state religious expenditures since they are not devoted to public religious provisions. I generally omit local governments' expenditures when not included in central state budgets (with the notable exceptions of Egypt's Provincial Councils and Turkey's local administrations mentioned below). They are typically an order of magnitude smaller than central state expenditures for the period under study. I also omit the expenditures of the Bayt al-Mal (a fund with a definite religious character constituted by the revenues of the *jizya* when it was in force, along with some religious endowments and unclaimed inheritances of Muslims), which, despite their symbolic importance, were comparatively small. Also, earlier in my dataset, some public waqfs might not have been included in the central Waqfs Administrations' accounts I examined, due, for instance, to unfinished centralization.

I ascribe state religious expenditures to four fixed categories in my analysis: worship, sharia justice, Islamic education (in modern schools as well as in specialized Islamic tracks, defined below), and public works and assistance (when under the purview of the waqfs), although their aims can overlap. For instance, I generally count payments to descendants of the Prophet as worship, unless they are explicitly labeled as public assistance. Also, I count as expenditures on Islamic education the entire al-Azhar budget in Egypt (excluding expenditures devoted to its modern faculties) although, besides al-Azhar University and Institutes, this budget also sustains other activities (notably since

---

well as on religious expenditures such as worship, Islamic education, and public assistance (which were eventually dwarfed by those of the ministry). From 1962 to 1965 there were two ministries, a Ministry of Waqfs and a Ministry of Islamic Affairs, which were subsequently merged.

4. Al-Azhar had a separate budget until 1961, when it was integrated into the state budget after the reform law of 1961. It was published in *Al-Waqāʾiʿ al-Miṣrīya* starting in 1927, with its extrabudgetary revenues starting only in 1931–1932.

5. The Zaytuna Grand Mosque had a separate budget from that of the Djemaia until 1904 (and so did the foundations for the Ḥaramayn, the Qur'an reciters, and the muezzins). It was then included in the Djemaia's budget until 1947, and then had its own budget, annexed to that of the central state, until shortly after independence. From 1960 onward, its expenditures were either entirely, or almost entirely from 1970 onward, subsumed under those of the University of Tunis. It was only in 2015, after the Arab Spring, that the published state budget listed all the expenditures of the Zaytuna University.

al-Azhar, like other madrasas such as the Zaytuna and the Qarawiyin, is also a mosque). On the religious vs. nonreligious distinction, I count as religious the expenditures devoted to, say, hospitals when they are run by waqfs administrations but as nonreligious when they are run by ministries of health.

To estimate the state expenditures devoted to Islamic instruction in modern schools, I multiply the aggregate expenditures devoted to modern schools in the state budget by (1) the fraction of the Muslim students' curriculum dedicated to Islamic education and (2) the percentage of total school enrollments Muslim students represent. When possible, I estimate separately the expenditures incurred in different levels of schooling or types of school, which might have a different cost structure, or might only receive subsidies. I also strive to subtract user fees such as the tuition that might be paid by students in public schools. To estimate state expenditures devoted to specialized Islamic tracks when they do not have their own budget or their own line in the state budget, I multiply the aggregate expenditures devoted to education in the state budget by the percentage their enrollments constitute, distinguishing secondary and higher education (which generally costs more per student) from other levels, when possible.

For each of the countries under examination (Egypt, Tunisia, Turkey, and Morocco), I used or consulted detailed annual central state budgets, often several hundred pages each. I generally use provisional, as opposed to realized, budgets (except for Turkey). I include recurrent expenditures as well as nonrecurrent ones (such as capital expenditures), debt service expenditures (including those handled by an administration whose budget might not be included in that of the central state, such as, in the early years of my dataset, the Commission Financière in Tunisia, or the Administration de la Dette Marocaine in Morocco), public social security expenditures (including those kept out of the central state budget), and any other expenditure included in or annexed to the state budget. I strive to avoid double counting expenditures by identifying gross transfers from one part of the budget to another. While fiscal years vary from country to country and year to year, I use, when possible, the budget for the fiscal year with the largest overlap with the calendar year displayed in tables 1, 2, and 3 (see exceptions below). When the fiscal year of the Waqfs Administration does not coincide with that of the central state budget, I use the fiscal year with the greatest overlap. Given the challenge of finding detailed budgets for every year, whenever necessary, I simply interpolated between the closest available years or displayed figures for the closest year available (see below).

More work could be done to improve the precision of my estimates of aggregate religious and nonreligious state expenditures and their comparability over time and from country to country. Moreover, there is great uncertainty around GDP and price level estimates for the more distant past as well as for recent years[6] (since new economic activities might not be immediately accounted for and since data commonly used for international comparisons rely on National Accounts figures produced by governmental statistical offices and constitute a political stake). Hence, the estimates I rely on for the quantities and the ratios displayed in tables 1, 2, and 3 might not allow for too fine-grained comparisons. However, they allow me to accurately capture the gist of the broad trends, country-to-country differences, and historical fluctuations analyzed in chapter 5.

For enrollments and hours of instruction, I only include schools that are administered by any part of the state (including local governments such as the Provincial Councils in Egypt), whether the state funds them entirely or only in part, and those that are state-subsidized. For instance, I do not consider Qur'anic schools (*kuttābs*) in Tunisia, although they were (lightly) regulated by the state. Few *ḥabūs* were generally devoted to them, families generally directly paid the teachers (*mu'addibs*), and the timid attempts that were made to modernize them and include them in a project of public schooling during the French protectorate failed. However, in Egypt, I do consider the Qur'anic schools that were modernized and put under the purview of the Ministry of Education in the late nineteenth century (and also later under the purview of the Provincial Councils) or subsidized in exchange for accepting governmental inspection and adhering to some standards. These schools were initially labeled *kuttābs* in official statistics, sometimes *maktabs*, and later elementary schools (*madāris awwalīya*). I also consider the "compulsory elementary schools" (*madāris ilzāmīya*) established after the 1923 Constitution made elementary school compulsory for boys and girls, and which had a distinct (and shorter) schedule and curriculum. I strive to keep track of their enrollments separately for the purpose of computing aggregate hours of religious (and nonreligious) instruction. I also include the Écoles Coraniques Modernes (ECM) in Tunisia and the renovated *msids* in Morocco since they were, over time, subsidized by the state.

I call "modern schools" those established in the modern period for the primary purpose of teaching imported European knowledge (including traditional structures, such as Qur'anic schools, when they were repurposed to this end—e.g., elementary schools in Egypt and renovated *msids* in Morocco). I call "specialized Islamic tracks" the institutions whose primary purpose is the

6. Pamuk (2018, chapter 2).

teaching of the Islamic sciences, be it the madrasas or modern incarnations thereof (such as the Imam-Hatip schools in Turkey). Notwithstanding their difference of purpose, more often than not, religious subjects are taught in modern schools and nonreligious ones in madrasas. During the period under study, specialized Islamic tracks are as follows: in Turkey, the Imam-Hatip schools and, at the university level, the Islamic Higher Institutes and Ilahiyat Faculties; in Morocco, "original schooling" (*ta ʿlīm aṣlī*, also called *aṣīl*) at the primary and secondary level, the Islamic Centers in Tangiers, Meknes, and various other cities, the Qarawiyin in Fes (with its primary, secondary and higher levels), the Ibn Yusif madrasa in Marrakesh, the Qarawiyin University system (in Fes, Agadir, Tetouan, and Marrakesh), the Faculty of Sharia at Samara, Dar al-Hadith, and the Islamic Studies departments in modern universities; in Egypt, the al-Azhar system with its primary and secondary institutes and al-Azhar University, excluding its modern faculties; and in Tunisia, the Zaytuna system (pre-university and university levels). These were not the only Islamic institutions transmitting knowledge, although they were the largest in terms of enrollment. More research needs to be done to estimate enrollments in other madrasas, especially before the twentieth century. However, including them would not significantly alter the broad trends I analyze in chapter 5.

While the Turkish Statistical Institute (Turkstat) has produced a retrospective series of school enrollments by level of education in Turkey since 1923, constructing such series for more than a century in Egypt, Tunisia, and Morocco is challenging. It can be difficult to disaggregate levels of education, particularly for the indigenous Muslim population during the French protectorate in Morocco and Tunisia. In addition, available data can be messy for the period of transition to independence in Egypt, Tunisia, and Morocco. For earlier years, the definition of higher education in the sources is not always clear, especially in specialized Islamic tracks. I made assumptions and I explain them below when applicable. For years when data is missing, I generally interpolate using information from nearby years or related data for that year (such as the number of graduates). By convention, academic year n/n+1 is labeled as year n in tables 4a, 4b, 4c, and 4d. I have not included preschools in my enrollment estimates, nor doctoral programs in higher education, whenever a distinction was possible.

In Tunisia, Morocco, and Egypt the enrollment statistics I use provide a breakdown by religion only until the 1960s or the 1970s, and in Egypt only starting around 1900. I therefore made some coarse assumptions for the rest of the period displayed in tables 4a, 4b, 4c, and 4d (see below). While they prevent too granular comparisons, they are sufficient to estimate Muslim student enrollments and to grasp the gist of the broad trends, country-to-country differences, and historical fluctuations analyzed in chapter 5.

For curricula, I count as Islamic instruction subjects explicitly labeled as such (e.g., *tarbiya Islāmīya*) or religious subjects such as *ḥadīth, kalām, fiqh*, or *uṣūl al-fiqh*. Even when taught in madrasas, and although they are often understood as instruments for religious sciences, I do not count grammar, belles lettres, or general history as "religious." Finding curricula for modern schools and specialized Islamic tracks over more than a century for the four countries under study is challenging, especially for earlier years, and the data is often sparse. I have projected back my earliest observation when necessary, and I have assumed that curricula remained unchanged between observations. It is also important to note that official curricula are often aspirational, or guidelines that are not always fully implemented on the ground. They also sometimes confirm a reality that was in effect for some time or, on the contrary, they take some time to be implemented. As explained in chapter 5, in the earlier years of my dataset there might not be official curricula or instruction guidelines or, if they exist, they might not specify the number of hours of religious instruction with precision. In some cases, I relied on the number of classes taught or on the specialization of teachers, using official reports or anthropological observations. Although a comprehensive assessment of all curricular variations is unrealistic, this dataset captures the gist of the broad trends, country-to-country differences, and historical fluctuations in the quantity of Islamic instruction dispensed in Egypt, Tunisia, Morocco, and Turkey in the period under study.

Yearly Budgets (Central States, Public Waqfs, And Other Religious Institutions)

An Abbasid Court Budget in Hilal al-Sabi's Kitāb al-Wuzarāʾ

Busse (1967) analyzed this budget based on the Gotha manuscript #1756, also mentioned by Kremer (1887). Hilal al-Sabi's *Kitāb al-Wuzarāʾ* was edited and published in Arabic by Amedroz (1904). It was again edited and published in Al-Ṣābī (1958), using a manuscript from al-Azhar in Cairo. Although I used this printed edition for my analysis, I did not find differences of any consequence with Busse (1967). An incorrect sum therein of daily expenditures (6,981 dinars instead of 7,000 claimed by Hilal al-Sabi) seems to be due to Busse (1967) missing the fact that Hilal al-Sabi listed aggregate daily amounts for paragraphs 23 and 32 without adding the supplemental incomes he mentions (50 and 500 dinars, respectively) in his description of the monthly sums. Once the supplemental incomes are counted and converted into daily expenditures using a thirty-day month, I find that total daily expenditures add up to 6,999⅓ dinars.

Central State Budgets (Egypt)

I used select detailed provisional Egyptian state budgets from 1898 to 2020 published by the Ministry of Finance (see the bibliography under "Egypt") as well the budget laws in *Al-Waqāʾiʿ al-Miṣrīya* and *Al-Jarīda al-Rasmīya.* Since detailed budgetary information is challenging to locate for the period 1990–2005, I use the lower granularity annual budget laws published in *Al-Jarīda al-Rasmīya* to display total state expenditures as a percentage of GDP in table 1 for those years. For the period after fiscal year 2005–06, I use the annual Egyptian budgets published online by the Egyptian Ministry of Finance (http://www.mof.gov.eg). For fiscal years 1969–70, 1975, and 1980–81, I use the total state expenditures in El-Baradei (1986, 130) to correct for what appear to be unaccounted-for gross transfers in the budget laws of these years. A large part of state expenditures on education are incurred at the provincial level and not entirely included in the state budget in the early years of my dataset. For those years, I took them from *Statistique scolaire de l'Egypte* and *Annuaire statistique de l'Egypte.* I was unable to estimate state religious expenditures for 1980, 1995, and 2000 in tables 2 and 3. With some exceptions due to transitions from one time frame to the other, fiscal years have run from July 1 to June 30 since 1950, with a hiatus between 1973 and 1979 when they followed the calendar year. From 1915 to 1949 they ran from April 1 to March 31, and followed the calendar year before that. I generally display state expenditures for fiscal year n-1/n for year n in tables 1, 2, and 3. There are exceptions (either to maximize the overlap with the calendar year or because of data unavailability): 2005 (fiscal year 2005–06), 1990 (fiscal year 1988–89), 1980 (fiscal year 1980–81), 1945 (fiscal year 1945–46), 1920 (fiscal year 1920–21), 1930 (fiscal year 1930–31), 1925 (fiscal year 1925–26), and 1915 (fiscal year 1915–16).

Central State Budgets (Tunisia)

For my incursion into eighteenth-century Tunisian state expenditures, I analyze in detail a 1730–31 register of central state revenues and expenditures (ANT, Register #11). For aggregate state revenues and expenditures in 1800 and 1850, I used figures in Chater (1984). For the year 1880, I used MAE, *Mémoires et documents,*

Tunis, Documents financiers (1868–1882), and I added the debt service expenditures handled by the International Financial Commission (*Commission Financière Internationale*) at the time. For the years 1884 to 1899, I used realized budgets from Régence de Tunis (1903). For 1900 onward, I used select published detailed provisional Tunisian state budgets: Régence de Tunis, Protectorat Français (1901 to 1956–57), and République Tunisienne (1957–58 to 2020). When I could not find a detailed budget, I used the less granular provisional budget laws in *Al-Rāʾid al-Tūnisī* and *Al-Rāʾid al-Rasmī li-l-Jumhūrīya al-Tūnisīya*, in combination with the more granular budgetary information I was able to locate regarding administrations of interest for my estimates. For the 2008–2016 period, I used the detailed budgetary data of the World Bank BOOST initiative.[7] Also, thanks to the important efforts of the civil society organization Al-Bawsala, post-2011 detailed state budgets have been made available online.[8] I was unable to estimate state religious expenditures for 1885 in tables 2 and 3. With some exceptions due to transitions from one time frame to the other, fiscal years ran from mid-October to mid-October before 1892, and then followed the calendar year except for 1931, 1932, and 1949 to 1960, when they ran from April 1 to March 31. I display state expenditures for the fiscal year with the largest overlap with the year shown in tables 1, 2, and 3, except for 1880 (fiscal year 1880–81), 1915 (fiscal year 1914), 1960 (fiscal year 1959), 1975 (fiscal year 1974), and 1985 (fiscal year 1984).

Central State Budgets (Turkey)

I used the realized state budgets provided by Turkey's Ministry of Finances from 1924 to 2020,[9] as well as the annual state budget laws published in the *Resmî Gazete*. I also used or consulted *1999–2023 Genel Devlet Toplam Gelir ve Harcamaları*,[10] *2011–2021 Yılları Sosyal Güvenlik Kurumları Bütçe Harcamaları*,[11] *1995–2017 Cari Fiyatlarla Sosyal Güvenlik Kuruluşları Gelir-Gider Dengesi*,[12] International Labour Office (1958–1995), and the OECD Social Expenditure Database (SOCX)[13] to estimate the expenditures of the public social security apparatus that are not in the state budget. I also include the contribution of local administrations to school expenditures listed in *İstatistik Yıllığı* for the period 1924–1950.

7. http://www.mizaniatouna.gov.tn.

8. http://www.finances.gov.tn.

9. https://www.hmb.gov.tr/bumko-butce-buyuklukleri-ve-butce-gerceklesmeleri.

10. https://www.sbb.gov.tr/yillar-bazinda-genel-devlet-istatistikleri.

11. https://muhasebat.hmb.gov.tr/sosyal-guvenlik-kurumlari-butce-istatistikleri.

12. https://www.sbb.gov.tr.

13. OECD.Stat.

Central State Budgets (Morocco)

I used select published detailed annual provisional Moroccan state budgets for the period 1914–15 to 2020: Empire Chérifien, Protectorat Français, *Budget de l'exercice* (from 1914–15 to 1956); Royaume du Maroc, *Budget de l'exercice* (1957 to 1963), *Loi de finances pour l'année* (from 1964 to 1972, and from 2007 to 2020). Since detailed budgetary information is difficult to locate for the period 1973–2007, for those years I used the less granular annual budget laws published in the *Bulletin officiel*. For 1915, I estimated the part of debt service expenditures handled by the Administration of the Moroccan Debt (*Administration de la Dette Marocaine*) from data in *Annuaire économique et financier du Maroc* of 1918–1919. Some earlier budgets do not include the revenues and expenditures of the Spanish-controlled zone, a small fraction of the overall budget. For figures displayed in Pesetas Hassani in early budgets, I use the conversion rate to francs found in the same budget. With some exceptions due to transitions from one time frame to the other, fiscal years followed the calendar year, except for 1913 to 1917 (May 1 to April 30), 1931 and 1932 (April 1 to March 31), and 1996 to 2000 (July 1 to June 30). I display state expenditures for the fiscal year with the largest overlap with the year shown in tables 1, 2, and 3, except for 1980 (fiscal year 1979) and 2000 (fiscal year 1999–2000).

Public Waqfs Budgets (Egypt)

I used annual public waqfs budgets (*Khayrī*, and *Ḥaramayn* when reported separately) for the period from 1926–27 to 1957–58 from *Al-Waqāʾiʿ al-Miṣrīya* and for 1958–59 from *Al-Jarīda al-Rasmīya*. After that, the budget of the Waqfs Ministry is included in the central state budget, as is the budget of the Waqfs' Organization (*Hayʾat al-Awqāf*), which manages the revenue-generating assets of the public waqfs. For select earlier years, I used or consulted *Al-Waqāʾiʿ al-Miṣrīya*; Sékaly (1929); Al-Ḥukūma al-Miṣrīya, Al-Jamʿīya al-Tashrīʿīya (1914); *Al-Ahrām*, March 18, 1916; House of Commons Parliamentary Papers, Reports by His Majesty's High Commissioner on the Finances (1920 and 1921); *Annuaire statistique de l'Egypte* (various years); and Al-Dawla al-Miṣrīya, Majlis al-Nuwwāb (1924–1952).

Al-Azhar Budgets (Egypt)

I used annual al-Azhar budgets from *Al-Waqāʾiʿ al-Miṣrīya* from 1927–28 to 1957–58, and from *Al-Jarīda al-Rasmīya* from 1958–59 to 1960–61. For the period 1924–1952, I also used the budgets of al-Azhar published in Al-Dawla al-Miṣrīya, Majlis al-Nuwwāb (1924–1952). For earlier years, I used or consulted Calame (1903), Bayram (1903), Majlis al-Azhar al-Aʿlā (1913, 1915, 1916–1917, 1918, 1919–1920), Lajnat Iṣlāḥ al-Azhar al-Maʿmūr (1910), Sékaly (1927–1928), Majlis al-Nuwwāb (1927), ʿInān (1958), Rajab (1946), Abū al-ʿUyūn (1949), and Khafājī (1954). When applicable, in the early years of my dataset, I added estimates of al-Azhar's extrabudgetary revenues and expenditures. After 1961, al-Azhar's budget is in the central state budget.

Public Waqfs Budgets (Tunisia)

I used the annual Djemaia budgets for Tunisia's public *ḥabūs* for the period 1875–1956 from ANT SC C26, D1-1 to D1-75, which also contain the budgets of the Zaytuna, the *Ḥaramayn,* the Qur'an reciters, and the muezzins, when they were kept separate from the Djemaia's budget.

Public Waqfs Budgets (Turkey)

In the Republic of Turkey, the Budget for the General Directorate of Foundations (*Vakıflar Genel Müdürlüğü*) is included in the central state budget, and I used it in combination with the detailed yearly General Directorate of Foundations budget laws published in the *Resmî Gazete.*

Public Waqfs Budgets (Morocco)

I used, for select years, the Moroccan public *Ḥabūs* Administration budgets for the period of French occupation (1912–1956) and 1957 from ANOM, Fonds Luccioni, CADN 1MA-200-754, CADN 1MA-200-755, CADN 1MA-1-123, and Al-Iyāla al-Sharīfa, Wizārat ʿUmūm al-Aḥbās (1916). These budgets are generally those of "Occidental Morocco" and do not include "Oriental Morocco" and the "Tangiers Region," which both represented a small fraction of the "Occidental Morocco" *Ḥabūs* budgets—for example, about 5 percent in 1930. For the 1958–1979 period, I used or consulted the *Ḥabūs* Administration budgets published in *Annuaire statistique du Maroc,* and for 1963 and 1964 those published in Al-Mamlaka al-Maghribīya, Wizārat ʿUmūm al-Awqāf (1964). After 1979, I only found information about the Waqfs "specific budget" (which lists the revenues and expenditures of their revenue-generating assets as well as their public religious provisions, which are distinct from those of the Ministry of Waqfs and Islamic Affairs) for the years 2009 and 2010 in Al-Mamlaka al-Maghribīya,

Wizārat al-Iqtiṣād wa-l-Mālīya (n.d.), and in Al-Mamlaka al-Maghribīya, Majlis al-Nuwwāb (2009). The 2009 Waqfs specific budget allowed me to verify that the fraction of total state religious expenditures it was able to sustain was still very small (about 5 percent compared to 9 percent in 1979) and I therefore ignored its contribution in my calculations after 1979. I used *Ḥabūs* expenditures for the fiscal year with the largest overlap with the year shown in tables 1, 2, and 3, except for 1980 (fiscal year 1979), 1940 (fiscal year 1941), 1935 (fiscal year 1352H, i.e., April 1933 to April 1934), 1925 (interpolation of fiscal years 1342H, i.e., August 1923 to August 1924, and 1345H, i.e., July 1926 to June 1927), and 1920 (interpolation of 1334H, i.e., November 1915 to October 1916, and 1342H, i.e., August 1923 to August 1924).

School Enrollments and Curricula

Enrollments and Religious Education Hours (Egypt, 1865–2020)

For modern school enrollments, I used Sāmī (1917), the annual *Statistical Yearbook of Egypt* (1909 to 2020), and *Statistique scolaire de l'Egypte* (1907–08 to 1959–60, published every three years or so). I included the *maktabs*, also called *kuttābs* or elementary schools (*madāris awwalīya*) in official statistics, that were administered or subsidized by the Ministry of Education, the Provincial Councils, and other departments of the state. Before 1914–15, I also included those that were only inspected by the Ministry of Education since they were aspiring to be subsidized. I did not include "free" *maktabs* until 1951–52, after which elementary schools were folded into the primary school system. For the rest, I start with counting what Sāmī (1917) calls "governmental schools" (*madāris ḥukūmīya*). They include the primary schools called "*amīrīya*" (state schools), primary schools called "*ahlīya*" (Egyptian schools the creation of which was spearheaded by the ruler and received a combination of funds from private donors and the state), the primary schools under the Waqfs Administration, technical schools (*ṣināʿīya*), specialized schools (*khuṣūṣīya*), secondary schools (*thānawīya*), and higher schools (*madāris ʿāliya*). They exclude private Egyptian and foreign schools. After 1914, the end of Sāmī's (1917) data set, I continue with the state and state-subsidized schools listed in the *Statistique scolaire de l'Egypte*: they include schools (at the primary, preparatory, secondary, and higher levels) administered or subsidized by the Ministry of Education, the Provincial Councils, the Ministry of Waqfs, other departments of the state and the royal waqfs. The available data for modern schools in 1920 is insufficient to populate tables 4a, 4c, and 4d. After 1954–55, I do not include any private school (there are no subsidized private schools reported). From 1961–62 to 2000–2001, the *Statistical Yearbook of Egypt* does not provide a separate count of private school enrollments. I gradually excluded from overall reported enrollments an increasing portion of them starting in 1970, to account for the apparently hidden presence of private schools in official statistics until the year 1999–2000, and to match reported governmental schools' enrollments in 2000–2001.

For total enrollments at al-Azhar in the early years of my dataset, I used or consulted *Statistique scolaire de l'Egypte*, Vollers's article on al-Azhar in *EI*[1], Levernay (n.d.), Ministère de l'Intérieur (1879), Al-Zayyātī (1902), Bayram (1903), Heyworth-Dunne (1939), Salama (1939), A. Ḥusayn (1945), Abū al-ʿUyūn (1949), Khafājī (1954), Dodge (1961), Ḥasanayn (1997), and ʿAbd al-Karīm (1945). I used Sékaly (1928) for enrollments at each level of the al-Azhar system from 1916 to 1928; after that, the *Statistique scolaire de l'Egypte* and the *Statistical Yearbook of Egypt*, complemented for select years by Al-Ḥuṣrī (1949–1957), Matthews and Akrawi (1950), ʿInān (1958), Rajab (1946), Maṭar (1939), Wizārat al-Tarbiya wa-l-Taʿlīm (1970), Farhūd (1983), Ḥasanayn (1997), and Yasn (2010).

For the early years of my modern higher education enrollments dataset, I closely followed Sāmī (1917) and included the following institutions, most of which were established in the nineteenth century (notwithstanding name changes and temporary closures): the School of Medicine and Pharmacy, the School of Engineering, the School of Administration and Law, the Teachers' School (al-Tawfīqīya), the School of Languages (al-Alsun),[14] the Higher School of Agriculture of Gizeh, the Higher School of Commerce (est. 1911), as well as Dār al-ʿUlūm. I also included the School of Midwives and the School of Veterinary Medicine but did not include the police and military schools. I later included the School of Dentistry (est. 1925), the Institute of Pedagogy (Maʿhad al-Tarbiya, est. 1929), and the Egyptian University (est. 1925) to which some of the aforementioned schools were annexed. From the 1950s I follow the *Statistical Yearbook of Egypt* nomenclature, and I include all universities, the colleges and higher institutes that are not part of the universities (the few I omitted from my calculations earlier on, such as the École Supérieure des Beaux-Arts, had comparatively small enrollments), as well as the government technical institutes (above the intermediary level). For al-Azhar, I used

14. It appears in official statistics under various names such as Madrasat al-Muʿallimīn al-Khidyāwīya (Khedivial Training College) or Madrasat al-Muʿallimīn al-Sulṭānīya (Sultanieh Training College) and later Madrasat al-Muʿallimīn al-ʿUlyā (Higher Training College).

the fraction of students enrolled at the higher education level reported in Sāmī (1917) for the year 1875 and kept it constant from 1865 until 1914. I also counted the higher section of the School of *Qāḍīs* (est. 1907) as part of the higher education specialized Islamic tracks.

I used a fraction of Muslim students for (1) the elementary schools (*maktabs*), (2) the rest of the government school system (excluding higher education), and (3) higher education (universities and high institutes), derived from *Statistique scolaire de l'Egypte*. Prior to 1896 for higher education, 1907 for elementary schools, and 1900 for other schools, I was not able to distinguish Muslim student enrollments from total enrollments. I therefore used for earlier years the first percentage of Muslim students available in the sources, which is a coarse approximation. After 1960, I was not able to distinguish Muslim student enrollments from total enrollments either, and I simply extrapolated for the next twenty years the prior twenty years' convergence trend between Muslims and non-Muslims (rather than rely on inferences based on censuses). I assumed that the School of *Qāḍīs*, Dār al-ʿUlūm, and al-Azhar have a 100 percent fraction of Muslim students.

For hours of Islamic education in modern schools, I used or consulted: Niẓārat al-Maʿārif al-ʿUmūmīya (1899), Ministry of Public Instruction (1902), Egyptian Government Schools (1907), Gélat (1911, vol. 5, 655–663), Sāmī (1917), Galt (1936), Wizārat al-Tarbiya wa-l-Taʿlīm (1936), Boktor (1936, 1937, 1963), Maṭar (1939), Salama (1939), Matthews and Akrawi (1949), El-Koussy (1952), Al-Ḥuṣrī (1957, vol. 5), Saif (1959), Wizārat al-Tarbiya wa-l-Taʿlīm (1972), Aroian (1983), Massialas and Jarrar (1983, 1991), Arab Republic of Egypt (2000), Salmoni (2002), Maḥmūd (2009), International Bureau of Education (2010–2011), and *Al-Waqāʾiʿ al-Miṣrīya*. For the specialized Islamic tracks curricula, I used or consulted: Sékaly (1928), Al-Jāmiʿ al-Azhar wa-l-Maʿāhid al-Dīnīya al-ʿIlmīya al-Islāmīya (1931), Salama (1939), Al-Jāmiʿ al-Azhar (1954, 1958, 1959), Dodge (1961), Jāmiʿat al-Azhar, al-ʿAlāqāt al-ʿĀmma (1992), and Yasn (2010). I counted the modern faculties of al-Azhar as modern higher education (rather than specialized Islamic tracks), with 10 percent of religious instruction, an average calculated using Jāmiʿat al-Azhar, al-ʿAlāqāt al-ʿĀmma (1992).

Enrollments and Religious Education Hours (Tunisia, 1865–2020)

For modern school enrollments at all levels, I used or consulted *Oeuvre scolaire (1881–1930)*, *Rapport au Président de la République sur la situation de la Tunisie*, *Annuaire statistique de la Tunisie* (under various names and incarnations), *BEP*,

BODIP, Macken (1974), Arnoulet (1991), Mechri-Bendana (1991), and Derouiche-Ben Achour (1996). For the Écoles Coraniques Modernes (ECMs) specifically, I also used or consulted CADN 1TU-1V-2074, CADN 1TU-1V-2077, ANT AP1 C1 D5-10, ANT SM6 C1 D703, and Ayachi (2003). Starting in 1967 (by which time almost all students were Muslim), I was not able to distinguish Muslim student enrollments from total enrollments at the pre-university level. I therefore assumed that the fraction of Muslims was 100 percent. For enrollments at the Zaytuna, I used or consulted ANT SH C63 D728 & 737 & 738, ANT SD C36 D1-1 & D1-2 & D1-3 & D1-10 & D3-7, ANT SL C11 D1, ANT SG-SG9 C274 D3, CADN 1TU-1V-2074, CADN 1TU-1V-2821, CADN 1TU-1V-2822, *Rapports au Président de la République sur la situation de la Tunisie*, *Annuaire statistique de la Tunisie*, Foncin (1882), Bayram V (1884–1894, vol.1), Machuel (1889, 1897, 1906), Van Krieken (1976), Green (1978), Abdelmoula (1984), Abdessamad (1985), ʿAyāshī (2003), recent data from http://www.mes.tn, and figures provided to me by the Zaytuna's administration. Starting in 1975, official statistics do not provide enrollments in the Zaytuna secondary tracks, only numbers of graduates; I used these to estimate their enrollments until 1989, when their mention disappears altogether from the *Annuaire statistique*. In the early years of my dataset, I used (and kept constant between observations) fractions of higher-level enrollments found, for select years, in ANT SD C36 D1-1 to D1-5, ANT SD C36 D5, as well as in Abdelmoula (1984, 130–132), for my estimate of specialized Islamic tracks higher education enrollments. I assumed a 100 percent fraction of Muslim students at the Zaytuna, the ECMs, and the Sadiki School.

I start counting modern higher education enrollments in 1910–1911, when the École Supérieure de Langue et de Littérature Arabes was created to replace the Chaire Publique d'Arabe (est. 1884). I do not consider enrollments in the Centre d'Études de Droit de Tunis (est. 1922), which prepared students for formal French law examinations, until it was folded into the Institut des Hautes Études de Tunis (IHET) at its creation in 1944–1945 (before that, it does not seem to have been attended by many Muslim students). However, I do consider the *cours de droit tunisien*, also called *cours de législation tunisienne*, after it became part of the École Supérieure de Langue et de Littérature Arabe in 1922. The latter was also folded into the IHET at its creation. I start counting students in the higher education tracks of the École des Beaux-Arts (est. 1923) and of the Conservatoire de Musique (est. 1896) in 1944–45, and those of the Higher School of Agriculture (the successor of the École Coloniale d'Agriculture, est. 1898) in 1956–1957. Before that, these schools were attended by very few Muslim students. After independence, in addition to the university (which opened in

1960 succeeding the IHET), I also included the various professional schools that sprang up under the label "specialized education." Starting in 1976 (by which time almost all students were Muslim), I was not able to distinguish Muslim student enrollments from total enrollments in higher education. I therefore assumed that the fraction of Muslims was 100 percent.

For the number of hours of Islamic instruction in modern schools, I used or consulted Machuel (1906), *BOEP*, *BODIP*, ANT AP1 C1 D5-9, ANT SH C64 D750, ANT AP1 C1 D5-10, CADN 1TU-1V-2074, CADN 1TU-1V-1359, République Tunisienne, Secrétariat d'Etat à l'Education Nationale (1958–1959), Lelong (1971), Sraïeb (1967, 1974), Tarifa (1971), Ayachi (2003), Charfi and Redissi (2010), *JORT*, International Bureau of Education (2006–7 and 2010–11), and printed material I obtained from Tunisia's Ministry of Education. For specialized Islamic tracks, I used or consulted *Al-Rāʾid al-Tūnisī*, Machuel (1897, 1906), ANT SE C262 D13-2, ANT SE C262 D13-5, ANT SD C36 D5, ANT AP1 C1 D5-2, ANT SG-SG5 C301 D5, ʿAyāshī (2003), and *Revue de l'IBLA* (no. 99, 1962; nos. 101–102, 1963; no. 133, 1974).

Enrollments and Religious Education Hours (Turkey 1925–2020)

For modern school enrollments between 1925 and 2012, I used *İstatistik Göstergeler* (2013), and for the period 2013–2020, *Millî Egitim İstatistikleri, Örgün Eğitim, 2020–21*. For Imam-Hatip schools for the period 1925–2000, I used *İstatistik Yıllığı*. For the period 2001–2020, I relied on the yearly *Millî Eğitim İstatistikleri, Örgün Eğitim*. For a few select years, I also relied on Öcal (1999). I also consulted Çakmak (2009). For Ilahiyat Faculties and Islamic Higher Institutes, I used *İstatistik Yıllığı* for the period 1925–1964. For the period 1965–1978, I used Jacob (1982). After that, I used *Millî Eğitim İstatistikleri*, and *Yükseköğretim İstatistikleri* until 2012. For the period 2013–2020, I used data from the Ministry of Higher Education's website.[15] Since I restrict myself to the period of the Republic of Turkey, I assume that all students are Muslim, which is an approximation, of course.

For hours of religious education in modern schools, I used or consulted Jacob (1982), Salmoni (2002), and *Tebliğler Dergisi*. For specialized Islamic tracks, I used or consulted Parmaksizoğlu (1966), Jacob (1982), Koştaş (1990), Pacaci and Aktay (2006), Çınar (2013), Nazıroğlu (2016), Sobi (2020), and the *Resmî Gazete*. For the Ilahiyat faculties in recent years, I also used or consulted

15. https://istatistik.yok.gov.tr.

data from their websites,[16] and for Imam-Hatip schools, information from the website of the General Directorate of Religious Education.[17]

Enrollments and Religious Education Hours (Morocco 1915–2020)

For enrollments in modern schools at the primary and secondary levels, I used or consulted *Annuaire statistique du Maroc* (1925 to 2022) as well as Protectorat de la République Française au Maroc, *Historique,* (*1912–1930*). For the renovated *msids* specifically, I used or consulted Gaudefroy-Demombynes (1928), Paye (1957), Gruner (1949), Damis (1970), CADN 1MA-300-107, CADN 3MA-900-43, Luccioni (1982), and *Annuaire statistique du Maroc.* For modern higher education enrollments, I have included the *enseignement juridique et administratif* starting from when it became part of the newly created Institut des Hautes Études Marocaines (IHEM) in 1920. It became the Centre d'Études Juridiques in 1930 (still part of the IHEM) and the Faculty of Law (Faculté de Droit) in 1958. Starting in 1921, I have also included the newly created *enseignement supérieur franco-musulman,* also under the IHEM. At the IHEM, I have not included the Arabic and Berber classes (*langue arabe et dialecte berbère*), the public lectures (*conférences*), distance learning (*préparation par correspondance*), and the training of official translators (*cours à l'usage des élèves interprètes civils*). In aggregate, it seems that these were mostly attended by (mainly French) auditors rather than students enrolled in a formal program of studies, although some prepared for formal examinations. Starting in the 1940s, I have included the newly created Centres d'Études Supérieures Littéraires et Scientifiques, which became the Faculty of Letters and Faculty of Sciences (Faculté des Lettres and Faculté des Sciences) in 1958. For enrollments until 1958, I have used or consulted Protectorat de la République Française au Maroc, *Historique (1912–1930)*; *Annuaire statistique du Maroc*; *BEP*; Direction de l'Instruction Publique au Maroc (1950); *Annuaire économique et financier*; *Rapport sur l'activité des Services du Protectorat*; Gaudefroy-Demombynes (1928); and Vermeren (2002). After 1958 higher education enrollments are drawn from *Annuaire statistique du Maroc, Statistiques universitaires, Maroc universitaire,* and *Annuaire statistique de l'enseignement supérieur au Maroc.* Breakdown by religion in higher education only appears in official statistics in a systematic fashion in the mid-1940s. Enrollments of Muslim students prior to that are rough approximations. Starting in 1967 (by which

16. Such as https://ilahiyat.omu.edu.tr.

17. https://dogm.meb.gov.tr.

time almost all students were Muslim), I was not able to distinguish Muslim student enrollments from total enrollments at any level. I therefore assume that the fraction of Muslims is 100 percent. I also assume a 100 percent fraction of Muslims in all specialized Islamic tracks and in the renovated *msids*.

I include in specialized Islamic tracks the Qarawiyin in Fes (with its primary, secondary and higher tracks after the reform of 1933); the Islamic Centers in Marrakesh (the Madrasa Ibn Yusif), Tangiers (est. 1943), and Meknes; and, after independence, "original education" (*ta ʿlīm aṣlī*) at the primary and secondary levels. For higher education, I include the Madrasa Ibn Yusif and the Qarawiyin system. After 1963 it included four faculties (the Sharia Faculties in Fes and Agadir, the Theology Faculty in Tetouan, and the Faculty of Arabic Language in Marrakesh). I also include Dar al-Hadith (est. 1965), the Islamic Studies departments in various Faculties of Letters in modern universities starting in 1982–83, and the Sharia Faculty of al-Samara starting in 2012–13. For enrollments in the Qarawiyin system and the various Islamic centers under the protectorate, I used or consulted CADN 1MA-300-107; CADN 1MA-300-108; CADN 1MA-300-110; CADN 1MA-300-111; CADN 1MA-300-113; Delphin (1889); Protectorat de la République Française au Maroc, *Historique (1912–1930)*; Gaudefroy-Demombynes (1928); Gruner (1949); Paye (1957); and Luccioni (1982). For the Qarawiyin University system and other Islamic higher institutes such as Dar al-Hadith after independence, I used Mouvement éducatif au Maroc (1957–1958), Centre National de Documentation (1960), Ministère de l'Education Nationale (n.d.), *Statistiques universitaires, Maroc universitaire, Annuaire statistique de l'enseignement supérieur au Maroc*, and *Annuaire statistique du Maroc*. Since I could not find data on enrollments in the higher level of the Qarawiyin system before 1952–53, I applied the fraction found for that year to earlier years' total enrollments. For enrollments in "original education" (*ta ʿlīm aṣlī*), I used *Annuaire statistique du Maroc, Bulletin économique et social du Maroc*, Royaume du Maroc (July 2004), information found at http://www.assiljadid.com, Al-Mamlaka al-Maghribīya, Wizārat al-Tarbiya al-Waṭanīya (2013–14), and data I obtained from the Ministry of National Education. For 2018–19, I relied on the intervention of the minister of national education in Parliament on May 13, 2019, in *Mudāwalāt Majlis al-Nuwwāb, Dawrat* April 2019, session 156, p. 44. For enrollments in the Islamic Studies departments of modern universities, I used or consulted Tozy (1999), *Maroc universitaire*, and *Annuaire statistique de l'enseignement supérieur*.

I omitted "traditional education" (the common translation of *ta ʿlīm ʿatīq*) overseen by the Ministry of Waqfs and Islamic Affairs. This would-be system of specialized Islamic tracks was put under the responsibility of the ministry in the mid-2000s and has gradually expanded. However, these schools are mainly financed by private associations and private gifts and only in part by the ministry and local authorities. In 2004–2005, only 2 percent of them were financed entirely by state funds, and 12 percent by a mix of private and state funds (Al-Mamlaka al-Maghribīya, 2004–2005). Hence, students in the state and state-subsidized "traditional" (ʿ*atīq*) sector only represented less than 20 percent of the state "original" (*aṣlī*) sector.

For hours of Islamic education in modern schools, I used or consulted: CADN 1MA-300-107, CADN 1MA-300-112, CADN 1MA-300-113, CADN 3MA-900-75, CADN 3-MA-900-90, *Bulletin officiel, Bulletin administratif de la Direction de l'instruction publique, BEP*, Gaudefroy-Demombynes (1928), Paye (1957), Damis (1970), *Al-ʿAlam* (June 2, 1957), L'enseignement au Maroc depuis l'indépendance (1971), Jābirī (1978), Le mouvement éducatif au Maroc (1978–1980, 1984–1986, 1988–1990, 1990–1992), Merrouni (1983), International Bureau of Education (2010–2011), Lahjomri et al. (1987), Al-Kitāb al-Abyaḍ (2002), data from www.men.gov.ma, and data I obtained from Morocco's Ministry of Education. For specialized Islamic tracks, I used or consulted CADN 1MA-300-113, Le mouvement éducatif au Maroc (1984–1986), Riʾāsat Jāmiʿat al-Qarawīyīn (1990), Al-Kitāb al-Abyaḍ (2002), data from www.assiljadid.com and www.men.gov.ma, and data I obtained from Morocco's Ministry of Education.

Population, GDP, And Prices

For historical population estimates in Tunisia, Egypt, Morocco, and Turkey in tables 1, 2, 4a, 4b, 4c, and 4d, I used Tabutin et al. (2001), and the Maddison Project Database, version 2020 (Bolt and van Zanden 2020) as well as World Bank data for population growth in recent years. I also used or consulted the various Tunisian censuses and *Dénombrements* since 1921, in addition to the various censuses cited in the book and to Seklani (1974). For GDP estimates in 1990 U.S. dollars adjusted for purchasing power parity, following Pamuk (2018, chapter 2) I start with the Maddison Project Database, version 2014 (Bolt and van Zanden 2014), with the adjustments made for Egypt and Turkey by Pamuk (2006, 2018) and Karakoç, Pamuk, and Panza (2017). I also used World Bank data for real growth in recent years, and—for interpolation purposes—Amin (1966) for Tunisia and Morocco, and Hansen and Marzouk (1965) and Yousef (2002) for Egypt. For Turkey's nominal GDP (i.e., in local currency at current prices), I used the GDP time series produced by Turkstat and harmonized as in Pamuk (2018, 31).[18] For

18. I thank Şevket Pamuk for his guidance with Turkstat GDP series.

Egypt, Tunisia, and Morocco after 1960, 1965, and 1966, respectively, I used World Bank data. For Egypt before 1966, I used Hansen and Marzouk (1965) and Yousef (2002). For Tunisia from 1914 to 1964, and for Morocco from 1914 to 1965, I estimated nominal GDP based on price indices in *Annuaire statistique de la Tunisie* and in *Annuaire statistique du Maroc.* For the period between 1827 and 1914, I estimated Tunisia's nominal GDP based on the price index for France in Sauvy (1952), the French Franc pure silver content in Allen (2001), and the Tunisian piastre pure silver content in Candia de Farrugia (1933, 1934, 1935) and Fenina (2003). For the period between 1730 and 1827, I estimated Tunisia's nominal GDP using a composite silver price index based on the silver price indices in Allen (2001) for various European cities and in Pamuk (2000b) for Istanbul, and the Tunisian piastre pure silver content in Candia de Farrugia (1933, 1934, 1935) and Fenina (2003). My resulting composite price index roughly matches the change in commodity prices reported in Valensi (1977, Figure 9) over this period in Tunisia. I use a common deflator for GDP, total state expenditures, and state religious expenditures.

BIBLIOGRAPHY

Archival Collections and Libraries Consulted

Archives Nationales de Tunisie, Tunis, Tunisia
Bibliothèque Nationale de Tunisie, Tunis, Tunisia
Centre de Documentation Nationale, Tunis, Tunisia
Institut Supérieur d'Histoire de la Tunisie Contemporaine, Manouba, Tunisia
Archives du Ministère des Affaires Etrangères, La Courneuve, France
Archives Nationales d'Outre-Mer, Aix-en-Provence, France
Archives Nationales de France, Pierrefitte-sur-Seine, France
Bibliothèque Nationale de France, Paris, France
Centre des Archives Diplomatiques de Nantes, Nantes, France

Periodicals And Printed Documents

Tunisia

Al-Jamʿīya al-Tūnisīya li-l-Qānūn al-Dustūrī. (1986). *Al-Majlis al-Qawmī al-Taʾsīsī, Aʿmāl Multaqā Ayyām 29–30–31 May 1984*. Tūnis: Markaz al-Dirāsāt wa-l-Buḥūth wa-l-Nashr.

Al-Jumhūrīya al-Tūnisīya. (1968). Kitābat al-Dawla li-l-Shuʾūn al-Thaqāfīya wa-l-Akhbār. *Buyūt Adhina Allāh an Turfaʿ*. Tūnis: Al-Dār al-Tūnisīya li-l-Nashr.

Al-Jumhūrīya al-Tūnisīya, Majlis al-Nuwwāb. (2009). *Munāqashāt al-Majlis al-Qawmī al-Taʾsīsī*. 2 vols. Bārdū: Markaz al-Buḥūth wa-l-Dirāsāt al-Barlamānīya.

Al-Rāʾid al-Rasmī li-l-Jumhūrīya al-Tūnisīya. Tūnis: al-Maṭbaʿa al-Rasmīya li-l-Jumhūrīya al-Tūnisīya (1957–).

Al-Rāʾid al-Tūnisī. Tūnis: Maṭbaʿat al-Dawla al-Tūnisīya (1860–1957).

Commission de codification des lois tunisiennes. (1899). *Code civil et commercial tunisien, Avant-Projet discuté et adopté au rapport de M. D. Santillana*. Tunis: Imprimerie générale J. Picard et Compagnie.

Depincé, C. (1909). *Congrès de l'Afrique du Nord tenu à Paris du 6 au 10 octobre 1908: Compte rendu des travaux*. 2 vols. Paris: Comité d'organisation du Congrès.

Grandchamp, P. (1935). *Documents relatifs à la révolution de 1864 en Tunisie*. 2 vols. Tunis: Imprimerie J. Aloccio.

Institut National de la Statistique. (2012). *Emploi et chômage, Premier trimestre 2012*. Tunis.

International Bureau of Education. (2006–2007). *World Data on Education, Tunisia*, 6th edition.

International Bureau of Education. (2010–2011). *World Data on Education, Tunisia*, 7th edition.

Journal officiel tunisien (1882–1957).

Journal officiel de la République tunisienne (1957–).

Lāʾiḥat Majallat al-Aḥkām al-Sharʿīya. Mustamadda min Uṣūl al-Madhhabayn al-Ḥanafī wa-l-Mālikī. (n.d.). Tūnis: Maṭbaʿat al-Irāda.

Loi organique ou code politique et administratif du royaume tunisien. Traduction de l'Arabe. (1861). Gênes: Imprimerie et litografie Faziola.

Qānūn al-Dawla al-Tūnisīya. (1861). Tūnis: Maṭbaʿat al-Dawla al-Tūnisīya.

Rapport au Président de la République sur la situation de la Tunisie. Paris: Imprimerie nationale. (1881–1925).

Régence de Tunis, Protectorat Français, Direction Génerale des Finances. (1903). *Budget général de la régence: Gestion budgétaire du protectorat depuis 1884 jusqu'en 1902 inclusivement*. Tunis: Imprimerie Borrel.

Régence de Tunis, Protectorat Français. *Budget de l'Etat* (select years from 1901 to 1956–57).

Régence de Tunis, Protectorat Français. *Bulletin officiel de l'enseignement public* (1887–1919).

Régence de Tunis, Protectorat Français. *Bulletin officiel de la Direction de l'instruction publique* (1919–1954, with some minor title variations over time).

Régence de Tunis, Protectorat Français, Direction générale de l'Intérieur. *Dénombrement de la population en Tunisie*, 1911, 1921, 1926, 1931 (2 vols.), 1936. Tunis, Imprimerie Rapide.

Régence de Tunis, Protectorat Français (1913–1956). *Statistique génerale de la Tunisie*, or *Annuaire statistique*.

République Tunisienne (1956–). *Annuaire statistique de la Tunisie*.

République Tunisienne. *Budget de l'Etat* (select years from 1957–58 to 2020).

République Tunisienne, Ministère des Affaires Religieuses. (2008). *Le Code du statut personnel. Enracinement dans l'islam et modèle de partenariat effectif*. Tunis: Editions Ministère des Affaires Religieuses.

République Tunisienne, Secrétariat d'Etat à l'Education Nationale. (1958–1959). *Nouvelle conception de l'enseignement en Tunisie*. Tunis: n.p.

Zeys, P. (1901). *Code annoté de la Tunisie: Recueil de tous les documents composant la législation écrite de ce pays au 1er janvier 1901*. 2 vols. Nancy: Berger-Levrault.

Turkey

Bianchi, T. X. (1856). *Khaththy Humaïoun ou charte impériale ottomane du 18 février 1856*. Paris: Typographie orientale de Madame Veuve Dondey-Dupré.

Budgets of the Republic of Turkey, 1924–2020, https://www.hmb.gov.tr/bumko-butce-buyuklukleri-ve-butce-gerceklesmeleri.

Charte des Turcs. (1840). *Journal asiatique*, January 5–29.

Güran, T. (2003). Osmanli Malî İstatiskleri Bütçeler 1841–1918, *Tarihi İstatiskler Dizisi*, Cilt 7. Ankara: State Institute of Statistics.

Öğrenci Seçme ve Yerleştirme Merkezi. *Yükseköğretim İstatistikleri* (various years).

Türkiye Cumhuriyeti. *İstatistik Yıllığı* (1928–2020).

Türkiye Cumhuriyeti. *Resmî Gazete*. (1925–2020).

Türkiye Cumhuriyeti, Millî Eğitim Bakanlığı. *Millî Eğitim İstatistikleri, Örgün Eğitim* (various years).

Türkiye Cumhuriyeti, Millî Eğitim Bakanlığı. *Tebliğler Dergisi* (1925–2020).
Turkstat. (2013). *İstatistik Göstergeler* (1923–2012).
Turkstat. (2015). *Ekonomik ve Sosyal Göstergeler* (1950–2014).

Levant

Haut Commissariat en Syrie et au Liban. (1922). *Recueil des actes administratifs du haut-commissariat de la République française en Syrie et au Liban*, vol. 3. Beyrouth: Imprimerie Jeanne d'Arc.
Palestine. *Report and General Abstracts of the Census of 1922, Taken on the 23rd of October, 1922*, compiled by J. B. Barron, Superintendent of the Census. Jerusalem: Greek Convent Press.
République Française. Ministère des Affaires Etrangères. *Rapport sur la situation de la Syrie et du Liban*. Paris: Imprimerie nationale (1922 to 1938).
The Syrian Republic, Ministry of National Economy. *Statistical Abstract of Syria for 1951 and 1952*. N.p.: n.d.

Egypt

Al-Dawla al-Miṣrīya, Majlis al-Nuwwāb. (1924–1952). *Majmū ʿat Maḍābiṭ*. Al-Qāhira: Al-Maṭbaʿa al-Amīrīya.
Al-Ḥukūma al-Miṣrīya, Al-Jamʿīya al-Tashrīʿīya. (1914). *Majmū ʿat Maḍābit Dawr al-In ʿiqād al-Awwal, 1913–1914*. Al-Qāhira: Al-Maṭbaʿa al-Amīrīya.
Al-Ḥukūma al-Miṣrīya, Lajnat al-Dustūr. (1924). *Maḥḍar Lajnat Waḍʿ al-Mabādiʾ al-ʿĀmma*. Al-Qāhira: Al-Maṭbaʿa al-Amīrīya.
Al-Ḥukūma al-Miṣrīya, Lajnat al-Dustūr. (1927). *Majmū ʿat Maḥāḍir al-Lajna al-ʿĀmma*. Al-Qāhira: Al-Maṭbaʿa al-Amīrīya.
Al-Jāmiʿ al-Azhar wa-l-Maʿāhid al-Dīnīya al-ʿIlmīya al-Islāmīya. (1931). *Khuṭṭa wa-Manhaj al-Dirāsa li-l-Qism al-Thānawī*. Al-Qāhira: Al-Maṭbaʿa al-Amīrīya.
Al-Jāmiʿ al-Azhar. (1954). *Khuṭṭa wa-Manhaj al-Dirāsa li-l-Qism al-Thānawī ʿalā al-Niẓām alladhī Wuḍiʿa li-l-Manāhij bi-l-Maʿāhid al-Dīnīya, Sanat 1954*. N.p.: Maṭbaʿat al-Azhar.
Al-Jāmiʿ al-Azhar. (1958). *Khuṭṭa wa-Manhaj al-Dirāsa li-l-Qism al-Ibtidāʾī ʿalā al-Niẓām alladhī Wuḍiʿa li-l-Manāhij bi-l-Maʿāhid al-Dīnīya, Sanat 1954*. N.p.: Maṭbaʿat al-Azhar.
Al-Jāmiʿ al-Azhar. (1959). *Al-Minhāj al-Muʿaddal al-Muqarrar ʿalā Ṭullāb al-Qismayn al-Ibtidāʾī wa-l-Thānawī, Sanat 1959–1960*. N.p.: Maṭbaʿat al-Azhar.
Al-Jarīda al-Rasmīya (1958–).
Al-Jumhurīya al-ʿArabīya al-Muttaḥida, Wizārat al-Khizāna al-Markazīya. *Mīzānīyat al-Iqlīm al-Janūbī* (1959–60, 1962–63).
Al-Jumhurīya al-ʿArabīya al-Muttaḥida, Wizārat al-Mālīya. *Al-Muwāzana al-ʿĀmma li-l-Dawla* (title may vary). (1964–65, 1965–66, 1966–67, 1969–70, 1973, 1974, 1975, 1977, 1984–85, 1986–87, 1988–89, years 2005–06 to 2019–20 downloaded from the website of the Egyptian Ministry of Finance, mof.gov.eg).
Al-Muʾtamar al-Miṣrī. (1911). *Majmū ʿat Aʿmāl al-Muʾtamar al-Miṣrī al-Awwal, al-Munʿaqad bi-Hilyūbūlīs min Yawm al-Sabt 30 Rabīʿ al-Thānī Sanat 1329 (29 Abrīl Sanat 1911) ilā Yawm al-Arbiʿāʾ 5 Jumādā al-Ūlā Sanat 1329 (4 Māyū Sanat 1911)*. Al-Qāhira: Al-Maṭbaʿa al-Amīrīya.

Al-Waqāʾiʿ al-Miṣrīya (1828–).

Aʿmāl Majlis Idārat al-Azhar, 1894–1904. (1905). Al-Qāhira: n.p.

Arab Republic of Egypt, National Center for Educational Research and Development. (2000). *National Report 1990–2000*.

Commission de la Réforme de l'Université d'El-Azhar (1328–1910). (1911). *Projet de réforme*. Le Caire: Imprimerie nationale.

Egyptian Census, 1917.

Egyptian Congress. (1911). *Minutes of the Proceedings of the First Egyptian Congress Assembled at Heliopolis from Saturday 29 April 1911 to Wednesday 4 May 1911*. Alexandria: Imprimerie d'Alexandrie.

Egyptian Government Schools. (1907). *Syllabus of the Primary Course of Study*. Cairo: National Printing Department.

Gélat, P. (1911). *Répertoire général annoté de la législation et de l'administration égyptiennes*, vol. 5. Alexandria: Imprimerie J. C. Lagoudakis.

Jāmiʿat al-Azhar, Al-ʿAlāqāt al-ʿĀmma. (1992). *Taqwīm Jāmiʿat al-Azhar*. N.p.

Lajnat Iṣlāḥ al-Azhar al-Maʿmūr. (1910). *Mashrūʿ Muqaddam li-Ṣāḥib al-ʿUṭūfa Muḥammad Saʿīd Bāshā*. Miṣr: Al-Maṭbaʿa al-Amīrīya.

Levernay, F. (n.d). *Guide-annuaire d'Egypte, Année 1872–1873*. Le Caire: Typographie française Delbos-Demouret.

Majlis al-Azhar al-Aʿlā. (1913, 1915, 1916–1917, 1918, 1919–1920). *Majmūʿat Maḥāḍir wa-Qarārāt al-Majlis*. Miṣr: Maṭbaʿat al-Nahḍa.

Majlis al-Nuwwāb. (1927). *Taqrīr Lajnat al-Awqāf wa-l-Maʿāhid al-Dīnīya ʿalā Mashrūʿ Mīzānīyat al-Jāmiʿ al-Azhar wa-l-Maʿāhid al-Dīnīya al-Islāmīya, li-Sanat 1927–1928 al-Mālīya*. Al-Qāhira: Al-Maṭbaʿa al-Amīrīya.

Majlis al-Shuyūkh. (1940). *Al-Dustūr: Taʿlīqāt ʿalā Mawaddihi bi-l-Aʿmāl al-Taḥḍīrīya wa-l-Munāqashāt al-Barlamānīya*. Al-Qāhira: Maṭbaʿat Miṣr.

Ministère de l'Intérieur, Bureau de la Statistique. (1879). *Essai de statistique générale de l'Egypte*. Le Caire: Typographie de l'état-major égyptien.

Ministère des Finances. *Budget du gouvernement égyptien pour l'exercice* (1898, 1899, 1900, 1904, 1905, 1910, 1913, 1915).

Ministry of Finance, Egypt. *Budget of the Egyptian Government* (1917–18, 1918–19, 1920, 1921–22, 1922–23, 1923–24, 1924–25, 1925–26, 1926–27, 1927–28, 1928–29, 1929–30, 1930–31, 1932–33, 1934–35).

Ministry of Public Instruction. (1902). *Code of Regulations Relating to the Organization and Discipline of the Kuttabs under the Management of the Ministry of Public Instruction*. Al-Qāhira: National Printing Department.

Niẓārat al-Maʿārif al-ʿUmūmīya. (1899). *Taqrīr ʿan al-Katātīb allatī Tudīruhā Niẓārat al-Maʿārif al-ʿUmūmīya min Shahr Yūlyū 1889 ilā Nihāyat 1898*. Būlāq: Al-Maṭbaʿa al-Amīrīya.

Publications du Bureau International d'Education. (1932). *L'Instruction publique en Egypte*. Genève: Bureau International d'Education.

Reports by His Majesty's High Commissioner on the Finances, Administration and Condition of Egypt and the Soudan (1920 and 1921).

Sharīf, M. (1938). *ʿAlā Hāmish al-Dustūr*. Miṣr: Maṭbaʿat al-Iʿtimād.

Statistical Yearbook of Egypt (yearly, from 1909 to 2020), also titled *Annuaire statistique de l'Egypte* and *Al-Iḥṣāʾ al-Sanawī al-ʿĀm*, or *Al-Kitāb al-Iḥṣāʾ al-Sanawī*.

Statistique scolaire de l'Egypte (1907–08, 1912–13, 1914–15, 1921–22, 1924–25, 1930–31, 1933–34, 1936–37, 1939–40, 1945–46, 1948–49, 1950–51, 1955–56, 1959–60).

Wizārat al-Mālīya. *Mīzānīyat al-Dawla al-Miṣrīya* (1943–44, 1946–47, 1954–55).

Wizārat al-Shu'ūn al-Ijtimā'īya. (1964?). *Taqwīm al-Jam'īyāt wa-l-Mu'assasāt al-Ijtimā'īya*. N.p.

Wizārat al-Tarbiya wa-l-Ta'līm. (1936). *Syllabus of the Secondary Course of Study for Boys*. Bulaq: Govt. Press.

Wizārat al-Tarbiya wa-l-Ta'līm. (1970). *Taqrīr 'an Taṭawwur al-Tarbiya wa-l-Ta'līm fī al-Jumhūrīya al-'Arabīya al-Muttaḥida, al-'Ām al-Dirāsī 1969–70*. Al-Qāhira: n.p.

Wizārat al-Tarbīya wa-l-Ta'līm, Markaz al-Tawḥīd al-Tarbawī. (1972). *Khiṭaṭ al-Dirāsa bi-Mukhtalif Marāḥil al-Ta'līm wa-Anwā'ihi bi-Jumhūrīyat Miṣr al-'Arabīya*. Al-Qāhira: Al-Idāra al-'Āmma li-l-Wathā'iq al-Tarbawīya, Markaz al-Tawthīq al-Tarbawī.

Morocco

Al-Iyāla al-Sharīfa, Wizārat 'Umūm al-Aḥbās (1916). Taqrīr Majlis al-Aḥbās. N.p.

Al-Mamlaka al-Maghribīya, Majlis al-Nuwwāb. (2009). *Taqrīr Lajnat al-Khārijīya wa-l-Difā 'al-Waṭanī wa-l-Shu'ūn al-Islāmīya*. N.p.

Al-Mamlaka al-Maghribīya, Wizārat 'Umūm al-Awqāf. (1964). *Al-Mīzānīya al-Ḥabsīya li-Sanat 1964*. Al-Ribāṭ: n.p.

Al-Mamlaka al-Maghribīya, Wizārat al-Awqāf wa-l-Shu'ūn al-Islāmīya. (1972). *Al-Awqāf fī Ẓill Ṣāḥib al-Jalāla al-Malik al-Mu'aẓẓam Mawlānā al-Ḥasan al-Thānī: Munjazāt 'Ashr Sanawāt 1961–1971*. Al-Ribāṭ: Wizārat 'Umūm al-Awqāf wa-l-Shu'ūn al-Islāmīya.

Al-Mamlaka al-Maghribīya, Wizārat al-Awqāf wa-l-Shu'ūn al-Islāmīya. (1975). *'Ishrūn Sana min al-'Amal: 1955–1975*. Al-Ribāṭ: Wizārat al-Awqāf wa-l-Shu'ūn al-Islāmīya.

Al-Mamlaka al-Maghribīya, Wizārat al-Awqāf wa-l-Shu'ūn al-Islāmīya. (1992). *Al-Tanmiya al-Waqfīya wa-l-Shu'ūn al-Islāmīya, 1984–1991*. Al-Ribāṭ: Wizārat al-Awqāf wa-l-Shu'ūn al-Islāmīya.

Al-Mamlaka al-Maghribīya, Wizārat al-Awqāf wa-l-Shu'ūn al-Islāmīya. (2004–2005). *Iḥṣā'īyāt al-Madāris al-'Aṭīqa*.

Al-Mamlaka al-Maghribīya, Wizārat al-Awqāf wa-l-Shu'ūn al-Islāmīya. (2018–2019). *Iḥṣā'īyāt Mu'assasat al-Ta'līm al-'Atīq*.

Al-Mamlaka al-Maghribīya, Wizārat al-Iqtiṣād wa-l-Mālīya. (n.d.). *Mashrū' Qānūn al-Mālīya li-Sanat 2009*. Al-Ribāṭ: Wizārat al-Awqāf wa-l-Shu'ūn al-Islāmīya.

Al-Mamlaka al-Maghribīya, Wizārat al-Tarbiya al-Waṭanīya. (2002). *Al-Kitāb al-Abyaḍ. Lijān Murāja'at al-Manāhij al-Tarbawīya al-Maghribīya li-l-Ta'līm al-Ibtidā'ī wa-l-Thānawī al-I'dādī wa-l-Ta'hilī*. 8 vols. N.p: Maṭba'at Wizārat al-Tarbiya al-Waṭanīya.

Al-Mamlaka al-Maghribīya, Wizārat al-Tarbiya al-Waṭanīya. (2013–2014). *Kharīṭat al-Ta'līm al-Thānawī al-I'dādī al-'Umūmī al-Aṣīl*. N.p.

Centre National de Documentation. (1960). *Enseignement supérieur 1957–1958*.

Direction de l'Instruction Publique au Maroc. (1950). *Bilan: 1945-1950*. Rabat: École du Livre.

Empire Chérifien, Protectorat Français. *Budget de l'exercice* (select years from 1914–15 to 1956).

Empire Chérifien, Protectorat de la République Française au Maroc. *Bulletin de l'enseignement public*, various years.

Empire Chérifien, Protectorat de la République Française au Maroc (1912–1956) & Royaume du Maroc (1956–). *Bulletin officiel*.

Gouvernement Chérifien, Protectorat Français au Maroc. *Annuaire économique et financier*, various years.

Gouvernement Chérifien, Protectorat de la République Française au Maroc (1917–1956) & Royaume du Maroc (1956–). *Annuaire statistique du Maroc* (yearly, from 1917 to 2020).

Gouvernement Chérifien, Protectorat de la République Française au Maroc. *Bulletin administratif de la Direction générale de l'instruction publique, des beaux-arts, et des antiquités au Maroc*, various years.

International Bureau of Education. (2010–2011). *World Data on Education, Morocco*, 7th ed.

L'enseignement au Maroc depuis l'indépendance. (1971). *Souffles*, no. 2021, Nov.–Dec., 4–11.

Ministère de l'Education Nationale, Direction de la Planification et des Objectifs. (1973). *Études sur l'organisation, les méthodes et la présentation des statistiques scolaires, 1ère et 2ème parties.*

Ministère de l'Education Nationale, Direction de la Planification. (n.d.). *Statistiques de l'enseignement supérieur 1974–1975.*

Protectorat de la République Française au Maroc, Direction de l'Instruction Publique, des Beaux-Arts et des Antiquités. (n.d.). *Historique (1912–1930).*

Résidence Générale de la République Française au Maroc. *Rapport sur l'activité des Services du Protectorat*, various years.

Riʾāsat Jāmiʿat al-Qarawīyīn. (1990). *Dalīl Jāmiʿat al-Qarawīyīn.* N.p.

Royaume du Maroc. *Aperçu sur le système éducatif marocain*, July 2004.

Royaume du Maroc. *Budget de l'exercice* (select years from 1957 to 1963).

Royaume du Maroc, Haut Commissariat au Plan. (2011). *Enquête nationale auprès des Institutions Sans But Lucratif (ISBL) (exercice 2007), Rapport de synthèse.*

Royaume du Maroc. *Loi de finances pour l'année* (select years from 1964 to 1972).

Royaume du Maroc, Ministère de l'Education Nationale. *Le mouvement éducatif au Maroc*, (1957–58, 1962–63, 1963–64, 1978–79 & 1979–80, 1984–85 & 1985–86, 1990–91 & 1991–92).

Royaume du Maroc. Ministère de l'Enseignement Supérieur, *Maroc universitaire* (2002–03 to 2016–17), *Annuaire statistique de l'enseignement supérieur au Maroc* (2017–18, 2019–20), *Statistiques universitaires* (2020–21).

Société d'études économiques, sociales, et statistiques. *Bulletin économique et social du Maroc.* Various years.

Miscellaneous

House of Commons Parliamentary Papers, Reports by his Majesty's High Commissioner on the Finances, Administration, and Condition of Egypt and the Soudan (1920 and 1921).

International Bureau of Education. (2010–2011). *World Data on Education*, 7th ed.

Maʿhad al-Dirāsāt al-ʿArabīya al-ʿĀliya. (1955). *Dasātīr al-Bilād al-ʿArabīya: Nuṣūṣ Jamīʿ al-Dasātīr allatī Ṣadarat fī Tawārīkh Mukhtalifa fī Kull min al-Urdun wa-Sūriyā wa-l-ʿIrāq wa-Lubnān wa-Lībiyā wa-Miṣr.* N.p: Jāmiʿat al-Duwal al-ʿArabīya, Maʿhad al-Dirāsāt al-ʿArabīya al-ʿĀliya.

Articles, Books, and Reference Works

ʿAbd al-Karīm, A. (1945). *Tārīkh al-Taʿlīm fī ʿAṣr Muḥammad ʿAlī.* Miṣr: Maṭbaʿat al-Naṣr.

ʿAbd al-Rāziq, ʿA. (1925). *Al-Islām wa-Uṣūl al-Ḥukm.* N.p.: Maṭbaʿat Miṣr.

Abdelmoula, M. (1984). *L'université zaytounienne et la société tunisienne*. N.p.

Abdelmoula, M. (1987). *Jihad et colonialisme: La Tunisie et la Tripolitaine, 1914–1918*. Tunis: Ed. Tiers-Monde.

Abdel Nour, A. (1982). *Introduction à l'histoire urbaine de la Syrie ottomane (XVIe-XVIIIe siècle)*. Beyrouth: Librairie orientale.

Abdesselem, A. (1973). *Les historiens tunisiens des XVIIème, XVIIIème et XIXème siècles: Essai d'histoire culturelle*. Tunis: Publications de l'Université de Tunis, Faculté des lettres et sciences humaines.

Abdesselem, A. (1983). *Ibn Khaldun et ses lecteurs*. Paris: Presses universitaires de France.

Abdessamad, H. (1985). La résidence face à la question de la réforme de l'enseignement zaytounien 1930–1933. In *Mouvements politiques et sociaux dans la Tunisie des années 1930*. Sidi Bou Said: n.p., 799–816.

Abū Ghāzī, ʿI. (2000). *Taṭawwur al-Ḥiyāza al-Zirāʿīya fī Miṣr: Zaman al-Mamālīk al-Jarākisa: Dirāsa fī Bayʿ Amlāk Bayt al-Māl*. Al-Jīza: ʿAyn li-l-Dirāsāt wa-l-Buḥūth al-Insānīya wa-l-Ijtimāʿīya.

Abu-Uksa, W. (2016). *Freedom in the Arab World: Concepts and Ideologies in Arabic Thought in the Nineteenth Century*. Cambridge: Cambridge University Press.

Abū al-ʿUyūn, M. (1949). *Al-Jāmiʿ al-Azhar: Nubdha fī Tārīkhihi*. N.p.: Maṭbaʿat al-Azhar.

Afsaruddin, A. (2014). Politics and Governance in Pre-Modern Islamic Thought. *Storia Del Pensiero Politico*, (3), 381–398.

Agrama, H. (2010). Secularism, Sovereignty, Indeterminacy: Is Egypt a Secular or a Religious State? *Comparative Studies in Society and History*, 52(3), 495–523.

Agrama, H. (2012). *Questioning Secularism: Islam, Sovereignty, and the Rule of Law in Modern Egypt*. Chicago: University of Chicago Press.

Ahmed, D., & T. Ginsburg. (2014). Constitutional Islamization and Human Rights: The Surprising Origin and Spread of Islamic Supremacy in Constitutions. *Virginia Journal of International Law*, 54, 615–733.

Ahmed, H. (2018). The Nahda in Parliament: Taha Husayn's Career Building Knowledge Production Institutions, 1922–1952. *Arab Studies Journal*, 26(1), 9–33.

Ahmed, J. (1960). *The Intellectual Origins of Egyptian Nationalism*. London: Oxford University Press.

Ahmed, M. (1968). *Muslim Education and the Scholars' Social Status up to the 5th Century Muslim Era*. Zürich: Verlag "Der Islam."

Ahmed, S. (2016). *What Is Islam? The Importance of Being Islamic*. Princeton, NJ: Princeton University Press.

Ahmed, S., & N. Filipovic. (2004). The Sultan's Syllabus: A Curriculum for the Ottoman Imperial Medreses Prescribed in a Fermān of Qānūnī I Süleymān, Dated 973 (1565). *Studia Islamica*, (98/99), 183–218.

Aksit, B. (1991). Islamic Education in Turkey: Medrese Reform in Late Ottoman Times and Imam-Hatip Schools in the Republic. In R. Tapper (ed.), *Islam in Modern Turkey: Religion, Politics and Literature in a Secular State*. London: I. B. Tauris, 145–170.

Al-ʿAẓma, ʿA. (1998). *Al-ʿIlmānīya wa-l-Mujtamaʿ al-Madanī*. Markaz al-Dirāsāt wa-l-Maʿlūmāt al-Qānūnīya li-Ḥuqūq al-Insān.

Al-Azmeh, A. (2020). *Secularism in the Arab World: Contexts, Ideas and Consequences*. Edinburgh: Edinburgh University Press.

Al-Bannā, Ḥ. (1965). *Majmūʿat Rasāʾil al-Imām al-Shahīd Ḥasan al-Bannāʾ*. Bayrūt: Dār al-Andalus.

Al-Dijwī, Y. (1914). *Kitāb Sabīl al-Sa ʿāda*. Al-Qāhira: Maṭbaʿat al-Nahḍa al-Adabīya.

Al-Dijwī, Y. (1929 or 1930). *Kalima fī al-Salafīya al-Ḥāḍira*. Dimashq: Maktabat al-Qudsī wa-l-Budayr.

Al-Dijwī, Y. (2006). *Maqālāt wa-Fatāwā al-Shaykh Yūsuf al-Dijwī*. Al-Qāhira: Dār al-Baṣāʾir.

Al-Dijwī, Y. (n.d.). *Ṣawā ʿiq min Nār fī al-Radd ʿalā Ṣāḥib al-Manār*. Al-Qāhira: Maktabat al-Taqaddum al-Tijārīya.

Al-Ghazālī, A. (1904–1906). *Kitāb al-Mustaṣfā min ʿIlm al-Uṣūl*. 2 vols. Būlāq: Al-Maṭbaʿa al-Amīrīya.

Al-Ḥakīm, Y. (1966). *Sūrīya wa-l-ʿAhd al-Fayṣalī*. Bayrūt: Al-Maṭbaʿa al-Kāthūlīkīya.

Al-Ḥuṣrī, S. (1949–1957). *Ḥawlīyat al-Thaqāfa al-ʿArabīya*. 5 vols. Al-Qāhira: Maṭbaʿat Lajnat al-Taʾlīf wa-l-Tarjama wa-l-Nashr.

Al-Jabartī, A. (1879–1880). ʿAjāʾib al-Āthār fī al-Tarājim wa-l-Akhbār. 4 vols. Būlāq: n.p.

Al-Mājrī, Ḥ. (2014). *Min Ta ʿlīm al-Ṣibyān ilā al-Ta ʿlīm al-Ibtidā ʾī fī Madīnat Tūnis fī al-ʿAhd al-ʿUthmānī*. Tūnis: Arabesque.

Al-Maʿrūfī, M. Ṣ. (1988). *Ḥawla al-Dīn wa-l-Dawla*. N.p.

Al-Ṣābī, H. (1958). *Al-Wuzarāʾ, Aw Tuḥfat al-Umarāʾ fī Tārīkh al-Wuzarāʾ*. Al-Qāhira: Dār Iḥyāʾ al-Kutub al-ʿArabīya.

Al-Sanūsī, M. (1983). *Musāmarāt al-Ẓarīf bi-Ḥusn al-Ta ʿrīf*. Tūnis: Dār Bū Salāma li-l-Ṭibāʿa wa-l-Nashr wa-l-Tawzīʿ.

Al-Sayyid, L. (1945). *Al-Muntakhabāt*. Al-Qāhira: Maṭbaʿat al-Muqtaṭaf wa-l-Muqaṭṭam.

Al-Sayyid Marsot, A. L. (1972). The Ulama of Cairo in the Eighteenth and Nineteenth Centuries. In N. Keddie (ed.), *Scholars, Saints, and Sufis: Muslim Religious Institutions in the Middle East since 1500*. Berkeley: University of California Press, 149–166.

Al-Sayyid Marsot, A. L. (1973). The Political and Economic Functions of the 'Ulama' in the 18th Century. *Journal of the Economic and Social History of the Orient*, 16(1), 130–154.

Al-Sayyid Marsot, A. L. (1977). *Egypt's Liberal Experiment, 1922–1936*. Berkeley: University of California Press.

Al-Sharif, S. (1916). *La vérité au sujet de la guerre sainte*. Bern: Ferd Wyss.

Al-Ṭayyif, A. (2015). *Kharīf al-Qurā: Asbāb Intifāḍat al-Sāḥil al-Tūnisī Sanat 1864*. Mannūba: Jāmiʿat Mannūba, al-Maʿhad al-ʿĀlī li-Tārīkh Tūnis al-Muʿāṣir.

Al-Tūnisī, K. (1867). *Kitāb Aqwam al-Masālik fī Ma ʿrifat Aḥwāl al-Mamālik*. Tūnis: Maṭbaʿat al-Dawla.

Al-Tunisi, K. (1868). *Réformes nécessaires aux États musulmans: Essai formant la première partie de l'ouvrage politique et statistique intitulé la plus sûre direction pour connaître l'état des nations*. Paris: Imprimerie administrative de Paul Dupont.

Al-Tūnisī, K. (2000). *Kitāb Aqwam al-Masālik fī Ma ʿrifat Aḥwāl al-Mamālik*. 2 vols. Tūnis: Bayt al-Ḥikma.

Al-Ṭurṭūshī, M. (1872). *Kitāb Sirāj al-Mulūk*. Al-Iskandarīya: Al-Maṭbaʿa al-Waṭanīya.

Al-Zayyātī, S. (1902). *Kanz al-Jawhar fī Tārīkh al-Azhar*. N.p.

Allagui, A. (2016). *Juifs et Musulmans en Tunisie: Des origines à nos jours (Histoire partagée)*. Paris: Tallandier.

Alleaume, G. (1993). L'école polytechnique du Caire et ses élèves: La formation d'une élite technique dans l'Egypte du XIXème siècle. Thèse de doctorat d'Etat, Université de Lyon II.

Allen, R. C. (2001). The Great Divergence in European Wages and Prices from the Middle Ages to the First World War. *Explorations in Economic History*, 38(4), 411–447.

Amedroz, H. F. (1904). *The Historical Remains of Hilâl al-Sâbi: First Part of Kitab al-Wuzara (Gotha Ms. 1756) and Fragment of His History 389–393 A.H. (B.M.Ms. add. 19360)*. Beirut: Catholic Press of Beirut.

Amīn, M. (1980). *Al-Awqāf wa-l-Ḥayāh al-Ijtimā ʿīya fī Miṣr, 1250–1517*. Al-Qāhira: Dār al-Nahḍa al-ʿArabīya.

Amin, S. (1966). *L'économie du Maghreb*. Paris: Editions de Minuit.

Amor, A. (1974). La Constitution tunisienne de 1861. *Servir, Revue tunisienne du service public*, (14), 51–69.

ʿAmur, ʿA., & Q. Saʿīd. (1987). *Nuṣūṣ wa-Wathā ʾiq Siyāsīya Tūnisīya*. Tūnis: Kullīyat al-Ḥuqūq wa-l-ʿUlūm al-Siyāsīya.

Amri, N. (2000). L'occupation par un saint de Tunis (ixe/xve siècle) de sa future zâwiya, d'après les manâqib d'Ahmad b. ʿArûs. In R. Chih & D. Gril (eds.), *Le saint et son milieu*. Le Caire: Institut Français d'Archéologie Orientale, 117–136.

Anderson, J. (1958). The Tunisian Law of Personal Status. *International and Comparative Law Quarterly*, 7(2), 262–279.

An-Naʿim, A. (2008). *Islam and the Secular State: Negotiating the Future of Shariʿa*. Cambridge, MA: Harvard University Press.

Armitage, D. (2012). What's the Big Idea? Intellectual History and the Longue Durée. *History of European Ideas*, 38(4), 493–507.

Arnoulet, F. (1984). Les Tunisiens et la première guerre mondiale (1914–1918). *Revue des mondes musulmans et de la Méditerranée*, 38(1), 47–61.

Arnoulet, F. (1991). Les problèmes de l'enseignement au début du protectorat français en Tunisie (1881–1900). *IBLA*, 54 (167), 31–62.

Aroian, L. (1983). *The Nationalization of Arabic and Islamic Education in Egypt: Dar-Ulum and Al-Azhar*. Cairo: American University in Cairo.

Arslān, S. (1937). *Al-Sayyid Rashīd Riḍā, aw, Ikhā ʾ Arba ʿīn Sana*. Dimashq: Maṭbaʿat Ibn Zaydūn.

Asad, T. (1993). *Genealogies of Religion: Discipline and Reasons of Power in Christianity and Islam*. Baltimore: Johns Hopkins University Press.

Asad, T. (2003). *Formations of the Secular: Christianity, Islam, Modernity*. Stanford, CA: Stanford University Press.

Atassi, K. (2018). *Syria, the Strength of an Idea: The Constitutional Architectures of Its Political Regimes*. Cambridge: Cambridge University Press.

ʿAwwād, M. (1964). *Rusūm Dār al-Khilāfa, Ta ʾlīf Abī al-Ḥusayn Hilāl Ibn al-Muḥassin al-Ṣābi ʾ*. Baghdād: Maṭbaʿat al-ʿĀnī.

Ayachi, M. (2003). *Écoles et société en Tunisie, 1930–1958*. Tunis: CERES.

Ayadi, T. (1986). *Mouvement réformiste et mouvements populaires à Tunis: 1906–1912*. Tunis: Publications de l'Université de Tunis, Faculté des lettres et sciences humaines.

Ayalon, Y. (2009). Revisiting Ṭāhā Ḥusayn's *Fī al-Shi ʿr al-Jāhilī* and Its Sequel. *Die Welt des Islams*, 49(1), 98–121.

ʿAyāshī, M. (2003). *Al-Zaytūna wa-al-Zaytūnīyūn fī Tārīkh Tūnis al-Mu ʿāṣir, 1883–1958*. Tūnis: Jāmiʿat al-Zaytūna, Markaz al-Nashr al-Jāmiʿī.

Bachrouch, T. (1989). *Les élites tunisiennes du pouvoir et de la dévotion: Contribution à l'étude des groupes sociaux dominants, 1782–1881*. Tunis: Publications de l'Université de Tunis, Faculté des lettres et sciences humaines.

Bachrouch, T. (2008). *La médina de Tunis avant le protectorat*. Tunis: CERES.

Baer, G. (1962). *A History of Landownership in Modern Egypt, 1800–1950*. London: Oxford University Press.

Baer, G. (1997). The Waqf as a Prop for the Social System (Sixteenth–Twentieth Centuries). *Islamic Law and Society*, 4(3), 264–297.

Baina, A. (1981). *Le système de l'enseignement au Maroc*. 2 vols. N.p.: Editions maghrébines.

Bakhīt, M. (1925). *Ḥaqīqat al-Islām wa-Uṣūl al-Ḥukm*. Al-Qāhira: Al-Maṭbaʿa al-Salafīya.

Barbar, K., & G. Kepel. (1982). *Les waqfs dans l'Egypte contemporaine*. Le Caire: Centre d'études et de documentation économiques, juridiques et sociales.

Bargaoui, S. (2003). Débats identitaires et logiques territoriales: L'administration de la justice malikite à Tunis à l'époque moderne. *Studia Islamica*, (97), 121–153.

Bargaoui, S. (2015). Le waqf: Redéfinitions des appartenances et inscriptions sociales. In S. Bargaoui et al. (eds.), *Appartenance locale et propriété au nord et au sud de la Méditerranée*. Aix-en-Provence: IREMAM, 122–141.

Barkan, Ö. (1939). Les problèmes fonciers dans l'empire ottoman au temps de sa fondation. *Annales d'histoire sociale*, 1(3), 233–237.

Barnes, J. (1986). *An Introduction to Religious Foundations in the Ottoman Empire*. Leiden: E. J. Brill.

Barro, R., & R. McCleary. (2005). Which Countries Have State Religions? *Quarterly Journal of Economics*, CXX(4), 1331–1370.

Bashrūsh, T. (1991). *Rabīʿ al-ʿUrbān: Aḍwāʾ ʿan Asbāb Thawrat ʿAlī Ibn Ghadhāhim, Sanat 1864*. Qarṭāj: Al-Muʾassasa al-Waṭanīya li-l-Tarjama wa-l-Taḥqīq wa-l-Dirāsāt, Bayt al-Ḥikma.

Bashrūsh, T. (1999). *Mawsūʿat Madīnat Tūnis*. Tūnis: Markaz al-Dirāsāt wa-l-Buḥūth al-Iqtiṣādīya wa-l-Ijtimāʿīya.

Bayat, A. (1996). The Coming of a Post-Islamist Society. *Critique: Critical Middle Eastern Studies*, (9), 43–52.

Bayram I, M. (2016). *Al-Risāla al-Bayramīya fī al-Siyāsa al-Sharʿīya*. Markaz al-Dirāsāt al-Islāmīya bi-l-Qayrawān. Tūnis: Dār Saḥnūn li-l-Nashr wa-l-Tawzīʿ.

Bayram V, M. (1884–1894). *Kitāb Ṣafwat al-Iʿtibār bi-Mustawdaʿ al-Amṣār wa-l-Aqṭār*. 5 vols. Al-Qāhira: Al-Maṭbaʿa al-Iʿlāmīya.

Bayram, M. (1903). *Tārīkh al-Azhar*. Miṣr: Maṭbaʿat al-Tamaddun.

Bdira, M. (1978). *Relations internationales et sous-développement: La Tunisie 1857–1864*. Stockholm: Almqvist & Wiksell International.

Beck, C. J. (2009). State Building as a Source of Islamic Political Organization. *Sociological Forum*, 24(2), 337–356.

Behrens-Abouseif, D. (1994). *Egypt's Adjustment to Ottoman Rule: Institutions, Waqf and Architecture in Cairo, 16th and 17th Centuries*. Leiden: E. J. Brill.

Behrens-Abouseif, D. (2009). The Waqf: A Legal Personality? In A. Meier et al. (eds.), *Gottes Eigentum für alle Zeiten? Islamische Stiftungen von den Anfängen bis zur Gegenwart*. Berlin: Akademie-Verlag, 55–60.

Bein, A. (2006). Politics, Military Conscription, and Religious Education in the Late Ottoman Empire. *International Journal of Middle East Studies*, 38(2), 283–301.

Bein, A. (2011). *Ottoman Ulema, Turkish Republic: Agents of Change and Guardians of Tradition*. Stanford, CA: Stanford University Press.

Bel, A. (1938). *La religion musulmane en Berbérie: Esquisse d'histoire et de sociologie religieuses. T. 1: Etablissement et développement de l'Islam en Berbérie du VIIe au XXe siècle*. Paris: P. Geuthner.

Ben Achour, M. A. (1977). Les ulamas à Tunis aux XVIIIe et XIXe siècles. Thèse de Doctorat de 3ème cycle, Université de Paris Sorbonne (Lettres et Civilizations) Paris IV.

Ben Achour, M. A. (1989). *Catégories de la société tunisoise dans la deuxième moitié du XIXème siècle: Les élites musulmanes*. Tunis: Ministère des affaires culturelles.

Ben Achour, M. A. (1992). Le habous ou waqf: L'institution juridique et la pratique tunisoise. In S. Ferchiou (ed.), *Hasab wa nasab: Parenté, alliance et patrimoine en Tunisie*. Paris: Editions du Centre national de la recherche scientifique, 51–78.

Ben Achour, S. (2007). Le code tunisien du statut personnel, 50 ans après: Les dimensions de l'ambivalence. *L'Année du Maghreb*, 2(II), 55–70.

Ben Achour, Y. (1985). Justice des madhalim et justice administrative moderne. *International Review of Administrative Sciences*, 51(2), 109–119.

Ben Achour, Y. (2016). *Tunisie, une révolution en pays d'Islam*. Tunis: Cérès éditions.

Ben Ismail, Y. (2014). The Political Rise of Ennahdha's Women: Changing the Markers of Legitimacy. MA thesis, Center for Middle Eastern Studies, Harvard University.

Ben Ismail, Y. (2021). Sovereignty across Empires: France, the Ottoman Empire, and the Imperial Struggle over Tunis (ca. 1830–1920). PhD dissertation, Harvard University.

Ben Slimane, F. (2012). Entre deux empires: L'élaboration de la nationalité tunisienne. In N. Amara (ed.), *De la colonie à l'Etat-nation: Constructions identitaires au Maghreb, Maghreb et sciences sociales*, 107–118.

Benton, L. (2002). *Law and Colonial Cultures: Legal Regimes in World History, 1400–1900*. Cambridge: Cambridge University Press.

Bercher, L. (1972). En marge du pacte fondamental: Un document inédit. *Les Cahiers de Tunisie*, (79–80), 243–260.

Berger, M. (1970). *Islam in Egypt Today: Social and Political Aspects of Popular Religion*. Cambridge: Cambridge University Press.

Berkes, N. (1964). *The Development of Secularism in Turkey*. Montreal: McGill University Press.

Berkey, J. P. (2014). *The Transmission of Knowledge in Medieval Cairo*. Princeton, NJ: Princeton University Press.

Bernard, A. (1926). *L'Afrique du Nord pendant la guerre*. Paris: Les Presses universitaires de France; New Haven, CT: Yale University Press.

Bilici, F. (1993). Sociabilité et expressions politiques islamistes en Turquie: Les nouveaux vakifs. *Revue française de science politique*, 43ème année, no. 3, 412–434.

Bilici, F., ed. (1994). *Le "waqf" dans le monde musulman contemporain (XIXe–XXe siècles): Fonctions sociales, fonctions économiques; Actes de la table ronde d'Istanbul, 13–14 novembre 1992*. Istanbul: Institut français d'études anatoliennes.

Bilici, F. (2006). *Islam institutionnel, Islam parallèle: De l'empire ottoman à la Turquie contemporaine, XVIe–XXe siècles*. Paris: Éditions Isis.

Bilmuqaddam, R. (1993). *Awqāf Miknās fī ʿAhd Mawlāy Ismāʿīl: 1082–1139 H/1672–1727 M*. Fās: Al-Mamlaka al-Maghribīya, Wizārat al-Awqāf wa-l-Shuʾūn al-Islāmīya.

Bodin, D. (2002). L'ordre public: Limite et condition de la tolerance; Recherches sur le pluralism juridique. Thèse de doctorat. Université Paris I, Panthéon Sorbonne.

Boissevain, K. (2013). Des conversions au christianisme à Tunis. *Histoire, monde et cultures religieuses*, 28(4), 47–62.

Boktor, A. (1936). *School and Society in the Valley of the Nile*. Cairo: Elias Modern Press.

Boktor, A. (1937). Egypt. In *Educational Yearbook of the International Institute of Teachers College, Columbia University*, 115–143.

Boktor, A. (1963). *The Development and Expansion of Education in the United Arab Republic*. Cairo: American University at Cairo Press.

Bolt, J., & J. L. van Zanden. (2014). The Maddison Project. Collaborative Research on Historical National Accounts. *Economic History Review*, 67(3): 627–651.

Bolt, J., & J. L. van Zanden. (October 2020). *The Maddison Project: Maddison Style Estimates of the Evolution of the World Economy; A New 2020 Update*. https://www.rug.nl/ggdc/historicaldevelopment/maddison/releases/maddison-project-database-2020.

Borrmans, M. (1977). *Statut personnel et famille au Maghreb: De 1940 à nos jours*. Paris: Mouton.

Borrmans, M. (1988). L'Islam de certains manuels et catéchismes contemporains. *Studia Missionalia*, 37, 103–140.

Bourdieu, P. (1971). Genèse et structure du champ religieux. *Revue française de sociologie*, 12(3), 295–334.

Braun, C. (2006). A quoi servent les partis tunisiens? *Revue des mondes musulmans et de la Méditerranée*, 111(111–112), 15–62.

Brooke, S., & N. Ketchley. (2018). Social and Institutional Origins of Political Islam. *American Political Science Review*, 112(2), 376–394.

Brown, L. C. (1967). *The Surest Path: The Political Treatise of a Nineteenth-Century Muslim Statesman*. Cambridge, MA: Harvard University Press.

Brown, L. C. (1974). *The Tunisia of Ahmad Bey, 1837–1855*. Princeton, NJ: Princeton University Press.

Brown, L. C. (2005). *Consult Them in the Matter*. Fayetteville: University of Arkansas Press, 2005.

Brown, N. (2002). *Constitutions in a Nonconstitutional World: Arab Basic Laws and the Prospects for Accountable Government*. Albany: State University of New York Press.

Brown, N. (2012). *When Victory Is Not an Option: Islamist Movements in Arab Politics*. Ithaca, NY: Cornell University Press.

Brown, N., & M. Revkin. (2018). Islamic Law and Constitutions. In *The Oxford Handbook of Islamic Law*, chapter 27. Oxford: Oxford University Press.

Brown, N., & A. O. Sharif. (2004). Inscribing the Islamic Sharia in Arab Constitutional Law. In Y. Haddad & B. Stowasser (eds.), *Islamic Law and the Challenges of Modernity*. Walnut Creek, CA: AltaMira Press.

Brunner, R. (2009). Education, Politics, and the Struggle for Intellectual Leadership: Al-Azhar between 1927 and 1945. In M. Hatina (ed.), *Guardians of Faith in Modern Times: 'Ulama' in the Middle East*. Leiden: E. J. Brill, 109–140.

Brunschvig, R. (1931). Quelques remarques historiques sur les médersas de Tunisie. *Revue tunisienne*, 262–285.

Bsoul, L. (2008). *International Treaties (mu'āhadāt) in Islam: Theory and Practice in the Light of Islamic International Law (siyar) According to Orthodox Schools*. Lanham, MD: University Press of America.

Bulliet, R. (1972). *The Patricians of Nishapur: A Study in Medieval Islamic Social History*. Cambridge, MA: Harvard University Press.

Burgat, F. (2003). *Face to Face with Political Islam*. London: I. B. Tauris.

Busse, H. (1967). Das Hofbudget des Chalifen al-Mu'taḍid billāh. *Der Islam*, 43(1), 11–36.

Cachia, P. (1956). *Ṭāhā Ḥusayn: His Place in the Egyptian Literary Renaissance*. London: Luzac.

Çakmak, D. (2009). Pro-Islamic Public Education in Turkey: The Imam-Hatıp Schools, *Middle Eastern Studies*, 45(5), 825–846.

Calame, G. 1903. La mosquée-Université El-Azhar, *Revue internationale de l'enseignement*, (juillet–décembre 1903), 481–503.

Candia de Farrugia, J. (1933). Monnaies husseinites-II (1847–1859). *Revue tunisienne*, 1er et 2ème trimestre, nos. 13–14, 215–230.

Candia de Farrugia, J. (1934). Monnaies husseinites-III, Monnaies frappées de l'année 1196 à l'année 1262 hég. (1782 à 1846). *Revue tunisienne*, 1er trimestre, no. 17, 73–92.

Candia de Farrugia, J. (1935). Monnaies husseinites: Monnaies frappées de l'année 1117 à l'année 1196 hég. (1705 à 1782). *Revue tunisienne*, 1er semestre, no. 21, 15–36.

Cantori, L. J. (1966). The Organizational Basis of an Elite Political Party: The Egyptian Wafd. PhD dissertation, University of Chicago.

Carré, O. (1979). *La légitimation islamique des socialismes arabes: Analyse conceptuelle combinatoire de manuels scolaires égyptiens, syriens et irakiens*. Paris: Presses de la Fondation nationale des sciences politiques.

Carré, O. (2003). *Mysticism and Politics: A Critical Reading of Fi Zilal al-Qur'an by Sayyid Qutb (1906–1966)*. Leiden: E. J. Brill.

Carré, O., & G. Michaud (1983). *Les Frères musulmans: Egypte et Syrie, 1928–1982*. Paris: Gallimard.

Carter, B. L. (1986). *The Copts in Egyptian Politics*. London: Croom Helm.

Chamberlain, M. (1994). *Knowledge and Social Practice in Medieval Damascus, 1190–1350*. Cambridge: Cambridge University Press.

Charfi, M., & H. Redissi. (2010). Teaching Tolerance and Open-Minded Approaches to Understanding Sacred Texts. In J. E. Cohen & M. B. Malin (eds.), *International Perspectives on the Goals of Universal Basic and Secondary Education*. New York: Routledge, 145–175.

Charrad, M. (2001). *States and Women's Rights: The Making of Postcolonial Tunisia, Algeria, and Morocco*. Berkeley: University of California Press.

Chater, K. (1975). Le constitutionalisme en Tunisie au 19ème siècle. *Revue tunisienne de sciences sociales*, 12(40), 243–272.

Chater, K. (1978). *Insurrection et répression dans la Tunisie du XIXème siècle: La méhalla de Zarrouk au Sahel, 1864*. Tunis: Publications de l'Université de Tunis, Faculté des lettres et sciences humaines.

Chater, K. (1984). *Dépendance et mutations précoloniales: La régence de Tunis de 1815 à 1857*. Tunis: Publications de l'Université de Tunis, Faculté des lettres et sciences humaines.

Chekir, H. (2006). Les sources d'inspiration de la constitution tunisienne de 1861. In P.-J. Luizard (ed.), *Le choc colonial et l'islam*. Paris: La découverte, 71–88.

Chenoufi, M. (1968). Les deux séjours de Mohamed Abdouh en Tunisie. *Les Cahiers de Tunisie*, (61–64), 57–96.

Chérif, M.-H. (1970). Expansion européenne et difficultés tunisiennes de 1815 à 1830. *Annales: Histoire, sciences sociales*, 25(3), 714–745.

Chérif, M.-H. (1973). L'Etat tunisien et les campagnes au XVIIIème siècle. *Cahiers de la Méditerranée*, 1(1), 9–22.

Chérif, M.-H. (1986). Les documents de Bayt al-Mal dans les archives de l'ancienne direction des Habous (en Tunisie). In A. Temimi (ed.), *La vie économique des provinces arabes et leurs sources documentaires à l'époque ottomane*, vol. 3. Zaghouan: Centre d'études et de recherches sur les provinces arabes à l'époque ottomane, 209–212.

Chérif, M.-H. (1994). Ben Dhyâf et les Juifs tunisiens. *Confluences méditerranéennes*, (10), 89–96.

Chérif, M.-H. (2008). *Pouvoir et société dans la Tunisie de Husayn bin 'Ali: 1705–1740*. 2 vols. Tunis: Centre de publications universitaire.

Chih, R. (2021). The Social Role of Ṣūfīs. In A. Papas (ed.), *Sufi Institutions*. Boston: E. J. Brill, 187–217.

Çınar, F. (2013). 1924'ten 2000'e Kadar Uygulanmış Olan Imam Hatip Lisesi Öğretim Programlarının Analizi ve Karşılaştırılması. *Millî Eğitim Dergisi*, 43(197), 180–208.

Çizakça, M. (1995). Cash Waqfs of Bursa, 1555–1823. *Journal of the Economic and Social History of the Orient*, 38(3), 313–354.

Çizakça, M. (2000). *A History of Philanthropic Foundations: The Islamic World from the Seventh Century to the Present*. İstanbul: Boğaziçi University Press.

Clancy-Smith, J. (2011). *Mediterraneans: North Africa and Europe in an Age of Migration, c. 1800–1900*. Berkeley: University of California Press.

Clark, J. (1995). Islamic Social Welfare Organizations in Cairo: Islamization from Below? *Arab Studies Quarterly*, 17(4), 11–28.

Clayer, N. (2015). An Imposed or a Negotiated Laiklik? The Administration of the Teaching of Islam in Single-Party Turkey. In M. Aymes et al. (eds.), *Order and Compromise: Government Practices in Turkey from the Late Ottoman Empire to the Early 21st Century*, 97–120.

Cloarec, V. (1996). Politique musulmane, question arabe et Grande guerre. *Maghreb-Machrek*, 152, 13–18.

Cohen, M. (2008). *Under Crescent and Cross: The Jews in the Middle Ages*. Princeton, NJ: Princeton University Press.

Cook, B. J. (2000). Egypt's National Education Debate. *Comparative Education*, 36(4), 477–490.

Cook, M. (2000). *Commanding Right and Forbidding Wrong in Islamic Thought*. Cambridge: Cambridge University Press.

Cook, M. (2014). *Ancient Religions, Modern Politics: The Islamic Case in Comparative Perspective*. Princeton, NJ: Princeton University Press.

Crecelius, D. (1972). Nonideological Responses of the Egyptian Ulama to Modernization. In N. Keddie (ed.), *Scholars, Saints, and Sufis: Muslim Religious Institutions in the Middle East since 1500*. Berkeley: University of California Press, 167–209.

Crone, P. (2004). *God's Rule: Government and Islam*. New York: Columbia University Press.

Crone, P., & M. Hinds. (1986). *God's Caliph: Religious Authority in the First Centuries of Islam*. Cambridge: Cambridge University Press.

Crozet, P. (2008). *Les sciences modernes en Egypte: Transfert et appropriation, 1805–1902*. Paris: Geuthner.

Cuno, K. (1999). Ideology and Juridical Discourse in Ottoman Egypt: The Uses of the Concept of Irṣād. *Islamic Law and Society*, 6(2), 136–163.

Dabbab, M. (1980). *Les délégations destouriennes à Paris*. Tunis: Maison tunisienne de l'édition.

Dakhlia, J. (1998). *Le divan des rois: Le politique et le religieux dans l'islam*. Paris: Aubier.

Dallal, A. (2000). Appropriating the Past: Twentieth-Century Reconstruction of Pre-Modern Islamic Thought. *Islamic Law and Society*, 7(3), 325–358.

Dallal, A. (2018). *Islam Without Europe: Traditions of Reform in Eighteenth-Century Islamic Thought*. Chapel Hill: University of North Carolina Press.

Damis, J. J. (1970). The Free-School Movement in Morocco, 1919–1970. PhD thesis, Fletcher School of Law and Diplomacy, Tufts University.

David, P. (1923). *Un gouvernement arabe à Damas: Le congrès syrien*. Paris: M. Giard.

Davis, E. (1984). Ideology, Social Class and Islamic Radicalism in Modern Egypt. In S. A. Arjomand (ed.), *From Nationalism to Revolutionary Islam*. London: Macmillan, 134–157.

Davison, R. (1963). *Reform in the Ottoman Empire, 1856–1876*. Princeton, NJ: Princeton University Press.

Debbasch, C. (1959). L'assemblée nationale constituante tunisienne. *Revue juridique et politique d'Outre-Mer*, 13, 32–54.

Debbasch, Y. (1957). *La nation française en Tunisie, 1577–1835*. Paris: Sirey.

DeGeorges, T. (2006). Bitter Homecoming: Tunisian Veterans of the First and Second World Wars. PhD dissertation, Harvard University.

Deguilhem, R. (1986). History of Waqf and Case Studies from Damascus in Late Ottoman and French Mandatory Times. PhD dissertation, New York University.

Deguilhem, R. (1995). *Le waqf dans l'espace islamique: Outil de pouvoir socio-politique*. Damas: Institut français de Damas.

Deguilhem, R., & A. Hénia., eds. (2004). *Les fondations pieuses (waqf) en Méditerranée: Enjeux de société, enjeux de pouvoir*. Koweït: Fondation publique des awqaf du Koweït.

De Jong, F. (2000). *Sufi Orders in Ottoman and Post-Ottoman Egypt and the Middle East*. Istanbul: ISIS Press.

De Lavergne, N. (2004). L'Etat et le kuttab: Une analyse de la statistique scolaire égyptienne naissante (1867–1915), *Annales islamologiques*, (38), 371–404.

De Lavergne, N. (2007). La modernization des kuttâb en Egypte au tournant du XXème siècle, *Cahiers de la Méditerranée*, 75, 74–89.

Delgado, J. (2022). The Ties That Bind: Child Custody in Andalusi Mālikism, 3rd/9th–6th–12th c. PhD dissertation, Harvard University.

Dellagi, M. (2013). *Abdelaziz Thaalbi: Naissance du mouvement national tunisien*. Carthage: Editions cartaginoiseries.

Delphin, G. (1889). *Fas, son université et l'enseignement supérieur musulman*. Paris: E. Leroux; Oran: P. Perrier.

Demeerseman, A. (1996). *Aspects de la société tunisienne d'après Ibn Abî l-Dhiyâf*. Tunis: IBLA.

De Montety, H. (1927). *Une loi agraire en Tunisie*. Cahors: Imprimerie Typographique Coueslant.

Derouiche-Ben Achour, S. (1996). Aux sources du droit moderne tunisien: La législation tunisienne en période coloniale. Thèse pour le doctorat d'état en droit. Tunis: Université de droit économie et de gestion de Tunis, Faculté des sciences juridiques, politiques et sociales de Tunis.

Dodge, B. (1961). *Al-Azhar: A Millennium of Muslim Learning*. Washington, DC: Middle East Institute.

Dodge, M. (2013). From the Streets to the Ballot Box: Political Parties and the Foundation of a Tunisian Democracy. Senior thesis, Harvard College, March 2013.

Doumani, B. (1998). Endowing Family: Waqf, Property Devolution, and Gender in Greater Syria, 1800 to 1860. *Comparative Studies in Society and History*, 40(1), 3–41.

Doumato, E. A., & G. Starrett. (2007). *Teaching Islam: Textbooks and Religion in the Middle East*. Boulder: Lynne Rienner.

Duqqī, N. (1999). *Ḥarakat al-Shabāb al-Tūnisī*. Tūnis: Jāmiʿat Tūnis al-Ūlā, Al-Maʿhad al-Aʿlā li-Tārīkh al-Ḥaraka al-Waṭanīya.

Duran-Angliviel, A. (1921). *Ce que la Tunisie demande à la France*. Paris: Jouve.

Eccel, C. (1984). *Egypt, Islam and Social Change: Al-Azhar in Conflict and Accommodation*. Berlin: K. Schwarz.

Eickelman, D. (1976). *Moroccan Islam: Tradition and Society in a Pilgrimage Center*. Austin: University of Texas Press.

Eickelman, D. (1992). Mass Higher Education and the Religious Imagination in Contemporary Arab Societies. *American Ethnologist*, 19(4), 643–655.

El Ayadi, M. (2004). Entre islam et islamisme. *Revue internationale d'éducation de Sèvres*, 36.

El-Baradei, M. (1986). Government Expenditure in Egypt, Kuwait, Saudi Arabia and Jordan. In G. Luciani (ed.)., *Public Finance in the Arab Countries*. N.p.: International Development Research Center.

Elboudrari, H. (1985). Quand les saints font les villes: Lecture anthropologique de la pratique sociale d'un saint marocain du XVIIe siècle. *Annales: Histoire, sciences sociales*, 40(3), 489–508.

El-Ghobashy, M. (2005). The Metamorphosis of the Egyptian Muslim Brothers. *International Journal of Middle East Studies*, 37(3), 373–395.

El-Ghoul, Y. (2009). *Naturalisation et nationalisme en Tunisie de l'entre-deux-guerres*. La Manouba: Centre de publication universitaire.

El-Koussy, A. (1952). Egypt. *The Yearbook of Education*, 1952, 445–457.

Elloumi, M. (2014). Les terres domaniales en Tunisie. *Études rurales*, (192), 43–60.

El-Mabkhout, M. (1980). Les habous publics au Maroc: Mémoire du cycle supérieur. Rabat: École nationale d'administration.

El-Méchat, S. (2002). *Le nationalisme tunisien: Scission et conflits, 1934–1944*. Paris: L'Harmattan.

El-Rouayheb, K. (2015). *Islamic Intellectual History in the Seventeenth Century: Scholarly Currents in the Ottoman Empire and the Maghreb*. New York: Cambridge University Press.

El-Rouayheb, K. (2019). *The Development of Arabic Logic (1200–1800)*. Basel: Schwabe Verlag.

Elston, M. (2020). Reviving Turath: Islamic Education in Modern Egypt. PhD dissertation, Harvard University.

Emerit, M. (1949). Les crises des finances tunisiennes et les origines du protectorat. *Revue africaine*, 93(3–4), 249–276.

Enayat, H. (2013). *Law, State, and Society in Modern Iran: Constitutionalism, Autocracy, and Legal Reform, 1906–1941*. New York: Palgrave Macmillan.

Fabbe, K. (2019). *Disciples of the State? Religion and State-Building in the Former Ottoman World*. Cambridge: Cambridge University Press.

Fakhfākh, M. (1990). *Mūjaz al-Dafātir al-Idārīya wa-l-Jibāʾīya bi-l-Arshīf al-Waṭanī al-Tūnisī*. Tūnis: Manshūrāt al-Arshīf al-Waṭanī al-Tūnisī.

Faour, M. (1991). The Demography of Lebanon: A Reappraisal. *Middle Eastern Studies*, 27, 631–641.

Farag, I. (1999). La construction sociale d'une éducation nationale: Enjeux politiques et trajectoires éducatives (Egypte—première moitié du XXème siècle). Thèse de doctorat, École des hautes études en sciences sociales, Paris.

Farhūd, M. (1983). *Al-Azhar: Tārīkhuhu wa Taṭawwuruhu*. Al-Qāhira: Al-Amāna.

Faroqhi, S. (1976). The Tekke of Haci Bektaş: Social Position and Economic Activities. *International Journal of Middle East Studies*, 7(2), 183–208.

Feldman, N. (2020). *The Arab Winter*. Princeton, NJ: Princeton University Press.

Fenina, A. (2003). *Les monnaies de la régence de Tunis sous les husaynides: Études de numismatique et d'histoire monétaire, 1705–1891*. Tunis: Université de Tunis, Faculté des sciences humaines et sociales de Tunis.

Ferchiou, S., ed. (1992). *Hasab wa nasab: Parenté, alliance et patrimoine en Tunisie*. Paris: Editions du Centre national de la recherche scientifique.

Fernandes, L. (1988). *The Evolution of a Sufi Institution in Mamluk Egypt: The Khanqah*. Berlin: Klaus Schwarz.

Feuer, S. (2018). *Regulating Islam: Religion and the State in Contemporary Morocco and Tunisia*. Cambridge: Cambridge University Press.

Fierro, M., & J. Tolan, eds. (2013). *The Legal Status of Ḏimmī-s in the Islamic West*. Turnhout: Brepols.

Findley, C. (2008). The Tanzimat II. In R. Kasaba (ed.), *The Cambridge History of Turkey*. Cambridge: Cambridge University Press, 9–37.

Findley, C. (2010). *Turkey, Islam, Nationalism, and Modernity: A History, 1789–2007*. New Haven, CT: Yale University Press.

Fitoussi, E. (1901). *L'État tunisien, son origine, son développement et son organisation actuelle (1525–1901): Étude d'histoire politique, de droit public et de droit international*. Tunis: Imprimerie générale (J. Picard et cie).

Fogarty, R. (2008). *Race and War in France: Colonial Subjects in the French Army, 1914–1918*. Baltimore: Johns Hopkins University Press.

Foncin, P. (1882). L'enseignement en Tunisie. *Revue internationale de l'enseignement*, Deuxième année, no. 11, 401–418.

Fortna, B. (2000). Islamic Morality in Late Ottoman "Secular" Schools. *International Journal of Middle East Studies*, 32(3), 369–393.

Fortna, B. C. (2002). *Imperial Classroom*. Oxford: Oxford University Press.

Foucault, M. (1969). *L'archéologie du savoir*. Paris: Gallimard.

Foucher, L. (1897). *De l'évolution du protectorat de la France sur la Tunisie*. Paris: Larose.

Fox, J. (2008). *A World Survey of Religion and the State*. Cambridge: Cambridge University Press.

Fox, J. (2011). Building Composite Measures of Religion and State. *Interdisciplinary Journal of Research on Religion*, 7.

Fox, J. (2015). *Political Secularism, Religion, and the State: A Time Series Analysis of Worldwide Data*. Cambridge: Cambridge University Press.

Freeden, M. (2003). *Ideology: A Very Short Introduction*. Oxford: Oxford University Press.

Fregosi, F. (2003). *La régulation institutionnelle de l'Islam en Tunisie: Entre audace moderniste et tutelle étatique*. Paris. IFRI Policy Paper no. 11.

Frémeaux, J. (2006). *Les colonies dans la grande guerre: Combats et épreuves des peuples d'Outre-Mer.* Soteca: 14–18 Editions.

Galt, R. (1936). *The Effects of Centralization on Education in Modern Egypt.* Cairo: American University at Cairo.

Ganiage, J. (1959). *Les origines du protectorat français en Tunisie (1861–1881).* Paris: Presses universitaires de France.

Ganiage, J. (1960). *La population européenne de Tunis au milieu du XIXème siècle: Étude démographique.* Paris: Presses universitaires de France.

Ganiage, J. (1968). *Les origines du protectorat français en Tunisie (1861–1881).* Tunis: Maison tunisienne de l'édition.

García-Arenal, M. (2006). *Messianism and Puritanical Reform: Mahdīs of the Muslim West.* Leiden: E. J. Brill.

Gaudefroy-Demombynes, R. (1928). *L'oeuvre française en matière d'enseignement au Maroc.* Paris: P. Geuthner.

Gavison, R. (2011). Can Israel Be Both Jewish and Democratic? In A. Maoz (ed.), *Israel as a Jewish and Democratic State.* Liverpool: Jewish Law Association, 115–148.

Genç, M. (2018). Values Education or Religious Education? An Alternative View of Religious Education in the Secular Age, the Case of Turkey. *Education Sciences,* 8(4), 220.

Gershoni, I., & J. Jankowski. (1986). *Egypt, Islam, and the Arabs: The Search for Egyptian Nationhood, 1900–1930.* New York: Oxford University Press.

Gesink, I. (2010). *Islamic Reform and Conservatism: Al-Azhar and the Evolution of Modern Sunni Islam.* London: I. B. Tauris.

Ghānim, I. B. (1998). *Al-Awqāf wa-l-Siyāsa fī Miṣr.* Al-Qāhira: Dār al-Shurūq.

Ghānim, I. B. (2007). *Wizārat al-Awqāf.* Al-Qāhira: Markaz al-Dirāsāt al-Sīyāsīya wa-l-Istrātījīya bi-l-Ahrām.

Ghannūshī, R. (1988). *Maqālāt.* Tūnis: n.p.

Ghannūshī, R. (2001). *Min Tajribat al-Ḥaraka al-Islāmīya fī Tūnis.* London: Al-Markaz al-Maghāribī li-l-Buḥūth wa-l-Tarjama.

Ghazaleh, P. (2011). *Held in Trust: Waqf in the Islamic World.* Cairo: American University in Cairo Press.

Gibb, H., & J. Kramers. (1953). *Shorter Encyclopaedia of Islam.* Leiden: E. J. Brill.

Goldberg, E. (1991). Smashing Idols and the State: The Protestant Ethic and Egyptian Sunni Radicalism. *Comparative Studies in Society and History,* 33(1), 3–35.

Goldschmidt, A. (2000). *Biographical Dictionary of Modern Egypt.* Boulder: Lynne Rienner.

Goldstein, D. (1978). *Libération ou annexion: Aux chemins croisés de l'histoire tunisienne, 1914–1922.* Tunis: Maison tunisienne de l'édition.

Gran, P. (1979). *Islamic Roots of Capitalism: Egypt, 1760–1840.* Austin: University of Texas Press.

Grangaud, I. (2004). Les dotations de la mosquée Sîdî al-Kittânî (Constantine au XVIIIème siècle). In R. Deguilhem & A. Hénia (eds.), *Les fondations pieuses (waqf) en Méditerranée: Enjeux de société, enjeux de pouvoir.* Koweït: Fondation publique des awqaf du Koweït 79–98.

Grangaud, I. (2015). Le Bayt al-mâl, les héritiers et les étrangers. Droits de succession et droits d'appartenance à Alger à l'époque moderne. In S. Bargaoui et al. (eds), *Appartenance locale et propriété au nord et au sud de la Méditerrannée.* Aix-en-Provence: IREMAM, 122–141.

Grangaud, I., & M. Oualdi. (2014). Does Colonialism Explain Everything in North Africa? What Historians Can Bring to the Table. *L'Année du Maghreb,* 10, 233–254.

Gratien, J.-P. (2006). *Marius Moutet: Un socialiste à l'Outre-Mer*. Paris: L'Harmattan.
Green, A. (1976). A propos d'un document inédit de Béchir Sfar. *Revue d'histoire maghrébine*, (5), 87–92.
Green, A. (1978). *The Tunisian Ulama 1873–1915: Social Structure and Response to Ideological Currents*. Leiden: E. J. Brill.
Gruner, R. (1949). L'enseignement libre au Maroc. *Mémoire du CHEAM*, no. 1627, vol. 61.
Guellaty, H. (1909). *La justice tunisienne*. Tunis: Imprimerie Rapide.
Guezmir, K. (1978). Les élites tunisiennes et le protectorat français, 1881–1914. *Revue tunisienne de sciences sociales*, 15(52), 67–94.
Güldüren, C. (2017). The Conscription of Religious Students in the Ottoman Empire. Master's thesis, Koç University.
Haddad, M. (1997). Arab Religious Nationalism in the Colonial Era: Rereading Rashīd Riḍā's Ideas on the Caliphate. *Journal of the American Oriental Society*, 117(2), 253–277.
Haddad, M. (1998). ʿAbduh et ses lecteurs: Pour une histoire critique des "lectures" de M. ʿAbduh. *Arabica*, 45(1), 22–49.
Haddad de Paz, C. (1977). *Juifs et Arabes au pays de Bourguiba*. Aix-en-Provence: P. Roubaud.
Hagège, C., & B. Zarca. (2001). Les Juifs et la France en Tunisie: Les bénéfices d'une relation triangulaire. *Le Mouvement social*, (197), 9–28.
Ḥajjī, L. (2004). *Būrqība wa-l-Islām: Al-Zaʿāma wa-l-Imāma*. Tūnis: Dār al-Janūb li-l-Nashr.
Hallaq, W. (1997). *A History of Islamic Legal Theories: An Introduction to Sunnī Uṣūl al-Fiqh*. Cambridge: Cambridge University Press.
Hallaq, W. (2009). *Sharīʿa: Theory, Practice, Transformations*. Cambridge: Cambridge University Press.
Hallaq, W. (2013). *The Impossible State: Islam, Politics, and Modernity's Moral Predicament*. New York: Columbia University Press.
Hammoudi, A. (1980). Sainteté, pouvoir et société: Tamgrout aux XVIIe et XVIIIe siècles. *Annales: Histoire, sciences sociales*, 35(3/4), 615–641.
Hansen, B., & G. A. Marzouk. (1965). Development and Economic Policy in the UAR (Egypt). Amsterdam: North-Holland.
Harrak, F. (1989). State and Religion in Eighteenth Century Morocco: The Religious Policy of Sidi Muhammad B. Abd Allah 1757–1790. PhD thesis, School of Oriental and African Studies, University of London.
Ḥasanayn, M. S. (1997). *Tārīkh wa-Niẓām al-Taʿlīm fī Miṣr*. Ṭanṭā: Dār al-Khalīfa.
Hassan, M. (2016). *Longing for the Lost Caliphate: A Transregional History*. Princeton, NJ: Princeton University Press.
Hatina, M. (2000). On the Margins of Consensus: The Call to Separate Religion and State in Modern Egypt. *Middle Eastern Studies*, 36(1), 35–67.
Hatina, M. (2010). *Ulama, Politics, and the Public Sphere: An Egyptian Perspective*. Salt Lake City: University of Utah Press.
Hefner, R. (2000). *Civil Islam: Muslims and Democratization in Indonesia*. Princeton, NJ: Princeton University Press.
Hénia, A. (1999). *Propriété et stratégies sociales à Tunis à l'époque moderne: XVIème–XIXème siècles*. Tunis: Université Tunis I, Faculté des sciences humaines et sociales de Tunis.
Hénia, A. (2004). La gestion des waqfs khayrî en Tunisie à l'époque moderne: Du monopole privé au monopole public. In R. Deguilhem & A. Hénia (eds.), *Les fondations pieuses (waqf)*

en Méditerranée: Enjeux de société, enjeux de pouvoir. Koweït: Fondation publique des awqaf du Koweït, 283–316.

Heyd, U. (1973). *Studies in Old Ottoman Criminal law*. Oxford: Clarendon Press.

Heyworth-Dunne, J. (1939). *An Introduction to the History of Education in Modern Egypt*. London: Luzac.

Himadeh, S. B. (1936). *Economic Organization of Syria*. Beirut: American Press.

Hoexter, M. (1998). *Endowments, Rulers, and Community: Waqf al-Ḥaramayn in Ottoman Algiers*. Leiden: E. J. Brill.

Hoexter, M. (2002). The Waqf and the Public Sphere. In M. Levtzion (ed.), *The Public Sphere in Muslim Societies*. New York: State University of New York Press, 119–138.

Hokayem, A. (1996). *La genèse de la constitution libanaise de 1926: Le contexte du mandat français, les projets préliminaires, les auteurs, le texte final*. Antélias: Les Editions universitaires du Liban.

Hourani, A. (1962). *Arabic Thought in the Liberal Age, 1798–1939*. London: Oxford University Press.

Hourani, A. (1983). *Arabic Thought in the Liberal Age, 1798–1939*. Cambridge: Cambridge University Press.

Ḥusayn, A. (1945). *Al-Taʿlīm al-ʿArabī al-Jāmiʿī*. Miṣr: Maṭbaʿat al-Tawfīq.

Ḥusayn, Ṭ. (1926). *Fī al-Shiʿr al-Jāhilī*. Al-Qāhira: Maṭbaʿat Dār al-Kutub al-Miṣrīya.

Ḥusayn, Ṭ. (1938). *Mustaqbal al-Thaqāfa fī Miṣr*. 2 vols. Miṣr: Maṭbaʿat al-Maʿārif wa-Maktabatuhā.

Ḥusayn, Ṭ. (1958). *Min Baʿīd*. Al-Qāhira: Al-Sharika al-ʿArabīya.

Ḥusayn, Ṭ. (2002–2004). *Turāth Ṭāhā Ḥusayn: Al-Maqālāt al-Ṣuḥufīya min 1908–1967*. 4 vols. Al-Qāhira: Maṭbaʿat Dār al-Kutub wa-l-Wathāʾiq al-Qawmīya bi-l-Qāhira.

Ibn Abī al-Ḍiyāf, A. (1963). *Itḥāf Ahl al-Zamān bi-Akhbār Mulūk Tūnis wa ʿAhd al-Amān*. 8 vols. Tūnis: Al-Maṭbaʿa al-Rasmīya li-l-Jumhūrīya al-Tūnisīya.

Ibn ʿAddāda, A. (2003). *Al-Fikr al-Iṣlāḥī fī ʿAhd al-Ḥimāya: Muḥammad Ibn al-Ḥasan al-Ḥajwī Namūdhajan*. Al-Dār al-Bayḍāʾ: Al-Markaz al-Thaqāfī al-ʿArabī.

Ibn al-Azraq, M. (1977). *Badāʾiʿ al-Silk fī Ṭabāʾiʿ al-Mulk*. 2 vols. Tūnis: Al-Dār al-ʿArabīya li-l-Kitāb.

Ibn al-Khūja, M. (1939). *Tārīkh Maʿālim al-Tawḥīd fī al-Qadīm wa-l-Jadīd*. Tūnis: Al-Maṭbaʿa al-Tūnisīya.

Ibn ʿĀshūr, M. Ṭ. (1967). *A-Laysa al-Ṣubḥ bi-Qarīb*. Tūnis: Al-Sharika al-Waṭanīya li-l-Tawzīʿ.

Ibn Bilghayth, S. (2005). *Jamʿīyat al-Awqāf wa-l-Istiʿmār al-Faransī fī Tūnis 1914–1943*. Ṣafāqis: Maktabat ʿAlāʾ al-Dīn.

Ibn Qayyim al-Jawzīya, M. (1899–1900). *Al-Ṭuruq al-Ḥukmīya fī al-Siyāsa al-Sharʿīya*. Al-Qāhira: Maṭbaʿat al-Ādāb wa-l-Muʾayyad.

Ibn Yūsuf, M. (1998). *Al-Mashraʿ al-Mulkī fī Salṭanat Awlād ʿAlī Turkī*. Tūnis: Al-Maṭbaʿa al-ʿAṣrīya.

Ibn Zaydān, ʿA. (1937). *Al-Durar al-Fākhira bi-Maʾāthir al-Mulūk al-ʿAlawīyīn bi-Fās al-Zāhira*. Al-Ribāṭ: Al-Maṭbaʿa al-Iqtiṣādīya.

Ibrahim, S. (1980). Anatomy of Egypt's Militant Islamic Groups: Methodological Note and Preliminary Findings. *International Journal of Middle East Studies*, 12(4), 423–453.

Imber, C. (1997). *Ebu's-su'ud: The Islamic Legal Tradition*. Stanford, CA: Stanford University Press.

ʿImrānī, M. (2016). *Jāmiʿat al-Qarawīyīn wa-l-Ḥimāya, 1912–1934*. Al-Ribāṭ: Manshūrāt al-Ribāṭ.

İnalcık, H. (1976). The Rise of the Ottoman Empire. In M. Cook (ed.), *A History of the Ottoman Empire to 1730*. Cambridge: Cambridge University Press, 10–53.

İnalcık, H., & D. Quataert. (1994). *An Economic and Social History of the Ottoman Empire, 1300–1914*. Cambridge: Cambridge University Press.

ʿInān, M. (1958). *Tārīkh al-Jāmiʿ al-Azhar*. Al-Qāhira: Maṭbaʿat al-Taʾlīf wa-l-Tarjama wa-l-Nashr.

International Labour Office. (1958–1995). *The Cost of Social Security*. Geneva: International Labour Office.

Jābirī, M. (1978). *Aḍwāʾ ʿalā Mushkil al-Taʿlīm bi-l-Maghrib*. Al-Dār al-Bayḍāʾ: Dār al-Nashr al-Maghribīya.

Jacob, X. (1982). *L'enseignement religieux dans la Turquie moderne*. Berlin: K. Schwarz.

Jamal, A. (2012). *Of Empires and Citizens: Pro-American Democracy or No Democracy At All?* Princeton, NJ: Princeton University Press.

Jazi, D. (1971). *Les origines des parlementaires en Tunisie*. Paris: Université de Paris, Faculté de droit et des sciences économiques. Mémoire pour le diplôme d'études supérieures de science politique.

Jerad, M. (2012). Traités et accords conclus entre la Tunisie et les puissances occidentales (1626–1955). *Cahiers des archives*. Tunis: Archives Nationales de Tunisie.

Jerad, M. (2018). Enjeux marchands et intérêts de pouvoir autour de la jurisdiction contentieuse des consuls de France à Tunis. In A. Bartolomei et al. (eds.), *De l'utilité commerciale des consuls: L'institution consulaire et les marchands dans le monde méditerranéen (XVIIe-XXe siècles)*. Madrid: École française de Rome.

Jerfel, K. (2012). De grands acteurs économiques: Les négociants européens dans les villes ports de la côte Est de la régence de Tunis au XIXème siècle. *Mawarid, Revue de la faculté des lettres et des sciences humaines de Sousse*, (17), 121–180.

Johansen, B. (1967). *Muhammad Husain Haikal: Europa und der Orient in Weltbild eines ägyptishen Liberalen*. Beirut: In Kommission bei F. Steiner, Wiesbaden.

Johansen, B. (1988). Des institutions religieuses du Maghreb. *Arabica*, 35(3), 221–252.

Johansen, B. (1999). *Contingency in a Sacred Law: Legal and Ethical Norms in the Muslim Fiqh*. Leiden: E. J. Brill.

Johansen, B. (2008). A Perfect Law in an Imperfect Society: Ibn Taymiyya's Concept of "Governance in the Name of the Sacred Law." In P. Bearman, W. Heinrichs, & B. G. Weiss (eds.), *The Law Applied: Contextualizing the Islamic Sharia*. London: I. B. Tauris, 259–294.

Julien, C. A. (1952). *L'Afrique du Nord en marche: Nationalismes musulmans et souveraineté française*. Paris: R. Julliard.

Karakoç, U., Ş. Pamuk, & L. Panza. (2017). Industrialization in Egypt and Turkey, 1870–2010. In K. O'Rourke & J. Williamson (eds.), *The Spread of Modern Industry to the Periphery since 1871*. Oxford, 2017; online edition, Oxford Academic, March 23, 2017.

Karaman, K., & Ş. Pamuk. (2010). Ottoman State Finances in European Perspective, 1500–1914. *Journal of Economic History*, 70(3), 593–629.

Karaman, K., & Ş. Pamuk. (2013). Different Paths to the Modern State in Europe: The Interaction between Warfare, Economic Structure, and Political Regime. *American Political Science Review*, 107(3), 603–626.

Karoui, H. (1973). *La régence de Tunis à la veille du protectorat français: Débats pour une nouvelle organization, 1857–1877*. Thèse de troisième cycle. Paris: École Pratique des Hautes Études.

Karpat, K. (2001). *The Politicization of Islam: Reconstructing Identity, State, Faith, and Community in the Late Ottoman State.* New York: Oxford University Press.

Kattānī, I. (1982). *Al-Niẓām al-Tarbawī fī al-Maghrib Ba ʿd Rub ʿ Qarn min ʿAhd al-Istiqlāl, 1956–1982.* Al-Ribāṭ: Nādī al-Fikr al-Islāmī.

Keddie, N., ed. (1972). *Scholars, Saints, and Sufis: Muslim Religious Institutions in the Middle East since 1500.* Berkeley: University of California Press.

Kedourie, E. (1968). The Genesis of the Egyptian Constitution of 1923. In P. Holt (ed.), *Political and Social Change in Modern Egypt: Historical Studies from the Ottoman Conquest to the United Arab Republic.* London: Oxford University Press, 347–361.

Kennedy, H. (2004). *The Court of the Caliphs: The Rise and Fall of Islam's Greatest Dynasty.* London: Weidenfeld & Nicolson.

Kepel, G. (1985a). *The Prophet and Pharaoh: Muslim Extremism in Egypt.* London: Al Saqi Books.

Kepel, G. (1985b). Les oulémas, l'intelligentsia et les islamistes en Egypte: Système social, ordre transcendantal et ordre traduit. *Revue française de science politique*, 35(3), 424–445.

Kepel, G. (2002). *Jihad: The Trail of Political Islam.* Cambridge, MA: Harvard University Press.

Khadar, H. (1989). La révolution française, le Pacte Fondamental et la première constitution tunisienne de 1861. *Revue du monde musulman et de la Méditerranée,* (52–53), 132–137.

Khafājī, M. (1954). *Al-Azhar fī Alf ʿĀm.* Al-Qāhira: Al-Maṭba ʿa al-Munīrīya.

Khairallah, C. (1938). *Le mouvement évolutionniste tunisien: Notes et documents.* Tunis: Editions de l'imprimerie de Tunis.

Khalfaoui, M. S. (2012). Le parti démocrate progressiste. In H. Redissi, A. Nouira, & A. Zghal (eds.), *La transition démocratique en Tunisie: Etat des lieux.* Tunis: Diwen éditions, vol. 1, 71–110.

Khoury, P. (1981). Factionalism among Syrian Nationalists during the French Mandate. *International Journal of Middle East Studies,* 13(4), 441–469.

Khūrī, Y. Q. (1989). *Al-Dasātīr fi-l- ʿĀlam al- ʿArabī.* Bayrūt: Dār al-Ḥamrā ʾ.

Koçunyan, A. (2018). *Negotiating the Ottoman Constitution 1839–1876.* Paris: Peeters.

Kogelmann, F. (2009). The Reform of Pious Islam in Morocco during the French Protectorate. *Quaderni Storici,* XLIV(132[3]), 727–760.

Köprülü, F. (1942). L'institution du vakouf, sa nature juridique et son évolution historique. *Vakıflar Dergisi,* no. 2, 3–48.

Koştaş, M. (1990). Ankara Üniversitesi İlâhiyat Fakültesi (Dünü Bugünü). *Ankara Üniversitesi İlâhiyat Fakültesi Dergisi,* 31(1), 141–184.

Kraïem, A. (1986). Le premier procès de Abdelaziz Thaalibi (juillet 1904). *Revue d'histoire maghrébine,* 13(41–42), 101–116.

Kraïem, M. (1973). *La Tunisie précoloniale.* 2 vols. Tunis: Société tunisienne de diffusion.

Kraïem, M. (1976). *Nationalisme et syndicalisme en Tunisie, 1918–1929.* Tunis: UGTT.

Krämer, G. (2010). *Hasan al-Banna.* Oxford: Oneworld.

Kremer, A. (1887). *Ueber das Einnahmebudget des Abbasiden-reiches vom Jahre 306 H. (918–919).* Wien: Denkschriften der Kaiserlichen Akademie der Wissenschaften.

Kuran, T. (2001). The Provision of Public Goods under Islamic Law: Origins, Impact, and Limitations of the Waqf System. *Law and Society Review,* 35(4), 841–897.

Kuran, T. (2011). *The Long Divergence: How Islamic Law Held Back the Middle East.* Princeton, NJ: Princeton University Press.

Kuru, A. (2009). *Secularism and State Policies Toward Religion: The United States, France, and Turkey*. Cambridge: Cambridge University Press.

Ladhari, N. (1956). *Les conventions franco-tunisiennes du 3 juin 1955*. Tunis: n.p.

Lahjomri, A., et al. (1987). *La grande encyclopédie du Maroc*. Tome 2: *Education*. Rabat: GEM.

Lajili, M. (2007). Le Bayt al-Mal en Tunisie (1842–1957): Entre anachronisme et caractère anodin des réformes. *Rawafid, Revue de l'institut supérieur d'histoire du mouvement national*, no. 12, 9–34.

Lalouette, J. (2005). *L'Etat et les cultes 1789–1905–2005*. Paris: La Découverte.

Landau, J. (1953). *Parliaments and Parties in Egypt*. Tel-Aviv: Israel Pub. House.

Langohr, V. (2005). Colonial Education Systems and the Spread of Local Religious Movements: The Cases of British Egypt and Punjab. *Comparative Studies in Society and History*, 47(1), 161–189.

Lapidus, I. (1975). The Separation of State and Religion in the Development of Early Islamic Society. *International Journal of Middle East Studies*, 6(4), 363–385.

Larguèche, A. (1990). *L'abolition de l'esclavage à travers les archives, 1841–1846*. Tunis: Alif.

Larguèche, A. (1999). *Les ombres de la ville: Pauvres, marginaux et minoritaires à Tunis, XVIIIème et XIXème siècles*. Manouba: Centre de publications universitaire, Faculté des lettres de Manouba.

Laroui, A. (1977). *Les origines sociales et culturelles du nationalisme marocain, 1830–1912*. Paris: Maspero.

Latiri, K., & M. Zeghal, with T. Hermassi. (Forthcoming). Socio-Economic and Religious Cleavages and Electoral Choices after the Arab Spring: The Case of the Tunisian Elections of October 23, 2011. Working Paper.

LaTowsky, R. (1997). *Egypt's NGO Sector: A Briefing Paper*. Education for Development Occasional Papers Series 1, Number 4. Education for Development. Reading, England.

Lau, M. (2012). Islam and the Constitutional Foundations of Pakistan. In R. Grote & T. Röder (eds.), *Constitutionalism in Islamic Countries: Between Upheaval and Continuity*. Oxford: Oxford University Press.

Laurence, J. (2021). *Coping with Defeat: Sunni Islam, Roman Catholicism, and the Modern State*. Princeton, NJ: Princeton University Press.

Laurens, H. (1996). La politique musulmane de la France: Caractères généraux. *Maghreb-Machrek*, (152), 3–13.

Lauzière, H. (2015). *The Making of Salafism*. New York: Columbia University Press.

Lelong, M. (1971). Le patrimoine musulman dans l'enseignement tunisien après l'indépendance. Thèse présentée devant l'université de Provence I.

Le Pautremat, P. (2003). *La politique musulmane de la France au XXème siècle, de l'Hexagone aux terres d'islam: Espoirs, réussites, échecs*. Paris: Maisonneuve et Larose.

Lerner, H. (2011). *Making Constitutions in Deeply Divided Societies*. Cambridge: Cambridge University Press.

Levtzion, N., & J. Voll. (1987). *Eighteenth-Century Renewal and Reform in Islam*. Syracuse, NY: Syracuse University Press.

Lewis, B. (1984). Siyasa. In A. H. Green (ed.), *In Quest of an Islamic Humanism*. Cairo: American University in Cairo Press, 3–14.

Lewis, M. (2014). *Divided Rule: Sovereignty and Empire in French Tunisia, 1881–1938*. Berkeley: University of California Press.

Lia, B. (1998). *The Society of the Muslim Brothers in Egypt: The Rise of an Islamic Mass Movement, 1928–1942*. Reading, UK: Ithaca Press.

Lombardi, C. B. (2013). Constitutional Provisions Making Sharia "a" or "the" Chief Source of Legislation: Where did they Come from? What do they Mean? Do they Matter? *American University International Law Review*, 28(3), 733–774.

Lombardi, C. B., & N. Brown. (2006). Do Constitutions Requiring Adherence to Shari'a Threaten Human Rights? How Egypt's Constitutional Court Reconciles Islamic Law with the Liberal Rule of Law. *American University International Law Review*, 21(3), 379–435.

Luccioni, J. (1982). *Les fondations pieuses "habous" au Maroc: Depuis les origines jusqu'à 1956*. Rabat: Imprimerie royale.

Lust-Okar, E. (2007). *Structuring Conflict in the Arab World*. Cambridge: Cambridge University Press.

Lybarger, L. (2007). *Identity and Religion in Palestine: The Struggle between Islamism and Secularism in the Occupied Territories*. Princeton, NJ: Princeton University Press.

Machuel, L. (1889). *L'enseignement public dans la régence de Tunis*. Paris: Imprimerie nationale.

Machuel, L. (1897). L'enseignement musulman en Tunisie. *Revue tunisienne*, no. 16, 385–398.

Machuel, L. (1906). *L'enseignement public en Tunisie (1883–1906)*. Tunis: Société anonyme de l'imprimerie rapide.

Macken, R. (1974). Louis Machuel and Education Reform in Tunisia during the Early Years of the French Protectorate. *Revue d'histoire maghrébine*, no. 1, 45–55.

Maddison, A. (2007). Historical Statistics for the World Economy, 1-2005. Paris: OECD Development Center.

Maghraoui, A. (2006). *Liberalism without Democracy: Nationhood and Citizenship in Egypt, 1922–1936*. Durham, NC: Duke University Press.

Mahjoubi, A. (1977). *L'établissement du protectorat français en Tunisie*. Tunis: Publications de l'Université de Tunis, Faculté des lettres et sciences humaines.

Mahjoubi, A. (1982). *Les origines du mouvement national en Tunisie (1904–1934)*. Tunis: Publications de l'Université de Tunis, Faculté des lettres et sciences humaines.

Mahjoubi, A., & H. Karoui. (1983). *Quand le soleil s'est levé à l'ouest: Tunisie 1881, impérialisme et résistance*. Tunis: Cérès productions.

Mahmood, S. (2005). *Politics of Piety: The Islamic Revival and the Feminist Subject*. Princeton, NJ: Princeton University Press.

Mahmood, S. (2016). *Religious Difference in a Secular Age: A Minority Report*. Princeton, NJ: Princeton University Press.

Maḥmūd, B. (2009). *Taʿaddudīyat al-Taʿlīm al-Ibtidāʾī fī Miṣr*, 1923–1993. Al-Qāhira: Al-Hayʾa al-Miṣrīya al-ʿĀmma li-l-Kitāb.

Makdisi, G. (1961). Muslim Institutions of Learning in Eleventh-Century Baghdad. *Bulletin of the School of Oriental and African Studies*, 24(1), 1–56.

Makdisi, G. (1981). *The Rise of Colleges: Institutions of Learning in Islam and the West*. Edinburgh: Edinburgh University Press.

Makdisi, U. (2000). *The Culture of Sectarianism: Community, History, and Violence in Nineteenth-Century Ottoman Lebanon*. Berkeley: University of California Press.

Maktabi, R. (1999). The Lebanese Census of 1932 Revisited: Who are the Lebanese? *British Journal of Middle Eastern Studies*, 26(2), 219–241.

Mantran, R. (1959). Les relations entre la Tunisie et l'Empire Ottoman du XVIème au XIXème siècle. *Les Cahiers de Tunisie*, 7(26–27), 319–333.

Manūnī, M. (1985). *Maẓāhir Yaqẓat al-Maghrib al-Ḥadīth*. 2 vols. Bayrūt: Dār al-Gharb al-Islāmī.

Maoz, Z., and E. A. Henderson. (2013). The World Religion Dataset, 1945–2010: Logic, Estimates, and Trends. *International Interactions*, 39(3), 265–291.

March, A. (2015). What Can the Islamic Past Teach Us About Secular Modernity? *Political Theory*, 43(6), 838–849.

March, A. (2019). *The Caliphate of Man*. Cambridge, MA: Harvard University Press.

Marglin, J. (2022). *The Shamama Case: Contesting Citizenship Across the Modern Mediterranean*. Princeton, NJ: Princeton University Press.

Marrūnī, M. (1996). *Al-Iṣlāḥ al-Ta ʿlīmī bi-l-Maghrib, 1956–1994*. Al-Ribāṭ: Al-Mamlaka al-Maghribīya, Jāmiʿat Muḥammad al-Khāmis, Kullīyat al-Ādāb wa-l-ʿUlūm al-Insānīya bi-l-Ribāṭ.

Marsans-Sakly, S. (2010). The Revolt of 1864 in Tunisia: History, Power, and Memory. PhD dissertation, New York University.

Maʿrūfī, M. S. (1988). *Ḥawla al-Dīn wa-l-Dawla: Muḥāwala li-Tarḥ al-Niqāsh min Dākhil al-Tārīkh al-ʿArabī*. Tūnis: n.p.

Marzouki, I. (1988). Le voile des colonisées: Tunisie, 1924–1936. *IBLA* 51(61), 59–89.

Masoud, T. (2014). *Counting Islam: Religion, Class, and Elections in Egypt*. New York: Cambridge University Press.

Massialas, B., & S. Jarrar. (1983). *Education in the Arab World*. New York: Praeger.

Massialas, B., & S. Jarrar. (1991). *Arab Education in Transition: A Source Book*. New York: Garland.

Maṭar, ʿA. (1939). Al-Taʿlīm wa-l-Mutaʿaṭṭilūn fī Miṣr. Al-Iskandarīya: Matbaʿat Madrasat Muḥammad ʿAlī al-Ṣināʿīya.

Matthews R., & M. Akrawi. (1950). *Education in Arab Countries of the Near East*. Washington, DC: American Council on Education.

Mayeur-Jaouen, C. (2002). Les débuts d'une revue néo-salafiste: Muhibb al-Dîn al-Khatîb et Al-Fath de 1926 à 1928. *Revue des mondes musulmans et de la Méditerranée*, 95(98), 227–255.

Mecham, R. Q. (2017). *Institutional Origins of Islamist Political Mobilization*. Cambridge: Cambridge University Press.

Mechri-Bendana, K. (1991). L'Institut des Hautes Études de Tunis (1945–1950). In La *Tunisie de l'après-guerre (1945–1950)*. Tunis: Faculté des sciences humaines et sociales de Tunis, 119–132.

Merrouni, M. (1983). Le collège musulman de Fes, 1914 à 1956. Thèse de doctorat, Université de Montréal.

Merrouni, M. (1993). *Le problème de la réforme dans le système éducatif marocain*. Rabat: Okad.

Mestiri, A. (2011). *Témoignage pour l'histoire*. Tunis: Sud éditions.

Mezghani, A. (2011). *L'Etat inachevé: La question du droit dans les pays arabes*. Paris: Gallimard.

Mezghani, A. (2012). Tunisie: Une révolution, une élection et des malentendus. *Le débat*, 168(1), 168–177.

Michel, N. (1996). Les rizaq iḥbāsiyya, terres agricoles en mainmorte dans l'Egypte mamelouke et ottomane: Étude sur les Dafātir al-Aḥbās ottomans. *Annales islamologiques*, vol. 30, 105–198.

Mitchell, R. (1969). *The Society of the Muslim Brothers*. London: Oxford University Press.

Mo, K. (2014). Contested Constitutions: Constitutional Development in the Sudan 1956–2005. Master's thesis in history, University of Bergen.

Moaddel, M. (2005). *Islamic Modernism, Nationalism, and Fundamentalism: Episode and Discourse*. Chicago: University of Chicago Press.

Moalla, A. (2004). *The Regency of Tunis and the Ottoman Porte, 1777–1814: Army and Government of a North-African Ottoman Eyâlet at the End of the Eighteenth Century*. London: Routledge.

Monchicourt, C. (alias Rodd Balek). (1920). *La Tunisie après la guerre: Problèmes politiques*. Paris: Publication du comité de l'Afrique française.

Montana, I. (2013). *The Abolition of Slavery in Ottoman Tunisia*. Gainesville: University Press of Florida.

Mottahedeh, R. (1997). The Transmission of Learning: The Role of the Islamic Northeast. In N. Grandin & M. Gaborieau (eds.), *Madrasa: La Transmission du Savoir dans le Monde Musulman*. Paris: Ed. Arguments, 64–73.

Moustafa, T. (2018). *Constituting Religion: Islam, Liberal Rights, and the Malaysian State*. Cambridge: Cambridge University Press.

Mubārak, ʿA. (1886–1889). *Al-Khiṭat al-Tawfīqīya al-Jadīda li-Miṣr al-Qāhira wa-Mudunihā wa-Bilādiha al-Qadīma wa-l-Shahīra*. 20 vols. Al-Qāhira: Al-Maṭbaʿa al-Kubrā al-Amīrīya.

Mzali, M., & J. Pignon. (1971). *Khérédine, homme d'état: Documents historiques annotés*. Tunis: Maison tunisienne de l'édition.

Naqqāsh, S. (1994). *Miṣr li-l-Miṣrīyīn*, vol. 4. Al-Qāhira: Maṭābiʿ al-Hayʾa al-Miṣrīya al-ʿĀmma li-l-Kitāb.

Nasīra, H. (2006). *Maḥmūd ʿAzmī: Rāʾid Ḥuqūq al-Insān fī Miṣr*. Al-Qāhira: Markaz al-Qāhira li-Dirāsāt Ḥuqūq al-Insān.

Nāṣirī, M. (1992). *Al-Aḥbās al-Islāmīya fī al-Mamlaka al-Maghribīya*. Al-Ribāṭ: Al-Mamlaka al-Maghribīya, Wizārat al-Awqāf wa-l-Shuʾūn al-Islāmīya.

Nasr, S. (2001). *Islamic Leviathan: Islam and the Making of State Power*. New York: Oxford University Press.

Nataf, C. (2008). L'exclusion des avocats juifs en Tunisie pendant la seconde guerre mondiale. *Archives juives*, 41, 90–107.

Nataf, C. (2013). Les Juifs de Tunisie et les négociations d'autonomie interne. In A. Danan & C. Nataf (eds.), *Juifs au Maghreb, mélanges à la mémoire de Jacques Taïeb*. Paris: Editions de l'éclat, 187–199.

Nazıroğlu, B. (2016). *Türkiye'de İlahiyat Eğitimi*. Ankara: STS Yayıncılık.

North, D., & B. Weingast. (1989). Constitutions and Commitment: The Evolution of Institutions Governing Public Choice in Seventeenth-Century England. *Journal of Economic History*, 49(4), 803–832.

Nwīra, A. (2012). Al-Ḥarakāt al-Islāmīya fī Tūnis wa-l-Intiqāl al-Dīmūqrāṭī. In H. Redissi, A. Nouira, & A. Zghal (eds.), *La transition démocratique en Tunisie: Etat des Lieux*. Tunis: Diwen éditions, vol. 1, 127–168.

Öcal, M. (1999). Kuruluşundan Günümüze Imam-Hatip Liseleri. *Din Eğitimi Araştırmaları Dergisi*, vol. 6, 201–254.

Öcal, M. (2007). From the Past to the Present: Imam and Preacher Schools in Turkey—An Ongoing Quarrel. *Religious Education*, 102(2), 191–205.

Olson, C. (2020). Creed, Belief, and the Common Folk: Disputes in the Early Modern Maghrib (9th/15th–11th/17th c.). PhD dissertation, Harvard University.

Ostrorog, L. (1901). *El-ahkâm es-soulthânîya: Traité de droit public musulman d'Abou 'l-Hassan Alî ibn Mohammed ibn Habîb, el-Mâwerdî*. Paris: E. Leroux.

Oualdi, M. (2011). *Esclaves et maîtres: Les Mamelouks des beys de Tunis du XVIIème siècle aux années 1880*. Paris: Publications de la Sorbonne.

Oualdi, M. (2020). *A Slave between Empires: A Transimperial History of North Africa*. New York: Columbia University Press.

Oualdi, M. (2022). *Salah Ben Youssef et les youssefistes: Au tournant de l'indépendance tunisienne (1955–1956)*. Tunis: Cérès éditions.

Pacaci, M., & Y. Aktay. (2006). 75 Years of Higher Religious Education in Modern Turkey. In I. M. Abu Rabi' (ed.), *The Blackwell Companion to Contemporary Islamic Thought*. Malden, MA: Blackwell Publications, 122–144.

Pamuk, Ş. (2000a). *A Monetary History of the Ottoman Empire*. New York: Cambridge University Press.

Pamuk, Ş. (2000b). *İstanbul ve Diğer Kentlerde 500 Yıllık Fiyatlar ve Ücretler, 1469–1998*. Ankara: T.C. Başbakanlık Devlet İstatistik Enstitüsü.

Pamuk, Ş. (2006). Estimating Economic Growth in the Middle East since 1820. *Journal of Economic History*, 66(3), 809–828.

Pamuk, Ş. (2018). *Uneven Centuries: Economic Development of Turkey since 1820*. Princeton, NJ: Princeton University Press.

Parmaksızoğlu, I. (1966). *Türkiye 'de Din Eğitimi*. Ankara: Millî Eğitim Basımevi.

Pascon, P. (1983). *Le Haouz de Marrakech*. 2 vols. Rabat: Centre universitaire de la recherche scientifique.

Pascon, P. (1984). *La maison d'Illigh et l'histoire sociale du Tazerwalt*. Rabat: SMER.

Pascual, J. (1983). *Damas à la fin du XVIème siècle: D'après trois actes de waqf ottomans*, tome I. Damas: Presses de l'IFPO.

Paye, L. (1957). *Introduction et évolution de l'enseignement moderne au Maroc (des origines jusqu'à nos jours)*. Thèse d'Etat. Paris: La Sorbonne.

Peaslee, A. (1950). *Constitutions of Nations*. Concord, NH: Rumford Press.

Pehlivan Ağırakça, G. (2013). *Mekteplerde Ahlak Eğitim ve Öğretimi (1839–1923)*. Istanbul: Çamlıca Yayınları.

Pellissier de Reynaud, H. (1853). *Description de la régence de Tunis*. Paris: Imprimerie impériale.

Perkins, K. (2014). *A History of Modern Tunisia*. New York: Cambridge University Press.

Peters, R. (1999). Administrators and Magistrates: The Development of a Secular Judiciary in Egypt, 1842–1871. *Die Welt des Islams*, 39(3), 378–397.

Petry, C. (1983). A Paradox of Patronage. *Muslim World*, 73(3–4), 182–207.

Petry, C. (1994). *Protectors or Praetorians? The Last Mamlūk Sultans and Egypt's Waning as a Great Power*. Albany: State University of New York Press.

Philpott, D. (2007). Explaining the Political Ambivalence of Religion. *American Political Science Review*, 101(3), 505–525.

Planel, A. (2015). *Du comptoir à la colonie: Histoire de la communauté française de Tunisie, 1814–1883*. Paris: Riveneuve.

Plantet, E. (1899). *Correspondance des beys de Tunis et des consuls de France avec la cour, 1577–1830*. Paris: F. Alcan.

Polat, A. (2015). Subject to Approval: Sanction and Censure in Ottoman Istanbul (1889–1923). PhD dissertation, University of Chicago.

Poncet, J. (1962). *La colonisation et l'agriculture européennes en Tunisie depuis 1881: Étude de géographie historique et économique*. Paris: Mouton.

Porter, B. (1984). *The Lion's Share: A Short History of British Imperialism, 1850–1983*. London: Longman.

Powers, D. S. (1990). Fatwas as Sources for Legal and Social History: A Dispute over Endowment Revenues from Fourteenth-Century Fez. *Al-Qanṭara*, 11(2), 295–341.

Prévost, F. (1862). *La Tunisie devant l'Europe*. Paris: E. Dentu.

Qabādū, M. (1875–1879). *Dīwān Shiʿr*. 2 vols. Tūnis: n.p.

Qindīl, A., & S. Ibn Nafīsa. (1994). *Al-Jamʿīyāt al-Ahlīya fī Miṣr*. Al-Qāhira: Markaz al-Dirāsāt al-Siyāsīya wa-al-Istrātījīya, al-Ahrām.

Rabbath, E. (1982). *La constitution libanaise: Origines, textes et commentaires*. Beyrouth: Librairie orientale.

Rabbath, E. (1986). *La formation historique du Liban politique et constitutionnel: Essai de synthèse*. Beyrouth: Librairie orientale.

Rajab, M. (1946). *Al-Azhar bayn al-Māḍī wa-l-Ḥādir*. Al-Qāhira: Maṭbaʿat al-Muqtaṭaf wa-l-Muqaṭṭam.

Raymond, A. (1953). British Policy towards Tunis (1830–1881). PhD dissertation, University of Oxford.

Raymond, A. (1955). Les tentatives anglaises de pénétration économique en Tunisie (1856–1877). *Revue historique*, 214(1), 48–67.

Raymond, A. (1964). La France, la Grande-Bretagne et le problème de la réforme à Tunis (1855–1857). In P. Marthelot & A. Raymond (eds.), *Études maghrébines: Mélanges C. A. Julien*. Paris: Université de Paris, 137–164.

Raymond, A. (1985). *Grandes villes arabes à l'époque ottomane*. Paris: Sindbad.

Raymond, A. (1998). Les grands waqfs et l'organisation de l'espace urbain à Alep et au Caire à l'époque ottomane (XVIème–XVIIème siècles). In A. Raymond (ed.), *La ville arabe, Alep, à l'époque ottomane*. Damas: Presses de l'IFPO, 141–160.

Raymond, A. (2009). La réforme dans le monde ottoman au XIXe siècle: Istanbul, Le Caire, Tunis; Influences croisées. In O. Moreau (ed.), *Réforme de l'Etat et réformismes au Maghreb (XIXe–XXe siècles)*. Paris: L'Harmattan, 27–36.

Raysūnī, A. (2014). *Al-Waqf al-Islāmī: Majālātuhu wa-Abʿāduhu*. Al-Qāhira: Dār al-Kalima li-l-Nashr wa-l-Tawzīʿ.

Reid, D. (1990). *Cairo University and the Making of Modern Egypt*. Cambridge: Cambridge University Press.

Reinhart, C., & K. Rogoff. (2009). *This Time Is Different: Eight Centuries of Financial Folly*. Princeton, NJ: Princeton University Press.

Riḍā, M. R. (1922). *Al-Khilāfa aw al-Imāma al-ʿUẓmā*. Al-Qāhira: Maṭbaʿat al-Manār.

Riesebrodt, M. (2010). *The Promise of Salvation: A Theory of Religion*. Chicago: University of Chicago Press.

Rivet, D. (1988). *Lyautey et l'institution du protectorat français au Maroc, 1912–1925*. Paris: L'Harmattan.

Rodríguez-Mañas, F. (1996). Encore sur la controverse entre soufis et juristes au moyen âge: Critique des mécanismes de financement des confréries soufies. *Arabica*, 43(3), 406–421.

Rollman, W. J. (1983). The "New Order" in a Pre-Colonial Muslim Society: Military Reform in Morocco, 1844–1904. PhD dissertation, University of Michigan.

Rosefsky Wickham, C. (2002). *Mobilizing Islam: Religion, Activism, and Political Change in Egypt*. New York: Columbia University Press.

Rosefsky Wickham, C. (2013). *The Muslim Brotherhood: Evolution of an Islamist Movement*. Princeton, NJ: Princeton University Press.

Rosenthal, F. (1967). *The Muqaddimah: An Introduction to History*. 3 vols. Princeton, NJ: Princeton University Press.

Rosenthal, F. (2007). *Knowledge Triumphant: The Concept of Knowledge in Medieval Islam*. Boston: E. J. Brill.

Roy, O. (1994). *The Failure of Political Islam*. London: I. B. Tauris.

Rustow, Marina. (2013). The Legal Status of Ḏimmī-s in the Fatimid East: A View from the Palace in Cairo. In M. Fierro and J. Tolan (eds.), *The Legal Status of Ḏimmī-s in the Islamic West*. Turnhout: Brepols, 307–332.

Rutherford, B. (2013). *Egypt after Mubarak: Liberalism, Islam, and Democracy in the Arab World*. Princeton, NJ: Princeton University Press.

Sabra, A. (2000). *Poverty and Charity in Medieval Islam: Mamluk Egypt, 1250–1517*. Cambridge: Cambridge University Press.

Safran, N. (1961). *Egypt in Search of Political Community: An Analysis of the Intellectual and Political Evolution of Egypt, 1804–1952*. Cambridge, MA: Harvard University Press.

Sahli, H. (1982). La publication intégrale du Rapport Baron. *Revue d'histoire maghrébine*, 9(27–28), 295–339.

Said, E. (1978). *Orientalism*. New York: Pantheon Books.

Ṣaʿīdī, ʿA. (1965). *Tārīkh al-Iṣlāḥ fī al-Azhar wa-Ṣafaḥāt min al-Jihād fī al-Iṣlāḥ*. Miṣr: Maṭbaʿat al-Iʿtimād.

Saidouni, M., & N. Saidouni. (2009). Il "waqf" in Algeria e l'amministrazione francese: Il caso della fondazione degli "Haramayn" (Algeri 1830–1873). *Quaderni Storici*, 132(3), 687–726.

Saif, P. (1959). Public Education in Egypt: Practice and Theory. PhD dissertation, University of Connecticut.

Sakka, A. (1917). *De la souveraineté dans le droit public musulman sunnite*. Paris: Jouve.

Salama, I. (1939). *L'enseignement islamique en Egypte*. Le Caire: Imprimerie Nationale.

Saleh, M. (2015). The Reluctant Transformation: State Industrialization, Religion, and Human Capital in Nineteenth-Century Egypt. *Journal of Economic History*, 75(1), 65–94.

Saleh, M. (2016). Public Mass Modern Education, Religion, and Human Capital in Twentieth-Century Egypt. *Journal of Economic History*, 76(3), 697–735.

Salem, N. (1984). *Habib Bourguiba, Islam, and the Creation of Tunisia*. London: Croom Helm.

Salmoni, B. A. (2002). Pedagogies of Patriotism: Teaching Socio-Political Community in 20th-Century Turkish and Egyptian Education. PhD dissertation, Harvard University.

Salomon, N. (2016). *For Love of the Prophet: An Ethnography of Sudan's Islamic State*. Princeton, NJ: Princeton University Press.

Sāmī, A. (1917). *Al-Ta'līm fī Miṣr fī Sanatay 1914 wa-1915 wa-Bayān Tafṣīlī li-Nashr al-Ta'līm al-Awwalī wa-l-Ibtidā'ī bi-Anḥā' al-Diyār al-Miṣrīya, Mumahhadan lahu bi-Shadharāt min Kitāb al-Ta'līm*. Al-Qāhira: Maṭba'at al-Ma'ārif.

Sanhuri, A. (1926). *Le califat: Son évolution vers une société des nations orientales*. Paris: P. Geuthner.

Sauvy, A. (1952). Variation des prix de 1810 à nos jours. *Journal de la société statistique de Paris*, tome 93, 88–104.

Sbaï, J. (1996). Organismes et institutions de la politique musulmane. *Maghreb-Machrek*, 152, 22–33.

Sbaï, J. (2018). *La politique musulmane de la France: Un projet chrétien pour l'islam? 1911–1954*. Paris: CNRS.

Schacht, J. (1960). Problems of Modern Islamic Legislation. *Studia Islamica*, 12, 99–130.

Schielke, S. (2012). Being a Nonbeliever in a Time of Islamic Revival: Trajectories of Doubt and Certainty in Contemporary Egypt. *International Journal of Middle East Studies*, 44(2), 301–320.

Schölch, A. (1981). *Egypt for the Egyptians! The Socio-Political Crisis in Egypt, 1878–1882*. London: Ithaca Press.

Schriber, A. (2021). The End of Shari'a? The Structural and Epistemological Evolution of the Shari'a Judge in Colonial-Era Morocco. PhD dissertation, Harvard University.

Schulze, R. (1990). Das Islamische Achtzehnte Jahrhundert. *Die Welt des Islams*, 30(1–4), 140–159.

Schulze, R. (2000). *A Modern History of the Islamic World*. New York: New York University Press.

Schwedler, J. (2011). Can Islamists Become Moderates? Rethinking the Inclusion-Moderation Hypothesis. *World Politics*, 63(2), 347–376.

Sebag, P. (1991). *Histoire des Juifs de Tunisie: Des origines à nos jours*. Paris: L'Harmattan.

Sebag, P. (1998). *Tunis: Histoire d'une ville*. Paris: L'Harmattan.

Sékaly, A. (1927–1928). L'Université d'El-Azhar et ses transformations. *Revue des études islamiques*, parts 1 to 4.

Sékaly, A. (1929). Le problème des waqfs en Egypte. *Revue des études islamiques*, parts 1 to 4.

Seklani, M. (1974). *La population de la Tunisie*. Tunis: Presses de la société tunisienne des arts graphiques.

Şen, A. T. (2021). The Sultan's Syllabus Revisited: Sixteenth-Century Ottoman Madrasa Libraries and the Question of Canonization. *Studia Islamica*, 116(1), 198–235.

Sewell, W. (2005). *Logics of History: Social Theory and Social Transformation*. Chicago: University of Chicago Press.

Shahrastān, M. (2000). *Al-Mu'tamar al-Sūrī al-'Āmm, 1919–1920*. Bayrūt: Dār Amwāj.

Shalabī, K. (1972). *Muḥākamat Ṭāhā Ḥusayn: Naṣṣ Qarār al-Ittihām Ḍidd Ṭāhā Ḥusayn Sanat 1927 Ḥawla Kitābihi* Fī al-Shi'r al-Jāhilī. Bayrūt: Al-Mu'assasa al-'Arabīya li-l-Dirāsāt wa-l-Nashr.

Shatzmiller, M. (1976). Les premiers Mérinides et le milieu religieux de Fes: L'introduction des médersas. *Studia Islamica*, (43), 109–118.

Shatzmiller, M. (2001). Islamic Institutions and Property Rights: The Case of the 'Public Good' Waqf. *Journal of the Economic and Social History of the Orient*, 44(1), 44–74.

Shaw, S. (1962). *The Financial and Administrative Organization and Development of Ottoman Egypt, 1517–1798*. Princeton, NJ: Princeton University Press.

Shaw, S., & K. Shaw (1977). *History of the Ottoman Empire and Modern Turkey*, vol. 2. Cambridge: Cambridge University Press.

Shepard, W. E. (2003). Sayyid Qutb's Doctrine of Jahiliyya. *International Journal of Middle East Studies*, 35(4), 521–545.

Sicard, H. (1965). Les effets sociologiques et économiques de la suppression des habous en Tunisie. In J. Berque & J.-P. Charnay (eds.), *De l'impérialisme à la décolonisation*. Paris: Editions de Minuit, 227–261.

Şimşek, E. (2013). Çok Partili Dönemde Yeniden Din Eğitimi ve Öğretimine Dönüş Süreci (1946–1960). *A. Ü. Türkiyat Araştırmaları Enstitüsü Dergisi*, 49, 391–414.

Singer, A. (2008). *Charity in Islamic Societies*. Cambridge: Cambridge University Press.

Skovgaard-Petersen, J. (1997). *Defining Islam for the Egyptian State: Muftis and Fatwas of the Dār al-Iftā*. Leiden: E. J. Brill.

Slama, B. (1967). *L'insurrection de 1864 en Tunisie*. Tunis: Maison tunisienne de l'édition.

Smida, M. (1970). *Khereddine ministre réformateur, 1873–1877*. Tunis: Maison tunisienne de l'édition.

Smith, C. (1983). *Islam and the Search for Social Order in Modern Egypt: A Biography of Muhammad Husayn Haykal*. Albany: State University of New York Press.

Sobi, E. (2020). 1997–2019 yılları arasında Türkiye'de yüksek din öğretimi. PhD dissertation, Ondokuzmayıs University, Samsun, Turkey.

Somel, S. (2001). *The Modernization of Public Education in the Ottoman Empire, 1839–1908: Islamization, Autocracy, and Discipline*. Leiden: E. J. Brill.

Soumille, P. (1975). *Européens de Tunisie et questions religieuses (1892–1901): Étude d'une opinion publique*. Paris: Editions du centre national de la recherche scientifique.

Sourdel, D. (1958). L'originalité du *Kitāb al-Wuzarā*ʾ de Hilāl al-Ṣābiʾ. *Arabica*, 5, 272–292.

Souriau, C. (1979). Quelques données comparatives sur les institutions islamiques actuelles du Maghreb. *Annuaire de l'Afrique du Nord*, 34(18), 341–379.

Spillmann, G. (2011). *Esquisse d'histoire religieuse du Maroc: Confréries et zaouïas*. Rabat: Publications de la Faculté des lettres et des sciences humaines de Rabat.

Sraïeb, N. (1967). Mutations et réformes de structures de l'enseignement en Tunisie. *Annuaire de l'Afrique du Nord*, 6, 45–113.

Sraïeb, N. (1974). *Colonisation, décolonisation et enseignement: L'exemple tunisien*. Tunis: Institut national des sciences de l'éducation.

Sraïeb, N. (1987). Elite et société: L'invention de la Tunisie de l'Etat-Dynastie à la nation moderne. In M. Camau et al. (eds.), *Tunisie au présent: Une modernité au dessus de tout soupçon?* Paris: CNRS, 65–69.

Sraïeb, N. (1992). Khérédine et l'enseignement: Une nouvelle conception du savoir en Tunisie. *Revue des mondes musulmans et de la Méditerranée*, 63(1), 203–210.

Sraïeb, N. (1995). *Le collège Sadiki de Tunis, 1875–1956: Enseignement et nationalisme*. Paris: CNRS.

Starrett, G. (1998). *Putting Islam to Work: Education, Politics, and Religious Transformation in Egypt*. Berkeley: University of California Press.

Steingass, F. (1882). *English-Arabic Dictionary*. London: W. H. Allen.

Stepan, A. (2012). Tunisia's Transition and the Twin Tolerations. *Journal of Democracy*, 23(2), 89–103.

Stilt, K. (2011). *Islamic Law in Action: Authority, Discretion, and Everyday Experiences in Mamluk Egypt*. Oxford: Oxford University Press.

Stilt, K. (2015). Contextualizing Constitutional Islam: The Malayan Experience. *International Journal of Constitutional Law*, 13(2), 407–433.

Stöber, G. (1986). *'Habous Public' in Marokko: Zur wirtschaftlichen Bedeutung religiöser Stiftungen im 20. Jahrhundert*. Marburg/Lahn: Im Selbstverlag der Marburger Geographischen Gesellschaft.

Stolz, D. (2018). *The Lighthouse and the Observatory: Islam, Science, and Empire in Late Ottoman Egypt*. Cambridge: Cambridge University Press.

Sullivan, W. (2005). *The Impossibility of Religious Freedom*. Princeton, NJ: Princeton University Press.

Tabutin, D., et al. (2001). L'histoire de la population de l'Afrique du Nord pendant le deuxième millénaire, Communication présentée à la conférence "The History of World Population in the Second Millennium," organisée à Florence du 28 au 30 juin 2001 par le Comité de Démographie Historique de l'UIESP et la Società Italiana di Demografia Storica.

Tamimi, A. (2001). *Rachid Ghannouchi: A Democrat within Islamism*. Oxford: Oxford University Press.

Tarifa. C. (1971). L'enseignement du premier et du second degré en Tunisie. *Population*, 26e année, no. 1, 149–180.

Tawfīq, A. (1978). *Musāhama fī Dirāsat al-Mujtamaʿ al-Maghribī fī al-Qarn al-Tāsiʿ ʿAshar: Īnūltān Min 1850 ilā 1912*. Al-Ribāṭ: n.p.

Tāzī, ʿA. (1972). *Jāmiʿ al-Qarawīyīn: Al-Masjid wa-l-Jāmiʿa bi-Madīnat Fās*. 3 vols. Bayrūt: Dār al-Kitāb al-Lubnānī.

Terras, J. A. (1899). Essai sur les biens habous en Algérie et en Tunisie: Étude de législation coloniale. Thèse pour le doctorat, Université de Lyon, Faculté de droit.

Tessler, M. (2015). *Islam and Politics in the Middle East: Explaining the Views of Ordinary Citizens*. Bloomington: Indiana University Press.

Thaalibi, A. (1920). *La Tunisie martyre: Ses revendications*. Paris: Jouve.

Thompson, E. (2015). Rashid Rida and the 1920 Syrian-Arab Constitution: How the French Mandate Undermined Islamic Liberalism. In C. Schayegh & A. Arsan (eds.), *The Routledge Handbook of the History of the Middle East Mandates*. London: Routledge/Taylor & Francis Group.

Thompson, E. (2020). *How the West Stole Democracy from the Arabs: The Syrian Congress of 1920 and the Destruction of Its Historic Liberal-Islamic Alliance*. New York: Atlantic Monthly Press.

Thompson, L. (2022). Who Speaks for the Sacred? The Politics of Blasphemy in Tunisia from the Nineteenth Century to the Present Day. PhD dissertation, Harvard University.

Tlili, B. (1973). Au seuil du nationalisme tunisien: Documents inédits sur le panislamisme au Maghreb. *Africa*, 28(2), 211–236.

Tlili, B. (1978). La SFIO de Tunisie et les questions islamiques (1919–1925). In R. Gallisot (ed.), *Mouvement ouvrier, communisme et nationalismes dans le monde arabe*. Paris: Les éditions ouvrières, 57–90.

Tlili, B. (1979). *Crises et mutations dans le monde islamo-méditerranéen contemporain, 1907–1918.* Tunis: Publications de l'Université de Tunis, Faculté des lettres et sciences humaines.

Toronto, J. A. (1992). The Dynamics of Educational Reform in Contemporary Egypt. PhD dissertation, Harvard University.

Toumi, M. (1989). *La Tunisie de Bourguiba à Ben Ali.* Paris: Presses universitaires de France.

Tozy, M. (1999). *Monarchie et islam politique au Maroc.* Paris: Presses de la Fondation nationale des sciences politiques.

Tyan, E. (1938). *Histoire de l'organisation judiciaire en pays d'islam.* Paris: Librairie du Recueil Sirey.

Ubicini, A. (1853–1854). *Lettres sur la Turquie.* 2 vols. Paris: J. Dumaine.

Valensi, L. (1967). Esclaves chrétiens et esclaves noirs à Tunis au XVIIIe siècle. *Annales: Histoire, sciences sociales,* 22(6), 1267–1288.

Valensi, L. (1969a). Islam et capitalisme: Production et commerce des chéchias en Tunisie et en France aux XVIIIème et XIXème siècles. *Revue d'histoire moderne et contemporaine,* 16(3), 376–400.

Valensi, L. (1969b). *Le Maghreb avant la prise d'Alger, 1790–1830.* Paris: Flammarion. (English Translation, 1977: *On the Eve of Colonialism: North Africa before the French Conquest.* New York: Africana First).

Valensi, L. (1977). *Fellahs tunisiens: L'économie rurale et la vie des campagnes aux 18ème et 19ème siècles.* Paris: Mouton. (English Translation, 1985. *Tunisian Peasants in the Eighteenth and Nineteenth Centuries.* Cambridge: Cambridge University Press; Paris: Editions de la Maison des sciences de l'homme.)

Valensi, L. (1981). The Tunisian Fellaheen in the Eighteenth and Nineteenth Centuries. In A. L. Udovitch (ed.), *The Islamic Middle East, 700–1900: Studies in Economic and Social History.* Princeton, NJ: Darwin Press, 709–724.

Valensi, L. (1994). Espaces public, espaces communautaires aux 19ème et 20ème siècles. *Confluences,* (10), 97–109.

Van der Haven, E. (2006). The Bey, the Mufti and the Scattered Pearls: Sharia and Political Leadership in Tunisia's Age of Reform, 1800–1864. PhD dissertation, University of Leiden.

Van Krieken, G. (1976). *Khayr al-Dîn et la Tunisie, 1850–1881.* Leiden: E. J. Brill.

Vermeren, P. (2002). *La formation des élites marocaines et tunisiennes: Des nationalistes aux islamistes, 1920–2000.* Paris: La Découverte.

Waines, D. (1977). The Third-Century Internal Crisis of the Abbasids. *Journal of the Economic and Social History of the Orient,* 20, 282–306.

Walzer, M. (2015). *The Paradox of Liberation: Secular Revolutions and Religious Counterrevolutions.* New Haven, CT: Yale University Press.

Weideman, J. (2021). Islamic Reform on the Margins of Colonialism: Political Economy, Social History, and Intellectual Life at the Zaytuna Mosque-University in 20th Century North Africa. PhD dissertation, Princeton University.

White, B. (2011). *The Emergence of Minorities in the Middle East: The Politics of Community in French Mandate Syria.* Edinburgh: Edinburgh University Press.

Wiktorowicz, Q. (2001). *The Management of Islamic Activism: Salafis, the Muslim Brotherhood, and State Power in Jordan.* Albany: State University of New York Press.

Winder, R. B. (1954). The Establishment of Islam as the State Religion: A Muslim Brotherhood View in Syria. *Muslim World,* 44(3–4), 215–226.

Windler, C. (2002). *La diplomatie comme expérience de l'autre: Consuls français au Maghreb (1700–1840)*. Genève: Droz.

Womble, T. (1997). Early Constitutionalism in Tunisia, 1857–1864: Reform and Revolt. PhD dissertation, Princeton University.

Wood, L. (2011). Reception of European Law, Origins of Islamic Legal Revivalism, and Foundations of Transformations in Islamic Legal Thought in Egypt, 1875–1960. PhD dissertation, Harvard University.

Wood, L. (2016). *Islamic Legal Revival: Reception of European Law and Transformations in Islamic Legal Thought in Egypt, 1875–1952*. Oxford: Oxford University Press.

Wood, L. (2018). Legislation as an Instrument of Islamic Law. In A. M. Emon & R. Ahmed (eds.), *The Oxford Handbook of Islamic Law*. Oxford: Oxford University Press, 551–584.

Wyrtzen, J. (2015). *Making Morocco: Colonial Intervention and the Politics of Identity*. Ithaca, NY: Cornell University Press.

Yarbrough, L. B. (2019). *Friends of the Emir*. Cambridge: Cambridge University Press.

Yasn, D. (2010). *Al-Taʿlīm al-Azharī qabl al-Jāmiʿī Bayn al-Māḍī wa-al-Ḥāḍir: Tawajjuhāt li-Taṭwīrihi*. Al-Qāhira: Dār al-Fikr al-ʿArabī.

Yazidi, B. (2005). *La politique coloniale et le domaine de l'Etat en Tunisie: De 1881 jusqu'à la crise des années trente*. Mannouba: Faculté des lettres, des arts, et des humanités.

Yediyıldız, B. (1990). *Institution du vaqf au XVIIIème siècle en Turquie: Étude socio-historique*. Ankara: Edition Ministère de la culture.

Yerasimos, S. (1994). Les waqfs dans l'aménagement urbain d'Istanbul au XIXème siècle. In F. Bilici (ed.), *Le "waqf" dans le monde musulman contemporain (XIXème–XXème siècles): Fonctions sociales, fonctions économiques*. Istanbul: Institut français d'études anatoliennes, 43–49.

Yıldız, H. (2017). Dârü'l-Hilâfeti'l-Aliyye Medresesi'nde Eğitim ve Öğretim. PhD dissertation, University of Istanbul.

Yousef, T. (2002). Egypt's Growth Performance under Economic Liberalism: A Reassessment with New GDP Estimates, 1886–1945. *Review of Income and Wealth*, series 48, no. 4, December, 561–579.

Zaman, M. Q. (1997a). The Caliphs, the ʿUlamāʾ, and the Law: Defining the Role and Function of the Caliph in the Early ʿAbbāsid Period. *Islamic Law and Society*, 4(1), 1–36.

Zaman, M. Q. (1997b). *Religion and Politics under the Early ʿAbbāsids: The Emergence of the Proto-Sunnī Elite*. New York: E. J. Brill.

Zaman, M. Q. (2002). *The Ulama in Contemporary Islam: Custodians of Change*. Princeton, NJ: Princeton University Press.

Zaouche, A. (1906). *La propriété indigène et la colonisation*. Tunis: Imprimerie rapide.

Zarcone, T. (1994). Waqfs et confréries religieuses à l'époque moderne: L'influence de la réforme des waqfs sur la sociabilité et la doctrine mystique. In F. Bilici (ed.), *Le "waqf" dans le monde musulman contemporain (XIXème-XXème siècles)*. Istanbul: Institut français d'études anatoliennes, 237–248.

Zarrūq, A. (1992). *Qawāʿid al-Taṣawwuf*. Bayrūt: Dār al-Jīl.

Zarzūr, ʿA. M. (2000). *Muṣṭafā al-Sibāʿī: Al-Dāʿiya al-Mujaddid*. Dimashq: Dār al-Qalam.

Zayn, A., & M. Mājid. (1995). *Maḥāḍir Munāqashāt al-Dustūr al-Lubnānī wa-Taʿdīlātihi, 1926–1995*. N.p.

Zeghal, M. (1996). *Gardiens de l'islam: Les oulémas d'al-Azhar dans l'Egypte contemporaine.* Paris: Presses de Sciences Po.

Zeghal, M. (1999a). État et marché des biens religieux: Les voies égyptienne et tunisienne. *Critique internationale*, 5(1), 75–95.

Zeghal, M. (1999b). Religion and Politics in Egypt: The Ulema of Al-Azhar, Radical Islam, and the State (1952–94). *International Journal of Middle East Studies*, 31(3), 371–399.

Zeghal, M. (2005). La constitution du Conseil Français du Culte Musulman: Reconnaissance politique d'un Islam français? *Archives de sciences sociales des religions*, 129, 97–113.

Zeghal, M. (2008a). Réformismes, islamismes et libéralismes religieux. *Revue des mondes musulmans et de la Méditerranée*, 123, 17–34.

Zeghal, M. (2008b). *Islamism in Morocco: Religion, Authoritarianism, and Electoral Politics.* Princeton, NJ: Markus Wiener.

Zeghal, M. (2011). Public Institutions of Religious Education in Egypt and Tunisia: Contrasting the Post-Colonial Reforms of Al-Azhar and the Zaytuna. In O. Abi-Mershed (ed.), *Trajectories of Education in the Arab World: Legacies and Challenges.* Florence, KY: Routledge, 111–124.

Zeghal, M. (2012). Veiling and Unveiling Muslim Women: State Coercion, Islam, and the "Disciplines of the Heart." In A. Filali-Ansary & A. Esmail (eds.), *The Construction of Belief: Reflections on the Thought of Mohammed Arkoun.* London: Saqi Books, 127–149.

Zeghal, M. (2013a). The Implicit Sharia: Established Religion and Varieties of Secularism in Tunisia. In W. F. Sullivan and L. G. Beaman (eds.), *Varieties of Religious Establishment.* London: Ashgate, 107–130.

Zeghal, M. (2013b). Competing Ways of Life: Islamism, Secularism, and Public Order in the Tunisian Transition. *Constellations*, 20(2), 254–274.

Zeghal, M. (2016). Constitutionalizing a Democratic Muslim State without Sharia: The Religious Establishment in the Tunisian 2014 Constitution. In R. Hefner (ed.), *Shari'a Law and Modern Muslim Ethics.* Bloomington: Indiana University Press, 107–134.

Zeghal, M. (2022). The Shaping of the 1857 Security Pact in the Regency of Tunis: A Reappraisal of the Nineteenth Century Constitutional Reforms. *Studia Islamica*, 117(2), 275–334.

INDEX

Italic pages refer to figures and tables

A NOTE ON THE TYPE

This book has been composed in Arno, an Old-style serif typeface in the classic Venetian tradition, designed by Robert Slimbach at Adobe.